Teaching Language Arts

A Student- and Response-Centered Classroom

Second Edition

Carole Cox

California State University, Long Beach

Allyn and Bacon

Boston London Toronto Sydney Tokyo Singapore

To my father,
Gordon D. Shirreffs,
and the memory of my mother,
Alice Shirreffs

Senior Editor: Virginia Lanigan
Editorial Assistant: Nihad Farooq
Senior Marketing Manager: Kathy Hunter
Production Administrator: Annette Joseph
Editorial-Production Service: Susan Freese
Text Design/Electronic Page Makeup: Denise Hoffman
Composition Buyer: Linda Cox
Manufacturing Buyer: Megan Cochran
Cover Administrator: Linda Knowles
Cover Designer: Studio Nine

A Simon & Schuster Company
Needham Heights, Mass. 02194

Library of Congress Cataloging-in-Publication Data

Cox, Carole.
Teaching language arts : a student- and response-centered classroom / Carole Cox. — 2nd ed.
p. cm.
Includes bibliographical references and index.
ISBN 0-205-17488-4 (case)
1. Language arts (Elementary)—United States. 2. Reading (Elementary)—United States. I. Title
LB1576.C755 1996
372.6'044—dc20 95-49413
CIP

Printed in the United States of America

10 9 8 7 6 5 4 3 2 1 00 99 98 97 96 95

Text Credits: p. 88, adapted from "The Role of Primary Language Development in Promoting Educational Success for Language Minority Students," by J. Cummins, 1981, in *Schooling and Language Minority Students: A Theoretical Framework* (p. 39), Los Angeles: California State University, Bilingual Training Center, School of Education. Copyright 1981 by California State University. Reprinted with permission; **pp. 219–224,** adapted from "Shakespeare and Company: The Best in Classroom Reading and Drama," by C. Cox, 1980, *Reading Teacher, 43,* pp. 542–545, and "Stirring Up Shakespeare in the Elementary School," by C. Cox, 1985, *Literature—News That Stays News: Fresh Approaches to the Classics,* edited by C. Carter. Reprinted with permission of the International Reading Association and the author; **pp. 249–250,** from *The Child as Critic,* Glenna Sloan, 2nd ed., Teachers College Press, 1984, pp. 104–106; p. 283, reprinted with permission of Atheneum Books for Young Readers, an imprint of Simon & Schuster, from *May I Bring a Friend?* by Beatrice Schenk de Regniers. Text copyright © 1964 Beatrice Schenk de Regniers. By permission also of Marian Reiner for the author in the case of de Regniers; **p. 459,** "Film Preference Instrument," Carole Cox, in *Measures for Research and Evaluation in the English Language Arts* (Vol. 2), William T. Fagan, Charles R. Cooper, and Julie M. Jensen, Eds., National Council of Teachers of English, 1985. Reprinted with permission; **pp. 463–467,** from "Young Filmmakers Speak the Language of Film," by Carole Cox, *Language Arts, 60* (March 1983): 296–304, 372. Adapted with permission.

Contents

Part II Spoken Language

Chapter 5 Listening and Talking 157

Chapter 6 Drama in the Classroom 193

Part III Literature and Reading

Chapter 11
Language Conventions: Grammar, Talking, and Writing 387

Chapter 12
Language Conventions: Spelling, Punctuation, and Handwriting 419

Part V Integrated Teaching

Appendix
Activities for the Schoolyear 523

Indexes 545

Preface

Teaching Language Arts, Second Edition, is designed for use as a main text in undergraduate and graduate language arts methods courses. This second edition takes a consistent student- and response-centered approach to literature-based teaching in today's culturally and linguistically diverse classroom. It's firmly grounded in current social constructivist learning theory combined with a reader-response perspective toward teaching with literature.

I hope to bring this vision of a classroom to life not only through clear explanations of these guiding principles but through examples of real teachers in real classrooms with real children, applying the ideas that have shaped the development of this second edition. Along with real-life examples, I've provided graphic organizers called "ripple effects," which demonstrate response-themed learning across the curriculum. Above all, I hope I've created a readable, student friendly, engaging, and practical text with a strong theoretical and research base.

Content of the Text

Teaching Language Arts is divided into five parts: Part I, Constructing a Foundation for Teaching Language Arts (Chapters 1–4); Part II, Spoken Language (Chapters 5–6); Part III, Literature and Reading (Chapters 7–8); Part IV, Written Language (Chapters 9–12); and Part V, Integrated Teaching (Chapters 13–14). In addition to the coverage of topics usually found in language arts texts, I've included separate chapters on drama and media literacy. In doing so, I've aimed to provide as broad a picture as possible of what it means to teach language arts in today's classroom. The content has also been enhanced with updated references and lesson and unit plans and strong coverage of reading and writing workshops and response-centered teaching with literature.

New to This Edition

Several new chapters have been added:

- **Chapter 3, Language and Cultural Diversity,** is devoted to teaching language arts in today's culturally and linguistically diverse classroom; it provides extensive discussion of second-language acquisition theory, teaching limited–English proficient students, and multicultural education.

• **Chapter 4, Emergent Literacy,** addresses first- and second-language and literacy development as a basis for teaching emerging readers and writers.

• **Chapter 10, Reading and Writing,** focuses on the connections between the reading and writing processes; five other chapters are also devoted to reading and writing.

An appendix has also been added, **Activities for the Schoolyear,** providing teaching ideas, lesson plans, and lists of children's books that coincide with seasons, events, holidays, and themes. Monthly units are included for September through June, carrying teachers and students through the schoolyear. Readers are encouraged to *remove* the appendix from this text and use it as a portable resource for planning and implementing creative classroom practice.

In addition to Chapter 3, readers will find that **linguistic and cultural diversity** are discussed throughout the text. Topics covered include emergent biliteracy, literature-based instruction for language-minority students, second-language acquisition and reading and writing, diversity and media literacy, and content-based English language development and sheltered instruction.

Special Features

• **Snapshots** give glimpses into real classrooms, showing the practical application of material discussed in the chapter and how ideas can be transformed into actions.

• **Lesson Plans and Teaching Ideas** offer specific suggestions and can readily be put into practice in the elementary classroom.

• **Chapter-opening questions** raise basic issues about the chapter topic. Following these questions, students are asked to write a Reflective Response, drawing on their own experiences and ideas. **Chapter-ending answers** go back to the same questions, providing summaries of chapter content.

• An **Assessment** section has been provided near the end of each chapter, addressing topics such as standardized versus authentic assessment, contextualized performance assessment, and student portfolios.

• **Looking Further,** another end-of-chapter feature, suggests opportunities for exploring chapter content more deeply: discussion questions, group activities focused on understanding how language is used, suggestions for observing and interacting with children, and ideas for participation and teaching applications to try out in the classroom.

• **Marginal notes** provide teaching tips, definitions, expanded explanations, citations of children's books, suggestions for further reading, and extensive cross-references to related sections of the book.

- **"Ripple Effects"** serve as graphic organizers of response-themed learning, offering extensive teaching ideas and lists of children's books. Each is related to chapter content and based on actual classroom experiences.

- **Visuals** richly illustrate the book, showing samples of children's drawings and writing and photos of actual teachers and children actually discussed in the text.

- Over 800 **children's books** are mentioned throughout as they're used in literature-based teaching. They're also listed in a separate References section at the end of each chapter and in a separate index, as well.

Acknowledgments

I've learned so much from the children I taught as an elementary teacher in Los Angeles, California, and Madison, Wisconsin, and from the preservice university students and inservice teachers I've taught and whose classrooms I've visited as a professor at Louisiana State University, in Baton Rouge, and at California State University, Long Beach. My special thanks goes to those I've written about in this book: Marjorie Abbott, Shelly Abesa, Paul Boyd-Batstone, Phyllis Crawford, Jaqui Denenberg, Audrey Eldridge, Avril Font, Phyllis Fuglaar, Marion Harris, Jennifer Howard, Gene Hughes, Mauretta Hurst, Sheila Kline, Lynn Lastrapes, Kathy Lee, Orlena MacKenzie, Margaret Mattson, Nora Miller, and Willa Richardson.

I've also written about the language and literacy development of my own three children—Wyatt, Gordon, and Elizabeth. Watching them grow has provided me an education not available through books or university classes. My husband, Stuart Spates, took all the photographs in this book, and our discussions about what we saw in elementary classrooms added another dimension to my writing. My family has always given me the support I've needed during the time it took to write both the first and second editions of this book. I especially liked it when they cheered when I came home after a long day at the computer.

Many reviewers have made excellent and insightful comments and suggestions and have done much to shape the content of this text. I especially thank those who said that the first edition of *Teaching Language Arts* had deeper, broader coverage of current practices in language arts education than other texts. They felt this book was slightly ahead of its time *then* but right in the mainstream *now*. My thanks go to Victoria Chou, University of Illinois–Chicago; Maggie Kirwin, College of St. Rose; Janet McClain, University of Northern Iowa; Karen F. Robertson, University of South Carolina; and Marie Schilling, Lancaster Bible College.

Reading Louise Rosenblatt's transactional theory gave me the explanatory power I needed to articulate my own classroom experiences and those of others with regard to teaching with literature, and her friendship and support for my research and writing efforts at putting theory into practice have also been much appreciated. I also acknowledge the California State University for funding my ongoing longitudinal research on the development of children's response to literature over a 7-year period.

Thanks also to Virginia Lanigan and Nihad Farooq of Allyn and Bacon, for the personal encouragement to be myself and for expert advice and support throughout the development of this second edition of *Teaching Language Arts*.

Carole Cox and her children (left to right): Wyatt, 25; Elizabeth, 11; and Gordon, 13.

Chapter 1

Learning and Teaching Language Arts

Questions about Learning and Teaching Language Arts

1. *What are the language arts?*
2. *How do children learn language arts?*
3. *How do you teach language arts?*

Reflective Response: What Are the Language Arts?

Think about the questions above, and jot down your ideas. Take a chance. Write whatever comes to mind in response to the term *language arts*. When you've finished, perhaps compare your response with those of other students in small groups or in a whole-class discussion with your instructor. Keep your ideas in mind as you read this chapter.

What Are the Language Arts?

The *language arts* have often been defined in elementary teaching as "listening, speaking, reading, and writing." But this definition is merely the tip of the iceberg. When I first thought about the questions you just responded to, I pictured the students I had when I was an elementary teacher, using language in the classroom. Sometimes, their use of language was audible and visible: talking in small groups or class discussions, writing in their journals or working together on a movie script, drawing illustrations for a book they were writing, constructing costumes or props for a play, singing, dancing, dramatizing, or laughing at each other's jokes. Other times, my students' language use was silent and invisible: listening as I read aloud, reading independently, or staring off into space, thinking about what they would write next.

In addition to the four topics commonly mentioned, the language arts also include language conventions: spelling, punctuation, grammar usage, and handwriting. And newer skills such as word processing are part of the language arts, as well. An important goal of teaching language arts is achieving literacy for all children. *Literacy* has often been defined in elementary teaching as "reading and writing." This is another narrow definition. Today, the meaning of literacy may include a range of abilities, from biliteracy (the ability to read and write in more than one language) to computer and media literacy.

As an elementary teacher, you will also face the exciting task of integrating all the language arts across the curriculum. Whatever subject or grade you teach, the medium of communication used will be language, in any one of its many forms. It would be an oversimplification, however, to suggest that the importance of language arts in school is simply as a vehicle to learn other subject matter. Language is a system of communicating that offers countless possibilities for representation, expression, and thought. It's certainly much more than a tool. It permeates human thought and life.

TABLE 1.1 The Language Arts

Oral Language	*Literacy*
Listening and speaking	Reading and writing
sharing	literature
planning	newspapers
conversations	environmental print
dialogues	journals
discussions	drawings
conferences	stories
reading aloud	research
drama	reference books
singing	written reports
storytelling	conventions: spelling, punctuation, grammar usage
oral reports	handwriting
media listening and viewing	word processing and computer literacy

Accordingly, language arts is more than just a subject. It's part of everything that happens in the classroom. You are a language arts teacher all day long. Table 1.1 is a simple list of the content of the language arts. You should jot down any other ideas you have and continue to do so as you read this book and think about the question: What are the language arts?

SNAPSHOT: A Day in Avril Font's Fourth-Grade Class

Let's take a look into one teacher's classroom to see how she teaches language arts all day long. It's an April morning, and the schoolday has just begun in Avril Font's fourth-grade class at Ryan Elementary School in the small community of Scotlandville, just outside Baton Rouge, Louisiana. As you read this Snapshot, note *when* and *how* you think Avril is teaching language arts.

9:00–9:15 Business (Teacher) and Journals, Newspapers, and Books (Students)

While Avril takes care of business like taking attendance, making the lunch count, and talking to a parent, the children choose to do one of three language and literacy experiences:

1. write in their journals
2. read the newspaper
3. read a book

Everyone in Avril Font's fourth-grade classroom enjoys sharing time.

9:15–9:45 Sharing with the Whole Class

Avril tells the class to meet her in the reading center. It's a comfortable place, surrounded with bookshelves. There's a big rug on the floor, which is covered with pillows for the children, and there are two old recliners—one for Avril, the other for students. After everyone settles in, Avril and the children talk about things that are important to them:

Avril: OK, let's share.
Child: Mrs. Font, my Paw Paw made things out of acorns for a craft show. I'll bring them in to show.
Avril: That's a neat idea for a story. Why don't you get your writing folder and jot down some ideas?
Child: OK.
Child: I got an idea of something to write about. I put a glass on the door to listen to my older sister talk on the phone. But I couldn't hear.
Avril: Try putting it on the wall. I bet that will work.

(One child reads from a book that's often used during sharing. It tells what's special about each day.)

Child: Hey, it says here that it's William Shakespeare's birthday today.
Avril: Who is he?
Child: A famous writer.
Child: He wrote poetry.
Child: He wrote literature.
Avril: Right. He wrote plays and poetry. Have you ever heard of *Romeo and Juliet?*
Child: Yeah.
Child: Over Easter, I watched Channel 27, and they had *Romeo and Juliet*, scene 2.

The words *Paw Paw* are commonly used in Southern Louisiana to mean "grandfather."

How to Make a Writing Folder
For each student, use a ready-made manila folder or create one by folding a piece of 11" × 18" construction paper in half. Staple a piece of paper inside to jot down "Ideas to Write About." Have the student decorate the cover and add a title like "My Writing." Keep all the student's works in progress in it.

The Book of Days (Donaldson & Donaldson, 1979)

9:45–10:00 Planning the Day

During sharing time, Avril observed children's responses to topics of interest that emerged. Now, she thinks about ways to center learning experiences around those responses and to merge them with subjects suggested in the curriculum guide as well as with seasonal and special events. Note that the way in which she provides for children's responses as they plan the day together helps them organize into groups for different subjects that will become integrated through language arts and literacy activities.

Avril picks a student to be Secretary of the Day, whose job is to record ideas on the chalkboard under the regular headings "Language Arts and Reading" and "Social Studies and Science," written in colored chalk. Children will do these activities throughout the day during several group workshop times. Not everyone will do the same activities at the same time, but they each will do all the subjects sometime during the day. Avril believes that this approach helps students learn to take control and responsibility for their work and time.

Avril: What are we doing in language arts?
Child: I'm going to start a story about pizza.
Avril: Why?
Child: 'Cause my mama works in a pizza place.

(Other children also talk about what they're writing about.)

Avril: Good. All of you keep writing on your own stories. Shane might want to start a story about his Paw Paw and the acorns. We'll get them ready to make into books. Sign up for turns on the computer. Write in your journals. What about reading?
Child: I have a new library book about sharks. How they eat people.
Avril: Sounds terrific. We'll have sustained silent reading (SSR) after recess, and you can get started reading it. Those of you who have finished your basal reader story can take the test. Continue to read your library books, and everyone read the newspaper. After lunch, I'll read the next chapter of *The Wind in the Willows* aloud.

Avril's district requires students to take basal tests, so she has them read the stories and take the tests; however, she doesn't do direct instruction with basal readers. Avril's students do well on these tests. She was named Louisiana Reading Teacher of the Year in 1992.

Here's what Edreka, the Secretary of the Day, has written on the chalkboard:

Language Arts and Reading

Write own stories. Use computer.
Journals.
Bookmaking.
SSR after recess.
Take basal test if finished basal reader story.
Read library book.
Read newspaper.
Mrs. Font reads The Wind in the Willows.

St. George and the Dragon (Spenser, 1984), a Caldecott Award–winning book illustrated by Trina Schart Hyman.

Next, Avril and the class will plan social studies and science together. The children will work together in small groups. Note the many ways in which language arts integrate the content:

Avril: OK, let's plan social studies for today. Who would like to go to the library and research William Shakespeare? (Several hands go up.) When you come back, talk about what you find with each other and begin to think about how you might share your research with everybody else. What else are we doing in social studies?

Child: St. George and the dragon. We're working on making a big dragon costume for our play of when St. George kills the dragon. We read about it in this book.

Avril: You're doing a terrific job with your research and play. What else?

Child: The maypole group. We have to practice the maypole dance. We did well yesterday.

Avril: Yes, you really did. I brought the maypole ribbons. Aren't they great? What about your science research and reports and posters on animals?

Child: Me and him want to do guppies. My cousin got 'em in an aquarium.

Avril: Why don't you two see if you can find out how to make an aquarium?

Child: OK! Can we go to the library?

Avril: Yes. Take some notes, get some books, and we'll make plans to do it.

Avril and her students also discuss plans for mathematics. Again, students will work in small groups, using their math books and a lot of manipulatives and games. Avril will monitor their progress and work with several small groups during the day. Here's what Edreka has written on the board for social studies and science:

Social Studies and Science

New Shakespeare group to library.
St. George and dragon group work on play.
Maypole dance practice.
Animal reports and posters.
New guppy group to library.

Avril helps the children plan which activity they'll do in the first-hour block of group workshop after recess. Some will go to the writing center, some to the library, and some will work on social studies, science, and mathematics activities. The children will rotate to other subjects during the afternoon group workshop time.

10:00–10:15 Recess

10:15–11:15 Group Workshop

As the children work, Avril moves among the small groups, interacting with them as she guides and monitors their progress. She does many on-the-spot conferences with individual children or groups, as needed. But for the most part, she expects the children to be self-directed.

Writing Center. The writing center is a long table that has space for six children to sit and write together. (The other children write alone at their desks.) Plastic tubs hold student writing folders and supplies, including many types of paper, pencils, and erasers. The writing center is located near a bulletin board, which provides space to display student writing, and a chalkboard, which comes in handy for group brainstorming and outlining of ideas. The computer center is next to the table in the center.

Several students are writing and discussing their stories with each other and Avril:

> *Child* (reading aloud, savoring the sound): "My Day at the Movies," by Lestreca.
>
> *Avril:* May I read it? (Reads story.) I like it. It seems a bit long in places, though. Read it to me and see what you think.

While Lestreca and Avril talk about the story, Mina works on her book, *My Mom the Seamstress.* She asks Avril to help her think of other words for *seamstress.* Together, they look in the thesaurus and find the word *couturiere.* Mina chooses it because she remembers that's what her mother was called in Japan, where she went to school and learned to sew without using patterns.

Students use language and learn together in group workshops.

Social Studies Groups. Avril moves among the groups, who are working on different topics. One group is preparing to do the maypole dance and write a report on it:

Avril: Where is the maypole gang? (Several children are on the floor, arranging the ribbons for the dance and reading books about countries that celebrate May Day.)
Child: Mrs. Font, what's this word?
Avril: Czechoslovakia. It's a country in Europe.
Child: Yeah. I was gonna say that. (Spelling aloud.) C-z-e-c-h-o-s-l-o-v-a-k-i-a. (Snapping her fingers as she says each syllable. Czech- (snap) o- (snap) slo- (snap) vak- (snap) i- (snap) a- (snap)! Right?
Avril: Right!
Child: Look. It says in this book that in Czechoslovakia, boys put trees under their sweetheart's window on May Day.
Child: Mrs. Font, there was an article about the maypole dance in the newspaper, but it didn't explain why it's danced.
Child: They don't know much.
Child: They could read about it in the encyclopedia or these books.
Avril: You read a lot. I'm impressed.

Next, Avril moves to the group doing a play of the story of "St. George and the Dragon." They're reading and talking about how to make a dragon costume:

Child: Mrs. Font, me and him want to know, were there really dragons?
Avril: Try looking up what we call "dragons" today. I think there are some big reptiles on the Galapagos Islands. Try the atlas.
Child: I thought everything was in the dictionary.
Child: No, 'cause it's the name of a place.

The students talk some more and tell Avril what kinds of supplies they need to make the dragon costume: big pieces of cardboard, twine, colored butcher paper, and poster paint and brushes. And they figure out that talcum powder, coming out of the dragon's snout, will look like smoke. Avril tells the group that they should bring up their plans during sharing and planning tomorrow to see if anyone in the class might have some of these things.

The Shakespeare group has just returned from the library with books, and they're very excited. They've been reading, taking notes, and talking about Shakespeare's life. They continue talking about how to share what they find out about this author with the rest of the class:

Child: Mrs. Font, it says he served with a company of actors. (She makes a "V for victory" sign.) I want to be an actress.
Child: It says here that he wrote "Mary Had a Little Lamb."
Avril: Are you sure?

Child: Uh-hmm. It says!
Avril: Read it again.
Child (reading): Oh. It says his plays were written as stories for children by Charles and Mary Lamb.
Avril: That's how I read Shakespeare when I was young (see Lamb & Lamb, 1957). Why don't you see if you can find that book in the library? And look for other books that tell the stories of his plays.

Tales from Shakespeare (Lamb & Lamb, 1957). See Chapter 6, Drama in the Classroom, for more children's books on Shakespeare.

Science Groups. The children tell Avril about their research on different animals and the posters they're making to share what they find with the rest of the class. The new guppy group has just returned from the library, and they're looking forward to making an aquarium:

Child: Mrs. Font, we got some books on aquariums. They tell how to make one, so we're gonna read and start working on our own.
Child (reading about animals in a book): Mrs. Font, what does *droppings* mean? It says, "But their presence is revealed by their tracks and droppings."
Avril: Try looking it up in the dictionary.
Child (returning with dictionary): Mrs. Font, I still don't get it.
Avril: I'll tell you what it is: It's when animals go to the bathroom, the little brown things they leave behind. *Excrement.*
Child: You mean like dog doo?
Avril: Yes.

11:15–11:45 Sustained Silent Reading

Everyone reads a book of his or her choice, including Avril. They all get comfortable. Some sit at desks, and some sit in the two recliner chairs. Others are nestled in bean bag chairs or stretched out on the rug. It's absolutely quiet. Everyone's reading.

11:45–12:15 Lunch

12:15–12:30 Read Aloud

As mentioned earlier, during read-aloud time, Avril reads from Kenneth Grahame's (1980) classic book *The Wind in the Willows.* Students can respond or ask questions, and Avril does, too. It's a great time to listen to and enjoy literature, respond openly to it, and talk about words, ideas, characters, and events in the book.

12:30–1:30 Group Workshop

This afternoon group workshop is similar to the morning session except that the children rotate subjects and activities. Once again, Avril observes and has conferences with students. Today, the maypole group is practicing outside the room, getting ready for a Friday visit from the local newspaper, who will take pictures and write an article.

1:30–2:00 Physical Education

2:00–3:00 Group Workshop

In this session, the children either rotate and work in a new area or continue with a big project. The "St. George and the Dragon" group started to build the dragon costume in the last group workshop and made a big mess. (They were practicing blowing talcum powder out of the dragon's snout.) Since they already had all their materials out, the group has continued working on the costume.

The day ends at 3:00.

Key Ideas for Learning and Teaching Language Arts

After school, I asked Avril, "What beliefs and knowledge guide your teaching of language arts?" Here's her answer:

> I believe that teaching language arts should be student and response centered. Children should be actively engaged in using language and focused on meaning. It should stem from the ideas, interests, language, and unique talents of each child. Why Shakespeare? Because someone noticed it was his birthday when reading *A Book of Days* (Donaldson & Donaldson, 1979), which they like. It was the same place they found out about St. George and the dragon and the maypole and decided they wanted to learn how to do the maypole dance. It was relevant to their interests, and I used their responses as a guide. Why read and write and draw and make books and build things like aquariums? The texts are boring. I love science and believe that children learn by doing. We do all hands-on science. We construct things and dramatize during social studies. We learn to read by reading and to write by writing. We use literature as texts and children's response to literature as a basis for activities. We work as a collaborative team. Students work together in groups, but their work is individual, stemming from their own ideas, interests, and responses. They just spend a lot of time sharing, planning, discussing, and helping each other.

Avril's beliefs and knowledge about how children learn language arts reflect a *social constructivist* point of view. Her beliefs about children's experiences with literature reflect the *transactional model* of the reading process. These theories also underlie the approach to teaching recommended in this book. The key ideas of that approach are:

- Learning language arts is:

  an active, constructive process that takes place when students are engaged in what they are doing and focused on the discovery of meaning

  a social, interactive process that takes place when students work collaboratively with each other and the teacher

  a transactional process between the reader and a text during each experience with literature

- The student's role involves:

  choice, voice, control, and responsibility

- The teacher's role involves:

  initiation, observation, demonstration, and expectation

- The curriculum is founded on:

  response-themed learning, in which transactions among learners, resources, and experiences are recognized and integrated in teaching all subject areas

We will look at each of these key ideas later in this chapter. They are summarized in Table 1.2, including examples of classroom experiences.

Learning Language Arts

An Active, Constructive Process

The constructivist theory of learning or cognitive development put forth by Jean Piaget (1973, 1977) maintains that learning is an active process in which the learner constructs meaning. This idea is also behind John Dewey's (1938) famous expression "learning by doing," which means that we discover or construct concepts by actively participating in our environments.

Piaget believed that children are able to construct a view of reality that's based on what they learn as they mature and also what they experience in their lives. In other words, they learn throughout their lives by exploring and discovering new things. Learning is a process of adding new bits of information to what they already know. Given this, the teacher's role is (1) to be aware of how children learn and develop and (2) to provide an environment and initiate experiences that help children engage in the active construction of meaning and knowledge about themselves and the world.

According to Piaget (1973, 1977), young children learn to organize their experiences and adapt to the environment through the processes of assimilation, accommodation, and equilibration. *Assimilation* is classifying an object into an already existing mental category or operation. Have you ever watched a baby try to put anything and everything into its mouth, including its feet? Piaget would say that the baby is assimilating new objects through the old process of

TABLE 1.2 Key Ideas for Learning and Teaching Language Arts: Classroom Experiences

Learning Language Arts	***Student's Role***	***Teacher's Role***	***Curriculum***
Active, constructive process: focused on meaning; learn by doing (listening, speaking, reading, and writing); hands-on experiences	*Choice:* books to read, writing topics, research topics, and student groups	*Initiation:* plans sharing, organizes groups, literature lessons, builds on student's responses	*Response themed:* content based on topics of interest to students and curriculum guides and seasonal events
Social interactive process: collaboration, sharing, planning, group workshops, and conferences	*Voice:* open discussions, personal journals, own stories, response to books, and drama	*Observation:* listens and watches; holds conferences (on the spot, scheduled, individual, and group)	*Integrated:* language used across the curriculum; read and write to learn in other subjects (social studies, science, math, and arts)
Transactional process: between reader and text; open response to literature and other texts	*Control:* topics of interest, monitor progress, make decisions about what and how to learn	*Demonstration:* reads aloud, shows needed skill or strategy	
	Responsibility: to read and write daily, to manage time	*Expectations:* to stay focused, to read and write, and to work cooperatively	

eating. That is, the baby is using something it already knows how to do—eating—to try to put unknown things into an existing mental category—things that can be put into its mouth. When my son Gordon was just learning to speak, he saw the beautiful French film *The Red Balloon* (1956); after that, he called every balloon a "red balloon." He also called every small animal a "kitty" in those early days. These are examples of assimilation, or classifying an object into an already existing mental category or operation.

Accommodation is adjusting a mental category or operation to include new objects and experiences in the environment. Gordon had to adjust his mental category of "balloons" one day when he was asked if he wanted a yellow, pink, or blue balloon at the grand opening of a toy store. He responded "red balloon," but the clerk said they didn't have any red ones and offered the other colors again. Gordon was temporarily in a state of disequilibrium, unable to fit this new information into what he already knew. He looked confused and longingly at the balloons, thought about it, and finally said that he wanted a yellow, pink, *and* blue balloon. He had adjusted, or accommodated, his existing category of "balloons" to include not only red balloons but a new phenomenon: balloons of different colors.

Equilibration is the self-regulatory process by which a balance is achieved between assimilation and accommodation. Through the ongoing, interacting processes of assimilation and accommodation, children construct increasingly sophisticated understandings of their environments. They continually add new information to their existing base of ideas. For example, after Gordon visited a petting zoo and had the chance to hold and pat some rabbits, he stopped calling all small animals "kitties" and learned to call rabbits "bunnies."

The concepts that are constructed during the ongoing processes of assimilation, accommodation, and equilibration are called *schemata*. Schemata are already existing knowledge structures. Think of them as comprising a sort of organizational chart or map, to which new details are constantly being added. Gordon was constructing schemata for balloons and small animals as he added what he learned about each from new experiences to his prior knowledge base. After learning that "bunnies" weren't "kitties," he continued to add new information to his existing schema about small animals by looking at pictures and books and taking more trips to the zoo.

Piaget's great contribution to learning theory, which was later supported by schema theory (Anderson, 1977; Rumelhart & Ortony, 1977), was to identify the importance of connecting new experiences to prior knowledge and organizing that new information. We make those connections through schemata. Children learn when they connect what they already know with what they discover through new experiences.

Piaget's theories and stages of development will be explained further in Chapter 2, Children and Language.

The *psycholinguistic theory* of the reading process, espoused by Kenneth Goodman (1972), adds to what we know about how children learn to use language. Goodman believes that by building on what they already know, children anticipate or make predictions about what will happen next, finally achieving an equilibrium and constructing new meaning. This theory is clearly linked to Piaget's notion of the disequilibrium that's necessary to encourage children to wonder about new things and to adapt them to existing schemata. Recall Gordon's initial confusion and then understanding when he figured out that balloons come in different colors and that there's more than one kind of small animal.

In practical terms, Goodman's psycholinguistic theory suggests that while reading, children should be encouraged to make guesses about what will happen next in a story and then to test those guesses against what they already know. In doing so, children discovering the meaning of the story for themselves. Goodman stresses the need for children to have time to read whole, meaningful texts in order to draw on the rich combination of graphic, syntactic, and semantic cueing systems of language.

Frank Smith (1988) maintains that "children learn when they have opportunities and reason to use language and critical thinking personally, . . . from what is demonstrated to them, from what they see others doing" (p. 55). With regard specifically to reading, Smith (1992) believes that the student's knowledge of the world is what brings meaning to the printed page.

A Social, Interactive Process

The social interactionist theory of Lev Vygotsky (1962) proposes that children learn through meaningful interactions with their environments and other people and that these are essential factors in the development of new knowledge. Whereas Piaget suggested that children's learning is an individual, internalized cognitive process that does not depend on adult support, Vygotsky emphasizes the social, contextual nature of learning and language. For example, children learn to talk by listening to their parents, siblings, and others and eventually talking back. Similarly, children learn to read and write by having others read to them, by participating in shared storybook readings and writing events, and by eventually reading and writing on their own.

See Chapter 4, Emergent Literacy, for much more on how young children learn to read and write.

A key idea in Vygotsky's (1978) theory is the *zone of proximal development:* "the distance between the actual developmental level as determined by independent problem solving and the level of potential development as determined through problem solving under adult guidance or in collaboration with more capable peers" (p. 76). This means that children learn when they are supported by others who know more than they do—for instance, teachers, parents, and even peers. (We'll discuss the zone of proximal development more in Chapter 2.)

Vygotsky's theories with reference to language development will be further explained in Chapter 2, Children and Language.

Jerome Bruner (1983) describes the support that adults give children as a "scaffold" for building new knowledge, moving children from one level of development to another. This support, or scaffolding, is only temporary, however; it's withdrawn as children develop and grow. But then it's replaced by new scaffolding: that is, by new knowledge that's been constructed through meaningful social interaction. The teacher—whether the classroom instructor or an advanced student peer—takes into account what the student already knows and uses that as a basis for providing support in new problem-solving situations. This represents a true interaction between the learner and the teacher. The teacher uses what the learner already knows as a foundation, and the learner builds on the scaffold provided by the teacher to gain knowledge.

A social constructivist framework also takes into account the unique cultural aspect of each classroom (Spindler, 1982) as well as the role of the family and the cultural and linguistic background of each child (Heath, 1983). Based on this framework, learning occurs in a particular context, which will vary from class to class and year to year (Green & Meyer, 1990). For instance, ideas and expectations will never be exactly the same. It's important for the teacher to initiate, observe, demonstrate, and set expectations based on the uniqueness of each child, group, and class.

Experiencing Literature

Literature-based teaching is currently considered an excellent approach to teaching language arts, developing literacy, and integrating the curriculum through the use of rich and authentic works of art, such as children's picture books and fiction and nonfiction tradebooks (Cox & Zarrillo, 1993; Cullinan,

1987, 1992; Huck, Hepler, & Hickman, 1993). We will consider many possible ways to approach teaching with literature in this book, especially in Chapters 7 and 8 on literature and reading, respectively.

A Transactional Process

The *transactional model* of the reading process, developed by Louise Rosenblatt (1938/1983), focuses on the active role of the reader in creating meaning from text. Rosenblatt is the reader-response theorist who first challenged the idea that meaning can be found solely in the text or that the reader's job is to figure out what the author means. Rather, Rosenblatt and other reader-response theorists (Bleich, 1975; Britton, 1970) believe that the reader and the text/author construct meaning together. According to Rosenblatt (1986), making meaning while reading and responding is "a complex, to-and-fro, self-correcting transaction between reader and verbal signs which continues until some final organization, more or less complete and coherent, is arrived at and thought of as corresponding to the text. The 'meaning'—whether, e.g., poem, novel, play, scientific report, or legal brief—comes into being during the transaction" (1986, p. 123).

Rosenblatt describes this process as a "two-way transaction" or "live circuit" between the reader and text. Actually, she borrowed the term *transaction* from John Dewey, who defined it as a reciprocal relationship among the parts in a single situation; this is in contrast to the term *interaction,* which involves two separate entities acting on one another. "Language . . . should not be seen as a self-contained, ungrounded, ready-made code of signifiers and signified, but as embodied in transactions between individuals and their social and natural context" (Rosenblatt, 1986, p. 122).

Obviously, this point of view not only gives young readers more choice and control and an opportunity to use their voices in response to literature; it also gives them more responsibility. Although the teacher may initiate experiences with literature, he or she will not set predetermined outcomes, such as having everyone agree on what the author meant in the story or doing a book report that must include setting, plot, character, mood, and theme. Rather, the teacher will encourage children to respond openly, drawing on their own fund of prior experiences and impressions while reading to construct a meaningful interpretation of the text. The focus of learning and teaching is on the students' responses or personal evocations of the text, not on the teacher's ideas (which are often based on teachers' guides prepared by somebody else) or even on the text itself.

In transactional teaching, teachers demonstrate this focus by asking open questions—So what did you think of it?—and by sharing their own personal responses. Teachers also expect students to do the same and to extend their responses to the book and develop interpretations through further language and literacy experiences. Students share responsibility for their learning by making choices when responding, by using their own voices, and by gaining control over their ideas and language.

See Chapter 7, Teaching with Literature, for more on Rosenblatt's transactional theory.

Teaching Language Arts

A Student- and Response-Centered Classroom

In a student- and response-centered classroom like Avril Font's, you'll notice that children are active and that they learn by doing. Students learn to talk by talking, to read by reading, and to write by writing. The teacher's role is to help them gain control over their own ideas and language through active engagement with learning experiences that are focused on the construction of meaning. Student- and response-centered language and literacy experiences can be defined as those that originate with the ideas, interests, and language of children. This is the alternative that John Dewey (1943) described of creating schools to fit students, rather than making all students learn the same thing, in the same way. In this type of school, teachers make time to let children share and plan together, to listen to and observe children expressing their ideas, and to make plans based on these ideas.

You may be more familiar with the opposite approach, a more traditional teacher- and text-centered classroom. In fact, you may have spent many years in classrooms like this: sitting in rows, always raising your hand to speak, listening to the teacher give directions, doing the same worksheet as everyone else, and so on. Do you remember reading groups? Even though the groups had names like Lions, Tigers, and Bears, you and your classmates all knew that you were grouped by ability and who was in the high, medium, and low groups. And finally, do you remember spelling: folding your paper in thirds and copying the list of 20 spelling words three times, even though you already knew how to spell all the words (or if you didn't, you didn't care)?

This description is only a slight exaggeration of what can be characterized as a teacher- and text-centered classroom. This type of classroom reflects the psychological theory of *behaviorism* and a *transmission model* of teaching. Educational applications of behaviorist learning theory were made popular in the 1950s by B. F. Skinner. Early behaviorists, particularly Ivan Pavlov, conducted experiments with animals in laboratories. You may have heard of Pavlov's dogs, who salivated in response to a ringing bell that signaled meal time. Behaviorists believe that learning follows a formula of *stimulus-response conditioning,* according to which acceptable responses are reinforced.

Teaching based on the behaviorist view would resemble what went on in the traditional classroom just described. In that type of classroom, teaching language, specifically, was based on the belief that children learn through a process of environmental conditioning and by imitating adult models. Teachers conditioned students' learning by modeling behaviors that the students were to imitate. If the students imitated those behaviors correctly, they received *positive reinforcement,* such as praise or rewards. And if they didn't, they received *negative reinforcement,* such as criticism or even punishment.

According to this traditional behaviorist approach, language learning was not believed to be instinctive. Moreover, language was supposedly learned in small increments, called *skills.* Mastering those skills meant that an individual learned them, one by one, and built up a repertoire until he or she could read

In a student- and response-centered classroom, children are active and learn by doing.

and write. For example, children learned to read first by mastering the letters of the alphabet, then combining letters to master words, and then combining words to master sentences. Learning to read was thought to be a step-by-step, cumulative process, each step building on the previous one. The basal readers used to teach reading in this way had "scope and sequences" of these skills, prepared for each grade and building on the grade before.

This traditional view we've been discussing—based on behaviorism and transmission—is called a *top-down* or *part-to-whole* approach to learning to use language. It's quite different from the *bottom-up* or *whole-to-part* approach we'll follow in this book. According to that approach, children learn to use language by using it when they are surrounded by print and when they have many rich social interactive experiences with language that focus on meaning. This learning goes on from the time children are babies through their school years and beyond.

As mentioned earlier, this current view is based on theories of learning like those of Piaget and Vygotsky and literary theories like Rosenblatt's transactional model of the reading process. Research by Walter Loban (1976, 1979) has also demonstrated that the language modes function together as children learn to use and control language. In a longitudinal study of the language development of 338 children in grades K–12 (kindergarten through twelfth grade), Loban found a strong positive correlation among reading, writing, listening, and speaking abilities; that is, ability in one usually indicated the presence of ability in others. But according to Loban, the most important element in learning to use language is to use it: "The development of power and efficiency with language derives from using language for genuine purposes and not from studying about it. The path to power over language is to use it, to use it in genuinely meaningful situations, whether we are reading, listening, writing, or speaking" (1979, p. 485).

Many teachers today are making a transition from the transmission model to the constructivist model, often referred to as the *whole-language model.* (See, for example, Regie Routman's book *Invitations* [1991].) Avril Font and I have talked about the fact that some of us have *always* believed in the constructivist model, and it hasn't necessarily been easy. Yet when given the choice between students and their ideas versus textbooks and other curriculum materials in boxes, we've always chosen the students. For me, the constructivist approach intuitively provided the best way to watch how children learn and how engaged they are when they ask their own questions and try to find their own answers.

What's more, I never felt that adhering to the constructivist approach diminished my role as a teacher. To the contrary, I felt my role expanded tremendously as I continually observed and reflected on what my students were doing on a minute-to-minute basis. In a single week, I might spend hours conferencing with students; use recess and lunch hours to get on the phone and track down things students needed; arbitrate small-group discussions and dissensions; arrange for use of the auditorium or for the newspaper to cover something we're doing; solicit parents' help for drama productions or science activities; and note children's progress as I simultaneously watch for the initiative they take and the ideas they generate. The ideas that children have for themselves are always richer than those I have for them.

I put myself in the general "stew," too. I love reading and writing as well as art, music, dance, and drama. Even though my students, years ago, first suggested to me that we do Shakespeare, I evolved it into a citywide program in Madison, Wisconsin, that's still in existence. And it didn't take much for my students to convince me to play music and to dance in connection with whatever we were doing at the time. Art history books, posters, and slides were a regular part of my teaching, as well. So were walks, fieldtrips, and guest speakers—especially parents who had talents to share with students. I love movies, so we watched a lot of films and made them ourselves, just as we made books, wrote letters to the editor of the newspaper, and created play scripts to express our ideas. The "bottom line" for me, though, was my students' interests, ideas, and level of active engagement in response to whatever we were doing.

To help you picture the conceptual differences between a traditional, teacher- and text-centered classroom and a student- and response-centered classroom (like Avril's), the following lists compare what the teacher and student do in each:

Teacher- and Text-Centered Classroom

Teacher

- makes all decisions for what's to be learned
- uses textbooks and commercial materials

Student

- is a passive recipient of learning
- imitates what the teacher has modeled

- uses teachers' guides for text-book series
- emphasizes part-to-whole learning
- follows a sequence of skills to be mastered
- believes the product is more important than the process
- believes that motivation is external; uses rewards
- evaluates based on test questions that have single correct answers

- follows directions of the teacher or textbook
- is evaluated on mastery of skills in a hierarchical order
- is grouped by ability
- does the same assignments as other students
- is evaluated by comparing work to that of other students
- is competitive with other students

Student- and Response-Centered Classroom

Teacher
- initiates hands-on, direct experiences
- provides opportunities for independent learning
- uses children's literature and student writing
- believes that learning is whole to part
- believes that the process is more important than the product
- provides options and demon-strates possibilities
- groups students based on interests, which are flexible and may change
- incorporates time for sharing and planning
- conferences frequently with students
- observes and listens to students, honoring student voices
- uses ideas and interests of students as the basis of thematic learning
- recognizes that even though all children go through a similar process and stages, not all do so at the same pace or in same way
- encourages cooperation and collaboration among students

Student
- makes choices about what to read, how to respond, what to learn about
- learns by doing; active engagement
- explores and discovers things on own
- works with others in groups, which which are flexible and can change
- interacts, cooperates, and collaborates
- reads self-selected literature
- writes on topics of own choosing
- has intrinsic motivation
- is responsible for and has control over learning

The following sections look at ways to create a student- and response-centered classroom, addressing curriculum content, classroom environment and learning centers, scheduling and grouping, materials and resources, and the ripple effects of response-themed learning. Each section begins with an example from the Snapshot of Avril Font's class.

Curriculum Content

Avril Font uses three sources in planning curriculum content: (1) state and district curriculum guides; (2) seasonal and special events through the year; and (3) students' ideas and interests.

> In the morning, we come together as a class to share and plan. And of course, we have special subjects as a whole class: library, P.E., music, French, and guidance. But the rest of the day, students move through the different subjects individually and work primarily in small groups. The subjects we designate are reading, language arts, math, social studies, and science—traditional subjects. But we choose topics as a class or individually and integrate all subjects.

For example, animal study is recommended by state curriculum guides, learning the maypole dance was related to the spring season, and Shakespeare came up as a topic during sharing. All three subjects involve language and literacy experiences, however. Avril artfully blends them together, always leaving the way open for topics students are interested in:

> My favorite day or week is Do Nothing, something I reserve for when we don't have any particular topic. But something usually comes up. We had a great Hurricane Day this year. As we were wondering if the hurricane would hit us here in Louisiana, students wrote wonderful haiku and other poetry. We watched the weather change daily, tracked the hurricane on charts, and studied hurricanes in depth.

It's easy to find out about state and district curriculum suggestions and seasonal and special events. But how do you find out about your students' ideas and interests? Here are some practical ways:

- *Sharing:* Provide regular time every day for sharing at all grade levels. It's important to let children know that they can share significant experiences at school. These sharing periods will become a primary source of information for your teaching.

See Chapter 9, The Writing Process, for more on types of journals and books in journal format.

- *Journals:* Provide time for students to write every day. You should write, too. Some variations on keeping individual journals are dialogue journals (teachers, aides, or other students write back and forth) and community journals (in which anyone can write observations in a journal stationed by the window, aquarium, or pet cage, for example). Or read a book in journal format, such as *Three Days on a River in a Red Canoe* (Williams, 1981).

• *Star of the Week:* Have one child per week be the "star," who gets to create a bulletin board and table display to share things that are important to him or her. Provide time to share these things and answer questions from other students. Record students' questions and answers on chartpaper and display or videotape them. Or turn information about the "star" into a short biography; prepare it on the computer and print a booklet, which other students can illustrate and give to the individual. Students can also write fan letters to the star. The first week of school, have everybody bring a picture for a Class Stars bulletin board. The second week, do a display about yourself—baby pictures and all. Let the children ask you questions to model the procedure.

Star of the Week items: photographs, awards, letters, books, mementos, crafts, and so on.

• *Autobiographies:* Have students write autobiographies the first few weeks of school. Set aside a period to develop guiding questions together: Where and when were you born? Tell about your family. What are your hobbies? You should write one, too.

• *Memoirs:* Encourage students to write their personal memoirs, as writing based on students' personal experiences can be the richest kind. See, for example, Figure 1.1, which presents Benton's book *The Lie That Mrs. Font Told My Mommy,* in which he writes about a time that his mother came to talk to Avril.

• *Conferences:* Ask children about themselves during planning and writing conferences and conference with parents.

• *Interviews:* Pair students and have them interview each other; after that, have them share the information about their partners with the class. By having partners ask open, simple, and positive questions, all children should be able to create positive portraits of themselves. For instance: Tell me about yourself. What are your favorite things? What are you interested in?

Avril Font conferences with a student.

Cover

1

2

3

FIGURE 1.1
Student's Book, Written about a Personal Experience

Classroom Environment

Avril Font's classroom is an example of an environment that puts the principles of student- and response-centered teaching into practice (see Figure 1.2). We talked about the reading center earlier as a good place for getting comfortable during sharing, planning with a friend, or curling up with a good book.

Around the reading center are seven tables, formed by pushing four student desks together. Each of these tables can be a home base for four children working together. Two large tables are designated work centers, providing materials and space for group work in writing, science, and mathematics.

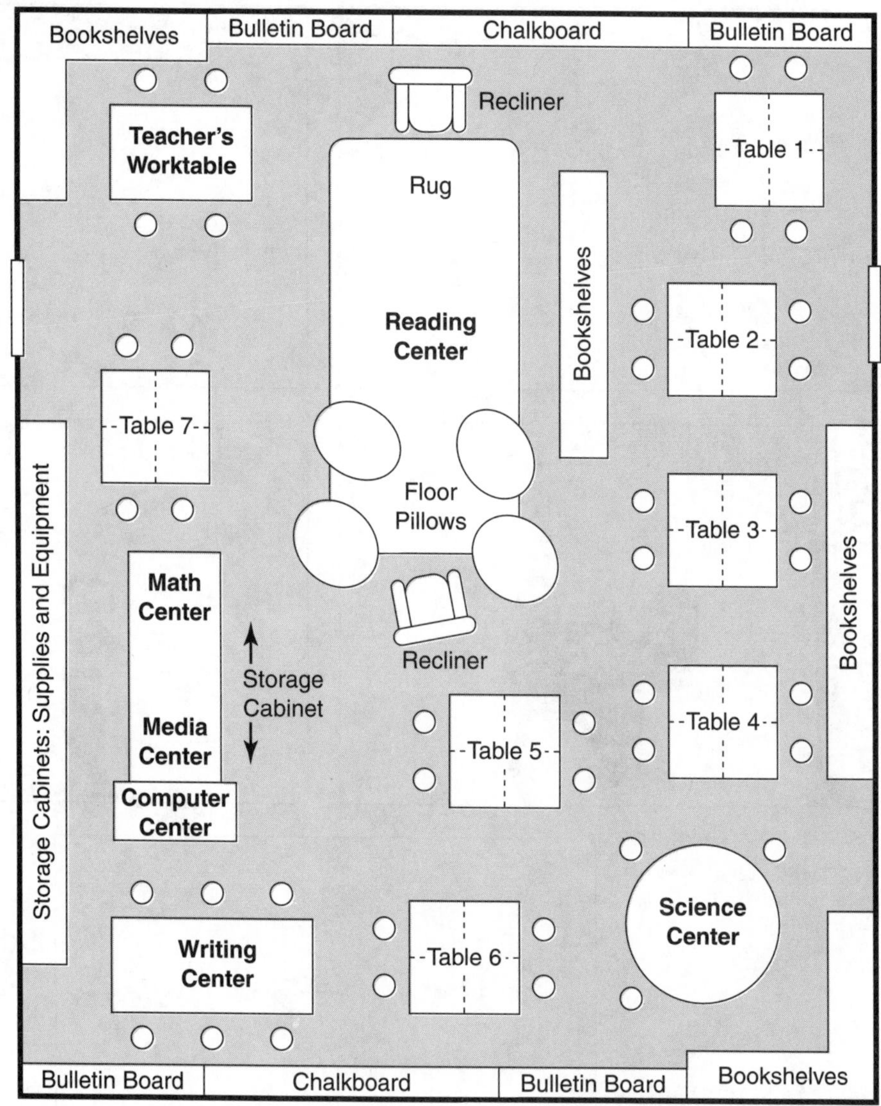

FIGURE 1.2 Diagram of Avril Font's Classroom

Two other qualities of Avril Font's classroom are important:

1. The classroom is a *print-rich environment,* full of children's literature—fiction and nonfiction, two daily newspapers, magazines, reference books, textbooks, and books and reports written by the children themselves. To create this kind of environment, your classroom should include a library, posters, bulletin boards, labels, and displays of children's writing and art.
2. The classroom is organized into a variety of *centers,* or work areas that are movable and flexible. There are clear table surfaces for large art

and construction projects, open floor spaces for movement and drama, tables and chairs that can be rearranged for discussion and group activities, and quiet corners for reading, talking, or planning. You should establish centers with materials for writing, art, media, and studying special topics and themes as well as research centers for looking into different subjects.

Scheduling and Grouping

Daily Schedule

Avril has developed a daily schedule that allows large blocks of time for individual and group work that emerges from students' ideas and interests:

9:00 Business (teacher) and journals, newspapers, books (students)
9:15 Sharing with the whole class
9:45 Planning the day
10:00 Recess
10:15 Group workshop
11:15 Sustained silent reading
11:45 Lunch
12:15 Read aloud
12:30 Group workshop
1:30 P.E.
2:00 Group workshop
3:00 Dismissal

Weekly Schedule

Avril Font's weekly class schedule, described in the Snapshot, is shown in Figure 1.3.

Monthly Schedule

The monthly schedule for Avril Font's class (again, as described in the Snapshot) is shown in Figure 1.4.

Flexible Scheduling

The truth is, schedules always look better on paper than they work in reality. For the teacher who follows a student- and response-centered approach to teaching, it's easy to get off schedule when children are actively engaged in what they're doing and thus allowed to continue as long as they stay involved. The teacher may have to shift the schedule each day, carry over exciting activities to the next day, or even follow different schedules on different days. When I did Shakespeare with children, we needed at least a $1\frac{1}{2}$ hour period to really rehearse. I scheduled rehearsals on alternating days, which increased the time spent on other days for other subjects. Many experiences like writing, drama, and art projects require larger chunks of time. You'll see the need to increase the flexibility of your schedule as your students grow in confidence and ability to take charge of their own learning experiences.

MONTH May WEEK 2 NAME

MONDAY	TUESDAY	WEDNESDAY	THURSDAY	FRIDAY
9:00 Student choice: Journals Newspapers Books 9:15 Sharing 9:45 Planning 10:00 Recess	→ → (Talk to custodian about cardboard for dragon costume.)	(Benton's mother) → → (Arrange for other 4th grades to watch Maypole dance.)	→ 9:30 Guidance (Call to confirm newspaper coming.)	School assembly: D.A.R.E. 9:15: Sharing 9:45 Planning
10:15 Sustained Silent Reading 10:45 Group Workshops Writing conferences Minilesson: quotation marks for script-writing 11:45 Lunch	→ Writing conferences Meet with Shakespeare group. 11:30 French (Aquarium group—call pet shop.)	→ Writing conferences Start aquarium Book binding (Cut cardboard for dragon costumes.)	→ Writing conferences Animal report presentations 11:30 French (Work on dragon costume)	→ Writing conferences Rehearse St. George play. Maypole, Shakespeare groups work together →( )
12:15 Read Aloud <u>Wind in the Willows</u> 12:30 Group Workshops Minilesson: Organizing information on animal posters. 1:30 P.E. 2:00 Group Workshops Start animal posters. Continue reports.	→ → Writing conferences Animal report posters Book binding → (Practice → Animal posters and reports. Book binding	12:15 Library 12:45 → Pet shop owner coming to talk to aquarium group. Animal posters. → Maypole Dance → Conference: Maypole group report.	12:15 Read Aloud <u>Wind in the Willows</u> → Minilesson: Prepare for interviews by newspaper on Maypole dance. → all week) → Minilesson: Mock interviews.	→ → Rehearse St. George play. Shakespeare group to library. → Do Maypole Dance for other 4th grades. Newspaper coming for pictures and interview.

(After School) Pick up free aquarium. Get more talcum powder for dragon smoke.

FIGURE 1.3 Schedule for a Week in Avril Font's Class

Grouping

In addition to organizing time, you must organize your students. You can do so in a variety of ways, usually in combination with one another:

- *Whole-Class Activities:* These can include sharing and planning; class discussions; initial experiences (e.g., talking about the hurricane headed your way); reading aloud by the teacher; talking about books; presenting new ma-

MONTH May NAME

WEEK #	1	2	3	4
Language Arts and Reading	Continue writing and binding books for Mothers or Special Person.	→ —————— Rehearse St. George and the Dragon play. Start to rehearse scenes from Shakespeare.	Rehearse scenes from Shakespeare. Present St. George and the Dragon play—invite other classes.	Present scenes from Shakespeare. Assemble final portfolios.
Social Studies and Science	Do Maypole Dance–for other 4th grade classes and newspaper on Friday. Animal reports and posters / start presentations to class.	Research fish and water environments. → ——————	Reports: Maypole St. George and Shakespeare together. Finish animal report and poster presentations.	Reports: Aquarium group. Timeline of Shakespeare's life.
Special needs / things to do.	Aquarium—find one. See if pet shop owner will come to talk to aquarium group. VCR to video animal reports.	Live fish for aquarium. Thrift shop for costume pieces for plays. More talcum powder for dragon smoke—BIG CAN of it!	VCR to video St. George and the Dragon play. Display animal posters in library. Invite parents to play.	VCR to video scenes from Shakespeare. Do St. George play and scenes from Shakespeare for whole school. Invite parents to scenes.

FIGURE 1.4 Schedule for a Month in Avril Font's Class

terials or identifying new topics or themes to investigate; getting organized to do so; and teaching initiating and demonstrating lessons. (We'll return to these types of lessons later in the chapter.)

• *Small-Group Activities:* Children work together in small groups on topics or themes of interest that are being pursued by the whole class (e.g., hurricanes), or that are of special interest just to them (e.g., Shakespeare or St. George and the dragon).

• *Individual Activities:* You should allow plenty of time for children to work alone, reading, writing, or pursuing topics of interest to them. Individual activities emerge from whole-class activities—for instance, one child writes a poem about hurricanes or studies an animal that interests him or her. Similarly, individual and group activities can be combined, such as finding out about Shakespeare's birthplace and sharing the information with another child in the group who found out about his education or one of his plays.

Materials and Resources

Avril's room is full of books, media, paper, and art supplies, all of which are readily available to the children. But in her student- and response-centered classroom, the real raw materials for teaching language arts originate with the children themselves: their experiences, thoughts, impulses, and language. Here are examples of materials you can use:

Students' Experiences

- *Shared Experiences:* Verbal, written, drawn, danced, or acted out descriptions of objects, people, or events created in or out of class
- *Home Experiences:* People, pets, sports, trips, movies, music, and things from home (books, pictures, awards, tapes, stories of experiences)
- *School Experiences:* Other classes (music, art, physical education), the library, assemblies, parties , fights on the schoolyard, and so on
- *Content Experiences:* Science experiments, social studies research, guest speakers, fieldtrips, and news items
- *Arts Experiences:* Art and music appreciation, creations, songs, dances, drama, and films
- *Organic Experiences:* Cooking and eating, growing things, animals and insects, and classroom nature collections
- *Cultural Experiences:* Traditions, holidays, events, celebrations, history, and social movements
- *Media Experiences:* Television, film, music, video, and computers
- *Your Experiences:* Share yourself with your students

Children's Literature

Your main source of reading and reference material should be good children's books. Develop a class library to provide resources in addition to those found in the school library. Borrow materials from school and public libraries, go to garage sales, and asks parents to donate. Ask your school and public librarians for help in identifying books on special topics. Here are several excellent sources of information about children's literature:

Children and Books (Sutherland & Arbuthnot, 1990)
Children's Literature in the Elementary School (Huck, Hepler, & Hickman, 1993)
Through the Eyes of a Child: An Introduction to Children's Literature (Norton, 1995)

Media

An assortment of the following media is essential for use in child and teacher creations, as instructional materials, and for self-expression and enjoyment. The new media include:

Computer with word-processing software, printer, and CD-ROM
Tape and CD player, blank tapes, earphones
Overhead projector, blank transparencies, and pens to write on them
Television and VCR, video camera, blank videotapes, videotapes

Some of the following older media are still readily available in schools and can be very useful:

Record player and records
Slide projector
35 mm camera and Polaroid camera for prints and slides
Filmstrip projector, filmstrips, and blank filmstrips
16 mm and Super-8 projector and film

Supplies

As you plan to stock your classroom, think about acquiring the following materials. Some will be provided by your school, but you'll have to come up with others by scrounging around and by getting parents involved:

Variety of paper: lined, unlined, art, wrapping and contact paper, butcher paper, paper bags
Stationery and envelopes
Pencils and crayons
Tools: rulers, scissors, staplers
Chart racks
Art materials for a variety of media
Science supplies and equipment
Cooking equipment and utensils
Rhythm and other musical instruments
Costumes and properties for drama
Puppet-making materials and stage
Dry-erase board and markers
Flannel board and material

Reference Books and Resources

Although your library will have reference books and resources, you should include as many as you can in your classroom, such as:

Dictionaries
Thesauruses
Encyclopedias
Atlases
File boxes for pamphlets, magazine clippings, articles
Electronic resources on CD-ROM

A Word about Language Arts Textbooks

Language arts textbooks provide descriptions of experiences and exercises in the language arts. They may be designed for whole-class, group, or individual activities. Even though these texts may present the picture of a total language arts program, using them for daily activities is not compatible with a student- and response-centered approach to teaching. Language arts textbooks should not provide the curriculum in a constructivist, meaning-centered classroom. However, they may be used selectively as one of many materials and resources in the following ways:

1. *To introduce a concept or skill needed by students for a particular purpose.* For example, most textbooks have a well-developed section on the basic form of a letter and variations for different letter-writing needs. If the class or a group of students has reason to write a letter and form is important, the textbook can be used to provide this information.
2. *To reinforce a skill or convention children have discovered themselves.* For example, punctuation skills develop naturally when children have many opportunities and reasons to write. But they may need to know an acceptable form or guideline in order to communicate more clearly. The textbook can provide answers to questions they may have about the proper uses of punctuation and other written conventions.
3. *To serve as a reference.* For example, students may have questions about the correct form for writing a play script if they want to use this form to create and present ideas of their own or to translate a story or book into dramatic form. Students can use a textbook for a reference on how to do this as they shape their ideas into a script.

"Ripple Effects" of Response-Themed Learning

At the beginning of the year, teachers can plan appropriate experiences and choose books and materials for the classroom based on their knowledge of how children learn language arts. In making these plans, teachers can use state and district curriculum guides and current and seasonal events as sources of curriculum content. Recall from earlier in the chapter that these are some of the sources that Avril Font uses, as well. This approach to curriculum planning has been called various names: *thematic units, theme cycles, language across the curriculum,* and *integrated* or *cross-curricular teaching.* Regardless of the name used, the approach involves beginning with an interesting focal point (such as "Our Community" or "Favorite Authors") or a question asked by the teacher or students (such as "What can we do to improve the environment?").

Throughout the schoolyear, teachers can continue to plan based on students' responses to those initial experiences. For instance, the teacher might observe children's delight in a special book or note an individual's interest in a topic or related prior experience. Given these observations, the teacher lets the children make choices about what they want to talk, read, and write about or even act out or research in the library. The students then collaborate with the teacher on what response-themed projects they will work on, how they will form groups to do so, and how they will share what they learn with others. Recall that Avril uses students' ideas and interests as a third source in planning curriculum content.

This kind of teaching results in what I call a "*ripple effect*" of learning themes that flow out of the initial experiences that teachers plan and the books and materials they choose. The focus of each ripple effect is an idea, experience, or subject that becomes a theme and opens up a wealth of instructional possibilities. Think about what happens when you throw a pebble into a pond or lake: It enters the water at a certain point and from there, creates an ever-widening circle of rings. In the classroom, these "rings" are the ongoing responses of the children: their spontaneous comments after you read aloud from a book, their sharing a similar experience they've had, their enthusiasm or questions about a new topic, and their ideas about how to learn more about it.

Several "pebbles" were tossed out in Avril Font's room on the day we read about in the Snapshot. For instance, Shakespeare became a hot topic for a group of children who read and wrote about him and published a book on his life. Another group who were interested in guppies researched aquariums, created one, and stocked it with fish, which they also studied. And the groups who were learning about "St. George and the Dragon" and the maypole dance connected these topics of English culture with what other children were learning about Shakespeare.

A great part of the joy of teaching is watching this ripple effect occur and thinking of how to enhance it—that is, to help children experience, explore, and discover new ideas and ways to use language and construct meaning. Once you begin, it's an adventure. You and your class can boldly go where no class has gone before! And this is when children reach and stretch and grow in their use and control of language as well as their understanding of themselves and the world.

Model and Example of a "Ripple Effect"

A ripple effect occurred in Avril's class at the beginning of the schoolyear that originated from a combination of a state curriculum requirement in social studies and questions that came up during sharing and planning one morning of the first week of school. Here's how it happened:

During morning sharing, it became apparent to Avril that many of the children in her class were not sure that Baton Rouge (the city they lived in) was actually the capital of Louisiana. Avril noted this and saw a teachable moment, since fourth grade is the year for which most states suggest a study of the local community and state history in social studies. Here was a chance for Avril to begin group workshops and for children to use language across the curriculum.

She began by asking them what they already knew about their community and state. They used the following KWL chart (Ogle, 1989) to begin the ripple effect, listing the things they already knew (K), what they wanted to learn (W), and what they learned (L, to be filled in later):

KWL Chart

K	W	L
What we know	What we want to learn	What we learned

Next, the students formed groups around topics that interested them and discussed how they could find out about these things. Avril suggested many ways the children could learn about their community, all of which were rich in opportunities for oral language, literacy, and cross-curricular experiences. Avril did some initiating lessons (like using an alphabet book as a frame for making an ABC book about Louisiana) and some demonstration lessons (like how to develop interview questions). (Again, we'll look at these types of lessons more closely in the next section.) But most of the students' works was done in small groups using a variety of children's literature, reference books, the newspaper, and their own writing—notes, memoirs, interview questions, and reports. Figure 1.5 shows a model for a ripple effect about "Our Community" that would work in any class using language arts across the curriculum.

For ideas on using alphabet books with middle-grade students, see Thompson (1992).

Lessons for Initiating and Demonstrating

In a student- and response-centered classroom, much of what happens takes place in group workshops and depends on students' ideas, interests, and abilities. However, the teacher will do *initiating lessons* to introduce a topic or type of literature and *demonstrating lessons* to teach students something they need to know to continue their work. Table 1.3 lists some examples of each type of lesson.

TABLE 1.3 Types of Lessons: Initiating and Demonstrating

Initiating	*Demonstrating*
Literature as a model for: writing personal responses reporting information memoirs	Notetaking Writing conventions: punctuation usage
Discussions of seasonal events	Report organization
Sensory experiences to talk and write about: science experiments cooking arts and crafts	Interview questions Script writing Bookmaking Mediamaking
Drama: sense training, improvisation, and story dramatization	Use of reference books Computer skills

FIGURE 1.5
"Ripple Effect" of "Our Community"

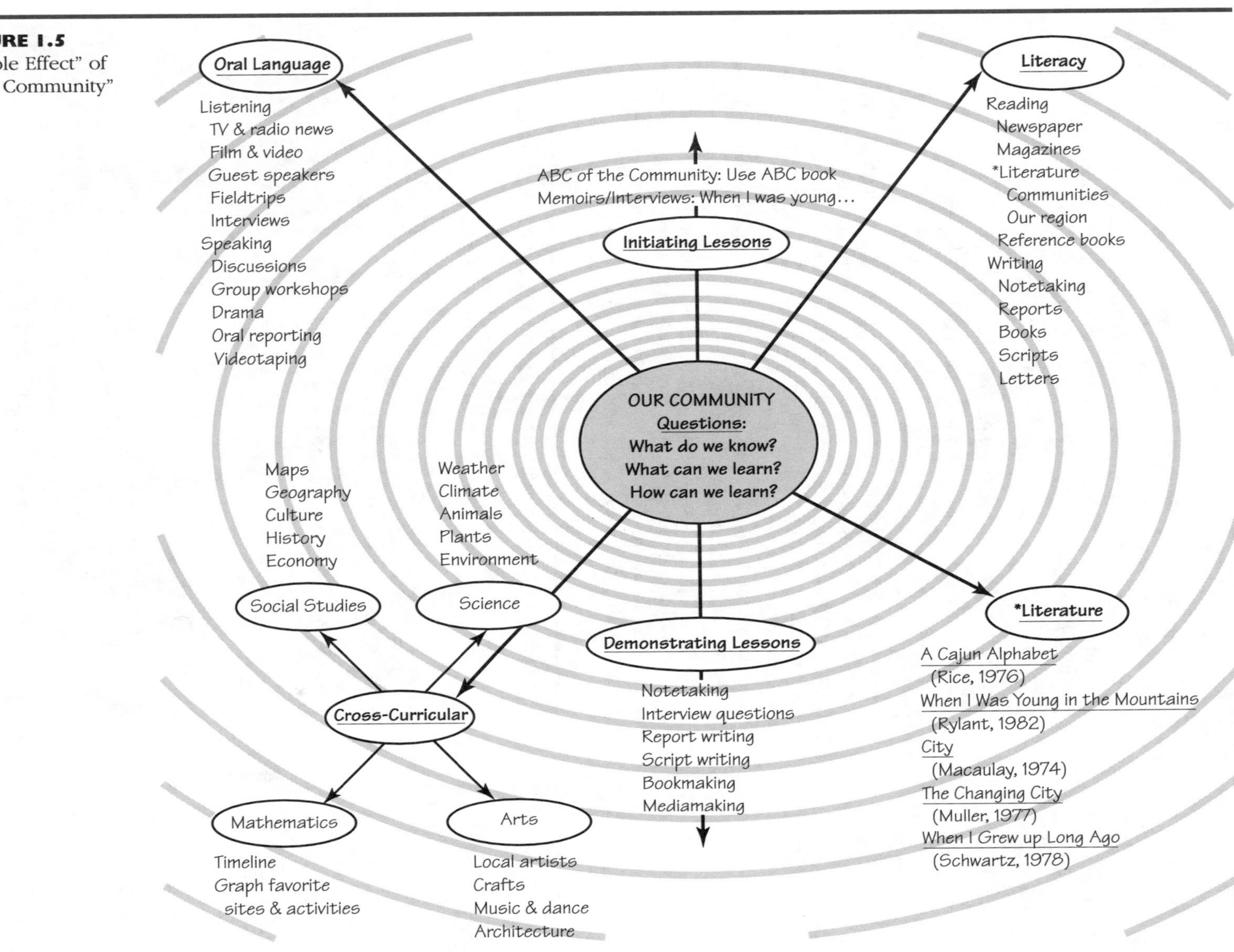

At the beginning of the year, the teacher should plan an initiating lesson about language and literacy experiences. The following Lesson Plan outlines such a lesson using an alphabet book. This book provides a source for reading and responding to literature as well as a frame for reporting on information learned across the curriculum on a topic like the community (Thompson, 1992).

Example of an Initiating Lesson

The alphabet books we have today are beautiful and exciting; they are definitely not "baby books." In fact, many are very sophisticated and appropriate for older students, including *The Z Was Zapped* by Chris Van Allsburg (1987). This is a predictable book. Each right-hand page shows a large illustration of a letter, having something done to it. Students can guess what's happening. The back of each page has a sentence about the letter: for instance, "The A was in an avalanche." What's nice about this book is that many interpretations are possible for each page.

Reading and talking about an alphabet book like this one can lead to lively discussions about the objects and images presented for the letters. Children can talk about their favorite image or other images that start with a certain letter of the alphabet, or they can reflect on what the book reminds them of. You could try this initiating lesson in your practice teaching or at the beginning of the schoolyear when you have your own class.

LESSON PLAN: Initiating Lesson Using Alphabet Books

The Z Was Zapped
by Chris Van Allsburg

Topic: Reading and writing in response to *The Z Was Zapped* by Chris Van Allsburg (1987)

Purpose: To listen to and enjoy literature through discussion and writing

Materials: *The Z Was Zapped;* paper; crayons; and pencils

Teaching Sequence:

1. Read *The Z Was Zapped* aloud. Ask children to predict what's happening to each letter. Encourage a variety of responses before you check to see what Van Allsburg wrote on the back of each page. Discuss *alliteration,* which is repeating the same letter or sound. (Note that the verb, or action word, in each sentence begins with the letter illustrated on that page.)

2. Discuss the book. Ask open-ended questions, which invite children to think about their own impressions while reading:
   "What did you think of the book?"
   "What was your favorite part?"
   "What things could happen to a letter?"
3. Record students' responses to the last question on chartpaper to create a "word wall" of their ideas. Pick one letter, or do several. Students could also do this activity in small groups after you demonstrate it with the whole class. Write this at the top of the chartpaper: "Word Wall for the Letter M."
4. Have each student pick a letter and draw and write something that's patterned after the book. Younger students or language minority students who are just learning to speak English could use the "word wall" for ideas. Or you could take dictation for them, writing their spoken words on their drawings.

Assessment:

1. Observe whether students listened to and enjoyed your reading the book aloud and responded to it during the discussion.
2. Note what students drew and wrote about in response to the book. Figure 1.6 is an example of student drawing and writing in response to *The Z Was Zapped.*

Extending Activities:

1. Encourage students to add alliterative sentences to their drawings and writings about certain letters. If they're interested, they could do more activities with alliteration.
2. Have students make a bulletin board with their work.

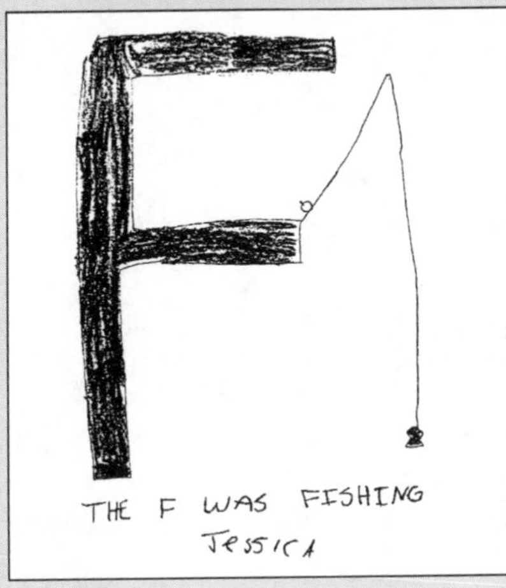

FIGURE 1.6
Student's Drawing and Writing in Response to *The Z Was Zapped*

(continued)

3. Bind the students' work into a class book, and place it in the class library.
4. Have the children dramatize the action for a certain letter by pantomiming it or creating a dialogue between two letters. Share this activity with the class.
5. Ask students to go to the library and find more books by Chris Van Allsburg:
   The Garden of Abdul Gasazi (1979)
   Jumanji (1981)
   The Polar Express (1985)
6. Have students go to the library and find more alphabet books that use alliteration:
   A, My Name Is Alice (Bayer, 1984)
   Animalia (Base, 1986)
   Aster Aardvarks Alphabet Adventures (Kellogg, 1987)
7. And here are more great alphabet books for students of different ages:

For Young Students: Grades K–2

A, B, See! (Hoban, 1982)
The ABC Bunny (Gag, 1933)
Brian Wildsmith's ABC (Wildsmith, 1962)
Chicka Chicka Boom Boom (Martin & Archambault, 1989)
Eating the Alphabet: Fruits and Vegetables from A to Z (Ehlert, 1989)
The Guinea Pig ABC (Duke, 1983)

For Older Students: Grades 3–5

Anno's Alphabet: An Adventure in Imagination (Anno, 1975)
Gretchen's ABC (Simpson, 1991)
The Handmade Alphabet (Rankin, 1991)
Hosie's Alphabet (Baskin, 1972)
Illuminations (Hunt, 1989)
The Ocean Alphabet Book (Pallotta, 1986)

For Students of Any Level

A, B, C's: The American Indian Way (Red Hawk, 1988)
Ashanti to Zulu: African Traditions (Musgrove, 1976)
A Cajun Alphabet (Rice, 1976)
The Calypso Alphabet (Agard, 1989)
A Caribou Alphabet (Owens, 1988)
A Peaceable Kingdom: The Shaker Abecedarius (Provensen & Provensen, 1978)

Classroom Management

Classroom management means many things: creating a classroom environment; establishing schedules and routines; organizing for group work and how to change groups when necessary; developing work habits, traffic patterns, duties; and so on. Discipline—often cited as the main issue of concern in public education—is also an essential part of classroom management.

Stages of Discipline Development

McDaniel (1984) suggests that classroom management and discipline develop as part of a teacher's overall professional competence according to three stages:

1. In the *instructional stage,* the teacher:
   - Knows the subject matter, methods, and means of assessment
   - Masters the elements of classroom instruction: organizing, sequencing, motivating, individualizing
   - Creates active involvement of students with content
   - Varies methods and materials: groups, media, drama, interaction as well individual activities
   - Communicates clearly with students
2. In the *behavioral management stage,* the teacher:
   - Establishes classroom structure, rules, consequences, and rewards that lead to an ordered learning environment
   - Works with students to develop rules for behavior
   - Reinforces students for appropriate behavior: praise, cues, modeling, and rewards (e.g., "I like the way . . .")
   - Sets limits in classroom encounters and enforces rules by action, not anger or threats (e.g., "I need you to . . .")
3. In the *humanistic stage,* the teacher:
   - Goes beyond teaching and control and demonstrates respect for students
   - Encourages student self-discipline, which is solution oriented
   - Facilitates a participatory democracy in rule-setting and problem-solving sessions and negotiations
   - Builds community and communication founded on mutual respect and reasonable expectations
   - States problems clearly and facilitates brainstorming

In a classroom based on the student-centered model of education, the emphasis will be on solution-oriented practices and personal relationships, democratic procedures, supportive decision-making techniques, and acknowledging the worth of each student.

Steps in Dealing with a Discipline Problem

Glasser (1986) suggests that students need to be in control of their own language and literacy experiences, rather than picturing themselves as inadequate learners. He recommends a *learning-team model,* rather than an individual assignment model, so that students have one another's support, work together to gain a sense of accomplishment, and take pride in their accomplishments together. This is called *collaborative* or *cooperative learning.*

See Chapter 3, Language and Cultural Diversity, for more on collaborative learning.

When problems occur, Glasser proposes that teachers ask a sequence of questions and propose actions that promote students' decision-making abilities and enable them to deal with discipline:

1. Ask "What are you doing?" in a nonthreatening, nonpunishing way.
2. Encourage students to confront the reality of their behavior and verbally analyze their decisions.
3. Ask "Did this help you or others?" to encourage students to evaluate their own behavior.
4. Ask "What should you be doing? Can you make a plan?" to help students come up with an alternative behavior as a solution.
5. Develop an action plan for the solution, and then monitor how well it's implemented.

Example of Dealing with a Discipline Problem

One afternoon in Avril Font's fourth-grade classroom, as students streamed in after P.E., several of them excitedly told Avril about an incident between Donald and Heather:

Child (pointing to Heather): Look! Donald did this to her.
Child: They were fist-fighting; then Heather slapped him in the face. Donald kept on messing with Heather.
Child: That boy kept messin' with her, and Heather slugged him.

Heather was flushed and hovered over her desk, writing intently in her journal. Donald came in and stood as close as he could to Avril without actually putting his head on her shoulder. He was close to tears. Avril put her arm around him and talked to him quietly. She addressed both Donald and Heather:

Avril: How did all this start? Tell me what was happening.
Donald: Well, before P.E. . . .
Heather (rushing up): See, when I was down here (points under the table) . . . and I accidentally kicked him.
Donald: Yeah, she accidentally kicked me hard, too.
Avril: Accidentally?
Heather: Well, he was bothering me, and I was trying to write in my journal, and he kept on bothering me and talking to me.
Donald: You was talking to me, too.

Avril: Did this help either one of you? Did it help to talk to her when she was writing? Did it help to kick him? (Silence.) What should you do next time something like this happens?

Heather: Next time you bother me, I'm gonna move to another table.

Donald: Next time she kicks me, I won't hit her and I'll be a big hero.

Assessing Language Arts

Assessing language arts means collecting, analyzing, summarizing, and interpreting information about students to appraise their performance and achievement.

Principles for Assessment Practice

The basic principles that should guide assessment include (Shanahan, 1994):

1. Assessment should account for the current theoretical shift in thinking about language, literacy, and learning.
2. Teacher judgment and student self-evaluation should be an integral part of the assessment process.
3. Test reliability should be verified by using multiple sources, rather than statistically manipulating the selection of test items.
4. Assessment information should be collected continuously and in a variety of contexts, rather than at one time or in a single situation.
5. Performance should be evaluated when students are actively engaged in authentic language and literacy experiences.
6. Collecting information during classroom instruction is likely to be more reliable and less disruptive than testing.
7. Assessment should monitor, guide, and support student learning and instruction.
8. Quality assessment should be dependable, consistent, and trustworthy and provide teachers, students, and parents with a clear understanding of students' progress and needs.

Assessment that aligns with the social constructivist theory of learning, described earlier in the chapter, focuses on meaningful language and literacy experiences. Such assessment follows these guidelines (adapted from Herman, Aschbacher, & Winters, 1992):

- *Learning is a process of personal construction of meaning.*

  Discuss new ideas and relate them to personal experience and prior knowledge.

  Encourage divergent thinking; there is no one right answer.

  Provide multiple modes of expression: role-playing, simulations, debates, explanations to others, and so on.

Emphasize critical thinking: analyze, compare, generalize, predict, and hypothesize.

- *Learning isn't a linear progression of acquiring separate skills.*

  Focus on problem solving.

  Don't make learning contingent on mastering routine, basic skills.

- *Learning varies according to student diversity.*

  Provide choices in tasks (not all reading and writing).

  Provide time to think, revise, and rethink.

  Include concrete experiences and link them to personal experiences.

- *Learning is affected by motivation, effort, and self-esteem.*

  Motivate students with meaningful tasks that are related to personal experiences.

  Encourage students to see the connection between effort and results.

  Have students self-evaluate: that is, to think about how they learn, why they like certain work, and how to set new goals.

- *Learning is social; group work is valuable.*

  Provide group work, and use heterogeneous groups.

  Encourage students to take on a variety of roles.

  Consider group products and processes.

Standardized Testing versus Authentic Assessment

Behaviorism is covered in more detail in Chapter 4, Emergent Literacy.

Standardized tests are based on a behaviorist model, which describes learning as a set of subskills that can be separated, taught, mastered, and tested. Multiple-choice tests reflect this model of learning. They can pinpoint what skill a student has difficulty with and make a reliable comparison of his or her ability with that of other students. But these types of tests cannot explain what went wrong in the learning process.

Language arts educators have come to believe that learning is a holistic process of the social construction of meaning. Students are actively engaged in authentic listening, speaking, reading, and writing experiences across the curriculum in the context of the classroom. This model of learning is reflected in *authentic assessment,* which is continuous, embedded in classroom contexts, and includes information from teacher observations, anecdotal records, checklists, conferences, and student work (e.g., art, writing, journals, reading records, projects, and portfolios) (Cambourne & Turbil, 1990; Johnston, 1992; Roderick, 1991). Authentic assessment situates a student's development over time in the classroom and relative to the whole-language learning process. Authentic assessment relies on information gathered by students and teachers during regular classroom activities, rather than on the results of paper-and-pencil tests.

Herman, Aschbacher, and Winters (1992) contrast the older behaviorist, transmission model of teaching and testing to the more current constructivist, holistic model:

> *No longer is learning thought to be a one-way transmission from teacher to students, with the teacher as lecturer and the students as passive receptacles. Rather, meaningful instruction engages students actively in the learning process. Good teachers draw on and synthesize discipline-based knowledge, knowledge of student learning, and knowledge of child development. They use a variety of instructional strategies . . . [and] involve their students in meaningful activities . . . to achieve specific learning goals. . . . Good teachers constantly assess how their students are doing, gather evidence of problems and progress, and adjust . . . accordingly.* (p. 64)

The following list compares the principles of standardized testing with those of authentic assessment:

Standardized Testing

- Information is gathered with paper-and-pencil tests.
- Tests are given only periodically.
- One test, given at a single point in time, determines evaluation.
- Specific problems can be identified but not in context.
- Subskills are the focus, rather than process.
- Forms include multiple-choice, true/false, matching, and short-answer questions.
- Teachers make no decisions about which tests are used.
- Attempts to "teach to the test" may not support learning.
- Testing disrupts the classroom schedule.

Authentic Assessment

- Information is gathered by teachers and students.
- Ongoing, daily observations are made.
- Multiple sources of information are used.
- Information is considered in the context of process.
- Artifacts (writing, art, journals, tapes) and rich descriptions (anecdotal records, checklists) are used.
- Teachers and students make decisions about assessment.
- Information is gathered as part of the classroom schedule.

Contextualized Performance Assessment

Authentic assessment in language arts means looking at students' performance over time in given classroom contexts. It does not rely on standardized test scores or standardized performance assessments (e.g., all students writing short essays on the same subject in a timed period). A key idea in authentic assessment is that students are active participants. They create or construct responses (e.g., writing in their daily journals), rather than merely choose from the options presented to them (e.g., the answer on a multiple-choice test). As mentioned earlier, with tests like these, there's no way of determining why students get answers right or wrong: Did they really understand the question? Did they make a careless mistake? or Did they just guess? Authentic, contextualized performance assessment requires that students demonstrate their knowledge, thereby showing whether they understand the process involved.

Students can demonstrate their understanding of language and literacy processes in several ways, and teachers can use these means to support, guide, and monitor students' learning. These methods are described here and illustrated with examples from Avril Font's fourth-grade class, which we looked at in the Snapshot at the beginning of this chapter. (Also note that each chapter of this book has a special section on assessment, with specific ideas about that aspect of learning and teaching language arts.)

- ***Observation:*** This is an ongoing, minute-to-minute technique used by teachers in student- and response-centered classrooms. Yetta Goodman describes observation using the wonderful term *kidwatching* (1985). Avril observes students continually. For example, in the Snapshot, she suggested that the student who shared about his Paw Paw should make things out of acorns or jot down the idea as something to write about. Similarly, Avril's observations prompted her to suggest that a group of students who showed interest in Shakespeare should go to the library to find out about him.

- ***Reading Logs, Learning Logs, Dialogue Journals:*** Students can use *reading logs* to keep records of books they have read and their responses to them. Students can then bring these logs to conferences with the teacher about their reading, and the teacher can keep anecdotal records of the conferences. Along the same idea, students can keep *learning logs* in other subjects. In *dialogue journals,* the teacher, aide, or another child writes in response to the student's daily journal entry. Avril uses all three methods—for example, discussing each child's self-selected reading, as noted in his or her reading log, during conferences held on a regular basis.

- ***Conferences:*** Teachers can confer with students in a variety of ways: having on-the-spot talks, regular reading or writing conferences, conferences with groups, scheduled conferences on an as needed basis, and informal conferences for special purposes. Recall from the Snapshot that Avril had a conference with the maypole group to make plans for their taped interview and videotaped session with a local television station. She also had a writing conference with Mina right before she was ready to publish her book about her mom's work as a seamstress.

- ***Anecdotal Records:*** Teachers make notes based on classroom observations, during conferences, or in interviews with students. These notes usually include not only what the students did but how the teacher interprets what they did, as well. Anecdotal records become the basis for further individualized instruction. They may be kept in notebooks with running entries, in computer files, on stick-on notes, or using a combination of these. Avril noted one child's interest in finding the meanings of words such as *droppings* and *excrement*.

• ***Developmental Checklists:*** Teachers can create checklists to cover a wide range of developing language and literacy behaviors or for specific individual or group projects. Avril created a checklist for students' reading and writing about animals, since each student was learning about an animal and making a poster about it to share with other students.

• ***Writing Samples:*** Samples of writing include a range of informal to formal writing, obtained at various stages. In Avril's class, students wrote daily in journals, wrote several drafts for books they published throughout the year, took notes and made outlines for research projects, and wrote letters, memos, and notes. All these provided suitable writing samples.

• ***Individual Projects:*** Individual projects demonstrate comprehensive skills or knowledge, are often cross-curricular in focus, and require students to take initiative and be creative. In Avril's class, one child read about sharks, made a chart graphing incidences of sharks eating people around the world, and told the class about it.

• ***Group Projects:*** Students demonstrate what they're learning by working collaboratively in groups. Some projects may be created by all the students, or each student may create part of a project in cooperation with others. In Avril's class, one group of students read about Shakespeare's life and wrote and illustrated a book about it.

• ***Oral Presentations:*** Sharing, interviews, storytelling, drama, puppets, and oral reports are all types of oral presentations. A group of students in Avril's class did the maypole dance and explained its origin and significance to a television news reporter who came to school to videotape the event. In doing so, they were using an oral presentation to demonstrate what they'd learned through reading, writing, and experiencing.

• ***Self-Evaluations:*** Students all evaluate themselves through notes they write to bring to conferences with the teacher or letters they write to the teacher or their parents about what they've done.

• ***Portfolios:*** Files or folders of students' work can be collected systematically and evaluated by both the teacher and the student over time. *Portfolios* represent individual students' performances. They're most commonly used in elementary school in the area of language arts, especially writing. If it's assumed that reading and writing involve the active construction of personal meaning, then individual portfolios of reading and writing habits, responses, and performances are valid assessment tools. There are several types of portfolios:

Portfolios are an essential part of authentic assessment.

See Chapter 10, The Writing Process, for more on writing portfolios.

See Chapter 9, Reading as a Language Art.

See Chapter 11, Reading and Writing.

Vermont's statewide portfolio assessment is looked at further in Chapter 10, The Writing Process.

1. *Writing portfolios* include examples of all the stages of writing: idea lists and clusters, drafts, revisions, final copies, and books.
2. *Reading portfolios* document reading habits and responses.
3. *Reading and writing portfolios* integrate information on reading and writing—for example, students' writing that uses literature as a model: poetry, stories in different genres, and longer narratives they publish as books.
4. *Portfolios across the curriculum* are used in some districts and states for subjects such as science, social studies, mathematics, and art in addition to reading and writing. Vermont and Michigan are among states using portfolios for assessment.

Answers to Questions about Learning and Teaching Language Arts

1. *What are the language arts?*

In simple terms, the language arts are listening, speaking, reading, and writing. In broader terms, they include everything based on language, which is a system of communicating that offers countless possibilities for representation, expression, and thought. Oral language—listening and speaking in the classroom—includes activities such as sharing and planning; having conversations and conferences; reading aloud; dramatizing, singing, and storytelling; and media listening and viewing. Literacy activities focus on both reading and writing in the classroom. Reading activities involve the use of a variety of materials, from literature to environmental print. Writing activities address the conventions of written language—spelling, punctuation, grammar, and usage.

Other literacy activities comprise handwriting, biliteracy, and word processing and computer literacy. Language arts provide a means to use language across the curriculum through integrated teaching.

2. *How do children learn language arts?*

Learning is an active, constructive process that takes place when students are truly engaged in what they're doing and focused on the discovery of meaning. The constructivist learning theory of Jean Piaget explains that children learn by adding new experiences to old and constructing new understandings of themselves and the world. To use John Dewey's expression, they "learn by doing."

It follows that children learn to use language by using it—listening, speaking, reading, and writing. Children must first explore and discover for themselves, which is essentially an individual and internalized process. And even though children all go through roughly the same stages of cognitive development, each child is unique and will develop personal understanding at his or her own rate. The teacher's job is to encourage and support this natural development by initiating hands-on experiences.

Learning is a social, interactive process that takes place when students work collaboratively with each other and the teacher. The social interactionist theory of Lev Vygotsky explains that children construct new knowledge by first interacting in context with adults, other children, and materials and tasks in the environment; then later, they internalize what they've learned. Teachers and more capable peers build "scaffolds," according to Jerome Bruner, to help learners construct new knowledge based on the foundation of what children already know. According to this view, the teacher's job is to observe, demonstrate, and support students' efforts and to organize instruction so as to include time for collaboration among students and with the teacher.

In literature-based teaching, Louise Rosenblatt's transactional theory explains that reading and writing are two-way transactions between a reader and a text, during which meaning is created. Readers draw on prior experiences, and the stream of these images and ideas flows through their minds while reading. In response-centered teaching, the teacher initiates experiences with literature but also observes each student's personal response to a story. The teacher will use these responses as a basis for extending experiences with literature and language and literature activities.

3. *How do you teach language arts?*

Teaching language arts in a student- and response-centered classroom means using a bottom-up or whole-to-part approach. That is, children learn to use language by using it when they are surrounded by print and participate in rich and social interactive experiences with language that always focus on meaning.

Curriculum content in this type of classroom comes from three sources: state and district curriculum guides; seasonal and special events through the year; and students' ideas and interests. Content is taught in "ripples" generated by response-themed learning, which emerge from topics of interest and student ideas. Lessons are used for initiating and demonstrating, but most of the time, the children are in a workshop atmosphere, in which they are in control of their own learning.

LOOKING FURTHER

1. Start a journal. You might focus on your thoughts while reading this text, on experiences in your college class and elementary classrooms, or on your ideas and plans for your future as a teacher.
2. Make a list of the things you would take to your class to demonstrate to your students how to be Star of the Week. What would you tell them about yourself? Why?
3. Review several language arts textbooks. Note their strengths and weaknesses, parts you would and wouldn't use.
4. Draw a floorplan of what you think your classroom might look like. Be sure to consider how you will create an environment for maximizing opportunities for student- and response-centered learning. Discuss your plan with others in your class, and compare yours to theirs.
5. Develop a plan for an initiating lesson using literature with a specific grade level. Use the initiating lesson example in this chapter as a model (see the Lesson Plan, pp. 34–36). Teach your lesson, if possible, and report to your class what happened.

RESOURCES

Goodman, K. S. (1986). *What's whole in whole language?* Portsmouth, NH: Heinemann.

Routman, R. (1991). *Invitations: Changing as teachers and learners K–12.* Portsmouth, NH: Heinemann.

REFERENCES

Anderson, R. C. (1977). The notion of schemata and the educational enterprise. In R. C. Anderson, R. J. Spiro, & W. E. Montague (Eds.), *Schooling and the acquisition of knowledge* (pp. 415–431). Hillsdale, NJ: Erlbaum.

Bleich, D. (1975). *Readings and feelings: An introduction to subjective criticism.* Urbana, IL: National Council of Teachers of English.

Britton, J. (1970). *Language and learning.* Harmondsworth, England: Penguin.

Bruner, J. (1983). *Child's talk: Learning to use language.* New York: Holt, Rinehart, & Winston.

Cambourne, B., & Turbil, J. (1990). Assessment in whole-language classrooms: Theory into practice. *Elementary School Journal, 90,* 337–349.

Cox, C., & Zarrillo, J. (1993). *Teaching reading with children's literature.* Columbus, OH: Merrill/Macmillan.

Cullinan, B. (Ed.). (1987). *Literature in the reading program.* Newark, DE: International Reading Association.

Cullinan, B. (Ed.). (1992). *Invitation to read: More children's literature in the reading program.* Newark, DE: International Reading Association.

Dewey, J. (1938). *Experience in education.* New York: Collier.

Dewey, J. (1943). *The child and the curriculum, the school and society.* Chicago: University of Chicago Press.

Glasser, W. (1986). *Control theory in the classroom.* New York: HarperCollins.

Goodman, K. S. (1972). The reading process: Theory and practice. In R. Hodges & E. H. Rudorf (Eds.), *Language and learning.* Boston: Houghton Mifflin.

Goodman, Y. (1985). Kidwatching: Observing children in the classroom. In A. Jaggar & M. T. Smith-Burke (Eds.), *Observing the language learner* (pp. 9–18). Urbana, IL: National Council of Teachers of English.

Green, J. L., & Meyer, L. A. (1990). The embeddedness of reading in classroom life: Reading as a situated process. In C. Baker & A. Luke (Eds.), *The sociology of reading* (pp. 141–160). Amsterdam, The Netherlands: Benjamins.

Heath, S. B. (1983). *Ways with words: Language, life and work in communities and classrooms.* New York: Cambridge University Press.

Herman, J. L., Aschbacher, P. R., & Winters, L. (1992). *A practical guide to alternative assessment.* Alexandria, VA: Association for Supervision and Curriculum Development.

Huck, C., Hepler, S., & Hickman, J. (1993). *Children's literature in the elementary school* (5th ed.). New York: Holt, Rinehart, & Winston.

Johnston, P. H. (1992). *Constructive evaluation of literate activity.* New York: Longman.

Loban, W. (1976). *Language development: Kindergarten through grade twelve.* Urbana, IL: National Council of Teachers of English.

Loban, W. (1979). Relationships between language and literacy. *Language Arts, 56,* 485–486.

McDaniel, T. R. (1984). Developing the skills of humanistic discipline. *Educational Leadership, 41*(8), 71–74.

Norton, D. (1995). *Through the eyes of a child: An introduction to children's literature* (4th ed.). New York: Merrill/Macmillan.

Ogle, D. (1989). The know, want to know, learn strategy. In K. D. Muth (Ed.), *Children's comprehension of text: Research into practice* (pp. 205–223). Newark, DE: International Reading Association.

Piaget, J. (1973). *To understand is to invent: The future of education.* New York: Grossman.

Piaget, J. (1977). *The development of thought: Equilibration of cognitive structures* (A. Rosin, Trans.). New York: Viking.

Roderick, J. A. (Ed.). (1991). *Context-responsive approaches to assessing children's language.* Urbana, IL: National Conference of Research on English.

Rogers, K. B. (1986). Do the gifted think and learn differently? A review of recent research and its implications for instruction. *Journal for the Education of the Gifted, 10*(1), 27–42.

Rosenblatt, L. M. (1983). *Literature as personal exploration.* New York: Modern Language Association. (Original work published 1938)

Rosenblatt, L. M. (1986). The aesthetic transaction. *Journal of Aesthetic Education, 20*(4), 122–128.

Routman, R. (1991). *Invitations: Changing as teachers and learners K–12.* Portsmouth, NH: Heinemann.

Rumelhart, D. E., & Ortony, A. (1977). The representation of knowledge in memory. In R. C. Anderson, R. J. Spiro, & W. E. Montague (Eds.), *Schooling and the acquisition of knowledge* (pp. 99–135). Hillsdale, NJ: Erlbaum.

Shanahan, T. (1994). Assessment, theory, and practice. In A. Purves (Ed.), *Encyclopedia of English studies and language arts* (Vol. 1). New York: Scholastic.

Smith, F. (1988). *Joining the literacy club: Further essays into education.* Portsmouth, NH: Heinemann.

Smith, F. (1992). Learning to read: The never ending debate. *Kappan,* 73(6), 442–447.

Spindler, G. (1982). *Doing the ethnography of schooling.* New York: Holt, Rinehart, & Winston.

Sutherland, Z., & Arbuthnot, M. H. (1990). *Children and books* (8th ed.). New York: HarperCollins.

Thompson, D. L. (1992). The alphabet book as a content area resource. *Reading Teacher, 46*(3), 266–267.

Vygotsky, L. S. (1962). *Thought and language.* Cambridge, MA: MIT Press.

Vygotsky, L. S. (1978). *Mind in society: The development of higher psychological processes.* Cambridge, MA: Harvard University Press.

CHILDREN'S BOOKS

Agard, J. (1989). *The calypso alphabet.* New York: Henry Holt.

Anno, M. (1975). *Anno's alphabet: An adventure in imagination.* New York: Crowell.

Base, G. (1986). *Animalia.* New York: Abrams.

Baskin, L. (1972). *Hosie's alphabet.* New York: Viking.

Bayer, J. (1984). *A, my name is Alice.* New York: Dial.

Donaldson, E., & Donaldson, G. (1979). *The book of days.* New York: A & W.

Duke, K. (1983). *The guinea pig ABC.* New York: Dutton.

Ehlert, L. (1989). *Eating the alphabet: Fruits and vegetables from A to Z.* San Diego, CA: Harcourt Brace Jovanovich.

Gag, W. (1933). *The ABC bunny.* New York: Coward, McCann.

Grahame, K. (1980). *The wind in the willows* (M. Hague, Illus.). New York: Holt, Rinehart, & Winston.

Hoban, T. (1982). *A, b, see!* New York: Greenwillow.

Hunt, J. (1989). *Illuminations.* New York: Bradbury.

Kellogg, S. (1987). *Aster aardvark's alphabet adventures.* New York: Morrow.

Lamb, C., & Lamb, M. (1957). *Tales from Shakespeare.* New York: Dutton.

Macaulay, D. (1974). *City.* New York: Houghton Mifflin.

Martin, B., & Archambault, J. (1989). *Chicka chicka boom boom.* New York: Simon & Schuster.

Muller, J. (1977). *The changing city.* New York: Atheneum.

Musgrove, M. (1976). *Ashanti to Zulu: African traditions.* New York: Dial.

Owens, M. B. (1988). *A caribou alphabet.* Brunswick, ME: Dog Ear Press.

Pallotta, J. (1986). *The ocean alphabet book.* Watertown, MA: Charlesbridge.

Provensen, A., & Provensen, M. (1978). *A peaceable kingdom: The Shaker abecedarius.* New York: Viking.

Rankin, L. (1991). *The handmade alphabet.* New York: Dial.

Red balloon, The [Film]. (1956). Available from Macmillan Films, Inc.

Red Hawk, R. (1988). *A, B, C's: The American Indian way.* Sacramento, CA: Sierra Oaks.

Rice, J. (1976). *A Cajun alphabet.* Gretna, LA: Pelican.

Rylant, C. (1982). *When I was young in the mountains.* New York: Dutton.

Schwartz, A. (Ed.). (1978). *When I grew up long ago: Older people talk about the days when they were young.* New York: Lippincott.

Simpson, G. D. (1991). *Gretchen's ABC.* New York: HarperCollins.

Spenser, E. (1984). *St. George and the dragon* (Retold M. Hodges; T. S. Hyman, Illus.). New York: Little, Brown.

Van Allsburg, C. (1979). *The garden of Abdul Gasazi.* New York: Houghton Mifflin.

Van Allsburg, C. (1981). *Jumanji.* New York: Houghton Mifflin.

Van Allsburg, C. (1985). *The polar express.* New York: Houghton Mifflin.

Van Allsburg, C. (1987). *The Z was zapped.* New York: Houghton Mifflin.

Wildsmith, B. (1962). *Brian Wildsmith's ABC.* New York: Franklin Watts.

Williams, V. B. (1981). *Three days on a river in a red canoe.* New York: Greenwillow.

Chapter 2

Children and Language

Questions about Children and Language

SNAPSHOT: ***Four Children Talking***

Language Acquisition

- Constructivist Theory
- Social Interactionist Theory

Language Systems

- Phonology
- Semantics
- Syntax
- Pragmatics
- Overview of Language Systems

Language Development

- An Active, Social, Individual Process
- Language Learning Adapted for All Students

Vocabulary and Concept Development in the Classroom

- Experiential Interaction
- Semantic Mapping

TEACHING IDEA: ***Semantic Maps with Limited–English Proficient (LEP) Students***

- Language Play

LESSON PLAN: ***Language Play and Literature***

Assessing Children and Language

Answers to Questions about Children and Language

Questions about Children and Language

1. *How do children acquire language?*
2. *What do we know when we know how to use language?*
3. *How does language develop?*
4. *How do teachers help support children's growing knowledge of language, concepts, and vocabulary?*

Reflective Response: Children and Language

How did you learn to talk? Who taught you? Jot down your ideas and think about them as you read this chapter.

SNAPSHOT: Four Children Talking

Let's take a look at four children of different ages and at different stages in their cognitive, language, and social development. Elizabeth is 9 months old, Gordon is 3 years old, Becky is 7 years old, and Wyatt is 14. Wyatt is taking care of his sister and brother, Elizabeth and Gordon, while his mother is at work writing a book in her home office. Becky, a neighbor, joins the group as Wyatt helps Gordon work a puzzle and tries to keep Elizabeth happy. Think about what each child is saying and why as well as how all the children interact.

Elizabeth (crying): Fafafafafafa.
Wyatt: How you doin', Elizabeth? (Singing.) Little Elizabeth. Pretty little lizard.

Interaction with older children greatly enhances children's language development.

Becky (to Wyatt about Elizabeth's crying): Maybe it was something we said?

Wyatt (laughing at Becky's remark and helping Gordon with the puzzle): Gordon, do you think you could help Becky work this puzzle? Do the puzzle, Gor.

Gordon: Where dis go? Dis go?

Wyatt: Do you want this one? This one goes right here. Here.

Becky: This one goes here. There.

Gordon (grabbing the piece from Becky): Dat my piece. My piece. My piece.

Wyatt: Do the puzzle, Gordon.

Becky: Did he do this? It's pretty good, though. Map of the world. If the world was that small, I know . . . I know how Christopher Columbus made it. But the world's flat. Hmm-mmm.

Gordon: Der. I di-i!

Wyatt: Gordon, did you do that puzzle? All by yourself?

Elizabeth: Ehehehehehehe!

Wyatt: Elizabeth? You want to work a puzzle sometime by yourself?

Gordon: Now I . . . goin' to find it. Becky (pushing her to put in a puzzle piece)!

Becky: Huh?

Elizabeth: (crying): Fafafafafafa.

Wyatt: Elizabeth (soothingly, picking her up, rocking her, and singing). Puff, puff, cocoa puff. Chocolate covered cocoa puffs.

Gordon: Oh, wow!

Wyatt: You have a little baby brother, Becky?

Becky: Yeah!

Wyatt: How old is he?

Becky: About fo— . . . he's . . . uhm . . . almost a month.

Wyatt: That's pretty small.

Becky: Yeah, real.

Wyatt: What's his name?

Becky: Patrick.

Gordon: Oh . . . we're missing dat piece!

Wyatt: You like him?

Becky: When he's happy! He gets happy!

Wyatt: He cries a lot?

Becky: Yeah, he's usually happy and like—"ooohhhhh" (imitating baby noise)—and sometimes he's only—and sometimes he, he—when he's in a sore mood—he always—and sometimes he's like this (imitates baby). Like he's ready to sock ya.

Wyatt (laughing): Ha-ha-ha-ha!

Becky: Once Mom goes "What you thinkin' about Patrick?" and he goes (makes face).
Gordon: Right . . . one here. One. Let's do other side.
Wyatt: Do the other side. Do the other side (of a double-sided puzzle).
Gordon: O–KAY!!!

Language Acquisition

You can easily see the differences in linguistic structures used by these children of different ages. But did you also observe the way in which each child used language and the importance of the meaning of what he or she was saying? The role of the oldest child, 14-year-old Wyatt, is especially important. He was obviously taking care of the two youngest children. What may not be so obvious is how he supported their language development by negotiating meaning with them.

Studies of children's language development (Cook-Gumperz, 1979; Hickman, 1985; Shugar, 1978; Snow, 1986; Wells, 1981) show that caretakers of young children—mothers, fathers, older children, and teachers—constantly negotiate meaning with them, responding to *what* they're trying to say more than *how* they say it. By doing this, caretakers help children develop what Hymes (1974) calls *communicative competence,* or the ability to really use language.

Let's take another look at the Snapshot of four children talking from a social constructivist perspective. As you may recall from Chapter 1, this perspective of learning language draws from the fields of psychology, linguistics, and sociology and is widely used to support child- and response-centered teaching. The social constructivist perspective merges ideas from two viewpoints about how children learn and acquire language: (1) the constructivist theory of Jean Piaget (1959) and (2) the social interactionist theory of Lev Vygotsky (1986). Each theory is described in a following section, including examples from the Snapshot and suggestions for teaching.

Constructivist Theory

Piaget's ideas on cognitive development were introduced in Chapter 1.

Jean Piaget (1959) held that language acquisition is an aspect of general cognitive development. Although he believed that thought (or cognition) and language were interdependent, he maintained that language development is rooted in the more fundamental development of cognition. In other words, conceptualization precedes language.

Piaget based this cognitive constructivist view on his observations of children at play. Through manipulating objects, they demonstrate that they understand concepts and can solve problems without verbalizing them. In the Snapshot, Gordon illustrated this understanding as he worked the puzzle.

Children learn to understand language as they first assimilate and then accommodate language symbols to their symbolic structures, or schema (as discussed in Chapter 1). In the search for meaning, children *symbolize* before they *verbalize*.

Piaget viewed the adult or other caretaker's role in teaching language as creating situations in which children discover meaning themselves. For example, Wyatt got out the puzzle for Gordon and encouraged him to work it. According to the constructivist view, language will follow experience. In order to support language development, teachers provide opportunities for self-discovery in the classroom, such as centers with materials for art, writing, and science. This isn't to suggest that language doesn't play a part in children's overall development. To the contrary, language is critical in children's social interaction with one another and adults, and this interaction is essential in order for children to grow and move away from a totally egocentric (self-focused) point of view.

Each child in the Snapshot falls into one of Piaget's stages of cognitive development. Let's look at the development of language in each stage.

Sensorimotor Stage (0–2 years): Preverbal—Elizabeth

Elizabeth is 9 months old and in the sensorimotor stage of cognitive development. She is crying and babbling—repeating one-syllable sounds, usually beginning with a consonant, such as "fafafafafa." She also says "Ma-ma," "Da-da," and "bye-bye." She will probably speak her first words at about 1 year old and two-word sentences at about 2 years old. Did you notice in the Snapshot that the only person to speak directly to her was her older brother, Wyatt? He included her in the conversation as though she was really part of it. This kind of talk—called "motherese" or "caretakerese"—is essential to further language development.

Elizabeth spoke these words between 9 months and 1 year: *Oh-oh, Wyee* (her brother Wyatt), *wa-* (water), *Hi!, Mama, Dada,* and *Bye-bye.*

Preoperational Stage (2–7 years): Vocabulary and True Language—Gordon

Gordon is 3 years old and in the preoperational stage. He can name things and use two-word, or *telegraphic,* sentences, and other simple sentences. He can't pronounce many words accurately, but he is able to make his meaning clear. He repeats a lot and is still pretty egocentric. In the Snapshot, he was focused on doing the puzzle that interested him and not very interested in anyone else, except when he thought that Becky was taking a puzzle piece away from him. Wyatt interacted with Gordon as a big brother/coach. He adjusted his speech according to what Gordon said in the same way that studies show mothers do with even very young children (Lindfors, 1987). Wyatt didn't correct Gordon's speech approximations; rather, he responded to the meaning of what he knew Gordon was trying to say. Wyatt offered guidance and suggestions. He used simple, short, concrete sentences and repetition, specific directions, and exaggerated intonation. He also offered encouragement while sharing in Gordon's attempts to work the puzzle and talk.

Gordon spoke these phrases and sentences between 18 months and 2 years: *All gone* (and twists hands), *Uh-oh hat* (when he dropped it), *Daddy fix* (when he broke a toy), *I'm tired,* and *Go car!*

Concrete Operational Stage (7–11 years): Logical Reasoning and Socialized Speech—Becky

At 7 years old, Becky is in the concrete operational stage. Her speech is remarkably like adult speech. Although her language will continue to develop in complexity of form and function, Becky has pretty much mastered her native language of English. You probably observed in the Snapshot that Becky was much more social than Gordon. She was primarily interested in talking to Wyatt, who would talk back to her, yet she still commented on Elizabeth and tried to interact with Gordon (who had only limited, self-serving interest in her). Note that Wyatt listened to Becky, laughed at her jokes, asked her a lot of questions, and invited her to talk about herself and family.

Formal Operations Stage (11–15): Abstract Reasoning and World of Symbols—Wyatt

Wyatt is 14 years old and in the formal operations stage. Essentially, his speech can't be differentiated from that of an adult, as illustrated by the ways he used language to interact with the three younger children. He acted as their coach: negotiating meaning with them and helping them interact with each other in ways that both accepted and expanded their individual levels of cognitive and language development. What Wyatt did naturally as a caretaker is a good model for teachers in the classroom who wish to support their students' language development.

Social Interactionist Theory

Environment plays a more prominent role in social interactionist theories than in cognitive constructivist theories. Social interactionist theory assumes that language acquisition is determined by the interaction of physical, linguistic, and social factors—any and all of which may vary greatly for each individual child. Lev Vygotsky (1978, 1986) believed that interaction with the environment, especially with adults and older children, plays a critical role in children's language development. As summarized by Vygotsky, "Language is a major stimulant for conceptual growth, and conceptual growth is also dependent on interaction with objects in the environment. Moreover, adults (and older children) have a role in stimulating language growth through a variety of means" (p. 11, quoted in Pflaum [1986]).

Zone of Proximal Development

This stimulation should take place in what Vygotsky (1978) calls the *zone of proximal development*. As defined in Chapter 1, this zone is the center around which the child forms *thought complexes* (similar to schema) or *symbolic structures*. Piaget (1973, 1977) also identified the importance of connecting new experiences to prior knowledge and organizing that new information. However, his ideas differ from those of Vygotsky in that Piaget believed children verbalize structures that have already developed through first-hand experiences with objects in their environments. Vygotsky sees the verbal interaction between the adult and child as the primary means by which children achieve potential meaning through language. He clearly puts great emphasis on the role of the caretaker or teacher in the cognitive and linguistic development of the child.

Wyatt's interaction with Elizabeth, Gordon, and Becky is an example of Vygotsky's theory. This interaction also illustrates what Jerome Bruner (1978) describes as a "scaffold," or a temporary frame for constructing meaning from language (see Chapter 1). When Wyatt talked to the younger children, he often repeated himself but used slightly more complex language than that of the children.

For more on "scaffolding," see Applebee and Langer (1983) and Cazden (1983).

Language Systems

What do children like Wyatt, Becky, Gordon, and Elizabeth actually know when they use the language they're acquiring? Language consists of interacting systems of sounds, meanings, sentence formation, and use. You know how to use these interacting systems when you know a language.

Phonology

When you know how to use a language, you're able to make sounds that have meanings and are able to understand the meanings of sounds that other people make. *Phonology* is the study of the patterns and systems of human language. *Phonetics* is a system of classifying these speech sounds. This term should not be confused with *phonics,* which is a method of teaching unfamiliar words in print that's supposedly based on the sound/letter correspondences in spoken language.

The phonology of each language includes a set of basic building blocks called *phonemes.* A phoneme is the smallest unit of sound that distinguishes between the meanings of words in a certain language—for example, *fan* versus *pan.* Only certain sequences of these segments make sense in a language. There are about 40 phonemes in the English language (although linguists don't always agree) but only 26 letters in the English alphabet to represent these sounds. In written language, sounds in words are represented by *graphemes.*

Semantics

When you know a language, you're also able to produce sentences with certain meanings and to understand the meanings of sentences that other people make. *Semantics* is the study of linguistic meaning. *Morphemes* are the smallest units of meaning in each language; they are sequences of phonemes that can't be divided without losing meaning. Morphemes combine to form *words,* which can be made up of more than one morpheme. For example, the word *puzzle* can't be reduced without losing meaning. It's called a *free morpheme,* because it functions as a unit of meaning by itself. To create the plural word *puzzles,* we add another morpheme: *-s*. The *-s* is called a *bound morpheme,* because it cannot function as a unit of meaning by itself.

When you know a language, you know the morphemes, their meanings, how they may be combined to form words, and how to pronounce them. The vocabulary of morphemes and words in a language is called the *lexicon*.

Syntax

Knowing a language also involves knowing the rules of *syntax*. When you know these rules, you can combine words in sentences that express your ideas and are able to understand the sentences produced by other people to express their ideas. Meaning in a *sentence* is partly determined by *word order,* one of the things that syntactic rules determine.

Pragmatics

When you know a language, you know how to use the rules that govern its use for different functions, which are called *conventions*. We can't discuss these conventions without referring to how language is used by specific people or in specific situations. For instance, you can probably think of examples of the manipulative use of language in commercial advertising and political rhetoric (sometimes called *doublespeak*). Language also can be used to used to perpetuate racial or gender bias, unknowingly or intentionally. You may have noticed in reading this book that whenever a personal pronoun is needed, *he or she* is used, rather than just *he*. The latter was considered conventional until recently, when the use of *he* by itself was acknowledged as sexist. Awareness of gender fairness in language has also led to the use of *police officer* instead of *policeman* and *chairperson* instead of *chairman*. Because these usages are considered appropriate in most situations today, they have become new conventions.

How language is used in given societies or cultures is studied by *sociolinguists*. One such scholar, Michael Halliday (1975), defines *language* as "'meaning potential,' that is, as sets of opinions, or alternatives, in meaning, that are available to the speaker-hearer" (p. 63). Based on that definition, Halliday has created a model that shows the functions of language that children have developed by the time they come to school. Table 2.1 lists these functions along with examples from the Snapshot of four children talking. The table also shows the types of language arts classroom experiences that can help children expand their "meaning potential."

Overview of Language Systems

You know a language when you know whether a sentence sounds right or not. You have a feel for the language, which is an underlying knowledge of the language systems. That underlying knowledge represents your linguistic

TABLE 2.1 Halliday's Model of Language Functions

Function	*Example*	*Classroom Experiences*
Instrumental: "I want" Language to get things done	"Dat my piece!"	Problem solving Gathering materials
Regulatory: "Do as I tell you" Language to control	"This one goes here."	Giving instructions Making rules, as in games
Interactional: "Me and you" Language in social relationships	"Let's do the other side."	Talking in groups Dialogue and discussion
Personal: "Here I come" Language to express individuality	"Oh, wow!"	Make feelings public Discovery through interaction
Heuristic: "Tell me why" Language as a means to learn	"Did he do this?"	Question/answer routines Metalanguage (language about language; words like question, answer, knowing)
Imaginative: "Let's pretend" Language to create and explore	"Puff, puff, cocoa puff."	Stories and dramatic games Rhymes, poems, and riddles Nonsense and word play Metalanguage (stories, make-believe, pretending)
Representational: "I'll tell you" Communication of content	"This one goes right here."	Telling about the real world Expressing propositions Conveying messages with specific references to real things (people, qualities, states, etc.)

competence. Competence in any language includes knowledge of the following systems:

- phonological rules, which specify the sound patterns of the language
- semantic rules, which characterize the meanings of words and sentences
- syntactic rules, which specify how to combine words in sentences
- pragmatic conventions, which define how language is used

Even very young children like Gordon know these principles. In fact, it's rather amazing how rapidly children acquire their first language before entering school. In the next section, we'll describe children's language development before and during elementary school years, using more examples of the speech of Elizabeth, Gordon, and Becky for illustration.

Language Development

By the time most children enter school at age 5, they are able to communicate effectively with others. This is a remarkable achievement, when you consider that most children only speak their first words at age 1. Even more remarkable is that by the time they are 3, most children already know many rules of language (grammar); can use it to express their needs, thoughts, and feelings; and are able to produce sentences like Gordon's: "Dat my piece."

An Active, Social, Individual Process

How does this remarkable amount of learning happen? And how can teachers use children's ideas, interests, and language to teach the language arts? Three key ideas, supported by social constructivist theory and research, provide answers to these questions.

Language Development Is an Active Process

Children are constantly forming and testing hypotheses about language structure, as suggested by Piaget's (1959) constructivist theory. Linguist Noam Chomsky's ideas about the nature of language are also relevant here (1957, 1965). His *generative theory of language* suggests that we each have an innate *language acquisition device* (*LAD*) that enables us to understand and produce sentences never heard before. Using a finite number of words, we can produce an infinite number of sentences. We do this by constantly testing hypotheses about our developing understanding of language, not merely by imitating the speech of others. Making errors is an important part of this process, because we are testing what we know about language. The errors children make show their basic underlying conceptualization of how language works, a notion already explained in Piaget's theory of child development.

Thus, language learning is an active process, in which the child repeatedly forms new hypotheses, tries them out or tests them, and corrects them as needed while gaining control over language. Chomsky's generative theory prompted great interest in psycholinguistic research in children's language development in the 1960s and 1970s, particularly regarding the stages and rate of acquiring language structures (Cazden, 1972; Chomsky, 1969; Menyuk, 1963; Strickland, 1962).

Language Development Is a Social Process

As Vygotsky's (1978, 1986) theories suggest, communicative interaction with others is also an important part of language development. Babies hear language used around them and begin to use language to communicate their needs. Caretakers are sensitive to children's needs and developing language and try to understand both, making their language understandable to children. Caretakers aren't concerned with pointing out errors or correcting them; instead, they pay attention to the meaning of what children are trying to communicate. Messages are important; mistakes are not. Caretakers therefore provide an environment in which children are willing to test new hypotheses about language structure and use through social interaction that's founded on a need to negotiate and establish meaning. Sociolinguistic research in the 1970s and 1980s began to focus more on this social aspect of language development (Cook-Gumperz, 1979; Halliday, 1975; Lindfors, 1987; Tough, 1977; Wells, 1981).

Language Development Is an Individual Process

Children progress through approximately the same stages in language development but at surprisingly different rates, as explained through Piaget's (1959) stages of cognitive and language development. Even though children basically know how to use their native language when they enter school around age 5, they continue to develop their ability to use and control language throughout the elementary school years (Loban, 1976; Strickland, 1962). For school-age children, experiences with print make a difference. Children who are read to or read independently may progress more rapidly through stages of linguistic development (Bissex, 1980; Durkin, 1966). Given this, teachers should read aloud frequently to children and provide books, time, and opportunities for children to read books of their own choice across a wide range of topics and genres.

Table 2.2 shows the relative stages of children's language development through age 12, roughly corresponding to the period from birth through the elementary school years. The table also shows how these stages compare to Piaget's stages of cognitive development, described earlier in this chapter. Although approximate ages are indicated for these stages, remember that children may vary greatly in the rates at which they acquire language. (They do tend to move through these developmental stages in the same relative order, however.)

Language Learning Adapted for All Students

Every class you teach will be made up of children with different backgrounds, interests, personalities, exceptionalities, and language-learning abilities. A series of federal laws have mandated that education be responsive to students who have special educational needs: namely, Public Law (PL) 94-142, the Education for All Handicapped Children Act (passed in 1975); PL 99-457, amendments to the Education of the Handicapped Act (1986); and PL 101–476, the Individuals with Disabilities Education Act, or IDEA (1990). In sum, these laws require educational accommodations and individualized educational planning that provide each exceptional student with the least restrictive environment for learning. Classrooms in which this approach is followed are generally described as being *mainstreamed* or *inclusive*.

The following sections discuss some of the most common types of exceptionalities that require adaptive education for language learning and ways to provide the special instruction needed in teaching language arts.

TABLE 2.2 Piagetian Stages of Cognitive and Language Development (ages 0–12)

Stage	*Age*	*Characteristics*
Sensorimotor	Birth–6 months	Crying: • undifferentiated and differentiated Babbling: • makes random sounds, then selective and repeated (e.g., "fafafafafa") • associates hearing and sound production • imitates sounds of self and others selectively (e.g., "eheheheh")
	12–18 months	One-word stage: • speaks and duplicates single syllables (e.g., "Ma-ma," "Da-da") • has communicative intent • speaks one-word (holophrastic) sentences (e.g., "Juice" means "I want juice") • 10-word vocabulary
Preoperational	18–24 months	Two-word stage: • meaningful expressive language • speaks telegraphically, using two or more, mainly content words (e.g., "bye-bye car" means "I want to go somewhere in the car—now!") • 150–300 word vocabulary; mainly nouns, verbs, and adjectives; adds plural *s*
	3–4 years	Simple and compound sentences, becoming more complex: • understands present and past tenses but may overgeneralize (e.g., uses *-ed* as in "He goed") • knows numerical concepts (*few* and *many; one, two, three*) • negative transformations • 1,000–1,500 word vocabulary, adding more adjectives, adverbs, pronouns, and prepositions
	5 years	Grammatically correct complex sentences: • has acquired most of basic rules of language • uses present and past tenses and pronouns correctly • 2,500–8,000 word vocabulary and growing
	6 years	Begins to read and write: • use adjectival and conditional clauses, beginning with *if*
Concrete operations	7 years	More symbolic language use: • understand concepts (e.g., time and seasons)
	8–10 years	Very flexible language use: • subordinates clauses beginning with *when, if, because* • articulates most sounds correctly
Formal operations	11–15 years	More complex sentences and subordination

Learning Disabilities

Students with learning disabilities have severe and unique learning problems due to the great difficulties they have in acquiring, organizing, or expressing specific academic skills or concepts. Their learning problems are generally caused by factors other than lack of educational opportunity, emotional stress in the home or school, difficulty adjusting to school, curricular change or temporary crisis situations, other disabling conditions, lack of motivation, and/or environmental, cultural, or economic disadvantage. The largest group of students with learning disabilities have conditions such as dyslexia, perceptual or memory disorder, or attention-deficit disorder (ADD).

Learning disabilities are typically manifested in school as significantly poor performance in such areas as reading, writing, spelling, arithmetic reasoning or calculation, oral expression or comprehension, and the acquisition of basic concepts. Students who are learning disabled often have difficulties in language processing and literacy learning; they are often referred to as poor readers, disabled readers, or as having specific or developmental language disabilities. Their reading and writing achievement is often significantly below their intellectual capacities.

A language and literacy program for students with learning disabilities should find ways that they can be successful and perceive themselves as learners. For example, the use of computers with word-processing software that checks spelling, grammar, and style gives students greater control over writing. Here are some other guidelines for creating such a program:

Adapting Language Learning

1. Focus on the meaning of language, rather than its parts.
2. Build on students' personal explanations of the world.
3. Use materials at the students' levels of interest.
4. Keep tasks short and at students' ability levels.
5. Emphasize students' intentions in writing over conventions like spelling and punctuation.
6. Use a variety of methods and materials.
7. Emphasize oral language experiences.

Mental Retardation and Below-Average Intelligence

Students with mental retardation are at a low level of intellectual functioning, with IQ scores of 70 or below, or two standard deviations below the mean. (Average intelligence is considered an IQ of 100.) These students are also characterized by deficits in adaptive behavior and limited language abilities, and they may have low levels of self-esteem and problems with social adjustment.

Students with below-average intelligence—called "slow learners"—have IQ scores between 71 and 85. Other characteristics are similar to those of students who are retarded but manifested to a lesser degree. Nonetheless, slow learners acquire information and skills much more slowly and/or have much more difficulty retaining what they've learned than is typical of students of the same age. A language and literacy program for students who are mentally retarded or who are slow learners should provide opportunities for success and be adapted for their special needs.

Adapting Language Learning

1. Immerse students in a language-rich environment.
2. Read aloud to students daily.
3. Provide opportunities for students to express themselves in writing according to their abilities.
4. Use the language experience approach and shared "big book" reading (see Chapter 9 on reading).
5. Demonstrate specific strategies—for instance, in book selection and writing conventions.
6. Build on students' prior knowledge.
7. Use concrete, hands-on experiences.
8. Use predictable books and language patterns for writing.
9. Use a variety of print materials, including environmental print, product packaging, and other functional materials.
10. Allow more time for students' to complete tasks.

Hearing and Vision Impairments

Students are considered to have hearing or vision impairments if their auditory sensitivity/acuity or visual acuity or both adversely affect their educational performance, even with correction. Students may have varying degrees of impairments. For instance, those with hearing impairments may be hard of hearing or deaf, and those with vision impairments may be partially sighted or blind.

These children will benefit greatly from proper diagnosis and the use of hearing aids, glasses, and other aids. Classroom procedures will benefit from these measures, too.

Adapting Language Learning: Hearing-Impaired Students

1. Seat students where they can see your lips move; for group work, seat students where they can see other students' lips move.
2. Speak loudly and clearly, facing students.
3. Make use of written directions on the board, charts, and the like.

Adapting Language Learning: Visually Impaired Students

1. Seat students in the best places for them to see.
2. Use small-group work, and have buddies read directions.
3. Provide materials with large print, paper with darkened lines, and so on.

Giftedness

The U.S. Office of Education defines *gifted* students as those "possessing demonstrated or potential abilities that give evidence of high performance capability in areas such as intellectual, creative, artistic, leadership capability, or specific academic fields, and who require services or activities not ordinarily provided by the school in order to fully develop such capabilities" (PL 97-35, 1981, sec. 582).

Children who are gifted often have verbal talents that are demonstrated by being perceptive, critical, sensitive, and able to see relationships. These characteristics *should* be valued in language arts education, but they can also pose problems—for instance, when students have ideas not anticipated by the teacher; appear critical, sarcastic, or argumentative; continually ask questions; focus on personal interests to the exclusion of classroom tasks; refuse to submit work that's less than perfect; or dominate class discussions. In a synthesis of 106 studies of giftedness, Rogers (1986) concludes that characteristics typically assigned to gifted students are not exclusive to them. "Rather, they are dimensions of ability, development and attitudes on which gifted students tend to be favored" (p. 31).

Adapting Language Learning

1. Focus on activities that require independence and synthesizing ideas, rather than structure and recall.
2. Use a variety of materials and media.
3. Work on high-level projects, individually or in groups.
4. Have students self-select literature and content materials to support their research on projects.
5. Explore a variety of genres in reading and writing.
6. Allow students to work at their own level and pace.
7. Encourage making connections among concepts, prior knowledge, and content.

Behavior Disorders

Children with behavior or emotional disorders show patterns of situationally inappropriate personal behavior over an extended period of time, including unhappiness, depression, withdrawal, and development of physical symptoms or fear associated with personal or school problems. Behavior and emotional disorders cannot be explained by intellectual, sensory, neurological, or general health factors.

Adapting Language Learning

1. Maintain a positive classroom atmosphere.
2. Establish close relationships with students' parents or caretakers.
3. Provide many ways for students to communicate ideas and feelings.
4. Team students with buddies.
5. Make directions clear, provide structure when needed, and monitor and follow up.

Language Disabilities

As children learn their first language, many language disabilities can develop, such as difficulties with articulation, word choice and selection, and morphological and syntactic skills. A common occurrence, for example, is incorrect pronunciation of the letters *r* and *s*. Young children also omit final consonants and simplify consonant clusters at the beginnings of words and ends of syllables.

Language disabilities may also involve communication or speech disorders such as stuttering, impaired articulation, or language or voice impairments. Disabilities such as these interfere with the development, formation, and expression of language. When a young child's language varies notably from that of peers, he or she may need to be assessed for a language disorder. Doing so is complex with young children, because what may appear to be a disorder may simply be a developmental delay. (Remember the broad age range of expected language behaviors in young children.) Other factors that may be confused with language disorders are different ways of speaking, social or regional dialects, or the child's primary language (if it's other than English).

Given these many variables, any tests of language disorders should be accompanied by assessment information that focuses on how children use language. Such information should be collected in context in the classroom, from families, and over time. In most school districts, speech therapists work with children who have language disabilities. The role of teachers is to recommend assessment and provide supportive classroom environments for language interactions.

Genishi (1994, p. 73) recommends the following guidelines when assessing potential language disorders:

Adapting Language Learning

1. Make sure that you completely understand the purpose of each type of assessment.
2. Determine that the procedure or test is really necessary and that the information obtained from it will be useful and beneficial enough to justify any possible stress placed on the child and parents.
3. Ensure that the child is observed—not tested—in as many situations as possible.

Vocabulary and Concept Development in the Classroom

Our discussion of social constructivist theory has illustrated that teachers can play a very important role in the children's development of vocabulary and concepts. One way to do so is to provide many interesting, hands-on experiences in the classroom, encouraging children to experiment with and discover things for themselves. Another way is to create many opportunities for interaction between the teacher and students and between students, as well.

Students are making their own movie cameras. Experiential interaction supports vocabulary and concept development in this classroom of limited-English proficient students.

Children develop increasingly sophisticated understandings of the world and language as they add to existing schema, or symbolic structures they have, for concepts and words. The vocabulary of a school-age child may range from 2,500 words (Crystal, 1987) to 8,000 words (Gleason, 1989) and will increase dramatically through the elementary years. Teachers can support vocabulary and concept development in the classroom through experiential interaction, semantic mapping, and language play.

Experiential Interaction

In a whole-language classroom, concepts and vocabulary develop naturally. We saw examples of this in Chapter 1, the Snapshot of Avril Font's classroom during sharing and group time. (Recall how one student learned the word *excrement.*) Here are things you can do as a teacher to promote such learning:

Experience Things

- *Sharing*—Let children talk about experiences they've had outside of school.
- *Hands-on classroom experiences*—Try cooking, science experiments, class pets, and so on.

Read Books

- *Read aloud*—Do so every day, even with upper-grade children.
- *Reading alone*—Provide time every day for children to read on their own.

Name Things

- *New words*—Introduce new words in the context of meaningful experiences.

Display language, such as these signs, in learning centers, where students can have hands-on experiences in developing concepts and vocabulary.

- *Word for the Day*—Let students choose words that pique their interest. Write each on the board and talk about it. Ask students to talk about it at home and share what they talk about in class the next day.

Show Words

- *Label things in the classroom:* Objects, centers, desks with children's names.
- *Display lists:* Days of the week, months, colors, seasons, holiday words, and the like.

Talk about Words

- *Give other words for words:* Synonyms, antonyms, compounds, and idioms.
- *Use reference books:* Introduce thesauruses and dictionaries to older students.

Try *A First Thesaurus* by Wittels and Greisman (1985).

Write Words

- *Personal dictionaries:* Make these to collect special and useful words, reserving a page for each letter of the alphabet.
- *Word file:* Record special words on file cards in a box or on small strips of heavy paper attached to a metal ring.

Semantic Mapping

Johnson and Pearson (1984) define *semantic maps* as "diagrams that help children see how words are related to one another" (p. 12). Other terms you'll encounter that describe this visual means of relating many ideas to a central one are *cluster, web*, and *"word wall."* (I use the last term throughout this book.) To create a semantic map, Johnson and Pearson suggest using the following strategy:

1. Choose a key word related to students' ideas, interests, or current studies.

2. Write the word in the middle of the chalkboard or a large piece of chartpaper.
3. Brainstorm other words that are related to the key word, and classify the new words in categories that you or the students suggest.
4. Label the categories that emerge.
5. Discuss the words and their relationships and meanings.

TEACHING IDEA

Semantic Maps with Limited–English Proficient Students

One of my students, Jennifer Howard, did a semantic mapping activity with a group of children who were primarily limited English proficient (LEP); they spoke Armenian as their first language. Jennifer read Mary O'Neill's (1961) book of color poems *Hailstones and Halibut Bones,* which she thought would be a good choice for an English language development activity.

See Chapter 10, Reading and Writing, for an entire thematic unit on color that began with this book.

Jennifer read the poems and talked about them with the students. She modeled a semantic map (or "word wall") by writing the word *yellow* in the middle of the chalkboard. Then she asked the students to mention all the other words for *yellow* they could think of and to name yellow things; she wrote down all these words. Next, each child wrote or drew in response to the poems. Aris did a semantic map for the word *green* because he said it was his favorite color (see Figure 2.1).

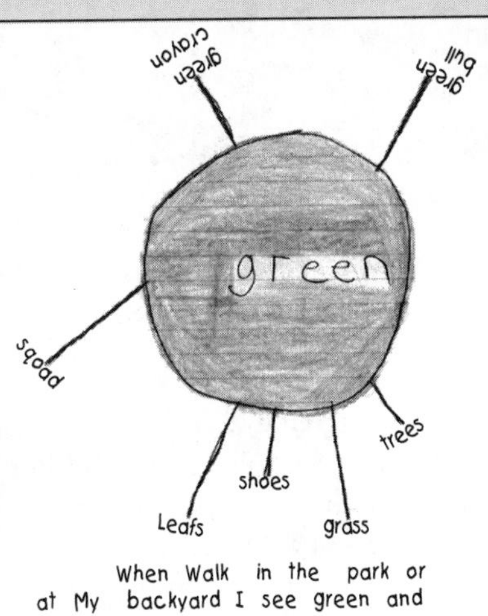

FIGURE 2.1
Semantic Map of Color Green

(continued)

Jennifer tells how the activity went:

I began reading, and they really liked the poems. They wanted to express their opinions about the colors and other objects they thought of that were the same color, such as each and every Power Ranger! We created a "word wall" around the color *yellow.* They loved it! They all stood up and encircled the "word wall" and me. They were excited to think up things that weren't in the original poem. Then they did their own semantic maps.

I was surprised at the level of writing of these LEP students. I think the more LEP students are exposed to books, reading, writing, and lots of discussion, the stronger their achievements will become. This lesson was good for LEP students because it was visual and hands on, two things that help lower the "affective filter" for them.

See Chapter 3, Culture and Language Diversity, to learn about the *affective filter,* which is the anxiety level of students learning English as a second language.

Students with limited proficiency in English benefit from literature-based instruction.

Language Play

See *Wordplay and Language Learning for Children,* by Geller (1985).

From infancy, children naturally play with language and words. Kornei Chukovsky, a Russian linguist, collected language samples from children for many years to support his claim that children are linguistic geniuses. Consider these examples from his book *From Two to Five* (1971): "A bald man has a barefoot head," "A mint candy makes a draft in your mouth," and "A grasshopper's husband is a daddy hopper" (p. 62).

Teachers who support this natural genius help children develop their own understanding and control over language. Teachers can do this by recognizing and valuing children's playful inventions; by providing time, books, and materials for language play; and by displaying children's written examples of language play. Here are some suggestions for encouraging playing with language and words:

See *Chortles: New and Selected Wordplay Poems* by Merriam (1989) and *Herds of Words* by MacCarthy (1991).

Synonyms

These are words that have the same or similar meanings.

- *Word search:* Make a game of searching for synonyms for color words. Places to look could be at home, in the crayon box, or on boxes of hair coloring at the store. (See the Teaching Idea for semantic mapping with color words above.)
- *Thesaurus:* Encourage older children to use a thesaurus for writing.

Antonyms

These are words that have opposite meanings.

- *Brainstorm lists:* Start with a good children's book of antonyms.
- *Children's books*
  - *Antonyms: Hot and Cold and Other Words That Are as Different as Night and Day* (Hanson, 1972)
  - *Fast-Slow, High-Low* (Spier, 1972)
  - *Opposites* (Wilbur, 1973)
  - *Push-Pull, Empty-Full: A Book of Opposites* (Hoban, 1972)

Homonyms

These are words that look the same (*homographs*) or sound the same (*homophones*) but have different spellings or meanings—for instance, *bear* (meaning "an animal" or "to carry") versus *bare* (meaning "uncovered").

- *Brainstorm lists: bear/bare, flour/flower, to/too/two*
- *Children's books*
  - *A Chocolate Moose for Dinner* (Gwynne, 1976)
  - *Eight Ate: A Feast of Homonym Riddles* (Terban, 1982)
  - *Eye Spy: A Mysterious Alphabet* (Bourke, 1994)
  - *The King Who Rained* (Gwynne, 1970)
  - *A Little Pigeon Toad* (Gwynne, 1988)
  - *The Sixteen-Hand Horse* (Gwynne, 1980)
  - *Two-Way Words* (Kudrna, 1980)
  - *What's a Frank Frank? Tasty Homograph Riddles* (Maestro, 1984)
  - *What's Mite Might? Homophone Riddles to Boost Your Word Power* (Maestro, 1986)
- *Cartoons:* Write and illustrate cartoons using the wrong word from a homophone pair.

Parts of Speech

- *Grammar:* Introduce students to the parts of speech through literature.
- *Children's books*
  A Cache of Jewels and Other Collective Nouns (Heller, 1987)
  Kites Sail High: A Book about Verbs (Heller, 1988)
  Many Luscious Lollipops: A Book about Adjectives (Heller, 1989)
  Seeing, Saying, Doing, Playing: A Big Book of Action Words (Gomi, 1994)
  Your Foot's on My Feet! and Other Tricky Nouns (Terban, 1986)

Onomatopoeia

These are words that sound like the sounds they describe—for example, *snap, crackle, pop.*

- *Word search:* Brainstorm a list of words in class, and then continue to add to it.
- *Children's books*
  Click, Rumble, Roar: Poems about Machines (Hopkins, 1987)
  Gobble, Growl, Grunt (Spier, 1971)
  Thump, Thump, Rat-a-Tat-Tat (Baer, 1989)
  Train Song (Siebert, 1990)

Palindromes

These are words or sentences that can be read forward and backward—for example, *Mom, Dad, and Bob* and *Able was I ere I saw Elba* (attributed to Napoleon).

- *Word search:* Start a list of palindromes in class, and add to it. One second-grade teacher started a palindrome craze in her school. Together, the children in the school found over 1,000 palindromes, which were displayed in long lists outside her class.
- *Children's books*
  Go Hang a Salami! I'm a Lasagna Hog! and Other Palindromes (Agee, 1992)
  Too Hot to Hoot: Funny Palindrome Riddles (Terban, 1985)
  Too Hot to Hoot: The Palindrome Puzzle Book (Stuart, 1977)

Similes

These are expressions that make comparisons using *like* or *as*—for instance, *eats like a bird* or *as blue as the sky.*

- *Children's books*
  As: A Surfeit of Similes (Juster, 1989)
  As Quick as a Cricket (Wood, 1982)

Riddles, Puns, and Conundrums

For more on riddles and puns, see Geller (1981).

Riddles are puzzling questions that are solved by guessing—for example, *What has four or more wheels and flies? A garbage truck.* Puns are plays on words using sounds and meanings, such as *Two coin collectors got together for old dime's sake.* A conundrum is a riddle based on an imagined likeness between things that are unlike: *What did the goblin say to the ghost? Spook for yourself.*

- Write and illustrate riddles, puns, conundrums. To get started, see:
  Funny You Should Ask: How to Make Up Jokes and Riddles with Wordplay (Terban, 1992)
- *Children's books*
  I Spy: A Book of Picture Riddles (Marzollo, 1992)
  Monika Beisner's Book of Riddles (Beisner, 1989)
  Spooky Riddles and Jokes (Rosenbloom, 1987)
  Sports Riddles (Rosenbloom, 1982)

Hink-Pinks

These use a question and answer form, with the answer patterned in rhyme and meter. Geller (1981) collected examples that were related to a class study of the Middle Ages: *What do you call a sad gargoyle? A pout spout.*

- Write or pantomime hink-pinks.
- *Children's books*
  Teapot, Switcheroo, and Other Silly Word Games (Tremain, 1979)

Sniglets

This word was coined by Rich Hall (1984), who defined it as follows: "*Sniglet* (snig´-lit): n. any word that doesn't appear in the dictionary but should. For example, *Alponium* (al-po´-neeum): n. (chemical symbol: Ap) Initial blast of odor upon opening a can of dog food" (p. 2).

- Children could collaborate on a book of their own Sniglets. My son Wyatt wrote these when he was 12:

  Spork (spork): n. The plastic eating utensil provided in fast-food restaurants which is a combination of the bowl of a spoon and the tines of a fork.

  Foon (foon): n. Another word for spork.

  Absenphoneomeonon (ab´-sen-fo-nom'i-non): n. Condition during which the phone call you've been waiting for all day comes during the only 5 minutes you are out of the house.

- *Children's books*
  Sniglets (Hall, 1984)

The importance of different language genres for language-minority students is discussed in Chapter 3, Language and Cultural Diversity, the section on sociocultural factors and self-esteem.

LESSON PLAN: Language Play and Literature

ANTics! An Alphabetical Anthology
by Cathi Hepworth

Level: Upper grade

Purpose: Children will listen to and enjoy good literature; discuss the book by responding to open, aesthetic questions and prompts; play with words and increase vocabulary; and draw and write in response to the book.

Materials:

1. *ANTics! An Alphabetical Anthology* by Cathi Hepworth (1992)
2. Chartpaper and marking pens for a "word wall."
3. Plain white paper and pencils or crayons.

Teaching Sequence:

1. Read the book *ANTics! An Alphabetical Anthology* aloud. It's a humorous book that uses ants to illustrate words from A to Z that all have an *ant* in them—for example, *There's E for Enchanter.*
2. Use aesthetic, open-ended questions and prompts to discuss the book. Ask students:
   "What did you think of the book?"
   "What was your favorite part?"
   "What did you notice that all the words in the book had in common?"
   "Can you think of other words the author/illustrator could have used?"
3. Create a "word wall" on chartpaper by writing down all the words the children suggest. Write "Ant Words" in the center.
4. Ask children to pick a word from the book or the "word wall" or to think of their own word to illustrate in a class book of *antics.*

Extending Activities:

1. Write and illustrate more *antics.*
2. Dramatize a short scene based on one of their *antics.*
3. Write and sing a song for an *antic.*
4. Make a list of words that all have another small word in them, such as *cat* in *caterpillar, catastrophe, catalyst, cataclysmic,* and so on.
5. Make all the small words possible by using the letters in a big word.

6. Read some more language play books, such as:
   Buggy Riddles (Hall & Eisenberg, 1986)
   Catch That Cat! A Picture Book of Rhymes and Puzzles (Beisner, 1990)
7. Read a book about ants, such as:
   All Upon a Sidewalk (George, 1974)
   Ant Cities (Dorros, 1987)
   If I Were an Ant (Moses, 1992)
   One Hundred Angry Ants (Pinczes, 1993)
   Step by Step (Wolkstein, 1994)
   Two Bad Ants (Van Allsburg, 1988)
8. Make a simple ant farm. Fill a large jar about two-thirds full with sifted dirt, and put some ants in it. Add a small piece of damp sponge for water and a little food (try sweets, seeds, other insects). Cover the jar with a lid with holes in it. Keep it in a dark place, but bring it into the light to watch ants.

Assessment:

1. Observe the children's reactions while you read the book. Did they listen and seem to enjoy it?
2. Were they able to play with words and brainstorm new *ant* words for the "word wall"?
3. Were they able to draw and write their own *antics* in response to the book?

More *ant* words: *antlers, buoyant, cantaloupe, contestant, deodorant, distant, elephant, elegant, fragrant, gigantic, hydrant, infant, lieutenant, nonchalant, panther, pants, quadrant, radiant, rant, servant, slant, tarantula, transplant, unpleasant, vacant,* and *want.*

FIGURE 2.2
Sample of Children's "Antics"

Assessing Children and Language

Teachers constantly assess children's language learning in the classroom through a variety of means:

1. ***Observation:*** Practice "kidwatching" as you observe and listen to children use language. Consider various aspects of language use, but focus primarily on ways children use language to create meaning.

2. ***Checklists:*** See Table 2.1, which shows Halliday's model of seven language functions; it also gives examples of children's language and related classroom experiences. You could make a checklist using these functions to note children's development of language as "meaning potential" (see Figure 2.3).

3. ***Semantic Maps:*** Check children's understanding of concepts and the words that go with them through semantic mapping activities. Give children a word and ask them to draw or write as many related pictures or words as they can.

FIGURE 2.3
Checklist of Language Functions

NAME ______________________ DATE/TIME __________

ACTIVITY ______________________ SITUATION __________

Language Function	*Observation*	*Interpretation*
Instrumental		
Regulatory		
Interactional		
Personal		
Heuristic		
Imaginative		
Representational		

4. ***Multiple Meanings of Words:*** Give students a word and challenge them to draw or write variations on it according to the acronym *SCAMPER:*

S Substitute
C Combine
A Adapt
M Modify
P Put to other use
E Elaborate
R Reverse

Answers to Questions about Children and Language

1. *How do children acquire language?*

The social constructivist perspective of how children acquire language merges ideas from two viewpoints: the cognitive-constructivist theories of Jean Piaget and the social interactionist theories of Lev Vygotsky. Piaget maintained that children learn language as they first assimilate and then accommodate language symbols to their already existing symbolic structures, or schema. They do this through a process of self-discovery and through direct, hands-on experiences, like working puzzles or playing with clay. Vygotsky maintains that language is learned through the interaction of physical, linguistic, and social factors and that adults and older children play an active role in stimulating younger children's language growth. This stimulation takes place in what Vygotsky calls the *zone of proximal development.* Basically, children acquire language through a process of interaction with the world and people around them, as they add increasingly sophisticated information about language to what they already know.

2. *What do we know when we know how to use a language?*

Language consists of four interacting systems: phonology (sounds), semantics (meanings), syntax (sentence formations), and pragmatics (use). Phonological information enables us to make sounds that have meanings and understand the meanings of sounds that other people make. Phonemes—the smallest units of contrasting sounds with different meanings—are the basic building blocks of the phonology of any language. Semantic information enables us to produce sentences with certain meanings and to understand those of others. Morphemes are the smallest units of meaning in each language; they cannot be divided without losing meaning. Syntactic information enables us to combine words in sentences to express our ideas and understand those of others. Word order is determined by the syntax of a language. Pragmatics is the set of the rules that govern the use of language for different functions, relating to other language users or specific situations. Halliday provides a good definition of language in terms of how people use it: as "'meaning potential,' that is, as sets of opinions, or alternatives, in meaning, that are available to the speaker-hearer" (1975, p. 64). We know a language when we have a feel for it, which is our underlying knowledge of the language systems.

3. *How does language develop?*

Children develop language very rapidly. They speak their first words at around 1 year, and by the time they enter school at age 5, they are able to communicate effectively with others. Three key ideas explain this development. First, language development is an active process. Children are constantly forming, testing, and correcting hypotheses about language structure, as Piaget's constructivist theory suggests; making errors is a natural part of this process. Second, language development is a social process. As Vygotsky's interactionist theory suggests, communicative interaction is an important part of language development. Children listen to language around them and begin to use language when they need to communicate to others around them. Third, language development is an individual process. Children progress through approximately the same stages in language development but at surprisingly different rates, as shown in Piaget's stages of cognitive and language development.

4. *How do teachers support children's growing knowledge of language, concepts, and vocabulary?*

In whole-language classrooms—where children are active, interact with others, and are allowed to progress at their own rate—teachers provide many opportunities for experiential interaction with hands-on experiences. In addition, teachers create a print-rich environment, putting words on display and doing semantic mapping activities (also called *webbing, clustering,* or *"word walls"*). Many books and writing materials are available in print-rich classrooms. Children are encouraged to self-select books, given time to read, and provided with many opportunities to work and write their own ideas. Time for sharing and group work are important, as well. Teachers also create opportunities for word play by reading books that focus on words and encouraging children to respond to them through talking, reading, drawing, and writing.

LOOKING FURTHER

1. Check your baby book and find out when you spoke your first words, phrases, and sentences and what they were. Have a group of children find out the same information, and talk about how we learn language.
2. Describe three learning activities for kindergarten: (a) one that strictly reflects Piaget's notion of how children acquire language, (b) another that reflects Vygotsky's ideas, and (c) a third that combines the two views.
3. Observe in a classroom, and record children's language as they interact in large or small groups. Analyze and classify their language and how they use it according to Halliday's model of children's language (see Table 2.1).
4. Develop a semantic map with others in your class or with a group of children. How could you use this map to plan further learning experiences?
5. Invent a sniglet.

REFERENCES

Applebee, A. N., & Langer, J. A. (1983). Instructional scaffolding: Reading and writing and natural language activities. *Language Arts, 60,* 168–175.

Bissex, G. L. (1980). *Gnys at work: A child learns to write and read.* Cambridge, MA: Harvard University Press.

Bruner, J. S. (1978). The role of dialogue in language acquisition. In A. Sinclair, R. J. Jarvella, & W. M. Levelt (Eds.), *The child's conception of language* (pp. 241–256). New York: Springer-Verlag.

Cazden, C. (1972). *Child language and education.* New York: Holt, Rinehart, & Winston.

Cazden, D. (1983). Adult assistance to language development: Scaffolds, models, and direct instruction. In R. Parker & F. Davis (Eds.), *Developing literacy: Young children's use of language.* Newark, DE: International Reading Association.

Chomsky, C. (1969). *The acquisition of syntax in children from 5 to 10* (Research Monograph No. 52). Cambridge, MA: MIT Press.

Chomsky, N. A. (1957). *Syntactic structures.* The Hague, The Netherlands: Mouton.

Chomsky, N. A. (1965). *Aspects of the theory of syntax.* Cambridge, MA: MIT Press.

Chukovsky, K. (1971). *From two to five.* Berkeley: University of California Press.

Cook-Gumperz, J. (1979). Communicating with young children in the home. *Theory Into Practice, 18,* 207–212.

Crystal, D. (1987). *The Cambridge encyclopedia of language.* Cambridge, England: Cambridge University Press.

Durkin, D. (1966). *Children who read early.* New York: Teachers College Press.

Geller, L. (1981). Riddling: A playful way to explore language. *Language Arts, 58,* 669–674.

Geller, L. (1985). *Wordplay and language learning for children.* Urbana, IL: National Council of Teachers of English.

Genishi, C. (1994). Assessment and achievement testing in the early grades. In A. Purves (Ed.), *Encyclopedia of English studies and language arts* (Vol. 1). New York: Scholastic.

Gleason, J. B. (Ed.). (1989). *The development of language,* (2nd ed.). Columbus, OH: Merrill/Macmillan.

Halliday, M. A. K. (1975). *Learning how to mean.* London, England: Edward Arnold.

Hickman, M. (1985). The implications of discourse skills in Vygotsky's developmental theory. In J. Wertsch (Ed.), *Culture, communication, and cognition* (pp. 236–257). Cambridge, England: Cambridge University Press.

Hymes, D. (1974). *Foundations in sociolinguistics: An ethnographic approach.* Philadelphia: University of Pennsylvania Press.

Johnson, D., & Pearson, P. D. (1984). *Teaching reading vocabulary* (2nd ed.). New York: Holt, Rinehart, & Winston.

Lindfors, J. W. (1987). *Children's language and learning* (2nd ed.). Englewood Cliffs, NJ: Prentice-Hall.

Loban, W. (1976). *Language development: Kindergarten through grade twelve.* Urbana, IL: National Council of Teachers of English.

Menyuk, P. (1963). Syntactic structures in the language of children. *Child Development, 34,* 407–422.

Pflaum, S. W. (1986). *The development of language and literacy in young children.* Columbus, OH: Merrill.

Piaget, J. (1959). *The language and thought of the child.* (3rd ed.). London, England: Routledge & Kegan Paul.

Rogers, K. B. (1986). Do the gifted think and learn differently? A review of recent research and its implications for instruction. *Journal for the Education of the Gifted, 10*(1), 12–20.

Shugar, G. W. (1978). Text analysis as an approach to the study of early linguistic operations. In C. Snow & N. Waterson (Eds.), *The development of communication.* Chichester, England: John Wiley.

Snow, C. E. (1986). Conversations with children. In P. Fletcher & M. Garman (Eds.), *Language acquisition: Studies in first language development* (2nd ed.). (pp. 69–89). Cambridge, England: Cambridge University Press.

Strickland, R. G. (1962). *The language of elementary school children* (Bulletin of the School of Education, No. 4). Bloomington: Indiana University.

Tough, J. (1977). *The development of meaning.* London, England: Allen & Unwin.

Vygotsky, L. S. (1978). *Mind in society.* Cambridge, MA: Harvard University Press.

Vygotsky, L. S. (1986). *Thought and language.* Cambridge, MA: MIT Press.

Wells, G. (Ed.). (1981). *Learning through interaction: The study of language development.* London, England: Cambridge University Press.

CHILDREN'S BOOKS

Agee, J. (1992). *Go hang a salami! I'm a lasagna hog! and other palindromes.* New York: Farrar, Straus, & Giroux.

Baer, G. (1989). *Thump, thump, rat-a-tat-tat.* New York: Harper Row.

Beisner, M. (1989). *Monika Beisner's book of riddles.* New York: Farrar, Straus, & Giroux.

Beisner, M. (1990). *Catch that cat! A picture book of rhymes & puzzles.* New York: Farrar, Straus, & Giroux.

Bourke, L. (1994). *Eye spy: A mysterious alphabet.* San Francisco: Chronicle Books.

Dorros, A. (1987). *Ant cities.* New York: Harper & Row.

George, J. (1974). *All upon a sidewalk.* New York: Dutton.

Gomi, T. (1994). *Seeing, saying, doing, playing: A big book of action words.* San Francisco: Chronicle Books.

Gwynne, F. (1970). *The king who rained.* New York: Windmill.

Gwynne, F. (1976). *A chocolate moose for dinner.* New York: Windmill.

Gwynne, F. (1980). *The sixteen-hand horse.* New York: Prentice-Hall.

Gwynne, F. (1988). *A little pigeon toad.* New York: Simon & Schuster.

Hall, K., & Eisenberg, L. (1986). *Buggy riddles* (S. Taback, Illus.). New York: Dial.

Hall, R. (1984). *Sniglets.* New York: Macmillan.

Hanson, J. (1972). *Antonyms: Hot and cold and other words that are as different as night and day.* New York: Lerner.

Heller, R. (1987). *A cache of jewels and other collective nouns.* New York: Grossett & Dunlop.

Heller, R. (1988). *Kites sail high: A book about verbs.* New York: Scholastic.

Heller, R. (1989). *Many luscious lollipops: A book about adjectives.* New York: Grossett & Dunlop.

Hepworth, C. (1992). *ANTics! An alphabetical anthology.* New York: Putnam's.

Hoban, T. (1972). *Push-pull, empty-full: A book of opposites.* New York: Macmillan.

Hopkins, L. B. (Comp.). (1987). *Click, rumble, roar: Poems about machines* (A. H. Audette, Illus.). New York: Crowell.

Juster, N. (1989). *As: A surfeit of similes.* New York: Morrow.

Kudrna, C. I. (1980). *Two-way words.* New York: Abingdon.

MacCarthy, P. (1991). *Herds of words.* New York: Dial.

Maestro, G. (1984). *What's a frank frank? Tasty homograph riddles.* New York : Clarion.

Maestro, G. (1986). *What's mite might? Homophone riddles to boost your word power.* New York: Clarion.

Marzollo, J. (1992). *I spy: A book of picture riddles* (W. Wicks, Photographer). New York: Scholastic.

Merriam, E. (1989). *Chortles: New and selected wordplay poems* (S. Hamanaka, Illus.). New York: Morrow.

Moses, A. (1992). *If I were an ant.* Chicago: Children's Press.

O'Neill, M. (1961). *Hailstones and halibut bones* (L. Weisgard, Illus.). Garden City, NY: Doubleday.

Pinczes, E. J. (1993). *One hundred angry ants.* Boston: Houghton Mifflin.

Rosenbloom, J. (1982). *Sports riddles.* New York: Harcourt Brace Jovanovich.

Rosenbloom, J. (1987). *Spooky riddles and jokes.* New York: Sterling.

Siebert, D. (1990). *Train song* (M. Wimmer, Illus.). New York: Crowell.

Spier, P. (1971). *Gobble, growl, grunt.* New York: Doubleday.

Spier, P. (1972). *Fast-slow, high-low.* New York: Doubleday.

Stuart, R. (1977). *Too hot too hoot: The palindrome puzzle book* (P. Ford, Illus.). New York: David McKay.

Terban, M. (1982). *Eight ate: A feast of homonym riddles.* New York: Clarion.

Terban, M. (1985). *Too hot to hoot: Funny palindrome riddles.* New York: Clarion.

Terban, M. (1986). *Your foot's on my feet! and other tricky nouns.* New York: Clarion.

Terban, M. (1992). *Funny you should ask: How to make up jokes and riddles with wordplay* (J. O'Brien, Illus.). New York: Clarion.

Tremain, R. (1979). *Teapot, switcheroo, and other silly word games.* New York: Greenwillow.

Van Allsburg, C. (1988). *Two bad ants.* Boston: Houghton Mifflin.

Wilbur, R. (1973). *Opposites.* New York: Harcourt Brace Jovanovich.

Wittels, H., & Greisman, J. (1985). *A first thesaurus.* Racine, WI: Western.

Wolkstein, D. (1994). *Step by step.* New York: Morrow Junior Books.

Wood, A. (1982). *As quick as a cricket* (D. Wood, Illus.). New York: Child's Play International.

Chapter 3

Language and Cultural Diversity

Questions about Language and Cultural Diversity

1. *How do children acquire a second language?*
2. *How can teachers support language-minority students' English language development?*
3. *What do teachers need to know about student cultural diversity?*
4. *How should teachers approach multicultural education?*

Reflective Response: Language and Cultural Diversity

Describe any experience you have had learning a second language, being with second-language learners, or living or working with people whose culture is different from your own. Jot down your ideas, and think about them as you read this chapter.

Stages of Language Proficiency

1. Listening comprehension, or prespeech
2. Early production
3. Extending production

SNAPSHOT: Language Arts with Language-Minority Students

Jaqui Denenberg, one of my students, taught a literature-based lesson as part of her field-experience requirement for my language arts methods course. She taught the lesson in a second-/third-grade combination class in which all the students were native Spanish speakers and classified as *limited English proficient* (*LEP*). (We'll discuss this term later in the chapter.) The classroom teacher, Linda Malone, had 2 years' experience and was not bilingual. Her entire curriculum was literature based.

Jaqui's assignment had two parts. First, she had to identify each child's stage of language proficiency according to Krashen's theories (Krashen & Terrell, 1987), which we'll look at more later in this chapter. Second, she had to teach a literature-based language arts lesson that involved listening, talking, reading, and writing and then describe what happened.

Jaqui taught her lesson using Wanda Gag's picture book *Millions of Cats* (1928/1956) to a group of 9 second-graders who varied considerably in English language proficiency, from the listening comprehension stage (or silent stage) to extending production in English. Although it's important to know each child's stage of language proficiency, it would be unrealistic to plan all language instruction around grouping students of similar proficiencies. Other factors are important to consider, as well, such as students' ideas and interests and cooperative learning in groups. Furthermore, language-minority students benefit from interaction with students who are slightly more advanced in language acquisition, working in groups in which there's a cooperative, constructive, and enjoyable atmosphere for learning.

After completing the lesson, Jaqui made the following observations about the students' stages of English language proficiency:

Reading literature aloud is a great way to support the language and literacy development of students with limited English proficiency.

1. ***Listening Comprehension, or Prespeech: Silent Stage, Active Listening (1 student)***

Veronica has a limited understanding of directions in English. She knows the meanings of words she has heard frequently or that have been discussed in class. She's very aware of what's going on in a story being read from a book that has pictures.

2. ***Early Production: Single Words or Short Phrases (4 students)***

Dixon can follow directions in English but has a limited understanding of a story being read to him in English from a book that doesn't have pictures. If the book has pictures, he can identify what's happening. Some of the English words he speaks are *cat, dog, bird,* and *fish*.

Juan V. understands directions in English, but he responds and writes in Spanish. He's curious about English words and always asks questions about their meanings.

Angeles understands directions in English and can pick out and say certain words that she's used to seeing in print. She's interested in listening to a story and then trying to relate what happened in it by looking at pictures in the book. While listening to *Millions of Cats,* she understood that "millions, and billions, and trillions of cats" was a large quantity of cats.

Mario understands directions in English and, like Angeles, can identify certain words in stories with the help of pictures. Once he understood what the story *Millions of Cats* was about, he was eager to share experiences he had with his dogs in Mexico.

3. ***Extending Production: Sentences and Longer Narratives (4 students)***

Magdalena understands English when it's read to her and understands what's happening in a story without looking at the pictures. But even though she understands English, she's not comfortable speaking it.

Juan L. understands English directions and will respond in a combination of English and Spanish when he doesn't know a word in English. He prefers to speak Spanish, however, because he's fluent in it and likes to talk. He cannot write in English.

Faviola can follow English directions and knows many English words. When she's comfortable in a learning situation, she will speak and write in limited English.

Oscar understands spoken English and responds to questions in English. He understood *Millions of Cats* and interpreted the story for other students while Jaqui was occupied answering questions. He was very proud when Jaqui made a "word wall" of responses with his answers in English. He prefers to write in Spanish because he's not yet confident writing in English, although he can. He spoke comfortably in English throughout the whole lesson.

LESSON PLAN: Literature and Learning English as a Second Language

Level: Primary-grade students with limited English proficiency (LEP)

Purpose: Children will listen to and enjoy good literature; respond to literature through a variety of means, drawing and writing in Spanish or English or both; and develop concepts and vocabulary in the context of a shared literature experience.

Materials:

1. *Millions of Cats* by Wanda Gag (1928/1956)
2. Props: stuffed animals (cats)
3. Pictures: photographs of real cats
4. Chartpaper and marking pens for a "word wall"
5. Plain white drawing paper and crayons and pencils

Teaching Sequence:

1. Read *Millions of Cats* aloud to students, using dramatic voice and facial expressions and gestures. Use illustrations from books and photographs of real cats to clarify the language. Use stuffed animals as props when cats are speaking in the story.
2. Use aesthetic, open-ended questions and prompts to discuss the book:

   "What did you think of the story?"
   "What was your favorite part of the story?"
   "What kind of pets do you have?"
   "Have you ever found a stray animal? What did you do?"
3. Discuss the children's responses and record them in marking pen on chartpaper, making a "word wall." In the center, write "Our ideas about *Millions of Cats*."

4. Give students the following response options after the discussion:
   a. Draw or write anything you want about the story.
   b. Reread *Millions of Cats* with the teacher or a buddy.
   c. Talk about the book in small groups.

Extending Activities:

1. Read other books by Wanda Gag:
   A B C Bunny (1933)
   The Funny Thing (1929)
   Gone Is Gone (1935)
2. Read other English language books about cats:
   Catch That Cat! A Picture Book of Rhymes and Puzzles (Beisner, 1990)
   The Fat Cat (Kent, 1971/1990)
   Have You Seen My Cat? (Carle, 1987)
3. Read Spanish language books about cats:
   El Gato Cui (Gonzalez de Tapia, 1984)
   El Gato Sabio de Juanito (Vanhalewijn, 1980)
   Gatos (Petty, 1991)
4. Dramatize part of *Millions of Cats.*
5. Do a puppet show using stuffed animal cats or student-made puppets.
6. Create a chart of everybody's pets.
7. Invite a pet store owner in the community to talk to the class about cats. Ideally, ask someone who speaks Spanish.
8. Read *How Much Is a Million?* by David Schwartz (1985) to develop concepts and vocabulary about large quantities like *millions, billions,* and *trillions.*

Jaqui described how the lesson went:

> The outcomes of this lesson were so overwhelming. I have been a substitute for 9 months, and it is amazing to see the differences in responses from the students when they are read to from a basal reader versus a literary book. It is always positive when a literary book is read. The students went on to so many different tangents and experiences from each of the stories, and even the shyest of students was sharing his experience with the dogs he had in Mexico. It was so exciting to hear all the different stories that the students had about themselves. They spoke in Spanish and English and helped each other out in English.
>
> They really responded in individual ways. Only one of their drawings had to do with the actual story. The rest all had to do with

experiences that they have had with their own animals. Juan V. did a wonderful drawing of his farm in Mexico, showing all the animals that were on the farm, including a cat that used to love to climb on top of him to sleep. Oscar and Juan L. decided to draw a picture of the class pet, Pumpkin the bunny. When they finished, they read the book the class had written earlier in the year about Pumpkin. Mario, the shyest student, started telling me about his dog, which helped him fight off other dogs one day when he was playing in Mexico.

What was so great about all this was that the students were learning new things about each other that they had not known all year long. I think it helped that I brought in a picture of my cat and stuffed animals. They were so eager to talk in English and Spanish. All the students wanted me to draw pictures of their pets.

Linda Malone, the classroom teacher, believes in using a lot of literature and hands-on experiences with her language-minority students, so she was very pleased that the children were so involved with the story. She praised Jaqui on bringing in props like stuffed animals and pictures to provide visual support and clues for understanding the story. Linda also praised the "word wall" technique (see Figure 3.1) and asked to see students' drawings and writings. She told Jaqui that these are the types of things she includes in students' portfolios for assessment or makes notes about in an anecdotal record she keeps about each student. Linda insists that portfolio assessment is much more accurate than taking tests. She can see students' progress with her own eyes.

See Chapter 9, The Writing Process, for more on portfolios.

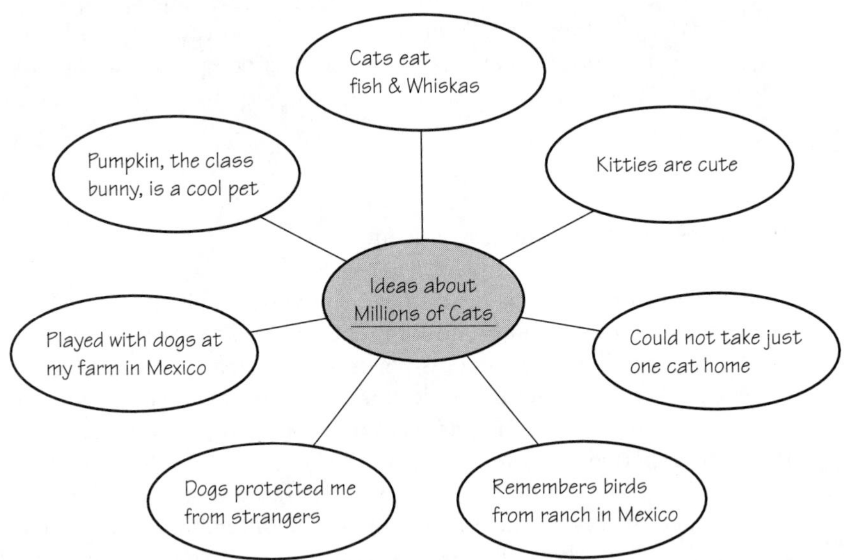

FIGURE 3.1 "Word Wall" for *Millions of Cats*

Learning English as a Second Language

Several important principles can be learned from Jaqui's lesson using literature for English language development:

1. Children learn a second language best when instruction draws on their prior experiences, which occurs naturally in response-centered, literature-based lessons.
2. Children will respond in different ways, no matter what their native language or level of English proficiency. They should be allowed to respond in their native language, in English, or using a combination of the two. What's important is that students are actively engaged in a learning experience (as explained by Piaget's [1973, 1977] cognitive-constructivist theories).
3. Children are empowered to use language for meaningful purposes when the teacher focuses on what they are trying to say (as explained in Vygotsky's [1962, 1978] social interactionist theories), rather than on a text, such as a basal reader.

Second-language theorist James Cummins (1981) calls this *context-embedded instruction,* which will be explained in the next section, Learning English as a Second Language.

See Chapters 1 and 2 for more on the theories of Piaget and Vygotsky.

Like the class that Jaqui taught, many students in the United States speak a first language other than English. These students are often referred to as *LEP,* or *limited English proficient.* Other related terms are *PEP* (*potentially English proficient*) and *ELL* (*English language learners*). LEP students become *FEP,* or *fluent English proficient,* when they reach an advanced level of English proficiency.

The United States is fast becoming a multilingual society. By the year 2000, language-minority students will make up 15 percent of the K–12 (kindergarten through twelfth grade) enrollment. By 2026, they will make up almost 25 percent of school enrollment. Given these increases, it's likely that you will teach language-minority students at some time during your career.

There is widespread agreement among educators regarding educational goals for language-minority students. They should be able to:

1. attain high levels of oral English proficiency
2. experience positive psychosocial adjustment to life in a complex, multicultural society
3. achieve success in academic areas, including mathematics, reading, and writing (California State Department of Education, 1981)

Another important goal in teaching language arts to language-minority children is *biliteracy*—the ability to read and write in two languages as well as to speak in two languages (which is *bilingualism*). Research has shown that language-minority children can successfully learn to read and write in English while learning to speak it. In fact, knowing how to read and write in a first language other than English supports literacy development (Edelsky, 1986; Zutell & Allen, 1988), and literacy experiences support language acquisition (Hudelson, 1984; Rigg, 1986; Urzua, 1987). Given these findings, children should continue to learn to read and write in their native language as much as possible (Goodman, Goodman, & Flores, 1979).

These are important goals for all students, whatever their primary languages. But when children come to school with little or no proficiency in English, how are these goals to be met? In recent years, second-language instruction has been guided primarily by the theories and research of two linguists: James Cummins and Stephen Krashen. We'll review their work in the following sections.

Dimensions of Language Proficiency

The theories and research of Canadian linguist James Cummins have greatly influenced the education of language-minority students in the United States. Cummins (1981) has identified two *dimensions* of language proficiency: communicative language skills and academic language skills. *Basic interpersonal communication skills* (*BICS*) are used daily in social speaking situations, such as children talking together on the playground. *Cognitive academic language proficiency* (*CALP*) involves those language skills used in school tasks, such as taking notes on a lecture and writing a report using the information.

The relationship between BICS and CALP is often illustrated using an iceberg and the old adage about being deceived in seeing only its tip. According to this metaphor, BICS are the tip of the iceberg (see Figure 3.2). In other words, we can see and hear basic communicative competence but can be misled in thinking that a student has also developed CALP, which is required for success in complex academic tasks.

Context-Embedded Communication

Proficiency in both dimensions of language is determined by the amount of contextual support present. Cummins (1981) calls this proficiency *context-embedded communication.* In it, meaning is actively negotiated between speakers and supported by many contextual clues, like when deciding whose turn it

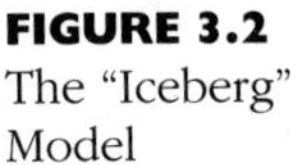

FIGURE 3.2
The "Iceberg" Model

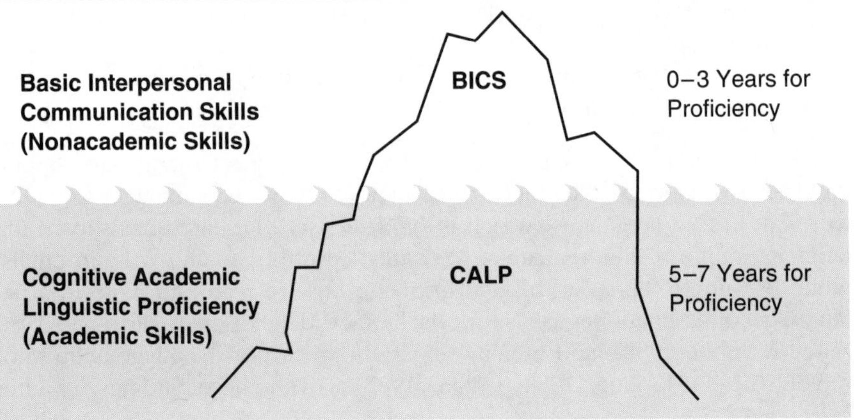

is in playing a game. In *context-reduced communication,* there are few clues as to meaning—for example, answering a teacher's questions after a lecture. Each type of communication task also has a level of cognitive demand. Little thought is required in cognitively *undemanding* tasks, such as taking your turn in a game. Cognitively *demanding* tasks (such as writing a 5-paragraph essay) are more difficult, however.

According to Cummins, "A major aim of schooling is to develop students' ability to manipulate and interpret cognitively-demanding context-reduced text. The more initial reading and writing instruction can be embedded in a meaningful communicative context (i.e., related to the child's experience), the more successful it is likely to be. The same principle holds for second language instruction" (1984, p. 136). Cummins cautions that achieving ability with cognitively demanding, context-reduced text takes a long time (sometimes 5 to 7 years) and should not be confused with the ability to use language in cognitively undemanding, context-embedded instructional situations (e.g., sharing time in class or playing a game at recess).

Cummins's theory is often explained using a figure divided into quadrants. See Figure 3.3, which shows the relationship between the cognitive demands of the task (from undemanding, or easy, to demanding, or difficult) and the contextual support for the task (from context embedded, or many clues, to context reduced, or few clues). The tasks shown in each quadrant—A, B, C, D—are determined by the interaction of the cognitive demands of the task and the amount of contextual support necessary to achieve it.

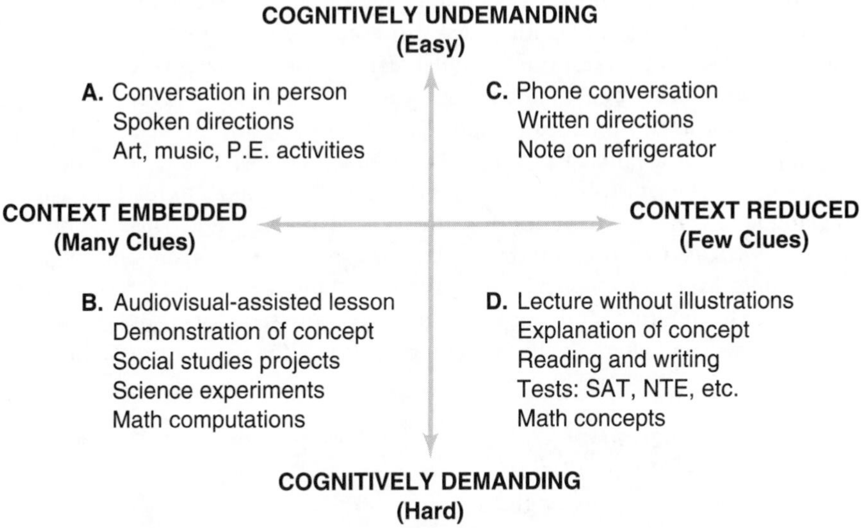

FIGURE 3.3 Cummins's Model of Language Proficiency

COGNITIVELY UNDEMANDING
(Easy)

A. Conversation in person
Spoken directions
Art, music, P.E. activities

C. Phone conversation
Written directions
Note on refrigerator

CONTEXT EMBEDDED (Many Clues) ⟷ **CONTEXT REDUCED (Few Clues)**

B. Audiovisual-assisted lesson
Demonstration of concept
Social studies projects
Science experiments
Math computations

D. Lecture without illustrations
Explanation of concept
Reading and writing
Tests: SAT, NTE, etc.
Math concepts

COGNITIVELY DEMANDING
(Hard)

Source: From "The Role of Primary Language Development in Promoting Educational Success for Language Minority Students," by J. Cummins, 1981, in *Schooling and Language Minority Students: A Theoretical Framework* (p. 12), Los Angeles: California State University, Bilingual Training Center, School of Education. Copyright 1981 by California State University, Los Angeles. Reprinted with permission.

Building a papier-mâché model of The Great Kapok Tree *(Cherry, 1990) while learning about tropical rainforests is an example of context-embedded instruction for second-language learners.*

Common Underlying Proficiency

To meet the goals of educating language-minority students, teachers must ensure that they're able to develop both communicative and academic language skills in English and in their primary language. This doesn't mean, however, that it will take twice as much time and effort. According to Cummins (1981), language-minority students are able to manage the linguistic demand of more cognitively difficult, context-reduced school tasks because a *common underlying proficiency* (*CUP*) underlies both languages. That is, developing the ability to perform cognitively demanding tasks in context-reduced situations in one language is a basis for performing similar tasks in another language.

For example, bilingual students who read well in one language usually also read well in the other language. They become good readers, and their skill applies to both their first and second languages. This is called *additive bilingualism*. The opposite is also true: Bilingual students who read poorly in one language generally read poorly in the other language, too. This is *subtractive bilingualism*. Cummins (1981) explains these tendencies using the *linguistic threshold hypothesis:* For bilingual students, the degree to which proficiencies in both the first and second languages are developed is positively associated with academic achievement, as follows (adapted from Cummins, 1981):

Level of Bilingualism	***Academic Effect***
1. *Proficient bilingualism:* High levels in both languages	Positive
2. *Partial bilingualism:* Nativelike ability in one of the languages	Neither positive nor negative
3. *Limited bilingualism:* Low levels in both languages	Negative

Language Acquisition versus Learning

The ideas of American linguist Stephen Krashen (1981) also have been important in the development of approaches to teaching language-minority students. His theory of second-language acquisition has five hypotheses:

1. *The Acquisition/Learning Hypothesis:* Second-language learning involves two distinct processes: (a) *language acquisition,* or the subconscious, natural way we learn language by using it for real communication, and (b) *language learning,* or conscious knowing about a language, as when we are able to describe its rules. We *acquire* a second language the same way we acquire a first language: through the successful communication of meaningful messages. People who travel or live in a foreign country often learn the local language without formal instruction by listening to it and using it on a daily basis in naturally occurring situations, such as going shopping or eating in restaurants. This is similar to how a child acquires a first language: picking it up naturally, as subconscious, implicit knowledge, which formal teaching doesn't help. We *learn* language, on the other hand, by studying its grammar and rules, which is how foreign language classes are taught. Thus, language learning is formal, conscious, explicit knowledge, which formal teaching does help.

2. *The Natural Order Hypothesis:* Grammatical structures are acquired in a predictable order—some early and some late. However, not everyone acquires these structures in exactly the same order, nor do they acquire them in a second language in exactly the same order they were acquired in the first.

3. *The Monitor Hypothesis:* Conscious learning about a language has a limited function in second-language performance. The rules of language we learn don't make us fluent but only serve to monitor (i.e., check or fix) what we've acquired. Fluency is the result of what we have acquired in natural communicative situations. In addition, in order to use the monitor function successfully, three conditions must be met:

- The speaker has to have time. If the conversation is rapid, thinking about the rules may disrupt or stop it.
- The speaker has to be thinking about the rule. Often, *what* is said is more important than *how* it is said.
- The speaker has to know the rule. Many people learn to use a language without conscious knowledge of its rules.

What is important about the monitor hypothesis is that language is not produced by knowledge of the rules but by acquisition. The monitor is only used for self-correction.

4. *The Input Hypothesis:* We acquire (not learn) language by understanding input that's a little beyond our current level of proficiency. Listening and reading are of primary importance, and speaking and writing come later.

Fluency in speaking, for example, isn't taught directly but emerges after we've built competence through comprehending input. To progress to the next stage in language acquisition, we need to understand language input that's somewhat more difficult than what we already know. (This idea is similar to Vygotsky's [1978] zone of proximal development.)

Krashen uses the term *comprehensible input* to describe the type of understandable language experiences that we need for second-language acquisition. Characteristics of comprehensible input include:

- involves language that's already known to the student together with some not yet acquired
- provides contextual clues, such as objects in familiar situations
- provides paralinguistic clues, such as gestures and facial expressions
- uses linguistic modification, such as intonation, repetition, paraphrasing, simplification, clear pronunciation, and reduced speed
- addresses a topic students have prior knowledge of
- is meaningful and interesting to students
- does not need to be grammatically sequenced

As summarized by Krashen:

> *We acquire when we obtain comprehensible input in a low-anxiety situation, when we are presented with interesting messages, and when we understand these messages. Comprehensible input has been the last resort of the language teaching profession: We have tried nearly every other possibility—grammar teaching, dialogue memorization, pattern drills, and expensive awkward teaching machines. None of these approaches attempts to provide the essential ingredient—comprehensible input.* (1985, p. 10)

The Input Hypothesis $i + 1$
Students move from i (their current level of competence) to $i + 1$ (the stage immediately following) with the help of comprehensible input.

Understanding meaning is the basis of language acquisition. If teachers are checking for understanding, children will acquire progressively more difficult language gradually and naturally, without direct instruction.

5. ***The Affective Filter Hypothesis:*** Comprehensible input is necessary but not sufficient for language acquisition to take place. Affective factors, called the *affective filter,* determine how much of the raw material of language (the comprehensible input) will be processed. Acquisition will be limited when the affective filter is high, as when students are nervous, not motivated to speak the new language, and lacking self-esteem. Acquisition will increase when the affective filter is low, as when students have low levels of anxiety but high levels of motivation and self-confidence.

Krashen's five hypotheses form the basis of a teaching method called the *natural approach,* which is designed to supply good comprehensive input and promote a low affective filter. (We'll discuss this approach later in the chapter.) Creating a positive, supportive school environment with opportunities for cooperative learning and interactions among minority students, majority students, and teachers will enhance language-minority students' language proficiency and academic achievement.

Teaching English as a Second Language

Classroom teachers who aren't bilingual should concentrate on methods of English language development when teaching language-minority students. This should be done in conjunction with primary language support for academic achievement in other subjects with a late-exit bilingual maintenance program (that is, classes taught in student's first languages, K–12) for maximum school success (Ramirez & Merino, 1990). While they learn English, students' first languages can also be maintained through the use of bilingual teachers, aides, paraprofessionals, and school staff; cross-age tutoring and grouping; and flexible scheduling and team teaching among bilingual and monolingual teachers in a school.

Historically, two types of approaches have been used in second-language education: grammar based and communicative based. *Grammar-based instruction* focuses on accuracy in grammar usage. It's been a successful instructional approach when the goal has been either to learn grammar or to produce grammatically correct sentences in a limited communicative context. Grammar-based instruction has not been helpful, though, in helping students function in normal communicative contexts. Krashen (Krashen & Terrell, 1987) calls this *language learning*. *Communicative-based instruction* focuses on meaning, or the student's ability to communicate messages. Krashen calls this *language acquisition*.

Here's a comparison of the two instructional approaches:

Language Learning (grammar based)	***Language Acquisition*** (communicative based)
1. Focus is on language forms.	1. Focus is on meaningful communication.
2. Success is based on mastery of language forms.	2. Success is based on using language to get things done.
3. Lessons are organized around types of language forms and structures: teacher-directed activities.	3. Lessons are organized around ideas and interests of students: student-/response-centered activities.
4. Error correction is essential for mastery.	4. Errors in form are acceptable.
5. Learning is a conscious process of memorizing rules, forms, and structures.	5. Acquisition is unconscious and occurs through exposure to comprehensible input.
6. Emphasis on production skills may result in anxiety in early stages.	6. Emphasis on letting language emerge naturally results in low anxiety.

Communicative-based (or language acquisition) approaches currently used in elementary classrooms apply methods relevant to the functional language needs of students who are learning to live in language environments different than that those of their homes. Examples of communicative-based approaches include Stephen Krashen and Tracy Terrell's (1987) *natural approach* and James Asher's (1977) *total physical response*. We'll look at each in the following section.

The Natural Approach

The natural approach is based on Krashen's theory of second-language acquisition and the basic premise that children acquire a second language the same way they acquire a first: in natural situations focused on the communication of meaningful messages—a natural approach. Think back to the Snapshot in Chapter 2, which presented a dialogue among four children of different ages. This is an example of how children acquire a first language: easily and naturally, with support from family members and friends who concentrate on what each child is trying to say or mean, not on correcting mistakes in pronunciation or grammar or usage.

See Chapter 2 for more on how children acquire a first language and how teachers can enhance their continued language development.

Principles of the Natural Approach

1. *The goal of the natural approach is communication skills.* It's important that students focus on the communication of messages in the language they're learning. In the long run, students will learn to speak more fluently and accurately because of the greater amount of comprehensible input received when the focus is on the meaning and the message, rather than grammatical accuracy.
2. *Production must be allowed to emerge in stages.* The first stage of language production is nonverbal communication, the next stage is speaking single words, and so on. In short, children will speak when they're ready to. Error correction is not important or advisable in these early stages. Instead, teachers should use the target language predominantly, create communicative situations, and provide comprehensible input that matches students' levels of language proficiency.
3. *Teaching must be based on language-acquisition activities.* Instruction should focus on students' ideas, interests, and experiences. Grammar will be acquired as students learn to communicate for real purposes in real situations.
5. *Activities should lower the affective filter.* The classroom atmosphere should be warm and friendly, and teachers should create activities that fully engage students. Here are some appropriate topics and situations on which to base language experiences that can lower the affective filter:

   Topics: Names, descriptions of students and family, numbers, clothing, colors, objects in the classroom, and pets

   Situations: Greetings, classroom directions, playing games and sports, and sharing home experiences

Stages of Language Proficiency

As mentioned in principle 2, second-language learners move through stages of language proficiency: from listening comprehension, or preproduction, to early production, to extending production (Krashen & Terrell, 1987). There is a silent period at the beginning, when students are focusing on comprehension but not yet speaking.

These stages were used to describe the students that Jaqui Denenberg taught in the Snapshot at the beginning of the chapter. However, these stages are not intended as a means of classifying children in similar stages. For one thing, it would be unrealistic to try to maintain such a structure in a self-contained, whole-language classroom, in which many other factors should determine grouping, such as students' interests and friendships. Moreover, children benefit from interaction with peers whose language proficiency is at least slightly more advanced than their own.

Nonetheless, you should be aware of the characteristics of each stage as you help emerging English speakers. Each stage is described in the following list, which also provides appropriate activities, suggested by Krashen and Terrell (1987). The children in Jaqui's group who are at each stage of proficiency are included, as well, to help you picture real students in each case.

1. ***Listening Comprehension, or Preproduction: Silent Stage, Active Listening:*** Veronica is at this stage of second-language proficiency. She knows the meanings of words she hears frequently and can follow a story in a book that has pictures.

Students should be allowed to go through a silent period, which can last anywhere from a few hours to several weeks or months. During this stage, the teacher will talk a lot, providing comprehensible input. Techniques from James Asher's (1977) *total physical response* (*TPR*) approach, mentioned earlier, may be used. These techniques only require that students move or gesture in response to directions the teacher speaks or acts out. The teacher does so first to demonstrate and then again with students. Finally, the students are able to follow the spoken direction only.

Total Physical Response Activities

- *Movement:* "Stand, sit, turn around, walk, stop, wave, . . ."
- *Body parts:* "Touch your head, eyes, nose, shoulders, . . ."
- *Classroom:* "Touch or point to the wall, floor, window, . . ."
- *Objects:* "Touch or pick up the pencil, book, paper, . . ."
- *Sequences:* "Stand, touch your head, point to the wall, . . ."

Comprehension Activities

- *Names:* "Walk to Retana."
- *Physical descriptions:* "Give the book to the person with brown hair."
- *Numbers:* "Pick up three pencils."
- *Colors:* "Touch the red book."
- *Clothing:* "Put on the sweater."
- *Sequences:* "Give Fabiola three yellow pencils."

Visual aids are also useful with these activities and can be combined with TPR and comprehension activities. Students can follow the teacher's lead, for example, by pointing to a type of clothing in a mail order catalogue. In addition, TPR techniques are often applied in combination with other activities and continue to be useful beyond the comprehension stage.

Visual Aids to TPR and Comprehension Activities

- *Pictures:* Photographs, posters, magazine and newspaper pictures
- *Media:* Slides, filmstrips, transparencies

Perhaps create a picture file according to concepts such as colors, animals, people, clothing, and food. Ask students to bring pictures from home that interest them, including family photographs or illustrations from magazines, catalogues, or newspapers.

2. ***Early Production: Single Words or Short Phrases:*** Dixon, Juan V., Angeles, and Mario are at this stage. They can understand directions in English, speak some words, and follow a story in a book through pictures.

This stage begins when students start to produce words and can last from a few months to a year or more. To support development, teachers should ask questions that require "yes" or "no" or one-word answers:

- *Yes/no questions:* "Are you a student?" "Am I a teacher?"
- *Either/or questions:* "Do I have blue eyes or brown eyes?"
- *One-word answer questions:* "What color eyes does Nam have?"

Answers to questions about students—for instance, about eye or hair color—can be graphed or displayed on a chart and used for further activities. What's more, these questions can build on and be combined with activities from the comprehension stage.

3. ***Extending Production: Sentences, Longer Narratives:*** Magdalena and Juan L. are both at this stage. Both can understand English and follow a story without pictures, but they speak only limited English. Oscar understands English, responds extensively in English, and can write in English.

During this stage, students becomes increasingly fluent and progress from producing one-word answers to short phrases. This development will occur gradually, taking up to 3 years. The teacher should expect errors and deal with them through indirect correction, such as repeating the child's message in correct English without drawing attention to the error or making him or her repeat what was said correctly. It's important that the teacher provide comprehensible input in an atmosphere of low anxiety.

Questions and dialogue at this stage should be open ended:

- *Open-ended sentences:* "My name is . . . I am wearing . . . After school I want to . . ."
- *Open-ended dialogues:*
  First speaker: "Hi, my name is . . . "
  Second speaker: "I'm glad to meet you. My name is . . ."

  First speaker: "I'm from . . . Where are you from?"
  Second speaker: "I'm from . . ."

Literature in Multilingual Classrooms

Good children's books can provide the basis for many language development activities in multilingual, whole-language classrooms (Allen, 1989; Elley & Mangubhai, 1983; Rigg, 1986). A teacher reading a good children's picture book aloud can cast a spell in the classroom. Even children who don't understand every word (or any of the words) will be spellbound by the sound of the teacher's voice—reading dramatically, speaking in different tones and pitches for different characters, using facial expressions and gestures, and so on. Children can also follow stories through their illustrations. Repeated-pattern books are excellent choices. Many other beautiful children's books have minimal text but compelling illustrations, which serve the same purpose as the pictures suggested in our discussion of the natural approach.

See Chapter 4, Emergent Literacy, for more on pattern books.

The keys to using literature with language-minority students are (1) to make the experience interesting and (2) to provide comprehensible input in a low-anxiety atmosphere. Good books that appeal to children have the potential to do both these things and more. In the following section, we'll look at some types of books and authors that complement the activities suggested in the natural approach and that provide children with experiences with good books.

Concept Books

These are also called *single-concept books* because they clearly focus on one concept that's useful and appropriate for primary-age children; they are also ideal for use with language-minority students. The following lists present books that are related to concepts frequently used with language-minority children. Also listed are books by some specific author/illustrators and author/photoillustrators who have specialized in concept books so you can ask for them by name.

Colors

My Very First Book of Colors (Carle, 1974)
Samuel Todd's Book of Great Colors (Konigsburg, 1990)
Color Dance (Jonas, 1989)
Color Zoo (Ehlert, 1990a)
Colors (Reiss, 1969)

Animals

Animal Alphabet (Kitchen, 1984)
Feathers for Lunch (Ehlert, 1990b)
My Hen Is Dancing (Wallas, 1993)
Whose Baby? (Yabuuchi, 1985)
Whose Footprints? (Yabuuchi, 1985)

Food

Anno's Faces (Anno, 1989)
Apples and Pumpkins (Rockwell, 1989)
Each Peach Pear Plum (Ahlberg, 1978)

Eating the Alphabet (Ehlert, 1989)
Potluck (Shelby, 1991)

Author/Illustrators of Concept Books
Donald Crews
Carousel (1982a)
Freight Train (1978)
Harbor (1982b)
School Bus (1984)
Truck (1980)

Brian Wildsmith
Brian Wildsmith's ABC (1962)
Brian Wildsmith's Birds (1967)
Brian Wildsmith's Circus (1970)
Brian Wildsmith's Fishes (1968)
Brian Wildsmith's Puzzles (1971)

Author/Photoillustrators of Concept Books
Tana Hoban
Big Ones, Little Ones (1976)
Circles, Triangles, and Squares (1974)
More Than One (1981)
Over, Under, Through, and Other Spatial Concepts (1973)
Shapes, Shapes, Shapes (1986)

Bruce McMillan
Becca Backward, Becca Forward: A Book of Concept Pairs (1986)
Growing Colors (1988)
Here a Chick, There a Chick (1983)
Mouse Views: What the Class Pet Saw (1993)
Super, Super, Superwords (1989)

Student Cultural Diversity

Culture has been defined many times by anthropologists through the years. Spradley (1980) offers a cognitive definition, which includes three fundamental aspects of human experience: what people do, what people know, and what people make and use (p. 5). Of these three, he emphasizes the importance of what people know, or *cultural knowledge*. He defines *culture* as "the acquired knowledge people use to interpret experience and generate behavior" (p. 6). In other words, culture is a system of knowledge that produces behavior and is used to interpret experience.

A given culture is shared by the people in a particular social group. Bullivant (1993) makes this important distinction, explaining that "culture is defined as a social group's design for surviving in and adapting to its environment" (p. 29). Given this definition, "one aim of multicultural education is to teach about the many social groups and their different designs for living in our pluralist society" (p. 29). *Multicultural education,* then, must go beyond a vague, general approach to teaching about different heritages and traditions to teaching about the cultures of specific social groups.

Student cultural diversity, as explained by Au (1993), has three distinguishing features:

1. *ethnicity:* national origin, such as African American, Asian American, Hispanic American, and Native American or, more specifically, Haitian, Cambodian, El Salvadoran, or Sioux
2. *class:* socioeconomic status, or parents' occupation and family income
3. *language:* whether a dialect of English, such as Black English, or a language other than English, such as Spanish

Current research and theory on the cultures of different social groups provides useful information for planning and teaching language arts in linguistically and culturally diverse classrooms.

Sociocultural Factors and Self-Esteem

Understanding how language is used in varying social and cultural contexts is equally important to understanding how language is acquired. The ideas of Shirley Brice Heath and John Ogbu are important here, as they provide teachers with ideas about raising students' self-esteem and thus their academic achievement, as well.

Language Genres

In her book *Ways with Words* (1983), Shirley Brice Heath reported the results of a study she did in South Carolina, which looked at the ways language was used in a poor, African American community and in a working-class European American community. She found differences in how language was used in the homes versus the schools in these communities.

To characterize these differences, Heath (1983) has identified what she calls *language genres,* or descriptive units into which different types of language events fit. Different cultural groups use certain genres more frequently, and not all groups use the same genres. The language of schooling has its own genres, and Heath argues that in order for children to succeed, they must be able to use these school language genres:

1. *Label Quests:* Teachers ask questions about the names and attributes of things: "What is this? What color is it?"
2. *Meaning Quests:* Teachers ask students to explain the meanings of words, pictures, and events: "What did the author mean?" (Heath says this occurs with books from "the basal to Shakespeare.")
3. *Recounts:* Teachers ask children to summarize information or recount facts they already know.

4. *Accounts:* Students can provide new information or new interpretations. Show-and-tell and creative writing are also accounts. (Schools generally allow for few accounts.)
5. *Eventcasts:* These are narratives of events that are happening or will occur. For instance, teachers tell students what will take place or how to solve a math problem or do a science experiment.
6. *Stories:* This is the most familiar language genre. It includes fiction in basal readers as well as children's literature.

Heath emphasizes that "critical to school success, however, is the extent to which all of these school-valued genre occur in the home—either in the minority language or English—repeatedly, around written materials, and with strong positive reinforcement" (1986, p. 171). In her study, she compared how these school-valued genres were used in the homes of Mexican Americans (who had come to the United States in the last 20 years) and Chinese Americans. The relative frequencies of use of school genres between the two groups are as follows:

School Genre	***Mexican American Homes***	***Chinese American Homes***
Label quests	Rarely	Frequently
Meaning quests	Rarely	Frequently
Recounts	Rarely	Infrequently
Accounts	Frequently	Frequently
Eventcasts	Almost never	Frequently
Stories	Very popular	Frequently

As we can see, many of the school-valued genres are not used frequently in Mexican American homes but are more so in Chinese American homes. Teachers should be aware of how language is used in the homes of their students. And in the classroom, Heath suggests that teachers do the following:

1. Children should have experiences with the full range of language genres typically used in school. Teachers should expand the number of language genres that students can use. Label quests, recounts, and eventcasts should receive emphasis. Children should practice their use in their primary language as much as possible and with the help of bilingual paraprofessionals such as aides.
2. Teachers should go beyond traditional school texts and use texts or types of narratives that are more familiar to children, such as jokes, comic books, and television.
3. Teachers should accept the use of children's native languages.
4. Teachers should not expect that children will learn to use genres in any kind of linear order. Some children will use certain genres better than others, and use and progress will differ among individuals.

Here are some popular joke books for children: *Clifford's Riddles* (Bridwell, (1974); *Invisible Oink: Pig Jokes* (Phillips, 1993); *Old Turtle's 90 Knock Knock Jokes and Riddles* (Kessler, 1991); and *Tyrannosaurus Wrecks: A Book of Dinosaur Riddles* (Sterne, 1979).

Heath (1983) draws our attention to the sociocultural context of language development and the cultural differences that may exist between the home and school. We know that the language genres of each setting are different. The school may demand language use that is not naturally occurring in the home. Teachers should not make assumptions and try to "fill in the gaps" in students' language use differences. Rather, teachers should model the use of language genres in the classroom.

Types of Minorities

John Ogbu's research (Ogbu & Matute-Bianchi, 1986) has focused on the knowledge, identity, and school adjustment of minorities. He distinguishes three types of minorities:

1. ***Autonomous Minorities:*** In the United States, people who are Amish, Mormon, and Jewish are autonomous minorities in a numerical sense, but they are not language minorities (because they speak standard English, for the most part). The experience of this type of minority is quite different from that of the other two.

2. ***Immigrant Minorities:*** Immigrants have come voluntarily to the United States and include Japanese, Chinese, Cuban, and Filipino Americans, among others. These groups may have been exploited and subordinated economically and politically in this country, but they don't have low opinions of themselves. Rather they are optimistic and consider themselves better off than if they had remained in their homelands. Immigrant minorities are motivated to do well in school, and their children are taught to accept the school's way of doing things.

3. ***Caste Minorities:*** Caste minorities have become incorporated into U.S. society more or less involuntarily through slavery, conquest, or colonization. Included in this group are African, Mexican, Puerto Rican, and Native Americans. People from these groups are often exploited economically primarily because they hold self-limiting and low-paying jobs. (They often lack the education or training to obtain other types of work.) Because caste minorities feel they can't succeed in the majority culture, they may reject its values. Ogbu explains the poor scholastic achievement of Mexican Americans in terms of their castelike status: "The school failure of Mexican-Americans, especially among older children, is due, in part, to inadequate effort or low academic effort syndrome, resulting from sociocultural factors created by caste-like barriers" (Ogbu & Matute-Bianchi, 1986, p. 117). Many such students are disillusioned with academic effort, since they feel it rarely leads to later success in life.

Raising Self-Esteem of Language-Minority Students

Heath and Ogbu each explain why many language-minority students don't have the same potential for academic success that other students do. Heath (1983) points to different language genres and how teachers can apply knowledge of them to recognize and use genres from the home and to reinforce school-use genres in the classroom. Ogbu's ideas (Ogbu & Matute-Bianchi, 1986) speak more directly to the idea of increasing students' self-esteem

Music, poetry, and song provide rich contextual support for second-language development as well as an opportunity for parent participation in this bilingual Spanish/English classroom.

through use of their primary languages, especially students who belong to castelike minorities. Here are ways teachers and schools can achieve these goals:

- Encourage parent participation in the classroom. Invite parents to help and share their experiences.
- Encourage community members who speak students' native languages to participate in the classroom and school.
- Prepare letters and memos that are to be sent home in both English and the student's primary language.
- Give announcements at assemblies and over the loudspeaker in multiple languages, as needed.
- Use trained paraprofessionals, such as aides, who speak primary languages.
- Use peer tutoring (involving students who speak primary languages other than English but who are at different levels of English proficiency) and cross-age tutoring (involving older students who are more English proficient in helping younger students).
- Team teach with teachers who speak or have knowledge of students' primary languages for English language development.

Language Variety, Dialect, and Register

A Language Community

Even among native English speakers, language varies in many ways. To identify the different ways we can look at each person's language, sociolinguists describe the phenomenon of a *language community*. Members of a language community regard themselves as speakers of the same language. Each speaker within the community has a personal speech pattern called an *idiolect*. Systematic variations in speech patterns among speakers that stem from differences in social status or geographic region are called *dialects*. A dialect can be either a regional variety of a language, such as Southern English in the United States, or a social variety of a language, such as African American vernacular English. When speakers choose from the range of varieties of use within a dialect, they are using a *register*.

Among the many factors that determine a person's idiolect, dialect, and register are age, gender, health, size, personality, emotional state, grammatical idiosyncrasies, profession, racial/ethnic heritage, family situation, geographic region, and social group. Recall Heath's (1983) research, which showed the differences between the language learned at home and at school by children from different socioeconomic communities. These findings were used to modify instruction in local schools to better address these differences.

Language Variation and Literacy

Sociolinguists in the 1960s and 1970s began to systematically describe certain dialects (particularly those of African Americans) and the relationship between dialectal difference and learning to read and write (Labov, 1972; Shuy, 1969). Ample evidence suggested that the use of a dialect didn't critically interfere with learning to read (Goodman, 1978; Ruddell, 1965). In fact, other studies suggested that teachers' limited knowledge of dialectal differences was perhaps what made the difference in students' literacy learning. Specifically, teachers with limited knowledge were more likely to mistake differences in pronunciation for reading errors (Cunningham, 1976–1977) and have lower expectations, estimates of intelligence, and ratings of performance for nonstandard dialect speakers (Harber & Beatty, 1978; Politzer & Hoover, 1977).

Some successful literacy programs have modified reading and writing instruction to be more congruent with local speech; for example, there's a reading program based on the Hawaiian "talk story" (Au, 1980; Au & Jordan, 1981). Other programs have successfully incorporated children's family values and life histories as the basis for literacy instruction (Diaz, Moll, & Mehan, 1986), and still others have used dialogue journals, in which writing isn't evaluated but serves as a natural form of communication between student and teacher (Staton, Shuy, Kreeft Payton, & Reed, 1988).

Language Variation and Teacher Attitude

Children are aware of and sensitive to teachers' attitudes to their speech and may be reluctant to use their natural dialects in teachers' presence (Lucas, 1983). Labov (1978) reminds teachers that progress in English language development and literacy may be less tied to language differences than to cultural conflicts between the child's own language and culture and those of the classroom. Teachers should be knowledgeable about language differences and variations and be able to make the fundamental distinction between a difference in pronunciation and a mistake in reading and writing (Farr & Daniels, 1986; Labov, 1978).

For more about teachers' attitudes toward students who are culturally and linguistically different, read Flores, Cousin, and Diaz (1991), "Transforming Deficit Myths about Learning, Language, and Culture," *Language Arts, 68*, 369–379.

Ethnosensitivity is the most important principle of effective literacy instruction for students from minority groups (Baugh, 1981). Teachers' attitudes toward students who are culturally and linguistically different are crucial to those students' academic success. As James Baldwin so aptly put it, "A child cannot be taught by anyone whose demand, essentially, is that the child repudiate his experience and all that gives him sustenance" (1981, p. 51).

Approaches to Multicultural Education

According to Grant and Sleeter (1993), *multicultural education* has "become the most popular term used by educators to describe working with students who are different because of race, gender, class, or disability" (p. 55). These authors state that the societal goals of multicultural education are "to reduce prejudice and discrimination against oppressed groups, to work toward equal opportunity and social justice for all groups, and to effect an equitable distribution of power among members of the different cultural groups. The multicultural education approach attempts to reform the total schooling process for all children, regardless of whether the school is an all-White suburban school or a multiracial urban school" (p. 55).

Levels of Integration of Multicultural Content

James Banks (Banks & Banks, 1993) describes four approaches to the integration of multicultural content into the curriculum that's occurred since the 1960s:

1. ***The Contributions Approach:*** This approach focuses on heroes and heroines, holidays, and discrete cultural elements. It's used as a first attempt to integrate ethnic and multicultural content into the curriculum. The mainstream curriculum remains unchanged; rather, ethnic figures and artifacts similar to those in the mainstream culture are inserted into it. For example, people are chosen for study because of their success within the mainstream, rather than the ethnic, community. The significance of artifacts such as food, music, and dance within the ethnic community is ignored.

2. ***The Additive Approach:*** In this approach, content, concepts, themes, and perspectives are added to the curriculum without changing its structure. For instance, books or units on ethnic content are added to the existing curriculum. However, as with the contributions approach, ethnic content is still seen from a mainstream perspective.

3. ***The Transformation Approach:*** The structure of the curriculum is changed in this approach to enable students to view concepts, issues, events, and themes from the perspectives of diverse ethnic and cultural groups. Students view issues and concepts from different ethnic perspectives, only one of which is the mainstream perspective. This approach goes beyond looking at how ethnic and cultural groups have contributed to mainstream culture and society, however. Instead, the emphasis is on how the common U.S. culture and society emerged from a complex synthesis and interaction of the diverse cultural elements that originated within the various cultural, racial, ethnic, and religious groups that make up U.S. society. Banks (Banks & Banks, 1993) calls this process *multiple acculturation,* which describes how various ethnic and cultural groups have been an integral part of shaping U.S. society.

4. ***The Social Action Approach:*** Following this approach, students make decisions on important social issues and take actions to help solve them. This goes beyond the transformation approach, educating students for social change and decision making. The result is a synthesis of knowledge and values.

In reality, these approaches are mixed and blended when applied in the classroom. A teacher might begin with the contributions approach and then move to other levels, for example. Or perhaps becoming aware of the importance of moving to higher levels of integrating multicultural content into the curriculum will help a teacher recognize opportunities when they occur.

SNAPSHOT: Students Discover Columbus and the Taino

This Snapshot illustrates an opportunity to integrate multicultural content into the curriculum. In Edison Elementary School, which has many language-minority students and several bilingual classrooms, teachers team teach and Hispanic bilingual and monolingual English students from different classes are combined regularly during the year to promote intercultural

Bilingual Spanish and monolingual English students discuss literature together in a group for better understanding of literature and each other.

Literature plans will be explained in Chapter 7, Teaching with Literature.

understanding. One of the third-grade bilingual teachers, Paul Boyd-Batstone, uses a literature-based, response-centered approach to language arts integrated across the curriculum. Students work in groups for 2- to 3-week periods, choosing books or themes of interest to them to form the basis of language and literacy activities developed through a literature plan.

In 1992, all the groups in Paul's class were reading books about the people, history, and culture of the Americas. At the time there was a lot of interest in the five-hundredth anniversary of Columbus's arrival. One of the groups had brought two books about Columbus back from the library: *Columbus* by the d'Aulaires (1955), written from a European perspective, and *Encounter* by Jane Yolen (1992), written from the first-person perspective of a Taino (the native people who lived on the island of San Salvador when Columbus landed there in October 1492).

On the day Elizabeth came to the group from a nonbilingual class, the group wanted to read *Encounter*. Paul suggested that Elizabeth read it aloud, since it was written in English and she was "an expert English user." Elizabeth read aloud to Paul's students: Antonio, Fabiola, Eddie, Sammy, Natalie, and Gerardo. During this time, Paul conferenced with other students about their writing. When Elizabeth finished reading *Encounter*, Paul told the group to take some time and talk about it—anything they wanted. (In Paul's class, students are encouraged to voice their own opinions about books they read.) Paul joined the group after a while (the discussion was in English, because Elizabeth doesn't speak Spanish):

Paul: Tell me about the book.
Antonio: It's a sad story. Columbus took the Taino people as slaves to Spain. Many died. Only one survived in the story.
Elizabeth: He was little. A child. The little boy had a bad dream about Columbus coming and he woke up. Nobody believed him when he said bad things would happen.
Antonio: He was sad because he had his people and his land taken away.
Paul: Have you ever had things taken from you?
Elizabeth: We were robbed. They took my Dad's tools and our bikes.
Eddie: My mom was washing, and they stole all the clothes from the line.
Fabiola (to Elizabeth): How did they get in your house?
Elizabeth: Don't know. But it's happened twice.

(Other children told about being robbed. Every child in the group had had such an experience.)

Paul: So you've all been robbed, and the boy in the story was robbed.
Elizabeth: Yeah, of his own people.
Gerardo: They took him away from his land.
Paul: Did he ever come back?
Natalie: No.

Then Paul read aloud the other book, *Columbus.* It didn't mention the Taino by name but referred to them as "red-skinned savages" and said, "The Spaniards did not mind being treated like gods by these gentle heathens to whom they had come to bring the Christian faith" (d'Aulaire & d'Aulaire, 1955, p. 40). This book didn't tell what happened to the Taino after Columbus left, either. A lively discussion followed, comparing the two different perspectives on Columbus and his visit to the New World. The students were most interested in what happened to the Taino described in *Encounter.* Paul recorded their ideas on a "word wall" (see Figure 3.4).

Later, Paul asked one of the other bilingual teachers who had studied the native people of Puerto Rico to come to his class and discuss the group's comparison of the same historical event presented from two different perspectives. The class had read other books about Columbus and the native people of the Americas. The question the students kept asking as they read these books was: "What happened to the Taino people when Columbus came to the Americas?" Depending on which perspective the book was written from, the information was presented differently. Antonio finally summed it up: "Somebody's lying."

Based on this experience, the students' understanding of history changed. They realized how important it is to look at people and events from multiple perspectives. The children wrote a report about what they learned, "La vida de los Indios Tainos" ("Life among the Taino Indians"). And they also wrote a script based on the book *Encounter,* which they presented as a play for the whole school to tell the story of Columbus's arrival in the Americas from the point of view of the Taino.

This Snapshot is a real-life illustration of how multicultural content can be integrated into the curriculum. What's more, it illustrates how a school can promote intercultural understanding and how a perceptive teacher can use a literature-based, response-centered approach to do this.

See Chapter 7, Teaching with Literature, for more children's books with different perspectives on multicultural topics.

FIGURE 3.4
"Word Wall" for Two Perspectives on History

What happened to the Taino people when Columbus came to the Americas?

In <u>Encounter</u> by Jane Yolen	In <u>Columbus</u> by the d'Aulaires
Taino welcomed Columbus with feast.	Didn't mind being treated like gods.
Took Taino's gold and gave them beads.	Thought gold was his to take for Spain.
Took Taino as slaves to Spain.	Thought Taino should be converted.
He lied to them.	They were cold in Spain.
They lost land, language, and religion.	Doesn't say what happened to them.
300,000 Taino in 1492—none today.	Taino didn't seem important to them.

TEACHING IDEA

Books with Multiple Perspectives on Multicultural Content

By locating children's books with various perspectives on multicultural content, you and your students can read, discuss, and compare different views on historical figures, events, and issues such as gender, race/ethnicity, disabilities, social class, and language and cultural diversity. Here are examples of children's books about Columbus and the native people of the Americas that offer three different points of view: the European perspective, Columbus's personal perspective, and the perspective of the Taino people.

European Perspective

Columbus by Ingri and Edgar Parin d'Aulaire (1955)—This well-illustrated picture book portrays the native Taino people as simple "heathens," who worshipped Columbus and his men as gods; the book also shows Columbus's intentions to convert the Taino to Christianity and to teach them Spanish. As mentioned earlier, this book doesn't tell what happened to the Taino after they were taken to Spain.

The Columbus Story by Alice Dalgliesh (1955)—This is another well-illustrated picture story book. It's only mention of the Taino says that Columbus "took with him some Indians."

Columbus's Perspective

I, Columbus: My Journal, 1492–1493 edited by Peter and Connie Roop (1990)—Adapted from a copy of Columbus's log, this short nonfiction book shows that he wanted the native people to develop a friendly attitude so they could be converted to Christianity, as they seemed to have no religion. Columbus wanted to take them to Spain so they could learn Spanish, even though he recognized that they had their own culture and language.

The Log of Christopher Columbus by Christopher Columbus, selections by Steve Lowe (1992)—In this picture book, also adapted from Columbus's log, the explorer mentions meeting friendly native people on arrival in San Salvador, which is where the book ends.

Taino Perspective

Encounter by Jane Yolen (1992)—This dramatically illustrated picture book shows that Columbus encountered native people who had an established culture and civilization, which challenges the idea that he "discovered" a new world. Events are seen through the eyes of a Taino boy, who escapes from Columbus's ship (which is taking his people to Spain) and lives to old age. During his life, he sees colonization by the Spanish result in the loss of his land, religion, language, and lifestyle.

Morning Girl by Michael Dorris (1992)—This short novel is a fictional perspective about what the community of Taino people that Columbus met in the fifteenth century might have been like. We meet Morning Girl and her family and see that they live in a community striving to co-exist with the natural world, not dominate it. The community also expects visitors to be friendly, not dangerous. The book ends with the arrival of Columbus.

Consult other books about Columbus to read and compare: *The First Voyage of Christopher Columbus 1492* (Smith, 1992); *Follow the Dream: The Story of Christopher Columbus* (Sis, 1991); *In 1492* (Marzollo, 1991); *A Picture Book of Christopher Columbus* (Adler, 1991a), also available in Spanish, *Un Libro Ilustrado Sobre Cristobal Colon* (Adler, 1991b); *Westward with Columbus* (Dyson, 1991); and *Where Do You Think You're Going, Christopher Columbus?* (Fritz, 1980).

Assessing Language and Cultural Diversity

It's important for teachers to consider whether assessment practices will be sensitive to the linguistic and cultural diversity of students. Questions related to authentic performance assessment include: Is a single set of standards appropriate for all students in the United States? Should certain standards be set in affluent districts (which can afford books, materials, computers, etc.) and others set in poor districts (which cannot)? Another relevant issue is whether assessment should be kept at the local level, which is contrary to the trend toward national standards. Some argue that local school districts are better able to address the diversity among their own students (Garcia, 1993).

Especially important is the linguistic demand that any assessment measure places on students who are learning English as a second language. Miller-Jones (1989) advises that teachers use "functionally equivalent tasks specific to the culture and instructional context of the individual being assessed" (p. 363). Any language assessment should be culturally sensitive—that is, responsive to students' social and cultural differences. Tests of language invariably reflect aspects of culture. In reality, no single test can encompass all aspects of the increasingly diverse cultures of American schools. Furthermore, many tests and assessment procedures have been written with white, middle-class children in mind.

Teachers, therefore, must focus on what individual students demonstrate about their own culturally based understanding of language and literacy. Here are some ways to do this:

1. ***Observing Culturally and Linguistically Diverse Students:*** This sort of observing must be rooted in an orientation to students' specific backgrounds and cultures as well as an understanding of second-language acquisition. Family members can provide such insight and should be involved in the assessment process. Remember that the so-called silent period of a student acquiring a second language may go on for weeks or even months, so his or her language development may not be apparent to the teacher. In such a case, the teacher should talk to the child's parents to find out whether he or she is using English at home.

2. ***Focus on Silent Reading:*** As students begin to read, they need plenty of time and opportunities to practice and develop fluency in reading meaningful and useful books. Rather than ask a developing English speaker to read aloud, the teacher should ask for a retelling of a story or a drawn or written response in order to assess the student's experience and understanding.

3. ***Take Dictation in Writing:*** As students begin to write, the teacher should provide support by taking dictation, using language experience and group-dictated stories. The focus should be on content and meaning in writing, rather than form.

4. ***Assessing English Language Proficiency:*** To assess students' instructional needs and placement in appropriate classes, commercial tests frequently are used. However, the sole use of such tests is not appropriate based on the current integrative, sociolinguistic view of language learning and assessment. According to this view, being proficient means demonstrating what Hymes (1974) calls *communicative competence:* knowing how to use a language for specific purposes in real-life situations. In terms of assessing proficiency, this means using naturalistic, communication-centered events that involve contextualized language use. Again, the emphasis is not on form but on the meaningful use of language.

Richard-Amato (1988) suggests that English language proficiency should be assessed by approximating normal classroom communicative situations, such as listening comprehension (e.g., a simple TPR activity, an interview, informal writing, and reading comprehension tests). The following descriptions of students' language behaviors at various levels of proficiency (adapted from Richard-Amato, 1988) will help teachers make observations and assessments:

Beginning Student

Low — Depends on gestures, facial expressions, objects, and pictures; understands words or phrases occasionally

Mid — Understands more if many clues are provided; uses concrete referents; speaks haltingly, if at all

High — Understands more in social conversation but with difficulty; speaks hesitantly; makes frequent errors in grammar, vocabulary, and pronunciation; is often silent

Intermediate Student

Low — Same as "High" description for "Beginning Student," described above

Mid — Possibly shows dramatic increase in vocabulary; has difficulty with idioms; makes frequent errors; is frequently misunderstood and often asked to repeat; gropes for words

High — Understands normal conversation but requires repetition; is gaining confidence; makes errors less frequently

Advanced Student

Low Same as "High" description for "Intermediate Student," described above

Mid Understands much of normal conversation; sometimes requires repetition; still finds idioms difficult; speaks more fluently but with errors; meaning is usually clear

High Understands normal conversation with little difficulty; understands most idioms; speaks fluently with few errors; meaning is clear; regresses occasionally

Answers to Questions about Language and Cultural Diversity

1. *How do children acquire a second language?*

James Cummins identifies two dimensions of proficiency in acquiring a second language: basic interpersonal communication skills (BICS), or informal, social speaking, and cognitive academic language proficiency (CALP), or language skills used in school tasks. Proficiency in both dimensions of language is determined by the amount of contextual support present, or context-embedded communication. The goal in educating language-minority students is for them to be able to use language in cognitively demanding, context-reduced instructional situations. A common proficiency underlies both languages, such that proficiency in the first language supports acquisition of the second.

Stephen Krashen distinguishes between language acquisition and language learning. He maintains that we acquire a second language the same way in which we acquire a first: through successful communication of meaningful messages. This is language acquisition. Language learning is knowledge about the language, such as grammar. Krashen maintains that a communicative-based approach is the best way for language-minority students to develop basic skills in a second language; they do so through what he calls comprehensible input. Students acquire a second language when they obtain comprehensible input in a low-anxiety setting.

2. *How can teachers support language-minority students' English language development?*

Communicative-based instruction is advocated today. It focuses on meaning, or students' ability to communicate messages, rather than on grammar, which was the instructional focus in the past. Learning English as a second language will be more successful when done in conjunction with primary language support, which involves maintaining students' first languages and cultures as they learn English. This support can come through the use of bilingual teachers, flexible scheduling, trained bilingual aides and paraprofessionals, cross-age tutoring, and team teaching between bilingual and English only teachers.

Krashen and Terrell's natural approach focuses on communication of meaningful messages in natural situations, involving comprehensible input in a low-anxiety environment. Activities are tailored to students' levels of language proficiency: listening comprehension, or preproduction; early production; and extending production. Children's literature should provide the basis for many English language development activities in multilingual, whole-language classrooms.

Techniques from James Asher's *total physical response* (*TPR*) approach are also useful in teaching English as a second language. Using these techniques, students move or gesture in response to directions the teacher has spoken or acted out, first imitating the teacher and eventually acting on their own.

3. *What do teachers need to know about student cultural diversity?*

A *culture* is a system of knowledge that produces behavior and is used to interpret experience. People in a particular social group share a culture. Student cultural diversity has three features: race/ethnicity, class, and language.

Understanding how language is used in varying social and cultural contexts is important to understanding how language is acquired. Shirley Brice Heath has identified language genres, or descriptive units into which certain language events fit. Different cultural groups regularly use different genres, and not every cultural group uses the same genres. The language of schooling has genres, which children must know how to use. Teachers should be aware of how language is used in students' homes, give students the full range of genres typically used in school, and accept students' use of native languages.

John Ogbu has identified three types of minorities: autonomous, immigrant, and caste. He explains that many language-minority students don't have the same potential for academic success that other students do and emphasizes the importance of increasing students' self-esteem by using their primary languages in school. Ethnosensitivity is the most important principle of effective literacy instruction for students from cultural and language minorities.

4. *How should teachers approach multicultural education?*

According to Grant and Sleeter, multicultural education means working with students who are different because of race/ethnicity, gender, class, or disability. The goal is to reduce prejudice and discrimination and provide equal opportunities for all students. Multicultural education attempts to reform the total schooling process for all children, whether at an all-white suburban school or a multiracial, multilingual urban school.

James Banks identifies four approaches to integrating multicultural content into the curriculum: the contributions, additive, transformation, and social action approaches. The latter approach is the highest level, which educates students for social change and decision making. In reality, the approaches are mixed and blended, but teachers should always be aware of the importance of moving to higher levels. When teaching language arts, children's books can be an important resource for presenting multiple perspectives on people and historical events.

LOOKING FURTHER

1 Do the following activity with a small group of language-minority students: (a) Ask the teacher to identify each child's stage of language proficiency. (b) Read a picture book, discuss it, and ask children to draw and write in response to it. (c) Describe what happened.

2 Interview someone in a school or district office who's responsible for identifying students' stages of language proficiency. Ask him or her to describe the procedures used for doing this.

3 Observe a teacher in a class with a high percentage of minority and multilingual students. How does he or she show awareness of Shirley Brice Heath's suggestion about the use of language genres or of John Ogbu's work about types of minorities and self-esteem?

4 Create an activity that would fit each of James Banks' four approaches to integrating multicultural content for either a primary (K–3) or upper-grade (4–6) class.

5 Find two children's books that present different perspectives on multicultural content (e.g., gender, disabilities, immigrant status, or ethnic/race relations).

RESOURCES

Au, K. H. (1993). *Literacy instruction in multicultural settings.* Fort Worth, TX: Harcourt Brace Jovanovich.

Banks, J. A., & Banks, C. A. M. (1993). *Multicultural education: Issues and perspectives* (2nd ed.). Boston: Allyn and Bacon.

Faltis, C. J. (1993). *Joinfostering: Adapting teaching strategies for the multilingual classroom.* New York: Merrill/Macmillan.

Krashen, S. D., & Terrell, T. D. (1987). *The natural approach: Language acquisition in the classroom.* Englewood Cliffs, NJ: Prentice-Hall.

Richard-Amato, P. A. (1988). *Making it happen: Interaction in the second language classroom.* White Plains, NY: Longman.

REFERENCES

Allen, V. (1989). Literature as support to language acquisition. In P. Rigg & V. Allen (Eds.), *When they all don't speak English: Integrating the ESL student into the regular classroom.* Urbana, IL: National Council of Teachers of English.

Asher, J. (1977). *Learning another language through actions: The complete teacher's guide.* Los Gatos, CA: Sky Oaks.

Au, K. H. (1980). Participation structures in a reading lesson with Hawaiian children. *Anthropology and Education Quarterly, 11,* 91–115.

Au, K. H. (1993). *Literacy instruction in multicultural settings.* Fort Worth, TX: Harcourt Brace Jovanovich.

Au, K. H., & Jordan, C. (1981). Teaching reading to Hawaiian children: Finding a culturally appropriate solution. In H. Trueba, G. Guthrie, & K. Au (Eds.), *Culture and the bilingual classroom.* Rowley, MA: Newbury House.

Baldwin, J. (1981). If black English isn't a language, then tell me what is? In M. Shugrue (Ed.), *The essay.* New York: Macmillan.

Banks, J. A., & Banks, C. A. M. (Eds.). (1993). *Multicultural education: Issues and perspectives* (2nd ed.). Boston: Allyn and Bacon.

Baugh, J. (1981). Design and implementation of writing instruction for speakers of non-standard English: Perspectives for a national neighborhood literacy program. In B. Cronnel (Ed.), *The writing needs of linguistically different students.* Los Alamitos, CA: Southwest Regional Laboratory Research and Development.

Bullivant, B. M. (1993). Culture: It's nature and meaning for educators. In J. A. Banks & C. A. M. Banks (Eds.), *Multicultural education: Issues and perspectives* (2nd ed., pp. 29–47). Boston: Allyn and Bacon.

California State Department of Education. (1981). *Schooling and language minority children: A theoretical framework.* Los Angeles: California State University.

Cummins, J. (1981). The role of primary language development in promoting educational success for language minority students. In *Schooling and language minority students: A theoretical framework* (pp. 3–49). Los Angeles: California State University.

Cummins, J. (1984). *Bilingualism and special education: Issues in assessment and pedagogy.* San Diego, CA: College-Hill.

Cunningham, P. M. (1976–1977). Teachers' correction responses to black dialect miscues which are nonmeaning changing. *Reading Research Quarterly, 12,* 637–653.

Diaz, S., Moll, L., & Mehan, H. (1986). Sociocultural resources in instruction: A context-specific approach. In *Beyond language: Social and cultural factors in schooling language minority students.* Los Angeles: California State University, Evaluation, Dissemination & Assessment Center.

Edelsky, C. (1986). *Writing in a bilingual program: Habla una vez.* Norwood, NJ: Ablex.

Elley, W. B., & Mangubhai, F. (1983). The impact of reading on second language learning. *Reading Research Quarterly, 19,* 53–67.

Farr, M., & Daniels, H. (1986). *Language diversity & writing instruction.* Urbana, IL: National Council of Teachers of English.

Flores, B., Cousin, P. T., & Diaz, E. (1991). Transforming deficit myths about learning, language, and culture. *Language Arts, 68,* 369–379.

Garcia, E. (1993). Director's note: Linguistic diversity and national standards. *Focus on Diversity, 1*(3), 1–2. University of California, Santa Cruz: National Center for Research on Cultural Diversity and Second Language Learning.

Goodman, K. S. (1978). *Reading of American children whose language is a stable rural dialect of English and a language other than English, Final Report.* Washington, DC: U.S. Department of Health, Education, and Welfare, National Institute of Education.

Goodman, K., Goodman, Y., & Flores, B. (1979). *Reading in the bilingual classroom: Literacy and biliteracy.* Rosslyn, VA: National Clearinghouse for Bilingual Education.

Grant, C. A., & Sleeter, C. E. (1993). Race, class, gender, and disability in the classroom. In J. A. Banks, & C. A. M. Banks (Eds.), *Multicultural education: Issues and perspectives* (2nd ed., pp. 48–67). Boston: Allyn and Bacon.

Harber, J., & Beatty, J. (1978). *Reading and the black English speaking child.* Newark, DE: International Reading Association.

Heath, S. B. (1983). *Ways with words: Language, life, and work in communities and classrooms.* Cambridge, England: Cambridge University Press.

Heath, S. B. (1986). Sociocultural contexts of language development. In *Beyond language: Social and cultural factors in schooling language minority students* (pp. 143–186). Los Angeles: California State University.

Hudelson, S. (1984). Kan yu ret an rayt en Ingles: Children become literate in English as a second language. *TESOL Quarterly, 18,* 221–238.

Hymes, D. (1974). *Foundations in sociolinguistics: An ethnographic approach.* Philadelphia: University of Pennsylvania Press.

Krashen, S. D. (1981). Bilingual education and second language acquisition theory. In *Schooling and language minority children: A theoretical framework.* Los Angeles: California State University.

Krashen, S. D. (1985). *Inquiries and insights: Essays in language teaching, bilingual education, and literacy.* Hayward, CA: Alemany.

Krashen, S. D., & Terrell, T. D. (1987). *The natural approach: Language acquisition in the classroom.* Englewood Cliffs, NJ: Prentice-Hall.

Labov, W. (1972). *Language in the inner city: Studies in the Black English Vernacular.* Philadelphia: University of Pennsylvania Press.

Labov, W. (1978). *The study of non-standard English.* Urbana, IL: National Council of Teachers of English.

Lucas, A. (1983). *Language diversity and classroom discourse (Final Report to NIE)*. Washington, DC: Center for Applied Linguistics.

Miller-Jones, D. (1989). Culture and testing. *American Psychologist, 44* (2), 360–366.

Ogbu, J. U., & Matute-Bianchi, M. E. (1986). Understanding sociocultural factors: Knowledge, identity, and school adjustment. In *Beyond language: Social and cultural factors in schooling language minority students*. Los Angeles: California State University.

Piaget, J. (1973). *To understand is to invent: The future of education*. New York: Grossman.

Piaget, J. (1977). *The development of thought: Equilibration of cognitive structures* (A. Rosin, Trans.). New York: Viking.

Politzer, R., & Hoover, U. (1977). *Teacher and pupil attitudes toward black English speech varieties and black pupil achievement*. Stanford, CA: Center for Education Research.

Ramirez, J. D., & Merino, B. J. (1990). Classroom talk in English immersion, early-exit and late-exit transitional bilingual education programs. In R. Jacobson & C. Faltis (Eds.), *Language distribution issues in bilingual schooling* (pp. 61–103). Clevedon, England: Multilingual Matters.

Richard-Amato, P. A. (1988). *Making it happen: Interaction in the second language classroom*. White Plains, NY: Longman.

Rigg, P. (1986). Reading in ESL: Learning from kids. In P. Rigg & D. S. Enright (Eds.), *Children with ESL: Integrating perspectives* (pp. 55–92). Washington, DC: Teachers of English to Speakers of Other Languages.

Ruddell, R. B. (1965). The effect of oral and written patterns of language structure on reading comprehension. *Reading Teacher, 18*, 270–275.

Shuy, R. (1969). Some language and cultural differences in a theory of reading. In K. S. Goodman & J. Fleming (Eds.), *Psycholinguistics and the teaching of reading*. Newark, DE: International Reading Association.

Spradley, J. (1980). *Participant behavior*. New York: Holt, Rinehart, & Winston.

Staton, J., Shuy, R., Kreeft Payton, J., & Reed, L. (1988). *Dialogue journal communication: Classroom, linguistic, social, and cognitive views*. Norwood, NJ: Ablex.

Urzua, C. (1987). "You stopped too soon": Second language children composing and revising. *TESOL Quarterly, 21*, 279–304.

Vygotsky, L. S. (1962). *Thought and language*. Cambridge, MA: MIT Press.

Vygotsky, L. S. (1978). *Mind in society* (M. Cole, Ed.). Cambridge, MA: Harvard University Press.

Zutell, J., & Allen, V. (1988). The English spelling strategies of Spanish-speaking bilingual children. *TESOL Quarterly, 22*, 333–339.

CHILDREN'S BOOKS

Adler, D. A. (1991a). *A picture book of Christopher Columbus* (J. & A. Wallner, Illus.). New York: Holiday House.

Adler, D. A. (1991b). *Un libro ilustrado sobre Cristobal Colon* (por J. Y. A. Wallner, Illus.). Traduccion de Teresa Mlawer. Madrid, Spain: Editorial Everest.

Ahlberg, J. (1978). *Each peach pear plum*. New York: Viking.

Anno, M. (1989). *Anno's faces*. New York: Philomel.

Beisner, M. (1990). *Catch that cat! A picture book of rhymes and puzzles*. New York: Farrar, Straus, & Giroux.

Bridwell, N. (1974). *Clifford's riddles*. New York: Scholastic.

Carle, E. (1974). *My very first book of colors*. New York: Crowell.

Carle, E. (1987). *Have you seen my cat?* New York: Picture Books.

Cherry, L. (1990). *The great Kapok tree*. New York: Harcourt Brace Jovanovich.

Columbus, C. (1992). *The log of Christopher Columbus*, selected by S. Lowe (R. Sabuda, Illus.). New York: Philomel.

Crews, D. (1978). *Freight train*. New York: Greenwillow.

Crews, D. (1980). *Truck*. New York: Greenwillow.

Crews, D. (1982a). *Carousel*. New York: Greenwillow.

Crews, D. (1982b). *Harbor*. New York: Greenwillow.

Crews, D. (1984). *School bus*. New York: Greenwillow.

Dalgliesh, A. (1955). *The Columbus story* (L. Politi, Illus.). New York: Scribner's.

d'Aulaire, I., & d'Aulaire, E. P. (1955). *Columbus*. New York: Doubleday.

Dorris, M. (1992). *Morning girl*. New York: Hyperion.

Dyson, J. (1991). *Westward with Columbus* (P. Christopher, Photographer). New York: Scholastic.

Ehlert, L. (1989). *Eating the alphabet.* New York: Harcourt Brace Jovanovich.

Ehlert, L. (1990a). *Color zoo.* New York: Lippincott.

Ehlert, L. (1990b). *Feathers for lunch.* New York: Harcourt Brace Jovanovich.

Fritz, J. (1980). *Where do you think you're going, Christopher Columbus?* (M. Tomes, Illus.). New York: Putnam's.

Gag, W. (1929). *The funny thing.* New York: Coward, McCann.

Gag, W. (1933). *ABC Bunny.* New York: Coward, McCann.

Gag, W. (1935). *Gone is gone.* New York: Coward, McCann.

Gag, W. (1956). *Millions of cats.* New York: Coward, McCann. (Original work published 1928)

Gonzalez de Tapia, G. (1984). *El gato Cui.* Mexico City, Mexico: Editorial Trillas, S.A.

Hoban, T. (1973). *Over, under, through, and other spatial concepts.* New York: Macmillan.

Hoban, T. (1974). *Circles, triangles, and squares.* New York: Macmillan.

Hoban, T. (1976). *Big ones, little ones.* New York: Greenwillow.

Hoban, T. (1981). *More than one.* New York: Greenwillow.

Hoban, T. (1986). *Shapes, shapes, shapes.* New York: Greenwillow.

Jonas, A. (1989). *Color dance.* New York: Greenwillow.

Kent, J. (1990). *The fat cat.* New York: Parent's Magazine. (Original work published 1971)

Kessler, L. (1991). *Old turtles 90 knock knock jokes and riddles.* New York: Greenwillow.

Kitchen, B. (1984). *Animal alphabet.* New York: Dial.

Konigsburg, E. L. (1990). *Samuel Todd's book of great colors.* New York: Atheneum.

McMillan, B. (1983). *Here a chick, there a chick.* New York: Lothrop, Lee, & Shepard.

McMillan, B. (1986). *Becca backward, becca forward: A book of concept pairs.* New York: Lothrop, Lee, & Shepard.

McMillan, B. (1988). *Growing colors.* New York: Lothrop, Lee, & Shepard.

McMillan, B. (1989). *Super, super, superwords.* New York: Lothrop, Lee, & Shepard.

McMillan, B. (1993). *Mouse views: What the class pet saw.* New York: Holiday House.

Marzollo, J. (1991). *In 1492* (S. Bjorkman, Illus.). New York: Scholastic.

Petty, K. (1991). *Gatos.* New York: Franklin Watts.

Phillips, L. (1993). *Invisible oink: Pig jokes.* New York: Viking.

Reiss, J. (1969). *Colors.* New York: Bradbury.

Rockwell, A. (1989). *Apples and pumpkins.* New York: Macmillan.

Roop, P., & Roop, C. (Eds.). (1990). *I, Columbus: My journal : 1492–1493* (P. E. Hanson, Illus.). New York: Avon.

Schwartz, D. (1985). *How much is a million?* (Steven Kellogg, Illus.). New York: Lothrop, Lee, & Shepard.

Shelby, A. (1991). *Potluck.* New York: Orchard.

Sis, P. (1991). Follow the dream: The story of Christopher Columbus. New York: Knopf.

Smith, B. (1992). *The first voyage of Christopher Columbus 1492.* New York: Viking Penguin.

Sterne, N. (1979). Tyrannosaurus wrecks: A book of dinosaur riddles. New York: Crowell.

Vanhalewijn, M. (1980). *El gato sabio de Juanito.* Madrid, Spain: Editorial Everest.

Wallas, K. (1993). *My hen is dancing.* Cambridge, MA: Candlewick.

Wildsmith, B. (1962). *Brian Wildsmith's abc.* New York: Watts.

Wildsmith, B. (1967). *Brian Wildsmith's birds.* New York: Watts.

Wildsmith, B. (1968). *Brian Wildsmith's fishes.* New York: Watts.

Wildsmith, B. (1970). *Brian Wildsmith's circus.* New York: Watts.

Wildsmith, B. (1971). *Brian Wildsmith's puzzles.* New York: Watts.

Yabuuchi, M. (1985). *Whose baby?* New York: Philomel.

Yabuuchi, M. (1985). *Whose footprints?* New York: Philomel.

Yolen, J. (1992). *Encounter* (D. Shannon, Illus.). New York: Harcourt Brace Jovanovich.

Chapter 4

Emergent Literacy

Questions about Emergent Literacy

SNAPSHOT: ***Apples and the First Week of First Grade***

How Young Children Become Literate

Family and Culture

Emergent Reading

Emergent Writing

Reading and Writing Emerge Together

Emergent Biliteracy

The Emergent Literacy Classroom

Seven Ways to Begin Teaching Reading and Writing

LESSON PLAN: ***Read, Talk, Draw, Write***

LESSON PLAN: ***Read, Talk, Draw, Write with Language-Minority Kindergartners***

Emergent Literacy in Kindergarten

SNAPSHOT: ***A Day in a Kindergarten Class***

Assessing Emergent Literacy

Answers to Questions about Emergent Literacy

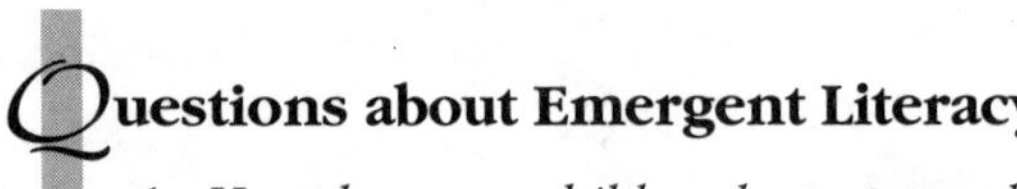

Questions about Emergent Literacy

1. *How do young children learn to read and write?*
2. *How can we teach young children to read and write?*

Reflective Response: What Is Emergent Literacy?

Write a brief memoir of your own experiences in learning to read and write at home or in school. Compare them to the experiences of the children described in this chapter.

SNAPSHOT: Apples and the First Week of First Grade

Marion Harris was in her second year of teaching first grade in Denham Springs, Louisiana, a small town near Baton Rouge. During the first week of school, some students brought her apples, which spontaneously provided active learning and literacy experiences for these emerging readers and writers. In reading this Snapshot, consider how Marion observed and listened to her students from day to day—their ideas, interests, and efforts at making meaning in reading and writing—and then used this information to plan further opportunities for meaningful literacy experiences. Take note of the teaching strategies she uses, which we'll return to later in this chapter in discussing ways to begin teaching young children to read and write.

Day 1. Apples for the Teacher during Sharing Time

It's the first day of school, and three of Marion's students bring her apples—really! She thanks the students and displays the apples prominently on her desk, but then she forgets about them. (Marion doesn't like apples.) During sharing time, when some of the children ask why she hasn't eaten the apples, Marion hedges slightly on the truth and says that she wants to share the apples in a special way. This gets the children excited. Marion listens as they speculate about what she means, and she begins to think about how she might really use the apples.

Day 2. Reading Aloud and Writing and Drawing in Small Groups

Marion has planned literacy experiences around apples. She's found a story riddle in a file that she developed during her student-teaching days. She gathers the children on the rug for reading aloud:

> ***An Apple Riddle Story***
>
> Once upon a time, there was a little star in the sky. This little star was not happy. It wanted to have a little, round, red house with no windows and no doors and a little, brown chimney. The star came

After reading aloud "An Apple Riddle Story," Marion Harris shows first-grade students the star-shaped seed pocket in an apple.

down to earth. It met a bear and asked, "Do you know where I can find a little, round, red house with no windows, no doors, and a little, brown chimney?" Mr. Bear said, "No, but why don't you ask Mr. Fox?" So the star asked Mr. Fox, "Do you know where I can find a little, round, red house with no windows, no doors, and a little, brown chimney?" Mr. Fox said, "No, but why don't you ask Mr. Owl?" So the star asked Mr. Owl, "Do you know where I can find a little, round, red house with no windows, no doors, and a little, brown chimney?" Mr. Owl said, "Don't you know, little star, of the perfect place you are looking for? Look under the big tree in the orchard."

This is a good flannel-board story. Use felt figures of the star, bear, fox, owl, apple tree, and apple that are big enough to fit over the star. Children can also dramatize the story or make puppets and props and tell it to others.

Marion tells the children that this is a riddle and they should guess the answer. A lively discussion follows, as the children try to guess the perfect place for the little star. Someone suggests an apple, but another child says that there aren't stars inside apples. Marion takes this as her cue to cut one of the apples in half horizontally and show the children the star-shaped seed pocket inside.

An apple has 5 seed pockets. An apple blossom also has 5 petals.

Next, Marion organizes the students in small groups, gives each group an apple, and asks each person to observe it: looking, touching, and smelling. After that, she asks the students to compare their observations with others in their group in order to come up with the most specific description possible. She tells them that if all the apples were together on the table, each group should be able to pick out its own.

Finally, Marion gives the children paper and pencils and an opportunity for writing and drawing by suggesting that they record their observations. The students excitedly begin to talk and look for things that will help them distinguish their own apples. They draw and write their observations, using combinations of pictures, letterlike forms, letters, and words to symbolize and record their experiences with apples (see Figure 4.1).

FIGURE 4.1
Children's Drawings about Apples

Day 3. Planning to Make Apple Pies and a Whole-Class Writing Activity

After collecting all the apples in a bag, Marion asks a child from each group to find that group's apple and discuss the choice with the rest of its members. To help them, the students use the drawing and writing they did the day before. After much discussing, sharing of ideas, and comparing of notes, each group reclaims the apple it agreed was its own.

See Chapter 8, Reading as a Language Art, for more on language experience charts.

Someone suggests making pies with the apples. Feelings are mixed on this issue, but those students in favor of making pies eventually win. So the class makes plans for the next day, talking about how to do it and what they'll need. Marion writes the list of materials on a piece of chartpaper. This *language experience chart* is a text of the children's spoken language. Language experience charts and stories are frequently used in emergent literacy classrooms.

Things We Need to Make Apple Pies

1. Knives to cut the apples
2. Bowls for mixing
3. A pot for cooking
4. Sugar and cinnamon
5. Oil for frying
6. A frying pan
7. Pie dough from the store

Day 4. Making Apple Pies and Writing and Reading

The apples simmer slowly with some cinnamon and sugar on a hot plate, while Marion and the class make plans to bake apple pies. Marion writes down what the children say on another language experience chart as they watch the apples cook:

Our Recipe for Apple Pies

Materials: Apples, sugar, cinnamon, pie dough, waxed paper, oil

Directions:

1. Cut up the apples and cook them in a pot with some sugar and cinnamon.
2. Mash the dough flat on waxed paper.
3. Put some cooked apples on it.
4. Pinch the dough together around the apples.
5. Fry the pies in oil.
6. Cool.
7. Eat.

Each child takes a piece of dough and some flour to keep it from sticking to his or her hands while flattening it out. The students talk in their small groups, and some of them start to imagine, rhyme, and play with the dough, flour, and language: "Yuck! Feels like Play-Doh. It's squishy. It's white. I like *flour* 'cause it's *powder*" (emphasizing the italicized words, as in a rhyme scheme).

Marion puts a dab of cooked apples on each child's piece of flattened dough. Then he or she folds the piece over, pinching its edges together. Next, each child cooks his or her pie in oil in a frying pan.

When the pies are cool, the children begin to eat them. Marion gets out more chartpaper to capture the children's ideas on a "word wall" of descriptive words that emerge from the children's experience of cooking and eating the little apple pies they've made themselves (see Figure 4.2). Marion

FIGURE 4.2
"Word Wall" for Apple Pies

Apple Pies

Colors	**Textures**	**Actions**	**Shapes**
brown	icky	squashing	circle
white	yucky	frying	ball
yellow	slimy	patting	clam
	like Play-Doh	spooning	crab
	sticky	cooking	oyster
	stiff	rubbing	long
	greasy	sprinkling	hot dog
	smushy		round
	hot		turtle shell
Feelings	**Sizes**	**Tastes**	**Sounds**
happy	small	good	popping
sad	little	yucky	bubbling
glad	big	yummy	snapping
good	large	great	crackling
smiling	huge	delicious	sizzling
great		terrific	
jumpy		100% good!	

Marion's students wrote this cinquain on a language experience chart about apple pies.

A cinquain follows this pattern:

- Line 1: Title
- Line 2: Description
- Line 3: Action
- Line 4: Feeling
- Line 5: Refers to title

sees that many of these words fit into a pattern for writing called a *cinquain*. She adapts the pattern for her first-graders, and together, they write a cinquain about apple pies:

Apple Pies
Snapping, sizzling
Floating in the grease!
Yummy, great, delicious
100% good!

Day 5. Apple Books, Drama, and Centers

Over the past few days, the children's active involvement with apples has created a rich context of ideas and spoken language, which has provided a basis for emergent reading and writing experiences: drawing and writing, sharing time, and making language experience charts. Marion has provided more emergent literacy experiences by reading aloud about apples; by creating a print-rich environment, with lots of books, posters, and labels in the room; by dramatizing; and by establishing learning centers.

Since Marion practices integrated teaching, she uses the children's experiences with apples to provide a "ripple effect" of opportunities. What began with language and literacy experiences centered around the theme of apples now spreads to other subjects: social studies, science, mathematics, and art. Some of Marion's ideas are shown in Figure 4.3. Many of these are excellent ways to begin the schoolyear, a time when some children still bring apples to their teachers—really!

October is officially known as the Apple Month.

FIGURE 4.3
A "Ripple Effect" of Apples

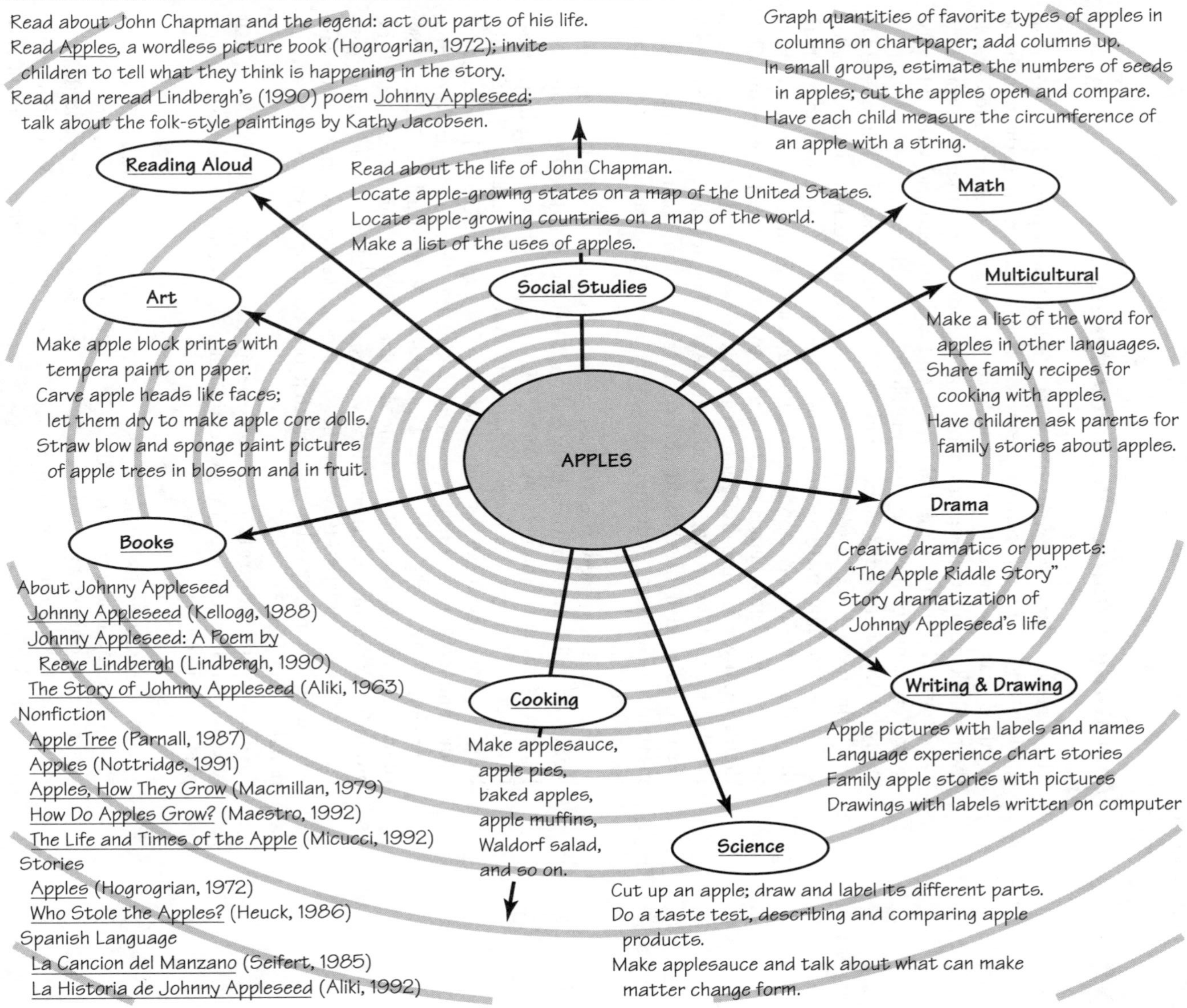

APPLES

Reading Aloud

Read about John Chapman and the legend: act out parts of his life.
Read Apples, a wordless picture book (Hogrogrian, 1972); invite children to tell what they think is happening in the story.
Read and reread Lindbergh's (1990) poem Johnny Appleseed; talk about the folk-style paintings by Kathy Jacobsen.

Social Studies

Read about the life of John Chapman.
Locate apple-growing states on a map of the United States.
Locate apple-growing countries on a map of the world.
Make a list of the uses of apples.

Math

Graph quantities of favorite types of apples in columns on chartpaper; add columns up.
In small groups, estimate the numbers of seeds in apples; cut the apples open and compare.
Have each child measure the circumference of an apple with a string.

Multicultural

Make a list of the word for apples in other languages.
Share family recipes for cooking with apples.
Have children ask parents for family stories about apples.

Art

Make apple block prints with tempera paint on paper.
Carve apple heads like faces; let them dry to make apple core dolls.
Straw blow and sponge paint pictures of apple trees in blossom and in fruit.

Drama

Creative dramatics or puppets: "The Apple Riddle Story"
Story dramatization of Johnny Appleseed's life

Books

About Johnny Appleseed
- Johnny Appleseed (Kellogg, 1988)
- Johnny Appleseed: A Poem by Reeve Lindbergh (Lindbergh, 1990)
- The Story of Johnny Appleseed (Aliki, 1963)

Nonfiction
- Apple Tree (Parnall, 1987)
- Apples (Nottridge, 1991)
- Apples, How They Grow (Macmillan, 1979)
- How Do Apples Grow? (Maestro, 1992)
- The Life and Times of the Apple (Micucci, 1992)

Stories
- Apples (Hogrogrian, 1972)
- Who Stole the Apples? (Heuck, 1986)

Spanish Language
- La Cancion del Manzano (Seifert, 1985)
- La Historia de Johnny Appleseed (Aliki, 1992)

Cooking

Make applesauce, apple pies, baked apples, apple muffins, Waldorf salad, and so on.

Writing & Drawing

Apple pictures with labels and names
Language experience chart stories
Family apple stories with pictures
Drawings with labels written on computer

Science

Cut up an apple; draw and label its different parts.
Do a taste test, describing and comparing apple products.
Make applesauce and talk about what can make matter change form.

The word *apple* in other languages: *pomme* (French); *manzana* (Spanish); *apfel* (German)

For information and materials on apples, contact the International Apple Institute, The Michigan Apple Committee, and the Washington State Apple Commission.

How Young Children Become Literate

The emergent literacy experiences that Marion Harris planned for her first-grade students reflect current views of how children in early childhood (birth–8 years) become literate. In addition to being involved and interested in their own learning, children use writing and reading for authentic purposes.

Young children have not always been taught to read and write this way, however. Views of how they become literate have changed over the years. A study by Morphett and Washburne in 1931 concluded that children needed to reach the mental age of $6^1/_2$ years before they could learn to read. So-called readiness teaching methods for young children were supposed to prepare them to read (Gates & Bond, 1936). Prerequisites included a range of skills, from knowing letter names to being able to walk on a balance beam. Children's writing was virtually ignored, as it was assumed that children had to be able to read before they could write. According to this perspective, children could read if they could accurately say the words in a simple basal preprimer or primer. Until then, they were merely prereaders, getting ready for real reading.

The readiness view wasn't challenged until the 1960s and 1970s, when studies of children who were early "natural" readers (Clark, 1976; Clay, 1967; Durkin, 1966) and writers (Clay, 1975; Graves, 1978) showed that literate behavior doesn't begin at a particular age but emerges continually. Specifically, literacy development begins with children's first experiences with print in the home and continues through preschool and the first few years of formal schooling (Clay, 1989; Goodman, 1986; Harste, Woodward, & Burke, 1984; Holdaway, 1979; Taylor, 1983; Teale & Sulzby, 1989). This research laid the groundwork for the emergent literacy perspective of how children learn to read and write. Sulzby (1989) defines *emergent literacy* as "the reading and writing behaviors of young children that precede and develop into conventional literacy" (p. 7).

Clearly, the old reading readiness perspective is quite different from that of emergent literacy, which is currently held. Let's compare the basic principles of the two:

Then: Reading Readiness	***Now: Emergent Literacy***
1. Reading instruction should begin only when children have mastered a set of prerequisite skills.	1. Reading and writing are language processes and thus learned like spoken language: through active engagement and the construction of meaning.
2. Children should learn to read before they write.	2. Young children have been actively engaged in functional reading and writing experiences in real-life settings before coming to school.

3. Reading is a subject to be taught, involving a sequenced mastery of skills. The focus should be on teaching the formal aspect of reading; its functional uses are generally not relevant.
4. It's not important what children know about language before they enter school and before formal teaching and practice of a sequence of skills begin.
5. Children should move through a scope and sequence of readiness and reading skills, and their progress should be measured with regular, formal testing.

3. The literacy experiences of young children vary across families, social classes, racial/ethnic groups, and age groups.
4. Young children actively construct concepts about reading and writing.
5. Reading and writing are interrelated and develop concurrently.

Family and Culture

Children know a great deal about literacy when they enter school. Most of this knowledge is acquired in the home from parents and family. Sulzby (1991) summarized research on the commonalties of literacy experiences among families (Anderson & Stokes, 1984; Heath, 1983; Taylor, 1983; Taylor & Dorsey-Gaines, 1988; Teale, 1986). In short, prior to entering school, all children are involved in literacy experiences in the home, regardless of the family's race/ethnicity, social class, or economic status. These literacy experiences are social and functional in nature and have a real purpose (i.e., they are not just for the sake of achieving literacy). Individual families have regular, recurring patterns of literacy experiences.

Teale (1986) classified the literacy events that are part of these patterns in a study of six low-income families from three ethnic groups (Anglo, Hispanic, and African American) living in the San Diego area. Literacy events were classified according to function into nine groups: daily living activities, entertainment, school-related activities, work, religion, interpersonal communication, participation in information networks, storybook time, and literacy for the sake of teaching/learning literacy.

Some of the differences in what children know about literacy can be explained by differences among families and cultures. Recall from Chapter 3 Shirley Brice Heath's (1983) well-known study of working-class black and white families as well as middle-class families, in which she documented varying storybook reading styles in families that differed according to social class, race/ethnicity, and age of child. For example, the working-class black families included children in literacy events but didn't read storybooks to them. The working-class white families read storybooks to their children but limited any active responding at about age 3 to low-level literal recall of just listening. The middle-class families read storybooks to their children and expected them to listen to longer stories at about age 3, but active, verbal, imaginative responses and interaction were still encouraged.

In addition to these differences across social and ethnic/racial groups, there may be broad differences within groups (Miller, Nemoianu, & DeJong, 1986). It would be a mistake to assume that literacy behaviors can be explained solely by membership in a group. Moreover, home and family literacy events are present in every cultural group, and children are always included in them. All children come to school showing some signs of emergent reading and writing.

Emergent Reading

The early reader studies (Clark, 1976; Durkin, 1966) clearly showed that young children are emerging as readers well before they come to school. Their early experiences with environmental print and storybook reading in the home or preschool are significant factors in their development of emergent reading.

Environmental Print

Children learn a great deal about print from the environment (Goodman, 1980; Harste, 1990; Hiebert, 1981; McGee, Lomax, & Head, 1988). Children as young as 3 years old from various racial/ethnic and socioeconomic backgrounds are aware of what words in their environments mean. What's more, they understand more of these words when they're presented in meaningful contexts (Goodman & Altwerger, 1981). For instance, Harste, Woodward, and Burke (1984) found that children understand complex concepts and words related to restaurants and common household containers and wrappers. These researchers explain that through understanding words in context, children develop the important expectation that language is meaningful.

My son Gordon demonstrated this expectation as a preschooler through his ongoing experiences playing with frozen yogurt containers. One day, he pointed at the lid, which had the acronym for the chain of stores on top—"TCBY!!" (i.e., "The Country's Best Yogurt")—and said, "Cream!" He had trouble saying "frozen yogurt," so he called it "i-cream" or "cream" for short.

Gordon's language learning continued. At $2^1/_2$, he pointed at the yogurt container and said, "Yogurt eleven." He was learning numbers and thought the two exclamation points were the number 11. At the age of 3, he called it "TCBY" and laughed at himself for having said "cream" and "yogurt eleven." When he was almost 4, Gordon could read the words *chocolate* and *vanilla* in the daily list of flavors posted at the store, but he couldn't tell for sure if they had his favorite: *strawberry*. By 4 years and 3 months, though, he could read all the flavors listed—from *strawberry* to *papaya* to *kiwi*. And by age 5, Gordon was reading the store's brochure, which outlined the rules for owning a TCBY!! franchise.

Storybook Experiences

Perhaps the most extensively documented research finding (Sulzby, 1991) about how young children learn to read is a deceptively simple one: that children learn about reading when adults read aloud and talk to them about stories. Children who are read to often at home imitate reading behaviors like turning the pages, holding and looking at the book in certain ways, touching pages, retelling the story in their own words, and using booklike language. This pretend reading, or readinglike behavior, is in fact the beginning of reading. Sulzby (1985) calls these episodes of pretending *emergent storybook readings* or *independent reenactments.*

Taylor and Strickland (1986) have shown that parents of varying backgrounds do many of the same things with their children during storybook reading:

- talking with the child to further understand the story, its content, and print
- relating new information to what the child already knows
- expanding vocabulary by providing synonyms, brief explanations, and examples of words
- augmenting the story when a problem in understanding is anticipated
- listening to the child and answering questions about the story line, characters, pictures, words, and letters

Laying this foundation is fundamental to emergent literacy. Research has shown that reading to children at home is associated with their later success in reading in school (Teale, 1984; Wells, 1985).

Emergent Writing

When given the materials and opportunities to write and an adult model to follow, young children experiment with and build a repertoire of knowledge about written language (Sulzby, 1985; 1992). They draw on this repertoire to create what Holdaway (1979) and Clay (1975) call "gross approximations" of what will gradually become more and more like conventional writing.

Stages of Children's Emergent Writing

Sulzby (1989) describes a sequence of the forms of writing that mainstream U.S. children typically use as they begin to write: scribbling, drawing, nonphonetic letterstrings, invented spelling, and conventional orthography. In the next few sections, we'll discuss these forms or stages of writing by looking at examples from three children between 1 and 8 years old, the period of early childhood. You may remember these children—Elizabeth, Gordon, and Wyatt—from the Snapshot in Chapter 2.

Scribbling: Elizabeth at 1 year. Under the old chestnut table on which her mother writes at home, Elizabeth finds a pad of the smallest Post-its. She makes a mark on one with a pencil she's also found on the floor, pulls the

Post-it off the pad, and sticks it to her arm. She repeats this process slowly until she's covered with notes, like a bird with square yellow feathers, each with its own curious marking. Then, as her mother watches with pride, she raises and flaps her paper-feathered arms and crows her pleasure in the marks she has made.

Elizabeth is symbolizing her experience by making these marks. Just as she learned to speak by hearing words spoken to her and interacting with others around her, she is learning to write by watching others and having materials available.

Drawing: Gordon at 2–3 years old. Under the same old chestnut table, Gordon scribbles on a piece of paper. He holds it up to show his mother and talks to her about it (see Figure 4.4):

Gordon: Look! Kite!
Mother: A cat?
Gordon: No. Dat a kite. Like up in da 'ky. (He points to the picture and points up.) Like Mary Poppins. Like little boy in Mary Poppins. (He pretends to fly a kite.)
Mother: I like that. (She writes the date in the corner of the paper as Gordon watches.)
Gordon: I like dat. You write *Gordon?*
Mother: Yes. (She writes *Gordon* in the corner of the paper as he watches.)
Gordon: What dat? What you write?
Mother: That's the date today: *November twentieth.*
Gordon: Oh. You put dat on window?
Mother: Yes. I'll put it on the window. (She tapes the drawing to the window next to some of her own papers.)
Gordon (admiring his work on the window): Give me 'nother paper, Mama.

FIGURE 4.4
Gordon's Writing at 2 Years Old: "Look! Kite!"

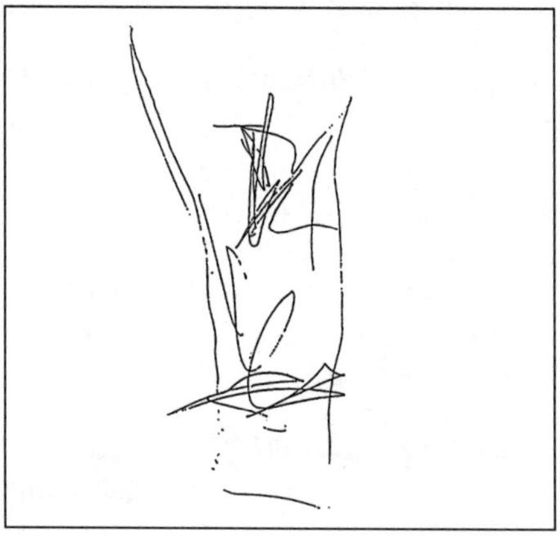

A year later, 3-year-old Gordon sits with his mother in a large armchair as she writes in a journal. He takes the pen out of her hand and vigorously makes marks on the page. He says, "Look, Mama. I write, too. I writing a building."

Gordon also takes pleasure in making symbols that signify his experience. He's able to tell his mother what his drawing means and to connect it to the story in a movie he's seen. He's also beginning to ask questions about writing. He reveals a *metalinguistic awareness* (Yaden & Templeton, 1986), which is the ability to talk about concepts of language by using the word *write* to describe what he's doing. Gordon shows that he understands some things about the writing process. For example, he knows that certain marks on a page mean something, like his name. He also wants to "publish" his writing, displaying it next to his mother's work on the window.

Vygotsky (1978) believes that when children engage in different types of symbol making, they do so by transforming shared social experience. This is true even of children as young as Elizabeth and Gordon. Piaget (1969) described this symbol-making function as "the ability to represent something—object, event, conceptual scheme—by means of a signifier—language, mental image, symbolic gestures" (p. 73).

Nonphonetic Letterstrings, Invented Spelling, and Conventional Orthography: Wyatt at 4–8 years old. At the age of 4, Wyatt draws pictures of his family. He then narrates what he's drawn to his grandmother while making large swirls with a red crayon next to the picture (see Figure 4.5). He tells her the swirls are writing.

At 5, Wyatt draws a picture that he says shows Alice in Wonderland's sister reading a book to her (see Figure 4.6). He draws a line around the picture and asks his mother for another piece of paper to glue next to it so he can make a book. He then carefully writes the letters and numbers he knows, explaining what's happening in the picture as he continues. Like other young children, he uses letter- and numberlike shapes to represent complex thoughts (Schickendanz, 1990). He tries many variations, experimenting with written language at this age. He can write his own name.

FIGURE 4.5
Wyatt's Writing at 4 Years Old: "My Family"

FIGURE 4.6 Wyatt's Writing at 5 Years Old: "Alice in Wonderland's Sister Reading a Book to Her"

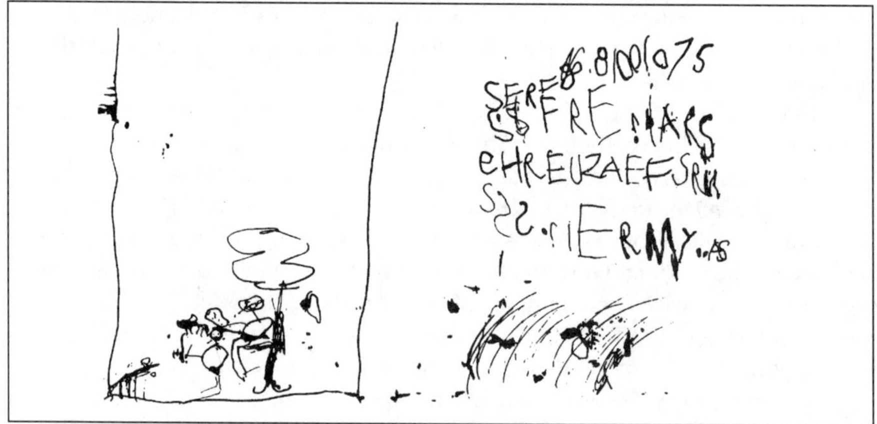

At age 6, as a first-grader, Wyatt writes about a trip to the zoo (see Figure 4.7). At 7, as a second-grader, he writes a story about his dog (see Figure 4.8). And at 8, as a third-grader, Wyatt writes about a family vacation.

Wyatt obviously learned a lot about writing over these 4 years. As a 4-year-old, he combined representational drawings and abstract swirls to tell a story. And as a 5-year-old, he used nonphonetic letterstrings and number shapes and gave meaning to his drawn and written symbols by talking about them. At age 6, Wyatt could write recognizable words and construct a story sequence. And at 7 and 8, he could write more elaborate stories and communicate his experiences to others using both invented spelling and conventional orthography.

by Wyatt
The Zoo.
I am at the zoo. it is fun at the zoo. about 100 animals. at the zoo.

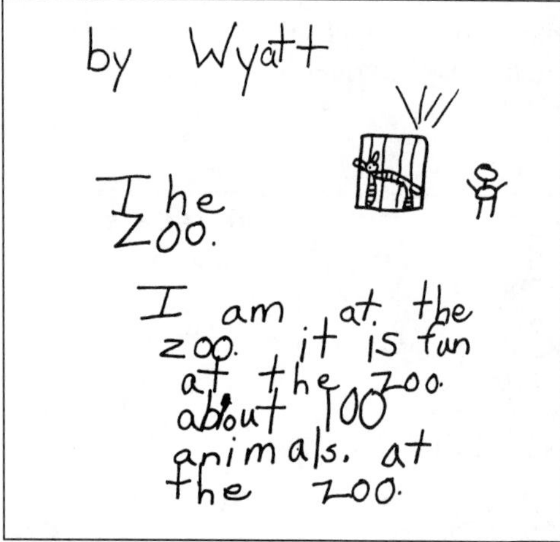

FIGURE 4.7 Wyatt's Writing at 6 Years Old: "The Zoo"

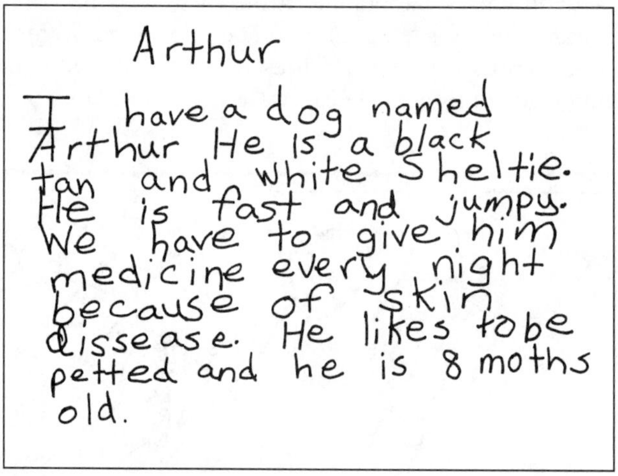

Arthur
I have a dog named Arthur He is a black tan and white Sheltie. He is fast and jumpy. We have to give him medicine every night because of skin dissease. He likes tobe petted and he is 8 moths old.

FIGURE 4.8 Wyatt's Writing at 7 Years Old: "Arthur"

Concepts about Print

As they discover the principles of written language, children's writing evolves, becoming more refined and conventional. Clay (1975) studied children's spontaneous experiments with writing to discover how it works. She describes the discoveries children make as *concepts about print,* which is characterized by these principles:

- ***The Sign and Message Concept:*** Children learn that signs carry messages and that spoken messages can be written; however, children don't always know whether what they write corresponds to what they have said.
- ***The Flexibility Principle:*** Children learn to experiment with letter forms and discover the boundaries of print conventions—that is, how far they can go before a letter will lose its identity as a language sign.
- ***The Recurrence Principle:*** Children repeat forms and patterns and begin to understand that certain elements recur in variable patterns, like the letters in the alphabet.
- ***The Generating Principle:*** Children learn the rules for arranging and combining the elements they already know in new and inventive ways. They also realize that this is a better way of learning to write than simply copying what others have written.
- ***The Contrast Principle:*** Children experiment with creating contrasts among shapes, meanings, sounds, and word patterns and learn that contrasts can be made between elements at several levels.
- ***The Direction Principle, Space Concept, and Page and Book Arrangement:*** Children learn that in the English language, the pattern of print moves from left to right and top to bottom and that spaces separate individual words. Children also learn how to use space on a line or page to accommodate their writing and how pages and books are typically formatted.

To summarize, Clay's (1975) research shows that young children are learning:

to understand that print "talks"
to form letters
to build up memories of common words they can construct out of letters
to use these words to write messages
to increase the number and range of sentences used
to become flexible in the use of sentences
to discipline the expression of ideas within the spelling and punctuation conventions of English (pp. 11–12)

Invented Spelling

As children discover these concepts and principles, they are moving toward writing that can be read and understood by others without spoken explanation. In doing so, they will use letters and create wordlike forms. Their knowledge of abstract phonological categories and relationships will result in unconventional spellings. Charles Read (1975) calls this *invented spelling*. His research demonstrates convincingly that kindergartners can make sophisticated auditory predictions about the spellings of words and that certain patterns occur frequently in their spellings. For example, he found that children often:

- use single letters to represent sounds of full letter names:
  PPL = people; BCAZ = because; LFNT = elephant
- omit nasal sounds before consonants:
  MOSTR = monster; NUBRS = numbers; PLAT = plant
- use single letters to stand for whole syllables:
  GRIF = giraffe; NHR = nature

One of the most revealing aspects of children's spelling that came out of Read's (1975) work is the sophisticated set of linguistic criteria children use for decoding which vowel sounds to use. Whereas adults are accustomed to the short/long vowel relationships found in spelling (e.g., the *a* in *nation* vs. *national*), children are more sensitive to phonetic relationships between vowel sounds. Consider the vowel sounds in *feel* and *fill,* which are formed similarly in the mouth. A child might spell both *FEL*. Similarly, *like* and *lock* might both be spelled *LIK*.

During early childhood, children internalize what they learn about language, creating some very flexible rules based on that knowledge and applying these rules as they begin to spell. This is a developmental, systematic, sequential, and very slow process—one that's far too complex to teach through simplistic strategies like making word lists or learning rules in spelling books. Learning to spell is clearly rooted in children's abilities to articulate as well as hear and segment speech sounds in words. Their invented spelling, therefore, is not random but systematic, even though it does not match conventional spelling.

Read (1975) suggests that teachers need to understand the underlying system of children's spelling in early childhood, to respect it, and to work with it, if only on an intuitive basis. Children move through relatively the same stages in learning to spell, and they know a great deal about English *orthography*. Using this knowledge, they create a hierarchy of concepts that guide their early spelling efforts. The sequence of stages children go through indicates that they're establishing internalized rules, moving from simple letter/sound correspondences to more complex phonological, syntactic, and semantic knowledge. They do this as they use spoken and written language in authentic, meaningful contexts: solving problems, testing hypotheses, and making mistakes as well as discoveries.

Orthography is the representation of sounds in a language by written or printed symbols; it's also the part of language study that deals with letters and spelling.

The stages of spelling through which children progress have been identified by several researchers (Beers & Beers, 1981 [summarizing Beers & Henderson, 1977]; Gentry, 1981; Henderson, 1980). Their different views are presented in Table 4.1. Next, we'll look more closely at the five stages identified by Gentry (1981):

TABLE 4.1 Stages of Spelling Development

Grade	Source: Gentry (1981)	Henderson (1980)	Beers & Beers (1981)
Preschool	***Deviant*** btBpA	***Preliterate*** ***Prephonetic*** dog candy bit Cinderella	***Prereading Stage*** 1. Prephonetic level ABDG—Wally 11 + 02—cat 2. Phonetic level WTBO—Wally KT—cat HM—home GT—get
Kindergarten and Beginning First	***Prephonetic*** MSR	***Preliterate Phonetic*** D or DJ K or KDE B or BT S	***Phonetic Stage*** GAT—get TREP—trip FRMR—farmer SCARD—scared JUPT—jumped
Midfirst	***Phonetic*** MONSTR	***Letter-Name Strategy*** DIJ KADE BET SEDRLI	
End First/ Beginning Second	***Transitional*** MONSTUR	***Vowel Transition*** DOG CANDE or CANDY BIT CINDARILA	***Orthographic Stage*** GAETF—gate MAIK—make SPATER—spatter RIDDER—rider SITTIN–sitting CANT—can't
Second–Fourth	***Correct*** MONSTER	DOG CANDY BIT CINDERELLA	
Fifth–Tenth			***Morphemic & Syntactic Stage*** 1. Control of doubling consonants. HAPPY SMATTERING 2. Awareness of alternative forms. MANAGERIAL manage REPETITION repeat 3. Awareness of syntactic control or key elements in words. SLOWLY SAVED PASSED RESTED FASTER SLEEPING

Source: Adapted from Gentry, 1981.

1. *Deviant Stage:* Children are becoming aware that speech can be recorded by means of graphic symbols, even though they don't have a clear, objective understanding of the relationships between sounds and letters in words or of what words really are. Children make drawings that gradually become more representational and are often accompanied by spoken explanations. These drawings are gradually replaced with letter- or numberlike shapes or actual letters and numbers, often scattered randomly over a page (see Figure 4.9). Some children at this stage can write their names.

2. *Prephonetic Stage:* Children are still unable to spell many words conventionally, and they're still unclear about the concept of what a word is; however, they do know that letters make words, and they don't invent symbols as substitutes for letters, as in the earlier stage. Children know that letter names stand for elements of words (usually consonants), and they make one-, two-, and three-letter representations of specific, individual words. They have more control over the sounds at the ends of words than they do over the middles and the beginnings. This development occurs around kindergarten age (5–6 years old) for many children.

3. *Phonetic Stage:* Spellings at this stage include all the sound features of words as children hear and articulate them. That is, the written form contains all the speech sounds, recorded in the same sequence (e.g., *CHROBLE* = *trouble*). Children pass through this stage between the first and third grades (6–8 years old).

4. *Transitional Stage:* Children include vowels in all recorded syllables and use familiar spelling patterns. Standard spellings are interspersed with in-

FIGURE 4.9 5-Year-Old's Drawing and Writing: Deviant Stage of Spelling

vented, phonetic spellings (e.g., *HIGHCKED* = *biked; TODE* = *toad*). Children seem to realize that it's necessary to spell words in order for them to be read and that all words have conventional spellings, used in print. Children also learn that there are various ways to spell many of the same speech sounds and that many words are not spelled entirely phonetically. This stage may occur around the end of first and the beginning of second grade (7–8 years old).

5. ***Correct Stage:*** The points of change are less clear in this stage. Children are mastering word roots, past tense, and short vowels, although they still have problems with consonant doubling, word affixes, and the positions of letters (e.g., the silent *e* that determines long vowel sounds). This stage occurs anywhere between the second and fourth grades (7–9 years old).

In order to connect research findings on emergent literacy and invented spelling with real children, let's look at examples of writing by Michael, Alisha, and Anita. All three wrote these stories during a writer's workshop at the beginning of first grade. See if you can identify each child's stage of spelling development based on the writing sample and what he or she said about it (see answers at page bottom):

- Michael reads his one-sentence story as "There is a plane." The words *is* and *a* are spelled correctly. He has written something to represent every word. Both *ThEHr/there* and *Plne/plane* include letters that represent some of the speech sounds heard in the word.

- Alisha reads her two-sentence story as "My cat is black and brown. He is cute." *Cat, black, and, he,* and *is* are spelled correctly, and the other spellings include all the sound features of the words: *mi/my, brwn/brown, cuty/cute.*

- Anita reads her four-sentence story as "My cat's name is Snow Paws. His last name is Fred. His middle name is Billy. And that is all." Most words are spelled correctly. Invented phonetic spellings use familiar patterns. A vowel is included in every recorded syllable: *Sno/Snow, Pous/Paws, mitul/middle, Bilee/Billy.*

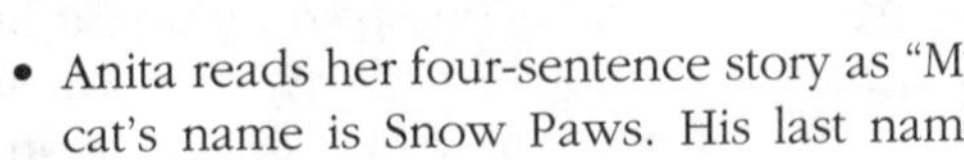

Answers: Michael is in the prephonetic stage, Alisha is in the phonetic stage, and Anita is in the transitional stage.

Reading and Writing Emerge Together

In studies of early natural readers (which inaugurated the current perspective of emergent literacy), both Durkin (1966) and Clark (1976) found that such children have usually been "paper and pencil kids," in Durkin's words. They drew pictures, copied letters, and wrote names of friends and family members before they could read. Chomsky (1971) suggests that writing precedes reading.

Interactive Nature of Reading and Writing

Literacy research has shown that reading and writing emerge together (Clay, 1975; Goodman & Goodman, 1983; Moffet & Wagner, 1993). De Ford (1981) has argued the importance of integrating language processes as a reflection of the "interactive nature of the reading and writing processes in literacy learning" (p. 653). She compared three classroom approaches—phonics, skills, and whole language—to early literacy instruction. In the whole-language classroom, the teacher used literature, experience centers, language experience charts, and integrated reading and writing activities. The children in this classroom scored higher on tests of comprehension of predictable stories, retelling of stories, and recalling story information than the children taught using the phonics and skills approaches.

The children in the whole-language program also produced a greater variety of writing forms: stories, informational prose, songs, poetry, and newspaper articles. And more of these students' stories were well crafted than those written by students in the other programs. De Ford (1981) concludes that supporting the interactive nature of reading and writing and encouraging children to use language for their own meaning-making purposes are the foundations of literacy.

The Author's Chair

Graves and Hansen (1983) have described what first-grade children know about the connection between reading and writing—both seen as acts of composing. These authors observed for a year in a first-grade class in which children read and wrote every day, saved their writing in portfolios, and published one of every four pieces as a bound book that became part of the classroom library. The teacher in this classroom also used an Author's Chair: a place where the teacher or student would read one of these books, ask questions, and discuss them. Graves and Hansen have identified three phases that characterize children's understanding of the author concept and the connection between reading and writing:

1. ***The Replication Phase: "Authors write books":*** As children watch others read and write, draw and write their own works, use invented spelling, and hold up a book and both tell the story and "read" it, they begin to grasp what readers and writers do.

2. ***The Transition Phase: "I am an author":*** Children learn what it means to be an author. They learn to identify with authors they have listened

to when the teacher reads aloud or have heard on tapes in the listening center. In addition, they learn to choose topics, become interested in print as a complement to drawing, and analyze what they write.

3. ***The Option-Awareness Phase: "If I wrote and published this book now, I wouldn't write it this way":*** Children begin to convey more information by way of implication, expecting the reader to contribute to the message; they also use different fictional forms more frequently and anticipate readers' reactions. As readers, children ask more questions and expect authors to be able to defend their choices of options. As writers, they exercise their own options and expect questions from their readers.

Graves and Hansen conclude, "Readers who are also writers develop a sense of authorship that helps them in either composing process" (1983, p. 183).

Emergent Biliteracy

Children who come to school speaking a language other than English should learn to read and write in both languages. As we discussed in Chapter 3, this is *additive bilingualism,* or building knowledge of a second language on the foundation of the first (Cummins, 1980)—including knowledge about reading and writing. Students who learn to read and write in their native language have a better chance of learning to read and write in English (Edelsky, 1986; Hudelson, 1987) and may even have an advantage over children who speak only English. From a summary of research on the cognitive consequences of bilingualism, Au (1993) concluded:

> *Bilingual children have an advantage over monolingual children in several areas of cognitive functioning. One of these areas, which has particular benefit to literacy learning, is called metalinguistic awareness, which involves the ability to analyze the forms of language. . . . Bilingual children have the opportunity to compare and contrast two languages, and so are more likely than monolingual children to develop an abstract understanding of how language works.* (pp. 146–147)

Language-minority students should have instructional support in their primary language in order to learn to read and write in it. Such support can be provided through bilingual programs, the use of bilingual paraprofessionals such as aides, flexible scheduling and team teaching among bilingual and monolingual teachers, and peer tutoring among students.

See Chapter 3, Language and Cultural Diversity, for more on second-language acquisition and education.

Emerging Reading in a Second Language

Many studies have shown the importance of teaching young children to read in their native language—the language they already know (Hudelson, 1987)—rather than a language they don't know well (Snow, 1990). Children's knowledge of spoken language supports reading, and reading experiences support language acquisition (Urzua, 1987). When learning to read other than their native language, children are more successful if they have early experiences with environmental print, background knowledge, and the type of text (Goodman, Goodman, & Flores, 1979; Hudelson, 1984). Familiar narrative forms such as folktales are most easily understood (Rigg, 1986).

Emerging Writing in a Second Language

Edelsky (1986) found that primary-grade children in a bilingual Spanish program used their knowledge of Spanish print to help them learn how to use English print; in fact, this knowledge enhanced learning English. Basically, second-language learners draw on their knowledge of print in their first language as they learn to write in the second language (Lanauze & Snow, 1989). For example, Hispanic students use their knowledge of Spanish orthography when spelling in English (Zutell & Allen, 1988). Hudelson (1984) suggests that bilingual students should be encouraged to explore English print before they have control over their native language.

Research findings suggest that children learning to read in Spanish should be taught according to the constructivist model advocated in this book, rather than the transmission, or skills-based, model traditionally used to teach children to read in English (Rigg, 1991). Using the constructivist approach is recommended despite the assumption that because Spanish has a one-to-one sound/symbol correspondence, phonics should be emphasized, not the construction of meaning (Barrera, 1983; Freeman, 1988). Young language-minority children should have many authentic experiences with print and well-written books as they learn to read and write (Allen, 1989). Support for their primary language should be provided.

Teachers in bilingual classrooms should provide comprehensible input and shape language to meet learners' needs. Teachers should simplify, slow down, use gestures, and link discussion to a strong context and situation. Opportunities should be provided for students to collaborate and interact frequently, and peer tutoring should be used when appropriate. Children should use language for a variety of *real* purposes. Creating "ripple effects," which link concepts and experiences across themes, is a useful way to organize instruction and provide support for language acquisition and literacy learning. Classrooms for young children that present language and literacy as authentic, integrated processes support second-language learners' efforts in becoming biliterate.

The Emergent Literacy Classroom

A summary of the research on emerging literacy suggests that a classroom for emerging readers and writings has these characteristics (Strickland & Feeley, 1991, summarizing Harste et al., 1984; Mason & Au, 1986; Schwartz, 1988):

1. Classrooms should provide a print-rich environment.
2. Children should have many opportunities to test their growing hypotheses about language in a risk-free atmosphere, with lots of interactive experiences with written language.

3. Reading and writing should be interrelated, integrated across the curriculum, and related to children's experiential backgrounds. Many direct experiences should occur in the classroom for concept and vocabulary development as well as for sheer enjoyment.
4. Children should be given many choices about what topics to read and write about along with opportunities to do so.
5. Meaning should be at the center of all language and literacy experiences. Children will learn about language and how to use it in authentic and meaningful situations.
6. Teachers should model reading and writing, showing that they are fun and dynamic processes.

Seven Ways to Begin Teaching Reading and Writing

The seven ways to begin to teach reading and writing that follow are founded on the assumption that, from the very beginning, children learn language holistically for authentic, meaningful purpose. Moreover, they should continue to learn this way in the early years of school, as they each develop the inner control necessary to work with print (Clay, 1991). Each of the following recommendations begins with an example from Marion Harris's first-grade room and the "ripple effect" of apples that emerged there.

A Print-Rich Environment

When Marion's students became more and more interested in apples, she found and displayed posters with information about apples:

Different Types of Apples: Delicious (Red and Golden), Macintosh, Granny Smith, Gala, and Fuji

Apple Parts: Leaves, stem, core, skin, seeds, and flesh

Apple Products: Sauce, jelly, vinegar, cider, pies, and juice

Seven Leading Apple-Growing States: Washington, Michigan, New York, California, Pennsylvania, Virginia, and North Carolina

Young children learn a lot about written language through exposure to print in their environment. The term *environmental print* means print that is visibly situated in a context that will help children understand it.

1. ***Signs, Labels, Lists, and Charts:*** These materials should be displayed prominently in the room, and the teacher should point to them when discussing what they label. Signs, labels, and the like should be functional, and children should be encouraged to use and read them. Examples:

The teacher's name and room number on the door
A "Welcome to Our Room" sign
Children's names on their desks
Labels for centers and supply storage

Calender with dates, school events, and birthdays
Poems, songs, and chants
Charts for classroom jobs
List of classroom rules
Daily schedule

See Chapter 3, Language and Cultural Diversity, for a list of single-concept books and authors who write and illustrate them.

2. *Books in the Classroom:* As many books as possible should be provided in the classroom. When you begin teaching, build your collection any way you can: Go to garage sales or request donations from parents, and use school and public libraries. Public library books should be kept on a separate shelf, and students should be involved in caring for them, keeping track of due dates, and so on. Teachers should look for books that that they will enjoy reading aloud and that children will enjoy looking at, such as great storybooks and single-concept books. For more ideas, also see the section on pattern books, later in this chapter.

For more information on print-rich environments, see two articles in *The Reading Teacher* by Dorothy Strickland and Leslie Morrow (1988, 1989).

3. *A Library/Reading Corner:* A place for books and reading should be created in a corner of the classroom, perhaps using bookshelves to define a space. Things to add might include a rocking chair or recliner for the teacher, a rug for the children to sit on while being read to, floor pillows, plastic crates for different types of books, plants, dolls or stuffed animals of characters from stories, and reading lamps.

Sharing Time

Sharing time was when Marion discovered her students' interest in apples and began to plan learning experiences around it. To get the most out of sharing time, consider these guidelines:

1. *When to Share:* Every day, time should be set aside for children to share what's important to them. Many teachers do so first thing in the day. By listening to the children, the teacher can find out more about them and thus come up with ideas for teaching.

See the Snapshot in Chapter 1 for a description of how Avril Font uses sharing time with fourth-grade students.

2. *Variations on Sharing*

- Teachers can share, too, both school-related items, like announcements and plans for the class, and personal information, like favorite poems and things that are important to them.
- Combine sharing time with other activities that begin the day, such as the calendar, weather, or thematic poetry, songs, or rhymes.
- Designate a student as Star of the Day or Week. Plan ahead to have that child bring in special things to share with the class (e.g., pictures, artwork, or mementos), and create a bulletin board around them.

Reading Aloud

After a few days of apple activities, Marion asked her school librarian to find books related to the apple theme. She read several aloud to the class; the first was Steven Kellogg's (1988) *Johnny Appleseed*. Here are suggestions for reading aloud:

1. *When to Read Aloud:* Teachers should read aloud to students several times every day, such as at the close of sharing time in the morning, before or after recess, to initiate a writing or drama activity, before or after lunch, or at the end of the day. In addition to serving a modeling purpose, reading aloud is one of the best ways to create a quiet, peaceful atmosphere in the classroom. Teachers who feel they need more control in the classroom should get out a good book and read it aloud to students.

2. *How to Read Aloud:* Teachers should share books they love. By doing so, they will be more likely to read dramatically and with enthusiasm. Others should be invited to read, too: principals, counselors, parents, and community members. Likewise, children should be encouraged to read aloud to each other (i.e., *buddy reading*), perhaps favorite books they have brought to share and even their own stories, read from the Author's Chair. Children learn to read by hearing stories read aloud and by reading aloud themselves. Time should be provided to do both often.

3. *Predictable Pattern Books:* Most predictable pattern books are based on familiar cultural sequences, like the alphabet, numbers, days of the week, or seasons. Other such books use repeated phrases that invite children to chime in. Remember "Sam I am, that Sam I am" from Dr. Seuss's *Green Eggs and Ham* (Seuss, 1988)? Some pattern books are cumulative tales, in which new parts of the story are continually added, as in the nursery rhyme "The House That Jack Built." Many pattern books are based on traditional rhymes, songs, or folktales; others are new and original. Predictable pattern books encourage children to participate in the reading experience by guessing what will happen next, by joining in a repeated phrase, or by repeating everything that's been said before. These books should be read often with young children.

Here are some examples of types of predictable pattern books:

Familiar Sequences

Numbers: *Over in the Meadow* (Keats, 1973)

Days: *The Very Hungry Caterpillar* (Carle, 1969)

Months: *Chicken Soup with Rice* (Sendak, 1962)

Repeated Phrases

Caps for Sale (Slobodkina, 1940)
The Little Red Hen (Galdone, 1973)
Mary Wore Her Red Dress (Peek, 1985)
Millions of Cats (Gag, 1928, 1956)
Whose Mouse Are You? (Kraus, 1970)

Rhyming Patterns

Chicka Chicka Boom Boom! (Martin & Archambault, 1989)
Green Eggs and Ham (Geisel, 1988)
Is Your Mama a Llama? (Guarino, 1989)
We're Going on a Bear Hunt (Rosen, 1989)
The Wheels on the Bus (Wickstrom, 1988)

Recurring Patterns
Are You My Mother? (Eastman, 1960)
Ask Mr. Bear (Flack, 1932)
Brown Bear, Brown Bear, What Do You See? (Martin, 1983)
The Doorbell Rang (Hutchins, 1968)
The Three Billy Goats Gruff (Brown, 1957)

Cumulative Patterns
I Know an Old Lady Who Swallowed a Fly (Hawkins & Hawkins, 1987)
If You Give a Mouse a Cookie (Numeroff, 1985)
The Mitten (Brett, 1986)
The Napping House (Wood, 1984)
Rooster's Off to See the World (Carle, 1972)

Chapter 8 on reading describes the shared "big book" method, offering a detailed example of how to do one.

4. *"Big Books" and Shared Reading:* New Zealand educator Don Holdaway (1979) introduced the idea of using "big books" (i.e., books with oversized pages and print) and shared reading in emergent literacy classrooms. The purpose for doing so is to replicate the bedtime story experience and the good feeling children have when a parent or caretaker sits close to them and reads aloud. Today, many publishers have enlarged popular children's books to the "big book" size. Teachers can also create "big books" by copying stories on paper large enough so that children can see the words from up to 20 feet away.

Drama

In the weeks after Marion Harris told the apple riddle story, small groups of students dramatized it by acting it out and using props and puppets to retell it. The story was a natural for dramatizing; with a narrator, five children could easily plan and act it out. Other recommendations for using drama to teach reading and writing include:

See Chapter 6 for much more on creative dramatics in the classroom.

1. *Story Dramatization:* After the teacher has read a story aloud several times (to the entire class or a small group) or after children have read it aloud to each other, they can discuss dramatization: choosing what events to act out, characters and who will play them, and costumes or props that will be needed. The children might also practice the dramatization several times before sharing it with others; this is always optional.

See Chapter 5, Listening and Talking, for more ideas on storytelling and puppetry.

2. *Props and Puppets:* A simple way to relive and retell a story is through the use of props or puppets. Students can make puppets out of construction paper, manila folders, or paper plates and attach tongue depressors to hold them up. Puppets can also be made out of paper bags and old (clean) socks. Dolls, stuffed animals, and real objects can be used as props. A box of prop and puppet supplies should be available in the room.

Writing and Drawing

Marion's students wrote and drew in small groups to describe their apples. And as a class, they also wrote a list of things needed to make apple pies, a recipe, and a cinquain. After Marion read *Johnny Appleseed*, the class discussed it; then she told them to draw or write anything they wanted about the story. Here's a simple strategy for doing this:

1. ***Read, Talk, Draw, Write:*** The teacher should read a good story aloud and simply talk about it with the children, asking aesthetic questions. After that, the teacher should give students paper, crayons, and pencils and ask them to draw or write anything they want about the story. Following is a step-by-step lesson plan for doing this with any book.

Aesthetic questions direct children to what they were thinking and feeling while reading. This and other types of questions are reviewed in Chapter 5.

LESSON PLAN: Read, Talk, Draw, Write

Purpose: Children will listen to and enjoy literature; actively participate in a shared reading experience; talk in response to open and aesthetic questions and prompts; and draw and write in response to literature.

Materials: Children's book; props and realia (i.e., real objects); paper, crayons, and pencils

Procedure:

1. ***Read***

- Select a good children's book, based on these criteria: What you like and think children will like; good illustrations; predictable patterns; and "big books."
- Read dramatically and slowly, vary intonation and voices for different characters, and use sound effects, facial expressions, and gestures.
- Use props and realia, such as objects from the story and stuffed animals or dolls representing story characters.
- Encourage participation in reading pattern books (e.g., repeating words or phrases).
- Reread if children ask you to do so.

2. ***Talk***

- Ask open and aesthetic questions after reading to elicit children's individual responses:
  "What did you think of the book?"
  "What was your favorite part?"
  "Has anything like this ever happened to you?"
  "How would you feel if you were a character in the story?"
  "Is there anything in the story you wondered about?"
  "Is there anything in the story you would change?"
- Base further questions and prompts on what the children say.
- Encourage children to interact with each other.

(continued)

- Write children's ideas down on a "word wall," displaying it on a chalkboard, chartpaper, butcher paper, dry-erase board, or overhead projector.

3. ***Draw***
   - Give children paper, pencils, and crayons.
   - Tell them, "You can draw anything you want about the story."

See Chapter 9, The Writing Process, for ways to publish children's writing and bookmaking.

4. ***Write***
   - Tell students to write, if they want to: their names, labels, captions, and so on.
   - Encourage all writing efforts (e.g., invented spelling).
   - Give assistance if students ask for it (e.g., write a word so they can copy it, take dictation for them, etc.).
   - Publish children's drawings and writings by sharing them, mounting them on the bulletin board, or making a group or class book.

Marjorie Abbott, one of my students in a language arts methods class, created a "Read, Talk, Draw, Write" lesson for use with a group of native Spanish–speaking kindergarten children at various levels of English language proficiency. She had a bilingual fifth-grader as an aide to provide primary language support in Spanish. Marjorie used the "big book" version of Audrey Wood's (1984) *The Napping House,* a cumulative story about a house and a bed. It has a lot of action, wonderful illustrations, and repeated phrases the children can join in on. Here's Marjorie's lesson plan, along with her descriptions of the activities:

LESSON PLAN: Read, Talk, Draw, Write with Language-Minority Kindergartners

The Napping House by Audrey Wood

Purpose: Children will listen to and enjoy an English, "big book" version of a pattern book; discuss the story; and draw and write in response to it.

Materials:

1. "Big book" version of *The Napping House* by Audrey Wood (1984)
2. Props to act out the story, including stuffed dolls and animals: a granny; Dalmatian dog; tiger-stripped kitty; doll; catnip mouse; flea made from dryer lint; small, white quilt with a red, heart-shaped pillow for the bed
3. White construction paper
4. Crayons

Procedure:

1. ***Read***

   I sit in a small chair holding the "big book," and the children sit on the floor in front of me. I show them the cover and read the title page and author's name. Next, I make a little bed in front of me and tell them the reason I'm making the bed is because the story is about napping or sleeping. The children listen quietly, watching my every move. I start reading the first page, and then, while reading the second page, I put "granny" in bed. As I read the book and turn the pages, I (quite miraculously) am able to stack all the stuffed animals and dolls on top of each other without a single spill! I pretend to snore when I refer to the "snoring granny." (My fifth-grade aide, Norma, really laughed at seeing me act so silly! It's fun, and I don't mind because the children are so engrossed.) I make my voice sound dreamy when I put the "dreaming child" on top of the "snoring granny." I "meow" when I place the cat on the dog, and "squeak" when I put the mouse on top of the cat. I had no sound effects for the flea—would you?

   Norma, who has heard the story, hurries to my side at the end, when it's time for all the characters to jump up and off one another as each is clawed, bitten, scared, or whatever! She helps with the dramatic ending, while I excitedly read (and laugh) and turn the remaining pages frantically. The children *get* this! They laugh and cheer and catch some of the flying animals, speaking mainly in Spanish. It's wonderful!

2. ***Talk***

   I first ask the children their favorite part of the story. Eric replies, "The house" in English. Norma interprets my question for other children, and their answers come in Spanish. I hear "el ratón," "el perro," "el gato," "la abuela," and "la casa" (which mean the "mouse," "dog," "cat," "grandmother," and "house," respectively).

3. ***Draw***

   I give the children paper and crayons and ask them to draw their favorite part or anything they want about the story. Norma, the aide, repeats these directions in Spanish. I go around to the students individually, asking what they've drawn, or I ask (imitating the aide), "Que es esto?" They usually answer with one word—in Spanish *or* English. If I don't understand, the aide translates.

4. ***Write***

   I ask the students to write their names on their drawings. Most of them also allow me to write, in English, a sentence about what's going on in their drawing. They also say it's all right for me to

(continued)

> write/spell the name of the object they have colored. Everyone thinks it's a good idea, *except* for Victor, who repeatedly says, "Nada, nada!" (i.e., "Nothing, nothing!"). He simply does not want *anything* written on his drawing! Eric has drawn all the animals and has me label each one and the granny. Then I ask him "Where's the child?" He answers in English, "Under Granny!"
>
> Marjorie continues:
>
> I see that this lesson could have expanded into the areas of the family and sleep, just to name a few. I was constantly aware of keeping the affective filter low, acting relaxed, friendly, and caring. The children behaved as if they felt safe and secure. With my heart pounding, and happy, I left the room where literacy in two languages was experienced by all.

2. *Writing and Drawing Center:* Materials for drawing and writing should be kept in boxes, files, and baskets in one central location in the classroom, on or adjacent to a table. If the location is near a bulletin board, it will provide a natural place for children to publish their work. This writing and drawing center can be used when children need it: during small-group activity; for special purposes, like writing letters; and for special themes, like holidays. Children can also go to the center to draw and write simply because they have something they want to say. Here are some ideas for things needed in the center, which the teacher can collect or ask people to donate:

New multicultural crayons are available, offering a range of skin colors.

Paper of any kind
Pencils: plain lead, colored
Erasers
Crayons and crayon sharpener (baskets of these work well)
Envelopes: legal, manila
Post-its
Stationery
Index cards (for notes, to make postcards)
Construction paper (save and use scraps)
Tape: invisible, masking, colored
Scissors
Glue and glue sticks
Hole punch (for joining paper)
Yarn (for joining paper, book making)
Paper clips

3. *Class Post Office:* Children should be encouraged to write notes and memos to each other and to "mail" them in class. A postal system can be created, with a mailbox for each child. Students' cubbies can be used, or mailboxes can be made out of clean, half-gallon, paper milk cartons. Cut off the tops, and staple the cartons together in stacks of five, with the open tops facing the same direction. Next, staple the five-carton stacks together, side by side, making enough so there's one for every child. Label the mailboxes with students' names.

4. *Language Experience Charts:* When Marion Harris made a list of what the children needed to make apple pies, recorded their recipe, and displayed the cinquain they wrote, she was using the language experience approach. Russell Stauffer (1970) and Roach Van Allen (Allen & Allen, 1968), among others, advocate this approach, which involves recording children's ideas and spoken language and displaying them as written text in the classroom. Doing so demonstrates to each student:

Again, the language experience approach is explained in more detail in Chapter 8, including a sample lesson.

- What I can experience and think about, I can say.
- What I can say, I can write or others can write for me.
- What I can write or others have written for me, I can read.

Language experience charts show children how written language works: that it involves words put on paper; that they're in order, from left to right; that letters have certain shapes and sounds; that when combined, letters make words; and that you can read what you've written. These charts become part of the print environment in the classroom or library. They can be displayed on bulletin boards or walls or bound into "big books."

Types of experiences that lend themselves to these charts include:

Cooking experiences	Science experiments
Holidays	Class pets
Fieldtrips	Weather
Classroom visitors	Responses to literature
Current events	Class stories

5. *The Author's Chair:* The Author's Chair is where children can sit when they read aloud a story they have written. Others can listen, ask questions, and make comments, discussing the story with its young author. This discussion can involve the whole class or just a small group during a writer's workshop.

Centers

In addition to the materials about apples in her writing center, Marion put tapes of the book *Johnny Appleseed* (Kellogg, 1988) in her listening center, materials for apple art in her arts and crafts center, and books and materials about growing things in her science center. All these types of centers provide many opportunities for reading and writing. Here's how each classroom center supports emergent literacy:

1. *Writing Center:* Given materials and opportunities, children can draw and write for authentic, specific purposes or simply to play and experiment with written language.

2. ***Listening Center:*** Tape recorders and earphones and tapes of stories and books provide opportunities for young children to listen as they follow along with the pictures and print in books.

3. ***Arts and Crafts Center:*** Art supplies for drawing; for constructing puppets, props, signs, and labels; and for specific activities, like making apple head dolls, encourage children to use visual symbols and print to express meaning.

4. ***Science Center:*** Children can use nonfiction books and magazines (e.g., *Ranger Rick*) or write in observation logs about science experiments or displays (e.g., the class pet, seeds growing, or a collection of different types of apples).

5. ***Thematic Center:*** Centers can be developed around special themes, such as apples. A Center for the Study of Apples, for example, could include materials related to the "ripple effect": apple books, children's language experience charts about apples, and materials for apple projects.

Some centers, like the writing or listening center, will be set up permanently in the classroom. Others, such as thematic centers, will be temporary. Centers can be combined sometimes—for instance, the writing center with the classroom library and reading corner or the arts and crafts and science centers. Centers like the latter, which can get messy, should be located on a table or counter near a sink, where you may also locate cooking activities.

Integrated Teaching

In Marion's class, apples became a unifying theme that resulted in a "ripple effect" of learning experiences across the curriculum. This sort of integrated teaching is a natural outgrowth of developmentally appropriate, child- and response-centered classrooms, in which children have opportunities to explore, experiment, and discover things for themselves through many hands-on experiences. Suggestions for integrated teaching include:

1. ***Natural "Ripple Effects":*** When teachers listen to children and note their ideas and interests, "ripple effects" occur naturally, as happened with the apples in Marion Harris's class. Other "ripple effects" stem from children's responses to literature, to seasons, or to what's going on in the world. Child-centered teachers notice these things, think about developmentally appropriate activities they can do in connection with them, and find a variety of resources to enhance the learning experience. Such teachers integrate these topics and activities with the ongoing classroom program of sharing, reading aloud, writing and drawing, drama, and learning centers.

2. ***Theme Cycles:*** Sometimes, teachers choose themes that are important and thus worth spending time on. But at other times, teachers select themes that lack a broad, conceptual base or that are trivial and not appropriate for extended study across the curriculum. For example, you could find ways to integrate the theme of teddy bears across the curriculum, but how important are teddy bears? (A kindergartner in a class loaded with teddy bears once confided to me, "I hope she can't find another bear book.") Instead, teachers should select themes that have big ideas behind them or that draw extensively on children's own experiences, such as:

All about me	Native Americans	Growing things
Home and family	Martin Luther King, Jr.	Animals and the zoo
The community		

Emergent Literacy in Kindergarten

Theory, research, and practice about emergent literacy are, in many ways, the same for teaching kindergartners as for teaching students in the first through third grades, the years of early childhood. Yet in other ways, supporting emergent literacy is different in teaching kindergarten. An excellent resource on this topic is Bobbi Fisher's *Joyful Learning: A Whole Language Kindergarten* (1991). Rather than describe how kindergarten and the primary grades are alike and different, let's look at a day in a kindergarten class that uses the ideas for supporting emergent literacy discussed in this chapter.

SNAPSHOT: A Day in a Kindergarten Class

Mauretta Hurst teaches an all-day kindergarten class in Baton Rouge, Louisiana. She explains her approach to teaching, saying, "I draw on the children's own experiences and then relate language, literature, and lots of drama experiences to them." Here's how she does it:

In many parts of the United States, children attend kindergarten for just a half day.

Schedule for a Day in Kindergarten

Theme: The zoo

9:00–9:30	Sharing time
9:30–10:55	Writing and drawing and language experience story
10:55–11:15	Recess
11:15–12:15	Centers: Reading/writing, blocks/social studies, math, art, listening
12:15–1:15	Lunch/recess/P.E.
1:15–2:30	Reading aloud and drama
2:30–3:15	Rest/read aloud/review

In planning the day, Mauretta incorporates all the ways to begin teaching young children to read and write described in this chapter. She also integrates learning experiences across the curriculum. Here's an expanded description of what she does in a day:

9:00–9:30 Sharing Time

Children share about any subject they choose. Then Mauretta asks them to share about the fieldtrip they took to the zoo the day before. They excitedly talk about their many impressions of this fieldtrip.

9:30–10:55 Writing and Drawing and Language Experience Story

Next, the children draw about their experiences on the zoo fieldtrip. Some write their names on their pictures, and others write words, labels, and captions using invented spelling. The children talk to each other while working, and Mauretta moves from table to table, helping them get their ideas down on paper. Then she gathers the children together on the rug and asks them to tell about their pictures. On a large piece of chartpaper, she makes a list of all the animals the children drew about. She notices that the most popular animal was the baby elephant and suggests that they write a story together about it. She encourages them to share more, discusses what they say, and asks for ideas for the story, which she writes down on another large piece of chartpaper. Together, the class writes "The Adventures of a Baby Elephant." After they have finished the story, they read it aloud together; some students volunteer to read it solo.

10:55–11:15 Recess

11:15–12:15 Centers: Reading/Writing, Blocks/Social Studies, Math, Art, Listening

Children go to these different centers in groups of six. They will rotate, going to the other centers on one or several days throughout the week. Mauretta has used the theme of the zoo in several centers in the room. Here's what's happening in each center:

1. ***Reading/Writing:*** Some children are gluing the drawings of animals they did earlier on bigger pieces of paper. Mauretta has provided yarn,

Mauretta Hurst's kindergarten class wrote a story, "The Adventures of a Baby Elephant," after taking a trip to the zoo, which she recorded on a language experience chart.

feathers, and scraps of fake fur to glue on their animal pictures, if they want to. Other children continue to draw and write, putting their names on their pictures and using scribbling, letterstrings, and invented spellings. Children can also give dictation to Mauretta or an aide, who records their ideas on their pictures, or copy the names of their animals from the list Mauretta wrote down earlier. Students share ideas about their drawing and writing as they work and tell or read their stories to others.

2. *Blocks/Social Studies:* Children are building a zoo with wooden blocks and boxes. They're putting stuffed and plastic animals in their zoo and playing with them, pretending to be visitors, zoo keepers, or animals.

3. *Math:* Children are working on a class graph of their favorite animals in the zoo. Each person tells what was his or her favorite animal and draws it. Then all the children glue the animals in columns on a large piece of chartpaper, noting on the bottom the names of their favorite animals and their own names next to the ones they've made. Each group will add to the chart, and when everyone has contributed, the class will add up the number of animals in each column and write it at the bottom.

4. *Art:* Children are working at the easels and painting: animals, the zoo, or whatever they choose.

5. *Listening Center:* Children are listening to a tape of the story of "The Three Billy Goats Gruff," following along with several copies of the book as they listen.

12:15–1:15 Lunch/Recess/P.E.

1:15–2:30 Reading Aloud and Drama

Mauretta reads aloud Marcia Brown's (1957) picture book *The Three Billy Goats Gruff.* She reads dramatically, with a lot of facial expressions and gestures. When she's finished, the children applaud and ask her to read it again. She does, using as much expression as she did the first time. During the second reading, she encourages the children to fill in whatever words they remember from the first reading. Since this is a predictable pattern book, with a repeated phrase, many students join in, chanting with the troll, "Who's that tramping over my bridge?" The children begin to imitate Mauretta's gestures, such as making a long nose with her hand for the troll and patting the floor to make the "trip-trap" sound as the billy goats cross the bridge, one by one. The children make this noise softly for the first and smallest billy goat and loudly for the last and biggest one.

After reading, the class talks about what happened in the story. Mauretta asks open-ended, aesthetic questions:

"What did you think about the story?"
"What was your favorite part?"
"Who was your favorite character?"

"Who's that tripping over my bridge?" Mauretta Hurst reads aloud The Three Billy Goats Gruff *(Brown, 1957), using a lot of expression and gestures.*

Next, the class dramatizes the story. First, the children spread out around the room and pretend to be the different characters, imitating one at a time. Mauretta says she will take one volunteer to act out each character. The rest of the students have rhythm sticks and will make the "trip-trap" sound effects. The scene is set with green carpet squares for grass and a bridge made of wooden blocks. A narrator is chosen to tell the story. The students dramatize the story this way several times. Mauretta promises she will read it again the next day, giving more children chances to play the characters.

2:30–3:15 Rest/Read Aloud/Review

After the children take a short rest, Mauretta reads aloud the language experience story they wrote earlier, "The Adventures of a Baby Elephant"; Brown's (1957) *The Three Billy Goats Gruff* again; and a new zoo book, *A Children's Zoo* by Tana Hoban (1985). The class ends the day by talking about their zoo trip, their favorite zoo animals, and what other things they can do around the theme of the zoo.

On following days, Mauretta continues the theme of the zoo in centers, dramatizing *The Three Billy Goats Gruff,* reading more books about animals, and drawing and writing. She integrates learning experiences through the unifying theme of animals and the zoo, an experience the children all shared and had many ideas and much enthusiasm about. Like Marion Harris did with her first-graders, Mauretta created a "ripple effect" in her kindergarten class.

Assessing Emergent Literacy

The National Association for the Education of Young Children (NAEYC, 1991) opposes the use of standardized tests for young children, except as a way of screening for development and special services. To assess emergent literacy, teachers of young children should employ a variety of means, relying heavily on observations of children's reading and writing in authentic, contextualized classroom situations (Genishi, 1992; Nurss, 1992). Specific means of assessment include:

1. ***Anecdotal Records:*** These records can be in the form of a journal, notecards for a file, or a grid for systematic recording of observations. Anecdotal records should include what was observed as well as an interpretation of what it means. For example, a kindergarten teacher might record her observations as follows:

Literacy Observation Grid

Date	Name	Observation	Interpretation
3/10	Anne S.	Played "mother," "memory reading" Mother Goose to "child" (doll); points to words she knows; asks "child" questions	Close to reading on her own; sees reading as social

Over time, anecdotal records will chart the development of children's emergent reading and writing and will be useful in planning, parent conferences, and evaluation.

2. ***Checklists:*** For teachers who work with many children, checklists provide a quicker, easier form of assessment. Checklists should be created by teachers to reflect children's current developmental levels and what's going on in the classroom. They should be flexible, evolving for use in different situations. To create a checklist, start with a blank checklist form, such as a photocopied list of children's names next to a grid. Leave spaces at the top of the checklist to write in different aspects of children's emergent literacy behavior. Here's an example:

Literacy Checklist

Literacy Behavior:	____________	____________	____________
Students' Names:	____________	____________	____________
	____________	____________	____________
	____________	____________	____________

For more ideas, see the *Primary Language Record* (Centre for Primary Language Education, 1988).

3. ***Storytelling and Drama:*** To assess children's understanding of stories structure and elements, language use, and responses to literature, teachers can keep anecdotal records, audiotapes, or videotapes of children's play, storytellings, creative dramatics, and story dramatizations.

See *The Boy Who Would Be a Helicopter: The Use of Storytelling in the Classroom* by Vivian G. Paley (1988).

4. *Drawing and Writing:* Samples of children's drawing and writing provide an essential source of information in describing and interpreting their emergent writing.

5. *Portfolios:* Portfolios provide a picture of young children's emergent literacy behavior and can include information collected through the types of informal, authentic assessment measures described here: anecdotal records, checklists, audio- and videotapes of storytelling and drama, and dated pieces of drawing and writing that are chosen by both children and teachers and collected over time.

Answers to Questions about Emergent Literacy

1. *How do young children learn to read and write?*

According to the emergent literacy perspective, young children learn to read and write as they use writing and reading for authentic purposes, actively constructing meaning. This view developed when studies of early natural readers challenged the previously held readiness view by showing that literate behavior does not begin at a certain age but is constantly emerging. Children know a great deal about literacy when they enter school, due to the influence of family and culture. Even though literacy experiences in the home may vary across families and cultures, all children have them. Important influences on emerging reading are environmental print and storybook experiences. Emergent writing develops in a series of predictable stages: scribbling, drawing, nonphonetic letterstrings, invented spelling, and conventional orthography. Children also go through predictable stages in spelling development: deviant, prephonetic, phonetic, transitional, and correct.

Reading and writing are interactive processes and emerge together. In order to become literate in English, language-minority students should learn to read and write in both English and their native language, acquiring additive bilingualism, which is building knowledge of the second language on that of the first.

2. *How can we teach young children to read and write?*

Seven ways to begin teaching young children to write include (1) creating a print-rich environment, (2) having a regular sharing time, (3) reading aloud, (4) dramatizing, (5) writing and drawing, (6) establishing centers, and (7) integrating teaching.

LOOKING FURTHER

1 Diagram a possible "ripple effect" of learning and teaching experiences for a specific grade level from kindergarten through third grade. Make sure that it's based on a worthwhile topic appropriate for that grade level and that it provides many opportunities for authentic reading and writing experiences.

2 Do a lesson plan for "Read, Talk, Draw, Write," described in this chapter, and try it out with a group of young children in grades K–3. Describe the experience.

3 Do a lesson plan for "Read, Talk, Draw, Write," and try it out with a group of language-minority children. Describe the experience.

4 Compare experiences in items 2 and 3, if you were able to do both lesson plans.

5 Observe in a kindergarten or primary-grade class while students are writing. Take note of their behaviors. After the children have finished, collect their writing samples and analyze them according to the stages of invented spelling. Report your findings to your college class.

6 Observe and participate in both a kindergarten and a first-grade class. In terms of their approach to emergent literacy, how were they alike? How were they different?

RESOURCES

Fisher, B. (1991). *Joyful learning: A whole language kindergarten.* Portsmouth, NH: Heinemann.

McGee, L. M., & Richgels, D. J. (1990). *Literacy's beginnings: Supporting young readers and writers.* Boston: Allyn and Bacon.

Strickland, D., & Morrow, L. (Eds.). (1989). *Emerging literacy: Young children learn to read and write.* Newark, DE: International Reading Association.

Teale, W. H., & Sulzby, E. (1986). *Emergent literacy: Writing and reading.* Norwood, NJ: Ablex.

REFERENCES

Allen, R. V., & Allen, C. (1968). *Language experience in reading.* Chicago: Encyclopaedia Britannica.

Allen, V. G. (1989). Literature as support to language acquisition. In P. Rigg & V. G. Allen (Eds.), *When they don't all speak English* (pp. 55–64). Urbana, IL: National Council of Teachers of English.

Anderson, A. B., & Stokes, S. J. (1984). Social and institutional influences on the development and practice of literacy. In H. Goelman, A. Oberg, & F. Smith (Eds.), *Awakening to literacy* (pp. 24–37). Portsmouth, NH: Heinemann.

Au, K. H. (1993). *Literacy in multicultural settings.* Fort Worth, TX: Harcourt Brace Jovanovich.

Barrera, R. B. (1983). Bilingual reading in the primary grades: Some questions about questionable views and practices. In T. H. Escobedo (Ed.), *Early childhood bilingual education: A Hispanic perspective.* New York: Teachers College Press.

Beers, C. S., & Beers, J. W. (1981). Three assumptions about learning to spell. *Language Arts, 58,* 573–580.

Beers, J. W., & Henderson E. H. (1977). A study of developing orthographic concepts among first graders. *Research in the Teaching of English, 11,* 133–148.

Centre for Primary Language Education, Inner London Education Authority. (1988). *Primary language record.* Portsmouth, NH: Heinemann.

Chomsky, C. (1971). Write first, read later. *Childhood Education, 47,* 296–299.

Clark, M. M. (1976). *Young fluent readers.* London, England: Heinemann.

Clay, M. M. (1967). The reading behavior of five-year-old children: A research report. *New Zealand Journal of Educational Studies, 2,* 11–31.

Clay, M. M. (1975). *What did I write?* Auckland, New Zealand: Heinemann.

Clay, M. M. (1989). Foreword. In D. S. Strickland & L. M. Morrow (Eds.), *Emerging literacy: Young children learn to read and write.* Newark, DE: International Reading Association.

Clay, M. M. (1991). *Becoming literate: The construction of inner control.* Portsmouth, NH: Heinemann.

Cummins, J. (1980). The cross-lingual dimensions of language proficiency: Implications for bilingual education and the optimal age issue. *TESOL Quarterly, 14,* 175–187.

De Ford, D. E. (1981). Literacy: Reading, writing, and other essentials. *Language Arts, 58,* 652–658.

Durkin, D. (1966). *Children who read early.* New York: Teachers College Press.

Edelsky, C. (1986). *Writing in a bilingual program: Habla una vez.* Norwood, NJ: Ablex.

Fisher, B. (1991). *Joyful learning: A whole language kindergarten.* Portsmouth, NH: Heinemann.

Freeman, Y. S. (1988). *The contemporary Spanish basal reader* (Occasional Paper No. 18). Tucson: Program in Language and Literacy, College of Education, University of Arizona.

Gates, A. I., & Bond, G. L. (1936). Reading readiness: A study of factors determining success and failure in beginning reading. *Teachers College Record, 37,* 679–685.

Genishi, C. (Ed.). (1992). *Ways of assessing children and curriculum: Stories of early childhood practice.* New York: Teachers College Press.

Gentry, J. R. (1981). Learning to spell developmentally. *Reading Teacher, 34,* 378–381.

Goodman, K., & Goodman, Y. (1983). Reading and writing relationships: Pragmatic functions. *Language Arts, 60,* 590–591.

Goodman, K., Goodman, Y., & Flores, B. (1979). *Reading in the bilingual classroom: Literacy and biliteracy.* Rosslyn, VA: National Clearinghouse for Bilingual Education.

Goodman, Y. (1980). The roots of literacy. In M. P. Douglass (Ed.), *Claremont Reading Conference 44th yearbook.* Claremont, CA: Claremont Graduate School.

Goodman, Y. (1986). Children coming to know literacy. In W. H. Teale & E. Sulzby (Eds.), *Emergent literacy: Reading and writing* (pp. 1–14). Norwood, NJ: Ablex.

Goodman, Y., & Altwerger, B. (1981). *Print awareness in preschool children: A study of the development of literacy in preschool children* (Occasional Paper No. 4). Tucson: University of Arizona Center for Research and Development, College of Education.

Graves, D. (1978). *Balance the basics: Let them write.* New York: Ford Foundation.

Graves, D., & Hansen, J. (1983). The author's chair. *Language Arts, 60,* 176–183.

Harste, J. C. (1990). Jerry Harste speaks on reading and writing. *Reading Teacher, 43,* 316–318.

Harste, J. C., Woodward, V. A., & Burke, C. L. (1984). *Language stories and literacy lessons.* Portsmouth, NH: Heinemann.

Heath, S. B. (1983). *Ways with words: Language, life and work in communities and classrooms.* Cambridge, MA: Harvard University Press.

Henderson, E. H. (1980). Word knowledge and reading disability. In E. H. Henderson & J. W. Beers (Eds.), *Developmental and cognitive aspects of learning to spell.* Newark, DE: International Reading Association.

Hiebert, E. H. (1981). Developmental patterns and interrelationships of preschool children's print awareness. *Reading Research Quarterly, 16*(2), 236–260.

Holdaway, D. (1979). *The foundations of literacy.* Portsmouth, NH: Heinemann.

Hudelson, S. (1984). Kan yu ret an rayt en Ingles: Children become literate in English as a second language. *TESOL Quarterly, 18,* 221–238.

Hudelson, S. (1987). The role of native language literacy in the education of language minority children. *Language Arts, 64,* 827–841.

Lanauze, M., & Snow, C. E. (1989). The relation between first- and second-language writing skills: Evidence from Puerto Rican elementary school children in the mainland. *Linguistics and Education, 1*(4), 323–338.

Mason, J. M., & Au, K. H. (1986). *Reading instruction for today.* Glenview, IL: Scott, Foresman.

McGee, L., Lomax, R., & Head, M. (1988). Young children's written language knowledge: What environmental and functional print reading reveals. *Journal of Reading Behavior, 20,* 99–108.

Miller, P., Nemoianu, A., & DeJong, J. (1986). Early reading at home: Its practice and meanings in a working class community. In B. Schieffelin & P. Gilmore (Eds.), *The acquisition of literacy: Ethnographic perspectives* (pp. 3–15). Norwood, NJ: Ablex.

Moffet, J., & Wagner, B. J. (1993). What works is play. *Language Arts, 70,* 32–36.

Morphett, M. V., & Washburne, C. (1931). When should children begin to read? *Elementary School Journal, 31,* 496–503.

National Association for the Education of Young Children (NAEYC). (1991). Guidelines for the appropriate curriculum content and assessment in programs serving young children ages 3 through 8. *Young Children, 46*(3), 21–38.

Nurss, J. R. (1992). Evaluation of language and literacy. In L. O. Ollila & M. I. Mayfield (Eds.), *Emerging literacy: Preschool, kindergarten, and primary grades.* Boston: Allyn and Bacon.

Paley, V. G. (1988). *The boy who would be a helicopter: The uses of storytelling in the classroom.* Portsmouth, NH: Heinemann.

Piaget, J. (1969). *The language and thought of the child.* London, England: Routledge & Kegan Paul.

Read, C. (1975). *Children's categorization of speech sounds in English.* Urbana, IL: National Council of Teachers of English.

Rigg, P. (1986). Reading in ESL: Learning from kids. In P. Rigg & D. S. Enright (Eds.), *Children with ESL: Integrating perspectives* (pp. 55–92). Washington, DC: Teachers of English to Speakers of Other Languages.

Rigg, P. (1991). Whole language in TESOL. *TESOL Quarterly, 25*(3), 521–542.

Schwartz, J. I. (1988). *Encouraging early literacy: An integrated approach to reading and writing in K–3.* Portsmouth, NH: Heinemann.

Schickendanz, J. A. (1990). *Adam's righting revolutions: One child's literacy development from infancy through grade one.* Portsmouth, NH: Heinemann.

Snow, C. E. (1990). Rationales for native language instruction: Evidence from research. In A. M. Padilla, H. H. Fairchild, & C. M. Valdez, *Bilingual education: Issues and strategies* (pp. 60–74). Newbury Park, CA: Sage.

Stauffer, R. C. (1970). *The language experience approach to teaching reading.* New York: Harper & Row.

Strickland, D. S., & Feeley, J. T. (1991). Development in the elementary school years. In J. Flood, J. M. Jensen, D. Lapp, & J. R. Squire (Eds.), *Handbook of research on teaching the English language arts* (pp. 286–302). New York: Macmillan.

Strickland, D. S., & Morrow, L. (1988). Creating a print rich environment. *Reading Teacher, 42,* 156–157.

Strickland, D. S., & Morrow, L. (1989). Environments rich in print promote literacy behavior during play. *Reading Teacher, 43,* 178–179.

Sulzby, E. (1985). Children's emergent reading of favorite storybooks: A developmental study. *Reading Research Quarterly, 20,* 458–481.

Sulzby, E. (1989). Assessment of writing and of children's language while writing. In L. Morrow & J. Smith (Eds.), *The role of assessment and measurement in early literacy instruction* (pp. 83–109). Englewood Cliffs, NJ: Prentice-Hall.

Sulzby, E. (1991). The development of the young child and the emergence of literacy. In J. Flood, J. M. Jensen, D. Lapp, & J. R. Squire (Eds.), *Handbook of research on teaching the English language arts* (pp. 273–285). New York: Macmillan.

Sulzby, E. (1992). Research directions: Transitions from emergent to conventional writing. *Language Arts, 69,* 290–297.

Taylor, D. (1983). Family literacy: *Young children learning to read and write.* Portsmouth, NH: Heinemann.

Taylor, D., & Dorsey-Gaines, C. (1988). *Growing up literate: Learning from inner-city families.* Portsmouth, NH: Heinemann.

Taylor, D., & Strickland, D. S. (1986). *Family storybook reading.* Portsmouth, NH: Heinemann.

Teale, W. H. (1984). Reading to young children: Its significance in the process of literacy development. In H. Goelman, A. Oberg, & F. Smith (Eds.), *Awakening to literacy* (pp. 110–121). Portsmouth, NH: Heinemann.

Teale, W. H. (1986). Home background and young children's literacy development. In W. H. Teale & E. Sulzby (Eds.), *Emergent literacy: Writing and reading* (pp. 173–206). Norwood, NJ: Ablex.

Teale, W. H., & Sulzby, E. (1989). Emerging literacy: New perspectives. In D. S. Strickland & L. M. Morrow (Eds.), *Emerging literacy: Young children learn to read and write* (pp. 1–15). Newark, DE: International Reading Association.

Urzua, C. (1987). "You stopped too soon": Second language children composing and revising. *TESOL Quarterly, 21,* 279–304.

Vygotsky, L. S. (1978). *Mind in society: The development of higher psychological processes.* Cambridge, MA: Harvard University Press.

Wells, C. G. (1985). Pre-school literacy related activities and success in school. In D. Olson, N. Torrance, & A. Hildyard (Eds.), *Literacy, language, and learning: The nature and consequence of literacy* (pp. 229–255). Cambridge, England: Cambridge University Press.

Yaden, D. B., & Templeton, S. (Eds.). (1986). *Metalinguistic awareness and beginning literacy: Conceptualizing what it means to read and write.* Portsmouth, NH: Heinemann.

Zutell, J., & Allen, V. (1988). The English spelling strategies of Spanish-speaking bilingual children. *TESOL Quarterly, 22,* 333–339.

CHILDREN'S BOOKS

Aliki. (1963). *The story of Johnny Appleseed.* New York: Prentice Hall.

Aliki. (1992). *La historia de Johnny Appleseed.* New York: Lectorum.

Brett, J. (1968). *The mitten.* New York: Putnam's.

Brown, M. (1957). *The three billy goats gruff.* New York: Harcourt Brace Jovanovich.

Carle, E. (1969). *The very hungry caterpillar.* Cleveland: Collins-World.

Carle, E. (1972). *Rooster's off to see the world.* Saxonville, MA: Picture Book Studio.

Eastman, P. D. (1960). *Are you my mother?* New York: Random House.

Flack, M. (1932). *Ask Mr. Bear.* New York: Macmillan.

Gag, W. (1956). *Millions of cats.* New York: Coward, McCann. (Original work published 1928)

Galdone, P. (1973). *The little red hen.* New York: Clarion.

Guarino, D. (1989). *Is your mama a llama?* New York: Scholastic.

Hawkins, C., & Hawkins, J. (1987). *I know an old lady who swallowed a fly.* New York: Putnam's.

Heuck, S. (1986). *Who stole the apples?* New York: Knopf.

Hoban, T. (1985). *A children's zoo.* New York: Greenwillow.

Hogrogian, N. (1972). *Apples.* New York: Macmillan.

Hutchins, P. (1968). *The doorbell rang.* New York: Morrow.

Keats, E. J. (1973). *Over in the meadow.* New York: Scholastic.

Kellogg, S. (1988). *Johnny Appleseed.* New York: Morrow.

Kraus, R. (1970). *Whose mouse are you?* New York: Macmillan.

Lindbergh, R. (1990). *Johnny Appleseed: A poem by Reeve Lindbergh.* Boston: Little, Brown.

Macmillan, B. (1979). *Apples, how they grow.* Boston: Houghton Mifflin.

Maestro, B. (1992). *How do apples grow?* New York: HarperCollins.

Martin, B. (1983). *Brown bear, brown bear, what do you see?* New York: Henry Holt.

Martin, B., & Archambault, J. (1989). *Chicka chicka boom boom!* New York: Simon & Schuster.

Micucci, C. (1992). *The life and times of the apple.* New York: Orchard.

Nottridge, R. (1991). *Apples.* Minneapolis, MN: Carolrhoda.

Numeroff, L. J. (1985). *If you give a mouse a cookie.* New York: HarperCollins.

Parnall, P. (1987). *Apple tree.* New York: Macmillan.

Peek, M. (1985). *Mary wore her red dress.* New York: Clarion.

Rosen, M. (1989). *We're going on a bear hunt.* New York: McElderry.

Seifert, J. (1985). *La cancion del manzano.* Madrid, Spain: Ediciones S. M.

Sendak, M. (1962). *Chicken soup with rice.* New York: Harper's.

Seuss, Dr. (1988). *Green eggs and ham.* New York: Random House.

Slobodkina, E. (1940). *Caps for sale.* New York: Harper & Row.

Wickstrom, S. K. (1988). *The wheels on the bus.* New York: Crown.

Wood, A. (1984). *The napping house.* San Diego: Harcourt Brace Jovanovich.

Chapter 5

Listening and Talking

Questions about Listening and Talking

1. *What kinds of listening and talking take place in elementary classrooms?*
2. *What is the relationship of critical thinking and literacy to listening and talking?*
3. *How can we teach listening and talking?*

Reflective Response: Do We Really Need to Teach Listening and Talking?

Listening and talking seem like such natural language acts. Babies listen before they speak, and young children come to school already speaking their native languages. Perhaps we don't really need to worry about teaching listening and talking when it's so important to teach reading and writing. What do you think? Jot down your ideas.

Listening and Talking in the Elementary Classroom

What kinds of listening and talking take place in the elementary classroom? Who does the listening, and who does the talking? How can listening and talking be taught? These questions are worth considering, because oral language (that is, listening and talking), thinking, and literacy are highly interrelated.

Learning Listening and Talking

Walter Loban's (1976, 1979) well-known longitudinal study of how children from kindergarten through grade 12 (K–12) use and control language had several significant findings. Namely, children who are proficient in oral language use more complex language and understand the conventions of language better, score higher on vocabulary and intelligence tests, and perform better in reading and writing than their less proficient peers. Research on the relationship between spoken language and learning to read confirms that children's experience with and knowledge of the linguistic organization of spoken language is basic to their ability to read (Cox, 1984; Sticht & James, 1984).

Listening and talking are integral to writing as well as reading. For young, emergent writers, writing is "as much an oral activity as a written one" (Dyson & Genishi, 1982, p. 126), since talking works in concert with expressing ideas in writing (Dyson, 1994). Writing is one aspect of the comprehensive process of language development, which also involves listening, talking, reading, and thinking. All these abilities develop simultaneously, not as isolated skills. James Britton's famous metaphor—"Writing floats on a sea of talk" (1970, p. 164)—helps us picture the importance of oral language as the basis for literacy.

However, other studies have shown that, despite the importance of oral language, opportunities for listening and talking in the elementary classroom may be much more limited than they are at home. Shirley Brice Heath (1983) has shown the frequent mismatches between language used at home and at school that are related to cultural differences. Schools do not always provide a linguistically rich environment, compared to homes, where children have more opportunities to learn through listening and talking (Wells & Wells, 1984).

Rankin's well-known 1928 survey showed that of the 68 percent of each schoolday spent in communication, listening is the most prevalent activity (45 percent), followed by speaking (30 percent), reading (16 percent), and writing (9 percent) (see Figure 5.1A). Later studies (Flanders, 1970; Wilt, 1974) showed that during the schoolday, someone is talking from one-half to two-thirds the time (which is more than twice the amount of time teachers estimated). Teachers talk more than all the students combined, and two-thirds of the time that someone is speaking, it's the teacher (see Figure 5.1B). Teacher talk tends to dominate activities involving explaining and evaluating, which limits children's oral language use in both quantity and meaningful purpose. As a result, children spend more time listening to teachers talk than engaged in active language interaction with either teachers or other students (Fox, 1983). Although perhaps limited, children's oral language use is nonetheless significant: They speak about twice as much as they read and three times as much as they write.

Teaching Listening and Talking

In the past, little attention has been paid to teaching how to listen, even though active approaches to teaching listening have been demonstrated to improve listening learning (Brent & Anderson, 1993; Devine, 1978). Possibilities for teaching listening and speaking have also been ignored because teachers tend to use reading and writing as measures of student achievement. However, research has shown that listening comprehension can be improved in a variety of ways when taught in the context of meaningful oral language experiences (Goodlad, 1984; Jalongo, 1991; Pearson & Fielding, 1982).

To focus on listening and talking skills as aspects of the language development process, teachers should:

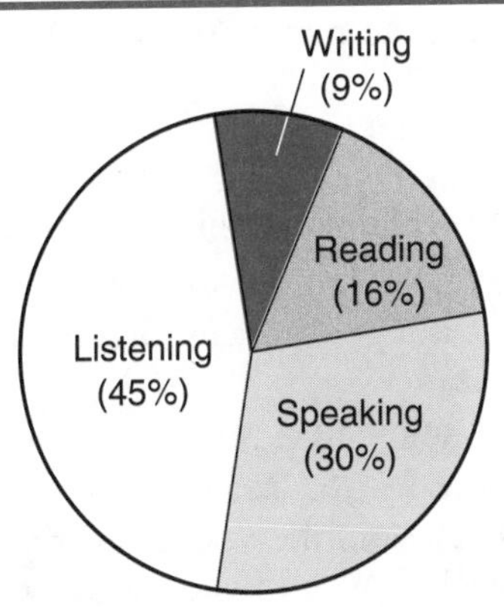

A. Time in Each Language Mode

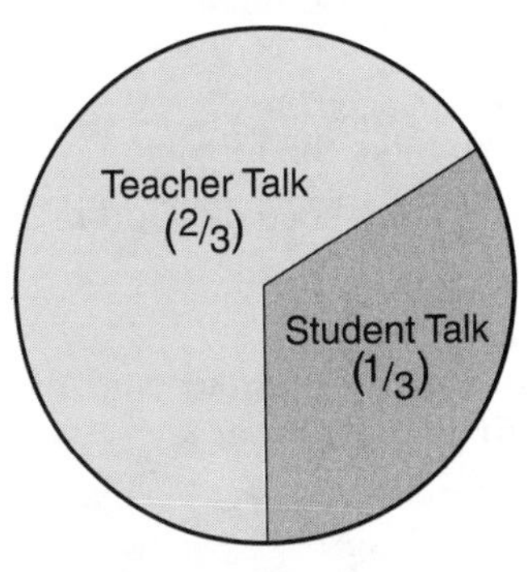

B. Teacher Talk vs. Student Talk

FIGURE 5.1
Part A: Amount of Classroom Day Spent in Language Modes (in percent)
Part B: Amount of Teacher Talk vs. Student Talk

1. Create a healthy climate for oral language to support reading and writing.
2. Emphasize certain aspects of spoken language most related to reading: expanding vocabulary development, using spoken language with flexibility, increasing sensitivity to conventions and varieties of language forms, raising metalinguistic awareness.
3. Help children understand and use connections among the language arts: listening, speaking, reading, writing, and thinking.
4. Build on children's prior experiences and linguistic and cultural heritages.
5. Take into account the native language abilities of bilingual and limited–English proficient students as well as those who speak nonstandard dialects; in addition, be aware that these differences don't critically interfere with learning to read and write.

Metalinguistic awareness means helping children realize what they know about language.

See Chapter 3, Language and Cultural Diversity.

Here are a number of effective approaches to teaching listening and talking:

1. Listen to literature being read aloud.
2. Prompt spoken responses during and after listening experiences.
3. Focus on meaning in listening and talking, as in reading and writing.
4. Do systematic teaching of listening and talking.
5. Plan student-led discussions, and teach skills in leading discussions.
6. Use open teacher questions and prompts (defined below) to extend thinking and participation.
7. Provide regular time for sharing.

Teachers must strike a balance between the power and potential of both self-discovery and interaction in children's development of thought and language. For teachers, knowing not only *when* but *how* to talk and *what* kinds of questions to ask are essential to the simultaneous development of oral language, literacy, and critical thinking. *Open* questions, which imply many possible answers, lead to richer language interactions and higher levels of thinking than *closed* questions, which imply only one possible answer, often yes or no (Barnes, 1976). For example, after watching the movie *The Wizard of Oz* (1939), the teacher might ask:

Closed Questions	***Open Questions***
Did you like the movie?	What did you think of the movie?
What color shoes did Dorothy have on?	Why do you think the Wizard of Oz is a good wizard or a bad wizard?
How many friends accompanied Dorothy on her journey?	How would you feel if you were: Dorothy? the Tin Man? the Cowardly Lion? the Scarecrow? or the Wicked Witch (who got melted)?

In planning for discussions with children, teachers should think about how they would answer each type of question: closed versus open. Which type of question elicits a more meaningful response? Clearly, open questions initiate and extend discussions, drawing out and linking children's thoughts and ideas.

Language Interaction Analysis

In the Snapshot that follows, we'll look at what kinds of listening, talking, and questioning activities went on in a second-grade class the week before Halloween, when teacher Kathy Lee read books and showed films about creatures and then led discussions with students. While reading that Snapshot, however, let's do simple analyses of several things: (1) the ratio of teacher talk to student talk and (2) the types of questions the teacher asked, closed versus open. Use Figure 5.2 to keep tallies of how many times the teacher and the students each spoke in the book and film talks as well as how many open and closed questions the teacher asked. We'll add up the totals and calculate ratios later, after reading the Snapshot, when we'll also discuss the implications of these observations.

FIGURE 5.2
Language Interaction Analysis Chart

DATE/TIME ____________________

ACTIVITY ____________________

	Type of Talk		**Type of Question**	
	Teacher	***Student***	***Open***	***Closed***
Book Talk 1				
Total	____	____	____	____
Ratio	____	____	____	____
Book Talk 2				
Total	____	____	____	____
Ratio	____	____	____	____
Film Talk 1				
Total	____	____	____	____
Ratio	____	____	____	____
Film Talk 2				
Total	____	____	____	____
Ratio	____	____	____	____

Use this form to analyze language interactions in a classroom or to monitor interactions in your own classroom when you're teaching.

SNAPSHOT: Talking about Books and Films about Creatures

Book Talk 1: *Where the Wild Things Are*

Kathy Lee read her second-graders Maurice Sendak's (1963) well-known Caldecott Award–winning book *Where the Wild Things Are,* which is about a little boy's adventures on an island with some wild, monstrous creatures. Kathy read the book in the way teachers often do with young children: reading the text, showing the illustrations, and asking questions about the story as she went along. While reading the book, she engaged the students in the following book talk (remember to analyze this language sample using Figure 5.2):

Teacher (points to title): What does it say?
Child (reading): Where the wild things are.
Teacher: That's right. And the picture looks like . . . ?
Child: A monster.
Teacher: What kind of feet does it have?
Child: Human feet.
Teacher: Maybe this can be for one of the days we're celebrating this month. What day is that?
Child: Columbus Day?
Teacher: Well, this (points to monster) can be for Halloween, and this (points to boat) can be for Columbus Day.

(Noise from the children.)

Teacher (reading): "The night Max wore his wolf suit and made mischief of one kind . . ." What is he doing?

Kathy continued to read the rest of the book in this way.

See Chapter 6, Drama in the Classroom, for a step-by-step approach to dramatizing this story with children.

Book Talk 2: *The Dragon of Santa Lalia*

This book, by Carol Carrick (1971), is about a little old lady who befriends a dragon that makes popcorn with its fiery breath. Kathy read as follows:

Teacher (points to title): What does it say?
Child (reading): The dragon . . . The dragon of the San–ta–la . . .
Teacher: You're pretty close.
Child: Lala?
Teacher (reading): The dragon of Santa Lalia.
Child (repeating): Lalia.
Teacher (reading): Do you see all that I just read?
Child: Uh-huh.
Teacher (reading): Can you see all that?
Child: Uh-huh.
Teacher (reading): Do you see it yet?

(Noise from children.)

Again, Kathy read the rest of the book in this way.

Film Talk 1: *The Dragon's Tears*

Kathy showed *The Dragon's Tears* (1962), a film about a little boy and a lonely dragon who become friends. After watching the film, the class talked about it:

Teacher: How were the story of *The Dragon of Santa Lalia* and this movie about dragons alike?
Child: They both had dragons in 'em.
Child: They both started alike, with the school out in front.
Child: Um, they were both dragons, and they both came from the hills, and, um, they both had fire.
Child: I know! This one, um, all the water came out of his ears, and all the popcorn started coming out of the other dragon's nose.
Child: One put flowers in the tree, and the other one made popcorn.
Child: That lady wasn't afraid of that other dragon, and the boy wasn't afraid of this dragon today.
Teacher: Very good! Would you be afraid of the dragon?
Many Children: NO!
Teacher: What would you do if you went out for recess now and saw a dragon on the playground?
Child: Uh, I'd make friends with it, and I'd feed it.
Child: I'd come in here and shut the door and get right under the desk.
Child: I would pet it.
Child: I'd make friends with it and call it with a whistle.
Teacher: Oh, like a dog?
Child: Ride it. Go over it and ride it and walk up his tail.
Teacher: Go up his tail? How big do you think these dragons were?
Child: Well, up to the ceiling.
Child: Uh, two times the height of, uh, one of, uh, how big was that? Uh, as high as . . . I mean to the middle of . . . that curtain. Two times as high as that. Two of those.
Child: Mrs. Lee, do you know what I'd do with the dragon?
Teacher: What would you do with the dragon?
Child: I'd use it for my popcorn popper.

Film Talk 2: *Clay*

Kathy showed the film *Clay: The Origin of the Species* (1964), a claymation, animated film in which things constantly change into other things at a frenzied pace. After the film was over, the class discussed it:

Teacher: Well, what did you think of it? What did you think of all those creatures?
Child: I liked the animals and people and boats and the Statue of Liberty.
Child: And a president. President Lincoln.
Child: A man eating. Something that eats everything that comes by. A lizard.

Child: And a whale and an elephant and a deer.
Child: Yeah, and a cow and a gingerbread boy.
Teacher: What do you think was the most unbelievable thing that happened in the movie? We saw a lot of funny things, but what really made you go "wow" or something?
Child: I know. When the dinosaurs were playing and they kissed.

(Many children laugh.)

Child: I like that, uh, that, um, one dinosaur, um, ate the other one.
Teacher: Do you think you could make things like you saw in the film?
Many Children: YEAH!
Teacher: What would you like to make?
Child: You could make anything you wanted to.
Child: Mrs. Lee, could we make something together?
Teacher: Would you like to make something together?
Child: Yeah. We'd like . . . two people to work in a group, you know, work together.
Child: Could we do it right now?
Teacher: I think maybe later on today we'll make some clay things.
Child: We're gonna make something good. We're gonna make a clown and a football player.
Child: See, I could bring a ball.
Child: We could make our own movie!
Child: Will we have prizes? Let's say they all get a prize.
Child: Yeah! Me included.
Child: We'll run the movie through again.
Child: We'll have prizes and show the movie and make our own movie and then we'll have it all together!

Now, add up your tallies (see Figure 5.2) and, for each discussion, calculate the ratios of (1) teacher to student talk and (2) open to closed questions. Also think about what the children said. Here's a comparison of students' responses in the closed-question book talks versus the open-question film talks:

Closed-Question Book Talks	***Open-Question Film Talks***
Read title, words	Compared book and film
Described pictures	Hypothesized what they would do if they saw a dragon
Answered with single words	Described parts they liked in the films and also the most unbelievable thing
Named holidays	Brainstormed ideas for making things out of clay
	Asked to watch the movie again
	Suggested they make a movie

Offered to work together in groups

Requested having prizes for their movie

Did you notice that during the book talks:

- Kathy talked more and asked more closed questions, and the students' responses were limited to one-word answers or trying to read words?
- In order to correctly answer the questions Kathy asked, the children just had to listen as she read the book? (The answers could be verified by the text.)
- The children didn't interact with each other, and they made noise unrelated to the book talk?

And did you notice that during the film talks:

- Kathy asked more open questions and did less talking—and consequently, more listening to what her students said?
- She invited more than one possible response and then built new questions on each one received?
- The students listened to and interacted with each other and led the discussion in new and interesting ways?

In sum, when Kathy asked closed questions, her teaching was teacher and text centered and the discussion was impoverished. As a result, very little happened in terms of developing language and possible "ripple effects" of ideas. When Kathy asked open questions, however, her teaching was student and response centered and the discussion was rich and full. She "scaffolded" on students' ideas, and the result was a "ripple effect" of language and literacy experiences that actually occurred in her room; for instance, the class made a clay animation film called *The Greatest Clay Movie on Earth*. Figure 5.3 shows the "ripple effect" about "creatures" that started with talking about films about creatures, dragons, and dinosaurs.

See Chapter 13, Media Literacy, for a demonstration lesson on storyboarding for filmmaking.

Critical Thinking and Communication

We can see from our review of the Snapshot that even in the same class, with the same teacher, the amount and quality of listening and talking can vary greatly, depending on the types of questions the teacher asks. We can also see that the types of listening and talking that go on in a classroom greatly influence students' critical thinking.

In looking at the relationship between critical thinking and communication, we first need to define *critical thinking*. The National Council of Teachers of English (NCTE) Committee on Critical Thinking describes it as "a process which stresses an attitude of suspended judgment, incorporates logical inquiry and problem solving, and leads to an evaluative decision or action" (Bosma, 1987, p. 2).

FIGURE 5.3
A "Ripple Effect" of Creatures

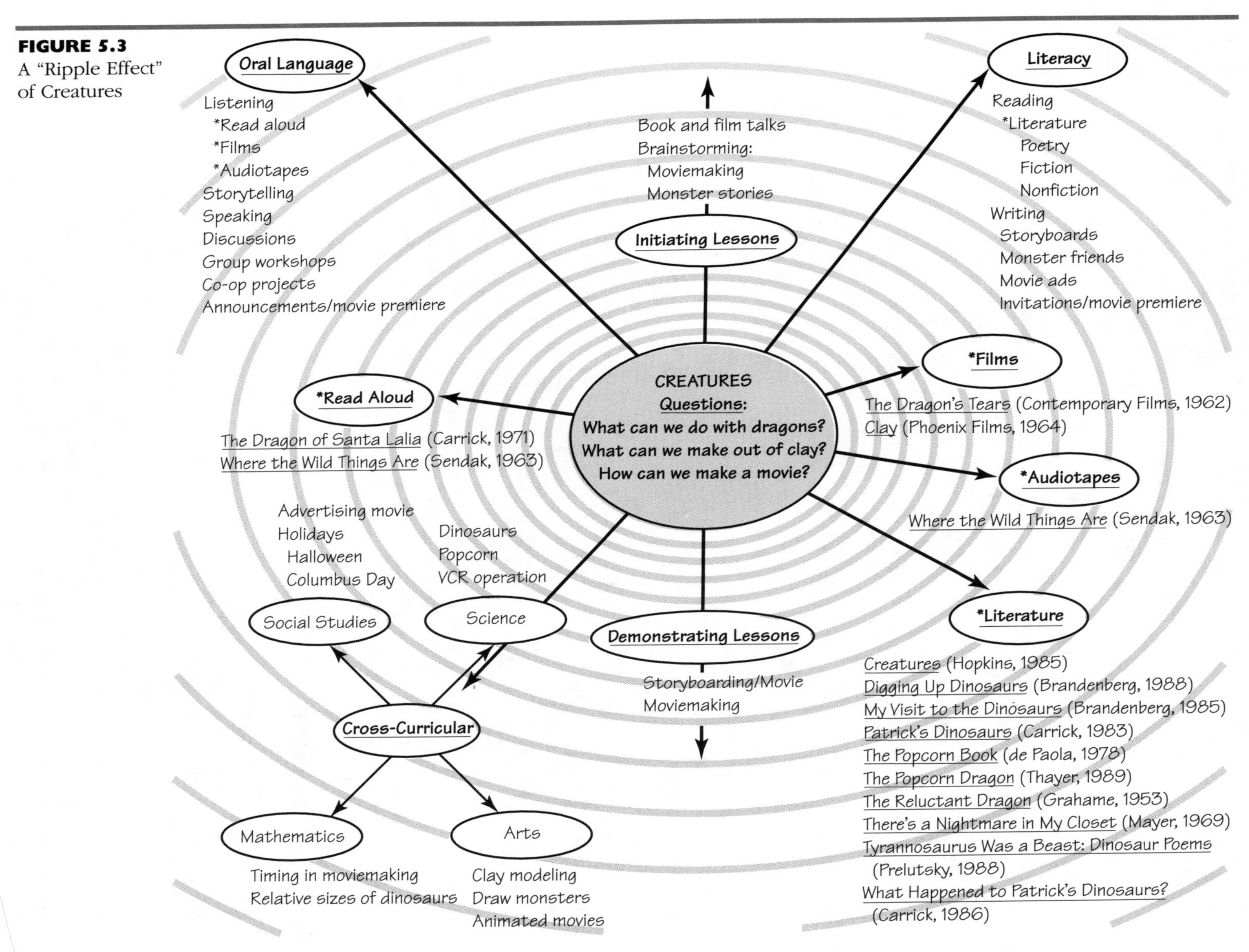

In a classroom grounded in the social constructivist perspective, children are encouraged to think through active engagement with others in literature and film discussions. In a classroom in which experiences with literature are response centered and transactional, children are encouraged to think through teacher questioning that's open and invites further discussion. Communicative situations such as discussions of literature and films are natural times for teachers to encourage children to challenge, question, wonder, doubt, evaluate, and seek meaning—that is, to think critically.

Research on young children's cognitive development shows that they acquire critical-thinking skills during successful learning experiences (Resnick & Klopfer, 1989). Thus, a focus on meaning and thinking should pervade the school curriculum at all levels, beginning in the first years. This approach to teaching should not be reserved for older students, who are supposedly reaching higher levels of cognitive development. The implication for teaching critical thinking and communication is that experiences should focus on the construction of meaning, rather than just the acquisition of information.

In the following sections, we'll review teaching strategies that support this approach: questions and prompts, problem solving and brainstorming, clustering and webbing, self-directed learning, cooperative learning, and instructional conversations.

Questions and Prompts

The kinds of questions and prompts teachers use are critical to the development of thinking and understanding. Given that, we might assume that teachers would most often choose to use open questions. But in *A Place Called School*, John Goodlad (1984) explains that this isn't the case:

> *A great deal of what goes on in the classroom is like painting-by-numbers—filling in the colors called for by numbers on the page. . . . [Teachers] ask specific questions calling essentially for students to fill in the blanks: "What is the capital city of Canada?" "What are the principal exports of Japan?" Students rarely turn things around by asking the questions. Nor do teachers often give students a chance to romp with an open-ended question such as "What are your views on the quality of television?"* (p. 108)

Open versus Closed Questions

What is the relative significance of closed versus open teacher questions? When Kathy Lee read books to her second-grade class, she used a closed questioning style, which has certain benefits in reading aloud. Most importantly, this structure resembles that of many other types of school lessons, in which a given book provides a topic, contextual support, and a focus for attention (Chomsky, 1972). However, Courtney Cazden (1983) cautions against being unresponsive to children's growing language competence by using closed or narrow questions in teaching about story structure, assuming that we'll leave students behind as we move on to more open, higher-level questions. She suggests using the same traditional structure across the grades but changing the content of the teacher's questions and students' answers, making them more complex. Peer dialogues should also be used, giving students opportunities to try the adult role of question asker.

Kathy Lee used a more open questioning style in discussing the films, perhaps because the discussion didn't take place during the film viewing. Moreover, films are not used as frequently and therefore not as subject to traditional teaching routines as books are. These open, student-centered questions and prompts have been shown to benefit students in language growth and thinking because of the control it gives them over their use of language. Students learn more and develop more positive attitudes toward the teacher and school in general when listening and talking in the classroom shifts from a narrow, teacher- and text-centered discussion, with a focus on finding one right answer to each question, to a more student- and response-centered discussion, in which the teacher is flexible and pays attention to students' responses.

Unfortunately, teachers spend more time engaging students in closed discussions than open ones. Wells and Wells (1984) suggest that the problem may be that we as teachers have a

> *less than wholehearted belief in the value that pupils' talk has for their learning. Many of us have years of being talked at as students and have probably unconsciously absorbed the belief that, as teachers, we are not doing our job properly unless we are talking, telling, questioning, or evaluating. But all the time we are talking, we are stopping our pupils from trying out their understanding in words. We are also depriving ourselves of valuable information about the state of their understanding and thus of an opportunity to plan future work to meet their specific needs.* (p. 194)

Efferent and aesthetic stances toward literature will be explained more fully in Chapter 7, Teaching with Literature.

Aesthetic versus Efferent Questions

The questions and prompts that teachers ask during and after reading aloud are extremely important, because they direct children's stance toward literature. According to Louise Rosenblatt's (1978) transactional theory, readers take a stance on a continuum of efferent to aesthetic responses. An *efferent* response focuses on information that can be taken away from the text—for instance, reading a story to learn facts. An *aesthetic* response focuses on personally experiencing the text—for instance, reading a story to examine personal values or attitudes. Rosenblatt (1980) suggests that children should be directed toward aesthetic stances during experiences with literature, rather than efferent ones.

Nonetheless, research on aesthetic versus efferent questions has shown that even teachers who describe themselves as literature based tend to direct children to take efferent stances (Zarrillo & Cox, 1992). This is the case even though studies with fifth-grade students (Cox & Many, 1992) and sixth- through eighth-grade students (Many, 1991) have shown that students who respond aesthetically to literature develop higher levels of understanding. Longitudinal research on young children's responses to literature has led to development of the types of questions and prompts that reflect children's natural aesthetic responses to literature (Cox, 1994). And classroom studies have demonstrated how efferent questions can follow and develop from the initial open, aesthetic questions and prompts, keeping instruction student and response centered (Many & Wiseman, 1992). Here are examples of both aesthetic and efferent questions (developing from aesthetic):

Aesthetic	***Efferent***
What do you think about the story?	What was the main idea of the story?
Tell anything you want about the story.	What did the author mean by —?
What was your favorite part? Tell about it.	Retell your favorite part. Tell the order of the story events.
Has anything like this ever happened to you? Tell about it.	Describe the main characters. Explain the characters' actions.
Does the story remind you of anything? Tell about it.	What other stories are like this one? Compare and contrast the stories.
What did you wonder about? Tell about it.	What was the problem in the story? How did the author solve the problem?
What would you change in the story?	How did the author make the story believable?
What else do you think might happen in the story?	Is it fact or fiction?
What would you say or do if you were a character in the story?	How do you think the characters felt?

Questions are among the most valuable tools teachers have to support understanding, thinking, and achievement for the following reasons (Christenbury & Kelly, 1983):

1. Students who ask questions learn more about subject matter.
2. Questions help students discover their own ideas and argue and sharpen critical-thinking skills.
3. Questions help children function as experts and interact among themselves.
4. Questions give the teacher valuable information about students' ability and achievement.

Problem Solving and Brainstorming

Brainstorming is a technique used by a group for the purposes of critical thinking and problem solving. The idea is to generate as many ideas as possible about a given topic, problem, or task. Brainstorming encourages imagination, flexibility, and a great deal of listening and talking. This technique can be used to explore any topic across the curriculum and is especially useful during planning sessions.

"How can we make it look like Godzilla is breathing fire?" These students are listening and talking while brainstorming ideas for making a videotape.

Brainstorming can be used during any of the stages of problem solving, as shown here (Parnes, Noller, & Biondi, 1977):

1. *Fact finding:* Considering problems, questions, and unorganized information and being aware of the information already in hand
2. *Problem finding:* Identifying the essence of the problem and working on it in a way that will help find a solution
3. *Idea finding:* Generating ideas
4. *Solution finding:* Proposing solutions and developing criteria to evaluate them
5. *Acceptance finding:* Developing a plan of action

Brainstorming sessions can be conducted with the whole class, having the teacher record students' ideas on chartpaper or the chalkboard, or students can work in small groups or individually. Here are guidelines for a planned brainstorming session:

1. Invite ideas.
2. Solicit all kinds of ideas.
3. Generate many ideas.
4. Suspend comments or judgments.
5. Record all ideas.
6. Encourage students to respond to each other's ideas.

As you may recall, clustering and webbing were discussed briefly in Chapter 2.

Clustering and Webbing

The children in Kathy Lee's class were brainstorming spontaneously when they thought of "all the things we could do with a dragon." The teacher can support spontaneous brainstorming like this (or even initiate it) and then use *clustering* and *webbing* to record children's ideas. To do so, the teacher simply writes down the focal point of the discussion at the top or in the center of a piece of chartpaper or the chalkboard and then records students' ideas for discussing and as a basis for further activities. For instance:

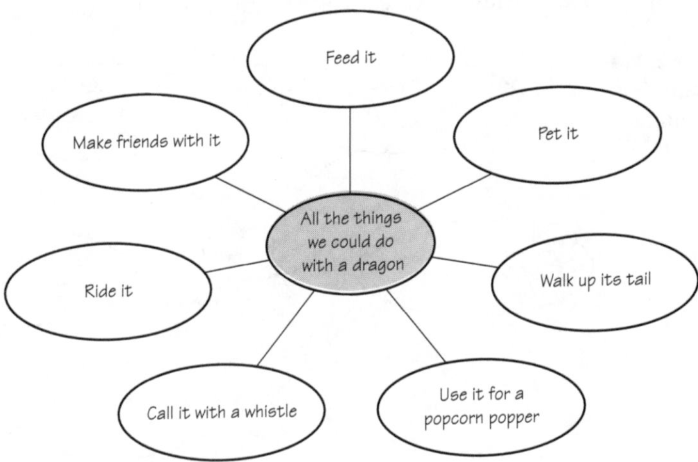

Types of Clusters and Webs

Different types of clusters and webs are useful for various purposes:

- *Spider:* This is the type shown above, in which connections among ideas are shown.
- *List:* Characteristics or steps are listed (in order, if appropriate).
- *Double List:* Characteristics or steps of two subjects or processes are listed in columns, side by side.
- *Venn Diagram:* Relationships among ideas or parts are shown by overlapping items or putting one inside another.
- *Flowchart:* The order of elements is indicated, showing cause and effect.

SNAPSHOT: Clustering in Literature Groups in a Bilingual Spanish Classroom

Paul Boyd-Batstone teaches a bilingual Spanish third-grade classroom in which all language arts and reading instruction is done in small literature groups. Sometimes, the whole class focuses on one book, one type of book, or books related to a theme. At other times, each small group picks a book it likes, reads it, and talks about it together; then they conference with Paul and plan their own "ripple effect" of extending experiences.

The two clusters shown in Figure 5.4 were created in such a group. The students had read *Maxie,* by Mildred Kantrowitz (1970), and clustered their ideas about the main character: a little girl who's alone and thinks nobody likes her. Doing the cluster made them think of the similarities of the story in the book to those of the popular films *Home Alone* and *Home Alone II.* The students brainstormed ideas for a Spanish language sequel, which they titled *Home Alone III.* In Paul's class, students are making the transition from English to Spanish and listen, talk, read, and write in both languages.

FIGURE 5.4
Clusters Created by Bilingual Students

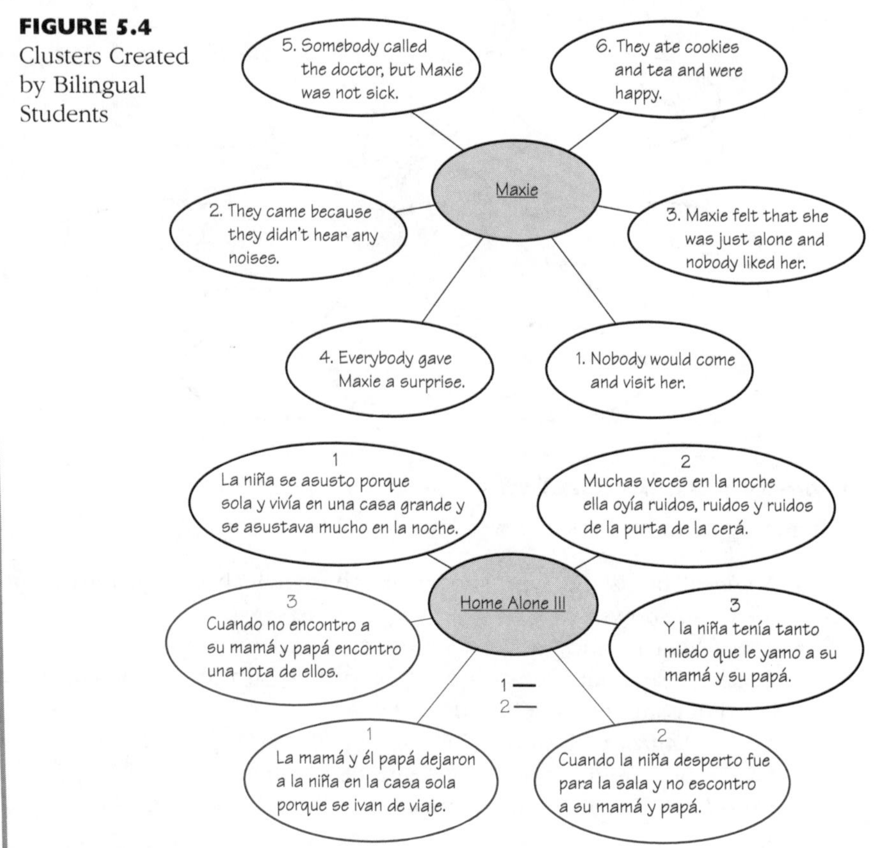

See Chapter 7, the Teaching Idea on literature plans (pp. 260–263), which explains how Paul uses color coding to help students organize their writing.

Self-Directed Learning

Manipulatives are tangible objects like blocks and balls that promote hands-on learning experiences.

Self-directed learning creates a rich context for teaching listening and talking. In this approach, the child plays the central role in learning experiences, and instruction and assessment are both individualized. Self-directed materials and activities are experience based and involve the use of multimedia and manipulatives. Critical thinking is encouraged along with independence, cooperation, and positive attitudes.

Teachers who organize their classrooms for self-directed learning design experiences around students' interests and responses that encourage listening and talking and the growth of language and thinking. Kathy Lee organized her classroom in this way when her students made their film about clay creatures. So did Avril Font, the teacher introduced in Chapter 1, whose students spend time every day sharing, planning, and working in small, cooperative group workshops.

Cooperative Learning

Cooperative learning is an instructional technique that uses students' own talk as a vehicle for learning. Kathy Lee used this technique when she formed her second-grade students into groups to work on some of the ideas that came from brainstorming "all the things we could do with a dragon." Students in one group read stories about dragons and made a list of all the different types they found, and students in another group popped popcorn, made a cluster of descriptive words, and wrote a poem.

Research has shown that cooperative learning improves students' academic achievement, social skills, and self-esteem (Sharan, 1990; Slavin, 1990). In teaching the language arts, cooperative learning groups provide a context and community for students who are listening and talking to one another in authentic communication with a real audience and a real purpose. The teacher functions as an organizer and facilitator, rather than a dispenser of information. Thus, cooperative learning groups reflect a student- and response-centered approach to teaching language arts.

Cooperative learning has five components (Johnson, Johnson, & Holobec, 1991):

1. *Positive interdependence:* The group must work together to earn recognition or reward.
2. *Face-to-face promotive interaction:* Students offer each other genuine communicative practice, including negotiating meaning.
3. *Individual accountability:* The group's success depends on the learning of each individual.
4. *Interpersonal and small-group skills:* Students get to know and trust one another, communicating accurately and unambiguously.
5. *Group-processing skills:* Group members must accept and support one another, resolving conflicts constructively.

Cooperative Learning Strategies

Several cooperative learning strategies have been developed (Kagan, 1985; Slavin, 1990):

1. *Jigsaw:* Students form teams, and each member of the team becomes an expert on one topic by working with members of other teams who are assigned the same topic. For example, if there are six teams and each has five members (A, B, C, D, E), topics would be assigned like this:

A How long ago and how long did dinosaurs live?
B Where and how did they live?
C What are the types of meat-eating dinosaurs?
D What are the types of plant-eating dinosaurs?
E Why did dinosaurs become extinct?

When students return to their original teams, they share what they learned about their respective topics. All members of the teams are assessed on all topics.

2. *Think-Pair-Share:* In this type of cooperative learning strategy, students think about a question or topic, pair up with partners to discuss it, and share their thoughts with the rest of the class (Kagan, 1985).

3. *Three-Step Interview:* Students working in this strategy also form pairs; each partner interviews the other and then shares what he or she has learned with the whole class (Kagan, 1985).

4. *Cooperative Projects, Co-op Co-op:* Students work together in small groups toward a single goal, but each individual must make an identifiable contribution. We've already seen several examples of this strategy in this book, including Avril Font's students working in group workshops to learn about the Maypole Dance or to build a dragon and dramatize the story of St. George and the Dragon. Kathy Lee's students provided another example when they worked on cooperative projects in groups and made animated claymation movies.

To work effectively, cooperative project groups should have the following features:

- Heterogeneous composition (ability, gender, race/ethnicity)
- Individual accountability
- Group goals (positive interdependence)
- Shared responsibility
- Emphasis on social skills

Instructional Conversations

Instructional conversations (*ICs*) are discussion-based lessons "geared toward creating richly textured opportunities for students' conceptual and linguistic development" (Goldenberg, 1993, p. 317). Even though the idea of simply holding a discussion may seem simple, students don't always have opportunities to engage in thoughtful, meaningful, student- and response-centered discussions. (Recall the research findings reviewed earlier in this chapter.) The instructional conversation, as explained by Claude Goldenberg, is an explicit instructional model designed to guide teachers in having discussions in the classroom that are interesting and engaging; are about focused, meaningful, relevant ideas; and have high levels of student participation not dominated by the teacher. Instructional conversations can be used for literature-based language arts and reading or in subject-matter across the curriculum.

Instructional conversations should be based on the following:

Instructional Elements

1. Identifying a thematic focus, a starting point to direct the discussion
2. Activating and using background and relevant schema (provided by the teacher)
3. Direct teaching, involving a skill or concept when necessary
4. Promoting more complex language and expression
5. Eliciting the bases for students' statements or positions (reasoning, text, pictures, etc.)

Conversational Elements

6. Asking more questions that have more than one possible answer
7. Being responsive to students' contributions
8. Connecting discourse, providing multiple, interactive, connected turns to talk
9. Establishing a challenging, nonthreatening atmosphere, in which the teacher is a collaborator, negotiating with students
10. Encouraging general participation, including self-selected turns, in which students volunteer; the teacher doesn't always determine who speaks

Linguistic and Cultural Diversity

Of the teaching approaches just described, cooperative learning and instructional conversations have been developed in linguistically and culturally diverse classrooms and are advocated as especially effective means to meet the needs of language-minority students and foster positive intercultural understanding. Let's look at each approach in the context of multicultural education.

Cooperative Learning: Most Collaborative, Least Competitive

Cooperative learning is an excellent approach to use with language-minority students and students of different racial/ethnic backgrounds. It's been proven an effective technique for improving proficiency in English for second-language learners (Watson & Rangel, 1989) as well for improving students' ethnic interactions and cultural awareness (Slavin, 1990). The four cooperative learning structures described (jigsaw, think-pair-share, three-step interview, and cooperative projects) are those that are the most collaborative and least competitive; thus, they are best suited to the purposes of second-language education and multicultural education.

Instructional Conversations: Application for Language-Minority Children

Goldenberg (1993) suggests that the perception that low-income, minority, and language-minority students only need to drill, repeat, and review in order to succeed academically means that classroom experiences for these students often fail to move beyond low-level skill and factually oriented instruction. According to Goldenberg, the instructional conversation model can make a difference for these students, because it assumes that intellectually challenging instruction is essential for *all* students. The instructional conversation model described earlier (Goldenberg, 1993) was developed in classrooms in order to help improve the academic achievement and literacy development of Hispanic students.

TEACHING IDEA

Teaching Listening and Talking in the Classroom

As a result of the rich film discussions that took place in Kathy Lee's class, a "ripple effect" was generated with a focal point of "Creatures" (see Figure 5.3). Using this ripple effect as an example, here is a model that can be used in many ways to teach listening and talking in the classroom. It moves through the steps of experiencing, sharing, discussing, and reporting—all of which provide rich contexts for listening and talking. Examples from Kathy Lee's class will be used to explain each step.

Step 1: Experiencing

See Chapter 1 for a list of shared experiences as a basis for teaching language arts.

In Kathy Lee's class, reading books and watching films initiated further opportunities for listening and talking. Any firsthand experience that stimulates children's senses, emotions, and ideas is good for listening and talking.

Guidelines

1. Plan many of these experiences—for instance, pets in the classroom, a resource unit in social studies or science, art or drama activities, and cooking.
2. Other experiences may arise spontaneously, but these can be the most welcome of all, sparking unexpected delight:
   - children sharing personal experiences
   - children connecting with other students
   - sudden weather changes
   - holiday or seasonal moods and magic

In the final analysis, an experience is only as good as the impact it has on children's feelings, ideas, and language.

Step 2: Sharing

Shared experiences, such as talking about books and films in Kathy Lee's class, can become the basis for shared meaning among children through listening and talking activities. This doesn't mean that every child will have the same experience or experience the same event in the same way. But considering that most teachers have 30-plus children in their classrooms, sharing becomes a basis for meaningful interaction and communication—listening and talking in a social context. Sharing is also important to create a sense of *esprit de corps* among the children—a sense of community as they live and learn together in the same classroom.

Teachers should set aside regular times for sharing, for several reasons. It may be the only official time children have to talk, and it may be their only opportunity to talk about important personal experiences.

What's more, sharing supports children's creations of personal narratives (Cazden, 1985).

Guidelines

1. Establish a regular time every day when children are free to share anything of interest to them.
2. Create sharing opportunities at other times, too, such as during book and media discussions, resource units in social studies, science experiments, singing and music activities, and visits from guest speakers.
3. Seize spontaneous moments for sharing, focusing on current or media events, class problem or conflicts that need to be resolved, or suggestions from children for special activities.

Step 3: Discussing

The students in Kathy Lee's class brainstormed ideas for activities and then discussed them in small groups with each other and the teacher.

Guidelines

Whole-Class Discussions

1. Discussions should be invitations for children to talk as well as listen.
2. Create a framework, ideally in collaboration between the teacher and students. (This is different than when the teacher decides to do an initiating or demonstrating lesson with the whole class.)
3. Create guidelines, such as:
   "Listen to each other."
   "Contribute your ideas."
   "Respond to what others are saying."
   "Take turns."
4. Direct students to respond to each other, instead of just to the teacher.

Small-Group Discussions

1. Encourage groups of students (not individuals), so they can interact with each other.
2. Plan groups for specific purposes and outcomes: research activities, science experiments, or preparing scenes for dramatic activities.
3. Plan groups for just talking, without specific purposes or outcomes: sharing experiences, discussing books or films, or talking about current events.

Dialogues

1. Solve problems in pairs, perhaps through research projects, constructing an aquarium or model, or puppet play.

(continued)

2. Conduct interviews:
   - Plan and develop questions for people in the community, school staff, parents, grandparents, and the like.
   - Have students interview each other and share what they learn with the rest of the class; this is a good activity for the beginning of the schoolyear. Topics for possible questions include:
     Name, birthdate, address
     Family: parents, siblings
     Pets, interests, and hobbies
     Favorites: subject, book, food, color, music, movie
   - Role-play characters from literature or history, such as sports or entertainment figures, characters from books or films, or historical or political figures.

Step 4: Reporting

In Kathy Lee's class, the students reported the results of experiencing, sharing, and discussing by reporting. They made up and told stories about dragons and monsters, dramatized the book *Where the Wild Things Are* (Sendak, 1963), created puppets to tell the story of *The Popcorn Dragon* (Thayer, 1989), and made an animated movie of clay creatures. The students did their reporting in a variety of ways:

Guidelines

Oral Reporting—Activities can include:

1. Describing what has occurred in a small group or problem-solving pair
2. Responding to literature, media, or storytelling
3. Reporting the results of social studies research or a science experiment
4. Playwriting in small groups
5. Doing committee work for a planned event or project, such as a class newspaper

Writing and Drawing—Activities can include:

1. Giving factual reports of research
2. Writing newspaper articles or letters to the editor
3. Making announcements and labels for projects
4. Creating posters and visual displays
5. Drawings, paintings, and murals
6. Illustrating, writing, and bookmaking

Dramatizing—Activities can include:

1. Storytelling
2. Puppetry
3. Pantomime and improvisation
4. Story dramatization
5. Reader's theater

Media Making—Activities can include:

1. Audio- and videorecordings
2. Transparencies
3. Films and filmstrips
4. Slide shows

Listening and Talking Activities

Listening and talking can be taught systematically and regularly throughout the schoolday and across the curriculum using a variety of activities (Funk & Funk, 1989; Winn, 1988). Teachers can help children use language for meaningful purposes as they listen and talk in classrooms by founding instruction on these principles (Halliday, 1973):

1. Use models of language that don't fall short of those of children.
2. Take into account each child's linguistic experiences and probe their richest potential.
3. Consider how children will use language in school and later in life.
4. Help children use language in meaningful ways in social contexts.

In the next few sections, we'll look at reading aloud, storytelling, puppetry, media centers, and oral histories as ideal ways of teaching listening and talking.

Reading Aloud

The benefits of reading aloud to children are well established: Young children whose parents have read to them gain in language development and literacy through expanded vocabulary, eagerness to read, and success in beginning reading in school (Sulzby, 1992). In school, teachers should read aloud every day, several times a day, to both younger and older students. Jim Trelease's (1989) book *The New Read-Aloud Handbook,* which is immensely popular with both educators and parents, reviews the benefits and pleasures, do's and don't's of reading aloud to children:

Read-Aloud Do's

1. Remember that the art of listening is an acquired one and must be taught and cultivated gradually.
2. Vary the length and subject matter of readings.
3. Follow through with readings. Don't leave the class dangling for several days between chapters and expect children's interest to be sustained.
4. Stop at a suspenseful spot each day.

5. If reading a picture book, make sure the children can see the pictures easily.
6. After reading, allow time for discussion and verbal, written, or artistic expression.
7. Don't turn discussions into quizzes or pry interpretations from children.
8. Use plenty of expression in reading, and read slowly.
9. Preview books before reading them to the class.
10. Bring the author to life by adding a third dimension when possible—for example, eat blueberries while reading *Blueberries for Sal,* by Robert McCloskey (1948).

Read-Aloud Don't's

1. Don't read stories that you don't like yourself.
2. If it becomes obvious that a book was a poor choice, stop reading it.
3. Don't feel that every book must be tied to something in the curriculum.
4. Don't be unnerved by students' questions during the reading. Answer and discuss them.
5. Don't use reading aloud as a threat or turn it into a weapon.

Selecting Read-Aloud Books

Trelease (1989) has also suggested selection criteria for a good read-aloud book. In sum, such a book should have:

1. A fast-paced plot, which quickly hooks the children's interest
2. Clear, well-rounded characters
3. Crisp, easy-to-read dialogue
4. Minimal long, descriptive passages

Trelease thinks the best read-aloud book is *James and the Giant Peach,* by Roald Dahl (1978). He also recommends the following:

Wordless Books

The Adventures of Paddy Pork (Goodall, 1968)
A Boy, a Dog, and a Frog (Mayer, 1967)

Picture Books

Alexander and the Terrible, Horrible, No Good, Very Bad Day (Viorst, 1976)
Frog and Toad Are Friends (Lobel, 1949)

Short Novels

The Reluctant Dragon (Grahame, 1953)
A Taste of Blackberries (Smith, 1976)

Novels

Bridge to Terabithia (Paterson, 1979)
The Lion, the Witch, and the Wardrobe (Lewis, 1970)

Poetry
The Golden Treasury of Poetry (Untermeyer, 1959)
Where the Sidewalk Ends (Silverstein, 1974)

Anthologies
The Fairy Tale Treasury (Haviland, 1980)
Zlateh the Goat and Other Stories (Singer, 1966)

Directed Listening Thinking Activity (DLTA)

The purpose of a DLTA is to focus attention on stories read aloud. And since similar kinds of reasoning take place in both listening and reading comprehension, DLTA is an important strategy for teaching reading, as well. In this activity, questions are used first to activate students' prior knowledge and encourage their predictions and then to focus their attention on the story to verify those predictions, helping students construct meaning from the text (Stauffeur, 1980).

TEACHING IDEA

Directed Listening Thinking Activity
***Where the Wild Things Are* by Maurice Sendak**

The teaching sequence outlined here presents sample questions using the book *Where the Wild Things Are* (Sendak, 1963); however, it can be used with any read-aloud story.

Before Reading

1. Introduce the book and tell something about it: "This is a book about a little boy and an adventure he had."
2. Encourage students to examine the cover and illustrations.
3. Discuss any experiences or concepts that come up.
4. Invite students to respond to the story while it's being read aloud with enthusiasm: "As I read, you can ask questions or share your ideas."

During Reading

1. Ask the children to make predictions about what will happen: "What do you think might happen to Max?"
2. Read but stop and give students opportunities to verify their predictions.
3. Continue to ask the children to make predictions and explain the reasons behind them: "What do you think will happen next? Why?"
4. Encourage students to respond openly to events, characters, and ideas in the book: "What do you think of Max, the Wild Things, or sailing away from home?"

(continued)

After Reading

1. Talk about the book: "What did you think of the book?"
2. Ask for personal responses to the story: "Did you like the book? Why or why not? What was your favorite part?"
3. Talk about interesting concepts or words that come up: "How would you describe a Wild Thing? What's a rumpus?"

Extending the Reading

1. Read related books, such as *In the Night Kitchen* (Sendak, 1970) or *There's a Nightmare in My Closet* (Mayer, 1969).
2. Encourage further response-centered activities: drawing pictures, writing stories, making monster masks, dramatizing the story, and so on.

Storytelling

Even with the number of books available for children today and the variety of stories they are exposed to on television and videos, children never seem to lose their fascination with storytelling. As one first-grade child put it, as I was about to read a picture book of a favorite folktale, "Tell it with your face!"

The tools of the storyteller are so deceptively simple and so basically human that storytelling is often neglected as a way of teaching listening and talking. It is, however, a powerful way for children to listen to and use spoken language (Nelson, 1989; Roney, 1989). It's also a wonderful way to share traditional literature and stories of the past, whether historical events or even your own life.

Stories are everywhere, and the most important storytellers are often family members. Young children love to hear stories told about when they were babies or when their parents or grandparents were young. My mother's tales of growing up in a German-speaking family on a farm in southern Illinois in the 1920s and 1930s never ceased to fascinate me. I especially liked the ones about stuffing peat moss in her little brother's knickers so he couldn't walk or putting frogs in the strawberry baskets and crow's eggs in the chicken egg cartons destined for sale in Chicago. And now I find that my own children like to listen to me tell about growing up in California in the San Fernando Valley in the 1950s.

Here are some good sources of stories for storytelling: *Homespun: Tales from America's Favorite Storytellers* (Smith, 1988) and *Look What Happened to Frog: Storytelling in Education* (Cooper & Collins, 1991).

Children should be encouraged to tell stories, too. When they do, they use *long language,* which reflects their growing knowledge of longer, more involved scripts and literary genres. Through the experience and practice they gain with storytelling and drama, students build up to creating the even more complex long language of discussions, reports, and fiction (Wolfe, 1984).

Teachers Telling Stories

1. ***Finding Stories:*** In addition to stories about personal experiences and those heard told by others, traditional folk literature is an excellent source for storytelling. Young children enjoy timeless tales, such as "The Three Billy

Can you guess which story this teacher is telling?

Goats Gruff," "The Three Pigs," and other tales of three. Tales like "Jack and the Beanstalk" and "The Gingerbread Man" are sure winners, too.

2. ***Starting a Storytelling File:*** Start a story file on 5" × 7" cards or in a loose-leaf notebook. Write down the name of each story and its source. Also identify the appropriate audience, props, resources (e.g., music), and related stories. Include space for an anecdotal record of responses and ideas for future tellings.

3. ***Telling Stories:*** Storyteller Ramon Royal Ross advises that above all, the storyteller should know the story very well. In addition, he suggests the following approach for actually telling the story, which works well for him (Ross, 1980):

a. Read the story aloud several times. Get a feel for its rhythm and style.
b. Outline the major actions in the story, identifying where one ends and another starts.
c. Picture the characters in the story carefully. Describe them to yourself.
d. Picture the setting. Make a map of it in your mind.
e. Search for phrases in the story that you'd like to work into telling it.
f. Start to tell the story aloud to yourself. Try different ways of saying things.
g. Practice gestures that add to the story.
h. Prepare an introduction and conclusion before and after the actual telling.
i. Practice telling the entire story—complete with intonation, colorful phrases, gestures, and sequence—in a smooth and natural fashion. Also, time your telling of the story as you practice.
j. Make an audio or videotape of yourself telling the story, and listen and look for areas in which you might improve.

4. ***Props:*** Even though props aren't necessary, some teachers like to use them for storytelling, especially with younger children. Props might be picture cards, flannelboards, puppets, or objects like a handful of beans for telling "Jack and the Beanstalk." Moodmakers like candles and incense and background music and noisemakers (e.g., rattles and tambourines) effectively enhance the telling, too.

5. ***Costumes:*** When used with props, costumes can create a dramatic impact. For instance, wearing a black cape and witch's hat adds drama to telling scary stories in autumn. Even simple costumes, like hats and shawls, can be used in many creative ways.

Children Telling Stories

After the teacher has modeled storytelling, children should be encouraged to try it themselves. One way to do so may be to suggest storytelling as a great way to tell others about a favorite book they have read. Children who like to tell stories may find this activity especially fun. Props, costumes, and other materials should be made available to students for storytelling.

Puppetry

Children are natural puppeteers. Watch any young child with a stuffed animal, toy car, or object that can become an extension of the body and voice, and you will see a born puppeteer. Rather than plan a specific, one-time puppet-making activity, teachers should make materials and books on puppets available in the classroom on a regular basis, seizing opportunities that arise in which puppet making is a perfect way for children to tell a story, respond to literature, or report on what they have learned.

Stories for Puppetry

1. *Basal reader stories:* Some of these stories are written as play scripts and may include suggestions for puppetry. Others can be developed into oral scripts, if they are stories students want to dramatize and puppetry seems a good way of doing so.
2. *Folktales:* These are an excellent source of puppetry ideas. The teacher may read a folktale aloud, or the children may find one they like in a book they are reading themselves.
3. *Picture books:* A favorite picture book is often one that children will act out anyway after repeated readings; puppetry is an excellent way to extend the reading experience.

See *Punch & Judy: A Play for Puppets* (Emberly, 1965), which is a picture storybook that includes a history of puppet drama along with a script for a puppet play.

Materials for Puppetry

Teachers should collect puppet-making materials themselves or ask for donations from students and parents. Many of the materials needed are everyday objects that would be discarded anyway. A box containing the following supplies should be made available to students and added to, as needed.:

1. Tools: scissors, tape, glue, paint, stapler
2. Bodies: fingers, hands, feet

3. Paper: construction, plates, bags, crepe, cups, envelopes, toilet paper roll
4. Cloth: scraps, yarn, socks, gloves, mittens, hats
5. Sticks: tongue depressors, ice cream sticks, twigs, dowels, old wooden spoons
6. Fancy things: buttons, feathers, beads, sequins, ribbons, old costume jewelry
7. Odds and ends: boxes, milk cartons, Styrofoam, cotton balls, ping pong balls, fruits and vegetables, gourds, leaves, moss, pine cones, egg cartons, plastic bottles

Making Simple Puppets

Making puppets should be kept simple and left up to students. They should use their imaginations in creating puppets; their ideas are so much better than those of adults. For instance, children don't need patterns to trace around, which produce puppets that all look alike. Rather, they should draw directly on materials like tongue depressors and ice cream sticks, creating fingers, hands, and feet.

These how-to puppet books provide many ideas: *Hanimals* (Mariolti, 1982); *Making Easy Puppets* (Lewis, 1967); *Puppets for Play Production* (Renfro, 1969); and *Puppet Making through the Grades* (Hopper, 1966).

To make simple puppets:

- *Stick puppets:* Attach a paper plate, cutout, or Styrofoam cup to a stick and decorate.
- *Paper bag puppets:* Draw directly on the bag and decorate.
- *Hand puppets:* Decorate a glove, mitten, sock, box, piece of fabric or handkerchief wrapped with rubber bands, or simply an envelope over the hand.

Staging Puppet Plays

A puppet stage is nice but not necessary to fulfill the real purpose of puppetry: to encourage children's thinking, listening, talking, and imagination as they create oral texts to share with others. Create a simple stage by:

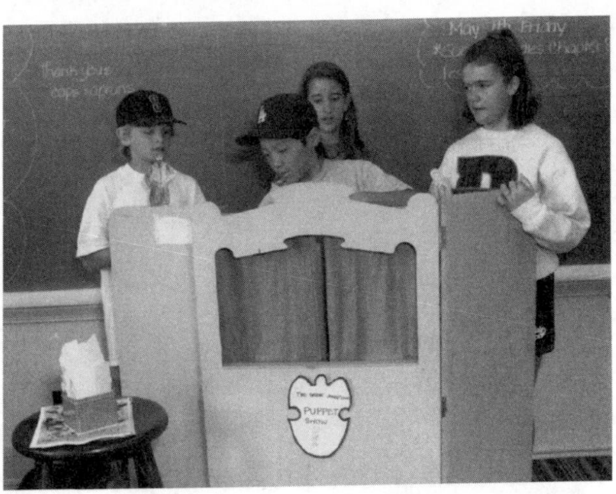

"The Great Jamestown Puppet Show," presented by fifth-grade early American "colonists"

1. Turning a table on its side and draping it with a dramatic-looking cloth
2. Having two reliable students hold a sheet or draping a sheet over a broomstick balanced on two chairs
3. Putting a cardboard box on a table, with the puppeteers seated behind it on low chairs

An excellent source of children's literature on media is *A Multimedia Approach to Children's Literature* (Hunt, 1983). For each book listed, it tells what media it's available in and the source. For example, *The Nutshell Library* is a collection of four books by Maurice Sendak (1962): *Alligators All Around*, an alphabet book; *One Was Johnny*, a counting song; *Pierre*, a moralistic tale; and *Chicken Soup with Rice*, about the months of the year. All are available on tape, videotape, and filmstrip. The poems in *Chicken Soup with Rice* have also been set to music and sung by Carole King.

Media Centers

A media center, offering listening and viewing activities, can be created in the classroom for use by small groups and individual children. In this center, children can listen to and view professionally recorded and filmed stories or their own media creations. Equipment needed includes:

- Tape/CD player with earphones
- Filmstrip projector and screen
- VCR and television monitor for videos

Extending Media Center Experiences

The only thing more joyful than listening to Carole King sing *Chicken Soup with Rice* would be to make hot chicken soup and eat it while listening, reading, and singing along. Other extending activities could be making puppets or dramatizing the poems, making costumes for use in presenting them, using them as patterns for more writing, or discussing how to make and eat chicken soup during a brainstorming session. Throughout these activities, students' ideas should be clustered and used as the basis for more extending activities.

Oral Histories

In preparing *oral histories,* students go to the source of history by interviewing people about the past: parents, grandparents, family members, or people in

A classroom media center—for enjoyment and learning

the community. Interviewing provides several benefits (Haley-James & Hobson, 1980):

1. Guests in the classroom increases interest in listening and talking.
2. Children enjoy the feeling of success and control they have when they interview others.
3. Interviews encourage a natural integration of the language arts and content area learning.
4. Children write more and use more specific vocabulary in conducting interviews.

Gathering Information

Students can identify, interview, and audio or video record members of their families or communities who have memories of special events in the past. In addition, students can research and collect artifacts, photographs, newspaper articles, and documents relating to the people they interview.

Reporting

Students can report their oral histories in writing or audio or video tape narration to go with recorded interviews. They can share their oral histories, along with any artifacts they may have collected, with wider audiences, such as the school or community, by publishing their accounts in the school or local newspaper or by creating their own newsletter or book.

The classic children's book *Caddie Woodlawn,* by Carol Ryrie Brink (1975), about a young pioneer girl in Wisconsin, is based on the author's recollections of her grandmother's childhood stories. Also see the *Foxfire* books by Eliot Wigginton (1972), which are excellent sources of ideas for experiences in oral history and cultural journalism.

TEACHING IDEA

A Model for Oral History
***Grandfather's Journey* by Allen Say**

Read aloud Allen Say's (1994) Caldecott Award–winning picture book *Grandfather's Journey,* a beautifully illustrated account of a Japanese grandfather's journeys to the United States and back to Japan over his lifetime. The story continues with the grandfather's child and grandchild. Discuss the book and make plans for children to write accounts of their grandparents' and parents' lives after interviewing them or other family members about them.

Children might also plan how they would interview other interesting persons about their lives or how they immigrated to the United States—for instance, famous or fictional figures from history. These oral histories could be written as stories, fictional journals, bound as books with illustrations, or recorded on audio- or videotape and presented to the class. Or children could write scripts and dramatize the lives of the people they've interviewed, dressing as them and playing scenes from their lives. The potential for cross-curricular teaching is obviously great here, extending to studies of U.S. immigration and history and even world geography and history.

Assessing Listening and Talking

Informal assessment based on observation of listening and talking makes the most sense in a student- and response-centered classroom. To do so means throwing out preplanned checklists of listening and talking behaviors and using artifacts: children's written and drawn work. Assessing listening and talking is more elusive, but the following approaches work:

1. ***"Kidwatching":*** Yetta Goodman's (1985) term is most appropriate here. It means careful, ongoing, and naturalistic observation of students in the classroom, engaged in a variety of activities. To assess listening and talking, the teacher must listen, observe, and interact with students on a daily basis in a variety of contexts: during sharing, planning, individual and group work, and conferences. The information the teacher gathers about each child is only important as a basis for planning further individualized experiences for that child.

2. ***Anecdotal Records:*** The teacher should keep a running log of his or her observations of children's listening and talking, noting problems, changes, and ideas for meeting each child's needs.

3. ***Conference Logs:*** Teachers should keep logs during their conferences with children.

4. ***Portfolio Items:*** Several of the learning experiences and activities described in this chapter would produce items that could be placed in a child's portfolio. Children should be encouraged to help determine what's put in their portfolios to document their progress in listening and talking:

- *Clusters and webs:* Group and individual
- *Collaborative group work:* Writing, drawing, and constructions
- *Personal writing:* Based on sharing, discussions, and group work
- *Collaborative writing:* Stories, storyboards, scripts, and advertisements
- *Media productions:* Films, filmstrips, and audio and video recordings
- *Art:* Puppets, murals, posters, and visual displays
- *Oral history projects:* Written or recorded accounts

Answers to Questions about Listening and Talking

1. *What kinds of listening and talking take place in elementary classrooms?*

Children listen more than they speak, read, or write in the classroom, yet most of the time, they're listening to the teacher. Schools do not always provide a linguistically rich environment compared to homes, in which children have more opportunities to actively listen and talk in authentic, meaningful interactions. In the classroom, teacher talk tends to dominate explaining and evaluating, which limits children's oral language use in both quantity and meaningful purpose. Little attention was paid in the past to teaching listening, but active approaches can improve listening learning. Listening and talking can be systematically taught.

2. *What is the relationship of critical thinking and literacy to listening and talking?*

Oral language (listening and talking), thinking, and literacy are highly interrelated. Loban's well-known longitudinal study of the uses and control of language by children in grades K–12 found that those who are more proficient in oral language use more complex language, understand the conventions of language better, score higher on vocabulary and intelligence tests, and perform better in reading and writing. Listening, talking, reading, writing, and thinking are part of a unified whole of language development.

The types of listening and talking that go on in a classroom greatly influence the kinds of thinking that occurs there, as well. In a classroom grounded in a social constructivist, response-centered, and transactional perspective, children are encouraged to think through active engagement with others and in response to teacher questioning that's open and aesthetic. Communicative contexts with active listening and talking are natural situations in which children can think critically. Research on young children's cognitive development shows that they acquire critical-thinking skills during successful learning experiences. A focus on meaning and thinking should pervade the school curriculum from the early grades on.

3. *How can we teach listening and talking?*

Important strategies for using listening and talking to teach critical thinking include asking open and aesthetic questions and prompts; problem-solving and brainstorming techniques; use of clustering and webbing; self-directed learning; cooperative learning strategies; and instructional conversations (ICs). In addition to these strategies, teachers can use a four-step model that includes experiencing, sharing, discussing, and reporting. Activities to use across the curriculum include reading aloud, directed listening thinking activity (DLTA), storytelling, puppetry, media center activities, and oral histories.

LOOKING FURTHER

1 Observe in a classroom and analyze a language sample according to the following criteria:

- Who talked and who listened? Count the number of times the teacher and children each talked during your observation period.
- How did the teacher talk and listen? Classify the questions the teacher asked as open or closed.

2 Pick a children's book, and develop a list of both aesthetic and efferent questions to ask about it. Read the book aloud to two different groups of children. Ask one group the aesthetic questions and the other group, the efferent questions. Compare responses from the two groups.

3 Poll several teachers across several grade levels as to whether they have a regular, planned time for sharing in their classrooms. If they do, ask why. If they don't, ask why not. List several ways you could plan sharing time in your schedule.

4 Plan and implement a brainstorming session on any topic with a group of children. Record their ideas, and develop a "ripple effect" of learning experiences, based on their responses.

5 Write and carry out an interview with another person in your class, and then let that person interview you. Each of you should share the results of your interview with the whole class.

6 Choose and prepare a story for storytelling, according to the guidelines suggested in this chapter. Create a simple prop or costume for your story. Tell the story to a group of children.

RESOURCES

Livo, N. J., & Reitz, S. A. (1988). *Storytelling: Process and practice.* Littleton, CO: Libraries Unlimited.

Trelease, J. (1989). *The new read-aloud handbook.* New York: Viking/Penguin.

REFERENCES

Barnes, D. (1976). *From communication to curriculum.* Hammondsworth, Middlesex, England: Penguin.

Bosma, B. (1987, November). *The nature of critical thinking: Its base and boundary.* Paper presented at the National Council of Teachers of English Annual Convention, Los Angeles.

Brent, R., & Anderson, P. (1993). Developing children's classroom listening strategies. *Reading Teacher, 47,* 122–126.

Britton, J. (1970). *Language and learning.* Hammondsworth, Middlesex, England: Penguin.

Cazden, C. (1983). Adult assistance to language development: Scaffolds, models, and direct instruction. In R. P. Parker & F. A. Davis (Eds.), *Developing literacy: Young children's use of language.* Newark, DE: International Reading Association.

Cazden, C. (1985). Research currents: What is sharing time for? *Language Arts, 62,* 182–188.

Chomsky, C. (1972). Stages in language development and reading exposure. *Harvard Educational Review, 42,* 1–33.

Christenbury, L., & Kelly, P. P. (1983). *Questioning: A path to critical thinking.* Urbana, IL: National Council of Teachers of English.

Cooper, P., & Collins, R. (1991). *Look what happened to Frog: Storytelling in education.* Scottsdale, AZ: Gorsuch-Scarisbuck.

Cox, C. (1984). Oral language development and its relationship to reading. In R. A. Thompson & L. L. Smith (Eds.), *Reading research review.* Minneapolis, MN: Burgess.

Cox, C. (1985). Filmmaking as a composing process. *Language Arts, 62,* 60–69.

Cox, C. (1994, April). *Young children's response to literature: A longitudinal study, K–3.* Paper presented at the American Educational Research Association Meeting, New Orleans.

Cox, C., & Many, J. (1992). Beyond choosing: Emergent categories of efferent and aesthetic stances. In J. Many & C. Cox (Eds.), *Reader stance and literary understanding* (pp. 103–126). Norwood, NJ: Ablex.

Devine, T. G. (1978). Listening: What do we know after fifty years of research and theorizing? *Journal of Reading, 21,* 296–304.

Dyson, A. H. (1994). *Social worlds of children learning to write in an urban primary school.* New York: Teachers College Press.

Dyson, A. H., & Genishi, C. (1982). Whatta ya tryin' to write? Writing as an interactive process. *Language Arts, 59,* 126–132.

Flanders, N. (1970). *Analyzing teaching behavior.* Reading, MA: Addison-Wesley.

Fox, S. (1983). Oral language development: Past studies and current directions. *Language Arts, 60,* 234–243.

Funk, H., & Funk, G. (1989). Guidelines for developing listening skills. *Reading Teacher, 42,* 660–663.

Goldenberg, C. (1993). Instructional conversations: Promoting comprehension through discussion. *Reading Teacher, 46,* 316–326.

Goodlad, J. (1984). *A place called school: Prospects for the future.* New York: McGraw-Hill.

Goodman, Y. (1985). Kidwatching: Observing children in the classroom. In A. Jaggar & M. T. Smith-Burke (Eds.), *Observing the language learner* (pp. 9–18). Urbana, IL: National Council of Teachers of English.

Haley-James, S., & Hobson, C. D. (1980). Interviewing: A means of encouraging the drive to communicate. *Language Arts, 57,* 497–502.

Halliday, M. A. K. (1973). *Explorations in the functions of language.* New York: Elsevier North-Holland.

Heath, S. B. (1983). *Ways with words: Language, life, and work in communities and classrooms.* Cambridge, England: Cambridge University Press.

Hopper, G. (1966). *Puppet making through the grades.* New York: Davis.

Hunt, M. A. (1983). *A multimedia approach to children's literature.* Chicago: American Library Association.

Jalongo, M. R. (199l). *Strategies for developing children's listening skills* (Phi Delta Kappa Fastback Series No. 314). Bloomington, IN: Phi Delta Kappa Educational Foundation.

Johnson, D., Johnson, R., & Holobec, E. (1991). *Cooperation in the classroom.* Edina, MN: Interaction Book.

Kagan, S. (1985). *Cooperative learning: Resources for teachers.* Riverside: University of California.

Lewis, S. (1967). *Making easy puppets.* New York: Dutton.

Loban, W. J. (1976). *Language development: Kindergarten through grade twelve.* Urbana, IL: National Council of Teachers of English.

Loban, W. J. (1979). Relationship between language and literacy. *Language Arts, 56,* 485–486.

Many, J. E. (1991). The effects of stance and age level on children's literary responses. *Journal of Reading Behavior, 21,* 61–85.

Many, J. E., & Wiseman, D. L. (1992). Analyzing versus experiencing: The effects of teaching approaches on students' responses. In J. E. Many & C. Cox (Eds.), *Reader stance and literary understanding* (pp. 250–276). Norwood, NJ: Ablex.

Mariolti, M. (1982). *Hanimals.* San Diego: Green Tiger Press.

Nelson, O. (1989). Story telling: Language experience for meaning making. *Reading Teacher, 42,* 396–390.

Parnes, S. J., Noller, R. B., & Biondi, A. M. (1977). *Guide to creative action.* New York: Scribner's.

Pearson, P. D., & Fielding, L. (1982). Research update: Listening comprehension. *Language Arts, 59,* 617–629.

Rankin, P. T. (1928). The importance of listening ability. *English Journal, 17,* 623–630.

Renfro, N. (1969). *Puppets for play production.* New York: Funk & Wagnalls.

Resnick, L. B., & Klopfer, L. E. (1989). Toward the thinking curriculum: An overview. In L. B. Resnick & L. E. Klopfer (Eds.), *Toward the thinking curriculum: Current cognitive research.* Arlington, VA: Association for Supervision and Curriculum Development.

Roney, R. C. (1989). Back to basics with storytelling. *Reading Teacher, 42,* 520–523.

Rosenblatt, L. M. (1978). *The reader, the text, the poem: The transactional theory of the literary work.* Carbondale: Southern Illinois University Press.

Rosenblatt, L. M. (1980). What facts does this poem teach you? *Language Arts, 57,* 386–394.

Ross, R. R. (1980). *Storyteller* (2nd ed.). Columbus, OH: Merrill.

Sharan, S. (1990). Cooperative learning: A perspective on research and practice. In S. Sharan (Ed.), *Cooperative learning: Theory and research.* New York: Praeger.

Slavin, R. (1990). *Cooperative learning: Theory, research, and practice.* Englewood Cliffs, NJ: Prentice-Hall.

Smith, J. N. (Ed.). (1988). *Homespun: Tales from America's favorite storytellers.* New York: Crown.

Stauffeur, R. G. (1980). *The language-experience approach to the teaching of reading* (2nd ed.). New York: Harper & Row.

Sticht, T. G., & James, J. H. (1984). Listening and reading. *Handbook of reading research.* In P. D. Pearson (Ed.), *Handbook of reading research* (pp. 293–318). New York: Longman.

Sulzby, E. (1992). The development of the young child and the emergence of literacy. In J. Flood, J. Jensen, D. Lapp, & J. Squire (Eds.), *Handbook of research on teaching the English language arts* (pp. 273–285). New York: Macmillan.

Trelease, J. (1989). *The new read-aloud handbook.* New York: Viking Penguin.

Watson, D., & Rangel, L. (1989). Can cooperative learning be evaluated? *School Administrator, 46*(6), 13–17.

Wells, G., & Wells, J. (1984). Learning to talk and talking to learn. *Theory Into Practice, 23,* 190–197.

Wigginton, E. (1972). *Foxfire.* New York: Doubleday.

Wilt, M. E. (1974). Listening: What's new? In J. de Stefano & S. Fox (Eds.), *Language and the language arts.* Boston: Little, Brown.

Winn, D. (1988). Develop listening skills as part of the curriculum. *Reading Teacher, 42,* 144.

Wolfe, D. (1984). Research currents: Learning about language skills from narratives. *Language Arts, 61,* 844–850.

Zarrillo, J., & Cox, C. (1992). Efferent and aesthetic teaching. In J. Many & C. Cox (Eds.), *Reader stance and literary understanding* (pp. 235–249). Norwood, NJ: Ablex.

CHILDREN'S BOOKS AND FILMS

Brandenberg, A. (1985). *My visit to dinosaurs.* New York: Crowell.

Brandenberg, A. (1988). *Digging up dinosaurs.* New York: Crowell.

Brink, C. R. (1975). *Caddie Woodlawn.* New York: Scholastic.

Carrick, C. (1971). *The dragon of Santa Lalia.* New York: Bobbs Merrill.

Carrick, C. (1983). *Patrick's dinosaurs.* New York: Houghton Mifflin.

Carrick, C. (1986). *What happened to Patrick's dinosaurs?* New York: Clarion.

Clay: The origin of the species [Film]. (1964). Available from Contemporary/McGraw-Hill Films.

Dahl, R. (1978). *James and the giant peach.* New York: Bantam.

de Paola, T. (1978). *The popcorn book.* New York: Holiday House.

Dragon's tears, The [Film]. (1962). Available from Contemporary/McGraw-Hill Films.

Emberly, E. (1965). *Punch & Judy: A play for puppets.* New York: Little, Brown.

Goodall, J. (1968). *The adventures of Paddy Pork.* New York: Harcourt Brace Jovanovich.

Grahame, K. (1953). *The reluctant dragon.* New York: Holiday House.

Haviland, V. (1980). *The fairy tale treasury.* New York: Dell.

Hopkins, L. B. (Ed.). (1985). *Creatures.* New York: Harcourt Brace Jovanovich.

Kantrowitz, M. (1970). *Maxie.* New York: Parent's Magazine.

Lewis, C. S. (1970). *The lion, the witch, and the wardrobe.* New York: Macmillan.

Lewis, S. (1967). *Making easy puppets.* New York: Dutton.

Lobel, A. (1979). *Frog and toad are friends.* New York: Harper & Row.

Mariolti, M. (1982). *Hanimals.* San Diego: Green Tiger Press.

Mayer, M. (1967). *A boy, a dog, and a frog.* New York: Dial.

Mayer, M. (1969). *There's a nightmare in my closet.* New York: Dial.

McCloskey, R. (1948). *Blueberries for Sal.* New York: Viking.

Paterson, K. (1979). *Bridge to Terabithia.* New York: Avon.

Prelutsky, J. (1988). *Tyrannosaurus was a beast: Dinosaur poems.* New York: Greenwillow.

Say, A. (1994). *Grandfather's journey.* New York: Houghton Mifflin.

Sendak, M. (1962). *The nutshell library.* New York: Harper & Row.

Sendak, M. (1963). *Where the wild things are.* New York: Harper & Row.

Sendak, M. (1970). *In the night kitchen.* New York: Harper & Row.

Silverstein, S. (1974). *Where the sidewalk ends.* New York: Harper & Row.

Singer, I. B. (1966). *Zlateh the goat and other stories.* New York: Harper & Row.

Smith, D. B. (1976). *A taste of blackberries.* New York: Scholastic.

Thayer, J. (1989). *The popcorn dragon.* New York: Morrow.

Untermeyer, L. (Ed.). (1959). *The golden treasury of poetry.* New York: Golden.

Viorst, J. (1976). *Alexander and the terrible, horrible, no good, very bad day.* New York: Atheneum.

Wizard of Oz, The [Film]. (1939). Available from MGM Los Angeles.

Chapter 6

Drama in the Classroom

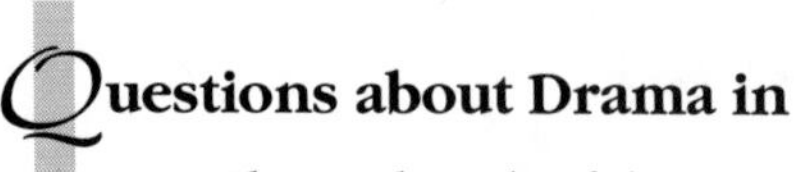

Questions about Drama in the Classroom

1. *What is the role of drama in education?*
2. *How should we teach drama?*

Reflective Response: What Are Your Experiences with Drama?

Jot down any memories you have of dramatic activities during your elementary school years. What did you do? How did you feel about it—then and now? How do you think you will use drama when you teach?

Drama in Education

Drama is an ancient art as well as a form of language and literature. The word *drama* comes from the Greek root word, meaning "to do or live through." Thus, the purpose of drama is to tell a story through the actions and speech of characters. In education, the use of drama reflects a social constructivist perspective (Piaget, 1962; Vygotsky, 1967), which emphasizes the experiencing of literature and drama as art forms in a student- and response-centered curriculum.

There are many reasons why drama should play a leading role in educating children and teaching language arts. As a living and learning experience for children, drama has the power to spark great enthusiasm and motivate students to participate in school activities. And through these activities, drama helps create a positive environment for learning and growing. It stimulates both critical and creative thinking and adds enjoyment and pleasure to learning and school. Drama also makes children feel good about themselves, as it helps establish a framework on which they can build positive self-images. Given all this, drama should play a central, rather than peripheral, role in education.

What kind of drama is used in elementary education? *Informal classroom drama* is described by the Joint Committee of the National Council of Teachers of English and Children's Theatre Association (1983) as "an activity in which students invent and enact dramatic situations for themselves, rather than an outside audience. This activity, perhaps most widely known as creative drama, . . . is spontaneously generated by the participants who perform the dual tasks of composing and enacting their parts as the drama progresses" (p. 3).

The Children's Theatre Association (Davis & Behm, 1978) explains the purpose of creative drama as follows: "Creative drama may be used to teach the art of drama and/or motivate and extend learning in other content areas. Participation in creative drama has the potential to develop language and communication. . . . Built on the human impulse to act out perceptions of the world in order to understand it, creative drama requires both logical and intuitive thinking, personalizes knowledge, and yields aesthetic pleasure" (pp. 10–11).

Drama across the Curriculum

The power of drama is its ability to give form to feeling. The subject of drama is the whole range of human experience—those emotions, ideas, and needs that may seem confusing in real life but can be organized, clarified, and understood through drama.

Drama embraces the visual arts—in fact, virtually all other arts and humanities. It forms a link with the past and with culture that children can understand and enjoy through their own dramatic experiences. As a mixed art, drama is a tool for integrated teaching. Consider for a moment the mixture of ingredients that can be introduced in a curriculum integrated through drama:

Language
Responding to and expressing experience
Organizing and clarifying experiences
Listening
Speaking
Reading
Writing
Nonverbal language

Content Areas
Content as the subject of drama:
- Multicultural education
- Social studies
- Science
- Mathematics
- Current events
- Physical education and dance

Literature
Responding to literature
Storytelling
Appreciating and understanding dramatic literature

The Arts
Music, dance, song
Theater and media arts:
- Costumes, set design, and properties
- Sound, lighting, and graphics

Conceptual Framework

Winifred Ward (1957), an early advocate of drama in the education of children, explains the important role that drama can play in education: "When one notes the eagerness with which children greet both creative and formal drama, he [or she] wonders how it can be that education has not long since made use of so deep-rooted an impulse. To ignore it seems a tremendous waste of power" (p. 15).

British educator Dorothy Heathcote explains why drama should be at the center of the elementary language arts curriculum: "All drama, regardless of the material, brings to the teacher an opportunity to draw on past relevant experience and put it into use; language, both verbal and non-verbal, is then needed for communication. . . . I am primarily in the teaching business, not the play-making business, even when I am involved in making plays. I am engaged first of all in helping children to think, talk, relate to one another, to communicate (Heathcote, 1981, pp. 80–81).

See also Heathcote (1983), "Learning, Knowing, and Language in Drama," *Language Arts, 60,* 695–701.

Other educators have also recognized the potential power of drama in education. In 1966, the Anglo-American Seminar on the Teaching of English brought together British and American educators at Dartmouth College. During their conference, the educators set forth the following rationale for the use of oral communication and drama to foster children's learning of language as an integral part of the English language arts curriculum (Duke, 1974):

1. *Drama and oral communication should become the centrality of pupil's exploring, extending, and shaping of experience in the classroom.*
2. *There is a definite urgency for developing classroom approaches stressing the vital, creative, dramatic involvement of young people in language experiences.*
3. *The importance of directing more attention to speaking and listening for pupils at all levels, particularly in those experiences which involve vigorous interaction among children, should be apparent.*
4. *The wisdom of providing young people at all levels with significant opportunities for the creative use of language—creative dramatics, imaginative writing, improvisation, role playing, and similar activities—has become increasingly evident.* (p. 30)

Geraldine Siks (1983) quotes Winifred Ward, noting that "drama comes in the door of a school with every child" (p. 3). Siks also expands on this notion: "Drama *does* come to school with children, but they don't know or even care that it is called 'drama.' What children care about are opportunities to join with others in actively expressing their thoughts, feelings, and imaginings. They want to act out some of their impressions about what they did, how they did it, and to reflect on the content—the heart of the enactments" (p. 3).

In particular, Siks focuses on "the importance of the art of drama to satisfy human needs and to foster the development and learning of children" (p. 3). Based on that notion, she has outlined the following principles as the core of a conceptual approach to drama in education:

1. *The art of drama is a way of learning and knowing about the self and the external world.*
2. *Drama in education, based in the expressive processes of children's dramatic play, is extended to their creative processes, enabling children to learn to give dramatic form to their feelings, perceptions, and imagingings.*
3. *Drama is taught as an art by employing and relating its basic processes and concept; it is used as teaching tool to integrate learning.*
4. *Drama is included, centrally, as an art in the language arts curriculum.*
5. *The teacher of drama should understand the nature of child development and learning and the nature of drama by experiencing its processes and concepts.* (p. 5)

Ward (1957) lists the following purposes of creative drama:

1. To provide children:
   - a controlled emotional outlet
   - an avenue of self-expression in one of the arts
   - opportunities to grow in social understanding and cooperation
   - experience in thinking on their feet and expressing ideas fearlessly
   - encouragement and guidance of creative imagination
2. To encourage children's:
   - initiative, resulting from encouragement to think independently and to express oneself
   - resourcefulness, from the experience with others in creating a play that is their own
   - freedom in bodily expression that comes from practice in expressing ideas through pantomime
   - growth in enjoyment of good literature and the beginning of appreciation for drama (pp. 3–9)

Developmental Perspective

Drama is central to the human experience. Since prehistoric times, humans have used drama to express feelings and ideas, recount past events, tell stories, and predict the future. In similar fashion, young children learn to express themselves through drama. From an early age, long before they actually speak, they use gestures and sounds to imitate things they observe in the environment. Piaget (1962) noted evidence of this innate tendency during the first few days of his own son's life, when he observed his newborn child cry upon hearing other babies in the hospital cry. Piaget also found that his son would cry in response to his imitation of a baby's cry but not to a whistle or other kinds of cries.

And just as the use of drama preceded literate attempts by humans to express and record their ideas and feelings in written language or other symbols, young children respond to and communicate with others by imitating life through sounds, gestures, and movements. Children are able to communicate successfully through dramatic means long before they can read and write. Thus, drama is a natural part of the evolution of thought and language—for individuals, in particular, and for humankind, in general.

Piaget (1962) explains that language development goes through three stages: (1) actual experience with an action or object, (2) dramatic reliving of this experience, and (3) words that represents this whole schema verbally.

Drama and Literacy

Dramatic play makes an important contribution to young children's language and literacy development (Christie, 1990; Martinez, 1993; Verriour, 1986). Drama, reading, and writing all involve language, perceptions, concept development, aesthetic appreciation, and ultimately, the whole range of experience itself. Drama, reading, and writing are all language arts and communication skills that can be integrated in many exciting ways and for a variety of purposes—from enhancing language and vocabulary development to applying comprehension and critical-reading skills. Summaries of research on the impact of drama in education show its particular importance in the development of oral language and literacy (Wagner, 1988, 1992).

The perspectives of Piaget (1962) and Vygotsky (1967) provide the foundation for the theory of the relationship of dramatic play and literacy development. Piaget explained that children learn to symbolize their experiences, first through play and imitation and later in writing. Vygotsky also saw play as essential in children's learning to manipulate symbols. Drama provides a framework within which to teach reading and writing as active, social processes. The emphasis in this approach is on *action:* young children acting out and reacting to stories through drama as they read, talk, listen, and write about what they're doing. Action is especially evident in the social interaction that takes place when children work in groups.

Drama and Reading

Research reinforces the notion of a positive relationship between action-centered experiences with drama and learning to read. For example, Yawkey (1980) found that reading readiness scores on the Gates-MacGinite Readiness Test were higher for a group of 5-year-old children who participated in role-playing activities that involved story dramatization and problem solving through dramatization (15 minutes a day, 5 days a week, for 7 months) than for a same-aged group that did cut-and-paste activities with minimal social interaction. In the first group, the children's understanding of story content and concepts was improved by role-playing, which encouraged them to think, feel, and act like the characters they were playing in the story.

Pellegrini and Galda (1982) found that among 108 children in kindergarten and the first and second grades, those who engaged in dramatic/thematic/fantasy play showed better story comprehension on a 10-item, criterion-referenced test after listening to the story of "Little Red Cap" than those children engaged solely in discussion or drawing activities. Based on these findings, researchers concluded that acting out the roles of major characters in the story—such as Little Red Cap, Grandma, the Hunter, and the Wolf—improved children's understanding because it involved them more actively with the events of the story. Other studies have reinforced the view that symbolization through play and drama supports literacy development (Galda, 1984; Pellegrini, 1985).

A *criterion-referenced test* measures performance against an established standard or expectation.

An important link with reading is formed as children experience drama in response to literature. The connections among reading, literature, and drama are demonstrated in the following sections. To illustrate each idea, examples are included using the story dramatization of the picture book *Where the Wild Things Are* (Sendak, 1963) for primary children and performing Shakespeare for middle- and upper-grade children.

Dramatization of Literature to Encourage Interest in and Motivation for Reading

Reader interest and motivation are essential to the effective teaching of reading. Consider, for a moment, a young boy, playing the part of Max in *Where the Wild Things Are.* How interested would he be in understanding how the wolf-suited Max confronted and tamed an island full of monsters? Consider also an older girl, playing the part of Juliet in Shakespeare's *Romeo and Juliet.* How interested would she be in reading her script or information about the Renaissance: costumes, the limited role of women in the theater, or how people behaved or danced at a masked ball? In both picture books and dramatic literature, there's something to capture everyone's interest. Especially appealing is the idea of playing exciting characters and sharing a story with others.

Dramatization of Literature to Expand Vocabulary

Teachers may become concerned with the difficulty levels of the vocabulary in books and plays. The readability level of *Where the Wild Things Are* is grade 3.2, and the vocabulary used in Shakespeare's plays is not usually considered within children's reach. Nonetheless, using the vocabulary of Sendak or Shakespeare provides an ideal way to teach difficult words to students, who will have real reason to understand and use these words in playing their parts.

Measures of readability are based on the difficulty of a given text, considering factors such as vocabulary, sentence length, and the like. A number is assigned, showing the approximate grade level (in years and months) at which someone should normally be able to read the text. For example, 3.2 means "third grade, second month."

A system of reciprocity is at work here: Students' interest in and need to understand words will be helped by their understanding the characters who are speaking the words and the story or play in which they are being spoken. Thus, comprehension supports word identification in the same way that word identification supports comprehension. Understanding a scene and dialogue will obviously help students understand words they haven't encountered before or don't fully understand.

Drama also provides a great opportunity to familiarize students with less common, abstract words when understanding these words is critical to playing a part. For example, how can students resist adding to their vocabularies words like *gnashed,* which signals the start of a wild monster rumpus in *Where the Wild Things Are,* or *tyrant,* which is uttered in *Macbeth* as a challenge and initiates a sword fight to the death?

Dramatization of Literature to Encourage the Development of Critical-Reading Skills and Comprehension

When dramatizing literature, students do more than repeat what has been written and read. They must interpret and transform their reading experiences as they become part of their dramatic experiences and even their lives. Through drama, a dialogue is initiated between the writer and the reader, as they both move the student toward creating the role.

To encourage the development of critical-reading and comprehension skills through drama, teachers can:

1. Provide a model for comprehension processes by reading and interacting with the story or play.

2. Stimulate guided discussions of stories and plays and practice questioning techniques to help students further understand what they have read so they can quite literally act on their reading.
3. Offer feedback pertinent to acting out a story to reinforce students' active reading, understanding, and responding to stories and scripts or information helpful to creating a play.
4. Manage the practice and development of certain skills that are ideally taught in the context of dramatizing literature, such as:
   - Paraphrasing what's been read through discussions of the motivation of characters, how scenes should be played, and what's actually happening during scenes
   - Identifying and distinguishing between the main idea of a play or scene and the details that are peripheral to the plot
   - Understanding story structure, plot, and narrative sequence, relying heavily on skills of ordering and understanding the sequence of action
   - Identifying cause and effect through analysis of character action as well as events in the story and their consequences
   - Identifying with characters, evaluating their traits, perceiving their relationships, and recognizing their emotional and motivational reactions
   - Recognizing, understanding, and appreciating figurative language and multiple meanings of words and passages
   - Encouraging the development of imagination, forming sensory impressions, and reacting to mood or tone
   - Interpreting and appreciating the symbolic use of language in literature

Drama to Encourage Guided, Extended Reading

Students become highly motivated to read and find out about anything that will help them play a part. Children who are dramatizing *Where the Wild Things Are* can extend their reading to other picture books about monsters, boats, and islands. And for older students, many Shakespeare-related topics will be of great interest: stagecraft, Renaissance costumes and weapons, and the man himself.

Drama to Encourage Lifetime Readers

One goal of reading instruction that can be easily lost in the daily shuffle of skills and drills is the creation of lifetime readers. Early experiences with dramatizing fine literature can develop readers who will continue to read, enjoy, and really experience literature and drama as adults.

Drama and Writing

The dynamic social nature of drama is the basis for its close connection with writing. Young children play, role-play, and act out ideas and feelings both before and as part of the writing process. In a kindergarten "store" center, they make grocery lists, and in the "home" center, they write notes to each other. Writing usually takes place in a rich, oral, social, and interactive context, in which listening, talking, gestures, and sound effects all play a part. Observe children who are writing about trucks, and you'll hear the sounds of engines. Observe children writing about superheroes, and you'll hear their challenges to villains and the sounds of their weapons.

Vygotsky (1978) suggests that writing is closely akin to speech and gesture. Research on young children's emergent writing shows its connection with gestures and dramatic play (Dyson, 1986) as well as the correlation of dramatic play in kindergarten with writing achievement, as measured by children's ability to write their own names, others' names, and the names of colors and objects (Pellegrini, 1984).

The following sections show the connections between drama and writing, again, using examples from a story dramatization of Sendak's (1963) *Where the Wild Things Are,* for younger children, and Shakespeare or scriptwriting, for older students.

Drama as Prewriting Experience

Just as children are better able to describe in writing an object they have looked at, smelled, held, or touched, so are they better able to write about an experience they have acted out. For example, by acting like "Wild Things" or feeling what it would be like to run away from home, as Max did, children gain tangible experiences from what would otherwise remain abstract concepts. Ideas generated by informal drama during role-playing, pantomime, or improvisation serve to further generate and clarify ideas for writing. Drama gives children a chance to try out ideas through speaking and actions that they later build on in constructing written texts and scripts for more formal drama.

Drama as a Means of Developing a Strong Voice and Sense of Audience in Writing

Students who put themselves in someone else's place—for instance, through role-playing a character in the context of a historical event—discover that person's voice, which they can use in writing with conviction about him or her. Activities like writing fictional journals of people immigrating to the United States or writing letters home from soldiers off at war are strengthened through drama experiences. Interestingly, students who have played characters like the witches in Shakespeare's *Macbeth* have amazing things to say in writing about evil.

Learning to Make Choices through Drama

Selection is as essential to drama as it is to writing. So for someone playing Max in *Where the Wild Things Are,* deciding exactly how to move to tame the "Wild Things" requires thinking through all the possibilities. This analysis and planning is similar to that a writer would do in deciding how to describe Max; only in writing, the decisions would be about word choice and sentence structure.

Learning to Organize Ideas through Drama

In acting out (especially in improvisation), children must pay careful attention to the order of events. Deciding what comes first, next, and last is essential to successfully portraying the story. The same is true in organizing ideas for writing of all kinds. In scriptwriting, as in informal drama, students learn that things are flexible and can change. Using drama to teach this concept to young children is especially effective, since movement, gesture, and speech are more familiar and less labor intensive than writing.

Visualizing through Drama

An essential skill for drama is *visualizing:* picturing what the character looks like, how he or she moves, where he or she is, what the mood is like, and so on. Visualizing is equally important in writing and reading. Being able to picture and imagine the setting of a story while reading it and writing about it are essential to the development of literacy.

Drama as a Revision Process

One of the best things about drama is its fluid nature: No two actions or readings will ever be exactly the same. Children quickly learn the freedom this offers and are encouraged to try out many possibilities. The same kind of flexibility and willingness to experiment should be encouraged in writing, too.

Teaching Drama

The Circle of Drama

We can picture the possibilities for teaching through drama by envisioning a circle (see Figure 6.1). A circle is appropriate because there is no particular linear order for using drama in the classroom. In addition, a circle is continuous, such that there is no beginning and end; rather, one thing follows from another.

In choosing dramatic activities, teachers should consider the grades they teach. For young children, the most appropriate drama experiences are creative dramatics. In addition, children in the middle grades will enjoy reader's theater and scriptwriting, and those in the upper grades can begin adaptations of dramatic literature. No matter which forms of drama teachers choose or how they decide to use them in the classroom and across the curriculum, their focus should always be on the children. Brian Way (1967) maintains that, as an educator, he is primarily "concerned with the development of people, not the development of drama. . . . Education is concerned with individuals; drama is concerned with the individuality of individuals, with the uniqueness of each human essence" (pp. 2–3).

Above all, Way emphasizes the importance of the role of the teacher in drama in the classroom. "The most important single factor in the use of drama as a genuine part of education is the teacher. . . . A really full, generous and

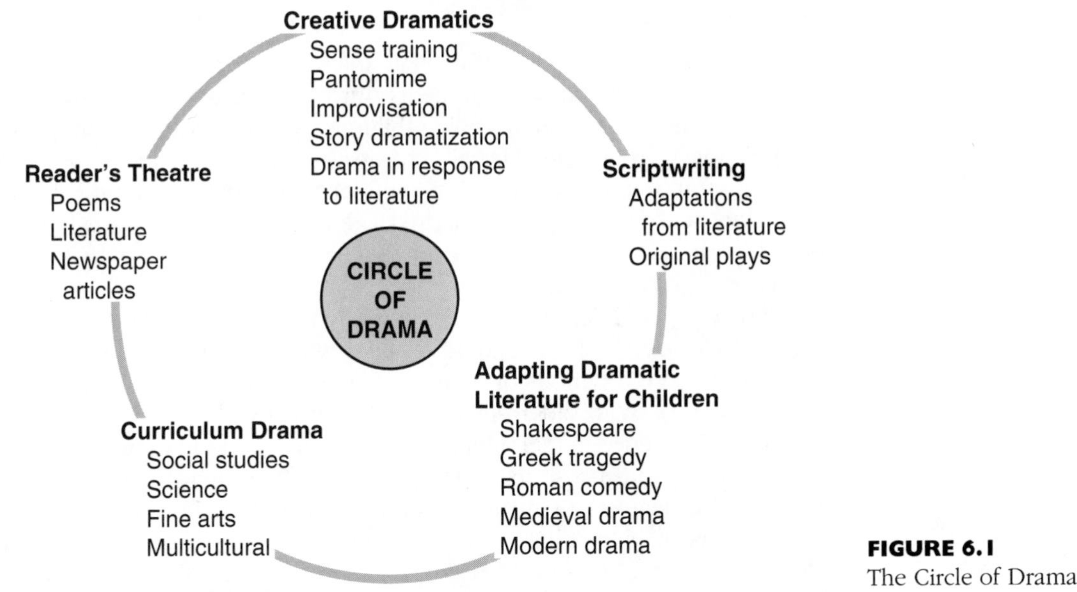

FIGURE 6.1
The Circle of Drama

compassionate interest in children, irrespective of academic ability or gift, is the first requisite; a knowledge of why to use drama is another; the freedom to approach the matter from where he or she feels happiest and most confident is another" (p. 8).

Way also makes the following suggestions for beginning to use drama in the classroom:

> *Start from where you yourself are happiest and most confident; this may be the telling of a story or it may be a simple discussion about appropriate behavior in certain situations; it may be the problems of the school play or a discussion of Hamlet's attitude toward Claudius; . . . it may be a simple concern with sharing physical space and material objects or the complex understanding of racial problems. Start from that point—where you yourself feel interested and confident. Keep reminding yourself that what you are concerned with is the development of everyone, of the manifold facets of human beings; a circle can start at any point on the circumference of the circle. Ultimately there may be only one goal, but the means of that goal are manifold and individual depending on where you, as teacher, are, and growing out of the particular bond you have made with the children or young people you are helping to develop.* (p. 9)

Creative Dramatics

Creative dramatics can be approached in many ways and be adapted to many age levels and instructional settings. It is a synthesis of sense training, pantomime and improvisation, and story dramatization.

Sense Training

Sense-training activities help individuals become aware of their senses and encourage creativity and self-confidence through expressing that awareness. The key is the concentration ability children develop as they communicate through nonverbal means: facial expressions, gestures, and movements. Teachers should emphasize creating confidence and enthusiasm for dramatic expression. Sense-training activities can be developed as warm-up exercises to help children evolve from simple movements to more elaborate forms of drama.

With younger children, sense-training activities can be expansions of their spontaneous play. Teachers should observe what the children are acting out during unstructured periods of dramatic play and build on these moments to lead into drama. With older children, sense training should begin slowly to give them confidence in their abilities to use their bodies to express their feelings and ideas and to use many language forms through drama. Older children will also develop an awareness of themselves as individuals as well as a sensitivity to others in communication events.

Here are some ideas for focusing warm-up activities on the four senses:

Touch. The teacher should have children sit on the floor, each individual doing his or her own activity. Dimming the lights may help create a secure atmosphere. The teacher should give the following directions (one activity at a time):

- "There is a balloon on the floor in front of you. Pick it up. Blow it up. Tie a knot in the end of it and attach a string. Let it float in the air as you watch."
- "There is a baby animal crouched behind you. It is frightened. Pick it up. Pet it and comfort it."
- "There is a blob of sticky, gooey clay in front of you. Pick it up. Make something from it."

Taste. For these activities, children should work in pairs, facing each other. The teacher should ask one partner to guess exactly what the other is pretending to eat:

- "Make your favorite sandwich and eat it."
- "Eat your favorite food."
- "Eat something you don't like."

Sight. Children should gather in small groups and sit in circles, everyone facing each other. The teacher tells them that there is a collection of something in the middle of the circle; then going around the circle, each individual takes out an item and pantomimes what he or she has selected. After everyone has finished, they should guess what one another did. Here are some ideas:

- "There is a trunk full of clothes in the middle of the circle. Take something out of it, and try it on. There is only one of each thing in the trunk."
- "There is a pile of presents wrapped in boxes in the middle of the circle. Choose one, open it, and take out and use what's inside."
- "Your favorite toy or game is in the middle of the circle. Pick it up and show how you play with it."

Sound. For these activities, children should stand in small groups (again, forming small circles). In response to the teacher's directions, each person should portray how a particular sound makes him or her feel. After everyone has finished, the students should try to tell what the others did. Here are some ideas:

- "I will make a sound. (Hit the table with a rhythmic beat.) Act out what it makes you think of."
- Give the same directions, but rub hands together to make a slithery sound.
- Give the same direction, but make a scraping sound with an object against the blackboard.

Pantomime and Improvisation

Pantomime and improvisation are natural extensions of sense training and may also follow from teachers' observations of children's spontaneous play. *Pantomime* uses facial expressions, body movements, and gestures to communicate instead of sounds and words, and *improvisation* adds speech to spontaneous movements and actions. These dramatic techniques may lead to more elaborate playing of scenes, story dramatization, or scriptwriting (Heinig, 1992).

A Pantomime File. Teachers should keep files of ideas to motivate pantomime activities related to children's experiences, literature, or other content areas. Some topics to focus on include:

- *Animals:* Movements, interactions between children and pets, interactions among animals, and so on
- *Play:* Sports, games, toys, and fun places to visit
- *Children's literature:* Nursery rhymes, poems, picture books, folktales, and stories
- *Cross-curricular:* Social studies, science, math, or fine arts

Teachers may also use costumes and other props to motivate children's pantomime (e.g., hats, capes, canes, buckets, baskets). Likewise, music provides a good source of motivation.

A Pantomime Play. Simple pantomime activities can lead into playing scenes. For example, children working in pairs could pantomime a short scene and lead into improvising a play, with one child speaking and the other communicating only through movement.

Improvised Scenes. When children have had experience with pantomime and added speech to their dramatic activities, they will move easily into improvised scenes. Some situations to improvise include:

- *Conversations:* On the telephone, between historic figures, or in role reversals (e.g., parent/child or teacher/student)
- *Imaginary journeys:* Riding in a car, bus, or plane
- *Responses to stories:* Original stories written by children or drawn from literature
- *Interaction with media:* Music, slide projections, or film

Story Dramatization

When children respond to a story through drama—portraying the actions as they play the characters—they are creating a *story dramatization.* This kind of drama is spontaneous and based on improvisation, but because it's based on an actual story, it follows a plot.

Not all children's stories are suitable for dramatizing, however. In selecting stories, teachers should look for the following qualities (Ward, 1957):

1. a worthy central idea or motive
2. a reasonable, limited number of incidents
3. a climax that's strong yet doesn't appeal too much to any single emotion
4. a quick and satisfying ending
5. genuine, believable characters, whether real or supernatural
6. dialogue that gives the impression of natural conversation

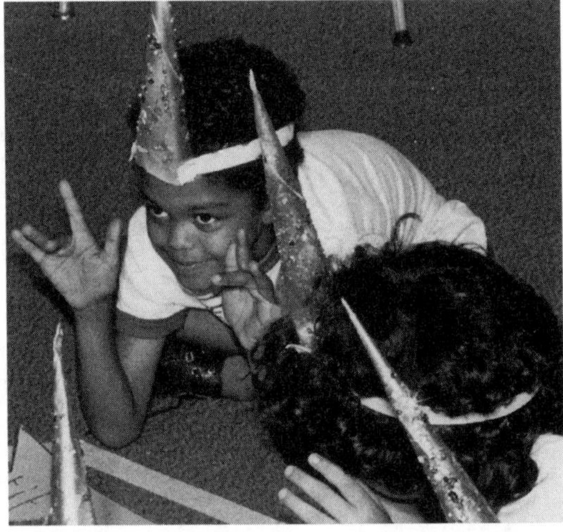

A story dramatization about a magic unicorn supports children's language and literacy development.

TEACHING IDEA

Dramatizing Literature

Here's an example of how all the elements of drama can be integrated progressively in experiences in response to Maurice Sendak's (1963) *Where the Wild Things Are:*

• ***Monster Masks:*** Making simple monster masks (see Figure 6.2) will set the mood and help children establish distance between their real selves and a monster selves. Making a mask will also help each student develop his or her own characterization for either Max or a "Wild Thing."

• ***Monster Mime:*** With masks in place, students can do sense-training, pantomime, and improvisational activities. After reading and discussing the book, the teacher should lead them through "A Day in the Life of a Monster," asking:

"Show me how you sleep, Monster, and how you wake up."

"What do you do when you wake up, Monster? Do you stretch, growl, do exercises, look mean?"

FIGURE 6.2 How to Make a Mask

Materials: Manila folder, scissors, stapler, glue, decorations

1. Cut the manila folder in half.

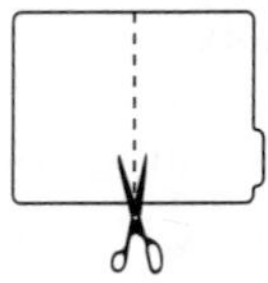

2. In one half, cut out an oval for the face to show through.

3. In the other half, cut out two strips on the diagonal.

4. Attach one strip to the back of the mask to fit around the head from side to side. Attach the other strip from the top center of mask to the other strip.

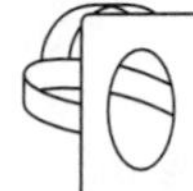

5. Decorate with scraps of manila folder, construction paper, feathers, scraps of cloth, pipe cleaners, yarn ribbons, and the like.

(continued)

"How do you get ready for a new day, Monster? Do you brush your teeth (or tooth)? comb your hair (scales, fur, or tentacles)? wear clothes?"

"How do you move around when you are ready for a new day, Monster? Do you creep, crawl, slither, lumber, galumph, stagger, stumble, or fall down frequently?"

In addition to the popular "Monster Mash," by Bobby "Boris" Pickett, try these other pieces of "monster music": *Abduction of the Bride* and *The Hall of the Mountain King* from *Peer Gynt,* by Edvard Grieg; *Danse Macabre,* by Camille Saint-Saëns; March of the Dwarves from *Huldigungmarsch,* by Edvard Grieg; *Night on Bald Mountain* and *Songs and Dances of Death,* by Modest Mussorgsky; and *The Sorcerer's Apprentice,* by Paul Dukas.

- ***Monster Dance:*** Using movements developed through mime, the "monsters" can dance. The teacher may suggest a series of movements for different types of monsters: walking, marching, jumping, crouching and pouncing, and so on. The teacher should experiment with a variety of music but let children choose their own preferred monster music.

- ***Story Dramatization:*** Maurice Sendak has said that the aesthetic problem he was attempting to solve when creating *Where the Wild Things Are* was that of capturing movement and dance on the pages of a picture book. He does this beautifully in the wordless sequence that starts when the young protagonist, Max—who has just been made "King of All Wild Things" by the "Wild Things" themselves—imperiously orders, "Let the wild rumpus start!"

This is a natural point of connection between the developmental sequence of drama activities focused around the theme of monsters and the dramatization of the story by the children. After they have heard the story, discussed and reacted to it, and crept inside the character of a monster (through masks, mime, movement, and dance), they need to take just a small step to try on the character of Max or a "Wild Thing." And after that, it's easy for children to jump inside this magical book and live it through story dramatization.

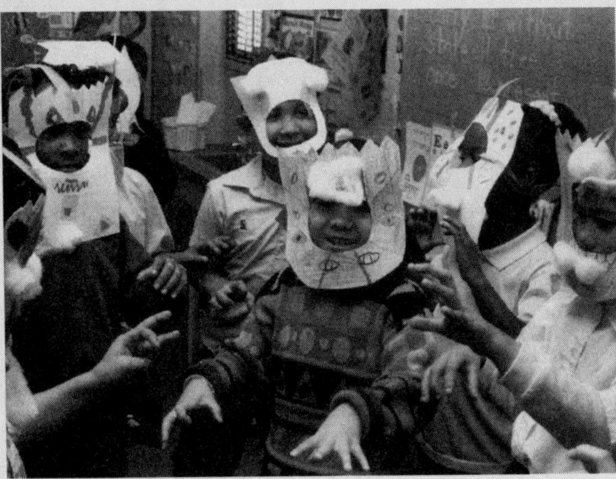

Second-grade limited–English proficient students make monster masks and do a story dramatization of Maurice Sendak's Where the Wild Things Are.

To do so (for this or any other story), follow this sequence of steps:

1. *Reread and discuss the book:* Ask children to note the number of characters, how they behaved, and the sequence of the events. Also note the most exciting parts, the climax, and the way the story ended (i.e., the resolution). After several readings, discuss these points and chart the story with the class for dramatization purposes on the board or chartpaper:

   Characters

   Narrator, Mother, Max, Dog, Wild Things, Other
   Inanimates: Trees, Boats, Ocean

   Sequence of Events

   (1) Max makes mischief. Mother sends to bed.
   (2) A forest grows. A boat comes by.
   (3) Max sails away to where the Wild Things are.
   (4) Max tames Wild Things. Max becomes King.
   (5) The wild rumpus (dance).
   (6) Max is lonely. He leaves Wild Things.
   (7) He sails home. His supper is still hot.

   Use a circle to help children understand the structure of the story in relationship to the sequence of events. Explain that this is a *circle story*: The setting and plot begin and end in the same place. Do this with the whole class on a "word wall," or let small groups or individuals do story maps (see Figure 6.3).

FIGURE 6.3 Story Map for *Where the Wild Things Are*

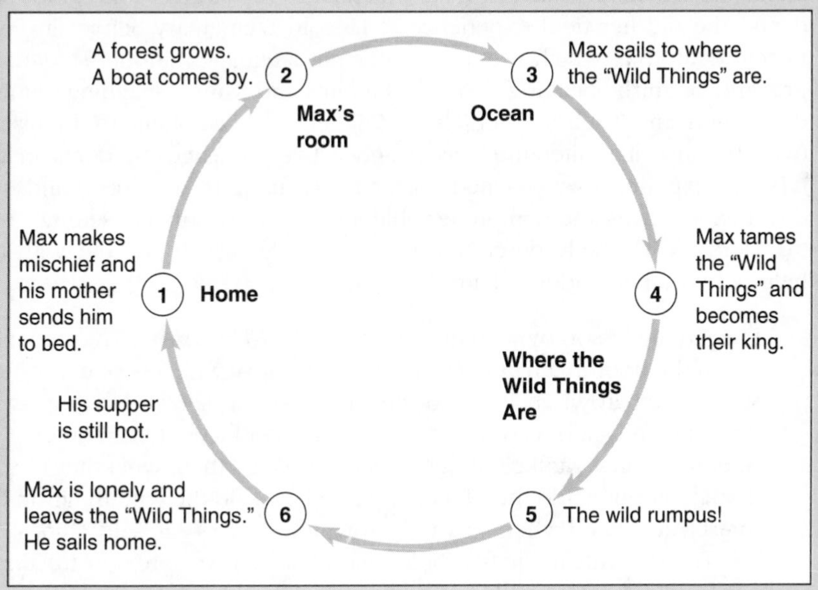

(continued)

2. *Take volunteers for the cast:* Delegate direction and leadership roles in the play to one child at a time. For example, begin with the narrator and rotate to other children.
3. *Have the cast plan how they will play the scene: who will do what action and where:* There are enough parts for trees, an ocean, a boat, and "Wild Things" to involve the entire class. Or half the students can play and the other half can watch; then reverse.
4. *Have the children play the scene:* Allow the narrator to provide direction for the story initially. Later, as the children play the scene several more times, this role will become less important.
5. *Discuss and evaluate after each playing with the children:* Everyone should become involved in this stage. Emphasize the positive by asking:

   What did you see that you liked?

   Who did something really interesting (or exciting, realistic, fantastic, etc.)?

   What can we do next time to make the play even better?

SNAPSHOT: Language-Minority Students Make Masks and Act Like "Wild Things"

Shelly Abesa, a student in a language arts methods class I teach, decided to dramatize *Where the Wild Things Are* (Sendak, 1963) with second-grade students. She did her field experience at Lincoln Elementary School in Long Beach, California, which is about 85 percent language-minority students—primarily Spanish-speaking Hispanic students and Khmer-speaking Cambodian Americans. Their teacher, Hope Zink, encouraged Shelly to do this activity because it is literature based and actively engages students in the types of experiences advocated for language-minority students: hands-on, direct experiences and comprehensible input in a low-anxiety setting.

Here's how Shelly described the experience, which she did with the help of two other students, Patricia and Rachel:

> I began my lesson by reading *Where the Wild Things Are.* The students sat on the floor in a half circle as I read the story with lots of expression. I even growled like a monster. The students showed their gnawing teeth and sharp claws as we made monster faces at each other. After reading, we talked about the story. I asked them what they thought about it and their favorite part. Many said the wild things in the forest. Alexi liked when Max was crowned "King of All Wild Things."
>
> The students made file-folder masks next. They tore construction paper, glued cotton balls and feathers on, and colored them with crayons. They enjoyed wearing them and showing them to each other.

Now we were ready to begin the drama. I said, "Here is a magic line. Once you cross the line, you become the character in the book." I had made large signs with the characters' names to hang around students' necks. I began narrating the story and then put the "Max" sign around Alexi's neck. One student was the "forest growing," others were the "water" and "boat." Everyone else was a "Wild Thing." Their favorite part was the "wild rumpus"; we danced to the Monster Mash. We had so much fun bringing the story to life.

The students tried new things. One girl began to show us a dance from Cambodia. When she realized everyone was watching, she became shy. Patricia reminded her that she wasn't herself anymore but a character from a book. She said "Oh, yeah!" and began to show us the dance again. The students asked to do the whole thing again. Chametra and Alexi wanted to wear their masks out to recess. Three girls gave me a hug. Ms. Zink said it was a great lesson. *I will definitely use drama with reading in my own class!*

Scriptwriting

As an extension of improvised, spontaneous drama in the classroom, children can create scripted drama (Chapman, 1984; Sklar, 1991). Preferably, these scripts should be those the children write themselves from original concepts or adaptations of fine children's books, basal reader stories, or dramatic literature. Children who write original scripts—perhaps in response to topics they're pursuing in school or recent events or experiences of high interest to them—have unique opportunities to put their feelings, thoughts, and language to work, as they draw on these responses as a source of inspiration.

Writing scripts for plays on subjects they choose puts students to work, building ideas by using language as a tool and constructing their own drama in written form. The real reward is when they are able to communicate their original ideas (which have gone through a period of revision and refinement through the composing process) to an audience of significant others. Through this experience, children literally act on what they know and bring their words and ideas to life, as they produce and perform their own play.

One approach to scriptwriting evolves from the entire class being interested in a topic and wanting to explore it further, learning what they know about it through selecting, organizing, elaborating, and dramatizing a script they have written (Cox, 1988). Follow these steps:

1. ***Select a topic:*** The suggestion to write a play for the first time may come from the teacher, *after* a topic of interest has emerged in the classroom. Some types of topics that may trigger playmaking include:

- Children's book read aloud to the whole class
- Social studies or science units of study
- Current events of interest
- Popular films and other media events
- Fieldtrips

2. ***Extend the response to the topic through writing:*** Younger children may dictate a group story to the teacher, who can record it as part of a language experience story, or students may write their own stories. Older students may come up with their own ideas and extend them through personal writing. Many ideas for scripts will also emerge from writing activities.

3. ***Share stories:*** At some point, children may choose to share what they are writing, and their stories may become a focal point for discussing and extending their ideas into a dramatic script.

4. ***Brainstorm ideas:*** Begin with small-group discussions of the focal idea, and then move to a whole-class sharing of these ideas.

5. ***Block a script:*** Again, begin with small-group discussions, followed by a whole-class discussion of group ideas. One way to organize these discussions is to group ideas under the following types of headings, writing them on the board or a large wall chart. These new terms may be defined and explained and added to children's growing vocabulary of drama and script terms:

Synopsis (story idea)
Plot
Setting
Characters
Sequence of actions and events

6. ***Record results:*** One child can record the ideas under one heading, and a small group can put them on a chart for the whole class to use as a framework for future discussions and writing.

7. ***Divide the sequence of events and actions into numbered acts:*** Then divide the class into groups according to their interests and ability to work together.

8. ***Write acts in small groups and add dialogue:*** This will be an extended period of discussing and revising until each group has a working draft it can share with the class. This is a good opportunity to introduce, teach, and reinforce the many specialized writing skills children will need to produce a working draft. For example:

- Ordering and sequencing events and actions
- Writing in a script form (scene notes, stage directions, narration, dialogue and quotation marks, etc.)
- Unity of time and place
- Consistency of character behavior and language

9. ***Come together as a large group to share act drafts:*** Read the drafts together, and discuss the sequencing of acts and ways to smooth transitions between them.

10. ***Revise the acts in multiple small groups:*** Groups should now collaborate on transitions between acts: the group for Act 1 with Act 2, Act 2 with Act 1 and Act 3, and so on.

11. ***Review and revise the script as a group:*** Leave a copy of the emerging working script available in a writing center, so that children can read and respond to it between periods of writing.

12. ***Synthesize the final script:*** Changes will undoubtedly occur as the play goes into production. Nonetheless, a working script, which has gone through an extended period of talking and writing, is the beginning point for producing a scripted play.

SNAPSHOT: Children Write and Perform "The Tale of an Unfair Election"

I had read aloud *The Mystery of the Haunted Mine* (Shirreffs, 1962), a book written by my father, to my third- and fourth-grade combination class, and it generated a "ripple effect" of ideas, interests, and activities. Working in small groups, my students created a play. Not only was the play a natural outgrowth of several interests that were organized, clarified, and communicated through dramatization; in addition, it demonstrated how natural it is to integrate the curriculum through writing and drama.

See Chapter 7, Teaching with Literature, for more about how I used *The Mystery of the Haunted Mine* across the curriculum.

My students were excited about the three main characters in the book—Gary, Tuck, and Sue—and were spontaneously playing them. I noticed somewhat uncomfortably that Sue began to take on mannerisms I knew were my own. (Children often "act out" their teachers, imitating voice and speech patterns when they don't think the teachers are listening.) These characters also began to appear in students' writing, so it seemed only natural to suggest scriptwriting and organizing these improvisational character sketches into dramatic form.

We began with the three main characters, but we still needed a setting, a plot, and a lot of action. Because the class was studying the moon and plants in science, the play's setting became another planet peopled by two races: the Plant People and the Humanoids. The conflict in the play came from another interest: a social studies unit on elections, since it was a presidential election year. The play began to take form when the children titled it "The Tale of an Unfair Election."

Here's the plot, as summarized in a promotional release for the performance:

> An election takes place on the planet Zot. The election has been rigged by the Humanoid presidential candidate, Taylor. The Humanoids are invaders from a dying planet and have enslaved the native Plant People. Trailing Arbutus, the other presidential candidate, sends his vice-presidential candidate, Leaf, to Earth for help to restore free elections for Plants and Humanoids alike.
>
> Leaf meets the Metzenberg children Gary, Tuck, and Sue, who take him to their father, a famous space scientist who is going on a scientific expedition to Zot. He takes Leaf along and promises to help.

The children stow away on the spaceship *U.S.S. Moonbeam* and join their father for many adventures on Zot.

The play was performed in-the-round on the floor of the gym. The audience sat in a circle of chairs around the action. Spaces were left at intervals in the circle for the entrances and exits of performers, who waited behind screens, outside the circle. To create an effect of deep space, the room was dark, except for spotlights on the action. During scenes with political rallies and revolt, the audience was invited to participate, becoming part of the crowd and the drama itself.

Although this play was special for everyone, one student in particular appeared to benefit. Jan was the shyest child in the class and often struggled to look people in the eye when she spoke. She was large for her age and self-conscious about it, which compounded her shyness and desire to remain unnoticed.

Surprisingly, Jan became extremely involved with her scriptwriting group. When we called for volunteers for the cast, she asked to play the important role of the presidential candidate of the Plant People, Trailing Arbutus. When Jan donned the imperial-looking robes of the leader of the Plant People—a long, flowing, hooded garment, covered with plastic leaves attached with safety pins—no one was prepared for the transformation that took place. She suddenly stood straighter, to the full advantage of her larger size. And as she gripped her robe and swished it about for emphasis, a voice emerged from inside the hood that none of us had ever heard before. It was similar to the voice of the quiet and very dignified Jan, but it had a new edge of authority and volume. Jan had become Trailing Arbutus!

Jan outdid herself in this role and came to relish all drama. The other children recognized her special talent and the transformation that took place when she worked on a script or put on a costume. For Jan, composing a play in the relative safety of a small group and then acting on it by assuming another persona was a special way to find her own voice—one barely audible during whole-class activities but strong and clear during dramatizations.

Reader's Theater

In *reader's theater,* participants read and interpret literature aloud from scripts adapted especially for this setting. The scripts can come from many types of literature: texts of picture books for younger children and novels for older children; folk- and fairy tales and other types of traditional literature (e.g., fables, myths, and legends); poetry and songs; stories and poems from anthologies and basal readers; and even nonfiction, too (Young & Vardell, 1993). In presenting reader's theater, children hold the scripts, which may be read or glanced at by the performing readers. No special costumes, sets, props, lighting, or music are required, so once the scripts have been developed, reader's theater can be practiced and performed almost instantly in the classroom.

Reader's theater serves many purposes:

- It helps children understand and appreciate literature through actively reacting to reading and sharing stories.
- It encourages retelling and sharing stories.
- It provides enjoyment from reading through the dramatization of a text.
- It expands students' oral language and sharpens their listening skills.
- It actively involves students in the reading process, as they reread, rethink, and act on what they've read.
- It improves comprehension by helping students interpret text.
- It involves all types of children, with all types of abilities.
- It enhances children's self-concepts.
- It integrates areas of the curriculum through using stories and texts related to other subjects.

In selecting stories for reader's theater, teachers should look for:

- dialogue and clear prose
- lively, high-interest, humorous stories, with children or personified animals as main characters
- a good balance of parts of nearly the same size
- short stories, especially the first time

Here are examples of stories that work well for reader's theater:

Folk Literature

For Younger Children

"Chicken Little"
"The Fisherman and His Wife"
"The Gingerbread Man"
"The Little Red Hen"
"The Three Billy Goats Gruff"
"The Three Wishes"

For Older Children

"Cinderella"
"East of the Sun, West of the Moon"
"The Frog King"
"Rumpelstiltskin"
"Snow White"
"The Tinder Box"

Books

For Younger Children

Amelia Bedelia (Parish, 1963)
The Case of the Scaredy Cats (Bonsall, 1971)
Fish Is Fish (Lionni, 1970)
Frederick (Lionni, 1967)
Horton Hatches the Egg (Seuss, 1940)
How the Grinch Stole Christmas (Seuss, 1957)
Leo the Late Bloomer (Kraus, 1971)
Owliver (Kraus, 1974)

Other sources for reader's theater: newspaper and magazine articles and advertisements, letters and memos, and textbooks.

For Older Children

The Lion, the Witch, and the Wardrobe (Lewis, 1950)
The Reluctant Dragon (Grahame, 1953)
Tales of a Fourth Grade Nothing (Blume, 1972)

See also other books by Crosby Bonsall and Judy Blume as well as others in the Narnia series by C. S. Lewis.

Poetry

A Light in the Attic (Silverstein, 1981)
Where the Sidewalk Ends (Silverstein, 1974)

Adapting a Story or Text for a Reader's Theater Script

1. Add narrator parts for the following: identification of time, place, scene, and characters. One narrator can be added for the whole story, or separate narrators can be added for different characters.
2. Delete lines that aren't critical to plot development, that are peripheral to the main action of the story, that represent complex imagery or figurative language difficult to express through gestures, that state characters are speaking (e.g., "He said . . ."), or whose meaning can be conveyed through characters' facial expressions or gestures, simple sound effects, or mime.
3. Change lines that are descriptive but could be spoken by characters or would move the story along more easily, if changed.

Putting Reader's Theater into Practice

This procedure may be used with a whole class, small group, or instructional group, such as a basal reading group:

1. ***Introduce the story:*** Read or tell the story aloud to young children, or let older children take turns reading the story aloud. Encourage an extended response period to the story through discussion involving all children. Questions to ask include:

- What did you think of this story? Why?
- How do you think some of the characters felt?
- Why did they act the way they did?
- How do you know?
- How did they express what they were feeling?

2. ***Explain reader's theater:*** If this is the first time students have done reader's theater, explain how it works: the physical arrangement and movements (turning in and out of the scene when not involved), the roles of narrators and characters, the uses of mime and expression, and the nature and use of scripts.

3. ***Cast the story:*** First, distribute prepared scripts: those the teacher has done alone or with children. An overhead projector is useful in displaying transparencies of the story and working through the adaptation with students. Revise it according to their suggestions as they watch on the overhead. Scripts can also be easily adapted by a few children or an individual using a word-processing program on the computer.

Next, take volunteers for all parts. In initial sessions, let many different children play each part. They should all become familiar with all the parts, as in improvised drama.

4. ***Develop script awareness:*** Read through the script with students. Stop periodically and discuss actions, characters, mood, and expression. Allow students to respond to the story with questions, comments, and reactions to other characters. Continue until they seem comfortable and secure with the script. Encourage them to continue reading, and react to their scripts each successive time. Emphasize reacting to the story, reading with expression, and communicating with an audience through voice, facial expressions, and gestures.

5. ***Block, stage, and practice playing the script:*** The teacher may plan the physical staging ahead with the group but should be ready to revise it according to how the script actually plays with the group. Suggestions for modifications should be accepted from students. Other guidelines are as follows:

- Narrators often stand, perhaps using a prop like a music stand for holding the script.
- Characters are usually seated on chairs, stools, or even tables.
- Floorplans should be decided ahead of time and changed as the play proceeds.
- There should be a minimum of movement around the floor in reader's theater.

6. ***Sharing reader's theater:*** By the time children have prepared and participated in reader's theater, they are so enthusiastic that they want to share it with others. To make this comfortable for them, avoid actual stages; instead, use a stage-in-the-round in the classroom or multipurpose room or library. Also, it's best to share with others in the classroom first, followed by classes of younger children and then classes of the same age. Work gradually toward sharing with adults, such as parents.

TEACHING IDEA

A Reader's Theater Script Prepared for Children

This script presents the a humorous tale about two infamous friends, Morris the Moose and Boris the Bear, from *Morris Has a Cold,* by Bernard Wiseman (1978).

Cast and Setting
Morris Narrator (standing)
Boris Narrator (standing)
Morris and Boris (both seated with their backs to the audience)

Morris Narrator: Morris the Moose said:
Morris (turning in): I have a cold. My nose is walking.
Boris Narrator: Boris the Bear said:
Boris (turning in): You mean your nose is running.
Morris: No. My nose is walking. I only have a little cold.
Boris: Let me feel your forehead.
Morris: Four heads! I don't have four heads!
Boris: I know you don't have four heads. But this is called your forehead.

(continued)

Morris: That is my ONE head.
Boris (growls): All right. Let me feel your one head.
Boris Narrator: Boris put his hand on Morris's forehead.
Boris: Your one head feels hot. That means you are sick. How does your throat feel?
Morris: Hairy.
Boris: No, no. I don't mean outside. How does your throat feel INSIDE?
Morris Narrator: Morris opened his mouth to feel the inside of his throat.
Boris (shouts): NO! NO! NO! Oh—just open your mouth. Let me look inside. Your throat is red. I know what is good for it. I will make you some hot tea.
Morris: Hot what?
Boris: TEA. Don't you know what tea is?
Morris: Yes. I know what it is. T is like A, B, C ,D . . .
Boris(yells): NO! NO! Tea is . . . Oh, wait—I will show you. This is tea.
Boris Narrator: Boris gave Morris some tea.
Boris: Drink it. It will make your throat feel better. But first, stick out your tongue.
Morris: I will not stick out my tongue. That is not nice.
Boris (shouts): Stick out your tongue!
Morris Narrator: Morris stuck out his tongue.
Boris (shouts): That is not nice!
Morris: I told you it was not nice.
Boris (growls): That is because you didn't do it the right way.
Boris: It is getting dark. Go to sleep. If your cold is better in the morning, I will make you a big breakfast.
Morris: A big what?
Boris: Breakfast. Breakfast is—OH! Go to sleep.
Morris Narrator: In the morning, Morris said:
Morris: My nose is not walking. My one head is not hot. My cold is better. Make me a big breakfast.
Boris: All right. But you have to do something for me.
Morris: What?
Boris: DON'T EVER GET SICK AGAIN!

Adapting Dramatic Literature for Children

Another way children can become involved with scripted drama is through adapting dramatic literature, like the works of Shakespeare. But some people question whether Shakespeare belongs in the language arts curriculum.

SNAPSHOT: "Doesn't He Know Who Shakespeare Is?"

A surprised principal once hastily posed the question "Does Shakespeare really belong in the language arts curriculum?" while leading a group of college students to observe language arts in my third-grade class. They arrived in the middle of our production of *Julius Caesar,* just as an active Roman mob came pouring out of the classroom, screaming "Burn, burn!" and "Kill, kill!" They had been fired up by Carolyn's impassioned delivery of Mark Antony's famous speech, "Friends, Romans, countrymen, lend me your ears," delivered over the dead body of Caesar (played by Bart).

Jeff, leader of the Roman rabble, heard the principal's question to the university students and stopped dead in his tracks. He turned to me dramatically and asked with amazement, "Mrs. Cox, doesn't he know who Shakespeare is?"

All Jeff really knew about Shakespeare was that he's considered a literary master and one of the world's greatest storytellers. All I really knew about doing Shakespeare with children was that it generated tremendous enthusiasm and extended possibilities for "ripple effects" across the curriculum. My third-grade class had already had extensive experiences with drama. When I added Shakespeare, I found that his language and ideas were not too difficult for the children to read and understand at their own level. They demonstrated this by their ability to perform his plays with great feeling, style, and energy.

No one will every grasp all of Shakespeare at one time; his plays are too rich in thought and emotion to be understood quickly and easily. But we can return to him at different times in our lives and always find new meaning. Children are able to find this meaning, as well. In fact, I can think of no way to make elementary-age children read, memorize, characterize, rehearse, and present a Shakespearean play without their understanding what they're doing or wanting to do it.

TEACHING IDEA

Shakespeare for Children

And just how do you do Shakespeare with children? Here's my approach (Cox, 1980, 1985):

- ***Adapting a Script:*** First, a script is needed. To prepare it, I work with a paperback copy of the play and underline what I think are the most important and manageable parts for the age of children who will use the script. I delete what will take the play beyond their reach (e.g., scenes and characters peripheral to the main plot, long soliloquies, etc.) but try not to underestimate the children. I am constantly amazed at

(continued)

I've adapted these Shakespearean plays for children: *A Comedy of Errors; Hamlet; Julius Caesar; Macbeth; A Midsummer Night's Dream; Richard III; Romeo and Juliet; The Taming of the Shrew; The Tempest;* and *Twelfth Night.*

For an excellent source, see *Shakespeare and Macbeth: The Story Behind the Play,* by Stewart Ross (1994).

their capacity to comprehend and act on Shakespeare's words. And I have never changed his words or thought that I should. Children love to roll the words and phrases of Shakespeare off their tongues. Reading and dramatizing Shakespeare is one way to develop children's taste for a gourmet vocabulary.

A script condensed for children should play about 30 minutes. (The original would run 2 or more hours.) While rehearsing, add or subtract lines. Many children will be able to add to their parts as the play and their confidence develop.

Here are examples of three scripts for the two witches' scenes from *Macbeth,* adapted for three levels: two versions of Act IV, Scene 1, for grades K–1 and 2–3, and one version of Act I, Scene 1, for grades 4 and above:

Grades K–1

Scene: A cavern. In the middle, a boiling cauldron. Thunder. Enter the three Witches.

First Witch: Round about the cauldron go.
All: Double, double, toil and trouble; Fire burn and cauldron bubble.
Second Witch: Fillet of a fenny snake, In the cauldron boil and bake.
All: Double, double, toil and trouble; Fire burn and cauldron bubble.
Third Witch: Scale of dragon, tooth of wolf; Witches' mummy, maw of the shark.
All: Double, double, toil and trouble; Fire burn and cauldron bubble.

Grades 2–3

Scene: A cavern. In the middle, a boiling cauldron. Thunder. Enter the three Witches.

First Witch: Round about the cauldron go; In the poison'd entrails throw.
All: Double, double, toil and trouble; Fire burn and cauldron bubble.
Second Witch: Fillet of a fenny snake; In the cauldron boil and bake. Eye of the newt and toe of frog; Wool of bat and tongue of dog.
All: Double, double, toil and trouble; Fire burn and cauldron bubble.
Third Witch: Scale of dragon, tooth of wolf; Witches' mummy, maw of the salt-sea shark; Root of hemlock digged i' the dark.
All: Double, double, toil and trouble; Fire burn and cauldron bubble.
First Witch: Cool it with a baboon's blood.
Second Witch: Then the charm is firm and good.
Third Witch: By the pricking of my thumbs; Something wicked this way comes; Open, locks, whoever knocks!

Grades 4 and Above

Scene: Scotland. A deserted place. Thunder and lightning. Enter three Witches.

First Witch: When shall we three meet again, In thunder, lightning, or in rain?
Second Witch: When the hurly-burly's done, When the Battle's lost and won.
Third Witch: That will be ere the set of sun.
First Witch: Where the place?
Second Witch: Upon the heath.
Third Witch: There to meet with Macbeth.
All: Fair is foul, and foul is fair; Hover though the fog and filthy air.

(Drum within)

Third Witch: A drum, a drum! Macbeth doth come.
All: The weird sisters, hand in hand; Posters of the sea and land; Thus do go about, about; Thrice to thine, and thrice to mine; And thrice again, to make up nine. Peace! the charm's wound up.

(Enter Macbeth and Banquo)

Macbeth: So foul and fair a day I have not seen.
Banquo: What are these, So wither'd and so wild in their attaire?
Macbeth: Speak, if you can: what are you?
First Witch: All hail, Macbeth! hail to thee, thane of Glamis!
Second Witch: All hail, Macbeth! hail to thee, thane of Cawdor!
Third Witch: All hail, Macbeth! thou shalt be King hereafter!
First Witch: Hail!
Second Witch: Hail!
Third Witch: Hail!
First Witch: Lesser than Macbeth and greater.
Second Witch: Not so happy, yet much happier.
Third Witch: Thou shalt get kings, though thou be none; So all hail, Macbeth and Banquo!
First Witch: Banquo and Macbeth, all hail!
Macbeth: Stay, you imperfect speakers, tell me more; I know I am thane of Glamis; But how of Cawdor? The thane of Cawdor lives, A prosperous gentle man; and to be king stands not within the prospect of belief; No more than to be Cawdor. Say from whence you owe this strange intelligence? Speak, I charge you.

(Witches vanish)

- ***Playing Scenes from Shakespeare:*** To play these scenes from *Macbeth,* read and discuss them with the class. Then begin to turn a corner of the room into a witches' cavern on a deserted heath in Scotland. Use murals and art created by the children and add a large black pot (a trash can works well); assorted rags, capes, hoods, and brooms; and childmade ingredients for the witches' brew (e.g., "eye of newt and toe of frog," etc.).

(continued)

Begin to move students through scenes of the play as the atmosphere develops and their interest mounts. With younger children, three witches can take turns saying their lines, as the rest of the class sit in a circle and chant the refrain for "All": "Double, double, toil and trouble; Fire burn and cauldron bubble." Here's one way to play the adapted witches' scene with an entire class in grades K–3:

1. Divide the whole class into three groups, and seat them in a semicircle around the cauldron.
2. Speak the lines to all the children, while they repeat them softly.
3. Practice chanting the lines softly and with expression until students are fairly comfortable with them. Enthusiasm and energy are important here, not exactness or enunciation. The lines can be divided such that students in the three groups recite the respective witches' lines together; the entire class can respond for the "All" lines.
4. Ask for a volunteer from each group to come forward to play a witch around the cauldron. Repeat the lines in step 3 again with all the children: the standing witches and their seated classmates.
5. When the children appear confident, let the standing witches say their lines alone, while the seated children chant the refrain along with them.

Fourth-grade students present their adaptation of Macbeth in a classroom setting.

6. After this succeeds, dim the lights and put dry ice in the pot. Have students add motions, gestures, and sound effects.
7. Repeat the above steps over several periods, continuing to add motions, gestures, and sound effects as well as costumes and props. Do so until every child who wants to be a witch has had the opportunity.

Fourth- through sixth-grade children can play the scene with the witches as well as the characters of Macbeth and Banquo. When children are not playing speaking parts, they can support the players by making sound effects, such as the beat of the drum. Every child should have the chance to play the role of a witch, Macbeth, or Banquo and to serve as a member of the chorus, crew, and audience.

- ***Casting an Entire Play Adapted from Shakespeare:*** Describe the play and each part while the children have scripts in hand. Ask them each to think about which part they would most like to play, if they could choose. Students usually have questions at this time:

How big is the part?
How many lines and how many scenes does the character play?
What kind of costume does the character wear?
What are some things the character does?

After discussing these issues, have students put their heads down and raise their hands as you call the name of the part they would most like to play. If no one else raises a hand, the part is theirs. Most parts can usually be cast in this way. If more than one student wants a certain part, give them a chance to pick one of the remaining parts. If they still want the same one, have them look over a few lines and read them on the spot for the rest of the class. The class can then vote secretly for the person they feel should have the part.

Children invariably want to play the parts they feel they're most suited for, and they all want to do their best and enjoy the experience. Letting them self-select parts virtually guarantees this. Furthermore, this means of selection helps develop children's tolerance for sharing and cooperating.

Perhaps understandably, the "heavy" parts aren't always the most desired. No one may select the role of Hamlet, for instance, although several may want to play his father's ghost. Likewise, it may require some coaxing to get someone to play Macbeth, but there's never a lack of volunteers to play the three witches. No distinction according to sex needs to be made when casting characters in Shakespeare. Some of my best Hamlets have been wonderfully intense girls, and Lady Macbeth was once a perfectly ruthless fourth-grade boy. Supernatural creatures—such as witches, fairies, ghosts, and monsters—are always open to both sexes, too.

(continued)

Safety Tips for Handling Dry Ice

1. Store it in a metal container.
2. Don't touch it with bare hands.
3. To create a bubble effect, slowly pour room temperature water over the ice.

One fourth-grader described what he liked about Shakespeare: "The things I like best is when swords bust or someone goes mad."

In the case of a large class, major parts can be split between students. Macbeth can be divided neatly in two: before and after the murder of King Duncan. Lady Macbeth, usually a highly desired part, can also be divided in two: before and after she goes mad. Splitting roles like this solves the problem of having more children than parts and gives more children the chance to play a meaty role.

In drama, *blocking* means staging the movements and positions of the characters.

- ***Rehearsal:*** Blocking the play relies heavily on working together as a group and making decisions. Children may also rehearse scenes in small groups and at different times, depending on the class schedule. It's not necessary to come together as a whole group at each rehearsal.

- ***Costumes, Sets, and Properties:*** Creating costumes, sets, and props requires that children research and read to get ideas from many sources. But when the information they're seeking will help them create a Renaissance ball gown for Juliet or a rapier for Tybalt, children are highly motivated to do extensive reading with attention to meaning. During this research, students glean ideas from a great range of sources and thereby extend their reading beyond the script of the play.

The children's imagination is perhaps the best resource in creating sets and costumes. Items found at home are more than enough to outfit a play. Children are quite adept at transforming materials like cardboard room dividers into an impenetrable castle and branches and twigs into the surrounding forest. Similarly, a pair of black tights and a belted blouse changes anyone into a Renaissance rake, whereas a child in leotard and tights decorated with colored nylon net becomes a midsummer fairy.

- ***Performances:*** When performance day arrives, the teacher can do several things to put the emphasis on children and their language, rather than on technical difficulties. As mentioned earlier, a real stage can be avoided. Children are visually lost and too far removed from the audience on a stage, and their voices don't carry well. The classroom, multipurpose room, or playground are ideal places to produce Shakespeare-in-the-round with room for chairs or sitting on the floor. Curtains are also unnecessary; a door or tree can be the exit/entrance. Shakespeare's theater was actually performed this way: curtainless, in the open, on a thrust stage with an entrance/exit or two in the rear. Prompting students during performance should be avoided, too. They should be encouraged to think on their feet. If someone forgets a line, he or she should improvise another to take its place.

A Renaissance festival may precede the play, with strolling performers in costume playing recorders or guitars and passing out flowers or pieces of gingerbread, an Elizabethan treat (see p. 227). Children will enthusiastically enter the time of William Shakespeare, throwing aside their inhibitions and fear of work. Or as one youngster exclaimed when asked what he thought about doing Shakespeare, "I liked everything about it except for when we took breaks."

Other Types of Dramatic Literature to Adapt for Children

In addition to Shakespeare, many other types of dramatic literature can be adapted for children:

Greek Tragedy
Antigone (Sophocles)
Electra (Sophocles)
Prometheus Bound (Aeschylus)

Roman Comedy
The Crock of Gold (Plautus)
The Haunted House (Plautus)
Menaechmi (Plautus)

Medieval Drama
Saint George, A Christmas Play (Anonymous)

English Passion Plays
Adam, or Man's Disobedience and the Fall of Man (Anonymous)
The Deluge: Noah and His Sons (Anonymous)
The Second Shepherd's Play (Anonymous)

English Morality Play
Everyman (Anonymous)

Renaissance Drama
Ralph Roister Doister (Nicholas Udall)
Plays of William Shakespeare

Seventeenth and Eighteenth Centuries
The Imaginary Invalid (Molière)
The Physician in Spite of Himself (Molière)
Tartuffe (Molière)

Nineteenth and Twentieth Century
Androcles and the Lion (George Bernard Shaw)
Cyrano de Bergerac (Edmond Rostand)
Mary Stuart (Friedrich von Schiller)
Saint Joan (George Bernard Shaw)

Curriculum Drama

Drama is a powerful means to enrich, enliven, and expand learning across the curriculum (Nelson, 1988; Putnam, 1991). *Curriculum drama* is a term used to "describe a method by which potentially dramatic moments within required studies are identified and developed in order to heighten emotionally the students' response to the curriculum, thus deepening the learning experience" (Kelly 1981, p. 102).

Potentially dramatic moments in the curriculum could include:

- problems of social living in the classroom
- contemporary social problems and current events
- reliving events in history
- stepping into the lives of people of other cultures
- becoming characters in favorite books
- dramatizing biographies of famous people

For more on these examples see: Chapter 1, Learning and Teaching Language Arts (group workshops), and Chapter 4, Emergent Literacy (*Three Billy Goats Gruff* in kindergarten and *Johnny Appleseed* in first grade). Later in the book, see Chapter 8, Reading as a Language Art (reader's theater of *Pig Pig Rides*), and Chapter 10, Reading and Writing ("ripple effect" of colors in third and fourth grades).

- bringing myths, legends, and folktales to life
- writing and adapting scripts of fantasy or spin-offs from subjects in the content areas

In this text, we've looked at several examples of such moments of curriculum drama and drama as an integrating force in the curriculum :

- Avril Font's fourth-grade class dramatizing the life of St. George, creating a TV documentary on Shakespeare's life, and dancing around the Maypole as part of their social studies small-group study
- Marion Harris's first-grade class acting out the life of Johnny Appleseed after she read a biography of his life, which was done in conjunction with a study of how things grow and what foods we eat
- Mauretta Hurst's kindergarten class story dramatization of the *The Three Billy Goats Gruff* after reading the book by Marcia Brown (1957) and in connection with a visit to the zoo and a study of animals

In this chapter, examples of such integrating drama across the curriculum have included young children's story dramatization and art-making experiences after reading *Where the Wild Things Are* (Sendak, 1963), middle elementary school students' writing inspired by literature and content-area study in social studies and science in the fantasy "The Tale of an Unfair Election"; and adaptations of dramatic literature, such as Shakespeare. The latter is an example of how to integrate learning in all subjects throughout an entire school.

All these activities were generated by "ripple effects," as one discussion or activity led to another and another. At times, though, teachers need to give initiating or demonstrating lessons to help students acquire specific knowledge or skills needed for further activities. Here are some ideas for both kinds of lessons:

Initiating Lessons	***Demonstrating Lessons***
Sense-training exercises: Hold a baby animal (individual) Pass a basket of fruit (group)	*Prepare a story for dramatization:* Identify characters and sequences of events Make a story map
Pantomime and improvisation: Telephone conversation (individual) Imaginary journey (group)	*Scriptwriting:* Blocking ideas and sequencing dialogue and revision
Literature discussions for dramatization Music, movement, dance, art making Reading dramatic literature, such as Shakespeare Clustering/webbing ideas for curriculum drama	*Reader's theater:* How to adapt a script Blocking action for a play, such as Shakespeare Research and report writing

SNAPSHOT: Back to the Renaissance

One year, I directed a cross-curricular study of the Renaissance in an entire school at the invitation of the principal, Orlena MacKenzie, a strong believer in the arts in education. The result was 2 weeks of concentrated schoolwide and classroom activities that culminated in a Renaissance Fair, held in conjunction with the school Book Fair. The gym was decorated with the children's art and writings, and teachers, children, and parents came to the fair in Renaissance dress. Renaissance theater treats of mead and gingersnaps were served, and a Renaissance recorder group from Louisiana State University played.

Recipe for Gingersnaps

1. Cream $^3/_4$ cup shortening and 1 cup sugar (brown or white).
2. Add 1 egg and 4 tablespoons molasses.
3. Sift and add 2 cups flour, 2 teaspoons baking soda, 1 teaspoon each ginger, cloves, and cinnamon.
4. Roll into balls and then in sugar.
5. Arrange evenly on a cookie sheet.
6. Bake at 350–375° for 10–12 minutes.

During the fair, each class presented what they had learned about the Renaissance or a scene from a Shakespearean play. For instance, fourth-grade classes presented reports on William Shakespeare and Renaissance weapons, complete with displays, murals, and demonstrations. A fifth-grade class reported on Renaissance music and did a recorder demonstration. Dramatic presentations included the witches scene from *Macbeth* (done by kindergarten, first-, and second-grade classes), the funeral oration scene from *Julius Caesar* (third grade), and various scenes from *Romeo and Juliet* and *Hamlet* (fourth and fifth grades).

The event was later featured as the lead article in the award-winning school newspaper *Paw Prints:*

> **Learning about the Renaissance**
> I love the exciting times of the Renaissance! I hope you like to get in touch with the Renaissance world like I do. Dr. Carole Cox Spates, a teacher from LSU, came to Walnut Hills. She showed us books, costumes, and great scenes by William Shakespeare, like Hamlet, which was acted out by students.

I used the adaptations of the witches scenes shown on pp. 220–221.

Children become interested in reading Shakespeare by dramatizing his plays.

> Then her husband, Mr. Spates, taught us how to use a sword, and how the people used the sword in Renaissance times. It was a lot of entertainment for me! But, the guy who was fencing against me won the fight.
>
> Thursday, February 16, I came with my parents to a Renaissance party at school. It was very exciting for me too, because I was wearing a Renaissance costume. —*A fifth-grader*

Articles by many children filled the pages of the school newspaper. Two of the children's written comments especially underscore the impact of this cross-curricular study of the Renaissance and Shakespeare:

> Shakespeare was a magnificent man. He was a play writer. He wrote plays such as Macbeth, Hamlet, Julius Caesar, and Romeo and Juliet. Feb. 16 we relived his plays. It was as if Shakespeare were inside us. Shakespeare will always live because of his plays. —*A fifth-grader*
>
> All around the school of Walnut Hills, kids and teachers have been talking about Shakespeare. Everyone knows he's a wonderful person, and he's been writing stories like Macbeth, Hamlet, and more. Even now he's gone, we still are looking back to his stories and enjoying them. —*A third-grader*

One teacher in particular, Lynn Lastrapes, was so enthusiastic about going back to the Renaissance that she wrote me a letter and we later talked about what happened in her class:

> I truthfully wondered how second-graders could understand some of the complicated plots and characterizations. Except for your talk to us, I never would have thought to try this myself. I didn't take to Shakespeare until after college, and I was an English major! I felt excited, stimulated, and good the whole week. I still do. I loved it for myself but even more for the way my class took to it. Even students who normally don't do very well loved it. They all seemed to relish the "meatiness" of the stories. There was so much going on. Their interest was thrilling.

Lynn discussed some of the many things that happened in her classroom after introducing Shakespeare:

- The class read 15 to 20 minutes of Shakespeare after lunch every day and completed four plays. The students were able to remember and compare things from all the plays.
- Vocabulary was greatly enhanced, with little effort from Lynn.
- The students could tell the play in their own words.
- Students imagined how various characters felt and shared how they would feel if they were certain characters.

- The class listened to music, like Mendelssohn's *A Midsummer Night's Dream* and Pavarotti singing the aria "O figli miei! Ah! la paterna mano," in which Macduff is thinking of how Macbeth murdered his children. (According to Lynn, "They were moved, I tell you! Even though it was in Italian, they felt the emotion.")
- During Brotherhood Week, the class used *Romeo and Juliet* as one of its stories and talked about the consequences of not being kind to one another.
- Several students thanked Lynn for letting them know about an LSU production of *Hamlet.* They went and loved it. (Lynn said, "Second-graders going to *Hamlet* is beautiful!")

Lynn told me, "The children are clamoring for more Shakespeare. I want to do *The Tempest* next year. *I* want more, too."

To learn more about Shakespeare and the Renaissance, try these children's books:

Bard of Avon: The Story of William Shakespeare (Stanley & Vennema, 1992)
Favorite Tales from Shakespeare (Miles, 1985)
Good Queen Bess: The Story of Elizabeth of England (Stanley & Vennema, 1990)
One Day in Elizabethan England (Kirtland, 1962)
Shakespeare and His Theatre (Brown, 1982)
Shakespeare Stories (Garfield, 1985)
Shakespeare and His Theatre (Stewart, 1973)
Shakespeare's England (Horizon Magazine Editors, 1964)
Shakespeare's Theatre (Hodges, 1966)
Stories from Shakespeare (Chute, 1976)
Tales from Shakespeare (Lamb & Lamb, 1979)
Will Shakespeare and the Globe Theatre (White, 1955)
William Shakespeare (Lepscky, 1988)
William Shakespeare and His Plays (Haines, 1968)
The World Awakes: The Renaissance in Western Europe (Brooks & Walworth, 1962)

Assessing Drama in the Classroom

Drama assessment is an ongoing process for teachers and children. This is also one of the important instances in which children can and should be involved as much as teachers in evaluating their own progress and that of the group. When children are involved in this way, assessment becomes a basis on which to build further instruction. Drama is student centered, not criterion referenced. Both teachers and students need to assess and understand what happened during Monday's session before planning and preparing for Tuesday's.

Another significant aspect of drama assessment is that the teacher, as the evaluator, is continually modeling important positive behaviors for students' self- and group assessments. What the teacher says and how he or she says it will affect how students evaluate and plan with each other, which is an integral part of all drama activities. Keep in mind that drama is always a cooperative group effort. In fact, one of the greatest benefits of drama is that it develops self-awareness and self-concept within an encouraging and supportive environment.

Four types of assessment are appropriate for drama:

1. ***Observations and Play Notes:*** The teacher should observe and take play notes during any type of drama session to provide the basis for follow-up discussions. Improvement, words of encouragement and praise, and questions and suggestions should all be jotted down for use during conferences.

2. ***Conferences:*** Conferences are a critical component of every type of drama session. The teacher must remember that he or she is a model of the type of constructive assessment the children will hopefully emulate. Conferences are essential to planning for the next drama session. Types of questions for leading these conference discussions include:

- What did you see that you liked?
- What did you enjoy doing or watching?
- Whom did you notice doing something really well (or interesting, imaginative, different, humorous)?
- Why did you like what they did?
- What do we need to work on next time? How can we do this?
- What should we concentrate on next time? (*Ideas:* concentration, cooperation, teamwork, movement, pace, energy, staying in character, dialogue, voice, gestures, using space, traffic patterns)

3. ***Anecdotal Records and Logs:*** Teachers should keep anecdotal records and logs to follow an individual's or group's progress. This type of information is useful for planning future drama experiences, pupil assessment, and parent conferences.

4. ***Student Self-Assessment:*** Teachers may develop forms or questionnaires for students, such as the one shown in Figure 6.4. Second-grader Ryan completed this form after playing several parts in *Macbeth*. His responses demonstrate the potential of drama in education for learning, living, and language. Forms such as this should include things that the teacher feels are important or pertain to the type of drama activity. These forms can be used during conferences; the teacher can write down young children's responses, and older students can record their own. This kind of informal self-assessment can provide insight into children's understanding of the narrative form and content of drama, of their parts in specific drama activities, and of their feelings about participating in drama.

NAME Ryan GRADE COMPLETED 2

Tell about the play by William Shakespeare.

It is about a man that was contro-
lied by witches. He takes over the
kingdom. And is killed bya brave
nobleman called Macduff

Whch character(s) do you play? Dun kin lennox docter sword

Tell about your character.

Dunkin is the kingof scot land.
Lennox is anodleman
The docter is a docter
Sword is the son of gener al Sword

What is the most important thing about the play?

Its Super natural

What is the most important thing about your character?

His king
nothing
Hes a docter
He fites macbeth

How did you feel about doing Shakespeare

happy

FIGURE 6.4 Student's Responses to Playing Shakespeare

Answers to Questions about Drama in the Classroom

1. *What is the role of drama in education?*

Drama should be central, rather than peripheral, in education. Piaget showed that children use imitation to learn and that they come to play and drama naturally as they learn to communicate with others. Drama reflects a social constructivist perspective of learning by doing through social interaction. Drama emphasizes the aesthetic, transactional experiencing of literature and drama as art forms in a student- and response-centered curriculum, in which language use is focused on meaning. Student's participation in drama provides great potential to develop language and literacy, communication in social contexts, learning in other content areas, and personal growth and development. As a mixed art, drama is ideal for integrated teaching across the curriculum.

2. *How should we teach drama?*

Drama experiences should always be student and response centered, "concerned with the development of people, not the development of drama" (Way, 1967. pp. 2–3). Appropriate experiences in drama that can be integrated across the curriculum include creative dramatics, a process-centered form of drama that consists of sense training, pantomime and improvisation, and story dramatization. Informal drama, such as creative dramatics, is an excellent activity for language-minority students, because it provides direct experience and offers rich, comprehensible language input in a low-anxiety setting. Scriptwriting can be done as a whole-class activity or in small groups, with children creating original scripts from their own experiences or in response to literature and other media. Reader's theater is a form of scripted performance in which students prepare and then read poems and stories for an audience. Dramatic literature, such as Shakespeare, may also be adapted, shared, and performed in the classroom. All forms of drama activities are ideal means for integrating learning across the curriculum, which is called *curriculum drama:* using potentially dramatic moments in all subject areas to heighten students' response to and understanding of the curriculum.

LOOKING FURTHER

1 Try out several of the sense-training activities with small groups of children. Brainstorm a list of other ideas for use with them.

2 List several stories suitable for dramatization with children. Choose one and develop an initiating lesson for a story dramatization. Try it out with children.

3 Identify several stories suitable for adaptation to a reader's theater script for a given grade level. Adapt one of them into a script, and play it with others in your college class. Then try it with children.

4 Adapt one scene from a Shakespearean play according to the suggestions in this chapter.

5 Play the witches' scene from *Macbeth* with a group of children.

RESOURCES

Cottrell, J. (1987). *Creative drama in the classroom: Grades 4–6.* Lincolnwood, IL: National Textbook.

Cottrell, J. (1987). *Creative drama in the classroom: Grades 1–3.* Lincolnwood, IL: National Textbook.

Heathcote, D. (1980). *Drama as context.* Aberdeen, Scotland: National Association for the Teaching of English.

McCaslin, N. (1990). *Creative drama in the classroom* (5th ed.). New York: Longman.

Stewig, J., & Buege, C. (1994). *Dramatizing literature in whole language classrooms.* New York: Teachers College Press.

Tarlington, C., & Verriour, P. (1991). *Role drama: A teacher's handbook.* Portsmouth, NH: Heinemann.

REFERENCES

Chapman, G. (1984). *Young playwrights.* Portsmouth, NH: Heinemann.

Christie, J. (1990). Dramatic play: A context for meaningful engagements. *Reading Teacher, 43,* 542–545.

Cox, C. (1980). Shakespeare and company: The best in classroom reading and drama. *Reading Teacher, 33,* 438–441.

Cox, C. (1985). Stirring up Shakespeare in the elementary school. In C. Carter (Ed.), *Literature—News that stays news: Fresh approaches to the classics* (pp. 51–58). Urbana, IL: National Council of Teachers of English.

Cox, C. (1988). Scriptwriting in small groups. In J. Golub (Ed.), *Student-to-student: Practice in cooperative learning* (pp. 32–39). Urbana, IL: National Council of Teachers of English.

Davis, J. H., & Behm, T. (1978). Terminology of drama/Theatre with and for children: A redefinition. *Children's Theatre Review, 27,* 10–11.

Duke, C. (1974). *Creative dramatics and English teaching.* Urbana, IL: National Council of Teachers of English.

Dyson, A. H. (1986). The imaginary worlds of childhood: A multimedia presentation. *Language Arts, 63,* 799–808.

Galda, L. (1984). Narrative competence: Play, storytelling, and story comprehension. In A. Pellegrini & T. Yawkey (Eds.), *The development of oral and written language in social contexts* (pp. 105–117). Norwood, NJ: Ablex.

Heathcote, D. (1981). Drama as education. In N. McCaslin (Ed.), *Children and drama* (2nd ed.). New York: Longman.

Heathcote, D. (1983). Learning, knowing, and languaging in drama. *Language Arts, 60.* 695–701.

Heinig, R. (1992). *Improvisations with favorite tales: Integrating drama into the reading/writing classroom.* Portsmouth, NH: Heinemann.

Joint Committee of the National Council of Teachers of English and Children's Theatre Association. (1983). Forum: Informal classroom drama. *Language Arts, 60,* 370–372.

Kelly, E. F. (1981). Curriculum drama. In N. McCaslin (Ed.), *Children and drama* (2nd ed.). New York: Longman.

Martinez, M. (1993). Motivating dramatic story reenactments. *Reading Teacher, 46,* 682–688.

Nelson, P. (1988). Drama, doorway to the past. *Language Arts, 65,* 20–25.

Pellegrini, A. D. (1984). Symbolic functioning and children's early writing: The relations between kindergartners' play and isolated word-writing fluency. In R. Beach & L. S. Bridwell (Eds.), *New directions in composition research* (pp. 274–284). New York: Guilford.

Pellegrini, A. D. (1985). The relations between symbolic play and literate behavior: A review and critique of the empirical literature. *Review of Educational Research, 55,* 107–121.

Pellegrini, A. D., & Galda, L. (1982). The effects of thematic-fantasy play training on the development of children's story comprehension. *American Educational Research Journal, 19,* 443–452.

Piaget, J. (1962). *Play, dreams, and imitation in childhood.* New York: Norton.

Putnam, L. (1991). Dramatizing non-fiction with emerging readers. *Language Arts, 68,* 463–469.

Rosenblatt, L. M. (1978). *The reader, the text, the poem: The transactional theory of the literary work.* Carbondale, IL: Southern Illinois University Press.

Siks, G. B. (1983). *Drama with children.* New York: Harper & Row.

Sklar, D. (1991). *Playmaking: Children writing and performing their own plays.* New York: Teachers and Writers Collaborative.

Verriour , P. (1986). Creating worlds of dramatic discourse. *Language Arts, 63,* 253–263.

Vygotsky, L. S. (1967). Play and its role in the mental development of the child. *Soviet Psychology, 12,* 62–67.

Vygotsky, L. S. (1978). In M. Cole, V. John-Steiner, S. Scribner, & E. Souberman (Eds.), *Mind in society: The development of higher psychological processes*. Cambridge: Harvard University Press.

Wagner, B. J. (1988). Research currents: does classroom drama affect the arts of language? *Language Arts, 65*, 46–55.

Wagner, B. J. (1992). Imaginative expression. In J. Flood, J. Jensen, D. Lapp, & J. Squire (Eds.), *Handbook of research on teaching the English language arts* (pp. 787–804). New York: Macmillan.

Ward, W. (1957). *Playmaking with children* (2nd ed.). New York: Appleton-Century-Crofts.

Way, B. (1967). *Development through drama*. New York: Humanities Press.

Yawkey, T. D. (1980). Effects of social relationships curricula and sex differences on reading and imaginativeness in young children. *Alberta Journal of Educational Research, 26*, 159–167.

Young, T., & Vardell, S. (1993). Weaving Reader's Theater and nonfiction into the curriculum. *Reading Teacher, 46*, 396–405.

CHILDREN'S BOOKS

Blume, J. (1972). *Tales of a fourth grade nothing*. New York: Dutton.

Bonsall, C. (1971). *The case of the scaredy cats*. New York: Harper.

Brooks, P., & Walworth, N. (1962). *The world awakes: The Renaissance in Western Europe*. New York: Lippincott.

Brown, J. R. (1982). *Shakespeare and his theatre*. New York: Lothrop, Lee & Shepard.

Brown, M. (1957). *The three billy goats gruff*. New York: Harcourt Brace Jovanovich.

Chute, M. (1976). *Stories from Shakespeare*. New York: New American Library.

Garfield, L. (1985). *Shakespeare stories*. New York: Schocken.

Grahame, K. (1953). *The reluctant dragon*. New York: Holiday House.

Haines, C. (1968). *William Shakespeare and his plays*. New York: Franklin Watts.

Hodges, C. W. (1966). *Shakespeare's theatre*. New York: Coward McCann.

Horizon Magazine Editors. (1964). *Shakespeare's England*. New York: American Heritage.

Kirtland, G. B. (1962). *One day in Elizabethan England*. New York: Harcourt Brace Jovanovich.

Kraus, R. (1971). *Leo the late bloomer*. New York: Windmill Books.

Kraus, R. (1974). *Owliver*. New York: Windmill Books.

Lamb, C., & Lamb, M. (1979). *Tales from Shakespeare*. New York: Dutton.

Lepscky, I. (1988). *William Shakespeare*. New York: Barrons.

Lewis, C. S. (1950). *The lion, the witch, and the wardrobe*. New York: Macmillan.

Lionni, L. (1967). *Frederick*. New York: Pantheon.

Lionni, L. (1970). *Fish is fish*. New York: Pantheon.

Miles, B. (1985). *Favorite tales from Shakespeare*. New York: Macmillan.

Parish, P. (1963). *Amelia Bedelia*. New York: Harper.

Ross, S. (1994). *Shakespeare and Macbeth: The story behind the play*. New York: Viking.

Sendak, M. (1963). *Where the wild things are*. New York: Harper.

Seuss, Dr. (1940). *Horton hatches the egg*. New York: Random House.

Seuss, Dr. (1957). *How the grinch stole Christmas*. New York: Random House.

Shirreffs, G. D. (1962). *The mystery of the haunted mine*. New York: Scholastic.

Silverstein, S. (1974). *Where the sidewalk ends*. New York: Harper.

Silverstein, S. (1981). *A light in the attic*. New York: Harper.

Stanley, D., & Vennema, P. (1990). *Good Queen Bess: The story of Elizabeth of England*. New York: Morrow.

Stanley, D., & Vennema, P. (1992). *Bard of Avon: The story of William Shakespeare*. New York: Morrow.

Stewart, P. (1973). *Shakespeare and his theatre*. London, England: Wayland.

White, A. T. (1955). *Will Shakespeare and the Globe Theatre*. New York: Random House.

Wiseman, B. (1978). *Morris has a cold*. New York: Dodd Mead.

Chapter 7

Teaching with Literature

Questions about Teaching with Literature

1. *How do readers respond to literature?*
2. *What is response-centered, integrated teaching with literature?*

Reflective Response

Think about a favorite book that you read as a child or that someone read to you. Jot down whatever you want about the book.

Reader Response to Literature

Literature-based teaching has been a major curricular development in recent years, particularly in whole-language instruction. There has been a shift from teacher- and text-centered approaches, which use basal readers and textbooks for other school subjects (e.g., social studies and science), to a student- and response-centered approach, which uses whole, meaningful texts, such as children's literature and own writing, for teaching with literature across the curriculum. For teachers, this shift has involved changing not only the types of texts they use but how they use them, as well (Langer, 1992). Reader-response theory has guided this shift (Beach, 1993).

A *text* is not just a textbook but anything you read: books, newspapers, menus, magazines, letters, advertising, road signs, and so on.

Reader-response theorists suggest that readers are actively engaged in constructing meaning while reading, not passively receiving meaning. In short, reading is an active process. It is the *creation* of meaning, rather than the *discovery* of it. And because meaning is created by individual readers, there is no single correct meaning of any text.

Transactions with Literature

See Chapters 1 (Teaching and Learning Language Arts), 5 (Listening and Talking), and 9 (The Writing Process) for more on the transactional theory, reading, and teaching.

Among reader-response theorists, Louise Rosenblatt's (1938/1978) *transactional model* of the reading process has especially interested whole-language elementary educators (Cox & Zarrillo, 1993; Goodman, 1992). She calls the reading process a transaction, during which a "live circuit" is created between the reader and text. According to Rosenblatt (1994), "Every reading act is an event, or a transaction involving a particular reader and a particular pattern of signs, a text, and occurring at a particular time in a particular context. Instead of two fixed entities acting on one another, the reader and the text are two aspects of a total dynamic situation. The 'meaning' does not reside ready-made 'in' the text or 'in' the reader but happens or comes into being during the transaction between reader and text" (p. 1063).

Although all reading occurs as experienced meaning, Rosenblatt suggests that readers assume a *stance;* that is, they focus their selective attention in different ways. A reader's stance represents the readiness to organize his or her thinking about what he or she is reading according to a more efferent or aesthetic framework. During a more *efferent* reading, the reader's focus is on the information he or she will take away from the text, or the more public as-

The word *efferent* comes from the Latin *effere,* which means "to take away."

pects—for example, reading the label on a medicine bottle to find out the correct dosage. During a more *aesthetic* reading, the reader focuses on the lived-through experience of the reading event, or the more private aspects—for example, reading a novel for enjoyment and picturing yourself as one of the characters. In sum, an efferent reading focuses strictly on what the book says, whereas an aesthetic reading focuses on the associations, feelings, attitudes, and ideas that the words in the book arouse in the reader.

Any text can be read more efferently or aesthetically, and readers move back and forth between these two extremes along on a continuum, eventually settling on one predominant stance (see Figure 7.1). For example, you could read *Gone with the Wind* efferently and learn about the Civil War and the post-war South, or you could read it aesthetically and imagine what it would be like to involved in a turbulent relationship like that of Scarlett O'Hara and Rhett Butler.

Rosenblatt maintains that for most experiences with literature, "our primary responsibility is to encourage the aesthetic stance" (1982, p. 275). Yet a study of teachers who made the shift from using a basal reader to literature-based reading found that they still use a teacher- and text-centered

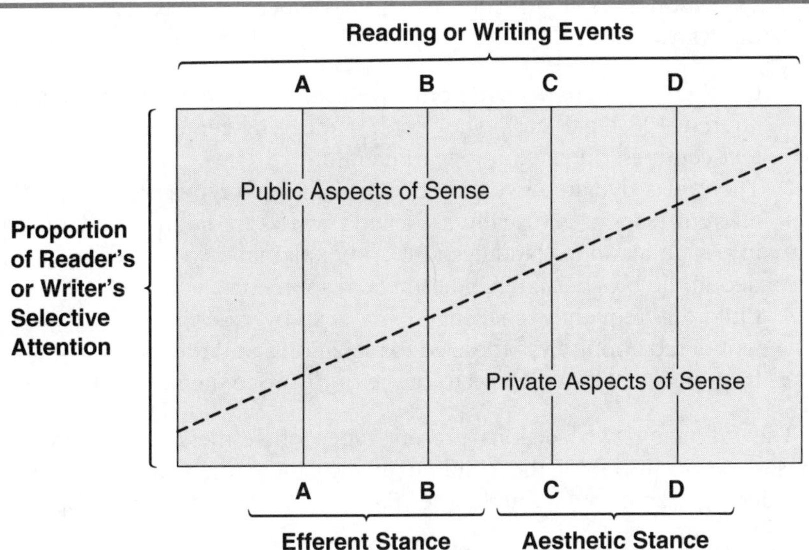

FIGURE 7.1 The Efferent-Aesthetic Continuum

Any linguistic activity has both public (lexical, analytic, abstracting) and private (experiential, affective, associational) components. Stance is determined by the proportion of each component admitted into the scope of selective attention. The efferent stance draws mainly on the public aspect of sense: the aesthetic stance includes proportionally more of the experiential, private aspect.

Reading or writing events A and B fall into the efferent part of the continuum, with B admitting more private elements. Reading or writing events C and D both represent the aesthetic stance, with C according a higher proportion of attention to the public aspects of sense.

Source: Figure 1 from "The transactional theory of reading and writing," Louise M. Rosenblatt, in *Theoretical Models and Processes of Reading*, 4th ed., Robert B. Ruddell, Martha Rapp Ruddell, and Harry Singer (Eds.), 1994. Reprinted with permission of Louise M. Rosenblatt and the International Reading Association.

(i.e., more efferent) approach (Zarrillo & Cox, 1992). These teachers changed the type of text but not how they used it.

For example, one teacher used a more efferent approach by asking students to read *Charlotte's Web* (White, 1952) and write down all the words they didn't know how to spell for their spelling words that week. A more appropriate aesthetic approach would be to first direct children to write what they thought about the story in their literature response journals and then to bring up these ideas in a literature discussion. Even though reading and responding to literature can certainly support spelling development, spelling should not be the first thing children's attention is directed to after they have experienced a beautifully written work like *Charlotte's Web.*

How Children Respond

A key to response-centered teaching with literature is knowing how children respond. This knowledge should provide the basis for asking questions and planning further experiences with literature. I have been collecting responses from the same group of children as they've moved from kindergarten to fifth grade. The results of this 6-year longitudinal study, involving analysis of the children's responses from a reader-response perspective (Cox, 1994a; 1994b), are as follows:

The following children's books were read in this study: *The Snowy Day* (Keats, 1963), *Make Way for Ducklings* (McCloskey, 1941), *Miss Rumphius* (Cooney, 1982), *Rosie's Walk* (Hutchins, 1968), *Umbrella* (Yashima, 1958), *Alexander and the Terrible, Horrible, No Good, Very Bad Day* (Viorst, 1972), *The Nicest Gift* (Politi, 1973), *Caps for Sale* (Slobodkina, 1947), *Ira Sleeps Over* (Waber, 1972), and *Nana Upstairs & Nana Downstairs* (de Paola, 1973).

1. Children's responses were primarily aesthetic (71.6 percent) rather than efferent (28.4 percent). They took a meaning-centered rather than a text-centered orientation toward literature.
2. There was dynamic interplay between the two types of stances. More efferent responses, usually associated with a traditional view of reading, such as understanding print and explaining, were always embedded in the broader-ranging aesthetic responses.
3. Children frequently challenged the text by questioning things they wondered about, hypothesized explanations, and drew on associations from personal experiences to prove or disprove them.

The following two sections present types of aesthetic and efferent responses (respectively) of the children in my study. Changes that occurred from kindergarten through third grade (K–3) are illustrated with examples:

Types of Aesthetic Responses: Focus on What the Text Aroused in the Reader

• ***Questioning:*** Children responded in this way when something puzzled them or made them wonder. For kindergartners, this meant addressing things that seemed peculiar or foreign. Questioning became more complex in first through third grades, as students questioned and explored ideas that could not be verified by the text. Here are examples of questions asked by students:

Kindergartner: What's a tropical island?
First-Grader: What kind of dinner is she having? Chicken? No. Not chicken. She is a chicken.

• ***Text Part:*** Students who responded in this way often began with "I like the part when . . ."—something specific had struck them. This response was frequently an opening for a more extended response, such as associating what happened in the story with a personal experience or explanation. This type of response changed little from K–3:

Kindergartner: I like the part when Mrs. Duck was crossing the street.
Third-Grader: Do you know my favorite page? Right here. Because I like bees.

• ***Associations:*** This type of reader response involved associating what was read with a personal experience, another story (i.e., intertextual), or a metaphor:

Kindergartner: I want a kitty but Dad's allergic.
First-Grader: It's like *Frosty the Snowman* on TV.

• ***Hypothesizing:*** Kindergartners who responded in this way predicted, speculated, retrospected, or extended the story. First- through third-graders hypothesized many possibilities while exploring anomalies they found in the story:

Kindergartner: Maybe her fairy godmother made her grow up.
Third-Grader: Ira shouldn't have been afraid to take his teddy bear, 'cause if Reggie's such a good friend, he shouldn't laugh. Sometimes I feel like laughing—but I don't.

• ***Performance:*** Students who responded like this were verbal and nonverbal, acted out, role-played by pretending to be characters or talking to characters, created sound effects, took action, and pantomimed. Kindergartners were more physical than first- and second-graders, and these behaviors had all but disappeared by third grade. For instance:

Kindergartner: Hi, Michael! Quack! Quack! (Flaps arms like a duck)
Second-Grader: Carlitos goes "Blanco, Blanco." (Mimes calling dog's name)

Types of Efferent Responses: Focus on Information to Take Away from the Text

• ***Explanations:*** Kindergartners looked at cause and effect, made generalizations, and drew conclusions. These responses become more extended through third grade and evolved from aesthetic responses, especially questioning. For example:

Kindergartner: Her hair's turning white because she's getting old.
Third-Grader: Reggie probably has a teddy bear too but just doesn't want to show Ira he's a scaredy cat and sleeps with a teddy bear.

• ***Print and Language:*** Kindergartners used letters, words, sentences, and rhyming patterns. First- and second-graders read words and phrases, joined in repeated language patterns, and read independently. By the third grade, children showed virtually no interest in print and language:

Kindergartner: This looks like a *T.* What does this say?
First-Grader: Want me to read this story to you? I know how. Let's try.
Second-Grader: (Read the whole text of *Rosie's Walk* [Hutchins, 1968].)

• ***Content:*** Retelling, listing, sequencing, or summarizing were common among kindergartners, but in no more than single sentences. Longer plot summaries were produced by first-graders, and students continued to retell and summarize through second grade but not by listing or sequencing. This response category had disappeared by third grade. Here are examples:

Kindergartner: He put the snowball in his pocket.
First-Grader: It was all about a fox and a hen.
Second-Grader: The monkeys keeped on copying him.

• ***Analysis:*** In kindergartners, analysis meant applying a critical framework: testing the story as facts against reality. Children in grades 1–3 made critical comments about the accuracy of facts, the author, and the writing style, illustrations, and book design. For instance:

Kindergartner: Could this be real? Ducks can't talk!
Third-Grader: Bernard Waber. He illustrated the pictures, too? They go really well with the story.

Children's Preferred Response Types

The following list shows children's preferred response types in order, from most to least used:

1. Questioning	19.0 percent
2. Text part	17.4 percent
3. Associations	15.0 percent
4. Hypothesizing	13.6 percent
5. Explanations	10.2 percent
6. Print and language	8.0 percent
7. Content	7.0 percent
8. Performance	6.8 percent
9. Analysis	4.1 percent

You can see that children's stances toward literature were primarily aesthetic.

Now think about your own response to literature: How would you describe the stance you took in thinking about your favorite children's book in the chapter-opening?

SNAPSHOT: How to Find a Lost Mine and Other Treasures in Children's Books

Student- and response-centered teaching with literature is a powerful means to actively engage children in experiences with literature and reading, to focus on the personal construction of meaning, and to integrate the curriculum. I discovered this almost by chance during my first year of teaching. As my fourth-grade class and I quietly pored over paperback book club order forms, three students approached me excitedly, saying, "Miss Shirreffs, there's a book in here with your name on it!" "Impossible," I countered, "No one has a name like that except my family." "It's true," they insisted, and they were right. My father is Gordon D. Shirreffs, an author of Western novels who has also written many books of historical and regional fiction for children and young adults.

See Cox (1986), "Gordon D. Shirreffs: An Interview with a Western Writer," *English Journal, 75,* 40–48.

More children's books about the Southwest by Gordon D. Shirreffs: *Mystery of Lost Canyon* (1963); *Mystery of the Lost Cliff Dwelling* (1968); *The Secret of the Spanish Desert* (1964) (sequel to *The Mystery of the Haunted Mine*); *Son of the Thunder People* (1957); and *Swiftwagon* (1958).

By now, the entire class was interested. Many students ordered their own paperback copies of *The Mystery of the Haunted Mine* (Shirreffs, 1962), a contemporary tale of mystery and adventure set in the rugged Arizona mountain country. In it, three young people search for an elusive lost Spanish gold mine that's supposedly been guarded by the spirit of the outlaw Asesino for over 50 years.

The day the books arrived was exciting for the children and significant for me in terms of how I began to perceive the role of literature in teaching language arts. Before this experience, I wasn't fully aware of how simultaneously easy and essential it is to base language and literacy learning across the curriculum on literature. Now, I can't imagine it any other way. And the children showed me how it should be done.

Here's a step-by-step review of what happened in this fourth-grade class and others that I taught, when one book set off a "ripple effect" of literature-based, response-themed learning:

1. ***Reading Aloud, Along, and Alone:*** I read a chapter of *The Mystery of the Haunted Mine* aloud every day, and it soon became the high point. Some students read along in their own copies (and some read ahead on their own, because they couldn't wait to find out what happened next). Others put their heads down on their desks and became lost in listening to the story of Gary, Tuck, and Sue, as they unraveled the mystery of the lost map and mine.

See Chapter 5, Listening and Talking, for more on reading aloud.

2. ***Talking Together:*** Time for talking after reading gave children the opportunity to reflect and respond, focus their thinking, clarify feelings, develop concepts, and share ideas as they thought aloud and talked with others—students and the teacher. I started each discussion with an open question: "What did you think?"

3. ***Writing in Literature Response Journals:*** Students wrote in their literature response journals each day when something about the book struck them, raised a question, or prompted a personal association. They could write while I read (or they read) or before or after our discussions. These journals became a record of each student's response to the book.

4. ***Response Options:*** In addition to talking and writing in literature response journals, I offered other options for response: talking in groups or with buddies; other types of writing; drawing, artmaking, or mediamaking; and drama. These optional responses became the basis for further integrated activities across the curriculum.

5. ***Focal Topics of Interest:*** The questions from students that emerged during whole-class discussions and other times gave us many ideas about how to extend literature reading and responding as well as experiences across the curriculum. I wrote down the following focal questions:

What would we do if we were Gary, Tuck, and Sue? How would we go about looking for the map and the treasure?
How would we feel if we were them?
Was there really a treasure? Whose was it?
What are the desert and mountains in Arizona like?
What were the Native Americans like there?
Are there other mines and treasures in Arizona?
Was this one really haunted?

Through further discussions and planning times, these questions became focal topics for more experiences.

6. ***Literature Groups:*** We formed literature groups to read and find out more about what questions interested students most. Each group developed their own questions and ideas for further learning experiences with literature across the curriculum.

7. ***Gathering Related Books and Resources:*** When one child brought in a map of Arizona, saved from a family trip, I invited others to do the same. Soon, a table and bookshelf were crowded with maps, postcards, rock collections, Native American artifacts, and a snakeskin and some real rattlesnake rattles. This area became our Center for Study of the Southwest United States. I began to look for related children's fiction and informational books and media to build our classroom study and literature center.

8. ***Wide Independent Reading:*** I learned to help students find books they were interested in or that related to the focal topic for wide independent reading. From discussions about the book, I discovered that some students had a real interest in mysteries; others, in stories about the supernatural; and still others, in adventure stories. I asked the school librarian for ideas and books lists.

9. ***Integrating Teaching across the Curriculum:*** Reading *The Mystery of the Haunted Mine* started a "ripple effect" of response-themed experiences about the Southwest United States that included social studies (history, geography, and Native American, Hispanic, and Anglo cultures), science (geology and ecology of the desert), the arts, and mathematics. Figure 7.2 shows the range of possible focal topics, learning experiences, and related books for research and wide independent reading by individuals or literature groups. Ever since my first experience with literature-based teaching, the beginning of any theme cycle or unit of study has been the time for me to gather a nucleus of good children's books—both nonfiction and fiction—around which to center opportunities for response-centered experiences related to students' interests. And well into the cycle or unit, I've continued to add books, based on my ongoing observation of students' responses.

Keep a record of theme-related books, making brief annotations on note cards or in a computer file.

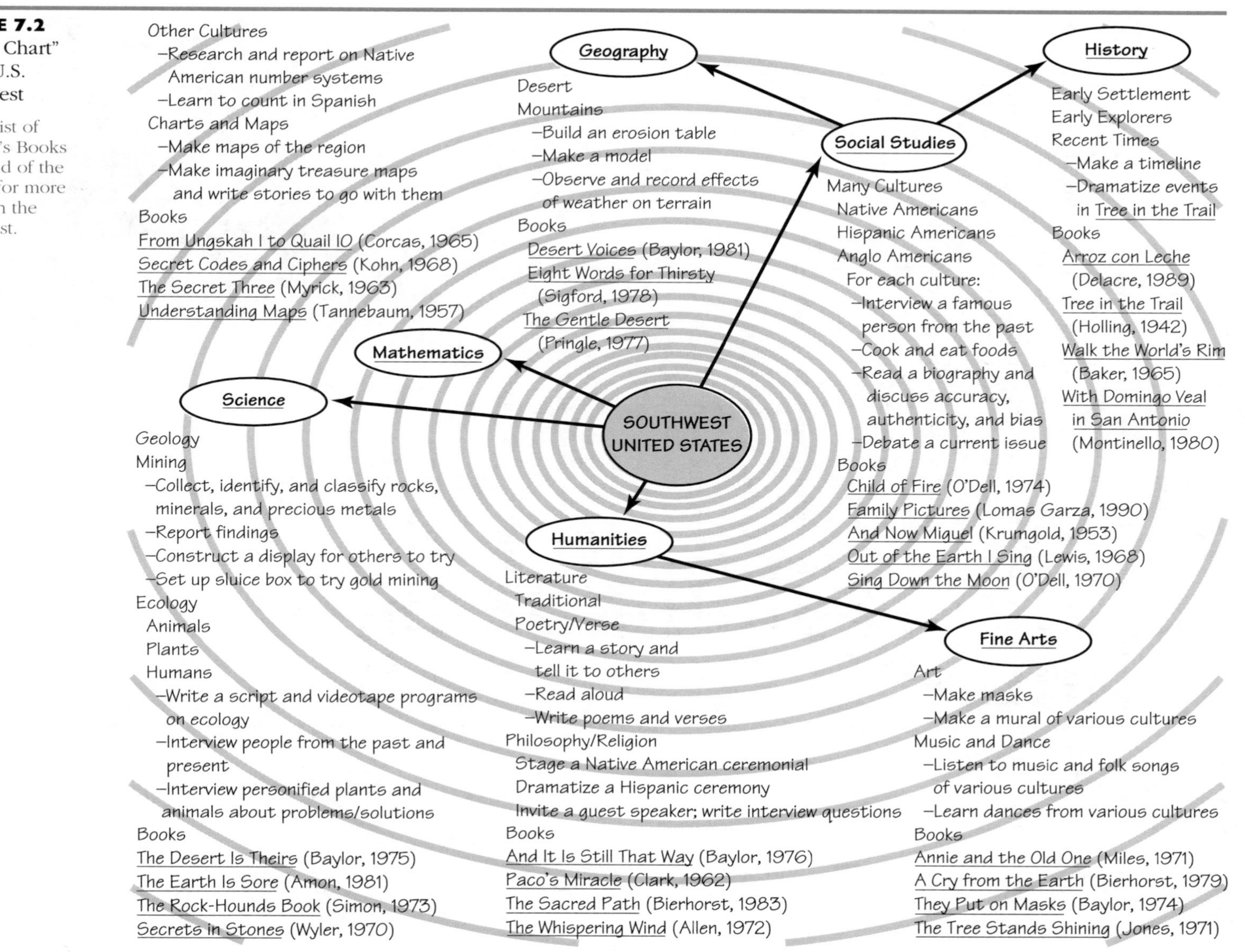

FIGURE 7.2
"Ripple Chart" of the U.S. Southwest

See the list of Children's Books at the end of the chapter for more books on the Southwest.

My father, Gordon D. Shirreffs, was the 1995 recipient of the Owen Wister Award, given by the Western Writers of America for lifetime contribution to the literature of the West.

A Visit from the Author

A highlight of the "ripple effect" that came from reading *The Mystery of the Haunted Mine* was a visit from the author (my father), Gordon D. Shirreffs. When he agreed to come and talk to my class, he warned me he wasn't going to answer impossible questions like "Where do you get ideas for your stories?" But he did just that as he told my students more stories drawn from his knowledge about the culture and history of the Southwest. From time to time during his narrative, he reached into an old shoebox full of arrowheads, old nails, and special rocks—things we'd found on family trips to the desert.

First, my father told the class the following seriously stated (but tongue-in-cheek) rules for how to find a lost mine:

1. Travel to a remote part of the Southwest desert that is unmapped and unexplored.
2. Be chased by bandits, desperadoes, or outlaws.
3. Lose your food and water.
4. Become completely lost.
5. Discover a gold mine but not a way of taking the gold with you.
6. Fill an empty tin can (shoe, canteen) with a few gold nuggets.
7. Head for civilization.
8. Be caught in a fierce desert sandstorm and stagger or crawl along.
9. Be found unconscious with the can (shoe, canteen) of gold nuggets clutched in your hand but unable to find your way to the gold mine.
10. You have found a lost mine!

Here's an old photo of my father, Gordon D. Shirreffs, along with my brother and me, doing research on a family trip.

More stories followed about mysterious mountains, strange glyphs and signs carved in rough canyon rock, and spirits of long-dead patrons. As my father spoke, he spirited these mesmerized fourth-grade students out of their classroom and over the twisting trails of the Southwest, sharing a curious blend of the truth and legend of the Native, Spanish, and Anglo American cultures. With my father as their beckoning guide, the children trudged through an imaginary desert, searching for gold.

My father also gave the children insight into the process of writing historical or regional fictional by telling them that everything in his books and stories was based on fact. For instance, he didn't create his formula for finding a lost gold mine out of his fertile imagination; rather, it grew from countless tales of prospectors about finding and losing mines under those very circumstances. And the Espectros Mountains, which appear in my father's books, are modeled closely after the Superstition Mountains in Arizona, the real site of many mysterious disappearances and unsolved murders documented in local records. Perhaps the most tempting nugget of Western lore that my father tantalized the children with was a description of the old Spanish miner's code: symbols that early miners carved in rock to mark their way back to mines. When he explained that these symbols were really used and might even still be out there—somewhere in the wild canyons and rugged foothills of the Southwest, just waiting to lead someone to a lost mine—many young eyes in the class lit up with a gleam that can only be described as "gold fever."

Espectros means "ghosts" in Spanish.

Keys to Response-Centered, Integrated Teaching with Literature

As curious as it may seem, the "ripple effect" of literature-based teaching just described in the Snapshot started when my students noticed a book written by an author with the same name as me, their teacher. From that initial show of interest in the author and the book, countless activities followed, involving not only the language arts but other content areas, as well.

From this experience with my first class, I learned that the power of literature is to capture the imagination for a moment, to take it where it's never been before—to other times and places and even other worlds. Through experiencing literature, we can empathize with others and discover their needs and pleasures, joys and fears. And above all, through literature, we can feel, see, and understand things that would otherwise have remained unknown—about ourselves and what it means to be human.

The importance of literature in a student- and response-centered classroom is that it provides a way of knowing about the world. Literature extends students' interests and encourages listening, thinking, talking, responding, and sharing. Literature also extends students' independent reading on a wide variety of subjects of interest to them. Finally, literature extends language learning across the curriculum, integrating the language arts with the content areas.

To establish a student- and response-centered program and make the most of children's literature, follow the content and teaching strategies described in the following sections. Note that each strategy expands on one of the steps described in the Snapshot.

Reading Aloud, Along, and Alone

Creating a literature-based classroom means setting up a room environment, selecting children's books, and scheduling time and opportunities for reading aloud, along, and alone.

Room Environment

- Set up a classroom library and book center. Designate space and shelves, displaying some books with the spines facing out and others with their covers showing (Morrow, 1992). Use furniture such as tables for displays of books and children's work.

- Provide comfortable chairs for reading (perhaps a rocker or recliner for the teacher) and other special reading places: floor pillows, beanbag chairs, or a homemade cave with a light in it.

- Set aside one bulletin board to promote literature and responses to it. Start by displaying book jackets or posters of them, and add information about authors or book genres (e.g., fairy tales, informational books, realistic fiction). Then continue to add samples of children's writing, art, or other responses to literature that can be shared on a bulletin board.

Selecting Children's Books

School librarians are willing to help teachers select books for their classrooms. Other ways of finding out about and choosing books are through journals, book lists, and specialized bibliographies, such as those selectively listed here:

- ***Journals:*** Include reviews of new books and articles about children's literature:

  Book List
  Bulletin of the Center for Children's Books
  Children's Literature in Education
  The Horn Book
  Language Arts
  The New Advocate
  The Reading Teacher
  School Library Journal

• ***Book Lists:*** Serve as general selection aids to children's literature:

Adventuring with Books: A Booklist for Pre-K—Grade 6 (Jett-Simpson, 1989)

Best Books for Children: Pre-school through Grade 6 (Gillespie & Naden, 1990)

The Elementary School Library Collection: A Guide to Books and Other Media (Winkel, 1990)

The Horn Book Guide (Horn Book, Inc., semiannual)

• ***Awards:*** Many awards are also given to children's books, which may guide your choices. For example, to honor the most distinguished contributions of literature for children published in the United States each year, the American Library Association gives the Caldecott Award to the illustrator of the best picture book and the Newbery Award to the author of the best text.

Scheduling Time and Opportunities to Read

Reading in the classroom can be promoted in many ways:

1. ***Reading Aloud:*** The teacher should read aloud several times a day to the whole class or to a group. Picture books are appropriate for primary-grade students as well as those at the middle- and upper-grade levels. For example, *Mojave* (Siebert, 1988) would be a great picture book to read to fourth-graders learning about the Southwest. For older students, read a chapter a day of a novel, either for sheer pleasure or in connection with a response-themed "ripple effect."

See Chapter 5. Listening and Talking, for a list of books to read aloud.

2. ***Reading Along:*** In reading along, or *shared reading,* students participate fully in reading by following along in their own copies of a chapter book,

Schedule time and opportunities and provide a comfortable environment for reading literature.

See Chapter 4, Emergent Literacy, for a list of predictable-pattern books, and Chapter 8, Reading as a Language Art, for an example of a literature-based lesson using a predictable-pattern book.

by reading the text of a "big book" guided by the teacher, or by reading a teachermade chart (e.g., of poems or songs) or sentence strips in a pocket chart. Predictable-pattern books are ideal for shared reading.

3. *Buddy Reading:* Students read in pairs during group workshop time or sustained silent reading (SSR) or when the teacher is conferencing with other students or groups. Students may read together to collect information for use in a project they're working on or simply because they like the same book and each other. Buddy reading is also a great way for students to share favorite books with friends.

See Chapter 8, Reading as a Language Art, for more on sustained silent reading.

4. *Sustained Silent Reading:* During this time, everyone in the class, including the teacher, reads a self-selected book silently.

5. *Wide Independent Reading:* Students self-select books and read widely for interest and enjoyment, or they read books on a theme of interest in the classroom, like students did when learning about the Southwest. Much independent reading can take place in group workshops.

See Chapter 10, Reading and Writing, for a description of a reading/writing workshop with many opportunities and time to read.

Teachers need to make sure to schedule sufficient time and opportunities for these types of reading. Here are suggested amounts of time and frequencies:

Type of Reading	*Amount of Time (per instance)*	*Frequency (per day)*
Reading aloud	15–30 minutes	2–3 times
Reading along (shared reading)	30–45 minutes	1–2 times
Buddy reading	15–30 minutes	1–2 times
Sustained silent reading	15–30 minutes	1–2 times
Independent reading	15–60 minutes	2–3 times

Talking Together

Teachers also need to provide time and opportunities to talk before, during, and after reading, involving the whole class, small groups, and individual students at various times. Peterson and Eeds (1990) describe these talks as "grand conversations." These moments are some of the richest times that students have to reflect on their own responses while reading and that teachers have to know more about those responses as a basis for planning further response-centered activities.

Questions: Aesthetic and Efferent

The types of questions teachers ask direct children to take aesthetic or efferent stances toward any text. Ideally, teachers should first direct students to take aesthetic stances toward literature. Think about the analysis of children's response types, described earlier. Their preferred types were aesthetic. They questioned, talked about favorite parts, hypothesized, and made associations.

Out of these broad, rich, aesthetic responses (which were focused on the development of personal meaning), more efferent concerns will emerge, such as developing explanations or attending to print and language, content, and analysis.

When developing questions and prompts for students, keep their preferred response types in mind. Remember to begin with aesthetic questions and prompts, which will lead students to efferent questions and prompts.

See also the list of aesthetic and efferent questions and prompts in Chapter 5, Emergent Literacy (p. 169).

Questions: Literary Elements

After students have had the opportunity to fully experience reading literature by responding aesthetically, teachers can also provide the opportunity to take a more critical, analytical approach. They can use efferent questions and prompts that emerge from responses to aesthetic questions and prompts (as just discussed). A framework for the critical analysis of a text can be developed by examining its literary elements.

Sloan (1984) suggests questions that teachers can use to guide children to better understanding the elements and structure of literature: namely, the story world and literary elements of setting and plot, characters, point of view, mood and theme, and finally, how these interrelate to create specific story structures:

1. ***Story World***
   - What signs indicate whether a story will be more fanciful than realistic: talking animals? exaggeration? strange, improbable situations, characters, or settings? beginning with "Once upon a time . . ."?
   - If the story world created by the author is far different from the world we know, how does the author make the story seem possible and believable?

2. ***Setting and Plot***
   - Where and when does the story take place? How do you know? If the story took place somewhere else or in a different time, how would it be changed?
   - What incident, problem, conflict, or situation does the author use to get the story started?
   - How is the story told or arranged: chronologically? by individual incidents? through flashbacks? through letters or diary entries?
   - Trace the main events of the story. Would it be possible to change their order? Could any of them be left out? Why or why not?
   - Suppose you thought of a different ending for the story. How would the rest of the story have to be changed to fit the new ending?
   - Did the story end as you expected it to? What clues did the author offer to prepare you for this ending? When you were reading or listening to the story, did you recognize these clues as being important?

3. ***Characters***
   - Who is the main character in the story? What kind of person is he or she? How do you know?
   - Do any characters change in the course of the story? If so, how? What made them change? Does the change seem believable?
   - Some characters play small but important roles. Pick out a "bit player." Why is this character necessary to the story?
4. ***Point of View***
   - Who is telling the story? How does this affect how it's told?
   - If one of the characters is telling the story, how does his or her personality or purpose influence what's told and how?
   - How might the story be different if told by an outside narrator?
5. ***Mood and Theme***
   - Does the story, as a whole, create a definite mood or feeling? What is the mood? How is it created?
   - Did you have strong feelings as you read the story? If so, what? How did the author make you feel that way?
   - What are the main ideas *behind* the story? How does the author get you to think of them?
6. ***Comparison to Other Stories***
   - Even though this story is different in content, is it like any other story you have read or watched? How so?
   - Does the story follow a pattern? If so, what is it?
   - Think about the characters in the story: Are any of them like characters you have met in other stories? What character types can you think of?

Questions: Story Structure

Story structure is a schema for stories, "an idealized, internal representation of the parts of a typical story and the relationship among those parts" (Mandler & Johnson, 1977, p. 111). The reader's mental image of a story structure must also be part of this definition.

When the goal is understanding a story's structure, teachers can develop questions for students based on their knowledge of elements of story structure, as shown when talking about books (Glenn & Stein, 1979; Rumelhart, 1975; Sadow, 1982). The elements of story structure are a setting, an initiating event, a response, an attempt to satisfy a goal, a consequence, and a reaction.

Teachers should follow these steps in developing questions based on elements of story structure:

1. Ask yourself generic questions, or frames, while reading, analyzing, and outlining a story.
2. Develop answers for these questions, based on the story.
3. Derive appropriate questions for classroom use, based on this information.

TEACHING IDEA

Story Structure Questions
Island of the Blue Dolphins by Scott O'Dell

Here's an example of a set of questions developed for Scott O'Dell's (1988b) *Island of the Blue Dolphins,* a book of historical fiction based on the real-life account of a young Native American woman who lived alone for 18 years on an island off the coast of California:

For Teacher's Use Only

Question Frames

1. *Setting:* Where and when does the story take place? Who are the characters involved?
2. *Initiating Event:* What starts the flow of events?
3. *Reaction:* How does the main character react to the initiating event?
4. *Action:* What does the main character do about it?
5. *Consequence:* What is the result of the main character's action?

Answers

1. *Setting:* The story takes place in the early 1800s on an island rich with otter, off the coast of California, where a 12-year-old Native American girl, Karana, lives with her people in the village of Ghalas-at.
2. *Initiating Event:* After many of the men in her village are killed by ruthless otter hunters, Karana's people seek a new home. They send a messenger, who sends a ship to take them to another island, but Karana's 6-year-old brother misses the sailing.
3. *Reaction:* Karana refuses to sail away and leave her brother.
4. *Action:* She dives into the stormy sea and swims to the island to find her brother.
5. *Consequence:* Since the ship does not return for her, Karana spends the next 18 years alone on the island, after her brother is killed by a pack of wild dogs. She learns to protect herself against the dogs and ruthless otter hunters, and she survives until a ship finally comes to the island.

For Use with Students

Classroom Questions

1. *Setting:* Who is Karana? Where and when did she live? What was her life like in the village of Ghalas-at?
2. *Initiating Event:* What happened to her village after the Aleut otter hunters came? Why did Karana's people seek a new home? What happened to her little brother when it was time to sail?
3. *Reaction:* How did Karana feel when she realized her brother wasn't on the ship?
4. *Action:* What did Karana do about it?
5. *Consequence:* What happened to her after she jumped into the sea to return to the island to find her brother?

Plot Patterns

Various types of plot patterns contain these story elements (Lukens, 1991). Here are the basic types of plot structures found in children's literature, along with examples of specific books:

1. ***Action builds and peaks with a final climax.***

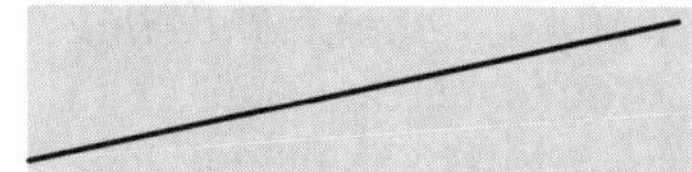

The Borrowers (Norton, 1953)—The family of little people who live in the baseboard of an old house must escape the dangers of ratcatchers and fumigators; it's unclear what happens to them at the end, however.

2. ***Action develops evenly through a series of related, interesting events.***

Little House in the Big Woods (Wilder, 1961)—The Wilder family's experiences are described from day to day, without major conflict or climax.

3. ***Action rises to a climax and then clearly concludes.***

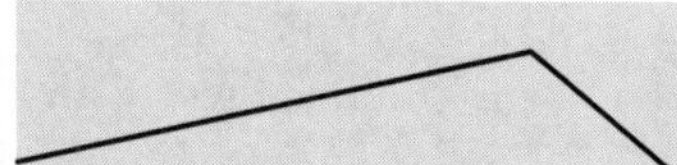

Roll of Thunder, Hear My Cry (Taylor, 1976)—In the rural south in the 1930s, the child of an African American family is nearly run down by a busload of white students; events continue to build tension in the story before coming to a resolution.

See also other books with tricks and twists by Chris Van Allsburg: *Jumanji* (1981), *The Mysteries of Harris Burdick* (1984), and *The Wreck of the Zephyr* (1983).

4. ***Action builds logically and ends with an unexpected twist.***

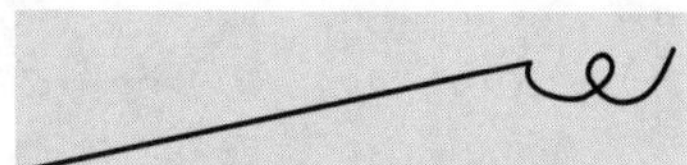

The Garden of Abdul Gasazi (Van Allsburg, 1979)—The reader is tricked at the end. (I hate to give it away.)

5. ***Action ends where it begins, after a series of events.***

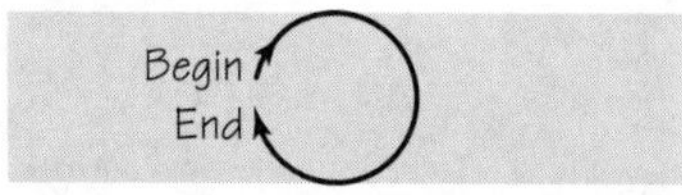

Hey, Al (Yorinks, 1986)—Al is unhappy at home. A large bird takes him to another world, and although he's happy at first, paradise goes sour and Al is happy to return home.

6. ***Action follows a repetitive, predictable pattern.***

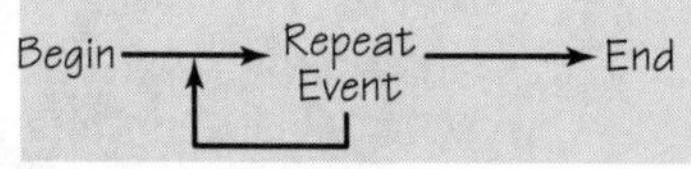

The Fat Cat: A Danish Folktale (Kent, 1971)—A hungry cat eats everyone he meets until he becomes very fat.

Teachers can model reading and share enthusiasm for literature in many ways.

Teachers can help students develop understanding of literary elements and story structures by providing various response options to literature, such as story maps, which will be described later in this chapter (see Response Options).

Scheduling Time and Opportunities to Talk

Teachers and students need time and opportunities to talk together about books. This can be done in whole-class discussions, in small groups during workshops, or in buddy reading. The following schedule suggests how much time should be provided each day for talking about books:

Type of Talking	***Amount of Time (per instance)***	***Frequency (per day)***
Whole-class discussion	30–45 minutes	1–2 times
Small-group workshops	30–60 minutes	2–3 times
Buddy reading	15–30 minutes	2–3 times

Writing in Response Journals

Response journals are an important component of response-centered teaching with literature. Students can write in them before, during, and after reading. These journals can also trigger discussions when talking together about books, during conferences with teachers, or during buddy reading.

Questions and Prompts for Response Journals

Make and post a list of questions and prompts in the classroom to suggest ways students can begin. These questions should be primarily aesthetic to encourage students to focus on the lived-through experience of the book. For example:

1. What were you thinking about while reading? Tell about it.
2. What was your favorite part of the story? Tell about it.
3. Was there anything you wondered about? Tell about it.
4. What else do you think might happen? Tell about it.
5. Has anything like this ever happened to you? Tell about it.
6. Write anything you want about the story.

Some teachers prefer to use double-entry journals: In one column, students write down the parts of the story that interested them, and in the second column, they write down what they thought about those parts. Figure 7.3 gives an example of a double-entry journal, written by a fourth-grader in a class reading *On My Honor,* by Marion Bauer (1986), together, a chapter at a time.

Response journals are important in assessing students' engagement with and understanding of literature. They provide an authentic, ongoing record of students' interests, responses, and experiences with literature.

Response Options

As mentioned earlier, it's important that teachers provide children with many options for responding to literature along with flexibility in using them. Some options will be done by everyone in the class, such as writing in literature response journals. But children will choose other options individually, because they are a good fit with the book they are reading and ideas they have about it.

Make a list of response options at the beginning of the year and post it in the classroom. Ask students for their ideas, too. Don't feel that after reading a book, children must always write or do a project about it. Probably the best thing to do after reading a book is to read another one.

Here are some response options:

- ***Read Another Book:*** If students enjoyed a book, talk to them about it and help them find another one with similar content, in the same genre, or by the same author. Adults and children alike are usually excited to find out that a book they loved is part of a series. To find more books, check with the librarian or do a search on the library computer, if that's possible.

FIGURE 7.3 Double-Entry Literature Response Journal

Left Side	***Right Side***
Interesting part of the book	Response to that interesting part
Example from *On My Honor*	
p. 33—"A single bird sang by a nearby tree. Shut up, Joel wanted to shout. You just shut up."	The bird's singing made me want to say what Joel wanted to say because his friend was gone and Joel was scared. And how can the bird sing at a time when his friend was gone?

Source: Adapted from Zarrillo & Cox, 1992

• ***Response Journals:*** Students make daily entries about their reading (see previous section).

• ***Read, Talk, Draw, Write:*** After the teacher reads aloud to the class or a group or one child reads to a buddy, students talk together about the book, draw a picture, and either write or give the teacher dictation.

See Chapter 3, Language and Cultural Diversity, for an example of using Read, Talk, Draw, Write with language-minority kindergartners.

• ***Literature as a Model for Writing:*** Children use the book as a model for their own writing. For example, after reading *When I Was Young in the Mountains* (Rylant, 1982), students might write about when they were young.

See Chapter 10, Reading and Writing, for examples of using literature as a model for writing, and Chapter 4, Emergent Literacy, for a list of pattern books that are excellent models for young children.

• ***Role-Playing:*** Students pretend to be characters in the book, either doing what the characters actually did or something the students think they might do. Books with two main characters are good for this, such as *Frog and Toad Are Friends* (Lobel, 1970).

• ***Story Dramatization:*** Students talk about the characters and how they act, analyze the story structure and decide which are the important events (in order), and play the story. Use the questions in the section on story structure, earlier in this chapter.

See Chapter 6, Drama in the Classroom, for a step-by-step approach for dramatizing *Where the Wild Things Are,* by Maurice Sendak (1963).

• ***Reader's Theater:*** Any printed text can be adapted for reader's theater, including both fiction and nonfiction. The poetry in Shel Silverstein's *A Light in the Attic* (1981) and *Where the Sidewalk Ends* (1986) is great for reader's theater.

See Chapter 6, Drama in the Classroom, for how to do reader's theater.

• ***Storytelling:*** Students retell the story in their own words and also use flannelboards, props, and music. Storytelling can be an individual or group project. Traditional tales, like *The Gingerbread Man* by Paul Galdone (1983), are excellent selections for storytelling.

See Chapter 5, Listening and Talking, for how to do storytelling and puppetry.

• ***Puppetry:*** By making puppets, students can play a part of or an entire story or create their own story based on a story's characters. Again, traditional tales are good choices, especially those with several characters, like *The Bremen-Town Musicians* (Plume, 1987).

• ***Filmstrip Making:*** Students enjoy creating filmstrips of the story or their version of it. Stories with simple plots and sequences of action work well for filmstrip making, such as *Rosie's Walk* (Hutchins, 1968).

Create filmstrips using the draw-on technique described in Chapter 13, Media Literacy.

• ***Videotaping:*** Students are motivated to respond to literature in a variety of ways by making videotapes—for example, role-playing characters, playing scenes or whole stories, creating their own versions of stories, or doing mock interviews with story characters. Books that present real conflicts, told from different points of view, are good candidates for videos. Consider using *The True Story of the Three Little Pigs* (Scieszka, 1989), which is told from the wolf's point of view.

• ***Dioramas:*** Students make three-dimensional constructions of the story world on a cardboard or Styrofoam base or in a box with one side cut away. They would have great fun creating a house for *Stuart Little* (White, 1954), the mouse child of normal-sized human parents.

See Chapter 9, The Writing Process, for how to make books in the classroom.

• ***Bookmaking:*** Students retell a story or make a new version of it by creating books out of construction paper or contact paper or by making fold-a-books or pop-up books. See *The Jolly Postman* (Ahlberg & Ahlberg, 1986) for a book made with letters and envelopes inside.

• ***Create a Character:*** Students talk about characters in a book and create characters of their own to write about. For example, fifth-grade students read *The Egypt Game* (Snyder, 1967), a contemporary story about a multicultural neighborhood, after they had also read and learned a lot about ancient Egypt. As a class, they created a web for different kinds of characters living in ancient Egypt. Then each student picked one type of person from ancient Egypt, did his or her own web, and wrote a story about that character (see Figure 7.4).

• ***Story Boxes:*** Students find or create objects related to the story and put them in boxes. The boxes can be made using origami techniques and should be decorated on the outside (see Figure 7.5). Then have each student use his or her box and the objects in it to tell others about the story. A good book for this activity would be *Angel Child, Dragon Child* (Surat, 1983), which

FIGURE 7.4
Create a Character: *The Egypt Game*
Part A: Class Web
Part B: Individual Web
Part C: Student's Story

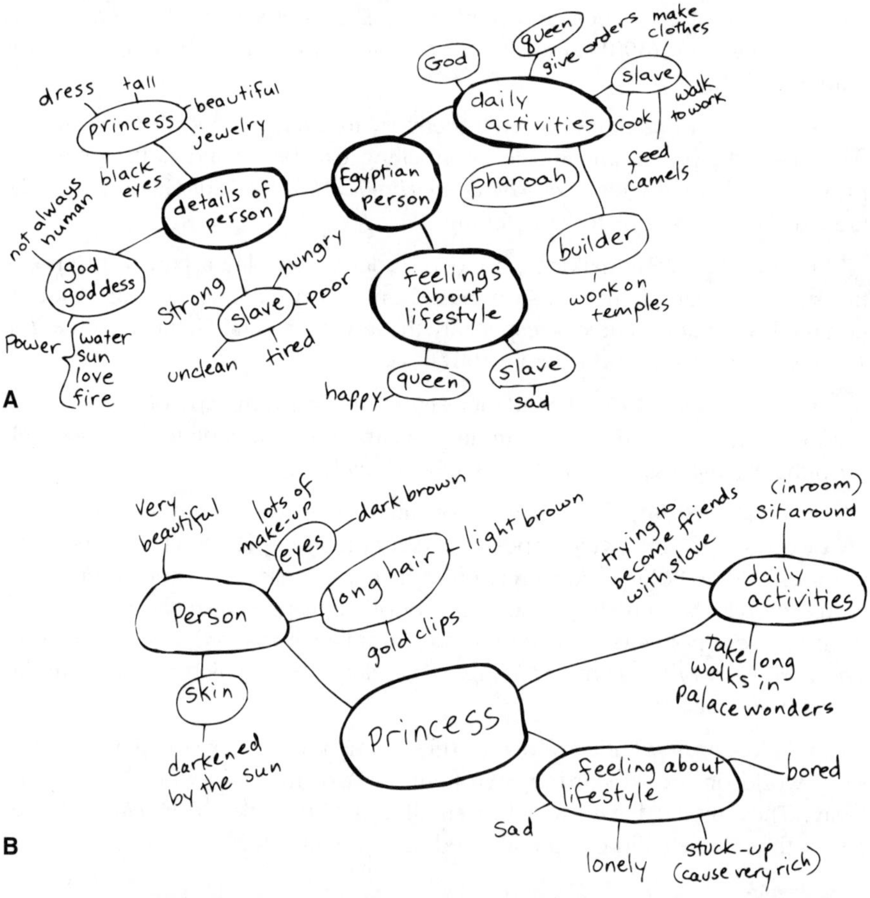

A

B

is about a young immigrant to the United States whose mother is still in Vietnam. The child carries a box with a picture and mementos of her mother.

• ***Story Maps:*** Students map the structure of a story or a character's journey through a story (see p. 250, Questions: Story Structure). Story maps can be created by the teacher with a class or group, or students can make their own.

• ***Make-Believe World Maps:*** Children create maps of their own make-believe worlds after reading a book set in a fictitious world that can only be entered in a special way—for instance, *Bridge to Terabithia* (Paterson, 1977) and *The Lion, the Witch, and the Wardrobe* (Lewis, 1986). In addition to drawing this world, children can also write about it, addressing these questions: What's your world like? Where is it? How do you get there? How do you get back? Why would you like to go there?

• ***Story Quilts:*** Children can draw pictures, for example, of their favorite parts of the story, glue them to construction paper for backing, punch holes around the edges, and weave them together with yarn. The result is a class quilt of responses to a story. For an example, look at Faith Ringgold's (1991) childhood memoir *Tar Beach,* which uses a quilt motif: books.

See the Appendix, March: Women's History Month, for more books with quilt motifs.

Soon Rava, the sun god would take the sun to the heavens. It was still dark when the young princess Tarfa a woke from her peaceful sleep. From the slave's eyes she saw the most beautiful person, her eyes as dark as the mud homes in the village. Tarfa hair was light brown just like the desert sand that laye out side. [She wore in her hair golden clips that sparkled in the sun.] Her skin was a creamy white but when Tarfa went out on her long walks. Her skin turned a light taned brown. Her father dispised of her and often scolded because she was not as pretty as her mother.

After her slave helped her on with a beautiful dress that had exotic colors. Then put her wig (made with other slaves hair.)

C

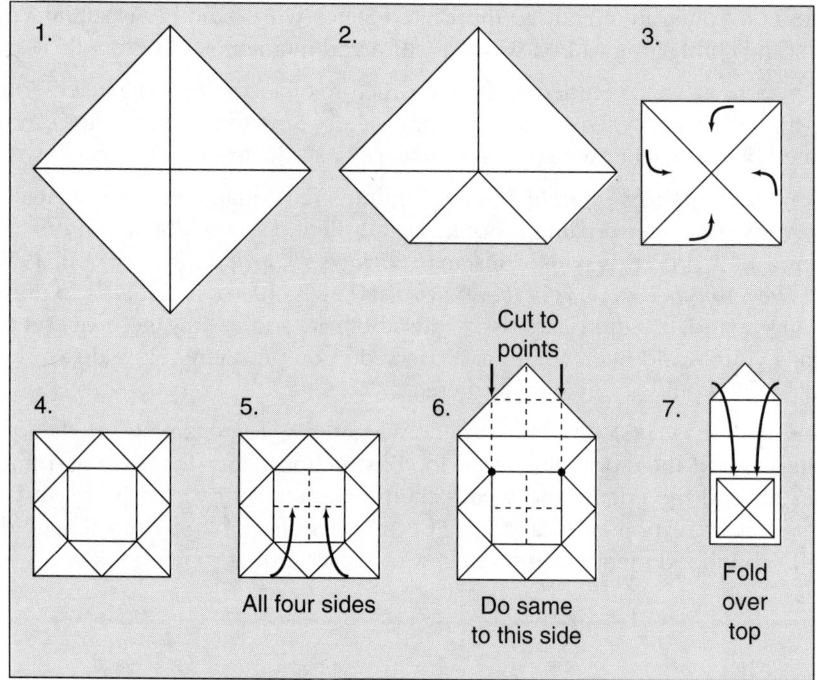

FIGURE 7.5
How to Make a Story Box

Focal Topics of Interest

Children's responses and questions during literature discussions often indicate focal topics of interest, or pebbles that will set off a "ripple effect" of learning experiences. Ideas from students' response journals may also be sources of worthy topics.

One easy way for teachers to develop focal topics is to start a running list of ideas and questions about a certain book on a piece of chartpaper. Another way is to do a cluster or web of ideas. Perhaps books that are related in some way will produce a theme, which might emerge by comparing the books with a Venn diagram. Examples of ways to develop focal topics from books are shown in Figure 7.6.

Literature Groups

See Chapter 1, Learning and Teaching Language Arts, for the example of Avril Font's class, in which all work is done in small, cooperative groups during workshops throughout the day.

Literature groups are formed when children have a common interest in a book or theme and enjoy working together. These groups can be formed temporarily to read, to write in response journals, or to discuss the book with the teacher (Peterson, 1987; Watson, 1988). Or they can be formed for longer periods of time—even several weeks or a month—for response-themed learning. Literature groups require self-direction by students, who take responsibility for their learning.

Literature groups are also sometimes called *literature circles* (Short & Pierce, 1990). Another similar concept is *book clubs,* in which small groups of

Book: *The Mystery of the Haunted Mine* (Shirreffs, 1962)

Way to Develop Topics: List of questions

1. What is the desert like?
2. What were the Native Americans like?
3. Are there still really mines and treasures?
4. How did the Spanish mine for gold?

Focal Topic: Life in the Southwest United States

Book: *Bridge to Terabithia* (Paterson, 1977)

Way to Develop Topics: Cluster/web diagram

Focal Topic: Imaginary worlds

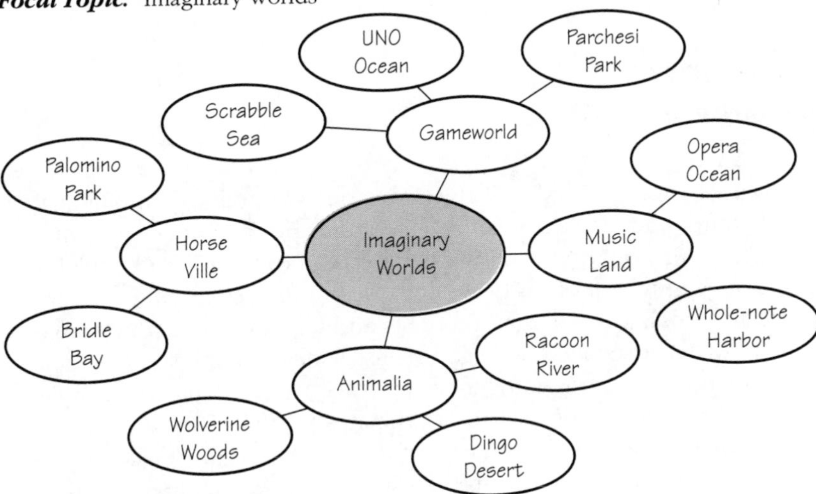

See Chapter 4, Emergent Literacy, for a "ripple effect" of apples and books about Johnny Appleseed.

Books: *Johnny Appleseed* (Kellogg, 1988) and *Miss Rumphius* (Cooney, 1982)

Way to Develop Topics: Venn diagram

Focal Topic: Making the world a better place

Johnny Appleseed
- Boy/man
- Planted apples
- Country
- Nonfiction
- Always traveling

Both
- Planted seeds
- Made world more beautiful
- Traveled
- Grew old

Miss Rumphius
- Girl/woman
- Planted lupines
- City
- Fiction
- Returned home

FIGURE 7.6
Ways to Develop Focal Topics from Books

Reader's workshop will be described more fully in Chapter 10, Reading and Writing.

children usually read, write, and talk about books without the teacher (Raphael, 1992). *Reader's workshop* is an entire approach to teaching reading and often writing in reading/writing workshops. All these types of groups share certain characteristics:

1. They are based on mutual interests: one book, several, or a theme.
2. They are flexible and can change in membership, the amount of time they meet, or focus.
3. They are social, cooperative, and collaborative.
4. They can be led by teachers or students.
5. They are student- and response-centered and allow ample time and opportunity to read, talk, write, plan, and carry out further experiences with literature.

TEACHING IDEA

Literature Plans

Here's an example of how Paul Boyd-Batstone, who teaches a bilingual Spanish third-grade class, organizes literature groups with a literature plan. (This idea could be used with any class, however.) Paul explains that this idea grew out of his desire to structure the classroom for listening and responding to students' thoughts and ideas, creating a rich environment for what second-language theorist James Cummins (1989) calls *context-embedded instruction*. Incidentally, Paul sees strong connections between Cummins's concept and Rosenblatt's (1938/1978) transactional theory, which affirms the importance of the reader and the ideas and experiences they bring to the classroom (Cox & Boyd-Batstone, in press).

Literature Plan Cycle

Here's how Paul outlines a literature plan cycle:

1. *Selection:* Students select what they want to read and form literature groups around the selected pieces.
2. *Reading:* Students spend the first week of the cycle reading and rereading their books by reading themselves (individually, in pairs, and in choral reading), by listening to the teacher read aloud, or by reading along with a taped version.
3. *Conferences:* Each group meets with the teacher to discuss the literature, focusing on that part of the story that gripped them. This is where the teacher listens for the background knowledge and prior experiences that the students bring to the text. Based on that point of contact between the text and the students' lives, writing is developed in the form of an essay, a poem, a song, a rewrite of the story, or a comparison of the text to another text or experience.

4. *Presentation:* At the end of the cycle, each literature group demonstrates their writing, poetry, music, and creative projects for the rest of the class. The parents are invited to be part of the audience, as the students show off their work. The students finish by writing an assessment of their own participation, what they would do differently to make it better, and what they learned from other groups.

Literature Plan Elements

Figure 7.7, Literature Plan Elements, shows the basic cluster for ideas generated by students in Paul's class:

1. *Writing:* The writing part of the plan is based on clustering students' responses to a book on a piece of chartpaper. Then they talk together and identify themes, circling the sentences that express similar ideas with colored markers. (Usually, more than one theme emerges from their responses.) Each color identifies sentences that will go in the same paragraph. The students talk about the order of the sentences within each color code and use the color-coded, clustered ideas as an organizer for writing a first draft. They take their work to another student to be edited, after which both editor and writer meet with the teacher for the final edit. The students finish by writing a final draft and illustrating their work. Three to four pieces of writing are usually generated this way during each literature group cycle.

2. *Creative Ideas* *:* As the teacher conferences with a group to talk about the story, ideas begin to germinate—the better the story, the richer the sharing of ideas. During this brainstorming, ideas rarely come to light

FIGURE 7.7 Literature Plan Elements

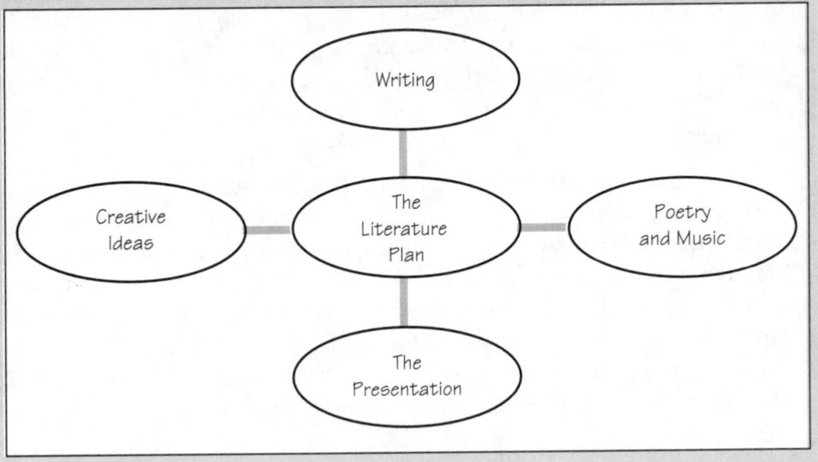

(continued)

Students in Paul Boyd-Batstone's bilingual Spanish/English class are actively engaged in experiences with literature during a literature plan cycle.

in sequential order. For example, a group might be discussing some aspect of a character, when suddenly a student will jump up and say, "Hey! Why don't we put on a puppet show?" The teacher can affirm the student's thinking by incorporating it into the literature plan on the spot. The creative ideas section is restricted only by the group's imagination of some project related to the story. The responsibility to produce the project, however, falls on the students' shoulders: how to make it, obtain the materials, and assign various tasks to complete the project. Some examples are making a "big book," putting on a play, painting a mural, and recording their version of the story.

See the Response Option section in this chapter for more ideas.

3. ***Poetry and Music:*** Poetry and music focus students' attention on the cognitively demanding features of language arts: metaphor, rhyme, meter, melody, and language play. Given their importance, students are required to find or compose poetry and music related to the story. They write the selected or composed poetry or music on chartpaper and teach the whole class their work.

4. ***Presentation:*** The culmination of the literature group cycle is a demonstration of the learning. Parents are invited to this presentation. Each student reads a selection of his or her writing and demonstrates creative idea projects, and they all teach the whole group their poetry and music. At this point, the students are the experts in the given area of study, so time is also set aside for questions and answers about their work. Students write an assessment of their group participation, what they have learned, and what improvements they would suggest for the next cycle.

Literature Plan Schedule

Here's a possible daily and weekly schedule for using a literature plan and literature groups with a whole-language classroom integrating teaching across the curriculum:

Daily	*Weekly*	*Focus*
1–2 periods	M 10:30–12:00, 1:00–2:00	Initiating writing
	Tu 10:30–12:00	Writing development
60–90 minutes each	W 10:30–12:00	Initiating projects
	Th 10:30–12:00	Project development
90–150 minutes total	F 10:30–12:00, 1:00–2:00	Closure to projects

The strength of using a literature plan framework for organizing literature-based language arts instruction is that by listening and responding to students' thoughts, context-embedded instruction occurs naturally. The role of the teacher changes from being the sole resource of knowledge to being a co-creator with students. Thus, the responsibility for learning is shared, rather than imposed. And while working with students on a literature plan, the teacher learns that they are the classroom's greatest resource.

Gathering Resources

When integrating teaching across the curriculum with literature, teachers can gather more resources in several ways:

- *School and public librarians:* The greatest resources for gathering related books and media will be the school and public librarians. They can offer a wealth of information about children's literature. Call library information services, and ask them for help.

- *Subject guides to children's literature:* Guides to finding children's books on particular subjects include:

A to Zoo: Subject Access to Children's Picture Books (Lima, 1989)
Eyeopeners! How to Choose and Use Children's Books about Real People, Places, and Things (Kobrin, 1988)
Index to Collective Biographies for Young Readers (Breen, 1988)
Index to Poetry for Children and Young People: 1982–1987 (Brewton, 1983)
The Museum of Science and Industry Basic List of Children's Science Books (Richter & Wenzel, 1988)
Subject Guide to Children's Books in Print (Bowker, annual)

For lists of *Notable Children's Trade Books in the Field of Social Studies* and *Outstanding Science Trade Books* chosen each year, write Children's Book Council, 67 Irving Place, New York, NY, 10003.

• *Parents and community members:* When a new theme cycle begins, let parents and community members know that their help is needed. They are a great resource of materials for the classroom. Children can write notes to take home, telling parents what you are doing and asking for their help.

Wide Independent Reading

Above all, teachers should encourage students to read widely and independently. Doing so is vital not to only reading achievement but to promoting wide experiences with literature.

Self-Selection

See Chapter 8, Reading as a Language Art, for more on self-selection as part of a literature-based reading program or comprehensive reading program.

The teacher chooses books that are to be read aloud, related to a theme, and for shared reading. However, students should also have many opportunities to self-select their own reading.

Genres of Children's Literature

Teachers should be familiar with various types or categories of children's literature, which are *genres*. In the following list, we'll look at basic genres of children's literature along with examples of what I call *popular classics:* books that are widely read, critically acclaimed, and popular. The classics listed for each genre include a picture book for younger children and a chapter book for older children (presented in that order).

• ***Poetry:*** Works of carefully chosen, condensed, and artfully arranged language that looks selectively at the world in unique and unusual ways:

Read-Aloud Rhymes for the Very Young (Prelutsky, 1986)
A Light in the Attic (Silverstein, 1981) and *Where the Sidewalk Ends* (Silverstein, 1986)

• ***Picture Books:*** Works in which illustrations and text combine equally to tell a story:

Where the Wild Things Are (Sendak, 1963)
Jumanji (Van Allsburg, 1981)

• ***Traditional Literature:*** Stories that have been told for many years, across many cultures, first orally and then written down:

Mufaro's Beautiful Daughters: An African Tale (Steptoe, 1987)
The People Could Fly: American Black Folktales (Hamilton, 1993)

• ***Fantasy:*** Stories told in the real or an unreal world, with characters or events that probably don't really exist and events that may depend on magic or the supernatural:

Sylvester and the Magic Pebble (Steig, 1988)
Charlotte's Web (White, 1952)

• ***Science Fiction:*** Stories that explore the possibilities of science in our lives through invention or extension of the laws of nature:

Dinosaur Bob (Joyce, 1988)
A Wrinkle in Time (L'Engle, 1976)

• ***Contemporary Realistic Fiction:*** Stories of real people, living here and now:

The Snowy Day (Keats, 1963)
Are You There God? It's Me, Margaret (Blume, 1972)

• ***Historical Fiction:*** Stories set in a real time and place in history but with some or all fictional characters:

Encounter (Yolen, 1992)
Sarah, Plain and Tall (MacLachlan, 1985)

• ***Biography*:** Stories about the lives of real people:

The Glorious Flight: The Story of Louis Bleriot (Provensen & Provensen, 1987)
Lincoln: A Photobiography (Freedman, 1987)

• ***Nonfiction:*** Books of information about a variety of topics in the real world:

Mummies Made in Egypt (Aliki, 1979)
The Way Things Work (Macaulay, 1988)

Integrating Literature across the Curriculum

Integrated teaching with literature is natural in whole-language classrooms, in which authentic texts—such as children's books and their own writing—are the true texts used. The "ripple effect" about the U.S. Southwest, described earlier, occurred spontaneously when students discovered that my father was an author. I can't take credit for planning this; it happened before I knew it because students responded with enthusiasm to my father's book. And as it turned out, this topic tied in beautifully with state curriculum guides for fourth-grade social studies and science, which emphasized state and regional history, geography, economy, environment and ecology, and related arts and mathematics.

Examples of other response-themed ripple effects I have seen emerge in classrooms (and the literature to go with them) follow:

See Chapter 14, Language across the Curriculum, for many examples of integrated "ripple effects."

Response Themes	***Literature***
Primary Grades (K–3)	
Dinosaurs	*Digging up Dinosaurs* (Aliki, 1988)
	Dinosaurs (Gibbons, 1987)
	Dinosaurs (Hopkins, 1987)
	Dinosaurs Are Different (Aliki, 1985a)
	My Visit to the Dinosaurs (Aliki, 1985b)

	Patrick's Dinosaurs (Carrick & Carrick, 1983)
	Tyrannosaurus Was a Beast: Dinosaur Poems (Prelutsky, 1988)
	What Happened to Patrick's Dinosaurs? (Carrick & Carrick, 1988)
Middle and Upper Grades (4–6)	
Survival	*Call It Courage* (Sperry, 1968)
	The Cay (Taylor, 1976)
	The Endless Steppe: Growing up in Siberia (Hautzig, 1968)
	Island of the Blue Dolphins (O'Dell, 1988b)
	Julie of the Wolves (George, 1974)
	My Side of the Mountain (George, 1991)

Multicultural Literature

Another important facet of teaching with literature should be the use of *multicultural literature,* which James Zarrillo (1994) defines as:

> 1. *Fiction with characters who are from cultural groups that have been underrepresented in children's books: African-Americans, Asian-Americans, Hispanic-Americans, Native Americans, and Americans from religious minorities;*
> 2. *Fiction that takes us to other nations and introduces readers to the cultures of people residing outside the United States; and*
> 3. *Information books, including biographies, that focus on African-Americans, Asian-Americans, Hispanic-Americans, Native Americans, Americans from religious minorities, and people living outside the United States.* (p. 2)

See Chapter 3, Language and Cultural Diversity, for more on approaches to multicultural teaching, including James Banks's (Banks & Banks, 1993) levels of integration of multicultural content in the curriculum.

An effective way to integrate multicultural content in teaching is through the use of multicultural literature or a variety of literature that presents—for example, a historical event from different perspectives. Recall from Chapter 3 how students read books about Christopher Columbus and the Taino Indians written from different perspectives: those of the Europeans, the Taino, and Columbus himself. The books presented conflicting accounts of what happened, which forced the children to think about them and develop their own conclusions, one of which was "Somebody's lying."

Teachers can begin using multicultural literature in any class by introducing the concept that people are both alike and different. An excellent children's selection to use for this purpose is Peter Spier's (1980) picture book *People.* It doesn't focus on one culture or even compare two different ones; instead, it takes a global look at diversity, showing how *all* people are alike and different. Students of all ages are fascinated with this book, and many adults are, as well. The following Lesson Plan presents an initiating lesson for reading, talking, drawing, and writing about human diversity.

LESSON PLAN: Examining Diversity with Literature

***People* by Peter Spier**

Topic: People are alike and different

Purpose: To listen to and respond to literature about diversity; to talk about how people are alike and different; to write about how each child is unique

Materials: *People,* by Peter Spier (1980); chartpaper; paper; crayons; pencils

Teaching Sequence:

1. Read *People* aloud. Encourage children to respond during the reading.
2. Discuss the book. Ask aesthetic questions that encourage students to think about their personal responses to the book.
   "What did you think about the book?"
   "What was your favorite part?"
   "How are we alike and how are we different in this class?"
   "What is special about you?"
3. Talk together about how students in the class are alike and different. Ask each individual to think of how he or she is special and unique.
4. Have students write in their literature response journals, using the following prompts:
   "Write anything you want about the book."
   "Tell about how people in this class are like and/or different."
   "Describe something about you that's special and makes you unique."
   "If you were going to write a book like *People,* what are some things you would put in it that Peter Spier didn't put in his book?"
5. Ask students to share their responses in literature groups.

Assessment:

1. Observe whether students listened to and responded to the book during reading aloud and talking about it.
2. Note students' written responses in their literature response journals.
3. Observe discussions in students' literature groups.

Extending Activities:

1. Students can draw a picture of themselves, identifying what's special about them.

(continued)

2. Students can make a bulletin board of their drawings.
3. Students can work in pairs and videotape themselves interviewing each other about what's special about them.
4. Read other books about how people are both alike and different, such as:
   Bread, Bread, Bread (Morris, 1989)
   Everybody Cooks Rice (Dooley, 1992)
   How My Parents Learned to Eat (Friedman, 1984)
   In the Beginning: Creation Stories from around the World (Hamilton, 1988)
   Straight Hair, Curly Hair (Goldin, 1966)
   This Is the Way We Go to School (Baer, 1990)

Types of Multicultural Literature

The list that follows presents examples of multicultural titles of cultural groups that have historically been underrepresented in children's literature. These books are divided into two categories: traditional and contemporary realistic fiction. This distinction has been made to encourage teachers to go beyond using just traditional tales, which depict Native Americans in ways of life that really don't exist anymore. It's also important to show Native Americans as they live today. Multicultural literature should include the present, as well as the past, which means looking at issues of racism, resistance, and violence, not just talking animals and happy villagers. Also, the books listed here come, as much as possible, from the experience of people in the Americas. For instance, traditional African tales are not included under the "African American" heading, because they are not representative of the African American experience.

This list of books provides a good start. Many of the titles mentioned have been used by my students when teaching with literature in field experiences. And I have annotated the list because some titles—like *Tar Beach* and *Amazing Grace*—don't really tell about the multicultural content of the book or how it might be used with children.

Traditional Tales

Native American

Doctor Coyote: A Native American Aesop's Fables (Bierhorst, 1987)—Mexican in origin, with a strong Spanish/Aztec influence, these tales could be compared to fables of Aesop, La Fontaine, and Native American trickster tales.

The Girl Who Loved Wild Horses (Goble, 1978)—A young Native American girl becomes one with nature and horses.

Also see other books about the Native American experience by Paul Goble.

The Legend of the Blue Bonnet (de Paola, 1983)—This is an original legend that tells of how the unselfishness of a child saved the Commanche people in Texas.

The Mud Pony: A Traditional Skidi Pawnee Tale (Cohen, 1988)—A retold Skidi Pawnee tale about people's relationship to nature and each other. The illustrator is Navajo.

Tonweya and the Eagles and Other Lakota Indian Tales (Yellow Robe, 1992)—These tales were told to the author by her father; both of them are Lakota.

African American

Flossie and the Fox (McKissack, 1986)—An African American folktale, retold for younger readers.

Jump! The Adventures of Brer Rabbit (Harris, 1986)—The trickster tales, retold with beautiful watercolor portraits of animals.

The People Could Fly: American Black Folktales (Hamilton, 1993)—A collection of 24 folktales from the African American experience, retold by the author.

The Talking Eggs (San Souci, 1989)—A Cinderella-type Creole tale from South Louisiana.

Wiley and the Hairy Man (Bang, 1976)—A tale of a boy and his mother who must outwit a "mighty mean man" by the laws of the Tombigbee Swamp, retold by the author.

Hispanic American

Arroz con Leche: Popular Songs and Rhymes from Latin America (Delacre, 1989)—Songs and poems from several Latin American cultures.

Borreguita and the Coyote (Aardema, 1991)—A clever little lamb outwits a wily coyote in this tale, originally from Mexico.

Brother Anansi and the Cattle Rancher (de Sauza, 1989)—A trickster tale from Nicaragua: The clever spider from West Africa and the Caribbean outwits a cattle rancher; in English and Spanish.

The Legend of El Dorado (Vidal, 1991)—The story of a "gilded man," El Dorado, in a tale originally from Colombia.

Tortillas para Mama and Other Spanish Nursery Rhymes (Griego, 1981)—Traditional rhymes in Spanish and English for younger readers.

Asian American

Tales from Gold Mountain (Yee, 1990)—Stories collected from those told by Chinese settlers in Vancouver, British Columbia, Canada.

Tales from the Rainbow People (Yep, 1989)—Stories the author collected from Chinese Americans in San Francisco, where he grew up.

Tongues of Jade (Yep, 1991)—More stories collected by the author from Chinese Americans, who told the stories not only to remind themselves of China but of how to survive in a new country.

Contemporary Stories and Biographies

Native American

Annie and the Old One (Miles, 1971)—Annie learns to accept the inevitability of her grandmother's death.

Black Star, Bright Dawn (O'Dell, 1988a)—An Eskimo girl competes in the grueling Iditarod dog sled race in Alaska.

Jimmy Yellow Hawk (Sneve, 1972)—The life of a boy growing up on a Sioux reservation in South Dakota today.

Knots on a Counting Rope (Martin & Archambault, 1987)—A young blind boy and his grandfather record the story of the boy's life.

Totem Pole (Hoyt-Goldsmith, 1990)—A photo essay about a boy whose father has kept alive the art of making totems.

African American

Amazing Grace (Hoffman, 1991)—Grace is a young African American girl with a lot of talent for acting; she perseveres to win the part of Peter Pan in the school play, despite resistance because of her race and gender.

M. C. Higgins, the Great (Hamilton, 1974)—A rich and complex novel about a boy in rural Ohio; won the Newbery Award in 1975.

The Patchwork Quilt (Flournoy, 1985)—A young girl and her grandmother make a quilt together.

Ragtime Tumpie (Schroeder, 1989)—The childhood of dancer Josephine Baker in St. Louis.

Tar Beach (Ringgold, 1991)—A childhood memoir of family and hot summer nights in the city on the roof, which is "tar beach."

Hispanic American

Baseball in April and Other Stories (Soto, 1990)—Short stories of young Hispanic children in California.

Family Pictures (Garza, 1990)—Paintings of the author's memories of the community she grew up in Brownsville, Texas; described in English and Spanish.

I Speak English for My Mom (Stanek, 1989)—A young Mexican American girl is her mother's link to an English-speaking community, until the mother goes back to school to learn English to get a better job.

Pelitos/Hairs (Cisneros, 1994)—A young girl describes her memories of her mother's hair.

Too Many Tamales (Soto, 1993)—A family Christmas dinner and losing mother's ring means that children eat too many tamales looking for it.

Asian American

Angel Child, Dragon Child (Surat, 1983)—A young immigrant struggles with separation from her mother (who's still in Vietnam) and lack of acceptance at school.

The Bracelet (Uchida, 1993)—The author writes about her experiences in an internment camp for Japanese Americans during World War II.

El Chino (Say, 1990)—A biography of a Chinese American who becomes a famous bullfighter.

I Hate English! (Levine, 1989)—Mei Mei resists learning English when she moves from Hong Kong to New York; she's proud of her ability to read and write Chinese.

The Journey: Japanese Americans, Racism, and Renewal (Hamanaka, 1990)—A factual account of the internment of Japanese Americans during World War II, written and illustrated by the descendant of an interned family.

Authors of Multicultural Literature

When choosing multicultural literature, note whether the author actually belongs to the culture he or she is writing about (Bishop, 1992). Until recently, that was not usually the case. Look for these authors, writing about these cultural groups:

Native American
Jamke Highwater
Virginia Driving Hawk Sneve

African American
Lucille Clifton
Eloise Greenfield
Virginia Hamilton
Patricia McKissack
Walter Dean Myers
Faith Ringgold
John Steptoe
Mildred Taylor

Hispanic American
Alma Flor Ada
Sandra Cisneros
Arthur Dorros
Carmen Lomas Garza
Nicholosa Mohr
Gary Soto
Victor Villasenor

Asian Americans
Betty Bao Lord
Allen Say
Yoshiko Uchida
Taro Yashima
Paul Yee
Laurence Yep
Ed Young

See Gary Soto's newest picture book, set in the contemporary barrio of East LA, *Chato's Kitchen* (1995).

Issues in Children's Literature

In addition to the multicultural issues already mentioned, children's books address sensitive topics such as divorce, death, or special needs. Be aware that these issues have not always been dealt with realistically, fairly, or humanely. In selecting books for use with children, judge each not only on interest and literary value but in terms of human value, as well.

Criteria to look for in selecting books that treat sensitive issues include (Rudman, 1984):

1. Realistic solutions to special problems such as divorce, adoption, racial and ethnic prejudice, and children with special needs
2. Realistic characters who behave plausibly, humanely, and responsively and are individuals, not rigid stereotypes
3. Bias-free language
4. Accurate and up-to-date information on subjects of a sensitive nature
5. Good writing and an avoidance of obvious sensational conflict or a too-obvious message
6. Appropriateness for a student's developmental level

Once again, the list of books that follows should be used as a starting point. I have annotated it because titles like *Hatchet* don't always reveal what sensitive issue is written about.

Divorce

Dear Mr. Henshaw (Cleary, 1983)—A boy writes to his favorite author about his parents' divorce.

Hatchet (Paulsen, 1988)—A boy faces his parents' divorce after he has survived in the Canadian wilderness.

Death

Bridge to Terabithia (Paterson, 1977)—A boy and girl share a special friendship and a make-believe play world until she dies and he must face her death.

On My Honor (Bauer, 1986)—A boy deals with his best friend's death.

Special Needs

The Pinballs (Byars, 1977)—Children who have experienced child abuse live together in a foster home.

Please Don't Tease Me (Madsen & Bockora, 1982)—A girl with a physical disability asks for tolerance.

An excellent source of more books is Rasinski and Gillespie (1992), *Sensitive Issues: An Annotated Guide to Children's Literature K–6.*

Assessing Teaching with Literature

Assessing students' authentic experiences with literature is an ongoing process, which can be done in a variety of ways in student- and response-centered classrooms:

1. ***Independent Reading Record:*** This record is a list of books that students have read. For each book, it could include the title, author, and date read and perhaps comments about it, too. An independent reading record shows the range and amount of the individual's reading.

2. ***Response Journals:*** As discussed earlier, these journals provide an ongoing, almost daily account of what students are reading, what attracts their attention, and how they are responding. These journals become even more important when used to talk about books and in literature groups.

3. ***Response Options:*** The activities students engage in after reading also provide information on their reading and responding. Teachers should keep annotated, anecdotal records of these projects.

4. ***Literature Conferences:*** Talking to students one on one provides a rich source of information. Teachers should keep logs of these conferences, noting things like what books students have read and when, what questions they asked, what comments they made, and any other observations.

5. ***Literature Groups: Student Self-Assessment:*** After working in literature groups, students should respond to these questions at the end of the cycle:

- "How would you evaluate your participation in the group?"
- "What did you learn in your group?"
- "What did you learn from other groups?"
- "What suggestions do you have for next time?"

NAME ____

1. Read *The Mystery of the Haunted Mine.* Yes/No
2. List other books you've read about the Southwest:
3. Write in your literature response journal. # of times ____
4. In your literature group:
   a. Work cooperatively.
   b. Talk together about books.
5. List projects you've done individually or in your literature group:
6. Describe what you've learned and how well you worked in your group:

FIGURE 7.8
Checklist for the Southwest

6. ***Literature Groups: Teacher Checklists:*** Teachers can develop checklists of what they expect students to do during literature-based "ripple effects." Figure 7.8 shows an example that could be used with the "ripple effect" of the Southwest, described earlier in the chapter.

Answers to Questions about Teaching with Literature

1. *How do readers respond to literature?*

Reader-response theorists explain that readers are actively engaged in constructing meaning while reading, not passively receiving it. Thus, reading is an active process. It involves the creation of meaning, rather than the discovery of it. And because meaning is created by individual readers, no text has a single correct meaning. Among reader-response theorists, Louise Rosenblatt's *transactional theory* has interested whole-language educators. She calls the reading process a transaction, during which a "live-circuit" is created between the reader and text. Meaning is discovered during this transaction.

Readers assume a *stance,* or focus their attention selectively in different ways, ranging between two points on a continuum. During an *efferent* reading, the focus is on the information to be taken away, or the more public aspects. During an *aesthetic* reading, the focus is on what the book arouses in the reader, or the more private aspects. Rosenblatt suggests that teachers' primary responsibility for most experiences with literature is to encourage children to take an aesthetic stance. Research has shown that children naturally assume a predominantly aesthetic stance toward literature. More efferent responses emerge from the richer, broader, more fluent aesthetic responses.

2. *What is response-centered, integrated teaching with literature?*

In this approach, teachers provide a classroom environment with many books, time, and opportunities for children to read or listen to books read aloud. Children have time to talk together, write in literature response journals, choose among response options, identify focal topics of interest, work in literature groups using related books and resources, and do wide independent reading. Literature is integrated across the curriculum and becomes the primary source of reading and information. Students' own responses determine much of what they will learn about.

LOOKING FURTHER

1. Keep a literature response journal to write about your own reading.
2. Read a book aloud to a group of children, and ask them what they think of it. Prompt them to draw or write anything they want in response to it. Analyze their responses to determine the stance they take toward literature: efferent or aesthetic.
3. Develop a literature plan for several theme-related books for use with a specific grade.
4. Use the lesson plan based on Peter Spier's (1980) *People* in this chapter, and try out some of the response options with children. Describe what happened. What would you do differently if you taught this lesson again?
5. Read several of the multicultural books listed in the chapter—some by authors who share the culture and some by authors who don't. Critique each book in terms of how realistic or genuine it seemed regarding multicultural content. Do you notice any differences among the books, depending on whether the author shared the culture? Write down your conclusions.

RESOURCES

Bromley, K. (1991). *Webbing with literature.* Boston, MA: Allyn and Bacon.

Zarrillo, J. (1994). *Multicultural literature, multicultural teaching: Units for the elementary grades.* Fort Worth, TX: Harcourt Brace Jovanovich.

REFERENCES

Banks, J. A., & Banks, C. A. M. (1993). *Multicultural education: Issues and perspectives* (2nd ed.). Boston: Allyn and Bacon.

Beach, R. (1993). *A teacher's introduction to reader-response theories.* Urbana, IL: National Council of Teachers of English.

Bishop, R. S. (1992). Multicultural literature for children: Making informed choices. In V. J. Harris (Ed.), *Teaching multicultural literature in grades K–8* (pp. 37–54). Norwood, MA: Christopher Gordon.

Bowker, R. R. (Annual). *Subject guide to children's books in print.* New York: Bowker.

Breen, K. (Ed.). (1988). *Index to collective biographies for young readers.* (4th ed.). New York: Bowker.

Brewton, J. E. (1983). *Index to poetry for children and young people.* New York: Wilson.

Cox, C. S. (1986). Gordon D. Shirreffs: An interview with a Western writer. *English Journal, 75,* 40–48.

Cox, C. (1994a, December). *Challenging the text: Case studies of young children responding to literature.*

Paper presented at the National Reading Conference, San Diego, CA.

Cox, C. (1994b, April). *Young children's response to literature: A longitudinal study, K–3.* Paper presented at the American Educational Reading Association Annual Meeting, New Orleans, LA.

Cox, C., & Boyd-Batstone, P. (in press). *Language development through literature in culturally and linguistically diverse classrooms.* Columbus, OH: Merrill/Macmillan.

Cox, C., & Zarrillo, J. (1993). *Teaching reading with children's literature.* Columbus, OH: Merrill/Macmillan.

Cummins, J. (1989). *Empowering minority students.* Sacramento: California Association for Bilingual Education.

Gillespie, J. T., & Naden, C. J. (1990). *Best books for children: Pre-school through Grade 6* (4th ed.) New York: Bowker.

Glenn, C., & Stein, N. (1979). An analysis of story comprehension in elementary school children. In R. Freedle (Ed.), *New directions in discourse processing* (Vol. 2, pp. 68–85). Hillsdale, NJ: Erlbaum.

Goodman, K. S. (1992). I didn't found whole language. *Reading Teacher, 46*(3), 188–199.

Horn Book, Inc. (Semiannual). *The Horn Book guide to children's and young adult books.* Boston: Horn Book, Inc.

Jett-Simpson, M. (Ed.). (1989). *Adventuring with books: A booklist for pre-K–Grade 6* (9th ed.). Urbana, IL: National Council of Teachers of English.

Kobrin, B. (1988). *Eyeopeners! How to choose and use children's books about real people, places, and things.* New York: Penguin.

Langer, J. A. (1992). *Literature instruction: A focus on student response.* Urbana, IL: National Council of Teachers of English.

Lima, C. W. (1989). *A to zoo: Subject access to children's picture books* (3rd ed.). New York: Bowker.

Lukens, R. J. (1991.) *A critical handbook of children's literature.* Glenview, IL: Scott, Foresman/Little, Brown.

Mandler, J. M., & Johnson, N. S. (1977). Remembrance of things parsed: Story structure and recall. *Cognitive Psychology, 9,* 111–151.

Morrow, L. M. (1992). *Literacy development in the early years: Helping children read and write.* Boston: Allyn and Bacon.

Peterson, R. (1987). Literature groups: Intensive and extensive reading. In D. Watson (Ed.), *Ideas with insights: Language arts K–6* (pp. 14–20). Urbana, IL: National Council of Teachers of English.

Peterson, R., & Eeds, M. (1990). *Grand conversations: Literature groups in action.* New York: Scholastic.

Raphael, T. (1992). Research directions: Literature and discussion in the reading program. *Language Arts, 69,* 54–61.

Rasinski, T. V., & Gillespie, C. S. (1992). *Sensitive issues: An annotated guide to children's literature K–6.* Phoenix: Oryx.

Richter, B., & Wenzel, D. (1988). *The museum of science and industry basic list of children's science books.* Chicago: American Library Association.

Rosenblatt, L. M. (1978). *The reader, the text, the poem: The transactional theory of the literary work.* Carbondale: Southern Illinois University Press. (Original work published 1938)

Rosenblatt, L. M. (1982). The literary transaction: Evocation and response. *Theory into practice, 21,* 268–277.

Rosenblatt, L. M. (1994). The transactional theory of reading and writing. In R. Ruddell, M. Ruddell, & H. Singer (Eds.), *Theoretical models and processes of reading* (4th ed., pp. 1057–1092). Newark, DE: International Reading Association.

Rudman, M. K. (1984). *Children's literature: An issues approach* (2nd ed.). New York: Longman.

Rumelhart, D. (1975). Notes on a schema for stories. In D. G. Bobrow (Ed.), *Representation and understanding: Studies in cognitive science* (pp. 85–107). New York: Academic.

Sadow, M. W. (1982). The use of story grammar in the design of questions. *Reading Teacher, 35,* 518–522.

Short, K. G., & Pierce, K. M. (Eds.). (1990). *Talking about books: Creating literate communities.* Portsmouth, NH: Heinemann.

Sloan, G. D. (1984). *The child as critic* (2nd ed.). New York: Teachers College Press.

Watson, D. (1988). What do we find in a whole language program? In C. Weaver (Ed.), *Reading process and practice* (pp. 13–21). Portsmouth, NH: Heinemann.

Weaver, C. (1988). *Reading process and practice: From socio-psycholinguistics to whole language.* Portsmouth, NH: Heinemann.

Winkel, L. (Ed.). (1990). *The elementary school library collection: A guide to books and other media* (17th ed.). Williamsport, PA: Brodart.

Zarrillo, J. (1994). *Multicultural literature, multicultural teaching: Units for the elementary grades.* Fort Worth, TX: Harcourt Brace Jovanovich.

Zarrillo, J., & Cox, C. (1992). Efferent and aesthetic teaching. In J. Many & C. Cox (Eds.), *Reader stance and literary understanding: Exploring the theories, research, and practice* (pp. 235–249). Norwood, NJ: Ablex.

CHILDREN'S BOOKS

Aardema, V. (1991). *Borreguita and the coyote.* New York: Knopf.

Ahlberg, J., & Ahlberg, A. (1986). *The jolly postman.* New York: Little, Brown.

Aliki. (1979). *Mummies made in Egypt.* New York: HarperCollins.

Aliki. (1985a). *Dinosaurs are different.* New York: HarperCollins.

Aliki. (1985b). *My visit to the dinosaurs.* New York: HarperCollins.

Aliki. (1988). *Digging up dinosaurs.* New York: HarperCollins.

Allen, T. D. (Ed.). (1972). *The whispering wind: Poetry by young American Indians.* New York: Doubleday.

Amon, A. (1981). *The earth is sore: Native Americans on nature.* New York: Atheneum.

Baer, E. (1990). *This is the way we go to school.* New York: Scholastic

Baker, B. (1965). *Walk the world's rim.* New York: Harper & Row.

Bang, M. (1976). *Wiley and the hairy man.* New York: Macmillan.

Bauer, M. D. (1986). *On my honor.* Boston: Houghton Mifflin.

Baylor, B. (1975). *The desert is theirs.* New York: Scribner's.

Baylor, B. (1981). *Desert voices.* New York: Scribner's.

Baylor, B. (1987). *And it is still that way.* Sante Fe, NM: Trails West.

Bierhorst, J. (1979). *A cry from the earth.* New York: Four Winds Press.

Bierhorst, J. (1983). *The sacred path: Spells, prayers and power songs of the American Indians.* New York: Morrow.

Bierhorst, J. (1987). *Doctor Coyote: A native American Aesop's fables.* New York: Macmillan.

Blume, J. (1972). *Are you there God? It's me, Margaret.* New York: Dell.

Byars, B. (1977). *The pinballs.* New York: HarperCollins.

Carrick, D., & Carrick, C. (1983). *Patrick's dinosaurs.* New York: Houghton Mifflin.

Carrick, D., & Carrick, C. (1988). *What happened to Patrick's dinosaurs?* New York: Houghton Mifflin.

Cherry, L. (1990). *The great Kapok tree: A tale of the Amazon rain forest.* New York: Harcourt Brace Jovanovich.

Cisneros, S. (1994). *Hairs/Politos.* New York: Knopf.

Clark, A. N. (1962). *Paco's miracle.* New York: Farrar, Straus, & Giroux.

Cleary, B. (1983). *Dear Mr. Henshaw.* New York: Morrow Jr. Books.

Cohen, C. L. (1988). *The mud pony: A traditional Skidi Pawnee tale.* New York: Scholastic.

Cooney, B. (1982). *Miss Rumphius.* New York: Viking.

de Paola, T. (1973). *Nana upstairs & Nana downstairs.* New York: Putnam's.

de Paola, T. (1983) *The legend of the blue bonnet.* New York: Putnam.

de Sauza, J. (1989). *Brother Anansi and the cattle rancher.* San Francisco: Children's Book Press.

Delacre, L. (1989). *Arroz con leche: Popular songs and rhymes from Latin America.* New York: Scholastic.

Dooley, N. (1992). *Everybody cooks rice.* Minneapolis: Carolrhoda Books.

Flournoy, V. (1985). *The patchwork quilt.* New York: Dial.

Freedman, R. (1987). *Lincoln: A photobiography.* New York: Houghton Mifflin.

Friedman, I. (1984). *How my parents learned to eat.* New York: Houghton Mifflin.

Galdone, P. (1983). *The gingerbread man.* New York: Houghton Mifflin.

Garza, C. L. (1990). *Family pictures.* San Francisco: Children's Book Press.

George, J. C. (1974). *Julie of the wolves.* New York: HarperCollins.

George, J. C. (1991). *My side of the mountain.* New York: Puffin Books.

Gibbons, G. (1987). *Dinosaurs.* New York: Holiday House.

Goble, P. (1978). *The girl who loved wild horses.* New York: Bradbury.

Goldin, A. (1966). *Straight hair, curly hair.* New York: HarperCollins.

Griego, M. C. (1981). *Tortillas para mama and other Spanish nursery rhymes.* New York: Holt, Rinehart & Winston.

Hamanaka, S. (1990). *The journey: Japanese Americans, racism, and renewal.* New York: Orchard.

Hamilton, V. (1974). *M. C. Higgins, the great.* New York: Macmillan.

Hamilton, V. (1988). *In the beginning: Creation stories from around the world.* Orlando, FL: Harcourt Brace Jovanovich.

Hamilton, V. (1993). *The people could fly: American black folktales.* New York: Knopf.

Harris, J. C. (1986). *Jump! The adventures of Brer Rabbit* (adapted by V. Parks & M. Jones). New York: Harcourt Brace Jovanovich.

Hautzig, E. (1968). *The endless steppe: Growing up in Siberia.* New York: Crowell.

Hoffman, M. (1991). *Amazing Grace.* New York: Dial.

Holling, H. C. (1942). *Tree in the trail.* New York: Literary Classics.

Hopkins, L. B. (Ed.). (1987). *Dinosaurs.* New York: Harcourt Brace Jovanovich.

Hoyt-Goldsmith, D. (1990). *Totem pole.* New York: Holiday House.

Hutchins, P. (1968). *Rosie's walk.* New York: Macmillan.

Joyce, W. (1988). *Dinosaur Bob.* New York: HarperCollins.

Keats, E. J. (1963). *The snowy day.* New York: Viking.

Kellogg, S. (1988). *Johnny Appleseed.* New York: Morrow.

Kent, J. (1971). *The fat cat: A Danish folktale.* New York: Parent's Magazine.

Kohn, B. (1968). *Secret codes and ciphers.* New York: Prentice-Hall.

Krumgold, J. (1953). *And now Miguel.* New York: Crowell.

L'Engle, M. (1976). *A wrinkle in time.* New York: Dell.

Levine, E. (1989). *I hate English!* New York: Scholastic.

Lewis, C. S. (1986). *The lion, the witch, and the wardrobe.* New York: Macmillan.

Lewis, R. (1968). *Out of the earth I sing.* New York: Norton.

Lobel, A. (1970). *Frog and toad are friends.* New York: HarperCollins.

Lomas Garza, C. (1990). *Family picture—Cuadros de familia.* New York: Children's Book Press.

Macaulay, D. (1988). *The way things work.* New York: Houghton Mifflin.

MacLachlan, P. (1985). *Sarah, plain and tall.* New York: Harper.

Madsen, J., & Bockora, D. (1982). *Please don't tease me.* New York: Knopf.

Martin, B., & Archambault, J. (1987). *Knots on a counting rope.* New York: Holt, Rinehart & Winston.

Martinello, M. L., & Nesmith, S. P. (1980). *With Domingo Leal in San Antonio, 1734.* San Antonio, TX: University of Texas, Institute of Texan Cultures.

McCloskey, R. (1941). *Make way for ducklings.* New York: Viking.

McKissack, P. (1986). *Flossie and the fox.* New York: Dial.

Miles, M. (1971). *Annie and the old one.* New York: Little, Brown.

Morris, A. (1989). *Bread, bread, bread.* New York: Lothrop.

Myrick, M. (1963). *The secret three.* New York: HarperCollins.

Norton, M. (1953). *The borrowers.* New York: Harcourt Brace.

O'Dell, S. (1970). *Sing down the moon.* Boston: Houghton Mifflin.

O'Dell, S. (1974). *Child of fire.* Boston: Houghton Mifflin.

O'Dell, S. (1988a). *Black star, bright dawn.* Boston: Houghton Mifflin.

O'Dell, S. (1988b). *Island of the blue dolphins.* New York: Dell.

Paterson, K. (1977). *Bridge to Terabithia.* New York: HarperCollins.

Paulsen, G. (1988). *Hatchet.* New York: Puffin Books.

Plume, I. (1987). *The Bremen-town musicians.* New York: HarperCollins

Politi, L. (1973). *The nicest gift.* New York: Scribner's.

Prelutsky, J. (1986). *Read-aloud rhymes for the very young.* New York: Knopf.

Prelutsky, J. (1988). *Tyrannosaurus was a beast: Dinosaur poems.* New York: Greenwillow.

Pringle, L. (1977). *The gentle desert.* New York: Macmillan.

Provensen, A., & Provensen, M. (1987). *The glorious flight: The story of Louis Bleriot.* New York: Puffin Books.

Ringgold, F. (1991). *Tar beach.* New York: Crown.

Rylant, C. (1982). *When I was young in the mountains.* New York: Dutton.

San Souci, R. (1989). *The talking eggs.* New York: Dial.

Sato, G. (1995). *Chato's kitchen.* New York: Putnam's.

Say, A. (1990). *El Chino.* Boston: Houghton Mifflin.

Schroeder, A. (1989). *Ragtime Tumpie.* Boston: Little, Brown.

Scieszka, J. (1989). *The true story of the three little pigs.* New York: Viking.

Sendak, M. (1963). *Where the wild things are.* New York: HarperCollins.

Shirreffs, G. D. (1957). *Son of the thunder people.* New York: Westminster.

Shirreffs, G. D. (1958). *Swiftwagon.* New York: Westminster.

Shirreffs, G. D. (1961). *The gray sea raiders.* New York: Chilton.

Shirreffs, G. D. (1962). *The mystery of the haunted mine.* New York: Scholastic.

Shirreffs, G. D. (1963). *Mystery of lost canyon.* New York: Chilton.

Shirreffs, G. D. (1964). *The secret of the Spanish desert.* New York: Chilton.

Shirreffs, G. D. (1968). *Mystery of the lost cliff dwelling.* New York: Prentice-Hall.

Siebert, D. (1988). *Mojave.* New York: Crowell.

Silverstein, S. (1981). *A light in the attic.* New York: HarperCollins.

Silverstein, S. (1986). *Where the sidewalk ends.* New York: Dell.

Simon, S. (1973). *The rock-hounds book.* New York: Viking.

Slobodkina, E. (1947). *Caps for sale.* New York: Harper & Row.

Sneve, V. D. H. (1972). *Jimmy Yellow Hawk.* New York: Holiday.

Snyder, Z. K. (1967). *The Egypt game.* New York: Macmillan.

Soto, G. (1990). *Baseball in April and other stories.* New York: Harcourt Brace Jovanovich

Soto, G. (1993). *Too many tamales.* New York: Putnam.

Sperry, A. (1968). *Call it courage.* New York: Macmillan.

Spier, P. (1980). *People.* New York: Doubleday.

Stanek, M. (1989). *I speak English for my Mom.* Niles, IL: Albert Whitman.

Steig, W. (1978). *Sylvester and the magic pebble.* New York: Windmill.

Steptoe, J. (1987). *Mufaro's beautiful daughters: An African tale.* New York: Lothrop, Lee, & Shepard.

Surat, M. (1983). *Angel child, dragon child.* Racine, WI: Carnival/Raintree.

Taylor, M. (1976). *Roll of thunder, hear my cry.* New York: Dial.

Taylor, T. (1976). *The cay.* New York: Avon.

Uchida, Y. (1993). *The bracelet.* New York: Putnam.

Van Allsburg, C. (1979). *The garden of Abdul Gasazi.* Boston: Houghton Mifflin.

Van Allsburg, C. (1981). *Jumanji.* Boston: Houghton Mifflin.

Van Allsburg, C. (1983). *The wreck of the Zephyr.* Boston: Houghton Mifflin.

Van Allsburg, C. (1984). *The mysteries of Harris Burdick.* Boston: Houghton Mifflin.

Vidal, B. (1991). *The legend of El Dorado.* New York: Knopf.

Viorst, J. (1972). *Alexander and the terrible, horrible, no good, very bad day.* New York: Atheneum.

Waber, B. (1972). *Ira sleeps over.* New York: Houghton Mifflin.

White, E. B. (1952). *Charlotte's web.* New York: HarperCollins.

White, E. B. (1954). *Stuart Little.* New York: HarperCollins.

Wilder, L. I. (1961). *Little house in the big woods.* New York: HarperCollins.

Wood, A. (1984). *The napping* house. New York: Harcourt Brace Jovanovich.

Yashima, T. (1958). *Umbrella.* New York: Viking.

Yee, P. (1990). *Tales from gold mountain.* New York: Macmillan.

Yellow Robe, R. (1992). *Tonweya and the eagles and other Lakota Indian tales.* New York: Dial.

Yep, L. (1989). *Tales from the rainbow people.* New York: Harper & Row.

Yep, L. (1991). *Tongues of jade.* New York: Harper.

Yolen, J. (1992). *Encounter.* New York: Harcourt Brace Jovanovich.

Yorinks, A. (1986). *Hey, Al.* New York: Farrar, Straus & Giroux.

Chapter 8

Reading as a Language Art

Questions about Reading as a Language Art

1. *What is reading, and what are the different models of the reading process?*
2. *What are the different methods and materials used to teach reading?*
3. *How should we teach reading in a student- and response-centered classroom?*

Reflective Response

What are your memories of reading in school? When, what, and how did you read? What methods and materials did your teachers use? Jot down your ideas and reflect back on them as you read the chapter.

Recommendations for Teaching Reading

Becoming a Nation of Readers: The Report of the Commission on Reading (Anderson, Hiebert, Scott, & Wilkinson, 1985) characterized reading as an integral part of the language arts. As stated in the report, "It cannot be emphasized too strongly that reading is one of the language arts. All of the uses of language—listening, speaking, reading, and writing—are interrelated and mutually supportive. It follows, therefore, that school activities that foster one of the language arts inevitably will benefit the others as well. Writing activities, in particular, should be integrated into the reading period."

For a critique of *Becoming a Nation of Readers*, see Davidson (1988), *Counterpoint and Beyond: A Response to Becoming a Nation of Readers*.

Becoming a Nation of Readers became an authoritative account of what we know about the theory and practice of teaching reading. Recommendations from the report for teaching reading included a greater focus on:

- getting meaning from print from the very beginning of school
- reading aloud to children
- providing a wide variety of experiences and talking together about them
- allowing more time reading self-selected books and writing and less time on worksheets
- developing better libraries
- providing more comprehensive assessment
- making more use of good literature in reading instruction

These recommendations came at a time when teachers were already making a shift to literature-based reading, which is planned by the classroom teacher, and away from basal reading programs, which emphasizes teaching separate skills and student workbook exercises (Shannon, 1990). This shift to literature-based reading is supported by the whole-language movement, which advocates a greater role for literature and teachers in reading instruction (Altwerger, Edelsky, & Flores, 1987; Goodman, 1986).

The Snapshot that follows describes an experienced teacher who had used a basal text for many years but decided to shift to literature-based reading. She had come to view reading as the construction of meaning while reading and literature as a means of personal exploration. As you read, think about your reading experiences in school and the recommendations of *Becoming a Nation of Readers.*

SNAPSHOT: A Literature-Based Lesson—Before, During, and After Reading

Nora Miller is about to teach a literature-based reading lesson to her first-grade class in Baton Rouge, Louisiana. She has the youngest first grade in the school, and two of her students are repeating this grade. As you read this Snapshot, note how she approaches teaching reading as a process of meaning construction. She is guided by a social constructivist perspective of learning: that children construct meaning when they're actively engaged in print and meaningful interaction with other students and the teacher. She is also guided by the transactional perspective of experiencing literature: the meaning of a work of literature comes into being during an active transaction between the reader and text. Here's what Nora does during this shared guided-reading experience—before, during, and after reading.

Before Reading

See Chapter 4, Emergent Literacy, for a list of predictable pattern books.

Beni Montresor won the Caldecott Award for illustrating *May I Bring a Friend?*

1. ***Choose Good Literature:*** Nora chooses the picture book *May I Bring a Friend?* by Beatrice Schenk de Regniers (1965). She believes her children will enjoy it and be motivated to join in the shared reading she has planned. This book is humorous and has a repeated pattern that students can predict and join in during the reading. The main character of the book is a child about the same age as Nora's students; other characters include

In her first-grade classroom, Nora Miller uses a flannelboard for a literature-based reading lesson on May I Bring a Friend?

zoo animals and a whimsical King and Queen, who keep inviting the child over to their house. The book is also colorful and has award-winning illustrations.

2. *Link to Students' Needs:* Nora's students have usually done poorly on recognizing the names of the days of the week and sequencing in the statewide minimum competency tests. Even though Nora doesn't believe that succeeding on this test is the best way to measure students' progress, in her school system, students must pass this test in order to move on to the next grade. Since many of her students are considered at risk, Nora planned this lesson to address their identified needs.

3. *Gather Materials: Flannelboard, Word Strips, and Pictures:* Nora has prepared word strips to use on the flannelboard. On them, she's written the names of the animals in the story and also the names of the days of the week. These word strips are scattered on the flannelboard next to her. She's also made pictures of all the animals and put these on the flannelboard, too.

4. *Set a Comfortable Mood:* Nora gets the book and gets comfortable in a chair next to the flannelboard. Then she invites the children to join her; they gather around her enthusiastically, settling on the floor. Nora reads aloud often and well. The mood is warm, and the setting is comfortable.

5. *Introduce the Book Enthusiastically:* Nora simply holds up the book and the children cheer. She's done repeated readings of this book (this is the third time this week), and her students enjoy it. It's like an old friend by now.

6. *Talk about Words:* The first two times Nora read this book, she simply read it and asked the children open and aesthetic questions: "What did you think of it?" and "What was your favorite part?" For this third reading, she wants the students to really join her, so she is drawing their attention to the words—animal names and names of the days of the week—and the order of both the appearance of the animals and the days of the week. She asks them if they remember the names of the animals, and as they call them out, she puts the animal word strips on the flannelboard. Then she asks if they remember the names of the days of the week, and as they call them out, she puts those words strips on the flannelboard, too. They talk about the words; some children read them, and some come to the flannelboard and touch them to show they recognize them.

During Reading

1. *Shared Repeated Reading:* Students join Nora in reading, chanting the parts of the story that they remember from the first two times she read it. They do this naturally and with pleasure. Here's the text of this rhyming book, which has a predictable pattern:

May I Bring a Friend?
by Beatrice Schenk de Regniers
The King and Queen
Invited me
To come to their house
On Sunday for tea.

I told the Queen
And the Queen told the King
I had a friend I wanted to bring.

The King told the Queen
"My dear, my dear,
Any friend of our friend
Is welcome here."

So I brought my friend . . .

2. ***Make Predictions:*** The page ends here, and before turning it, Nora dramatically asks the children to predict what will happen next:

Child: He'll bring a friend!
Nora: Do you know what friend he will bring?
Child: I know! A giraffe!
Nora: And what day of the week is it?
Child: Sunday?

3. ***Confirm Predictions:*** Nora turns the page slowly, mysteriously. The tension mounts. The children begin to bounce up and down in anticipation. Then they confirm their predictions when they see a picture of a giraffe. Nora continues reading:

The King said, "Hello."
He said, "How do you do?"
The Queen said, "Well!
Fancy meeting you!"

My friend sat down
Right next to me.
Then everyone had
A cup of tea.

4. ***Talk about the Story:*** Nora also asks the children aesthetic questions to encourage them to talk about the story and make more predictions:

Nora: Look at the picture of the king and queen. How do you think they're feeling?
Child: Sad.
Child: Amazed.
Nora: What do you think they'll do now? What would you do?
Child: I think she's gonna go (gestures with fist) wow! pow!

Nora: Why?
Child: She wouldn't take that. No way. I know I wouldn't.
Nora: Let's see what happens next.

Nora reads on, as the little boy brings a hippopotamus on Monday for dinner, monkeys for lunch on Tuesday, an elephant for breakfast on Wednesday, lions for Halloween on Thursday, a seal for Apple Pie Day on Friday, and on Saturday, they all go to the City Zoo for tea. As she reads, Nora asks the children to predict the story sequence, the day of the week, and the animal friend of the day. She also encourages them to respond aesthetically to the text and illustrations and discusses students' responses with them.

5. *Connect Ideas to Print:* After each new animal and day of the week, Nora asks a child to volunteer to find the name of that animal and day from among the word strips on the flannelboard. Each is placed in order on one side of the flannelboard.

After Reading

1. *Relive the Reading Experience:* Nora and her students talk about the experience of reading the book. Some of them chant parts of the story they remember. The children share their ideas and what they were thinking about while the story was being read. Nora encourages them to share all their ideas at this time, to listen to each other, and to interact. She does, too.

See Chapter 2, Children and Language, for more on semantic webbing and a Lesson Plan on finding words with *ant* in them.

2. *Talk about Words:* When one child announces that she knows how to spell *Sunday,* many others want to spell other days and animal names. Nora takes this as a cue to talk about what they remember about words. After a lot of spelling out loud, she asks if anyone notices a way in which all the day words are alike. Someone notices that they all have the little word *day* in them. They talk about this for a while, and Nora guides the students through a semantic web of words that have *day* in them (see Figure 8.1).

FIGURE 8.1 Semantic Web for a Day in First Grade

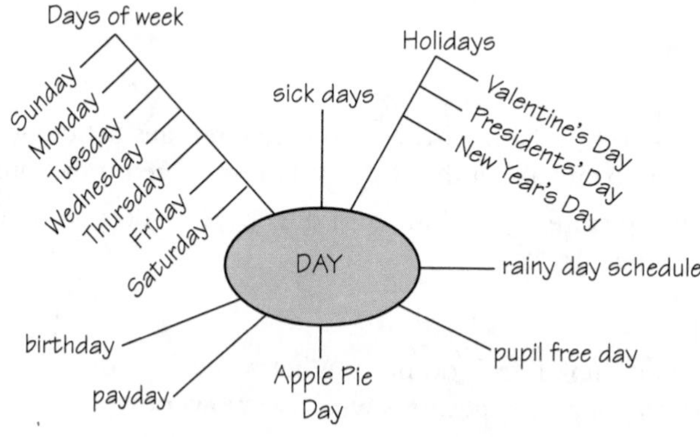

3. *Response Options: Drawing and Writing:* Nora asks what the students would like to do next with the story during group time, and together, they come up with the following list (based on the kinds of things they're used to doing after reading):

(1) Read the book again. Select another book to read.

(2) Draw a picture of a castle where the King and Queen lived.

(3) Make a castle collage out of pieces of construction paper cut in shapes: circles, triangles, squares, rectangles.

(4) Write a story about animals.

(5) Write an "If I Were" pattern about animals.

(6) Draw or write anything you want about the story.

The class had been talking about shapes in math.

"If I Were" Pattern
If I were a *lion*,
A *proud, loud, lion*,
If I were a *lion*,
This is what I would do:
I would *roar, roar, roar!*

4. *"Ripple Effect" Extending Activity:* The children had talked about what they would fix for the little boy in the story, if he were coming to their house. Peanut butter and jelly sandwiches were suggested. Nora asked the children if they'd like to make edible clay out of peanut butter the next day, and the response was "Yeah!" Nora brought the materials for edible clay and wrote the recipe in enlarged format on a piece of poster paper; she posted it on the wall above the table where they worked. She helped students make clay during group time, working with each group individually; students made all kinds of shapes with the clay. The other students continued to work on one of the response options they had started the day before or on other reading and writing activities.

Edible Clay
$^1/_2$ cup peanut butter
$^1/_2$ cup dry milk
$^1/_4$ cup honey
Mix and have fun!

Table 8.1 summarizes what Nora Miller did during this literature-based reading lesson and also offers other ideas for use with any children's book.

TABLE 8.1 Before, During, and After Reading

Before Reading	*During Reading*	*After Reading*
Choose good literature	Shared repeated readings	Relive reading experience
Link to students' needs	Make predictions	Talk about words
Gather materials:	Confirm predictions	Response options:
Flannelboard	Talk about story:	Drawing
Word strips	Aesthetic questions	Writing
Pictures	and prompts	Artmaking
Props	Connect ideas to print	Drama
Music		Constructions
Set a comfortable mood		Cooking
Introduce book enthusiastically		
Talk about words		

Reading as Meaning Construction

Reading is primarily the construction of meaning. This is not as simple as it sounds, however. Reading theory and research have wrestled for years with how to describe exactly how meaning is constructed during reading.

Models of the Reading Process

You should be familiar with several important models of the reading process as well as the methods and materials that reflect each model. When you read these models, think of what you wrote about how you read in school and how Nora Miller teaches. Where does your experience fit? Where does Nora's? Where do you think you will fit when you're teaching?

A Linear Model

The *linear model* of reading, familiarly called the *bottom-up model,* views reading as a part-to-whole process. First, the reader learns to recognize letters, followed by words, and then words in context, until he or she finally begins to understand what's read (Gough, 1976; LaBerge & Samuels, 1976). Thus, the reader's job is to figure out the meaning of the text as it was intended by the author.

The linear model is the theory behind the basal reader, sequential approach to teaching reading. According to this approach, the reading process is broken down into a series of smaller to larger subskills, which should be taught in a certain order. These skills are grouped under headings like *readiness, word recognition, word meaning,* and *comprehension*. The basal reader serves as both method and material reflecting this linear model. Namely, basal readers are graded sets of books that have hierarchies of objectives and activities. All students read the same stories, in the same order, and a teacher's manual guides the teacher step by step through the materials and sequence of skills.

An Interactive Model

The *interactive model* is based on schema theory (Rumelhart, 1984) and views the reading process as an interaction between the reader and text. *Schema theory* explains how learners acquire, store, and use knowledge in the form of schema, which are like scaffolding, giving structure to how knowledge is organized in the mind. The reader's job is to make meaningful connections between new information and prior knowledge (or *schemata*) and to use personal reading strategies—developed and adjusted for each individual purpose in reading—while constructing meaning from print. "In schema-theoretic terms, a reader comprehends a message when he [or she] is able to bring to mind a schema that gives a good account of the objects and events described in the message" (Anderson, 1985, p. 372).

This theoretical model allows for both bottom-up and top-down processes and is reflected in teaching approaches that emphasize direct reading instruction of word identification skills, vocabulary, and word meaning and comprehension. These strategies include activating prior knowledge and concept development, teacher-questioning strategies and reader self-questioning strategies, summarizing, graphically representing ideas to teach story structure, and using patterned books that encourage predictions on the part of the reader.

A Psycholinguistic Model

The *psycholinguistic model* developed by Kenneth Goodman (1976)—familiarly called the *top-down model*—views reading as part of language development and a process of hypothesis testing, in which the reader's job is to make predictions about the meaning of what's being read. Goodman uses the term "psycholinguistic guessing game" to describe the tentative information processing readers do while reading. Readers simultaneously test and accept or reject hypotheses as they create meaning. Goodman also introduced the notion of *miscue analysis* to point out that not all reading errors are equally important. He challenged the idea that language should be taught in pieces. This theoretical model is reflected in whole-language approaches (Goodman, 1986; Smith, 1971).

The Transactional Model

The *transactional theory* of the literary work developed by Louise Rosenblatt (1978, 1983, 1994) describes reading as a transaction between a particular reader and a particular text that occurs at a particular time and context. Meaning does not reside solely in the text or solely in the reader but comes into being during a transaction between the two. The reader is active; the text only consists of marks on the page until the reader transacts with it. The term *reader* implies a transaction with a text, and the term *text* implies a transaction with a reader. The two are not distinct entities but factors in a total situation. This view of the reading process has influenced approaches to teaching with literature that recognize the importance of the reader's response: student- and response-centered instruction, literature groups, response journals, and the use of more open, aesthetic questioning.

For more on applications of the transactional theory, see Chapter 1, Learning and Teaching Language Arts, and Chapter 7, Teaching with Literature.

Reading Methods Today

A variety of reading methods are used in the United States today. You should be familiar with them and how they reflect the various models of reading.

Basal Readers and Commercial Programs

The commercial basal reader program, which reflects the linear model of reading, has been the dominant method of reading instruction in elementary schools (Langer, Applebee, Mullis, & Foertsch, 1990). A basal reader program consists of a set of graded books used by a class or by groups within a class. All the books include selections of stories, which form the core of the reading lessons. The teacher follows directions in the teacher's guide for covering the separate subskills thought necessary in learning to read. Students complete workbooks and skillsheets to practice the skills taught during the teacher-directed lesson planned in the teacher's guide.

The method used with these materials is to form reading groups, usually on the basis of student ability. During a set reading period, the teacher works with one group at a time, while other groups do exercises in student workbooks or on skillsheets. The commonly used sequence of a teacher-directed lesson with a group is as follows:

1. *Prereading:* The teacher's manual provides a summary of the story, new vocabulary with suggestions for introducing words, background information to aid comprehension, and a prereading question for setting a purpose for reading.
2. *Silent reading:* Children read a set amount of text silently, and the teacher asks questions from the manual to check if they have understood what they read.
3. *Oral reading:* The teacher asks children to read aloud and asks more questions.
4. *Skill development:* Guided by the manual, the teacher gives direct instruction on decoding skills, word meaning, and comprehension. Students practice these skills in workbooks or on worksheets.

Patrick Shannon (1988), among others, has criticized basal readers because they have reduced reading to a kind of management system that certifies students' minimum reading competence. He maintains that they are widely used because schools want to show that they have a standardized way of judging reading competence. Commercial materials make this possible by using a sequence of testable objectives, a teacher's manual to guide instruction in meeting these objectives, and a test that demonstrates whether instruction has succeeded.

As a result, reading instruction often becomes nothing more than the use of a set of commercial basals throughout a district. This approach clearly diminishes the role of the teacher in deciding goals, methods, and pace of teaching, which is another criticism of basal reading systems. Their use clearly inhibits instructional innovations by predetermining teachers' instructional decisions. Similarly, basal reading systems limit the amount of attention paid to individual students, who have individual needs (Duffy, Roehler, & Putnam, 1987; Goodman, Shannon, Freeman, & Murphy, 1988).

A fundamental problem with basal reading systems was made clear by Durkin's research (1981), which showed that less than 1 percent of instructional time during basal reading lessons is devoted to comprehension, or understanding what's read. It's important to note, however, that newer basal reading systems have tried to emphasize meaning. In fact, the newest basal series have recognized the widespread use of literature-based reading and used excerpts or intact selections of children's literature. Nonetheless, they still direct teachers' decisions and don't focus on self-selected, voluntary reading (Morrow, 1992).

Questioning Strategies

Carefully planned questioning strategies for any kind of text—basal readers, children's literature, textbooks, or magazines—have developed from the interactive model of the reading process based on schema theory. The goal of this approach is to provide students with strategies that will help them become independent readers, who monitor their own thinking while reading and link their prior knowledge with the text they are reading. Many teacher-questioning strategies have been developed based on schema theory and the interactive model of the reading process. The *directed reading thinking activity (DRTA)* and *question-answer relationship (QAR)* can be used to help students monitor their own reading comprehension with any type of text.

Directed Reading Thinking Activity (DRTA). A directed reading thinking activity (DRTA) is a variation of a directed reading activity (DRA), such as those used in basal reading instruction. The main difference is that the DRA is carefully scripted, providing specific questions in the teacher's manual of a basal reading series. The DRTA (Stauffeur, 1975, 1980) focuses on active involvement with the text, as students make predictions and verify them as they read. Teachers use questions to activate prior knowledge, to introduce and expand vocabulary and word meaning, and to teach word identification skills and comprehension. Like the directed listening thinking activity (DLTA), the DRTA can be used with any text as an alternative to the basal reader or when making the transition from a basal reader to literature-based approach.

See Chapter 5, Listening and Talking, for more on DLTA.

Here are the steps in a DRTA:

1. ***Prereading***
   - Introduce the selection: show the cover or an illustration and read the title.
   - Ask for predictions about the story: What do you think the story is about? Why?
   - Ask what students already know about the subject. (This is especially useful for informational texts.)
   - Write ideas and predictions on the chalkboard or chartpaper.
2. ***Reading***
   - Direct children to read to verify their predictions.
   - Ask: What will happen next? Why do you think so?
3. ***Postreading***
   - Discuss verification of students' ideas and predictions.
   - Encourage children to find and read sections that prove or disprove predictions.
   - Encourage discussion of those predictions that can neither be proved nor disproved directly by the text but can be inferred.

Question-Answer Relationship (QRA). The premise underlying this approach is that students will understand more of what they read if they understand the question-answer relationship, or QAR (Pearson & Johnson, 1978; Raphael, 1982, 1986). Understanding the QAR will improve both literal and inferential comprehension that can be used with any type of text. The QAR is based on a system of categorizing a question depending on where the reader will find information to answer it. Here's an example:

The Text: *The beaver gnawed the tree. The tree fell to the ground.*

Three Types of Questions	***Question-Answer Relationship Where is the answer found?***
1. *Text-explicit question:* The answer is explicitly stated in the text. Q: "What did the beaver gnaw?"	1. *Right there:* The same words that make the question and the answer are found in the same sentence. A: "The beaver gnawed the tree."
2. *Text-implicit question:* The answer can be inferred from the text. Q: "Why did the tree fall?"	2. *Think and search:* The answer is there but not in the exact words used in sentence. A: "Because the beaver gnawed it."
3. *Script-implicit question:* The answer comes from the background knowledge of the reader. *Q:* "Why did the beaver gnaw the tree?"	3. *On my own:* The answer won't be found in the words in the story, but in your own mind. *A:*. . .

The teacher explains these three types of questions to students in practice lessons and encourages them to use the questions independently as they read any type of text.

Whole-Language, Literature-Based Reading

Whole language is not a method but a set of applied beliefs with regard to language development, curriculum, learning, teaching, and the community. Edelsky, Altwerger, and Flores (1991) describe it as a "professional theory in practice," drawing from the fields of psychology, child development, psycholinguistics and sociolinguistics, literary theory, composition theory, and the theory of literacy.

Kenneth Goodman (1986), whose psycholinguistic theory of the reading process is reflected in the whole-language approach, describes key ideas about whole language relevant to reading:

1. Literacy develops from whole to part during functional, meaningful, relevant language use.
2. Readers construct meaning while reading, drawing on their prior learning and experience.
3. Readers predict, select, confirm, and self-correct as they make sense of print.
4. Three language systems interact in written language: the graphophonic (sound and letter patterns), the syntactic (sentence patterns), and the semantic (meanings). They work together and can't be isolated for instruction.
5. Comprehension of meaning is always the goal of readers.

In a whole-language classroom, literature and other authentic texts—such as children's writing—are the material for reading, and the teacher makes decisions about how reading will be taught. Reading skills are not taught in isolation but in meaningful contexts and when students need them.

Second-Language Acquisition and Reading

Stephen Krashen has put forth a strong argument for learning to read by reading—especially what he calls *free voluntary reading* (*FVR*)—in his book *The Power of Reading* (1993). He maintains that this is true for students who are learning English as a second language and to achieve advanced second-language proficiency. According to Krashen, "Free reading is one of the best things an acquirer can do to bridge the gap from the beginning level to truly advanced levels of second language proficiency" (p. x). His review of the research shows that:

1. Free reading is a powerful tool in language education, a missing ingredient in first language arts and in second-language acquisition, as well.
2. Students who read more in their second language also write and spell better in that language.
3. Learning to read in one language helps students learn to read in a second language.
4. Reading provides knowledge of the world and subject matter knowledge that supports second-language acquisition.
5. Pleasure in reading the first language will transfer to pleasure in learning to read the second language.

Student- and Response-Centered Reading: Methods and Materials

In this section, we'll discuss the reading methods and materials most compatible with the theoretical underpinnings of this book. Namely, that includes the social constructivist perspective, which defines *learning* as an active, ongoing, constructive process that occurs in the social contexts of the classroom, home, and community, and the transactional perspective, which suggests that meaning is constructed during a transaction between the reader and text. In short, reading is acquired through use. Children learn to read by reading, and children's literature should be the main reading material, along with other authentic texts such as children's writing, language experience charts, magazines, newspapers, and environmental print.

Weaver (1988) has schematically shown how transactions between readers and texts occur in specific classroom contexts against the backdrop of the larger community and culture that students bring to school (see Figure 8.2). Methods and materials that reflect these perspectives are the language experience approach (LEA) and literature-based methods such as reading aloud, sustained silent reading (SSR), self-selected reading and reading conferences, shared reading and "big books," and literature units.

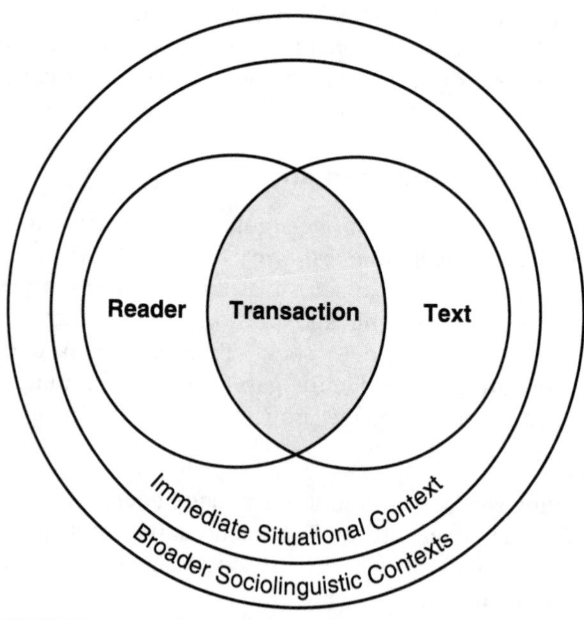

FIGURE 8.2
Reading in Context

Source: From *Reading Process and Practice: From Socio-Psycholinguistics to Whole Language,* by C. Weaver, 1988, Portsmouth, NH: Heinemann. Copyright 1988 by Heinemann Publishers. Reprinted with permission.

Language Experience Approach (LEA)

The language experience approach uses language experience charts, which are composed orally by the children and recorded by the teacher on a piece of chartpaper. We saw an example of language experience charts in Chapter 4, when first-grade teacher Marion Harris recorded students' descriptions of apples and kindergarten teacher Mauretta Hurst recorded the story "The Adventures of a Baby Elephant." Language experience charts based on interesting, shared experiences become part of the classroom print environment and student-composed texts for reading and rereading. These charts show the connection between reading, writing, experience, and meaning.

Here are the steps of the LEA:

See Chapter 2, Children and Language, for more on vocabulary and concept development, and Chapter 5, Listening and Talking, for more on clustering and webbing.

1. ***Use experiences to develop language and concepts.***
   - Use experiences as the basis for thinking and talking.
   - Develop concepts through talking, clustering ideas, and semantic webbing.
2. ***Build vocabulary.***
   - Focus on words children already know and use during discussions, and add new words along the way.
   - Record and display these words on word strips or chartpaper.

3. ***Children compose and teacher records on chartpaper.***
   - Choose a focal topic, such as an interesting classroom experience.
   - Discuss the topic and create a title. Record the title on top of the chart.
   - Continue to discuss; encourage children's comments; record them on the chart. Use questions like: "What else can you tell me?"
   - Children watch as the teacher writes their ideas on the chart and read while he or she is writing.
4. ***Children read the language experience chart.***
   - Read the chart with the children, pointing to words.
   - Take volunteers to read parts or all of the chart.
   - Let another child point to the words while others read.
5. ***Integrate skills.***
   - Skills can be taught in a meaningful context, as children read their own words.
6. ***Publish.***
   - Writing through language experience is published instantly, as it's recorded by the teacher.
   - Display charts on bulletin boards and walls or bind them together, creating class books for further reading and rereading.

TEACHING IDEA

LEA with At-Risk Readers

Here's an example of a teacher using the LEA with at-risk students who need motivation and help with reading. Their teacher, Gene Hughes, has found that LEA is a successful student- and response-centered method with students who have not succeeded with traditional reading instruction and who have low self-concepts of themselves as readers. Gene provides many interesting direct experiences, encourages students to talk about them, and uses LEA along with sustained silent reading, self-selected wide independent reading, and conferences. He builds vocabulary and teaches skills through these methods.

For example, Gene was given a baby crow, which he brought to school each day. Figure 8.3 shows the first language experience story the students wrote about Bart the Crow. Gene's students read this story many times and published it by posting it on the wall outside their room; an article about Bart, which appeared in the education section of the local newspaper, was posted in their classroom. Given their interest in Bart, the students read books about birds and how to care for them.

See *Cry of the Crow* by Jean Craighead George (1980).

When Bart had an accident, fracturing his leg, the students wrote a second language experience story about him and his injury. It's shown here using the step-by-step LEA sequence:

(continued)

BART THE CROW

Bart is a baby crow. He has black featnres. He is soft. Bart lives in a nest. The nest is a plastic pail filled with hay. Sometimes we take him outside so he can exercise and get fresh air. He has a good appetite. We feed him grapes, baby food, dog food, and puppy chow. He drinks water. He is a good bird and we care about him.

FIGURE 8.3
Students' First Language Experience Story

1. ***Share an Experience:*** Gene gathers the children together on the rug:

Teacher: When Bart comes out of his cage, he'll be excited.
Child: Here he comes!
Teacher: He needs to fly around for a while. His leg's doing better. He's not limping as badly as he was. What's he doing now?
Child: Taking a bath kinda like.
Teacher (picks Bart up and pets him soothingly): Just like a baby. Remember when he couldn't fly?
Child: Broken leg.
Teacher: Not exactly.
Child: Fractured.

2. ***Build Vocabulary:*** The students watch Bart walking around them:

Teacher: When babies are small their bones are . . .
Child: Tender.
Child: Soft.
Child: Weak.
Teacher: What did we do when he had the accident?
Child: Took him to the doctor.
Teacher: What do you call a doctor for animals?
Child: A vet.
Child: A veterinarian.
Teacher: What happened then?
Child: They took a picture of him.
Teacher: What's that called?

Child: I know! An x-ray.
Teacher: Let's talk about his accident. What happened?
Child: He had a fraction.
Child: No. He had a *fracture*.
Teacher: It didn't happen too long ago, so we could start our story with the word *recently*. That means something that happened just a little while ago.

3. *Write and Read:* Gene uses a marking pen to write the story on chartpaper as the students dictate it. He's working on the floor, with the students around him:

Teacher (writing and reading): "Recently Bart . . ."
Child: Had an accident.
Teacher: How do you spell that?
Child: A-c-c- . . .
Child: . . . i . . .
Child: A-c-c-i-d-e-n-t.
Child: Someone picked him up the wrong way.
Child: Bart fractured his leg.
Teacher: How did he act?
Child: He limped.
Child: He curled his toes up.
Teacher: What did we do to make him feel better?
Child: We took him to the vet at LSU.
Teacher: Let's read what we have so far.

(Student reads.)

Teacher: What happened next?

Students at risk for academic problems take turns holding Bart the Crow before writing a language experience story about their class pet.

(continued)

Child: The doctor gave him a shot.
Child: And x-rayed him.
Teacher: What did the doctor prescribe for him?
Child: The doctor said he needed rest.
Teacher: How is he doing now?
Child: Fine.
Teacher: Let's put a sentence to tell that.
Child: He's doing fine now.
Teacher: Will someone read the story?
(Student reads the story; see Figure 8.4.)

4. ***Integrate Skills:*** Gene and his students check the story and focus on skills:

Teacher: I see a little mistake. I wrote *need* here.
Child: Write *needed*. Add *-ed*.
Teacher: What should we add for a title?
Child: "Bart's Accident."
Teacher: This is an apostrophe. It means the accident happened to Bart. What does *LSU* stand for?
Child: Tigers!
Teacher: Yes, but the letters *LSU* are an abbreviation, or a short way to say something.
Child: Louisiana State University.
Child: *SU* is Southern University. Jaguars!
Teacher: What do we call letters like *SU?*
Child: Abbreviation.
Teacher: You did a great job on this story. What's the new word that tells when?
Child: *Recently.*
Teacher: There's also a word that tells the name of a doctor for animals.
Child: *Veterinarian.*

FIGURE 8.4
Students' Second Language Experience Story

BART'S ACCIDENT

Recently Bart had a little accident. Someone picked him up the wrong way. Bart fractured his leg. He limped and Curled his toes up. We took him to the vet at LSU. The doctor gave him a Shot and x-rayed his leg. The doctor Said he needs rest. He's doing fine now.

Teacher: Which word tells about a special picture?
Child: *X-ray.*

5. ***Publish:*** Gene talks with students about how to publish their story:

Teacher: Now let's sign our names. You're the authors.
Child: Let's put it in the hall so everybody can read it.
Child: Put it by our other ones and the story they wrote about us in the newspaper.

Literature-Based Reading

The use of literature-based reading is gaining momentum in the United States (Anderson, Hiebert, Scott, & Wilkinson, 1985; Goodman, Shannon, Freeman, & Murphy, 1988). In California, for example, the *English-Language Arts Framework, K–12* makes a literature-based curriculum a policy mandate. A number of very different perspectives have been proposed for using literature as part of reading instruction. Hiebert and Colt (1989) suggest that different approaches can be combined to form a comprehensive literature-based reading program:

> *Literature-based reading instruction, whether in the context of the literature of tradebooks or textbooks, can take a number of different forms. When teachers focus only on independent reading of student-selected material, they fail to consider the guidance that students require for becoming expert readers. A focus on teacher-led instruction fails to develop the independent reading strategies that underlie lifelong reading. A total reading program should contain various combinations of teacher and student interaction and selection of literature so that children develop as thoughtful, proficient readers.* (p. 19)

Figure 8.5 shows two dimensions of effective literacy programs (Hiebert & Colt, 1989), suggesting the possibilities on a continuum of instructional format. At one end of the continuum is teacher-led instruction with teacher-selected material, and at the other end is independent application with student-selected material. A variety of instructional formats are available between these extremes.

Instructional Format		
Teacher-led instruction	Teacher- and student-led interaction	Independent application
Teacher-selected material	Teacher- and student-selected materials	Student-selected material
Literature Selection		

FIGURE 8.5 Two Dimensions of Effective Literacy Programs

Source: From "Patterns of Literature-Based Reading Instruction," by E. H. Hiebert and J. Colt, 1991, *The Reading Teacher, 43*(1), 14–19. Reprinted with permission of the International Reading Association and E. H. Hiebert.

Reading Aloud

See Chapter 4, Emergent Literacy, for more on the importance of reading aloud and methods to use with young children; Chapter 5, Listening and Talking, for more on the benefits of reading aloud, read-aloud do's and don't's, books to read aloud, and how to do a DLTA; and Chapter 7, Teaching with Literature, for more on how to read aloud.

Reading aloud is an essential part of Nora Miller's literature-based approach to teaching reading. In the Snapshot, she was reading *May I Bring a Friend?* to her students for the third time. Summaries of research consistently show the power of reading aloud to children (Krashen, 1993).

In my own research on reading aloud to children and listening to their natural responses, I have found marked contrasts between the fluent, rich, and often rambling responses of students (sometimes up to an hour as early as kindergarten) and the way many students were taught reading in their classrooms, such that they were often silent and uncommunicative during this time (Cox, 1994a, 1994b). I have found that the more response-centered approach has consistently resulted in richer, more fluent discussions of a stories, words, authors' styles, and personal meaning than the text-centered approach. Here's a comparison of the two:

See Chapter 5, Listening and Talking, which discusses aesthetic and efferent questions and prompts, and Chapter 7, Teaching with Literature, which looks at aesthetic and efferent stances toward literature.

Response-Centered Reading Aloud	***Text-Centered Reading Lesson***
Child directed	Teacher directed
No formal introduction	Prepared questions asked: Word knowledge Prior knowledge Information on author
Child asks for words as needed	Teacher introduces words
Adult reads aloud	Child reads silently
Child initiates questions	Teacher initiates questions
Open, aesthetic responses	Closed, efferent questions
Child goes on tangents	Child directed to focus on text
Challenging/hypothesizing important	Retelling important
Explanations emerge from hypotheses	Teacher checks understanding
Child asks to read	Teacher decides who reads

Sustained Silent Reading (SSR)

Sustained silent reading is based on the constructivist idea that children learn to do things by doing them. Thus, they learn to read by reading. SSR means a period of uninterrupted reading of self-selected books and other reading materials in the classroom. The teacher reads, too. Other acronyms for SSR include *USSR* (uninterrupted sustained silent reading) and *DEAR* (drop everything and read).

SNAPSHOT: SSR in a First-Grade Classroom

Phyllis Crawford, a former classroom teacher and reading specialist (who's now a principal), explains the steps she used to initiate SSR in her first-grade classroom each year:

1. *Provide Reading Materials:* The only materials I use are good for reading at many levels and for many interests: picture books, chapter books, poetry, nonfiction, magazines, and newspapers, and so on. I like to have at least 100 different things to read in my room.

2. *Introduce Books to Whole Class:* I put a pile of 40 to 50 books on the rug in the reading center, with the children seated around the edge. I choose a book, read a few pages aloud, make a comment, and put the book back in the pile. I do this three to five more times and then read at least one entire book aloud. This takes 20 to 30 minutes.

3. *Introduce Approach:* I say, "Today we're going to read silently and we're going to sustain ourselves in silent reading. This means that you're going to spend some time with one book, paying attention only to it, reading and rereading it or looking at the pictures carefully."

4. *All Select Books:* All the children scramble into the middle of the pile and immediately grab the book I read all the way through; next, they choose the ones I've read a few pages from. After they all have books, they can go anywhere in the room to read. I find a book, too.

5. *All Read Silently:* No one can interrupt anyone, including the teacher. All the children must stay in the places they have chosen. If they finish looking at their books, they should reread or look at the illustrations.

6. *Share Books:* I signal the end of reading. (I note children's behavior to determine when to stop. If they are all absorbed in reading, I let them continue.) After SSR, I share something to give them an idea of how they might share about their book: what I thought about, my favorite part, how it relates to something in my life. I might read a passage aloud, share interesting words, phrases, ideas, or illustrations, or tell how I felt about reading it. Children then have a model for sharing their own books.

Usually four or five children share daily. I sometimes ask questions or invite other students to ask questions, which encourages them to think about and personalize their reading experience.

Self-Selected Reading

When Nora Miller's students suggested reading another book as a response option after the shared guided reading of *May I Bring a Friend?* they were doing *self-selected reading*. They also do this at other times during the day in Nora's class. In self-selected reading, students spend a lot of time during the day reading books of their own choice. This reading can take place during SSR and be blended with other student- and response-centered approaches to teaching with literature, such as literature groups, shared reading, and literature units. Self-selected reading is also known as *wide independent reading, voluntary reading* (Morrow, 1992), *free voluntary reading* (*FVR*) (Krashen,

See Chapter 7, Teaching with Literature, for more on literature groups.

1993), and the *individualized reading method* (which was popular in the 1950s and 1960s) (Stauffeur, 1980; Veatch, 1959, 1978).

Self-selected reading is based on the constructivist idea that children learn by doing. Thus, an important part of learning to read is spending time actually reading. Self-selected reading also incorporates the idea that choice and interest are important for developing readers who not only *can* but *want to* read. Self-selected reading is an important component of whole-language teaching. Some teachers use self-selected reading exclusively, whereas others use it to supplement literature units and other approaches (Zarrillo, 1989), including basal readers.

The advantages of the self-selected reading approach are that it provides for individual differences in interest and ability and emphasizes construction of meaning while reading actual texts. In addition, this approach allows teachers flexibility in planning. As Zarrillo (1989) has pointed out, however, teachers may be reluctant to try self-selected reading as a comprehensive format for a literature-based program because of several concerns: (1) absence of administrative support, (2) lack of books in the classroom, (3) fear of a chaotic environment, (4) uneasiness about tests scores, and (5) ignorance of how to implement it. Nonetheless, students in self-selected reading programs have become successful readers and writers and have succeeded on standardized tests (Bond & Dykstra, 1967; Duker, 1968; Krashen, 1993; Zarrillo, 1989).

Following are suggestions for implementing self-selected reading as a comprehensive program or as a supplement to literature-based or basal reading programs.

Classroom Library

Start to build a classroom library of 100 to 150 books of interest for the grade level. Supplement this selection with books from the school and public libraries. Good sources for inexpensive books are garage sales, flea markets, library book sales, PTA funds, and donations from parents. Children can bring books from home and order books from paperback book clubs. Add magazines, pamphlets, brochures, and other reading material of interest to students.

Students' Reading Interests

Studies of students' reading interests show (Purves & Beach, 1972):

To see which books children like best, see the October issue of *The Reading Teacher* each year for a list of "Children's Choices," based on a poll of 10,000 children across the United States.

1. Children prefer a literary to nonliterary presentation of materials, books that tell good stories with suspenseful plots and much action, and stories of others their own age.
2. Content (What's it about?) is the major determinant of reading interests.
3. Primary (K–3) students see reading as entertainment and like folk- and fairytales, stories with fantasy figures (often animals) representing childlike experiences.
4. Middle and upper (4–6) students also see reading as a way of finding out about the world and like stories of daily life as familiar experience, animals and nature, and adventure.

Opportunities for Extended Reading Periods

Students spend most of their time actually reading books of their choice. This can occur during SSR, group work or time designated for literature groups, or when students have finished work in other areas.

Response Options

Individual response options discussed with the teacher during conferences might include reading another book (by the same author or about the same subject or something totally new, writing in response journals, self-selected projects), writing, artmaking, drama, mediamaking, or working in a group with other students who share similar reading interests. The teacher should plan time for students to share ideas or projects about their reading with other students.

Conferences with the Teacher

An essential part of a self-selected reading program is to hold regular conferences between students and teachers. These can be scheduled in a variety of ways. A simple rotation system might be used, in which the teacher conferences with four or five students a day, or students can sign up to request conferences. The teacher may decide to conference more frequently with those students who seem to benefit more than others, or schedule conferences on an as-needed basis. It's good to check in with every student every 2 weeks or so.

During a reading conference, several things can occur:

1. The child reads to the teacher.
2. The teacher reads to the child.
3. Both ask questions of the other and talk about the book and their reading of it.
4. Both make plans for further reading or response options.
5. The teacher provides support for word recognition and meaning, author's style, or story structure, relating reading to the child's experience and cross-curricular connections.

SNAPSHOT: Reading Conferences with Second-Graders

Second-grade teacher Glynn Wink has used the basal reader but is making the shift to a self-selected reading program. She conferences with individual students while others read or work together in groups and centers. The child scheduled for a conference with Glynn brings in the book he or she is reading and his or her literature response journal. Teacher and student get comfortable at Glynn's desk or a table, and she asks general prompting questions, such as:

1. ***Reading Conference Questions and Prompts:***
   "Tell me about the book. What do you think about it?"
   "What do you like about the book? not like? Why?"

"What is happening now? What do you think about that?"
"What do you think will happen next? Why?"
"How would you feel or what would you do if you were a character in the book?"
"What are the characters like? What are they doing?"
"Would you like to read some of your book to me?"

2. ***Reading Conference Recordkeeping:***
   - *Teacher's Notebook:* Glynn keeps a notebook with space for the following information on a page for each student: book title, student's questions and comments about the book, her suggestions for further reading, observations about the student's reading, and the date.
   - *Student's Response Journal:* Each student keeps a running record of the books he or she is reading and responses to them. When Glynn conferences with each student, she goes to the last entry page, dates it, and writes a word of praise and encouragement with her initials. She also notes any suggestions that came out of her conference with the child.

Shared Reading and "Big Books"

Nora Miller used many aspects of a shared reading in her literature-based lesson *May I Bring a Friend?* This method is a natural outgrowth of the home bedtime story situation or the "lap method" of reading aloud and along with young children. Children are surrounded with books. An adult reads aloud to them, talks to them, answers their questions, and is willing to read favorite books over and over again. Shared reading and "big books" recreate the natural ways young children learn to speak and many learn to read.

Scholastic Books publishes many "big books."

The pleasurable social aspects of shared reading with an interested adult are important, as well. At 18 months old, my daughter Elizabeth demanded of anyone she thought could read, "Read to me!" To make her point, she would shove the book at her targeted reader. No one was exempt, including her 4-year-old brother Gordon, who had learned to read with the "lap method." This highly social and meaning-centered approach builds on the idea that children can learn to read in school the way many learn to read in literate homes, where there are books and people to read to them.

Donald Holdaway (1979) has described how this approach is used by teachers on a national scale in New Zealand. There, teachers have adapted the environment of the home bedtime story or lap reading situation to the classroom. The approach includes three elements:

1. Books should be those loved by children ages 5 through 7.
2. Books should have the same visual impact from 20 feet away (when used by a teacher with a group or class) that a regular book would have on the knee of a child.

3. Books should be presented by the teacher with joy—more as a performance than a lesson.

After instruction with this beginning reading method for the first 2 years of school, children in New Zealand proved equal or superior to those taught by traditional methods. Most significant was the highly positive attitudes among students considered at risk.

Here is a step-by-step sequence for shared "big book" reading (Holdaway, 1982):

1. *Opening Warm-Up:* Start with favorite poems, rhymes, and songs with enlarged text on chartpaper. Also teach new poems and songs.

2. *Old Favorite:* Share a favorite story in enlarged format. Teach skills in context and deepen students' understanding. Encourage unison participation, role-playing, and dramatization.

3. *Language Games:* Have fun with words and sounds in meaningful situations. Play alphabet games, recite rhymes, and sing songs using letter names.

4. *New Story:* This is the highlight of the session. A long story may be broken naturally into two or more parts. Discuss words in context and encourage students to participate in predicting the story, confirming new words.

5. *Response Options:* Children's response options can include self-selected reading from a wide selection of favorites; artmaking related to the new story; writing, often using structures from the new story; and playing "teacher" (in which several children enjoy their favorite story together, with one acting as the teacher).

During a shared reading experience, students role-play a favorite nursery rhyme, "There Was an Old Woman Who Lived in a Shoe."

Other books by Arnold Lobel: *Fables* (1980), *Frog and Toad Are Friends* (1970), and *Mouse Tales* (1972).

TEACHING IDEA

A Shared Reading

This Teaching Idea is all about pigs. It presents a shared reading following the step-by-step sequence outlined earlier:

1. ***Opening Warm-Up***
   - Read familiar nursery rhymes, such as "This Little Pig Went to Market," "Tom, Tom, the Piper's Son," and "Barber, Barber, Shave a Pig."
   - Read new poems, such as selections from *The Book of Pigericks* (Lobel, 1983).
2. ***Old Favorite***
   - Read *The Three Little Pigs* (Galdone, 1970), and ask children what they think of the story.
   - Teach skills in context: for example, words that begin with the letter *p* and words that rhyme with *pig*.
   - Deepen students' understanding of story structure. Identify story parts, such as the opening problem, the repetition of three encounters with the wolf, and the ending (see Table 8.2).
   - Ask students to recall other stories that follow a similar pattern, such as "The Three Billy Goats Gruff."
   - Do role-playing and story dramatizations, having students play each of the three pigs and the wolf.
   - Encourage unison participation, in which half the class play pigs and the other half play the wolf. Students chant:

     Wolf: Little pig, little pig, let me come in!
     Pig: Not by the hair on my chinny, chin, chin!
     Wolf: Then I'll huff, and I'll puff, and I'll blow your house in!
3. ***Language Games***
   - Using the *p* words shared during reading, create an alphabet pyramid pattern:

Alphabet Pyramid Pattern	Example about Pigs
noun	pigs
adj. noun	pink pigs
adj. noun verb	pink pigs prancing
adj. noun verb adverb	pink pigs prancing proudly

   - Create an alphabet rhyme, using words that rhyme with *pig:*

Alphabet Rhyme

This is a pig
This is a fig
This is a pig eating a fig.

TABLE 8.2 Story Structure for Repeated Pattern Stories

Story	*Beginning*	*Repeated Event*	*End*
"The Three Little Pigs"	Pigs build houses out of straw, sticks, and bricks	Wolf blows at houses but can't blow down bricks	Smart pig kills wolf
"The Three Billy Goats Gruff"	Goats cross bridge to eat grass	Troll challenges goats; lets first two cross	Big goat kills troll
"The Gingerbread Boy"	Gingerbread boy runs away	Gingerbread boy fools animals trying to eat him	Fox fools gingerbread boy and eats him
"The Little Red Hen"	Red hen plants wheat and needs help	Hen asks animals for help	Hen eats bread

4. ***New Story***
   - Introduce the new story: "*Pig Pig Rides* (McPhail, 1982) is about a young pig who tells his mother everything he is going to do that day, including jumping 500 elephants on a motorcycle. Predict what Pig Pig will do next."
   - Look at words like *elephants* and *motorcycle* in context.

5. ***Response Options***
   - Have students do self-selected reading of pig books, such as these:
     Paddy Pork's Evening Out (Goodall, 1973)
     The Pig's Wedding (Heine, 1979)
     Portly McSwine (Marshall, 1979)
     Roland the Minstrel Pig (Steig, 1968)
     A Treeful of Pigs (Lobel, 1979)
     The True Story of the Three Little Pigs (Scieszka, 1989)
   - Artmaking: Have students make thumbprint pigs by pressing their thumbs on an inkpad; add features and limbs to thumbprints to create pigs. Also consider the possibilities for pig pictures: drawings, paintings, or illustrations for stories.
   - Writing: Students should write anything they want. Perhaps they could write stories modeled after *Pig Pig Rides* or "The Three Little Pigs"; they could rewrite the latter from the wolf's point of view, as in Scieszka's (1989) book.
   - Playing "teacher" could involve shared reading in a group or taking turns reading the dialogue of Pig Pig and his mother.

For more "pig" literature and response options, see Joy Moss (1984), *Focus Units in Literature: A Handbook for Elementary School Teachers*.

See *Ed Emberly's Thumbprint Drawing Box* (Emberly, 1992) for ideas of things to make with thumbprints.

See *Perfect the Pig*, by Susan Jeschke (1981), which is about an artist who paints pictures of Perfect, a beautiful, flying pig.

Literature Units

For more on literature units, see *Teaching Reading with Children's Literature,* by Carole Cox and James Zarrillo (1993).

Literature units are the focus of reading instruction in the classroom (Cox & Zarrillo, 1993; Zarrillo, 1989). Using them is a way to organize teaching reading with literature. Three popular ways to do this are with core book units, author units, and genre units.

Core Book Units

Core book units focus on single books, "those selections that are to be taught in the classroom, are given close reading and intensive consideration, and are likely to be an important stimulus for writing and discussion" (California State Department of Education, 1990). Core book units are most appropriate for students in grades 2 through 6, although it's possible to use them with younger children, as well. James Zarrillo's research on teachers using the book model (Zarrillo, 1989; Zarrillo & Cox, 1992) showed the following characteristics of effective teaching with core books:

Aesthetic prompts and questions are described in Chapter 5, Listening and Talking, and Chapter 7, Teaching with Literature.

1. Instruction was response centered. Teachers built teaching around students' responses, using open and aesthetic questions and prompts.

2. Core books were placed in perspective; less than 25 percent of the year was devoted to them. Other literature units and self-selection were used, as well; children had substantial time to read self-selected books.

3. The teacher loved the book, and his or her interest and enthusiasm were communicated to students.

4. Core books were presented dramatically. Teachers read with flourish or presented books through reader's theater, using audiotaped versions read by professional actors, or through film or video. Children eagerly looked forward to each new chapter.

5. Children could read core books independently. Those who couldn't wait for the inclass reading could read ahead and then listen to or reread chapters; they could also read other books by the same author or books on related topics. Teachers did not try to hold anyone back from reading.

See Chapter 7, Teaching with Literature, which illustrates a "ripple effect" of the U.S. Southwest based on *Mystery of the Haunted Mine* (Shirreffs, 1962).

6. Core books led to independent reading and writing. Teachers paid attention to children's responses and provided response options of reading and writing, based on students' interests. Considerable time was spent just reading, rather than writing or making things after every chapter.

Here is a selection of core books for units, showing titles for primary, middle, and upper grades:

Primary Grades (K–2)	***Middle Grades (3–4)***	***Upper Grades (5–6)***
Madeline (Bemelamns, 1958)	*Charlotte's Web* (White, 1952)	*Bridge to Terabithia* (Paterson, 1977)

Make Way for Ducklings (McCloskey, 1943)
Millions of Cats (Gag, 1977)
Miss Rumphius (Cooney, 1982)
The Snowy Day (Keats, 1963)
The Indian in the Cupboard (Banks, 1982)
Ramona the Pest (Cleary, 1982)
Sarah, Plain and Tall (MacLachlan, 1985)
Tales of a Fourth Grade Nothing (Blume, 1976)
Dragonwings (Yep, 1975)
Treasure Island (Stevenson, 1947)
The Witch of Blackbird Pond (Speare, 1972)
A Wrinkle in Time (L'Engle, 1976)

SNAPSHOT: A Core Book Unit with Fourth- through Sixth-Graders

As a teacher of average- to high-achieving fourth-grade students, Margaret Mattson felt that using basal readers as the core of her reading program was inadequate: "Students never really got into the stories as one does with a really good book. The only rationale for using a certain story was to teach a certain skill. Although students were able to score well on skills tests after completing the prescribed activities, I never felt that they had learned anything that they actually integrated into their own personal reading processes. Rather, they learned the format, to give the expected answers. It is a superficial type of learning."

At the same time Margaret was struggling with the value of basal readers, she was aware that her students were not at all familiar with classic books. In addressing these two concerns, she decided not to use a basal reader but to teach reading through a core book unit on Robert Louis Stevenson's (1947) classic *Treasure Island.* Here's how she did it:

- *Selecting the Book:* Margaret chose *Treasure Island* because she loved it, none of her students had read it, and she felt a fantastic classroom environment could be created around it: pirates, mysterious maps, hidden treasure, and so on. She used PTA funds to order paperback copies for all students from a book club.

- *Planning the Unit:* Margaret tried to be discriminating. "I didn't want to dissect the book until its magic was gone, but I wanted it to be a productive learning experience." In addition to encouraging students to respond aesthetically, she felt this book would be a good one to discuss characterization, plot and story structure, setting, and point of view in literature.

- *Scheduling Reading and Activities:* Reading and activities were conducted during at least 1-hour blocks of time, three times a week. Students were also given 30 to 60 minutes a day to read the book; any unfinished reading was done at home. Impromptu sessions were also held as students' interest grew or when discussions or activities took longer than expected. The general schedule was as follows:

Daily	Students read book in class Unfinished reading at home	30–60 minutes
Weekly (3 times)	Whole class and group work	60–90 minutes
As needed	Impromptu sessions depending on interest or more time needed	30–60 minutes

• *Organizing Groups:* Students worked together in groups, which changed for different activities.

• *Creating a Classroom Environment:* Students drew a large map of Treasure Island on brown wrapping paper so it looked ancient. This map was displayed on one wall, a colorful paper parrot hung from the ceiling, and a bulletin board was covered with a labeled cross-section of a sailing ship, complete with a Jolly Roger. Each child had a paperback copy of the book.

Treasure Island was first published in installments entitled "The Sea Cook" in *Young Folks* magazine; it appeared in book form in 1883.

• *Initiating the Unit:* Margaret told students that Robert Louis Stevenson was a sickly person who felt the function of literature was to supply adventure to people who lead unexciting lives. She asked them to respond to that idea. She also told them that *Treasure Island* was the outcome of his adding a story to a map of an imaginary island drawn by his 12-year-old stepson. Stevenson entertained the boy and himself with stories of pirates and buried gold.

Here's a day-by-day description of what Margaret and her students did during the core book unit for *Treasure Island.*

Day 1. Reading Aloud and Talking Together

Margaret read the first 19 pages aloud. The story begins with a flashback and sets the mood with a vivid description of Billy Bones:

> *I remember him as if it were yesterday, as he came plodding to the inn door, his sea chest following behind him in a handbarrow; a tall, strong, heavy, nut-brown man; his tarry pigtail falling over the shoulders of his soiled blue coat; his hands ragged and scarred, with black, broken nails, and the saber-cut across one cheek a dirty, livid white.*

Margaret stopped and asked students what they thought about the story so far. They talked about the description of Billy Bones. One student remarked that she knew exactly what he looked like because she had seen the movie. This led to an interesting discussion about adapting books into movies and selecting actors to play the roles. Students talked about their feelings about Billy Bones and how the author created those feelings. They drew portraits of Billy Bones.

The only vocabulary Margaret talked about before reading were the words used on the labeled cross-section of the ship and a chart of nautical and geographical terms, which students added to throughout the unit. Vocabulary words were talked about after students read.

Reading for next day: The rest of Part I, "The Old Buccaneer," Chapters 1–4.

Day 2. Making Treasure Maps and Writing Summaries in Groups

Each group made a token treasure out of cardboard and hid it on the schoolgrounds; then they created maps to guide treasure seekers in other groups. Compasses and yellowed paper added authenticity. As Margaret had hoped, doing these activities was helping students get into the mood of the book. On their maps, they referred to Margaret as "One-Eyed Mattson" and the teacher next door as "Peg-Leg McGraw." Groups traded maps and went looking for treasure tokens. When the tokens were found, students traded them for real treasure: candy coins covered in gold foil.

Back in their groups, students talked together about the first four chapters and wrote summaries; then all the groups talked about the story. Margaret noted, "This was a clarifying experience for them and me. They really interacted and challenged each other. I find group activities to be very productive as it forces students to form an opinion and defend it."

Reading for next day: Part II, "The Sea Cook," Chapters 7–9.

Day 3. Recognizing and Discussing the Technique of Foreshadowing in Literature

The class talked about what they'd read and discussed foreshadowing (i.e., how authors give clues of what is to come) and how Stevenson used it.

Reading for next day: Part II, Chapters 10–12.

Day 4. Dramatizing a Scene from the Story

Groups picked scenes and planned dramatizations of them. Margaret noticed, "The room buzzed with the creative noise of students who were involved and excited about what they were doing, and a much deeper analysis of the story was occurring than any workbook or teacher's guide could inspire. One student said, 'Long John oughta be kind of like two different people, you know? All friendly and polite around the Captain but real mean and bragging when he's not.'" That student's group dramatized the scene with a trembling Jim hiding in the apple barrel while a freckle-faced Long John Silver boasted of his infamous past.

Students were very excited after their dramatizations and began to plan a play based on the whole story, which they wanted to perform on stage for the rest of the school.

See Chapter 6, Drama in the Classroom, for how to adapt a story for dramatization.

Reading for next day: Part III, "My Shore Adventure," Chapters 13–15.

Students in Margaret Mattson's class dramatize a scene from Treasure Island: *Jim Hawkins overhears Long John Silver plot to take over the Hispanola.*

Day 5. Painting and Writing Descriptions

Margaret reread the description of the island and asked students to close their eyes and imagine that they could really see it. They used watercolors to paint pictures of what they saw in their minds and wrote descriptions, as well.

Day 6. Discussing Cliffhangers

Margaret asked the children how many kept reading after Chapter 14, which ends in a cliffhanger. Many hands shot up, so she asked "Why? Isn't the end of the chapter a good place to stop?" They discussed how a cliffhanger makes you want to keep reading and how this writing technique is used elsewhere in the book, in other books they've read, and in film and television.

Reading for next day: Part IV, "The Stockade," Chapters 16–18.

Day 7. Discussing and Using Point of View in Writing

The three chapters the class read are told from the Dr. Livesly's point of view, rather than Jim Hawkins's. Groups talked about why Stevenson might have changed the point of view in the middle of the story. The whole class talked about advantages and disadvantages of first-person, omniscient, limited-omniscient, and objective points of view.

Students rewrote an episode in the book from a different point of view. One student wrote a journal for Long John Silver, complete with a tattered paper cover and blots of red ink (blood stains?) on the pages. Part of an entry reads:

> My Journal by Long John Silver
> Today me and my friends plotted to take over the Hispanola. But I said we're going to let them find the treasure and get it on board and wait till we're halfway back to England. Then we would take over. I was so happy just thinking how rich I was going to be.

Reading next day: Part IV, Chapters 19–21.

Day 8. Student-Selected Group Projects

Each group brainstormed ideas for a project and started it. Group 1 decided to make a papier-mâché model of the island, and group 2 created a board game based on the book. Group 3 wrote an etiquette book for pirates, and group 4 taped an interview with Long John Silver.

Reading next day: Part V, "My Sea Adventure."

Day 9. Discussing Jim's Character

Students discussed Jim's character in their groups: What kind of person was he? If he were transplanted to a different setting, like our classroom, what kinds of problems might he have? If we were transplanted to the setting of *Treasure Island*, what kind of problems might we have? Students also continued work on their projects.

Reading next day: Part VI, "Captain Silver."

Day 10. Group Projects

With the book finished, groups concentrated on their projects. They went back and mined the story for ideas:

Group 1: Island model: They skimmed the story for descriptions of the island, made a list of ideas, talked about them, and decided how their model would look.

Group 2: Game: They sequenced events in the story to lay out the game board.

Group 3: Etiquette book: They reread about pirates' actions and used informational books about real pirates and privateers to create a spoof, with chapters like "What to Do If You Receive the Black Spot."

Group 4: Interview with Long John Silver: They spent a lot of time rereading and talking about his complex character in preparation for writing the interview.

By tradition, duff was not properly cooked until it could be dropped from the cross-gallant crosstrees, the highest point on the ship, and not break.

A Recipe for Duff

Beat: 2 eggs well

Add & blend:
1 cup brown sugar
$1^1/_2$ cup raisins
$^1/_3$ cup shortening

Sift & add:
1 cup flour
$^1/_2$ teaspoon salt
1 teaspoon baking soda

Pour mixture into well-greased 1-quart mold (1-pound coffee can is ideal). Cover pudding with waxed paper and then cover can with double layer of aluminum foil, tied on tightly with string to prevent water from seeping in. Place can in large pot of boiling water, which should come $^3/_4$ of the way up the side of the can. Cover pot loosely and boil for $3^1/_3$ to 4 hours, adding more water as needed. Serve warm with whipped cream.

See Chapter 7, Teaching with Literature, for more on literature groups.

Days 11–15. Group Projects and Discussions

The groups continued to work on their projects, talk about the story, and respond to it. Margaret said they couldn't be stopped. Here are some of the things they did:

> ***Writing:*** Wrote accounts of the adventure for a Bristol newspaper, secret codes, journals for various characters, and sequels about another trip to the island to recover the remaining treasure. Students also adopted many of Stevenson's conventions in their writing.
>
> ***Artmaking:*** Made "Wanted" posters for pirates, designed book jackets for the story, and drew illustrations of unillustrated scenes.
>
> ***Dramatization and media*:** Added costumes and replayed the scenes they had created, dressed as pirates and had a pirate party; watched the Disney movie *Treasure Island* and acted like pirates; and ate duff (a dessert mentioned in the book).

Margaret is enthusiastic about teaching with literature because of the excitement and enthusiasm it generates, because she is able to teach all the language arts as an integrated whole, and because many of the skills associated with reading or critical analysis of literature occur naturally. In the *Treasure Island* core book unit, students learned new words, looked at idioms and figures of speech in context, identified and understood literary elements, and recognized and appreciated elements of style. After completing this unit, students formed literature groups, each of which chose a new book to read and explore.

Author Units

In an author unit, the unifying element is the author. The teacher reads aloud books by a single author, and students work together in groups and read books of their own choice independently. In picking an author, the teacher should choose one who has written a substantial number of books appropriate for the grade and of interest to many students. The following authors meet these criteria for primary, middle, and upper grades:

Primary Grades	*Middle Grades*	*Upper Grades*
Marcia Brown	Judy Blume	Lloyd Alexander
Eric Carle	Beverly Cleary	Betsy Byars
Tomie de Paola	Roald Dahl	Virginia Hamilton
Arnold Lobel	C. S. Lewis	Katherine Paterson
Dr. Seuss	Lois Lowry	Laurence Yep

Eric Carle is a good choice for a 1- to 2-week author unit in the primary grades. He's written many books, including predictable pattern books and books on topics like insects and animals, which lend themselves to cross-curricular activities. Here are some ideas for planning an author unit about Eric Carle, including a list of books, resources, and response options:

Books

Do You Want to Be My Friend? (1971)
The Very Busy Spider (1984)
The Grouchy Ladybug (1977)
The Very Hungry Caterpillar (1969)
The Very Quiet Cricket (1990)

Resources

- Kit to hatch butterfly eggs in the classroom
- Crickets in a cage
- Chart of names of days of week
- "Big book" versions of Eric Carle's books
- Tape recordings of the books
- Food from *The Very Hungry Caterpillar*
- Collage materials: paint, wrapping paper, tissue paper, yarn, fabric

Response Options

- Draw and write anything they want about the stories.
- Make collages using Eric Carle's illustrating style.
- Following the pattern of *The Very Hungry Caterpillar,* make a "big book" called *The Very Hungry Class,* with pages for all the children to draw or write what they would eat, on what day of the week, and so on.
- Act like a grouchy ladybug, a busy spider, a quiet cricket, and the like.
- Do a story dramatization of *Do You Want to Be My Friend?*
- Make a story map of *The Grouchy Ladybug.*
- Throw a "Hungry Caterpillar" party with food from the book; write a language experience story about it.

Genre Units

A genre of children's literature can also be used as the basis of a literature unit—for example, traditional literature, poetry, picture books, fantasy, science fiction, contemporary realistic fiction, historical fiction, biography, or nonfiction. Again, teachers choose and read aloud good examples of the genre and encourage children to form literature groups to read and respond through projects and to continue self-selected reading.

See Chapter 7, Teaching with Literature, for examples.

Successful Literature Units

James Zarrillo's (1989) research on literature units showed that successful implementation occurred when the teacher found a balance between activities involving all students and those that individual students selected themselves. All students usually participated when the teacher read aloud, planned response options for the read alouds, or taught lessons related to the unifying theme.

Zarrillo uses the example of a primary unit on fairy tales. All students listened to the same 10 stories read aloud and talked, wrote, drew, painted, or acted in response to them. The teacher presented lessons on fairy tale language patterns (e.g., "Once upon a time . . ."), characters, and settings. All students wrote letters to a fairy tale character, who wrote back (channeled through the teacher or aide). But in addition, students could choose from many response options to do on their own or in groups with common interests.

Assessing Reading as a Language Art

Assessing reading as a language art in a student- and response-centered classroom means using alternative means to standardized tests: that is, naturalistic, authentic, ongoing assessment by observing, interacting, and analyzing students' reading experiences. This kind of assessment should include five interactive components: "the observation, activity, test, or task must be relevant, authentic, and part of the teaching-learning process by informing the learner and furthering instruction" (Routman, 1991, p. 305). Here are types of naturalistic reading assessment:

1. ***Anecdotal Records:*** These are notes made by the teacher based on observations of students, usually including dated, informal, brief comments related specifically to reading and literacy. Over time, anecdotal records provide a picture of each child's progress and needs, which should form the basis for further planning. These records can be based on students' self-selected reading, participation in literature groups, response options to literature and work from literature units, and behavior in reading-aloud and shared-reading lessons.

2. ***Literature Response Journals:*** As described in Chapter 7, Teaching with Literature, these journals provide a rich, ongoing record of students' reading and responses.

3. ***Reading Conference Record*****:** This form can be adapted to keep track of reading conferences as part of ongoing assessment of a student's progress and to help plan further reading experiences for him or her. It should include information such as book titles and questions and comments, suggestions, and observations about them.

Answers to Questions about Reading as a Language Art

1. *What is reading, and what are the different models of the reading process?*

As explained in *Becoming a Nation of Readers,* reading is an integral part of the language arts. Reading is primarily the construction of meaning. Various theoretical models have been proposed to explain what that means. The *linear model* explains that reading is a bottom-up, or part-to-whole, process. The child first recognizes letters, then words, and then sentences; a sequence of smaller to larger subskills must be learned before the reader gets meaning from print. The *interactive model* is based on schema theory, which explains that learners acquire, store, and use knowledge in the form of *schema*. The reader makes meaningful connections between prior knowledge, or schemata, and uses personal reading strategies (developed and adjusted for each individual purpose in reading) while seeking to construct meaning from print. The *psycholinguistic model* views reading as part of language development and a top-down, or whole-to-part, process; the reader makes predictions about the meaning of what is read, testing and confirming hypotheses while reading. The *transactional model* describes each reading act as a transaction between the reader and text, occurring at a particular time and in a particular context. Meaning comes into being during the transaction, in which the reader is active.

2. *What different methods and materials can be used to teach reading?*

The basal reader approach, which reflects the linear model of reading, has been the dominant method of reading instruction in elementary schools. Basals are both method and material; they include a set of graded books with a scope and sequence of skills to be taught, a teacher's manual with directions for lessons, and workbooks or skillsheets for students. Basal readers offer a standardized way to teach reading but have been criticized because they don't pay enough attention to individual students or to teaching comprehension; in addition, basal programs take away the decision-making role of the teacher. Newer basal series have taken a meaning emphasis and used literature but still direct teacher's decisions and don't focus on self-selected, voluntary reading.

Questioning strategies—such as directed reading thinking activity (DRTA) and question-answer relationship (QAR)—are based on schema theory and can be used with many different types of texts, methods, and materials. Questioning strategies emphasize linking students' prior knowledge to reading and developing strategies for them to monitor their own reading and become independent readers.

Whole-language, literature-based reading is guided by the belief that literacy develops from whole to part during functional, meaningful language use. Comprehension of meaning is always the goal of readers. Whole-language methods use children's literature and other authentic texts for reading.

3. *How should we teach reading in a student- and response-centered classroom?*

A student- and response-centered classroom is based on the social constructivist perspective on learning (i.e., that learning is an active, ongoing process, which occurs in the social contexts of the classroom, home, and community) and the transactional perspective (i.e., that meaning is constructed during a transaction between the reader and text). Children learn to read by reading, and children's literature should be the main reading material used, along with children's writing and other authentic texts. Methods and materials that reflect this perspective and a whole-language view of literacy development include the language experience approach and literature-based methods such as reading aloud, sustained silent reading, self-selected reading, shared reading and "big books," and literature units (core book, author, and genre). Teachers are responsible for decision making and planning in student- and response-centered classrooms.

LOOKING FURTHER

1. With others in your class, describe, discuss, and compare memories of reading instruction in elementary school. Which of the models of reading did it most reflect? How so?
2. Pick a children's picture book you like, and make a list of things you would do before, after, and during reading.
3. Read a book aloud to a group of children, and ask them open and aesthetic questions: What did you think of it? What was your favorite part? Make a list of response options, based on what the children said.
4. Plan a shared reading lesson for the primary grades around a common theme; if possible, teach it. Share what happened with your college class.
5. In a group in your class, brainstorm ideas for literature units: core book, author, and genre. Pick one and expand it into a 1- to 3-week cycle for a class of a given grade level.

RESOURCES

Cox, C., & Zarrillo, J. (1993). *Teaching reading with children's literature.* Columbus, OH: Merrill/Macmillan.

REFERENCES

Altwerger, B., Edelsky, C., & Flores, B. M. (1987). Whole language: What's new? *Reading Teacher, 41,* 147–155.

Anderson, R. C. (1985). Role of the reader's schema in comprehension, learning, and memory. In H. Singer & R. Ruddell (Eds.), *Theoretical models and processes of reading.* Newark, DE: International Reading Association.

Anderson, R. C., Hiebert, E., Scott, J., & Wilkinson, I. (1985). *Becoming a nation of readers.* Washington, DC: National Institute of Education.

Bond, G. L., & Dykstra, R. (1967). The cooperative research program in first grade reading instruction. *Reading Research Quarterly, 2,* 1–42.

California State Department of Education. (1990). *Recommended readings in literature kindergarten through grade eight.* Sacramento, CA: State Department of Education.

Cox, C. (1994a, December). *Challenging the text: Case studies of young children responding to literature.* Paper presented at the National Reading Conference, San Diego, CA.

Cox, C. (1994b, April). *Young children's response to literature: A longitudinal study, K–3.* Paper presented at the American Educational Research Association, New Orleans, LA.

Cox, C., & Zarrillo, J. (1993). *Teaching reading with children's literature.* Columbus, OH: Merrill/Macmillan.

Davidson, J. L. (1988). *Counterpoint and beyond: A response to* Becoming a Nation of Readers. Urbana, IL: National Council of Teachers of English.

Duffy, G. G., Roehler, L. R., & Putnam, J. (1987). Putting the teacher in control: Basal reading textbooks and instructional decision making. *Elementary School Journal, 87,* 357–366.

Duker, S. (1968). *Individualized reading: An annotated bibliography.* Metuchen, NJ: Scarecrow Press.

Durkin, D. (1981). Reading comprehension instruction in five basal reader series. *Reading Research Quarterly, 16,* 515–544.

Edelsky, C., Altwerger, B., & Flores, B. (1991). *Whole language: What's the difference?* Portsmouth, NH: Heinemann.

Goodman, K. S. (1976). Reading: A psycholinguistic guessing game. In H. Singer & R. Ruddell (Eds.), *Theoretical models in processes of reading* (2nd ed.). Newark, DE: International Reading Association.

Goodman, K. S. (1986). *What's whole in whole language?* Portsmouth, NH: Heinemann.

Goodman, K. S., Shannon, P., Freeman, Y., & Murphy, S. (1988). *Report card on basal readers.* New York: Richard C. Owen.

Gough, P. B. (1976). One second of reading. In H. Singer & R. Ruddell (Eds.), *Theoretical models and processes of reading* (2nd ed.). Newark, DE: International Reading Association.

Hiebert, E. H., & Colt, J. (1989). Patterns of literature-based reading instruction. *Reading Teacher, 43*(1), 14–19.

Holdaway, D. (1979). *The foundations of literacy.* Sydney, Australia: Ashton Scholastic.

Holdaway, D. (1982, Autumn). Shared book experience: Teaching reading using favorite books. *Theory Into Practice,* 293–300.

Krashen, S. (1993). *The power of reading: Insights from the research.* Englewood, CO: Libraries Unlimited.

LaBerge, D., & Samuels, S. J. (1976). Towards a theory of automatic information processing in reading. In H. Singer & R. B. Ruddell (Eds.), *Theoretical models and processes of reading.* Newark, DE: International Reading Association.

Langer, J. A., Applebee, A. N., Mullis, I. V. S., & Foertsch, M. A. (1990). *Learning to read in our nation's schools: Instruction and achievement in 1988 at grades 4, 8, and 12.* Princeton, NJ: Educational Testing Service.

Morrow, L. M. (1992). Promoting voluntary reading. In J. Flood, J. M. Jensen, D. Lapp, & J. R. Squire (Eds.), *Handbook of research on teaching the English language arts.* New York: Macmillan.

Moss, J. F. (1984). *Focus units in literature: A handbook for elementary teachers.* Urbana, IL: National Council of Teachers of English.

Pearson, P. D., & Johnson, D. D. (1978). *Teaching reading comprehension.* New York: Holt, Rinehart & Winston.

Purves, A., & Beach, R. (1972). *Literature and the reader: Research in response to literature, reading interests and the teaching of literature.* Urbana, IL: National Council of Teachers of English.

Raphael, T. (1982). Question-answering strategies for children. *Reading Teacher, 36,* 186–190.

Raphael, T. (1986). Teaching question answer relationships, revisited. *Reading Teacher, 39,* 516–522.

Rosenblatt, L. M. (1978). *The reader, the text, the poem: The transactional theory of the literary work.* Carbondale, IL: Southern Illinois Press.

Rosenblatt, L. M. (1983). *Literature as exploration* (4th ed.). New York: Modern Language Association.

Rosenblatt, L. M. (1994). *The transactional theory of reading and writing.* In R. Ruddell, M. Ruddell, & H. Singer (Eds.), *Theoretical models and processes of reading.* Newark, DE: International Reading Association.

Routman, R. (1991). *Invitations: Changing as teachers and learners.* Portsmouth, NH: Heinemann.

Rumelhart, D. (1984). Understanding understanding. In J. Flood (Ed.), *Understanding reading comprehension* (pp. 1–20). Newark, DE: International Reading Association.

Shannon, P. (1988). *Broken promises: Reading instruction in 20th century America.* Granby, MA: Bergin & Garvey.

Shannon, P. (1990). *The struggle to continue: Progressive reading instruction in the United States.* Portsmouth, NH: Heinemann.

Smith, F. (1971). *Understanding reading.* New York: Holt, Rinehart & Winston.

Stauffeur, R. (1975). *Directing the reading thinking process.* New York: Harper & Row.

Stauffeur, R. (1980). *The language experience approach to the teaching of reading.* New York: Harper & Row.

Veatch, J. (Ed.). (1959). *Individualizing your reading program: Self-selection in action.* New York: Putnam.

Veatch, J. (1978). *Reading in the elementary school* (2nd ed.). New York: Wiley & Sons.

Weaver, C. (1988). *Reading process and practice: From socio-psycholinguistics to whole language.* Portsmouth, NH: Heinemann.

Zarrillo, J. (1989). Teacher's interpretations of literature-based reading. *Reading Teacher, 43*(1), 22–28.

Zarrillo, J., & Cox, C. (1992). Efferent and aesthetic teaching. In J. E. Many & C. Cox (Eds.), *Reader stance and literary understanding: Exploring the theories, research, and practice* (pp. 235–249). Norwood, NJ: Ablex.

CHILDREN'S BOOKS

Banks, L. R. (1982). *The Indian in the cupboard*. New York: Avon.

Bemelamns, L. (1958). *Madeline*. New York: Viking.

Blume, J. (1976). *Tales of a fourth grade nothing*. New York: Dell.

Carle, E. (1969). *The very hungry caterpillar*. New York: Philomel.

Carle, E. (1971). *Do you want to be my friend?* New York: Harper.

Carle, E. (1984). *The very busy spider*. New York: Philomel.

Carle, E. (1990). *The very quiet cricket*. New York: Philomel.

Carle, E. (1977). *The grouchy ladybug*. New York: HarperCollins.

Cleary, B. (1982). *Ramona the pest*. New York: Dell.

Cooney, B. (1982). *Miss Rumphius*. New York: Viking.

de Regniers, B. S. (1965). *May I bring a friend?* New York: Atheneum.

Emberly, E. (1992). *Ed Emberly's thumbprint drawing box*. New York: Little, Brown.

Gag, W. (1977). *Millions of cats*. New York: Putnam.

Galdone, P. (1970). *The three little pigs*. New York: Seabury.

George, J. C. (1980). *Cry of the crow*. New York: Harper & Row.

Goodall, J. S. (1973). *Paddy Pork's evening out*. New York: Atheneum.

Heine, H. (1979). *The pig's wedding*. New York: Atheneum.

Jeschke, S. (1981). *Perfect the pig*. New York: Henry Holt.

Keats, E. J. (1963). *The snowy day*. New York: Viking.

L'Engle, M. (1976). *A wrinkle in time*. New York: Dell.

Lobel, A. (1979). *A treeful of pigs*. New York: Morrow.

Lobel, A. (1983). *The book of pigericks*. New York: Harper & Row.

Lobel, A. (1970). *Frog and Toad are friends*. New York: HarperCollins.

Lobel, A. (1972). *Mouse tales*. New York: HarperCollins.

Lobel, A. (1980). *Fables*. New York: HarperCollins.

MacLachlan, P. (1985). *Sarah, plain and tall*. New York: Harper.

McCloskey, R. (1943). *Make way for ducklings*. New York: Viking.

McPhail, D. (1982). *Pig Pig rides*. New York: Dutton.

Marshall, J. (1979). *Portly McSwine*. New York: Houghton Mifflin.

Paterson, K. (1977). *Bridge to Terabithia*. New York: HarperCollins.

Scieszka, J. (1989). *The true story of the three little pigs*. New York: Viking.

Shirreffs, G. D. (1962). *The mystery of the haunted mine*. New York: Scholastic.

Speare, D. G. (1972). *The witch of Blackbird Pond*. New York: Dell.

Steig, W. (1968). *Roland the minstrel pig*. New York: Harper & Row.

Stevenson, R. L. (1947). *Treasure Island*. New York: Putnam.

White, E. B. (1952). *Charlotte's web*. New York: HarperCollins.

Yep, L. (1975). *Dragonwings*. New York: HarperCollins.

Chapter 9

The Writing Process

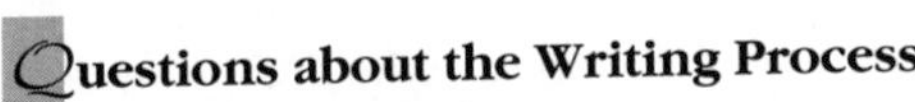

Questions about the Writing Process

Writing as a Process

Writing in a Second Language

Writing Workshop

SNAPSHOT: ***Writing Workshop in Sheila Kline's Fourth Grade***

A Process Approach to Writing

A Literate Environment

Modeling

Minilessons

Conferences

Journals

Writing across the Curriculum

Revising and Editing

Publishing

Scheduling

Assessing Writing

Authentic Assessment

Portfolios

Answers to Questions about the Writing Process

Questions about the Writing Process

1. *What is the writing process?*
2. *How should we teach writing as a process?*

Reflective Response

Choose one thing you remember about learning to write in elementary school and write about it. Think about how it might have influenced your feelings about yourself as a writer today and how you will teach writing.

Writing as a Process

The process approach to writing, which developed during the 1970s and 1980s, was based to a great extent on Donald Graves's (1983) influential book *Writing: Teachers and Children at Work.* With this approach, the focus of writing instruction shifted from the product to the process. The *process* of writing refers to what children do, which involves five stages: (1) prewrite, (2) draft, (3) revise, (4) edit, and (5) publish. And each of these stages involves children in a number of different activities:

Prewrite

Draw on their own experiences
Read or listen to stories read aloud
Generate ideas
Organize thinking
Talk over ideas with others
Choose what type of writing they'll do: journals, letters, expressive writing, literature as a model
Consider the audience they're writing for
Brainstorm ideas: make a list, cluster, quickwrite
Rehearse: draw, talk, map, plot, diagram, act out

Draft

Put their ideas down on paper
Focus on meaning, rather than conventions
Feel free to experiment
Understand that writing can change
Try out different possibilities
Talk over their draft with others
Rehearse some more

Revise

Reread during and after writing the draft
Rethink what they've written
Share with others in the reader's circle
Talk to the teacher in a conference
Change, add, delete, or modify their draft

Clarify meaning
Expand ideas

Edit

Proofread their revised piece
Talk to the teacher in an editing conference
Ask for help in a peer-editing conference
Rephrase and refine
Check: spelling, punctuation, capitalization, usage, form, legibility
Identify and correct their own pieces

Publish

Choose the form: book, displayed in room, drama, reader's theater, media, letter, "big book," newspaper, posters, advertisement
Share their published piece by reading aloud: reader's circle, author's chair, writing workshop

See Chapter 4, Emergent Literacy, for more on the author's chair.

Terms like *prewriting, drafting, revising, editing,* and *publishing* are useful for talking about the parts of the writing process, which don't necessarily occur in a fixed order for individual writers in specific situations. However, teachers shouldn't think of these terms as comprising steps in a rigid, linear fashion. Writing is a recursive process. Writers don't always do things in the same order. For instance, they may change the topic of a piece in the middle of writing it, rather than definitely deciding it at the beginning. They may think of an ending first and then add a beginning and middle. Or they may change ideas as they revise, in no particular order.

Graves suggests the idea of multiple starts in writing. Children may write down several possible opening sentences, with the understanding that only one or perhaps none of them will be used. They realize that first drafts can be tentative, and they can choose and change things at any time. Children need to know that they can take chances, make and test hypotheses, and experiment and that teachers will accept their approximations in writing (Cambourne & Turbill, 1987). To gain this confidence, children must be allowed to explore ideas through writing freely, to discover for themselves how the process works rather than follow a daily writing schedule, established by the teacher. Different aspects of the writing process occur simultaneously and even randomly. Teachers should exercise caution about turning a personal, creative, fluid, and even messy process like writing into a daily routine that must be followed.

Writing is a way of knowing, of discovering what you know as you put it down—not only in the form of words and phrases but of scribbles and drawings, ideas and images, and all the other wonderful stuff in your mind that may only become clear as you engage in the process of writing it down. Just as you may not know what you're going to say until you say it, so you may not know what you're going to write until you write it. Thus, as you write, writing becomes a way of knowing.

Viewed in this way, writing is a rather messy process. And as children freely use their innately human symbol-making power, they certainly make a lot of messes. They mark and scribble, gesture and talk and act out, draw and write and rewrite, crumple paper and make holes in it as they erase and break pencil points, and then write some more as they revise. All these activities are part of discovering what they know about the world and communicating it to others. Think of children as attempting to interpret the world by hypothesizing, taking chances, and testing new experiences.

Writing in a Second Language

See Chapter 3, Language and Cultural Diversity, for more on teaching language arts in culturally and linguistically diverse classrooms.

Teachers must be concerned about how to teach writing effectively to culturally and linguistically diverse students, which means viewing writing as a sociocultural act. In a student- and response-centered classroom, teachers pay attention to students' prior experience and situate writing in real and sensible contexts. And for nonnative English speakers who are learning to write in English as a second language, teachers must make careful plans to provide the kind of support and guidance these students need. In particular, this means frequent modeling of writing behaviors and needed skills related to language conventions (Reyes, 1991). It's also important to make expectations about writing clear to students (Delpit, 1988) and to connect the skill instruction and actual writing students do.

In a review of research on the writing development of students learning English as a second language, Hudelson (1986) found that their development parallels that of native English speakers. Given that, she makes five suggestions for teaching writing to these students:

1. Students can begin to write in English before they have complete control over all aspects of language conventions (e.g., grammar, spelling, and sounds). They're able to use what they know at the time to write.
2. Students can do different kinds of writing for different purposes and should have opportunities to do so (e.g., journals, dialogue journals, expressive writing, literature as a model for writing, and writing across the curriculum).
3. Students can revise their writing with feedback and support from teacher conferences and peer conferences. Their revision processes are similar to those of native English speakers, and they benefit from cooperative, collaborative peer revision and editing conferences.
4. Students are greatly affected by the teacher's attitude and classroom context for writing. A process approach to writing indicates to children that their experiences, ideas, and writing are important.
5. As is true with native English speakers, second-language students' writing development may vary greatly because of individual differences in ability as well as cultural background and language development.

Children who are learning to write in English as a second language can benefit from a process approach to writing, especially through the use of teacher modeling and minilessons in skills and language conventions, literature as a model for language, sharing and talking together, peer-response groups, cooperative and collaborative learning, dialogue journals (in which the teacher writes back), and drawing on their prior knowledge and experience.

Writing Workshop

Writing workshop is based on the ideas behind writing as a process (Atwell, 1987; Calkins, 1983; Graves, 1983) and reflects a social constructivist point of view about learning, as well. From a Vygotskian perspective, students collaborate with the teacher and other students to initiate writing. From a Piagetian perspective, they respond to tensions within themselves, within the environment, and with others to discover meaning.

The students' role is to exercise their choice of topics and genre in writing and time for writing. They use their own voices and learn to take control and responsibility for their own learning. The teacher's role is to provide a regular block of time for children to write and to initiate the process approach to writing in a student- and response-centered classroom. The teacher's role also involves modeling, observing students' activity and progress, demonstrating the writing process and needed skills, collaborating through conferences and serving as an audience for young writers, and expecting that children will succeed as writers. Teachers and other students respond to student writing to help them rethink, revise, and edit. Students write for real purposes and real audiences. Writing conventions and mechanics, or skills, are taught in the context of this real writing and adapted to meet individual needs.

See Chapter 1, Learning and Teaching Language Arts, for more on these key ideas.

Writing workshop may appear loosely structured, but it requires excellent organization, observation, and ongoing, authentic assessment on the part of the teacher. Part of students' responsibility is to learn the procedures of the writing process and writing workshop. Each session begins with a brief minilesson to initiate or demonstrate a procedure, concept, or skill relevant to students' writing and needs. This lesson is followed by a very brief planning period. The bulk of the period is reserved for writing, during which the teacher circulates, providing support, observing students' needs, and holding individual conferences. The teacher can also write during this time, modeling writing for students. The session can end with an open sharing in which students read their writing to the whole group and request feedback. Assessment is ongoing and authentic, and students do self-assessment. Students keep their work in progress in folders and use notebooks to jot down ideas to write about (Calkins, 1991).

Writing workshop is especially well suited to classrooms in which students' abilities vary. Likewise, this method is effective when students would seem to benefit from one-to-one conferences with the teacher and a cooperative, collaborative learning environment.

Parts of Writing Workshop
1. Minilesson
2. Writing status
3. Writing
4. Sharing

SNAPSHOT: Writing Workshop in Sheila Kline's Fourth Grade

Sheila Kline teaches fourth grade at Lincoln Elementary School, in which over 80 percent of the students are language minority or come to school speaking a language other than English. About half are Spanish speaking, and another half are Cambodian Khmer speaking; a few speak other languages.

Sheila Kline begins the writing workshop with a minilesson using literature.

Many of Sheila's fourth-grade students are still developing fluency in English and are emerging readers and writers. She uses writing and reading workshops every day because she believes in the writing process approach, takes a social constructivist perspective on learning and teaching language arts, and feels her language-minority students benefit greatly from the one-to-one individual conferences with her and the cooperative environment that exists.

See Chapter 3, Language and Cultural Diversity, for more on teaching language-minority students.

See Chapter 8, Reading as a Language Art, for more on reading workshops.

Sheila schedules hour-long writing workshops on Mondays, Wednesdays, and Fridays and reading workshops on Tuesdays and Thursdays, although reading and writing go on in both. Since two new students just joined Sheila's class, she's brought out handmade posters that describe writing workshop in her class and reviewed them with students (see Figure 9.1).

A Minilesson (7 minutes)

Sheila starts with a minilesson on expressive writing. She's made another poster to provide visual support for what she's saying and so students can refer to it later (see Figure 9.2). She goes over the ideas on the poster:

Sheila: I will do a minilesson to help make your writing stronger, more powerful. You're already doing lots of this. After we talk, you can look at the poster and think, "Oh, yeah! That's what I'm doing." Can you express yourself? Get those wonderful ideas out? From your brain to your hand and out your pencil? Sometimes it's *hard.* I know it is for me. Is it hard for any of you, too? (She raises her hand and several students do, too.)

In writing workshop, writers:

1. Think about what they want to write about. Use their idea list to find a subject.
2. Prewrite. Organize everything you want to say. Use a cluster, list, or outline.
3. Write a first draft.
4. Read the draft to at least two other people in reader's circle.
5. Revise. Make changes, add new information. Check to see if there is a topic, supporting details, and a conclusion. Writers listen to see if they used interesting sentences and good descriptions. Will the words put a picture in the reader's mind?
6. Read the piece in reader's circle.
7. Edit. Check your spelling, punctuation, margins, and indenting.
8. Turn in your paper for either an editing conference or a score.
9. Publish what is perfect!

FIGURE 9.1 Class Poster: Writing Workshops

Can you express yourself? Follow these easy steps, and you will succeed:

1. Introduction
   - Can you tell a little about the subject?
   - Why is this scene, person, object, or memory important? Give a clue or hint.
2. Body Paragraphs
   - Have you described the person, scene, object, or memory?
   - Have you told what you see, think, or feel about it?
   - Have you used details, names, and everything you can remember?
3. Conclusion
   - Tell again why this subject is important to you.

FIGURE 9.2 Class Poster: Minilesson for Expressive Writing

If you follow these steps I think it will help.

1. *Introduction.* Give a little clue or hint: "I'm going to tell you about something that changed my life" or "I'm going to tell you about the scariest thing." Throw out a fishing line with a little hook for the reader.
2. *Body Paragraphs.* Describe a lot. Now you have so much more to say than when we started school!

Child: In July, we knew a little. Now we know a lot.

Child: You could write more now.

Sheila: Check these off. Ask yourself, "What are your feelings?" Give details. Have you used names? What did he look like? Then . . .

Child: Conclusion. End.

Sheila: Yes! Wrap it up with a ribbon. "I told you about my plant because it's the neatest thing you've ever seen." Should you end with "the end" in 2 inch bubble letters?

Child: No. Write more.

Child: They'll be bored. Write more.

Sheila: Make it juicy!

Checking Writing Status (3 minutes)

To get organized, Sheila checks with each student to see what he or she is planning to do. She uses the Writing Status Checklist shown in Figure 9.3. Each student uses the same list as a record of what he or she has done and is going to do. Some answer with the symbols shown on the sheet or note other things they might be doing: "Rough draft on vacations," "Computer," or "Pen pal." Some of the symbols on the checklist correspond to a list Sheila has posted on a bulletin board, showing things children might do in the writing process: prewrite, draft, reader's circle, revise, edit, and publish.

Sheila's students correspond with pen pals at another school all year.

Establishing writing status this way means that each child knows what he or she is doing. Each child also knows that Sheila knows, and Sheila knows that he or she knows. This is an example of how the student's role in a whole-language classroom was described in Chapter 1—choice, voice, control, and responsibility. The teacher's corresponding role involves initiation, observation, demonstration, and expectation. These roles must constantly be negotiated, which they are each time a writing workshop takes place in Sheila's class.

Writing (45 minutes)

Everyone is getting ready to write or is already writing. Sheila circulates, talking to students about what they're doing, helping with questions, and finding things for them. Here are the things that happen during this writing workshop:

- ***Conference:*** Sheila conferences with one child who had placed a writing piece in one of the two files in the writing center: "Needs Editing" and "Grade." La Phin—an emerging speaker, reader, and writer in English—had placed hers in the "Needs Editing" file. Sheila took the story and went to La with an *editing strip:* a piece of lined paper cut in $2^1/_2$" strips. Sheila uses these strips to write comments on because she doesn't like to write on students' drafts. She wants them to do it on their own.

She asks La Phin to read her story (see Figure 9.4):

Sheila had read aloud *The Hundred Dresses,* by Eleanor Estes (1974), which is about a girl who's rejected by others. The class talked about whether that had ever happened to them or whether they'd seen it happen and what they did or would do.

FIGURE 9.3 Writing Status Checklist

NAME	MONDAY	TUESDAY	WEDNESDAY	THURSDAY	FRIDAY

Symbols to identify writing process:

PW = Prewrite	TC = Teacher Conference
D = Draft	ED = Editing
RC = Reader's Circle	FC = Final Copy

La Phin
The 100
Dressers
Janet H. got teas by Octavea.
She teas her and She said "you cant
play with us becuase you are Spanish."
It happened in November 23 1994.
It happened when it is reseshtime.
She felt Sad and angry. I whud
say, "Stop teasing her O.K. tease
sombody your Sise".

B

teased
sed
She
because
recess
would
Somebody

C

FIGURE 9.4 Student's (A) Prewrite Cluster, (B) Draft, and (C) Editing Strip

Sheila: What do you need here (where it says *teas*)?

La: *Teach.*

Sheila: Do you mean *tease?* (La nods.) OK, what do we need on the end?

La: A *d.*

Sheila: Do we need something else?

La: An *e.* (Sheila writes this on the editing strip.)

Sheila: Right! You have the rest of the word. Read the rest to me. (La reads very quietly; Sheila leans to listen.) That's good! You talked about feelings and what they did and how they needed to fix it. About Octavia, do we need something here? (La had started the second sentence with *teas*.)

La: *She*. (Sheila writes it next on the editing strip.)

Sheila: Yeah. Put a period and *she*. (Reading.) "She teased her and then she *said* . . ." What do you need to put around the words?

La: Marks. Quotation marks.

Sheila: Right. (Reading.) "You can't play with us because you are Spanish." When we write Cambodian, do we put a capital? (La nods.) Yes. It's an important name. We do the same for Spanish.

Sheila and La Phin continue through the story, both reading. Sheila helps La with several more things and ends the conference praising La:

Sheila: You spelled *teasing* just right. I like the way you told who got teased, where, how she felt, and when. Do you like it?

La: Yes. I like it.

Sheila: Me, too. I like it. You're in good shape. Make a final copy.

See Assessing Writing, near the end of the chapter, for the writing rubric Sheila has developed to score students' papers (see Figure 9.12).

Sheila notes that not all students request conferences. Those who don't put their writing in the "Grade" folder, and Sheila scores it.

• ***Reader's Circle:*** If students want to read their pieces to one another and get feedback, they put their names in a circle on the chalkboard. When there are at least two names, they meet and read to each other. Esther, Leosha, and Sonytha meet in a reader's circle, sitting on the floor. Esther reads her story "About My Vacation" while Leosha and Sonytha listen:

Leosha: I liked the part where you said *popcorn*. (To Sonytha.) What part did you like?

Sonytha: The conclusion. It was good. Do you need a capital here?

Sonytha reads her story, and Leosha—a native English speaker—helps her. Leosha then reads her story and talks about her self-portraits at the bottom of the page: "Me—Happy" and "Me—Sad."

• ***Publishing:*** Several students are at the writing center, making covers for their books, cutting and pasting their stories onto separate pages to illustrate them, and stapling pages together. Lately, they've been decorating their covers by punching holes around the edges and then tying pieces of colorful yarn through them. It gives their books a festive look that many children like.

• ***Collaborative Writing:*** Two students work together on a story that they'll illustrate and publish as a co-authored book. Another student illustrates a buddy's book. Two girls work on similar stories side by side, helping each other and drawing and writing on each other's papers.

• ***Individual Writing:*** Students do a variety of types of writing during the hour:

Make a list of ideas to write about
Cluster ideas for a story
Write: draft, revise, or edit
Write a letter to a pen pal

Collaboration and cooperative learning are important parts of the writing workshop.

Work at the computer
Conference
Reader's circle
Illustrate a story or book
Journal writing
Cut-and-paste editing for a book
Decorate a book cover
Read a story to the teacher or a friend

Sharing Published Pieces (5 minutes)

The writing workshop usually ends with students reading aloud things they have published.

Sheila's explains her beliefs about writing workshop as a part of learning and teaching language arts:

> In writing workshop, we don't move as a herd, doing everything the same at the same time. Today, some are writing to pen pals at another school, but others are doing different things. Sometimes, we are all over the place and my job is to coordinate. It's like a big, multilane freeway, where we shift lanes constantly. It's not linear but spiral, even amorphous. I do a lot of reading aloud, and we talk, and they might write about what I read and we talked about. I want to get the language flowing for my language-minority students. My aides provide primary language support in Spanish and Khmer. I throw out something each time in minilessons—procedure, terminology, types of writing, writing conventions—and some will use it right away and others take more time. Writing is like that. I find things to encourage them to put their "toe in" writing.

A Process Approach to Writing

Here are key ideas about teaching a process approach to writing, illustrated with examples from Sheila Kline's fourth-grade class of predominantly language-minority children.

A Literate Environment

Sheila has a writing center in her class as part of the literate environment she has created. There's a sign over it, "Writing Center," and this area contains materials for writing and bookmaking:

Stacking file with different kinds of paper: blank, lined, colored, stationary, note, Post-its
Paper clips and rubber bands
Paste and glue
Scotch tape, masking tape, wide tape for book binding
Pencils, colored pencils, crayons, and erasers
Scissors, staplers, hole punch, rulers
Construction paper for book covers
Decorations for book covers: yarn, wrapping paper, and so on

Organizing a Writing Center

Sheila uses a plastic file crate, divided in two, to contain the files "Needs Editing" and "Grade," in which students put their work. If they file a piece in "Needs Editing," Sheila knows they would like a conference with her, so she plans it. If they file a piece in "Grade," they've edited it themselves or with the help of other students in reader's circle.

Sheila has created a literate environment in her classroom in other ways, too. She has a large classroom library of books, including a file of books written by the students. The walls of the room are covered with student writing, posters made by Sheila about writing or other subjects, and labels, lists, and directions.

For more ideas on creating a literate environment in the classroom, see the section in Chapter 1, Learning and Teaching Language Arts, on classroom environment, and that in Chapter 4, Emergent Literacy, on a print-rich environment.

Modeling

Sheila Kline believes that modeling writing is an important part of teaching it. She models writing primarily as she responds to students' writing in conferences but also tries to find other times to do so. I once received a "love note" from a student, and at the bottom, she drew a picture with the caption: "Mrs. Cox's class writing books and Mrs. Cox writing report cards." I decided then that I didn't want children to think that teachers write report cards while children do the real writing. Many teachers consider themselves expert readers, but they might not think they are such good writers. What did you write about yourself as a writer at the beginning of the chapter, for example? Frank Smith (1981) says that it's a huge myth that "people who do not themselves enjoy and practice writing can teach children how to write" (p. 797).

Teachers can model the enjoyment and practice of writing just as they model the enjoyment and practice of reading:

1. *Provide examples:* Do so during minilessons or when the class is writing a language experience story. Share your ideas, ask questions about what's being written, and offer examples and options.
2. *Write your own pieces:* If you have used literature as a model or prompt for writing, write about it yourself. In October, when everyone else is writing Halloween stories, try it yourself.
3. *Keep a journal:* Start one now. It will become a thread that connects your future as a student teacher and teacher with your past, which will help you understand the present. Keep your journal going in your own classroom.
4. *Write curriculum:* Participate in professional writing like curriculum development, school self-study reports, inservice preparations, and other projects that require expository writing. You may find you have a great deal to say and learn when you're writing about children, teaching, and learning—things you know well.
5. *Write for publication:* Try it. Many of the journals of professional organizations, such as *Language Arts* (National Council of Teachers of English) and *The Reading Teacher* (International Reading Association), encourage classroom teachers to write articles.
6. *Join a writing project:* Through the National Writing Project, teachers participate in summer workshops, in which they learn to teach writing by writing themselves. Find out if your state has a writing project and become involved.

See Barbara Catroppa (1984), "Writing for Publication: Advice from Classroom Teachers," in *Language Arts, 61,* 836–841.

Minilessons

Minilessons is a term used in connection with writing workshops. Sheila Kline uses minilessons to initiate writing workshops. They usually last 5 to 10 minutes, focusing on procedures in the workshop, the writing process, and skills. On the day described in the Snapshot, Sheila did a minilesson on expressing yourself in writing. Here's the actual schedule of the minilessons she uses from July to January:

Sheila's school is on a year-round calendar, starting in July.

July

Procedural Lessons

Folders	Conduct in reader's circle
Idea list	When papers are turned in: where and how
How to make a cluster	Scoring rubric
Skills list	

September

9/8	Reviewed procedures
9/10	Main idea: reviewed questions to ask in reader's circle
9/12	Main idea and topic sentence

9/14	Conduct in reader's circle Who, what, when, where, and why/how should be covered in writing
9/16	Editing strips, "P" means to indent new paragraph
9/23	Reviewed editing strips, recopying for publication All week talked about feelings and making the reader see what the author saw
9/28	Margins
9/30	When do you publish? How do you publish?
October	
10/3–10/5	Publishing tips
10/7	All capitals for loud voices; review of quotation marks
10/10–10/31	Worked together to develop a Halloween scary story; emphasized topic, topic sentence, detail sentences, and conclusion
January	
1/4	Developed list of 9 items to check before turning in a piece
1/6	Reviewed parts of a paragraph
1/9	Reviewed scoring rubrics
1/11	Reviewed writing workshop procedures for new students

Sheila also uses class posters that summarize the ideas presented in minilessons so that children can refer to them. For example, see Figure 9.5, a class poster showing that a paragraph has four parts.

The following lists includes some of the many possibilities for minilessons for writing workshop:

FIGURE 9.5
Class Poster: Parts of a Paragraph

A paragraph has 4 parts:

1. Topic
   - Topic sentence
   - Ask a question, make a wish, state an opinion
2. Describe
   - Explain
   - Detail sentences
3. Support
   - Prove
   - Detail sentences
4. Conclusion
   - Repeat or restate topic sentence
   - Can be a WOW!

Procedures	***Writing***
Folders	Main idea
Idea list	Topic sentence
Clustering	Who, what, where, when, why
Reader's circle	Detail sentences
Reading as a source of ideas	Conclusion
Conferences	Making the reader see; describing
Filing papers	Feelings

Revising and Editing	***Publishing***
Editing strips	When do you publish?
Margins	How do you publish?
Capitals	Sharing writing
Parts of a paragraph	Illustrations
Parts of a sentence	Punctuation marks
Bookmaking	Computer publishing
Spelling	Drama and media
Editing checklist	Collaboration

Conferences

Teacher Conferences

Sheila Kline conferences with students during writing workshops when they put their pieces in the "Needs Editing" file, which she checks at the beginning of each workshop. She also holds on-the-spot conferences with students who ask for or appear to need them.

Conferences are an important part of the process approach to writing. Donald Graves's (1983) research has shown that language exists in meaningful contexts and that composing is an activity of literate communities for purposes of self-expression and communication, rather than the teaching of separate skills. Integral to this approach is the idea that teachers are knowledgeable adults who interact and guide children, who are the decision makers about their own writing (Bury, 1993).

Children use conferences as a means to do this, asking *responsive questions,* which Graves (1983) defines as those teachers don't know the answers to. Teachers guide students through the decision-making process needed to bring a text to publication during these conferences. Graves advises keeping conferences short by focusing on one thing, teaching only one thing per conference, avoiding rushing, and not talking too much. Here are other guidelines for teacher conferences:

See Chapter 5, Listening and Talking, for more on teacher questions.

1. ***Scheduling Conferences:*** Conferences can occur at any time—during writing workshop or writing in other subject areas. They can be scheduled by students (e.g., through signing up or placing their papers in a certain place) or occur spontaneously, as the teacher circulates while children write. With regard to scheduling conferences, Graves (1983) offers "answers to the toughest questions teachers ask about conferences":

- *"How do I find the time?"* You don't have to correct every paper for every child every time you meet. Writing and conferences are ongoing processes. A timetable for a 37-minute writing period, accommodating about 17 students, might look like this.
  - First 10 minutes: After reviewing writing folders, the teacher circulates the room and helps children who need it.
  - Next 15 minutes: The teacher holds regularly scheduled conferences with certain children.
  - Next 12 minutes: The teacher holds a conference either with a small group who are applying a common skill or with children who are at an important point in their writing.
- *"How often should I hold conferences?"* This will vary, but you should confer with each child at least once a week.
- *"What are the other children doing?"* The others should be writing, finding more things to write about as they do. It's important to create experience and interest centers in the classrooms to engage children, keep writing materials accessible, and keep children from interrupting. Class discussions will help children cope by themselves with certain problems, such as spelling, what to write about next, and so on.

2. *Questions for Writing Conferences:* Calkins (1983) lists questions for conferences that can apply to any kind of writing:

- "What is your favorite part?"
- "What problems are you having?"
- "How did you feel?"
- "Do your paragraphs seem to be in the right order?"
- "Can you leave out parts that repeat or that fail to give details about your subject?"
- "Can you combine some sentences?"
- "Can you use more precise verbs in some places?"
- "What do you plan to do next with this piece of writing?"

Peer Conferences

Children can work in groups to read and respond to each other's writing. As discussed earlier, Sheila Klein's class uses a *reader's circle* during writing workshop. Students write their names on the board inside a circle, and when several names are listed, students meet together to read what they have written to each other. The emphasis here is usually on listening and responding to the ideas and having an audience.

Another approach is *peer-editing groups,* in which children work together closely to edit each other's work, revising without teachers' help (Elbow, 1973). This may work best with older students. Here are some guidelines for peer-editing groups:

- Editors should make positive comments and emphasize strengths as well as places for improvement.
- Writers and editors should respect everyone in the group.

- Writers should not apologize or feel what they have written isn't good enough. The purpose of the group is to help.
- Rather than arguing, writers should discuss suggestions and then make their own decisions about revision.
- Writers should appreciate the comments and help offered by editors.

Students should follow these techniques for working in peer-editing groups:

- *Summarizing:*
  Give a one-sentence summary of what the writing is about.
  Give a one-word summary. Pick a word from the writing that best summarizes it, or pick a word of your own that you feel best describes it.
- *Pointing:*
  As you listen to the writer read, note words and phrases that make an impression on you.
  As you respond, point to the words and phrases.
- *Telling:*
  Tell the writer how you felt as you listened.

Students can also fill out forms during and after peer-editing groups (see Figure 9.6).

Journals

Students in Sheila Kline's class can write in their journals during writing workshop and also at other times during the day. Sheila sometimes writes in students' journals (as in a dialogue journal, described later) and sometimes dictates students' entries. Some entries are personal and some are about class activities, such as watching a bean plant grow. Many drawings are included, too. Here are some variations of journals:

• ***Personal Journals:*** Students can write in personal journals every day, both during a regular journal-writing period and throughout the day. All they need to get started is a notebook and support from the teacher.

FIGURE 9.6
Peer-Editing Response Form

The piece I read was ______________________________
by ______________________________.
The best thing about this piece is ______________________________
______________________________.
If the writer wanted to change something, I would suggest ______________
____
______________________________.

______________________ ______________________
Peer Editor Date

• ***Kindergarten Journals:*** Even the youngest students can write in journals. Kindergarten teacher Hipple (1985) has children write in journals during the first 30 minutes of every day, when they're eager to communicate. The journals she uses consist of five pieces of paper stapled together—a page for each day of the week. Children write their names and the date on each page (copied from the chalkboard). They all receive new journals every Monday, and the old ones are saved in their portfolios. Students can draw, write, dictate to the teacher, and talk about and share their journals with the rest of the class.

• ***Community and Content Journals:*** Not all journals are individual. Open, community journals may be kept in the room for all children to write in. Good places to keep these are at windows, encouraging children to write about what they see (e.g., the weather), or by class pets, helping children observe what they're doing. A first-grade teacher keeps the following community journals in her class (Mathews, 1984):

Journal Title	Topic
Smokey and Rockwell	Observations of the guinea pig and rabbit
Exploring	Science discoveries; science center
Things We Made	Art projects
Pretending	Plays and puppet shows
What We Did in Math	Math activities
Outside Our Window	Environmental observations

• ***Idea Journals:*** A journal can be a source of writing ideas and a place to test them out, or students can keep separate journals for writing ideas. For example, one of my fourth-grade students, Andrea, was a very private child. She wrote more than she talked and entered into classroom activities only reluctantly. Instead, she preferred to write in her journal, which soon became a loose-leaf notebook, bulging at the seams. Andrea began to write in the persona of a sorcerer's apprentice after listening to the music of Dukas in class and talking about the story. Eventually, she wrote a series of dialogues between herself, as the apprentice, and an imaginary sorcerer. She continued to write about herself and began referring to her journal as "her book." She took it home to write in, and years later, she told me she had continued the journal through high school.

• ***Literary Journals:*** Journals and diaries are an ancient form of recording the events in people's lives and have also become a literary form. Children who read books written in diary or journal form may choose to write in this form themselves. Read aloud one of the following books to introduce children to this form:

Anne Frank: The Diary of a Young Girl (Frank, 1952)
Diary of a Churchmouse (Oakley, 1987)
Diary of a Rabbit (Hess, 1982)
Diary of the Boy King Tut Ankh-Amen (Reig, 1978)
Dorrie's Book (Sachs, 1975)
The First Four Years (Wilder, 1971)
A Gathering of Days: A New England Girl's Journal, 1830–1832 (Blos, 1979)
Harriet the Spy (Fitzhugh, 1964)

I, Columbus: My Journal, 1492–1493 (Roop & Roop, 1990)
I, Trissy (Mazer, 1971)
Marco Polo: His Notebook (Roth, 1990)
My Side of the Mountain (George, 1959)
Nettie's Trip South (Turner, 1987)
Off the Map: The Journals of Lewis and Clark (Roop & Roop, 1993)
On the Frontier with Mr. Audubon (Brenner, 1977)
Pedro's Journal: A Voyage with Christopher Columbus (August 3, 1492–February 14, 1493) (Conrad, 1991)
Some of the Days of Everett Anderson (Clifton, 1970)
Three Days on a River in a Red Canoe (Williams, 1981)
Z for Zacahariah (O'Brien, 1975)

See Chapter 3, Language and Cultural Diversity, for more on reading about Columbus and the Taino Indians from several perspectives.

• ***Literature Response Journals:*** These are often double-entry journals, in which a student notes a part of the book that attracted his or her attention on one side and his or her response to that part on the other side.

See Chapter 7, Teaching with Literature, for ideas about journals for responding to literature.

• ***Dialogue Journals:*** Dialogue journals are written conversations. The children make journal entries on any topic, and the teacher writes back in response. These journals may be exchanged one or more times a week or on an individual basis. They are valuable because they make connections between thinking and language, speaking and writing, and teacher and child. In addition, dialogue journals help students unlock the literacy puzzle (Bode, 1989). Here are suggestions for dialogue journals (Staton, 1984):

Use small, bound notebooks (not spiral ones), which can be filled quickly enough so that children feel success when they get a new one to fill. Decorate the covers.
Establish regular places and times to turn in and pick up journals.
Teachers should write back immediately, taking the journals home to do so, if needed.
Writing more frequent, brief entries seem to work best.
Return journals first thing in the morning the day after students have written in them, and give students ample time to read and respond in return.

Teachers responding to journal entries of students for whom English is a second language (ESL) should indicate that the *meaning* of what they are saying is the most important thing, rather than language conventions like spelling or punctuation. Dialogue journals are nonthreatening and private types of writing, but teachers still need to model the writing process and use of language conventions (Peyton & Reed, 1990).

Writing across the Curriculum

Students in Sheila Kline's class wrote about bean plants because they were growing them as a science project. The emphasis in writing workshop was on using describing words to describe their bean plants, but they were also practicing writing across the curriculum.

One year, when I was teaching third/fourth grade, we studied the behavior of mealworms. They live burrowed in bran, can exist in small containers,

What's the class pet doing? Students record their observations in science journals in writing across the curriculum.

and can be taken out for observation of their behavior (e.g., life cycle, movement patterns, feeding, etc.). We used many different types of writing in the course of our study of the behavior of mealworms:

Live mealworms can be purchased at pet stores; they are used as food for birds.

- Signs and labels for setting up experiments
- Observation logs
- Graphs, tables, figures, charts, and diagrams
- Reports of findings of experiments
- Bibliographies
- Poems
- Fictional stories about mealworms
- Genre stories: "The Adventures of Superworm" and "Another Episode of Dragworm"
- Literary adaptations: "Wormeo and Juleworm," and "Abe and I," and "Swiss Family Worminson"
- Script for a class movie: *I Love You, Mealworm*
- Ads and publicity for the movie

Writing across the curriculum is a natural and useful way for children to understand and learn subject matter in science (Levine, 1985) and math (Evans, 1984), for example. Writing across the curriculum also helps improve the teaching of writing (Applebee, Langer, & Mullis, 1986). First, students need broad-based experiences in which reading and writing tasks are integrated into their work throughout the curriculum. In addition, instruction in the writing process needs to focus on teaching students how to think more effectively as they write.

Labels and Lists

The first label a child often learns to write is his or her name. Teachers of young children who write their names on drawings as the children watch are modeling. Older students can label anything for identification. They can collect lists of words in their personal spellers, with a single page for each letter. Students can also make lists of materials for science experiments, ingredients for cooking, books for research, or supplies for projects or parties.

Notes

Taking notes from discussions makes a link between talking and writing. Young children can dictate their ideas to teachers, and older students can take their own notes. The purpose for notes is to use writing as a means of observing, thinking, and recording, and to move away from the idea that collecting information is simply copying.

Observation Records

Science study encourages children to record observations of phenomenon and experiments. My third-/fourth-grade class observed and recorded the behavior of mealworms kept in boxes of bran as a means to test hypotheses.

Outlines and Layouts

Taking notes and keeping observation records lead to students creating more elaborate outlines and layouts for displaying findings or writing a newspaper.

Journals

Journals can be used across the curriculum in two ways: (1) as daily records of phenomenon or experiments and (2) for fictional writing by students who use what they have learned about historical events.

Reports

Reporting across the curriculum can mean writing straightforward written reports or other forms, such as a play (about a historical event), a videotaped talk show (interviewing a famous person in history or a famous scientist), or a newspaper (factual or fictional based on facts). Here are the steps in report writing, using the example of a fifth-grade class studying American history.

1. ***Identify Questions to Answer:*** These questions emerged during class discussions.

- What happened in this period of history? Why?
- What were the important events?
- What were the problems of the times?
- Who were the important people? Why?
- What was the daily life of the times like?
- What were beliefs of the people?

2. ***Gather Resources:*** A classroom resource center was established, providing books, magazines, maps, objects and artifacts, photographs, and other memorabilia from the library or home. Fieldtrips to historic sites in the area were another source of experience and information.

3. ***Take Notes for Group Discussion:*** Students took notes from man sources for discussions: fieldtrips, guest speakers, films and filmstrips, books and reference sources.

4. ***Research a Topic:*** Students took notes and began to write abou topics in depth, experimenting with different forms of writing. New question emerged during this period through further discussion, reading, and writing.

5. ***Report:*** Since these students had written newspapers for their class their school, and their community, it seemed only natural to go back in tim and report what they had found out about American history through a serie of newspapers, set in different historical periods (see Figure 9.7). Sometimes they made two newspapers, representing opposing political views; for in stance, "The Liberty Lion" and "George's Journal" voiced the Colonial an British point of views during the Revolutionary War. Students chronicle American expansion in the nineteenth century in "The Western Times." Th children also dramatized what they had researched and written about, givin speeches, holding debates, and recreating scenes. And their learning in severa content areas carried over into their fictional writing.

Revising and Editing

The writing process is as individual as a fingerprint. Some students write easil and prolifically; others write more slowly, spending more time revising. Revis ing and editing can be done in reader's circle in writing workshops, teache conferences, and peer-editing groups, all described earlier in this chapter. Stu dents can also do self-editing, relying on reminders in a poster like the on Sheila had over the writing center (see Figure 9.8) or using a self-editin checklist (see Figure 9.9).

While keeping in mind that revising and editing are not ends in them selves, consider the following guidelines for editing children's work:

1. *The self-image of the young writer:* How does the writer feel abou himself or herself? With some children—particularly young or reluctar writers—suggesting changes may discourage them from writing at al Teachers must consider the effects that their comments will have o students' feelings as well as their writing.
2. *The needs of the young writer:* Why is the child writing and for whom The more real writing is to students, the less they may need the teache to tell them what it might be like. Teachers should take their cue fror the degree of students' involvement in their writing.
3. *The purposes of the young writer:* What is the child's intent? Th teacher's suggestions for changes in a student's newspaper article, i which information needs to be clearly communicated, would be diffe ent from those made for a poem or some other personal piece.
4. *The style of the young writer:* What is the writer's approach? Some chi dren write factual stories based on their experiences and can easily ar swer questions about what really happened. Others prefer writing fic tion; fantasy emerges strongly in some students. When they're writin

The TIMES are
Dreadful
Diſmal
Doleful
Dolorous and
DOLLAR-LESS

Containing the freſeſt Advices, Foreign, and Domeſtick
To all my subſcribers and Benefactors who theſe my weekly
Journall By Mistreſſ Cox'ſ Dame School

BURGESSES DISCUSS COLONIES
Col. William Braxton
Jamestown, Virginia Colony, 1661

Last night the legislature and House of Burgesses met to discuss the colonies. Several burgesses made speeches about the people wanting to elect new representatives. Also about the people wanting more protection against the Indians.

Some members complained about the price of tobacco and said that Virginia should pass a law so that th there wouldn't be so much tobacco grown. Some people were afraid that Maryland wouldn't agree with Virginia but Maryland agreed and the Virginia House of Burgesses passed the law.

(assisting reporter-R. Rowley)

DEVELOPMENTS OF PHILADELPHIA

71 people came to Philidelphia in 10 families. The ship only comes twice a year. All of the people are Scots. They are not going to stay in Pennsylvania. They are going to move down to northern Virginia and the Carolinas.

Some people of the city think we should have a police force to watch the merchant's warehouses. Another idea was that we should have clear water. All our water is impure. There is a clear spring on a hill just outside the city. We ought to pipe to somewhere and make a well out of it. The merchants are going to form a company called the Philadelphia Water Company.

The Scientific and Literary → Club was thinking of having a bank but it wasn't a serious matter. One Merchant brought it up and decided to have a bank. It is called the Merchants Bank of Philadelphia.

J. Grinder

NEWS OF THE WITCHES ON TRIAL
Salem Village 1692

Mrs. Phillips will be tried for witchcraft on Saturday. She put apples in her dumplings <u>after</u> they were cooked.

Rev. Samuel Parrises slave, Tituba by name, will be tried for wi tchcraft on Sunday.

Two Indian slaves were hung for Witchcraft one week ago. They were said to have killed a crop.

D. Sternbach

LAWS OF THE BURGESSES PASSED

Last night the House of Burgesses decided on the law that one must pay a tax for protection from savage attack. One burgess said that Indians shall be treated fairly so our colony may live in peace.

It was decided that tobacco be sold at 18 pounds per barrel and if you do not work you shall be punished.

Ben Franklin and
Stan Metzenberg

AN EGG TODAY IS BETTER THAN A HEN TOMORROW. Ben Franklin

EARLY TO BED, EARLY TO RISE, MAKES A MAN HEALTHY, WEALTHY AND WISE.
Ben Franklin

FIGURE 9.7 Reporting on American History: Student Newspaper

Before I turn in a piece of writing for a score, I check to see if:

1. Paragraphs are indented.
2. Margins are correct.
3. Punctuation is correct: periods, commas, quotation marks, apostrophes, question marks, and exclamation points.
4. I used the right words.
5. Words are spelled correctly.
6. It has a topic sentence, detail sentences, and conclusion.
7. Capital letters are used correctly.
8. It is neat.
9. The prewrite and rough draft are stapled to it with one staple.

FIGURE 9.8
Class Poster: Self-Editing

about a person or place in their minds, which they may still be trying to visualize, it may be hard for them to explain it to someone else. The teacher can help by providing plenty of opportunities to discuss writing with others to clarify ideas.

My experience has been that when children care about what they are writing and have a strong sense of their purpose as well as their audience, they will readily seek revision as they need it. But keep in mind that not every piece needs revising or even finishing. When children have a wide audience in mind and the writing is important to them, they may want to make changes to make it as effective as possible. Their concern for conventions like spelling, punctuation, and grammar will reflect their concern for communicating with that audience.

Perhaps revision should be seen as answering the need for children to say clearly what they want to say, rather than answering the need for teachers to

FIGURE 9.9
Self-Editing Checklist

Name ______________________
Title ______________________
Date ______________

___ 1. Each sentence begins with a capital.
___ 2. Names of people and places are capitalized.
___ 3. Each sentence ends with a (.), (?), or (!).
___ 4. I have used (") to show when someone is talking.
___ 5. Each new paragraph is indented.
___ 6. I have corrected all misspelled words.
___ 7. I have chosen the words that best describe what I want to say.
___ 8. I have reread my writing and checked it.

have writing fit their own or someone else's model of the writing process. Consider yourself an active listener, a practice audience. Let children come to you to discover through rehearsal what they're trying to say.

Publishing

Publishing is an important part of establishing a sense of ownership for young writers as well as a feeling of authorship. Sheila Kline's students publish regularly: Stories they have written are displayed in the classroom and hallway, letters are exchanged with pen pals, and books they've made of their stories go in the classroom library. Children can publish their writing in countless ways, many of which we've already described.

See Chapter 4, Emergent Literacy, for more on language experience stories.

Bookmaking is another way of publishing students' work. It can be as simple as stapling a construction paper cover over a piece of writing or more involved. See Figure 9.10, which shows one type of bookmaking technique.

Scheduling

As mentioned earlier, Sheila Kline scheduled hour-long writing and reading workshops on alternating days of the week. Here's what the class does during each 60-minute period:

- *Minilesson (5–10 minutes maximum):* Procedures, process, skills, reading as a source of writing (ideas, clustering, chart stories).
- *Writing Status (5 minutes):* Uses a checklist of each child's focus; keeps terminology up; serves as an oral contract as part of management.
- *Writing (40–45 minutes):* Students work on their writing projects: individually, collaboratively, side by side. Also involves conferences with teacher and work in reader's circle.
- *Sharing (5 minutes):* Read published pieces aloud.

Children should also have opportunities to write throughout the day:

- *Journal Writing (15–30 minutes):* Writing in journals can take place first thing in the morning, even for children as young as kindergartners. A sustained period of writing like this can help get ideas flowing and identify topics to write about. Journal writing could also take place at any time during the day.
- *Writing Periods (30–60 minutes):* A whole class of younger children might work on a language experience chart with the teacher, whereas a class of older students might work on a group story, as they did in Sheila Kline's class at Halloween. Children in small groups can work on projects, newspaper articles, or play or media scripts. Individual children can work on stories, poetry, books, or literature response options.
- *Throughout the Day:* Children can continue working on pieces and projects when they are not directly involved with other subjects or whenever they have some time.

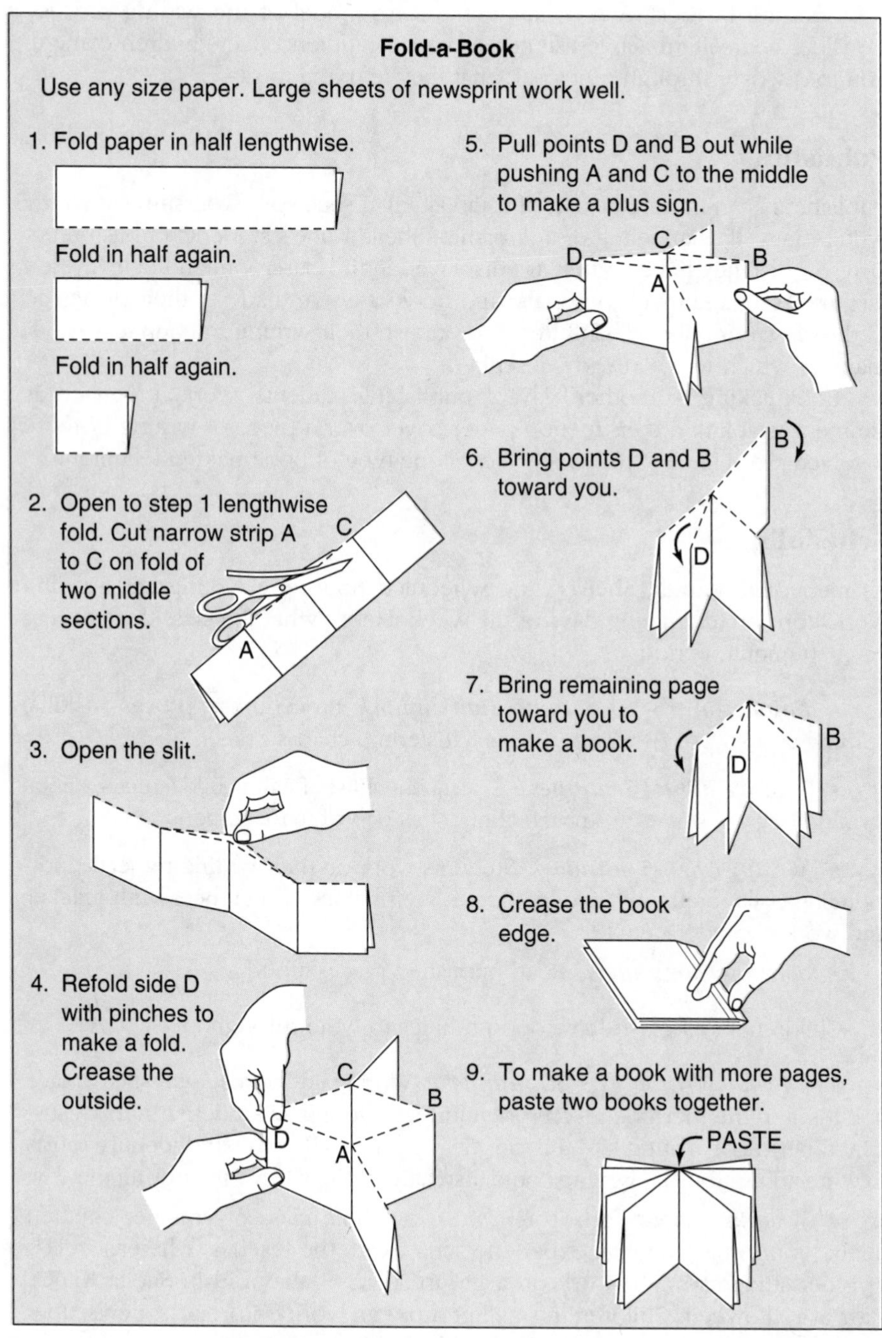

FIGURE 9.10
Steps to Bookmaking

Assessing Writing

The shift in elementary education to the process approach to writing has meant questioning traditional means of assessing writing: namely, multiple-choice tests based on questions and answers about subskills and timed essays that require specific prompts. Alternative means of writing assessment have emerged that more closely approximate the actual writing process—for instance, essay exams done in two sittings (one for prewriting and drafting and the second for revising and editing) and large-scale portfolio assessment.

The model of writing assessment used by many schools, districts, and states is based on the that of the Educational Testing Service (ETS). Students write on an assigned topic in a timed testing situation. Teachers score these pieces based on a rubric of scoring standards; usually more than one teacher reviews each paper. More than one writing test is often given. Similarly, national writing assessment is done through the writing portion of the National Assessment of Educational Progress (NAEP) for 9-, 13-, and 17-year-olds and the College Entrance Examination Board's Achievement Test in English Composition. They also evaluate short pieces of writing done in formal testing situations.

These more holistic testing and scoring procedures are an improvement over multiple-choice grammar tests and may help schools, districts, and states come to a consensus on what is good writing. However, these tests and procedures are not able to assess students' writing in real situations for real purposes on topics of their own choosing—the real goal of writing instruction. Constraints such as assigned topics (which may be of little interest or unfamiliar to students), a formal testing situation, and a short period of time are not conditions under which people really write.

Authentic Assessment

Students are involved in authentic assessment of writing, deciding which pieces should be edited and graded. Through this type of assessment, patterns of students' progress are revealed over time (Newkirk & Atwell, 1988). These patterns will not always be regular and will vary from child to child and among different types of writing.

Types of assessment include:

• ***Anecdotal Records:*** Keep a log for each child based on observations and conferences. Use a loose-leaf notebook, providing a page for each child; note the date, topic, and observation or score. Figure 9.11 shows the writing record Sheila Kline uses for pieces she scores.

• ***Holistic Scoring Rubrics:*** Teachers, schools, and districts have developed holistic scoring rubrics, which are used to look at a piece of writing as a whole and evaluate it on the basis of criteria with a scoring scale and a descriptor of what each point on the scale means. A rubric allows the teacher to look at a given student's progress compared to that of others whose writing

NAME	Date/Title	Date/Title	Date/Title	Date/Title
Albarron, Hugo 3/3	9/23 Mountain 3/3	9/19 School 3/3	10/17 Math Grade 3/3	
Barragan, Rolando 3/3	9/23 The Mall 3/3	10/17 Disneyland 3/3		
Caro, Taina 4/3	11/3 Babysitter 4/3	10/17 Chuck E Cheese 4/3		
Casarez, Hugo 2/3	9/16 Baseball 2/3			
Chann, Ry 2/3	9/23 Beach 2/3	9/23 Like to Write 2/3	10/17 Cats and Dogs Book 3/3	10/17 Like School 2/4
Chavez, Susana 4/4	9-17 Baby Cousin Fell 4/4	10/12 Window Hurt Finger 4/4	10/12 Mom in Hospital 4/4	10/17 Mexico 2/3
⋮				

FIGURE 9.11 Writing Record

has been scored by the same scale. Numbers can be attached to points on the rubric. Figure 9.12 shows the holistic scoring rubric Sheila Kline has developed to score her students' writing.

• ***Journals:*** These are ongoing records of students' fluency and flexibility in writing. For students who write in journals regularly, teachers can see changes in their writing. Journals are an important part of authentic, informal assessment in a process approach to writing.

Portfolios

For a review of recent books on portfolios, see Harry Noden and Barbara Moss (1994, October), "A Guide to Books on Portfolios: Rafting the Rivers of Assessment," *The Reading Teacher, 48.*

Portfolios are part of the movement toward more authentic assessment of student reading and writing. Interest in them as a means of authentic, ongoing, interpretive assessment is evidenced by the number of recent books on the subject (Clemmons, Laase, Cooper, Areglado, & Dill, 1993; D'Aoust, 1992; De Fina, 1992; Farr & Tone, 1994; Graves & Sunstein, 1992; Harp, 1993; Tierney, Carter, & Desai, 1991).

A *portfolio* is a representative collection of a student's work; it's sometimes called a *showcase portfolio* or an *active-writing folder.* Samples of writing should be kept throughout the year for use in planning and assessment. Portfolios are not simply folders of all student work nor are they collections of work considered most correct by adult standards. The contents of the portfolio are chosen to meet established criteria: What will be collected? under what conditions? for what purposes? and how will it be evaluated?

Both teachers and students select the pieces that go in portfolios and give reasons for their selections. This gives students choices as authors, such as planning the collection of work, making decisions about pieces they want to take all the way to the publishing stage, and deciding what and when to actually publish for evaluation. This type of assessment provides a more accurate picture of the individual writer in specific writing situations and in different contexts.

Compared to large-scale assessment, portfolios are driven by instruction, and decisions about creating and using them are made by teachers, schools,

WRITING RUBRIC						
CONTENT						
0	1	2	3	4	5	6
No attempt or impossible to decipher.	Collection of words with little sentence structure. Minimum of coherent organization.	Words and simple sentences. Mainly lists. No feelings or insight evident.	Fairly complete ideas. May use main idea sentence. Uses few supporting details. Writes with some feelings or sense of audience. Some descriptive language. Little evidence of insightful thinking.	Generally well thought out and arranged. Uses main idea/supporting details/conclusion formula. May have several supporting details. Writes with some evidence of feelings and sense of audience. Good clear descriptions. Some evidence of insight in place.	Well thought out and arranged. Many supporting details. Definite feelings and sense of audience. Clear, vivid descriptions. Much reflective, insightful thinking.	Well thought out and arranged. Many supporting details. Definite feelings and sense of audience. The overall impact of the piece is of a thoughtful, reflective author who has confidence in their writing.
CONVENTIONS						
0	1	2	3	4	5	6
No recognizable words.	Almost all spelling invented. Use of random upper-case and lower-case letters. Extremely hard to decipher. No margins.	Spelling mostly invented, interferes with reading the piece. Little sense of sentence or paragraph structure. May be written like a "list." Punctuation missing or randomly inserted. May use margins. Paragraphs may be indented.	Much invented spelling, but still easily readable. Some evidence of checking for correct spelling. Most common punctuation used correctly (, ' .). Uses fairly simple sentences. May use margins. Paragraphs may be indented.	Some invented spelling. Most words checked for correct spelling. Uses quotation marks, question marks, and exclamation points correctly most of the time (" ? !). Must use margins. Paragraphs are indented.	Almost all words spelled correctly. Most punctuation marks used correctly. Uses more complex sentences. Uses margins. Indents paragraphs.	Words have been checked and are spelled correctly. Punctuation is used correctly. Uses more complex sentences. Uses margins. Indents paragraphs.

FIGURE 9.12 Writing Rubric

Young writers proudly display their writing portfolios.

and even districts. This approach avoids the problem that teachers have had in the past of "teaching to the test," but it also makes it difficult to compare portfolios beyond the local context of the class, school, or district. Nonetheless, making portfolios more systematic has the potential of reducing their ability to fully characterize students' work and progress and thus their usefulness as a means of communicating this to parents.

Creating the Portfolio

Creating portfolios is part of the assessment process, or formative evaluation. Work is collected throughout the year, and students are essential to the process. Portfolios also provide a means of summative evaluation, as when a grade is finally given for the work and the portfolio created over a period of time. For example, because Sheila Klein saves samples of student writing all year, she's able to assess progress of students like Irene by comparing her writing at the beginning and end of the year. See Figure 9.13, which presents Irene's portfolio samples of writing about "My Friend" from the beginning and end of the year.

Here are the items that Sheila Kline's students collect in their portfolios:

1. Completed writing folder after all pieces have been scored
2. Student selection of best pieces, at least four in different modes: observation, expressive, expository, and persuasive
3. Writing across the curriculum: math, science, social studies
4. Published books

An Example of Portfolios

An example of the large-scale use of portfolios comes from Vermont, where all students in the fourth- and eighth-grades prepare showcase portfolios that are read by assessors (Vermont Assessment Program, 1991). The following items are in included in every child's showcase portfolio:

My Friend

My Friend is Julie. My friend has blonde hair. We were friends 6 months.
I met my friend in 4th ~~gerad~~ grade. I especially like my friend because She is helpful,
And because she is nice. I like my friend and I know she likes me too.

A

B

I have a friend and her name is Julie. She is funny. She makes me laugh a-lot.
I even copy her. She is very nice. When ever I need someone to help me
on things she is there. When ever she needs me I go to help her. We have
ben friends since we started 4th grade. She is White and I am Mexicin but
we don't care. She has blond hair and her eyes, I never seem to notice her
eyes, but I think her eyes are blueish greenish. I know that we are going to
be nice friends forever. We go to the Mall. But ther's problems sometime she
gets grachy or I get grachy. After that we get mad and start to fiat. But then
we bothe lough togeret. And then my ..

Irene Julie
friends

... other friends Lorena and Angelica come and the we are friends with a
hand shak and a haug.

FIGURE 9.13 Student's Portfolio Sample

Part A: Beginning of the Year

Part B: End of the Year

1. Table of contents of the portfolio
2. Dated "best piece"—one the student feels is representative of his or her best writing—chosen with the help of the teacher
3. Dated letter explaining why the student chose this piece and the process he or she went through in writing it
4. Dated poem, short story, play, or personal narration
5. Dated personal response to one of the following: a cultural, media, or sports event; a book or current issue of a magazine; a math or scientific problem
6. A dated piece of writing from any content area that is not language arts or English (one for fourth grade and three for eighth grade)

Student Choice

Students are expected to choose pieces to put in their portfolios. Sheila Kline has students fill out the form shown in Figure 9.14.

Name ____
Date ____________________

I chose this piece for my portfolio because

____

____.

Something special about this piece is

____

____.

I scored this piece with a ____ for rhetoric and a ____ for conventions.

My goal for the future in my writing is to:

___ Try a different type of writing, like poetry or fiction.
___ Spell more words correctly.
___ Write more sentences.
___ Write more interesting sentences.
___ Other ideas: ______________________________

FIGURE 9.14
Form for Student's Choice for Portfolio

Answers to Questions about the Writing Process

1. *What is the writing process?*

The *process approach* to writing, which developed during the 1970s and 1980s, is based on Donald Graves's influential book *Writing: Teachers and Children at Work* (1983). With this approach, the focus of writing instruction shifted from the product to the process. The stages of the writing process approach are prewriting, drafting, revising, editing, and publishing. These terms are useful for talking about the parts of the writing process, which don't necessarily occur in a fixed order for individual writers in specific situations. Teachers shouldn't think of these terms as comprising steps in a rigid, linear fashion. Writing is a recursive process.

2. *How should we teach writing as a process?*

The writing workshop is based on the principles of writing as a process and reflects a social constructivist point of view about learning, as well. The emphasis is on providing time and choices for students' writing. The teacher presents a short minilesson at the start of the workshop, students write individually or meet in reader's circles or conferences with the teacher, and share their writing briefly at the end.

Keys to a process approach to writing are creating a literature environment, teacher modeling, minilessons for procedures and language conventions, teacher and peer conferences, journal writing, writing across the curriculum, student-controlled revising and editing, publishing and establishing ownership and authorship, flexible scheduling, and authentic, ongoing, informal assessment (e.g., anecdotal records, holistic scoring rubrics, journals, and portfolios).

LOOKING FURTHER

1. Share with a small group of classmates what you wrote in the Reflective Response at the beginning of the chapter. Talk about your feelings about writing, how you were taught writing, and how you plan to teach writing.

2. Observe writing instruction in an elementary classroom. Compare what you saw with how the process approach to writing is described in this chapter.

3. Plan a minilesson for a writing workshop. Give the lesson to a group of students, if possible.

4. In your college class, write a short piece and share it in a reader's circle. Or conduct a peer-editing group, according to guidelines described in this chapter.

5. Collect several papers written by children and score them using Sheila Kline's writing rubric (see Figure 9.12). Then create a holistic scoring rubric you might use in your own class.

RESOURCES

Calkins, L. M. (1986). *The art of teaching writing.* Portsmouth, NH: Heinemann.

Farr, R., & Tone, B. (1994). *Portfolio and performance assessment: Helping students evaluate their progress as readers and writers.* Fort Worth, TX: Harcourt Brace Jovanovich.

Graves, D. (1983). *Writing: Teachers and children at work.* Portsmouth, NH: Heinemann.

REFERENCES

Applebee, A. N., Langer, J. A., & Mullis, I. V. S. (1986). *The writing report card: Writing achievement in American schools.* Princeton, NJ: National Assessment of Educational Progress.

Atwell, N. (1987). *In the middle: Reading and learning with adolescents.* Portsmouth, NH: Boynton/Cook.

Bode, B. (1989). Dialogue journal writing. *Reading Teacher, 42,* 568–571.

Bury, C. (1993). When all the right parts don't run the engine. *Language Arts, 70,* 12–13.

Calkins, L. M. (1983). *Lessons from a child: On the teaching and learning of writing.* Portsmouth, NH: Heinemann.

Calkins, L. M. (1991). *Living between the lines.* Portsmouth, NH: Heinemann.

Cambourne, B., & Turbill, J. (1987). *Coping with chaos.* Rozelle, Australia: Primary English Teaching Association.

Catroppa, B. (1984). Writing for publication: Advice from classroom teachers. *Language Arts, 61,* 836–841.

Clemmons, J. L., Laase, L., Cooper, D., Areglado, N., & Dill, M. (1993). *Portfolios in the classroom: A teacher's sourcebook.* New York: Scholastic.

D'Aoust, C. (1992). Portfolios: Process for students and teachers. In K. B. Yancy (Ed.), *Portfolios in the writing classroom* (pp. 39–48). Urbana, IL: National Council of Teachers of English.

De Fina, A. A. (1992). *Portfolio assessment: Getting started.* New York: Scholastic.

Delpit, L. D. (1988). The silenced dialogue: Power and pedagogy in educating other people's children. *Harvard Educational Review, 58,* 280–298.

Elbow, P. (1973). *Writing without teachers.* London, England: Oxford University Press.

Evans, C. S. (1984). Writing to learn in math. *Language Arts, 61,* 828–835.

Farr, R., & Tone, B. (1994). *Portfolio and performance assessment: Helping students evaluate their progress as readers and writers.* Fort Worth, TX: Harcourt Brace Jovanovich.

Graves, D. H. (1983). *Writing: Teachers and children at work.* Portsmouth, NH: Heinemann.

Graves, D. H., & Sunstein, B. (Eds.). (1992). *Portfolio portraits.* Portsmouth, NH: Heinemann.

Harp, W. (Ed.). (1993). *Assessment and evaluation in whole language programs.* Norwood, MA: Christopher-Gordon.

Hipple, M. L. (1985). Journal writing in kindergarten. *Language Arts, 62,* 255–261.

Hudelson, C. (1986). ESL children's writing: What we've learned, what we're learning. In P. Rigg & D. S. Enright (Eds.), *Children and ESL: Integrating perspectives.* Washington, DC: Teachers of English to Speakers of Other Languages.

Levine, D. S. (1985). The biggest thing I learned but it really doesn't have to do with science. . . . *Language Arts, 62,* 43–47.

Mathews, K. (1984). Community journals. *Livewire, 1,* 2–3.

Newkirk, T., & Atwell, N. (Eds.). (1988). *Understanding writing* (2nd ed.). Portsmouth, NH: Heinemann.

Noden, H., & Moss, B. (1994). A guide to books on portfolios: Rafting the rivers of assessment. *The Reading Teacher, 48,* 180–183.

Peyton, J. K., & Reed, L. (1990). *Dialogue journal writing with nonnative English speakers: A handbook for teachers.* Alexandria, VA: Teachers of English to Speakers of Other Languages.

Reyes, M. de la Luz (1991). A process approach to literacy instruction for Spanish-speaking students: In search of a best fit. In E. H. Hiebert (Ed.), *Literacy for a diverse society: Perspectives, practices, and policies* (pp. 157–171). New York: Teachers College Press.

Smith, F. (1981). Myths of writing. *Language Arts, 58,* 792–798.

Staton, J. (1984). Thinking together: Interaction in children's reasoning. In C. J. Thaiss & C. Suhor (Eds.), *Speaking and writing, K–12: Strategies and the new research.* Urbana, IL: National Council of Teachers of English.

Tierney, R., Carter, M., & Desai, L. (1991). *Portfolio assessment in the reading-writing classroom.* Norwood, MA: Christopher-Gordon.

Vermont Assessment Program. (1991). Montpelier, VT: Vermont Department of Education.

CHILDREN'S BOOKS

Blos, J. (1979). *A gathering of days: A New England girl's journal, 1830–1832.* New York: Scribner.

Brenner, B. (1977). *On the frontier with Mr. Audubon.* New York: Coward.

Clifton, L. (1970). *Some of the days of Everett Anderson.* New York: Holt Rinehart & Winston.

Conrad, P. (1991). *Pedro's journal: A voyage with Christopher Columbus (August 3, 1492–February 14, 1493).* Honedale, PA: Boyds Mills Press.

Estes, E. (1974). *The hundred dresses.* New York: Harcourt Brace Jovanovich.

Fitzhugh, L. (1964). *Harriet the spy.* New York: Harper & Row.

Frank, A. (1952). *Anne Frank: The diary of a young girl.* New York: Doubleday.

George, J. C. (1959). *My side of the mountain.* New York: Dutton.

Hess, L. (1982). *Diary of a rabbit.* New York: Scribner's.

Mazer, N. F. (1971). *I, Trissy.* New York: Delacorte.

O'Brien, R. (1975). *Z for Zacahariah.* New York: Atheneum.

Oakley, G. (1987). *The diary of a church mouse.* New York: Atheneum.

Reig, J. (1978). *Diary of the boy king Tut-Ankh-amen.* New York: Scribner.

Roop, P., & Roop, C. (Eds.). (1990). *I Columbus: My journal 1492–1493.* New York: Avon.

Roop, P., & Roop, C. (1993). *Off the map: The journals of Lewis and Clark.* New York: Walker.

Roth, S. L. (1990). *Marco Polo: His notebook.* New York: Doubleday.

Sachs, M. (1975). *Dorrie's book.* New York: Doubleday.

Turner, A. (1987). *Nettie's trip south.* New York: Macmillan.

Wilder, L. I. (1971). *The first four years.* New York: Harper & Row.

Williams, V. B. (1981). *Three days on a river in a red canoe.* New York: Greenwillow.

Chapter 10

Reading and Writing

Questions about Reading and Writing

1. *What is the relationship between reading and writing?*
2. *How should we teach reading and writing together and across the curriculum?*

Reflective Response

How were you taught reading in elementary school? How were you taught writing? Were they taught together? How do you think they are connected in language arts learning and teaching? Jot down your ideas in response to these questions, and think about them as you read this chapter.

Also pick a color and write about how you would portray it through pantomime.

The Reading and Writing Connection

In the past, reading and writing were often viewed as separate subjects. Reading instruction was teacher and text centered, and writing was primarily a supplement to reading activities. But today, reading and writing in student- and response-centered classrooms are integrally connected, merging these two aspects of literacy as a powerful tool for supporting thinking and learning (Tierney & Shanahan, 1990). So far in this text, we've looked at many teachers who have managed to do so successfully, integrating teaching reading and writing across the curriculum. These practices reflect current beliefs that learning and literacy development is a social and constructive process, that language is best learned when considered as a whole and used for authentic, meaningful purposes, and that listening, speaking, reading, and writing are interrelated and develop together.

Why should reading and writing be taught together (Tierney, 1994)?

1. To help students get closer to their own thinking and to allow others to get closer, as well.
2. To provide a means for students to have a voice, to jot down their ideas for themselves and others, and to share, compare, and rethink.
3. To offer students ways to experiment with ideas as well as to enlist different ways of expressing ideas.
4. To give students the opportunity to be authors, helping them realize that texts are written by people like themselves, not machines.
5. To provide students with opportunities to communicate with and collaborate in a variety of ways with others.
6. To enhance children's appreciation of what they read.
7. To ensure that students take advantage of texts and resources that can fuel and enhance the meanings they develop and to help them see their own experiences in this light, too.
8. To increase the amount of meaningful reading material available to students.

Students in a third-grade bilingual Spanish class connect reading and writing by working together in literature groups.

9. To contribute to a sense of community, in which members acknowledge and support each other.
10. To facilitate student-centered and meaning-oriented literacy activities and learning experiences that place a premium on the students' ideas and engagement.
11. To help ensure that reading and writing experiences merge individual and social learning opportunities, so that learning is simultaneously tailored to individual needs yet nourishing for the group.
12. To motivate students to think and learn for themselves, as they read and write their own texts and those of others.
13. To develop, learn, and apply reading and writing skills and strategies.

Reading and Writing Transactions

Louise Rosenblatt (1994) has discussed the similarities and differences between reading and writing in the context of her transactional theory. She maintains that reading and writing are not mirror images of each other; after all, a transaction that begins with a text written by someone else is not the same as one that occurs when a writer faces a blank page. Nonetheless, the teaching of one can affect the learning of the other. For example, reading provides the writer with the rich potential of language, whereas writing deepens the reader's understanding of the importance of paying attention to imagery or genre conventions.

The roles of the teacher and the classroom environment are critical to the development of reading and writing transactions. Because the transaction is a reciprocal relationship between reader and text (in the same way that people are always in some sort of transaction with an environment, context, or situation), neither the reader nor text is more important. Thus, teachers should not overemphasize either the text or the writing product (and associated skills, techniques, or conventions) or the process or personal aspects. As stated by Rosenblatt:

> *Hence the teaching of reading and writing at any developmental level should have as its first concern the creation of environments and activities in which students are motivated and encouraged to draw on their own resources to make "live" meanings. With this as the fundamental criterion, emphasis falls on strengthening the basic processes that we have seen to be shared by reading and writing. The teaching of one can then reinforce linguistic habits and semantic approaches useful to the other. Such teaching, concerned with the ability of the individual to generate meaning, will permit constructive cross-fertilization of the reading and writing (and speech) processes.* (1994, p. 1082)

Rosenblatt's work suggests several implications for teachers who wish to balance both the aesthetic and efferent responses and create these "live" meanings. Here are ways to create contexts for reading and writing transactions:

1. Enrich and make connections between the learner's reservoir of language and experiences.
2. Provide a sense of purpose as a guiding principle of selection and organization in both reading and writing.
3. Encourage:
   - purposive writing and reading that build on students' past experiences with life and language
   - the appropriate stance (efferent and aesthetic) for different types of reading and writing
   - dialogue about texts between teacher and students to develop insights as well as skills and conventions in meaningful contexts
   - peer reading and discussion of texts
   - comparison of different interpretations of texts

When teachers create contexts for collaborative interchange focused on reading and writing transactions, they no longer use commercial texts or teacher's guides written by other people, nor do they believe that there's only one interpretation of a text (their own or the one in the teacher's guide). Rosenblatt explains that "teaching becomes constructive, facilitating interchange, helping students to make their spontaneous responses the basis for raising questions and growing in the ability to handle increasingly complex reading transactions" (1994, p. 1084).

It's especially important that teachers encourage children to take a stance without guiding them to an inappropriate one. Rosenblatt frequently refers to a third-grade basal reader workbook that asks children to write in response to this question: "What facts does this poem teach you?" This request for facts (efferent information) is inappropriate in that, with regard to literature, children should be encouraged to take a predominantly aesthetic stance. On the other hand, Rosenblatt points out, this question is no more inappropriate than the example of the boy who complained that he wanted information about dinosaurs but his teacher only gave him "storybooks." A good read about dinosaur facts would mean taking an efferent stance.

While there should be a mix of aesthetic and efferent (i.e., private and public) in transactions with texts, Rosenblatt laments that schools have traditionally emphasized an efferent (information) orientation that overstresses analysis of literature: that is, terminology and procedures for categorizing literary elements or story structure. Given this focus, the importance of meaning and expressing feeling have been diminished.

Young children in particular should be encouraged to retain their delight in the sounds, rhythms, and imagery of poetic language—for example, as an experiential base for further efferent, analytical discussions of words, forms, or background information about authors. The aesthetic response becomes the rich, meaningful source of ideas, images, and feelings for sound, self-critical interpretations, and evaluation.

Modes of Writing

James Britton (1984) views language as a tool of social activity and has suggested that his spectator/participant continuum is similar to the aesthetic/efferent continuum. A *spectator* is someone who uses language to construct and manipulate an inner story world, which Britton compares to the aesthetic stance. A *participant* is someone who uses language to get things done, which Britton compares to an efferent stance. Rosenblatt (1985) disagrees with this comparison, maintaining that spectatorship is passive, whereas an aesthetic response is active.

For a discussion of reader-response theories, see Many and Cox (1992), *Reader Stance and Literary Understanding*, and Beach (1993), *A Teacher's Introduction to Reader-Response Theories.*

Britton's ideas are based on his research on the various modes of writing that students do in school (Britton, Burgess, Martin, McLeod, & Rosen, 1975). Essentially, there are three such modes:

1. *Expressive mode:* Writing that is close to the self; used to reveal personal experiences and feelings
2. *Transactional (or participant) mode:* Writing to get things done, such as recording or reporting information; used for decision making, action, and social interaction
3. *Poetic (or spectator) mode:* Writing that shapes ideas to receive an aesthetic effect; used for playing, dreaming, and storytelling

Britton's use of the term *transactional* should not to be confused with Rosenblatt's use regarding the transactional theory of language.

Britton found that the writing of young students is primarily expressive and resembles "written-down speech," telling about their experiences and feelings. Suzanne Langer (1967) describes this aspect of speech as a way for children to tell "the way things seem to us, the way we feel about things, the way things might be or we should like them to be" (p. 65). This is the type of language that will "undergo organization in the direction—ultimately—of verbal art, of poem, story, or play" (p. 65). Expressive writing, then, is an important source of ideas for poetic writing.

Britton also found that most of the writing students did in school was transactional (Britton et al., 1975). Students were expected to report information to people who knew more about it than themselves: teachers. Little importance was placed on expressive writing, in which students would know more than teachers about what they thought or felt. This devaluation of expressive writing illustrates the sort of practice in traditional education that Rosenblatt is critical of—namely, the focus on reading literature for information, not for the ideas, images, and feelings readers evoke in their personal transactions with texts.

Based on his research, Britton has suggested that as writers develop, they move from more expressive writing to other modes. Other researchers have found, however, that children can write freely across all modes (Bissex, 1980; Harste, Woodward, & Burke, 1984; Newkirk, 1984; Taylor, 1983). They can use the transactional mode to attempt to persuade, argue, make requests, and otherwise use writing to exercise power and control. They can also use language in the poetic mode, distancing language from the self and shaping it to achieve an aesthetic effect.

Children should have wide and varied experiences with all writing modes, from expressive to informational to persuasive to poetic. And they should have many opportunities to use their own voices in writing and to listen to the voices of authors using all three modes of language: expressive, transactional, and poetic. It follows that students should have many experiences reading and listening to children's literature in many genres, which occurs naturally in student- and response-centered classrooms, where language is used for real purposes across the curriculum.

Voice and Creativity

On any one day, students typically read different genres of literature and use different types of writing, and as they do, they learn to use their own voices in the writing. Creativity is part of the writing process in that it requires students to make choices, think of new ways to say old things, and flex and stretch the muscles of written voices. They will move beyond expressive writing about themselves to more functional writing, and they will also venture to express themselves through poetry and fantasy, letting their minds go free, visiting people and places they have never seen or looking at things from a completely new perspective.

Children can find their own voices in writing through any experience, in any subject, and for any reason. Thus, the choice of what they will say and how they will say it should be left open in order to let the sounds of their individual voices come through, clear and strong. For some students, writing will be most authentic when it's about experiences inside their heads—experiences that may be just as real to them as those that occur in the real world. Listen to a young child tell about the ghost downstairs at home that she chased away or the second-grader who comes late to class with a story about a monster he met on the way to school. If you listen carefully, you'll know that these experiences are every bit as real to these children as those that actually happened.

See Chapter 4, Emergent Literacy, for examples of Wyatt's writing at ages 7 and 8.

Children often roam the world in their minds or travel through time and space to play out their dreams and conflicts in countries of their minds. Wyatt—whose writing at ages 7 and 8 centered around his friends, pets, play, and family—began at age 11 to write about a "bracelet of power" in a mythical land. At the time, he was reading choose-your-own-adventure books, science fiction and fantasy, and playing Dungeons and Dragons and other fantasy adventure games with his friends. They chased each other around a lot with plastic swords, shouting things like "The treasure is mine!"

These interests showed in Wyatt's writing. He created an entire world, called Cesadie, including a landscape that he mapped in order to more carefully understand and explain the history of the place and events currently happening there. His writing voice came out of the mouth of a valiant young Prince Cesame, a character he'd created and chosen to use in writing about himself. Compared to the soft, flat, and somewhat weak voice he used in a teacher-assigned writing topic of what he thought his life would be like in the future, Wyatt's voice as Prince Cesame was strong and sure (see Figure 10.1).

There is also the issue of resistance in reading and writing in school, which occurs when teachers fail to recognize the importance of socioeconomic and racial/ethnic factors in influencing students' sense of the possibility for success or even understanding of the concept of a story (Heath, 1983). A young boy named Santiago illustrates this issue.

His teacher had planned a writing activity around chocolate chip cookies: how they looked, tasted, smelled, made you feel inside, and so on. She was interested in developing her students' observation skills and use of descriptive words in writing. Santiago resisted. He refused to write and caused problems while other students did write. The teacher talked to him and found that he

Years

10 years- 10 years from now I will be 21 and in college and almost be married.
25 years- 25 years from now I, will have a job and be married and have kids.
50 years- 50 years from now I will be old still married and my kids will be gone and almost married.

Bracelet Of Power

It Can make people breathe under water beacause the sea is wild, big storms, and at war they could see the ships. They go to war because of a bracelt that was given to Grakin from Eleo and was stolen from Ceside and the Princess is trying to stop the war, Since the Princess has the bracelt nobody can go under water, so Grakin launcham's an attack without the bracelt thinking that Ceside has the bracelt but they do not. So Grakin attacks with the ships but they lose half there army Some by storms, lighting, high tides and even sea creatures,

FIGURE 10.1 Comparison of Teacher-Assigned (left) vs. Student-Selected (right) Topics in Writing thought he was too mature to be writing about cookies and didn't want to appear to be a wimp. (Santiago was the biggest, most mature-looking boy in the class and a leader on the yard.) The teacher wisely told him to write about whatever interested him; the result was *Porsches* (see Figure 10.2). Santiago chose to write about Porsches and ended up publishing his own book. But this turnaround only came because the teacher observed his resistance and gave him the choice of writing about his own ideas and interests, rather than hers.

FIGURE 10.2
Writing on Student-Selected Topic

Cover

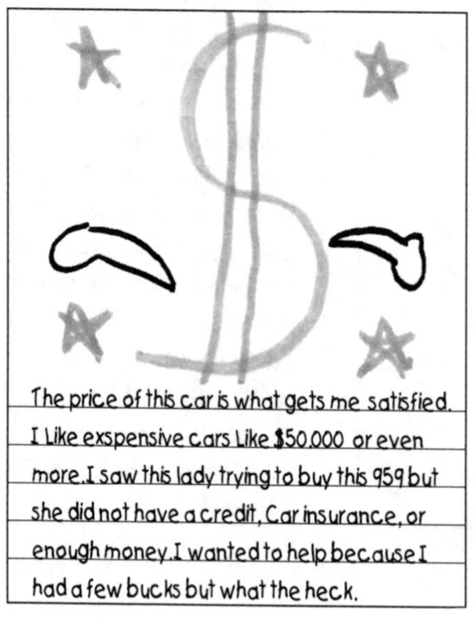

3

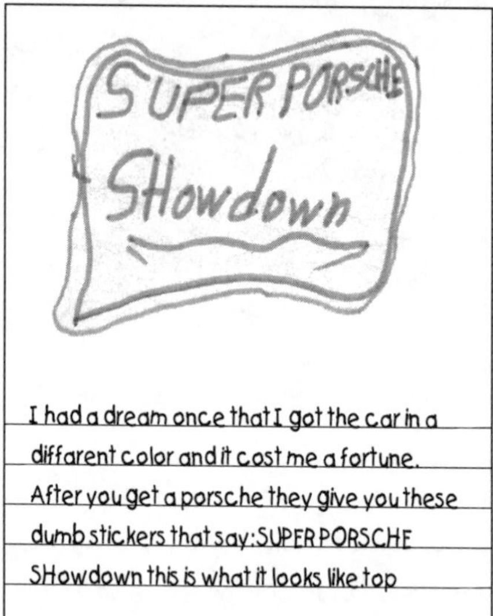

4

Creative Thinking

Creativity in education has sometimes been associated with certain subjects (e.g., art, music, drama, or writing fiction) or certain topics (e.g., fantasy, monsters, or space travel). Sometimes, certain children are perceived as being more creative because they show interest in fantasy themes, rather than science. The truth is, however, that creativity is important both for the child who enjoys reading and writing about imaginary adventures in space and the one who en-

1

2

5

6

Encouraging brainstorming and creative problem solving is an important part of reading and writing for self-expression.

joys reading and writing about astronomy. Separating the world of science facts from science fiction is one of the simplistic distinctions we make. Albert Einstein must have sensed this false dichotomy when he said, "The gift of fantasy has meant more to me than my talent for absorbing positive knowledge."

See Chapter 5, Listening and Talking, for ideas about creative problem solving and brainstorming.

Creative thinking and expression is a need as well as a prerogative of all children. Educators have identified and described creative thinking in its own right and shown its relevance to teaching any subject. Models for creative problem solving, which use techniques such as brainstorming, are important early lessons to help children think, speak, dramatize, draw, move, and read and write about subjects across the curriculum. Torrance (1962) has researched the meaning, teaching, and testing of creative behavior and describes an environment that supports the growth of creativity. That environment is characterized by these qualities and includes these activities:

1. ***Absence of serious threat to self: Willingness to risk***
   - Personal journal writing that's not evaluated but encouraged as a private place for recording ideas and feelings as sources for topics to write about
   - Rehearsing and drafting in writing (without editing or correcting) in order to try out new ideas
   - Withholding the teacher's immediate judgment of writing
   - Extensive self-selected reading
2. ***Self-awareness: Being in touch with one's feelings***
   - Choosing literature, topics and modes of writing to promote finding and speaking with strong voices
   - Extensive reading and writing on one topic or in one mode to fully explore it
   - Being aware of many forms (e.g., poetry), patterns for writing, and scripts
   - Having plenty of time, opportunities, and materials to experiment with reading and writing

3. ***Self-differentiation: Seeing the self as being different from others***
   - Sharing writing in a classroom in which all forms of writing, on all topics, are valued and appreciated
   - Highlighting the selected works of one published author or one young student author through Author of the Week displays
   - Trying a variety of publishing modes: charts, illustrated poems and stories, media, drama, and dance

4. ***Openness to the ideas of others: Confidence in one's own perceptions of reality or one's own ideas***
   - Discussing reading and writing with others
   - Reading and writing conferences: teacher, reader's circle, literature response groups, and book clubs
   - Working in peer-editing groups, in which ideas can be freely exchanged

5. ***Mutuality in interpersonal relations: Balance between an excessive quest for social relations and a pathological rejection of them***
   - Reading and writing in literature groups
   - Collaborative writing: newspapers, scriptwriting and performing, media scriptwriting and making
   - Compiling anthologies: collections of children's writing
   - Sharing language experience stories written by whole class

SNAPSHOT: Reading and Writing across the Curriculum

On one of those sparkling September days in the Midwest, when the light is so clear that everything seems suddenly to have come into sharper focus, I got "fall fever" and convinced myself that nothing could be gained by staying inside when it was so beautiful outside. My combination third-/fourth-grade class had been observing and talking about the changes in the colors of the leaves and the light and the seasons. So I divided the class into several groups and gave each a different colored piece of nylon net from the drama trunk.

Outdoors—surrounded by all the colors, smells, and textures of autumn—the children discussed ideas for acting out different colors. The groups communicated their ideas about colors wordlessly through pantomime, using movement and dance and the single prop of some slightly used nylon net. Blue was a waterfall; red was a sunset that suddenly appeared against the skyline between two old elm trees on the only hill on the playground; orange was a bonfire; green was a raucous, snapping, snarling dragon that moved among the trees around us. (By the way, compare what you wrote about acting out a color in your Reflective Response at the beginning of the chapter to what the children did that day.)

Once back indoors, we talked about colors, light, leaves, seasons, sunsets, dragons, and other related matters. We also started a "word wall" of words and phrases describing the experiences, feelings, and images of color the children had seen or imagined (see Figure 10.3). For the rest of the afternoon, the children wrote and talked about many of these and other feelings, ideas, and images they'd experienced that afternoon. I remembered a book of poetry about color called *Hailstones and Halibut Bones* (O'Neill, 1989), so after school, I went to get it from the library and asked the librarian to help me find other books related to color.

On the days following, we continued to work on color pantomimes and looked for music to add another dimension to the color movement and dance expressions. We took taped music outdoors to work on the pantomimes, which were turning into dances. The art teacher noticed the children outdoors and took colored slides of their dances, which she showed to the class. She also brought art history books of paintings and prints and talked to the students about the use of color in art. I read aloud from *Hailstones and Halibut Bones* every day. The children talked about the poems and began to look for color imagery in books they were reading.

The initial experience of looking at colored leaves one fall afternoon and pantomiming colors outside became the pebble that created a "ripple effect" of reading and writing about color across the curriculum. Actually, this effect continued through the entire schoolyear, expanding into every area of the curriculum: creative thinking, reading and writing, art and music, multicultural education, social studies, science and mathematics, and drama and dance. See Figure 10.4, which shows how this "ripple effect" happened and provides more ideas and many resources for using the theme of color for reading and writing across the curriculum.

FIGURE 10.3 Children's Images of Color

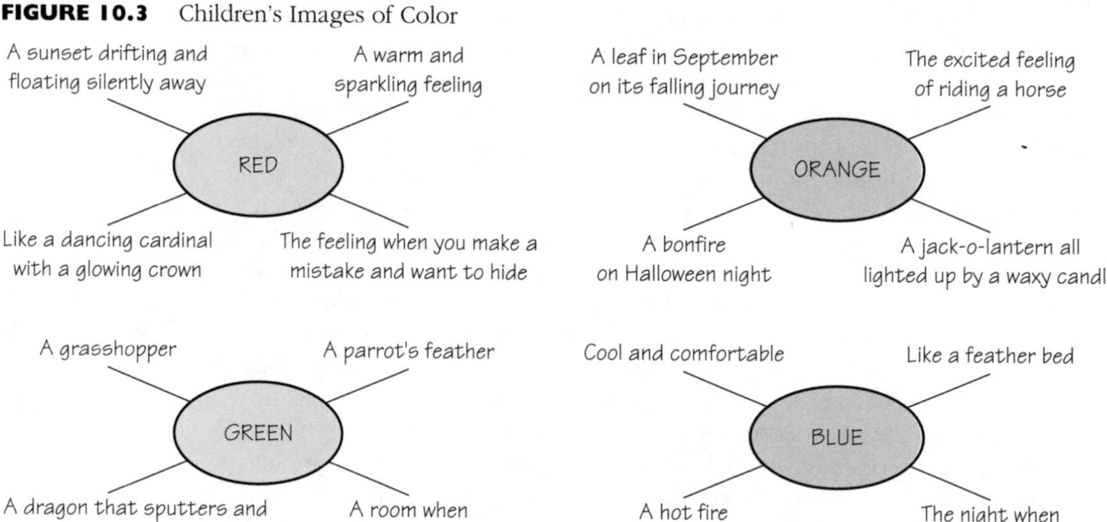

FIGURE 10.4
A "Ripple Effect" of Color

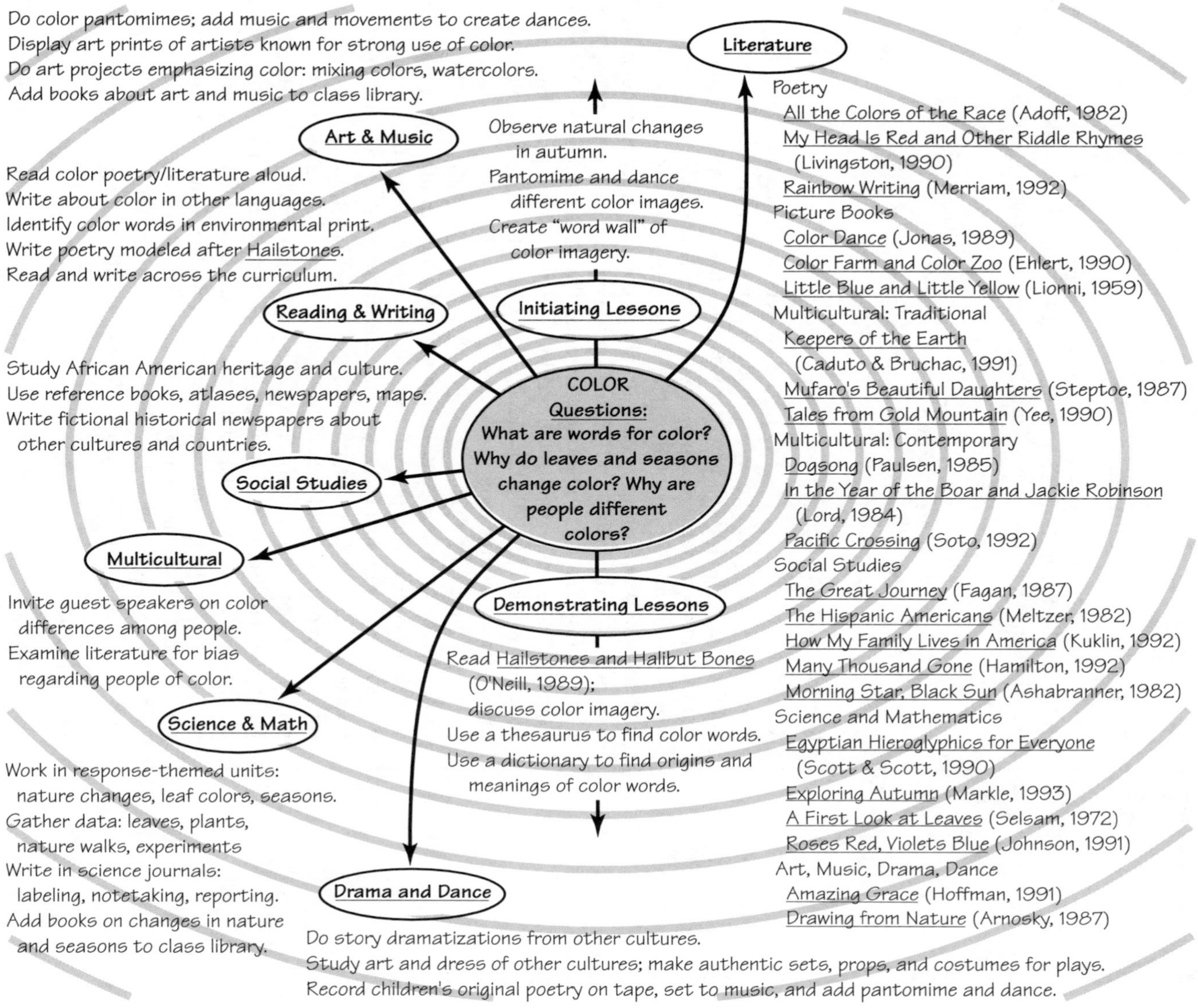

See the list of Children's Books at the end of the chapter for more books on color in art and nature.

COLOR
Questions:
What are words for color? Why do leaves and seasons change color? Why are people different colors?

Initiating Lessons

Observe natural changes in autumn.
Pantomime and dance different color images.
Create "word wall" of color imagery.

Demonstrating Lessons

Read <u>Hailstones and Halibut Bones</u> (O'Neill, 1989); discuss color imagery.
Use a thesaurus to find color words.
Use a dictionary to find origins and meanings of color words.

Art & Music

Do color pantomimes; add music and movements to create dances.
Display art prints of artists known for strong use of color.
Do art projects emphasizing color: mixing colors, watercolors.
Add books about art and music to class library.

Reading & Writing

Read color poetry/literature aloud.
Write about color in other languages.
Identify color words in environmental print.
Write poetry modeled after <u>Hailstones</u>.
Read and write across the curriculum.

Social Studies

Study African American heritage and culture.
Use reference books, atlases, newspapers, maps.
Write fictional historical newspapers about other cultures and countries.

Multicultural

Invite guest speakers on color differences among people.
Examine literature for bias regarding people of color.

Science & Math

Work in response-themed units: nature changes, leaf colors, seasons.
Gather data: leaves, plants, nature walks, experiments
Write in science journals: labeling, notetaking, reporting.
Add books on changes in nature and seasons to class library.

Drama and Dance

Do story dramatizations from other cultures.
Study art and dress of other cultures; make authentic sets, props, and costumes for plays.
Record children's original poetry on tape, set to music, and add pantomime and dance.

Literature

Poetry
- <u>All the Colors of the Race</u> (Adoff, 1982)
- <u>My Head Is Red and Other Riddle Rhymes</u> (Livingston, 1990)
- <u>Rainbow Writing</u> (Merriam, 1992)

Picture Books
- <u>Color Dance</u> (Jonas, 1989)
- <u>Color Farm and Color Zoo</u> (Ehlert, 1990)
- <u>Little Blue and Little Yellow</u> (Lionni, 1959)

Multicultural: Traditional
- <u>Keepers of the Earth</u> (Caduto & Bruchac, 1991)
- <u>Mufaro's Beautiful Daughters</u> (Steptoe, 1987)
- <u>Tales from Gold Mountain</u> (Yee, 1990)

Multicultural: Contemporary
- <u>Dogsong</u> (Paulsen, 1985)
- <u>In the Year of the Boar and Jackie Robinson</u> (Lord, 1984)
- <u>Pacific Crossing</u> (Soto, 1992)

Social Studies
- <u>The Great Journey</u> (Fagan, 1987)
- <u>The Hispanic Americans</u> (Meltzer, 1982)
- <u>How My Family Lives in America</u> (Kuklin, 1992)
- <u>Many Thousand Gone</u> (Hamilton, 1992)
- <u>Morning Star, Black Sun</u> (Ashabranner, 1982)

Science and Mathematics
- <u>Egyptian Hieroglyphics for Everyone</u> (Scott & Scott, 1990)
- <u>Exploring Autumn</u> (Markle, 1993)
- <u>A First Look at Leaves</u> (Selsam, 1972)
- <u>Roses Red, Violets Blue</u> (Johnson, 1991)

Art, Music, Drama, Dance
- <u>Amazing Grace</u> (Hoffman, 1991)
- <u>Drawing from Nature</u> (Arnosky, 1987)

Critical Creative Thinking

Experiences with color in the environment led to activities involving drama, music, and art, which developed into creative thinking and hypothesizing questions about colors. I wrote students' questions on a piece of chartpaper:

What is a color?
What would a color be if it were something else?
What are all the words for a color?
How do leaves and seasons change color?
Why are people different colors?

Reading and Writing

We added words and phrases to the clusters we had started about each color. They grew and grew, as children came up with new ideas about color concepts and vocabulary each day. I introduced the use of the thesaurus and dictionary in a minilesson so students could look for more words. I also reread all of the poems in *Hailstones and Halibut Bones* (O'Neill, 1989) and did a minilesson about color imagery in writing. The new words and phrases and images appeared in children's writing: journals, poems, patterns, and stories. I alerted the librarian to what we were doing, and she made available the color-related books of poetry and other literature we had identified. I added colored paper and pencils to the writing center for writing about colors.

I remembered the French poem "Voyelles" ("Vowels" in English), by Arthur Rimbaud, a nineteenth-century French poet. In this poem, he links vowels to colors with powerful imagery. He was also only 16 when he wrote it—not so much older than my students that they couldn't imagine themselves speaking with a poet's voice, as well. First, I read the poem in my best French and told the children some of my experiences living in Europe and what it was like to learn a second language. Then I translated the poem into English, writing it on a piece of chartpaper. We started a list of color words in French and added a list of Spanish and Japanese words, the two other languages spoken by students in my class. Mariko's mother came to school, and we had a minilesson on how to write in Japanese. We started more lists of other languages spoken by students in other classes, and we added foreign language dictionaries to the writing center.

Art and Music

When we found music to go with students' pantomimes of color, we added those records and tapes to the writing center. After the art teacher visited, we collected art prints and art history books, initially on loan from her but then supplemented by books provided by the librarian and others children brought from home. Certain artists—especially Picasso, Miró, Chagall, and the French Impressionists—captured students' interest because of their use of light and color. We talked about these artists, and students began to draw and color using their styles, illustrating their color poetry and stories. I added children's books about art, artists, music, and musicians to the class library.

Multicultural Education

The same autumn, the school district hired a consultant for multicultural education. Marlene Cummings, an African American registered nurse, drew on her medical background to speak to students: first about the physiology of color differences among people and then about multicultural issues. She was motivated by concern about her own three sons, who attended schools in which the majority of students were white; she felt racial differences might not be understood in these schools. After she explained the physiology of skin color, she played a game simulating prejudice and discrimination and then opened the discussion to questions from my students.

As she was leaving the class, Marlene noticed the book *Hailstones and Halibut Bones* in the writing center and told me about her reservations about O'Neill's poem "What Is Black?" Marlene felt it had more negative images than other poems to describe the color black—for instance, "things you'd like to forget," "run-down street," "broken cup," "soot spots," and "suffering." She wished the poet had used more images of beautiful things that were black.

I told students what Marlene said, and we talked about it. We decided to start a new list of color words and images with the title "Black Is Beautiful." The children drew pictures and brought in some from magazines from home. Everyone wrote a new poem, called "Black Is Beautiful." We sent these to Marlene Cummings, along with letters students wrote to thank her for visiting our classroom. Here's one of them:

> Dear Mrs. Cummings,
> You convinced me that black is beautiful. I am very glad you came to talk to us. Now I know what makes the skin black or white. Thank you for your time. Here is a poem I wrote about black.

Black Is Beautiful

Black is a racing horse, galloping full speed
Black is a tree trunk covered with leaves
Black is the ocean deep, deep down
Black is a blackbird's feathery crown
Black is a blackboard
Black is a cat
Black is a ringmaster's tall round hat

We made a bulletin board in the hall outside our room to display the students' poems and pictures. I found Ann McGovern's (1969) book of poetry *Black Is Beautiful* and read it aloud. We compared all the poems we had read and written.

A few months later, the school district published a book called *Dear Mrs. Cummings*, a collection of letters from the students who had written her that included all my students' letters and poems. The children were ecstatic. They were published letter writers and poets! The interest in color, reading and writing about colors, and the colors of races exploded in my classroom.

Social Studies

We started a thematic unit on cultural and racial diversity in the United States. An important focal topic was the heritage of African Americans: African history, culture, geography, and contemporary social and political structure. We went back in time to ancient Egypt and the early civilizations of West Africa. We learned about the history of African Americans from the time of slavery to the present, and we also studied race relations in the United States. Because many students of East Indian heritage attended our school, we added the history and culture of India to our investigations, as well.

The class read and wrote across the curriculum. Our reading involved a variety of genres: poetry and fiction, nonfiction and references books, and even newspapers and magazines. Our writing covered more poetry, stories, songs, and reports. The children reported much of what they learned in fictional historical and contemporary newspapers. One was written as though it took place in Ancient Egypt: *The Sphinx Speaks*. Others included *The Pan-African Press,* which was about Africa, and *Delhi's Daily,* which was about India.

Science and Mathematics

Our talk about how leaves change color led to a science unit on budding twigs. We used the inquiry, rather than the textbook, approach to science. Students used processes such as observation, classification, measurement, prediction, hypothesis, interpretation, and inference to gather data. Types of writing used were labeling, notetaking, and reporting in science journals. Students wrote about their observations of changes in trees, leaves, and plants in the neighborhood, from our classroom window, and on fieldtrips to a nearby arboretum with a naturalist guide. We conducted a series of experiments using branches cut and kept in water at intervals during the year. Keeping tallies and graphing these changes became a part of mathematics, as did reading about numerical systems and devices used in other cultures (e.g., hieroglyphics, the abacus) and trying them out in class.

Drama and Dance

As we learned about the cultures of ancient Egypt, Africa, and India, students read traditional tales, wrote scripts, and presented them as plays: "The Story of Ra" (Ancient Egypt), "Anansi the Spider" (Africa), and "Tales from the Ramayana" (India). The children studied the art and dress of each culture to make authentic sets, props, and costumes. They staged "The Story of Ra" as though it were from an ancient Egyptian frieze, in which everyone is facing sideways.

A *frieze* is a sculptured or highly ornamented band around the top or base of a building, common in Ancient Egyptian architecture.

Students' pantomimes, dances, and poetry about colors all came together in a performance called "Magic Colors." The children worked in groups, one color per group. Each wrote a collective color poem and recorded it on tape with music that went well with it. Then each group created pantomime and dance movements to the poem and music. The chil-

These girls are dancing a poem they wrote!

dren dressed in leotards or swimsuits of their group's color and used nylon net for props. The performance was given in a theater-in-the round (actually, the gym). The audience sat in a large circle of chairs, leaving several spaces at intervals for the children to enter and exit. After the audience had been seated and the room darkened, the children entered almost noiselessly, crouched behind the audience. As the tape recorder played each poem with music, spotlights were turned with filters to match the color of each group. Each group played out the pantomime/dance they had created. Marlene Cummings was a guest of honor and introduced the performance by telling about her visit to our class and reading some of the "Black Is Beautiful" poems the students had written.

Another activity that came from studying color, leaves, and culture was writing an original play, called "The Tale of an Unfair Election." See Chapter 6, Drama in the Classroom.

Connecting Reading and Writing in the Classroom

A Reading and Writing Day

Here's how a reading and writing day could look, providing time and opportunities for reading and writing, including reading and writing across the curriculum.

See Chapter 1, The Writing Process, for another way to organize the day in a writing workshop.

- *Reading Aloud (15–30 minutes):* The teacher reads poetry and literature that may become a model for writing, giving young readers and writers ideas.

- *Journal Writing (15–30 minutes):* Topics for writing may emerge, as journal writing encourages students to explore new experiences, feelings, and ideas.

• *Sharing (15–30 minutes):* Sharing encourages thinking out loud; students discover new ideas as they talk. The teacher can support and encourage these ideas as topics for writing.

• *Class Writing (20–30 minutes):* The teacher records shared experiences. Students can work together to write class stories or language experiences stories. Minilessons can be used to introduce writing forms: poems and patterns, genres of literature. Students can brainstorm ideas on a topic and plan future projects, writing lists, notes, and outlines.

• *Independent Writing on Topics of Choice (30–45 minutes):* Activities can include writing workshop, listing or clustering ideas for writing, writing drafts, revising , teacher conferences, reader's circle, peer conferences, editing, and illustrating and publishing.

• *Reading and Writing across the Curriculum (30–60 minutes):* Cross-curricular activities can overlap with independent writing. Students can use literary forms to explore and report content information: fictional journals, reports, stories, poems, and scripts. Collaborative reading and writing can involve writing reports or newspapers on a period in history. Dramatic writing activities include scriptwriting for drama, a media presentation, or publicity for a play or media performance.

• *Children Reading Their Own Writing (15–30 minutes):* This can be done through the author's chair, literature groups, the reader's circle in writing workshop, sharing published pieces, and rehearsing writing in groups with a buddy or the teacher.

Talk and Questions to Promote Thinking, Reading, and Writing

Talking and asking questions that promote creative thinking and encourage students to use their voices in writing are essential in creating a student- and response-centered reading and writing classroom (Calkins, 1983; Giacobbe, 1982; Graves, 1983; Jones, 1986; Murray, 1985; Smith, 1982, 1983). Here are strategies for accomplishing this:

1. ***Ask Questions to Promote Thinking:***
   - Ask students questions like these:
     What comes to your mind when . . . ?
     When you read . . . , what does it make you think about?
     If you think about . . . , what comes to mind next?
     What do you know about . . . ?
     What do you think that . . . means?
     How does that relate to . . . ?
     What does that mean for . . . ?
2. ***Talk to Rehearse and Expand Writing and Generate Thought:***
   - Hold peer, teacher, and group conferences, asking questions like:
     What can you tell me about (topic)?

What have you thought about your writing?
How will you begin?
- Arrange the classroom for mobility and flexible seating.
- Read aloud often.
- Read children's writing as if it's literature.
- Encourage children to share what they read and their impressions of it by asking questions like:
  What did you think of it?
  How do you suppose the author got that idea?
  What makes it work for you?
  Does this remind you of anything else you've read?

3. ***Talk to Verbalize Writing Strategies and Decisions:***
   - Hold peer, teacher, and group conferences, using questions like:
     How is it going?
     How can I help you in this conference?
     Why did you . . . ?
     I noticed that you (changed/added) . . . Why?
     When you started writing this piece, what were you thinking?
     Did anything surprise you about this piece?
   - Encourage children to share techniques that work for them: for getting started, choosing topics, getting unstuck, and the like.
4. ***Talk to Evaluate Efforts:***
   - Hold peer, teacher, and group conferences using questions like:
     What do you think of it so far?
     Which do you like best? Why?
     What would make it better?
     If you were going to work on this again, what would you do?
     Is there anything you would change?
   - Withhold judgment, including praise. Let the author be the ultimate critic.
5. ***Talking to Affirm Membership in the Reading and Writing Community:***
   - Treat children like authors. Assume they are capable of making their own decisions, and let them do so.
   - Demystify literature. Reinforce the idea that books are written by people and that some people simply have more experience than others.

Reading Workshop

The reading workshop is based on many of the principles of the writing workshop and also draws on Nancie Atwell's ideas about her own classroom, as described in *In the Middle* (1987). Reading workshop is an approach that recognizes the similarities of the reading and writing processes (Reutzel & Cooter, 1991). Namely, both readers and writers rehearse, draft, revise, and construct meaning while working with language.

Writing workshop is explained in Chapter 9, The Writing Process.

Like writing workshop, reading workshop requires a large block of time, most of which is for students to read self-selected books independently. Students also respond to what they're reading through dialogues and discussions, writing, or other response options, such as drama, art, or media. The organization of reading workshop is also similar to that of writing workshop, as follows:

Parts of Reading Workshop
1. Teacher sharing literature
2. Minilesson
3. Reading status
4. Self-selected reading and responding
5. Sharing

1. *Teacher Sharing Literature (5 minutes):* The teacher reads aloud a poem, picture book, or short story to introduce and interest children in a piece or type of literature.

2. *Minilesson (5 minutes):* The teacher does a brief lesson on some aspect of literature or literacy.

3. *Checking Reading Status (5 minutes):* The teacher checks what students are doing in reading and makes plans with them for the period. This could be done using a chart, like the one shown in Figure 10.5.

4. *Independent Self-Selected Reading and Responding (40 minutes):* This is the central activity of reading workshop and is based on the constructivist idea that children learn to read by reading. During self-selected reading, children may also write about their ideas and feelings in literature response journals. Teachers or other students may write in these journals, as well, responding to what each other has written and creating a dialogue. Students may also conference with the teacher, work in literature groups, choose response options, or discuss. The teacher meets with groups, holds conferences, and circulates to provide on-the-spot help and encouragement.

See Chapter 7, Teaching with Literature, for more on response journals, literature groups, and response options, and Chapter 8, Reading as a Language Art, for more on self-selected reading.

5. *Sharing Reading and Responding (5 minutes):* Students share something they've read, what they think about it, or how they've responded to it (e.g., writing, drawing, drama, etc.).

Reading workshop is based on the assumption that children learn to read by spending time reading real texts for real purposes, rather than listening to lessons on reading or doing skill drills. As such, reading workshop is an approach that can accommodate a wide range of interest and ability levels and address the needs of children in culturally and linguistically diverse classrooms.

FIGURE 10.5 Reading Status Checklist

NAME	MONDAY	TUESDAY	WEDNESDAY	THURSDAY	FRIDAY

Symbols to reading workshop activities:

SSR = Self-Selected Reading
TC = Teacher Conference
LG = Literature Group
RO = Response Options
J = Journal
D = Discussing

Literature as a Model for Writing

Introducing literature as a model for writing is a powerful means of connecting reading and writing and developing literacy in the classroom. In the following sections, we'll look at using poetry and other genres of literature; examples of appropriate children's literature are given for each.

Poetry

Children are natural poets and often speak metaphorically. Northrop Frye (1964) describes this as the way "the poet thinks, not in logical sequences, but in the most primitive and archaic of categories, similarity and identity. A is like B; A is B. These are categories that appear in poetry as simile and metaphor. 'Eternity is like unto a Ring,' says John Bunyan. 'Grandfather of the day is he,' says Emily Dickinson of a mountain" (p. 7). Frye urges teachers to "preserve a child's own metaphorical processes." That can be achieved by reading aloud poetry to children and encouraging them to try a variety of poetic forms in their own writing. See also Table 10.1, which gives examples of children's literature for each of the following poetic forms.

In *One at a Time: Poems for the Very Young,* David McCord (1977) shows young readers and writers how to write various poetic forms: couplets, quatrains, limericks, haikus, and others.

TABLE 10.1 Literature as a Model for Writing: Poetry

Similes & Metaphors
All the Small Poems (Worth, 1987)
As: A Surfeit of Similes (Juster, 1989)
As Quick as a Cricket (Wood, 1982)
Heartland (Siebert, 1989)
Mojave (Siebert, 1988)
Sierra (Siebert, 1991)

Rhymes
Couplets and Quatrains
Anna Banana: 101 Jump-Rope Rhymes (Cole, 1989)
A Gopher in the Garden and Other Animal Poems (Prelutsky, 1967)
I Met a Man (Ciardi, 1961)
A Light in the Attic (Silverstein, 1981)
One Sun: A Book of Terse Verse (McMillan, 1990)
The Owl and the Pussy Cat (Lear, 1991)
Tirra Lirra: Rhymes Old and New (Richards, 1932)
Where the Sidewalk Ends (Silverstein, 1974)
You Read to Me, I'll Read to You (Ciardi, 1962)

Limericks
The Complete Nonsense Book (Lear, 1846/1946)
The Hopeful Trout and Other Limericks (Ciardi, 1989)
The Book of Pigericks (Lobel, 1983)
Laughing Time (Smith, 1990)

Syllabic Patterns: Haiku, Senryu, and Tanka
Cricket Songs (Behn, 1964)
Haiku: The Mood of the Earth (Atwood, 1971)
In a Spring Garden (Lewis, 1964)
In the Eyes of the Cat: Japanese Poetry for All Seasons (Demi, 1992)
More Cricket Songs (Behn, 1971)
My Own Rhythm: An Approach to Haiku (Atwood, 1973)
The Seasons of Time (Baron, 1968)
Wind in the Long Grass: A Collection of Haiku (Higginson, 1991)

Predictable Patterns
Brown Bear, Brown Bear, What Do You See? (Martin, 1967)
A House Is a House for Me (Hoberman, 1982)
I Love My Anteater with an A (Ipcar, 1964)
The Important Book (Brown, 1949)

Concrete Poetry
Concrete Is Not Always Hard (Pilon, 1972)
Seeing Things: A Book of Poems (Froman, 1974)
Street Poems (Froman, 1971)
Walking Talking Words (Sherman, 1980)

Similes

A *simile* draws a comparison between dissimilar things using the connecting words *like* or *as*.

Saffron is a spice that also makes food vivid yellow.

- ***Color Similes:*** First-graders in Phyllis Crawford's class at Audubon School in Baton Rouge, Louisiana, wrote similes about *yellow* when talking about color words:

As yellow as . . . saffron rice
the sweltering sun
refreshing lemonade
a corpulent cat

- ***Sense Similes:*** Phyllis's first-graders were learning about the senses, too, so they thought of these similes:

Smell	As reeky as wrinkled, perspiring feet
Hear	As deafening as a hovering helicopter
See	As colorful as an enchanting sunset
Feel	As bumpy as a warted toad
Taste	As yummy as seasoned etouffé

Etouffé is a rice dish made in South Louisiana, usually with shrimp or crawfish.

- ***Synonym Similes:*** Students can start with a word, find a synonym in the thesaurus, and write a simile:

Word	*Synonym*	*Simile*
daisy	posy	like a little sun

See Figure 10.6, which shows illustrated similes done by third-graders.

FIGURE 10.6
Illustrated Similes by Third-Graders

Metaphors

A *metaphor* draws a comparison between two dissimilar things by naming one for the other. Aristotle felt this process of renaming was an indication of genius, since the ability to forge a good metaphor shows that the poet has an intuitive perception of what's similar in things that seem dissimilar at face value.

In his book *Wishes, Lies, and Dreams,* Kenneth Koch (1970) wrote about his experiences teaching poetry to children in New York City schools. In having his students write metaphors, he told them to use this process: First, think about one thing being like something else: for instance, *the cloud is like a pillow.* Then pretend that it really is the other thing; say *is* instead of *is like: the cloud is a pillow.* Koch gives this example of a metaphor by one of his students: "Mr. Koch is a very well-dressed poetry book walking around in shining shoes" (1970, p. 147).

Koch also recommends the use of *comparison poems,* which serve as frames to help students think in terms of similes and metaphors and use them in their writing. For example:

I used to . . . , but now I . . .
I am a . . . , but I wish I were . . .
If I were a . . . , I would . . .

Rhyme

Poetry doesn't have to rhyme but frequently does. To help children use rhyme in their poetry, introduce these simple rhyming patterns:

- ***Couplets:*** A *couplet* is a two-line, rhymed verse. The following couplet was written by a first-grader, who combined his impressions of learning a folk dance at school and taking a trip to the zoo:

A panther
Once was a folk dancer

The child's teacher said he first chanted the couplet aloud to himself and then wrote it down and illustrated it, showing a dancing panther with shoes.

- ***Quatrains:*** A *quatrain* is a four-line poem with a varied rhyme pattern. One of my fourth-grade students wrote this one when we were studying the behavior of mealworms in science:

A mealworm in bran
Is apt to expand
So give the mealworm
A helping hand

- ***Limericks:*** A *limerick* is a nonsense poem in which lines 1, 2, and 5 rhyme and lines 3 and 4 rhyme. Edward Lear popularized this form of verse around 1850. Here's one by a fourth-grader:

There once was a man from Mars
Who liked to eat the stars.
One day he ate twenty.
Oh, man, was he funny.
That silly old man from Mars.

Syllabic Patterns

Some forms of poetry follow a syllabic pattern, rather than a rhyme pattern. *Haiku* is a traditional form of Japanese poetry about nature, consisting of 17 syllables: 5 in line 1, 7 in line 2, and 5 in line 3. Here's an example written by a fourth-grader:

Shiny blue water
Ripples as the boy throws stones
Into the still sea.

Senryu follows the same pattern but is about topics other than nature. *Tanka* uses 31 syllables in five lines in a pattern of 7, 5, 7, 5, 7 and, like haiku, is about nature.

Predictable Patterns

See Chapter 4, Emergent Literacy, for a list of predictable pattern books to use as models for writing and an example of a cinquain pattern written about apples. See Chapter 11, Language Conventions: Grammar, Talking, and Writing, for examples of word patterns that can be used for writing.

Many predictable pattern books are based on familiar cultural sequences; some use repeated phrases or are cumulative tales; others are based on traditional rhymes, songs, or folktales; and still others are new and original. These books can provide excellent models for writing, as the pattern gives students a sort of framework to build on. For instance, after reading a predictable pattern book about the alphabet, a first-grader wrote:

Superman
I love my Superman with an S because he is superior
I dislike him with an s because he is strange
His name is Samson. He comes from space.
He lives on stars and suns. And he is a man of steel.

Concrete Poetry

In *concrete poetry,* the writing itself takes a representational form; that is, the words are written in the shape of whatever is being described. For example, a third-grade girl wrote a poem called "Moshiko" after a teacher of Israeli folk dances named Moshiko visited her. The words of the poem formed a winding, curving line, like the dancer's movements.

Other Genres

See Chapter 7, Teaching with Literature, for examples of books in different genres.

Other literary genres also provide excellent sources of children's literature for use in modeling and teaching writing. Read and discuss these genres and relate them to popular media genres. The following examples of children's books by genre are good choices for reading aloud or independent reading:

- ***Traditional Literature:*** Look for folktales with many variants, such as "Cinderella" and "The Gingerbread Man"; fables of Aesop and La Fontaine; Ancient Greek, Roman, and Norse myths as well as contemporary myths from other cultures; and hero tales, legends, and tall tales.

- ***Adventures:*** Try old classics like *Treasure Island* (Stevenson, 1947) or modern classics, like *Julie of the Wolves* (George, 1972), a story of survival on the Alaskan tundra.

- ***Mystery:*** Find series like the *Encyclopedia Brown* books (Sobol, 1982) or books like *The Westing Game* (Raskin, 1984).

- ***Fantasy:*** Try tales of other worlds, like Narnia in *The Lion, the Witch, and the Wardrobe* series (Lewis, 1961), Prydain in *The Book of Three* (Alexander, 1964), and Earthsea in *The Wizard of Earthsea* (Le Guin, 1968). Time fantasies include *A Wrinkle in Time* (L'Engle, 1962), *The Children of Green Knowe* (Boston, 1955), and *The Dark Is Rising* (Cooper, 1973). Younger students enjoy personified animals in *Winnie-the-Pooh* (Milne, 1926) and *Charlotte's Web* (White, 1952).

- ***Science Fiction:*** For older students, try books that look at the future, such as *The City of Gold and Lead* series (Christopher, 1967) and *The Giver* (Lowry, 1993) or stories of space by Robert Heinlein or *Enchantress from the Stars* (Engdahl, 1970).

TEACHING IDEA

Learning about Literary Elements and Story Structure through Popular Genres

A popular type of children's paperback book began with the choose-your-own-adventure series (first written by Edward Packard for Bantam), which cut across several popular genres: adventure, mystery, science fiction, and fantasy. Numerous other versions are offered by a number of publishers. The general idea behind all of them is that the reader makes choices at certain points in the plot, so that different versions of the story are possible.

I did a writing workshop with teachers using the basic idea of a choose-your-own-adventure story as a model for writing, which also required learning about story structure. We had a lot of fun writing these in groups; some selected adult genres to write in, like romances and soap operas. Regardless of the genre, here's the sequence I suggested:

(continued)

Look for paperback copies of choose-your-own-adventure books at garage sales and used book stores, and start a class collection.

1. ***Read Aloud (1–3 days):*** Read aloud one or several choose-your-own-adventure books to the class, and let them decide as a group about which way to go in the story. Encourage aesthetic responses by asking questions like: "What did you think of it?" "What was your favorite part?"

2. ***Group Reading (3–5 days):*** Children read to each other in groups, making decisions together. They can also read and just enjoy themselves (if they aren't already).

3. ***Minilesson on Story Structure (1 day):*** Identify and discuss literary elements and story structure. Use this lesson to get students started writing their own adventure stories, choosing from among the popular genres they're written in. Make and post charts of the following information; discuss these points and use them to guide students:

Choose Your Own Genre and Story Structure

1. ***Choose a genre:*** Folktales, adventure, mystery, fantasy, science fiction

2. ***Literary elements and story structure:***

Setting: When and where does story take place?
Time period: Past, present, or future?
Location: One or more than one place?
Changes: From one place to another?
Mood: Atmosphere or feeling of the place?

Characters: Who is in the story? Describe them.
Appearance: What do they look like?
Behavior: What kinds of things do they do?
Life history: Where are they from? What have they done?
Speech: How do they sound? How do they talk to others?
Protagonist/Antagonist: Is there a conflict between good characters and those that oppose them?

Plot: What happens in the story?
Sequence: What is the order of story events?
Problem: What is the conflict?
Patterns: Linear, circular, cumulative, flashbacks, foreshadowing, cliffhangers.
Climax: What is the high point of the story?
Solution: How is the problem resolved at the end?

Theme: What is the meaning of the story?
Main idea: A meaning obvious to everyone.
Subthemes: Other possible meanings.

Point of View:	Who is telling the story? Omniscient: Story is told from perspective of all characters. Limited omniscient: One character's perspective is most important. Objective: Just the facts in the story are told. First-person: *I* is used, as one character tells story.
Style:	How is language used in the story? Literary devices: Figurative language, metaphors, similes, personification, alliteration, symbols Tone: Irony, humor

4. ***Chart Ideas (2–3 days):*** Students can follow the charts and brainstorm ideas together or individually.

5. ***Drafting (2–3 days):*** Students can write descriptions and draw pictures of the setting and mood. They can do character sketches, telling about individuals' physical characteristics, behaviors, and life histories. Students can start a list of story events they would like to include, talk about the main idea and related subthemes, and discuss point of view.

6. ***Revising and Editing (5–7 days):*** Students can continue to work collaboratively on the same story in groups, or individuals can work on their own and later meet in peer-response groups to talk about their stories.

7. ***Publishing or Producing:*** The children's stories can be written, illustrated, and bound as books. And since the stories are of a popular genre, they also lend themselves to dramatic or media productions on video.

Phyllis Fuglaar, a published teacher/writer herself, tried this Teaching Idea with her combination fourth-/fifth-grade class in writing workshop. She told me that during the period they worked on these stories, her class generated many more ideas than usual in prewriting discussions. They also worked well in pairs and literature groups. The children became very involved in their stories and even got their parents involved by talking about them at home. The stories were longer and took more time to write than usual, perhaps because the children were motivated to get them right and worked more at editing each other's pieces. They were very eager to publish and read their books to the rest of the class. In fact, they were so proud of these books that they wanted to share them with other classes.

(continued)

Phyllis Fuglaar engages in a writing conference as her students work on choose-your-own-adventure stories.

Phyllis told me that this was the only project one child had finished so far that year. Another told me, "I liked writing this story because whenever I write a story, I always have lots of ideas for an ending, and doing this I can use all those ideas." Figure 10.7 shows excerpts from "Cave of the White Dwarves," one of the choose-your-own-adventure stories written in Phyllis Fuglaar's class.

FIGURE 10.7 A Fifth-Grader's Choose-Your-Own-Adventure Story

You walk home and get two sandwichs wrapped in foil, about 3 ft of rope, a flashlight, and a pocket knife. You put it all in a backpack and you walk back to the cave. You walk in and turn on your flashlight.
You see a tunnel in the corner of the cave and you walk towards it. You see letters carved in the stone. They are hard to read, but you still understand them-
DO NOT ENTER THE CAVE OF THE WHITE DWARVES

What should you do?
enter the tunnel? pg 6

Go back home? pg 5

Assessing Reading and Writing

Farr and Lowe (1991) recommend that teachers consider the following principles in assessing students' reading and writing:

- Students need to be engaged in acts of reading and writing that are real and have purpose—namely, those in which students are involved in the construction of meaning.
- Assessment should allow students to revise, solve problems, and make decisions, as would occur in real reading and writing situations.
- Assessment should be ongoing and provide a variety of opportunities to use reading and writing.
- The assessment process should consider the learner's own perception of his or her development; this is a rich source of information that teachers need to know more about.

It's also important to collection information about students' understanding of reading and writing across a variety of literary genres and types of texts. Teachers should use the following means to assess students' understanding of the relationship between reading and writing and their ability to read and write for a variety of purposes:

1. ***Writing Samples Based on Reading:*** Portfolios should include examples of students' writing that are based on their reading. Different types of literature should be represented, such as poetry, nonfiction, and fiction, including stories in a variety of genres.

2. ***Student Explanations of Writing Based on Reading:*** When students select pieces to include in their portfolios, they can write letters explaining why they chose these pieces and how these samples of writing might be related to reading.

3. ***Anecdotal Records:*** Teachers can keep records of how students' reading and writing are connected as a result of reading and writing across the curriculum. For instance, the teacher might explain how a piece of writing evolved from reading and experiences with literature as well as how the writing is connected to cross-curricular activities.

4. ***Read, Write, and Retell:*** Brown and Cambourne (1989) suggest a way to teach and assess reading and writing together in a collaborative group situation, with multiple possible interpretations of a text and using predicting, retelling, and revising. The basic plan includes:

- *Time to Predict:* On the basis of the title of a story, the teacher asks the children: "What do you think this might be about? Why?" The teacher has students do written predictions and share them in small groups.
- *Everyone Read:* The teacher reads aloud, and then students read silently. The teacher asks them to compare how their predictions are holding up with what they are reading.

- *Retell:* Students retell the story in writing.
- *Share and Compare:* Students talk to each other, reading and comparing their written retellings to identify similarities and differences.

5. ***Interviews:*** Hansen (1987) suggests interviewing students about their understanding and intent in reading and writing and encouraging them to evaluate themselves, using the following types of questions:

- What's something new you've learned to do as a reader/writer?
- What's something you'd like to learn so you can become a better reader/writer?
- How could you go about learning how to do this?

6. ***Portfolios:*** Portfolios should include anecdotal records of interviews and reading, writing, and retelling groups; samples of students' writing related to reading and reading and writing across the curriculum; students' explanations of their reading and writing; and teacher's comments. In addition, portfolios can include audio- and videotapes of students' performances of reading and writing, such as reader's theater and plays.

Answers to Questions about Reading and Writing

1. *What is the relationship between reading and writing?*

In the past, reading and writing were often viewed as separate subjects. Reading instruction was teacher and text centered, and writing was primarily a supplement to reading activities. But today, reading and writing classrooms are student and response centered and integrate reading and writing as a powerful tool for supporting thinking and learning. Louise Rosenblatt explains that reading and writing are both transactions. Reading provides the writer with the rich potential of language, and writing deepens the reader's understanding of the importance of paying attention to imagery and genre conventions. Teachers should create a rich context to enhance the development of reading, writing, and speech simultaneously. Children should be guided to take an appropriate stance when reading and writing: more aesthetic for reading literature, more efferent for reading information.

2. *How should we teach reading and writing together and across the curriculum?*

James Britton describes three modes of writing that students do in school: expressive, transactional, and poetic. According to his research, most writing done in school is transactional (i.e., "to get things done"); too little writing is expressive or poetic. However, other researchers have found that students read and write freely across all modes.

Reading across a range of genres can encourage students to discover and use their own voices. In a reading and writing classroom, a rich experiential environment can lead students to creative thinking and hypothesizing questions that connect different types of literature, writing, and subjects. Teachers should provide time and opportunities for reading and writing and promote talk and questions to enhance the development of thinking, reading, and writing. Reading workshops and using literature as a model for writing are effective approaches to doing so.

LOOKING FURTHER

1 Make a list or cluster of experiences that would be good for helping children write similes and metaphors.

2 Start a file of poems and patterns as models for writing in your classroom.

3 Ask to see three children's active-writing folders or portfolios. List the different types of stories each child wrote. Talk to the teacher about each child's reading. Do you see connections between these children's reading and writing?

4 Follow the steps in the Teaching Idea for writing a choose-your-own-adventure story. In your college class, write stories in small groups. Use an adult genre, if you'd like: murder mystery, detective story, or gothic romance.

5 Choose a poem you like and that you think children will like. Make a cluster of possible "ripple effects" that this poem might create for reading and writing across the curriculum. Share the poem with a class, and try some of your ideas.

RESOURCES

Atwell, N. (1987). *In the middle.* Portsmouth, NH: Boynton/Cook, 1987.

Calkins, L. M. (1983). *Lessons from a child.* Exeter, NH: Heinemann.

Graves, D. (1983). *Writing: Teachers and children at work.* Exeter, NH: Heinemann.

REFERENCES

Atwell, N. (1987). *In the middle.* Portsmouth, NH: Boynton/Cook, 1987.

Beach, R. (1993). *A teacher's introduction to reader-response theories.* Urbana, IL: National Council of Teachers of English.

Bissex, G. (1980). *GYNS AT WRK: A child learns to read and write.* Cambridge, MA: Harvard University Press.

Britton, J. N. (1984). Viewpoints: The distinction between participant and spectator roles in language in research and practice. *Research in the Teaching of English, 18,* 320–331.

Britton, J., Burgess, T., Martin, N., McLeod, A., & Rosen, H. (1975). *The development of writing abilities, 11–19.* London, England: Macmillan.

Brown, H., & Cambourne, B. (1989). *Read and retell.* Portsmouth, NH: Heinemann.

Calkins, L. M. (1983). *Lessons from a child.* Exeter, NH: Heinemann.

Farr, R., & Lowe, K. (1991). Alternative assessment in language arts. In C. Smith (Ed.), *Alternative assessment in the language arts.* Bloomington, IN: ERIC.

Frye, N. (1964). *The educated imagination.* Bloomington, IN: Indiana University Press.

Giacobbe, M. E. (1982). A writer reads, a reader writes. In S. Newton & N. Atwell (Eds.), *Understanding writing: Ways of observing, learning, and teaching.* Chelmsford, MA: Northeast Regional Exchange.

Graves, D. (1983). *Writing: Teachers and children at work.* Exeter, NH: Heinemann.

Hansen, J. (1987). *When writers read.* Portsmouth, NH: Heinemann.

Harste, J. C., Woodward, V. A., & Burke, C. L. (1984). *Language stories and literacy lessons.* Portsmouth, NH: Heinemann.

Heath, S. B. (1983). *Ways with words.* Cambridge, England: Cambridge University Press.

Jones, F. (1986). *Talk worth promoting in the writing classroom.* Paper presented at the National Council of Teachers of English, San Antonio, TX.

Koch, K. (1970). *Wishes, lies, and dreams.* New York: Random House.

Langer, S. (1967). *Mind: An essay on human feeling.* Baltimore, MD: Johns Hopkins University Press.

Many, J., & Cox, C. (Eds.). (1992). *Reader stance and literary understanding.* Norwood, NJ: Ablex.

Murray, D. (1985). *A writer teaches writing.* Boston: Houghton Mifflin.

Newkirk, T. (1984). Archimede's dream. *Language Arts, 61,* 341–350.

Reutzel, D. R., & Cooter, R. B. (1991). Organizing for effective instruction: The reading workshop. *Reading Teacher, 44,* 548–554.

Rosenblatt, L. M. (1985). Viewpoints: Transaction versus interaction—a terminological rescue mission. *Research in the Teaching of English, 19,* 96–107.

Rosenblatt, L. M. (1994). The transactional theory of reading and writing. In R. R. Ruddell, M. R. Ruddell, & H. Singer (Eds.), *Theoretical models and processes of reading* (4th ed., pp. 1057–1092). Newark, DE: International Reading Association.

Smith, F. (1982). *Writing and the writer.* New York: Holt, Rinehart & Winston.

Smith, F. (1983). Reading like a writer. *Language Arts, 60,* 558–567.

Taylor, D. (1983). *Family literacy.* Exeter, NH: Heinemann.

Tierney, R. J. (1994). Writing-reading relationships in instruction. *Encyclopedia of English studies and language arts* (Vol. 2). New York: Scholastic.

Tierney, R. J., & Shanahan, T. (1990). Research on the reading-writing relationship: interactions, transactions, and outcomes. In R. Batin, M. L. Kamil, P. Mostenthal, & P. D. Pearson (Eds.) *Handbook of reading research* (Vol. 2, pp. 246–280). New York: Longman.

Torrance, E. P. (1962). *Guiding creative talent.* Englewood Cliffs, NJ: Prentice-Hall.

CHILDREN'S BOOKS

Aardema, V. (1977). *Who's in Rabbit's house?* New York: Dial.

Adoff, A. (1982). *All the colors of the race.* New York: Lothrop, Lee & Shepard.

Alexander, L. (1964). *The book of three.* New York: Henry Holt.

Ancona, G. (1981). *Dancing is.* New York: Dutton.

Arnosky, J. (1987). *Drawing from nature.* New York: Lothrop, Lee & Shepard.

Ashabranner, B. (1982). *Morning star, black sun: The Northern Cheyenne Indians and America's energy crisis.* New York: Dodd, Mead.

Atwood, A. (1971). *Haiku: The mood of the earth.* New York: Scribner's.

Atwood, A. (1973). *My own rhythm: An approach to haiku.* New York: Scribner's.

Baron, V. (1968). *The seasons of time.* New York: Dial.

Behn, H. (1971). *More cricket songs.* New York: Harcourt Brace Jovanovich.

Behn, H. (Trans.). (1964). *Cricket songs.* New York: Harcourt Brace Jovanovich.

Boston, L. (1955). *The children of Green Knowe.* New York: Harcourt Brace Jovanovich.

Brown, M. W. (1949). *The important book.* New York: HarperCollins.

Caduto, M. J. , & Bruchac, J. (1988). *Keepers of the Earth: Native American stories and environmental activities for children.* New York: Fulcrum.

Christopher, J. (1967). *The city of gold and lead.* New York: Macmillan.

Ciardi, J. (1961). *I met a man.* Boston: Houghton Mifflin.

Ciardi, J. (1962). *You read to me, I'll read to you.* New York: Lippincott.

Ciardi, J. (1989). *The hopeful trout and other limericks.* New York: Houghton Mifflin.

Cole, J. (1989). *Anna Banana: 101 jump-rope rhymes.* New York: Morrow.

Cooper, S. (1973). *The dark is rising.* New York: Atheneum.

Davidson, R. (1993). *Take a look: An introduction to the experience of art.* New York: Viking.

Demi. (1992). *In the eyes of the cat: Japanese poetry for all seasons.* New York: Henry Holt.

Ehlert, L. (1989). *Color zoo.* New York: Lippincott.

Ehlert, L. (1990). *Color farm.* New York: Lippincott.

Engdahl, S. (1970). *Enchantress from the stars.* New York: Atheneum.

Fagan, B. M. (1987). *The great journey: The peopling of ancient America.* New York: Thames and Hudson.

Froman, R. (1971). *Street poems.* New York: McCall.

Froman, R. (1974). *Seeing things: A book of poems.* New York: Crowell.

George, J. C. (1972). *Julie of the wolves.* New York: HarperCollins

Hamanaka, S. (1994). *All the colors of the earth.* New York: Morrow Junior Books.

Hamilton, V. (1993). *Many thousand gone: African Americans from slavery to freedom.* New York: Knopf.

Higginson, W. (1991). *Wind in the long grass: A collection of haiku.* New York: Simon & Schuster.

Hirschi, R. (1990a). *Spring.* New York: Cobblehill.

Hirschi, R. (1990b). *Winter.* New York: Cobblehill.

Hirschi, R. (1991a). *Fall.* New York: Cobblehill.

Hirschi, R. (1991b). *Summer.* New York: Cobblehill.

Hoberman, M. A. (1982). *A house is a house for me.* New York: Penguin.

Hoffman, M. (1991). *Amazing Grace.* New York: Dial.

Ipcar, D. (1964). *I love my anteater with an A.* New York: Knopf.

Johnson, S. A. (1991). *Roses red, violets blue: Why flowers have colors.* Minneapolis: Lerner.

Jonas, A. (1989). *Color dance.* New York: Greenwillow.

Jones, H. (1995). *Big Star Fallin' Mama: Five women in black music.* New York: Viking

Juster, N. (1989). *As: A surfeit of similes.* New York: Morrow.

Kroll, V. L. (1992). *Masai and I.* New York: Four Winds.

Kuklin, S. (1992). *How my family lives in America.* New York: Bradbury.

L'Engle, M. (1962). *A wrinkle in time.* New York: Farrar, Straus, & Giroux.

Le Guin, U. (1968). *A wizard of Earthsea.* New York: Parnassus.

Lear, E. (1946). *The complete nonsense book.* New York: Dodd, Mead. (Original work published 1846)

Lear, E. (1991). *The owl and the pussy cat.* New York: Putnam.

Lepscky, I. (1984). *Pablo Picasso.* New York: Barron's.

Lewis, C. S. (1961). *The lion, the witch, and the wardrobe.* New York: Macmillan.

Lewis, R. (1965). *In a spring garden.* New York: Dial.

Lionni, L. (1959). *Little Blue and Little Yellow: A story for Pippo and Ann and other children.* New York: Obolensky.

Livingston, M. C. (1990). *My head is red and other riddle rhymes.* New York: Holiday House.

Lobel, A. (1983). *The book of pigericks.* New York: Harper & Row.

Lord, B. B. (1984). *In the year of the boar and Jackie Robinson.* New York: Harper & Row.

Lowry, L. (1993). *The giver.* New York: Houghton Mifflin.

Martin, B. (1967). *Brown bear, brown bear, what do you see?* New York: Henry Holt.

McCord, D. (1977). *One at a time: Poems for the very young.* Boston: Little, Brown.

McGovern, A. (1969). *Black is beautiful.* New York: Four Winds Press.

McMillan, B. (1990). *One sun: A book of terse verse.* New York: Holiday.

Meltzer, M. (1982). *The Hispanic Americans.* New York: Crowell.

Merriam, E. (1992). *Rainbow writing.* New York: Atheneum.

Milne, A. A. (1926). *Winnie-the-Pooh.* New York: Dutton.

Myers, W. D. (1991). *Now is your time! The African-American struggle for freedom.* New York: HarperCollins.

Myers, W. D. (1992). *The mouse rap.* New York: Harper & Row.

O'Neill, M. (1989). *Hailstones and halibut bones.* New York: Philomel.

Paulsen, G. (1985). *Dogsong.* New York: Puffin.

Pfister, M. (1992). *The rainbow fish.* New York: North-South Books.

Pilon, A. B. (1972). *Concrete is not always hard.* New York: Xerox.

Prelutsky, J. (1967). *A gopher in the garden and other animal poems.* New York: Macmillan

Raboff', E. (n.d.). *Art for children* (series). New York: Harper & Row.

Raskin, E. (1984). *The westing game.* New York: Avon.

Richards, L. (1932). *Tirra lirra: Rhymes old and new.* Boston: Little, Brown.

Scott, H. J., & Scott, L. (1968). *Egyptian hieroglyphics for everyone.* New York: Funk and Wagnalls.

Selsam, M. E., & Hunt, J. (1972). *A first look at leaves.* New York: Walker.

Sherman, I. (1980). *Walking talking words.* New York: Harcourt Brace Jovanovich.

Siebert, D. (1988). *Mojave. New* York: Crowell.

Siebert, D. (1989). *Heartland.* New York: Crowell.

Siebert, D. (1991). *Sierra.* New York: HarperCollins.

Sills, L. (1989). *Inspirations: Stories about women artists.* New York: Whitman.

Silverstein, S. (1974). *Where the sidewalk ends.* New York: Harper & Row.

Silverstein, S. (1981). *A light in the attic.* New York: Harper & Row.

Smith, W. J. (1990). *Laughing time.* New York: Delacorte.

Sobol, D. (1982). *Encyclopedia Brown.* New York: Bantam.

Soto, G. (1992). *Pacific crossing.* New York: Harcourt Brace Jovanovich.

Steptoe, J. (1987). *Mufaro's beautiful daughters: An African tale.* New York: Scholastic.

Stevenson, R. L. (1947). *Treasure Island.* New York: Putnam.

Taylor, M. (1976). *Roll of thunder, hear my cry.* New York: Puffin.

White, E. B. (1952). *Charlotte's web.* New York: Harper & Row.

Winter, J. (1991). *Diego.* New York: Knopf.

Wood, A. (1982). *As quick as a cricket.* New York: Child's Play International.

Worth, A. (1987). *All the small poems.* New York: Farrar, Straus, & Giroux.

Yee, P. (1990). *Tales from Gold Mountain: Stories of the Chinese in the New World.* New York: Macmillan.

Chapter 11

Language Conventions

Grammar, Talking, and Writing

Questions about Language Conventions

What Is Grammar?

Arguments for and against Teaching Grammar

Types of Grammar

SNAPSHOT: ***Arguing about Grammar in a Fifth-Grade Writing Workshop***

Grammar in Proper Perspective

How Children Learn to Use Language

Second Languages and Dialects

Learning to Use Language Conventions through Talking and Writing

Interacting with Others

Playing with Words and Sentences

Literature as a Model for Language Use

Written Style

Repeated Patterns

Playing with Stories

SNAPSHOT: ***Revising and Editing in a Fifth-Grade Writing Workshop***

Understanding Writing, Language Conventions, and Meaning

Assessing Language Conventions

Answers to Questions about Language Conventions

Questions about Language Conventions

1. *What is* grammar?
2. *How should grammar, talking, and writing be taught in a student- and response-centered classroom?*

Reflective Response

Write down your ideas about what you think *grammar* is. Then write any memories you have of learning grammar. What do you think you learned, and how did it affect your talking and writing?

What Is Grammar?

You may or may not have a firm idea of what *grammar* is, depending on how you were taught it. The role of grammar in instruction is an elusive and loaded concept, with a long history linking it to everything from philosophy, logic, and rhetoric during the time of the Ancient Greeks to literature, writing, and usage today. Few people agree on any one description.

Weaver (1979) has listed all the things the word *grammar* has meant to different people for different purposes and in different periods of history:

1. *Sentence Structure:* Grammar often simply refers to word order, the functions of words, and the grammatical endings of words in a language.
2. *Usage:* Socially acceptable and prestigious language use is often referred to as "good grammar"; "bad grammar" often means the use of language forms and constructions that are not acceptable to many people.
3. *Description:* Many linguists have attempted to classify and describe the syntactic structure of a language, which they call a "grammar."
4. *A Process:* Psycholinguists have tried to describe how people are able to create and understand sentences in a language; they refer to this process as "grammar."
5. *A Set of Rules:* In education, grammar has often been thought of as a set of rules for teaching students about some combination of the meanings above as well as pronunciation and whatever else teachers thought would help students speak and write "correctly."

Which of these descriptions best fits the definition of *grammar* you wrote down earlier? That likely depends on your age, the kind of school you went to, the English books you used, and the beliefs of your parents, English teachers, and school administrators regarding the purpose and importance of teaching grammar. Regardless, chances are that you were definitely taught something called "grammar." In reality, though, exactly what that was may have little to do with how educators now believe grammar should be taught.

Arguments for and against Teaching Grammar

Weaver (1979) has described the reasons people have given over the centuries as to the great importance of teaching grammar. The study of grammar is a way to learn:

- About and understand how to use a language
- How to approach other topics that require a scientific, investigative approach
- How to think, since language is a reflection of thought
- How to learn a second language more easily
- How to speak and write in a socially acceptable and even prestigious way
- How to become a better speaker and writer

The fact is, however, that researchers have explored these six reasons for teaching grammar and consistently failed to find support for them (Hillocks & Smith, 1991). Furthermore, researchers have shown that students don't even remember aspects of the formal study of grammar very long after they've been taught. Braddock asserts that "the teaching of formal grammar has a negligible, or, because it usually displaces some instruction and practice in actual composition, even a harmful effect on the improvement of writing" (Braddock, Lloyd-Jones, & Schoer, 1963, p. 38).

These research findings certainly support current social constructivist beliefs that children learn by doing, not by learning rules about doing. That is, children learn to speak by speaking, to read by reading, and to write by writing in meaningful transactions with others and texts they experience or compose themselves.

Research has failed to support the argument that learning formal rules of grammar transfers to learning actual language use or to knowledge in other subjects. Actually, research supports an argument *against* the formal teaching of grammar, since time spent learning these rules takes away from time spent using language for meaningful purposes. Furthermore, in an examination of compositions written by 9-, 13-, and 17-year olds as part of the National Assessment of Educational Progress (NAEP), Applebee, Langer, and Mullis (1987) found that "most students make only a few errors and the frequency of errors is less at the older ages" (p. 3).

So, if extensive, long-term research has failed to support the arguments for teaching grammar and even suggested that doing so has a negative effect, why do we persist in teaching it? Why is the subject even included in this book? Teachers must be aware of and able to deal with many historical, philosophical, social, cultural, and even political reasons in facing the issues of whether or not and how to teach grammar and usage. Consider the following:

- ***Teaching grammar has a long tradition:*** Of all the subjects, grammar has the longest unbroken tradition as an essential subject in school. This tradition goes back to the time of the Ancient Greeks and Romans, who taught rhetoric as a means to analyze and understand poetry and speak effectively in public, to the current generation of parents and teachers, who were taught grammar in schools and may have a deeply embedded belief that it was a necessary part of their education.

- ***Teaching grammar is viewed as a basic skill:*** Nationwide concern has arisen over teaching and learning what are called "basic skills," and in many people's minds, grammar is traditionally one of those skills. These people believe that grammar provides a foundation for learning correct language usage and writing, which are vital to success in school and the world. Again, this view is not supported by research.

- ***Teaching grammar is a part of textbooks:*** In a survey of representative elementary school English textbooks over a 60-year period, three major trends appeared: (1) less emphasis on writing, (2) more emphasis on oral language, and (3) no change for grammar and sentence construction exercises. The latter reflects "those nineteenth century die-hards, . . . plodding unerringly along, oblivious to changing times . . . and educational currents" (von Bracht Donsky, 1984, p. 797).

- ***Teaching grammar lends itself to testing:*** It's much easier to test and grade students' knowledge of rules of grammar using objective, multiple-choice tests than it is to test the quality of their actual writing or the sophistication level of their speech. Standardized tests of language are still used extensively as measures of students' success.

Types of Grammar

Given the long tradition of teaching grammar and the likelihood that it will remain an educational issue, teachers should know what it is and how to teach it. Their decisions as to how to approach teaching grammar should be based on information about grammar, grammar teaching, and language development and learning.

Grammarians have developed different models for explaining how language works. The three main types of grammar described in the following sections—traditional, structural, and transformational—have different histories and theoretical frameworks. Teachers should be familiar with them in order to put grammar in proper perspective. The following comparison considers the features of these three types of grammar, including a historical perspective, main characteristics, educational implications, and some terms, rules, and definitions.

Traditional Grammar

Traditional grammar began as a prescriptive grammar for teaching English in medieval times; its roots can be traced to the study of classical languages. Traditional grammar provided a commonly used terminology for talking about language and a tradition of analyzing and describing the grammar of a language. Eventually, however, traditional grammar became a set of rules for writing English correctly, based on rules that had been developed for writing

Latin. But English is not a Latin language; thus, Latin categories and terms don't fit English or accurately describe it.

During the eighteenth century, traditional language scholars classified the parts of English speech in the same way classical languages were classified. These parts of speech are still found in schoolbooks today. In the nineteenth century, linguists began to focus on describing how language forms, such as those that had been studied for centuries before, were related to language use.

Structural Grammar

Structural grammar was an attempt by linguists to distinguish between spoken and written language and to analyze the patterns unique to English, taking into account language differences among geographical regions and social classes, dialects of different groups, and individual idiolects. These linguists provided much information about how language is really used, in nonstandard as well as standard usage, and about the many varieties of language use, such as literary, formal, colloquial, and slang.

Anthropological interest arose when the structuralists described Native American languages, for example, and throughout the 1950s, as linguists sought to accurately describe how English was actually spoken. Unlike earlier linguists, however, these structuralists didn't relate meaning to their descriptions, given the impreciseness of the terms, and used categories (or form classes), rather than the traditional parts of speech, to classify relationships among words.

Transformational Grammar

Transformational grammar is a more recent attempt to describe not only how language is used but also what psycholinguistic processes are at work when we use it. This type of grammar also makes the most complete attempt to establish the relationship between sound and meaning in language. Noam Chomsky (1957) and other linguists challenged the structuralist view, which left meaning out of descriptions of language, citing examples such as *John is eager to please* and *John is easy to please.* These two sentences can't be explained without reference to their meanings.

The transformationalists were most interested in the intuitive knowledge that allows speakers—even very young ones—to create, use, and understand sentences that they have never heard before but that are nonetheless grammatical. The transformationalists maintain that grammar should be more than just a description of speech. It should be a description of the process of how language is produced.

Chomsky (1957) made an important distinction between *competence* and *performance. Competence* is what we know; *performance* is what we say. In order to explain this distinction, Chomsky described two levels of language:

1. Language competence is characterized by *deep structure,* or meaning: understanding the underlying propositions and relationships among them.

2. Performance is characterized by *surface structure,* or form: the string of sounds, letters, words, phrases, and clauses.

The transformationalists were not as interested in defining terms as they were in explaining the relationship between surface structure and deep structure. They were also concerned with understanding the innate "sentence sense" that tells us when a sentence in our native language is grammatical and when it is not—in other words, when it just "sounds right."

Transformational grammar is not a set of prescriptive rules of how to speak and write correctly (traditional grammar) or simple descriptions of the language (structural grammar). Instead, transformational grammar attempts to describe the relationship of form to meaning and how any speaker is able to produce language. Chomsky (1957) says that a grammar should explain how a language user is able to make infinite use of finite means. The rules should explain why speakers can create and use sentences they have never heard before and why others, who may never have heard these sentences either, will understand them. Even very young children are able to do this because they have internalized these rules of language. And even though children learn much about language through imitation, the process they draw on to use language is innate.

SNAPSHOT: Arguing about Grammar in a Fifth-Grade Writing Workshop

Faith and Barbara are in Phyllis Fuglaar's fifth-grade class. The girls are best friends and like to work together, but they often fight. I observed them one day during writing workshop. They were in a group with their friend Lillian, writing a rebus story they wanted to publish as a book and read aloud to the kindergarten classes. Barbara had misplaced several days' worth of ideas, notes, and drafts for the story. Faith was annoyed, Barbara was defensive, and Lillian was very quiet as the other two criticized each other's attempts to reconstruct the story and write a new draft.

In a *rebus story,* a letter, number, or picture replaces a word using the same sound (e.g., a picture of an eye = the word *I*) or meaning (e.g., a picture of an eye = the word *eye*).

As you read about the three friends arguing about grammar and writing, think about these key issues of language learning and literacy development:

1. The primary role of meaning in talking and writing
2. Children's intuitive knowledge of the rules underlying language production and of the formal rules of grammar
3. The teaching of talking, writing, and grammar

Barbara (reading a draft): "In Lancaster, Wisconsin, a small 8-year-old boy found a lost cat." *Found* is past tense.

During writing workshop, Faith and Barbara argue about the book they're writing, while Lillian tries to keep out of the crossfire!

Faith: I think it should be in the present tense because, see, he says, "How long will I have to stay?"
Barbara: How about "While they're gone, Tommy started walking around"?
Faith (sarcastically): Yeah. That's what we put on the draft *you* lost. (She makes a face at Lillian in front of Barbara.)
Barbara (visibly upset): It doesn't matter, Faith. You don't have to look at Lillian that way.
Faith (to Lillian): What do you like: past or present?
Lillian: I like 'em both.
Barbara: Oh, I hate it! Now she's gonna say majority rules 'cause she doesn't care. Faith, uh . . . how come you always use majority rules when you want to get your own way? OK, if we use present tense, how am I gonna say "You tripped over him"?
Faith: We had that part, and you were supposed to have proofread it, but now we don't know because you can't find it!
Barbara: There's no time to argue.
Faith (sarcastically): I'm sorry. OK. You can just redo it all again.

The conversation continues a little later, when they're adding rebus pictures to the story:

Faith: Draw an eye for *I.*
Barbara: *I* is a pronoun. I don't think kindergartners would think about an eye.
Lillian (quietly): Anybody have any marking pens?
Faith (loudly): I don't like the eye!

Barbara (more loudly): Then *you* change it!
Faith (loudest): OK! I'LL CHANGE IT!

They continue to talk—and argue—about the types of rebus pictures that kindergartners will understand the meanings of:

Barbara (reading back what she has just written): "The cats came back . . . came back . . . came back . . . came back?" Maybe we should say *returned.*
Faith: Come on, Barbara! They don't know what that means.
Barbara: OK. "Came back . . . accidentally."
Faith (sarcastically): *Accidentally?* Are they going to know what that means? What's another word for *accidentally?*
Barbara (laughing): *Not-on-purposely!* "The cats came back not-on-purposely."
Faith (sighing resignedly): Barabara. Please. Tomorrow, will you just bring your work?

Grammar in Proper Perspective

In order to put grammar in proper perspective in the context of teaching language arts, think about the girls in the Snapshot arguing about grammar and writing. They made references to grammatical terms and to many of the meanings associated with the word *grammar.* When I asked them, "What is *grammar?*" they gave the following answers:

Faith: Grammar is dots and things that make sense. So that it sounds right. Also so that people can understand what you wrote. I know spelling, periods, commas, colons, semicolons, pronunciation, exclamation points, question marks, quotations, parentheses, capital letters, paragraphs, complete sentences, adverbs, adjectives, subjects, noun predicate, verb, preposition, prepositional phrase, infinitive, gerund, present tense, past tense, participles, spaces, letters, punctuation, usage.
Barbara: Grammar is the way that you use words. Slang is bad grammar. I know the parts of speech, how to use words properly, when to use words.

How did the girls' answers compare to the one you wrote in the Reflective Response at the beginning of the chapter? Clearly, Barbara and Faith can define grammar and tell what they know about it. Both have had many years of instruction in the formal rules of grammar using textbooks and skill exercises, and they have been successful at completing such exercises on grammar tests. What's important to note, however, is that Barbara and Faith would be able to talk and write effectively *without* knowing how to define grammar, to tell about it, or do exercises or pass tests on it. Like all children, they come to school with an underlying intuitive knowledge of the rules that govern language production. They are able to communicate meaning.

To illustrate, let's examine what Faith and Barbara were really doing during their writing workshop:

- In arguing over whether to use the present or past tense, they were really talking about meaning: Will it make sense to the reader? Present and past were not the real issue. Rather, the issue was what they wanted their story to mean and how to communicate that to whomever reads it.

- When they were arguing about proofreading and paragraphs, the girls were checking for the organization of their ideas, the sequence of chunks of meaning—or paragraphs—and how they relate to one another.

- When they were arguing about using a drawn eye for an *I* and about nouns and pronouns, they were really talking about the ambiguities of word meanings in English, because many words that sound alike are written differently.

- When they were talking about word choice—for instance, whether to use *came back, return, accidentally,* or *not-on-purposely,* they were concerned about using the right words to say precisely what they meant and so others would understand them.

So even though Barbara and Faith used grammar terms in talking about their writing, the real focus of their session was on communicating meaning.

In teaching language conventions for talking and writing, teachers need to be especially careful not to assume that some of the terms or rules they use to talk about language are more important than the actual use of the language. The ultimate goal is to help children use language to think and learn and to make sense as they talk, write, and read. Unfortunately, the study of grammar has often been described in terms of knowledge about parts of speech, pronunciation, punctuation, and spelling. When that's the case, grammar is mistakenly viewed as anything that needs to be corrected by teachers: less prestigious forms of speech or slang, dialect and language differences, and language conventions in writing. From this perspective, grammar is a quick fix for whatever's wrong with speech or writing.

From a social constructivist and language development perspective, however, teaching grammar is not an effective way to help children develop their use of language in talking and writing. As mentioned earlier, research on the effectiveness of teaching grammar has even shown that doing so may have a negative effect on language learning, since it deprives students of some of the time they would spend actually using language: talking, writing, and reading. What experiences will help children grow in language fluency, flexibility, elaboration, and control over more and more complex grammatical structures?

Think again about what Barbara, Faith, and Lillian were doing while talking and writing together in writing workshop:

- They were learning to talk by talking and to write by writing.
- They were using talking, writing, and reading together in a group formed for a social purpose as well as a language purpose.
- Their writing had a purpose: to make a rebus book for kindergartners.
- They were exercising choices in their writing: they picked a topic and decided what to write about it.
- They were solving a problem: how to do a rebus story.
- They were focusing on meaning: how to tell the story.
- They were interacting: arguing and revising and editing their story.
- They were being creative and using their own voices: composing the story and playing with language by making up words like *not-on-purposely*.
- They were exercising control: revising and editing their story so it made sense.
- They were being responsible: they started a new draft when the old one was lost.

See Chapter 10, The Writing Process, for more on writing workshop and an example from a fourth-grade class.

Above all, the girls' thinking and language were focused on *meaning*. And by planning writing workshop, their teacher supported them in their efforts.

How Children Learn to Use Language

Chapter 2, Children and Language, explains how children acquire and develop language, and Chapter 3, Language and Cultural Diversity, explains how children acquire and develop second languages.

Before they come to school and without formal instruction, children have intuitive knowledge of the underlying grammar of the language they speak (Strickland, 1962). Moreover, they continue to build on that underlying knowledge of language production. Hunt (1965) found that "the average child in the fourth grade produces virtually all the grammatical structures ever described in a course in school grammar" (p. 156).

Carol Chomsky (1980) explains how children are continually in the process of constructing their internal language system:

> *Children of elementary age are still actively engaged in acquiring their native language. Language development is much slower than during the preschool years and not as noticeable in the earlier years, but studies show it continues in much the same manner as with younger children. School-age children continue to learn new constructions systematically on their own, using the language they hear around them. They are prepared to construct their own internal language system from inputs that come their way and they benefit from exposure to a rich and varied linguistic environment.* (p. 56)

For ways students can investigate language, see Judi Lesiak (1978), "The Origin of Words: A Unit of Study," *Language Arts, 55*, pp. 317–319.

This isn't to suggest that students shouldn't learn about language. They can use grammatical terms as a vocabulary to talk about language. But teachers can't assume that this is an essential part of learning to speak or write. Rather, children need to use language to fulfill real needs and purposes and to discover and create meaning. They will gain control over their vast underlying knowledge of grammar by putting it to use.

Second Languages and Dialects

Second Languages

The *monitor model* supports the idea that a second language is best learned using a communicative-based, natural approach. Based on that model, Stephen Krashen (1981; Krashen & Terrell, 1987) argues that learning the rules of grammar is only effective as a monitor of language use—and even then, the speaker or writer has to know the rule, be thinking about it, and have time to apply it. This happens infrequently in speaking and may not be effective in writing, either. What's most important is providing *comprehensible input* (i.e., language that's just a little bit beyond the child's current level of language acquisition) in a low-anxiety environment (what Krashen calls a *low affective filter*).

See Chapter 3, Language and Cultural Diversity, to review the difference between the *grammar-based* (language-learning) and *communicative-based* (language-acquisition) approaches to learning a second language.

The monitor model is important because it challenges the notion of teaching English as a second language with formal rules of grammar. Instead, the model suggests using language for real communication and meaningful purposes—a point of view that's compatible with the whole-language approach. Teaching suggestions include involving students in real communication about interesting and relevant topics, conducted in a low-anxiety atmosphere. The emphasis is on meaning rather than form.

Richard-Amato (1988) explains that this has been an effective approach to language acquisition, without ignoring the importance of learning about language or grammar. "Organizing interactional activities related to content, providing for a silent period, and allowing for the natural development of interlanguage require creativity, flexibility, and patience on the part of teachers" (p. 280). She also warns that "when such relatively noncommunicative activities become the focus of the curriculum . . . they can be detrimental to the progression of second language students in programs in which communication is the goal" (p. 280).

Dialects

Variations in use within the same language are found among different language communities in which unique speech standards have developed. For example, Labov (1972) describes what he calls *Black English Vernacular (BEV)* and argues that it's not a mass of errors in speaking Standard English. Instead, BEV is a "distinct subsystem within the larger grammar of English" (pp. 63–64), with it's own regular conventions and rules for language production. For example, "I been knowin' your name" means "I have known for a long time, and still know, your name" (pp. 53–55).

Heath (1983) has shown that a teacher's lack of knowledge of BEV rules can cause misunderstanding when interpreting what a student speaking in this dialect is saying:

> *A teacher asked one day: "Where is Susan? Isn't she here today?" Lem answered: "She ain't ride de bus." The teacher responded: "She doesn't ride the bus, Lem." Lem answered: "She do be ridin' de bus." The teacher frowned at Lem and turned away. Within the system of Black English Lem used,* ain't *was used as equivalent to* didn't, *the negative of the past tense of the auxiliary* do; *thus his answer had to be inter-*

> *preted as "She didn't ride the bus." The teacher heard the* ain't *as equivalent to* doesn't *and corrected Lem accordingly; he rejected this shift of meaning and asserted through his use of* do be ridin' *that Susan did indeed regularly ride the bus.* (pp. 277–278)

For teaching methods that are effective in culturally and linguistically diverse classrooms, see Chapter 3, Language and Cultural Diversity.

Labov's (1972) work has shown that BEV has an internal logic and its own language conventions. Nonetheless, Heath's (1983) work has shown that conflicting conventions in the language used within the same community can lead to misunderstanding for both teachers and students and thus failure to learn. Sensitivity to differences in native languages and dialects are essential to teaching language arts.

Learning to Use Language Conventions through Talking and Writing

The meaning of *grammar* most relevant to language learning and teaching in elementary school is that children have an underlying knowledge of language, which they draw on as they use it. Given that, classroom experiences should focus primarily on active language use. Teachers in student- and response-centered classrooms can provide that focus and help children develop awareness of the form and structure of language by using the following activities.

Interacting with Others

Rich experiences in talking and interacting with others are essential in order for children to continue to expand their ability to use language fluently and flexibly and to understand how language works. For example, Barbara and Faith learned about language as they used it to argue. Each was doing her best to convey her ideas and assert herself, carefully choosing words, organizing sentences and arguments, emphasizing them with inflections, making facial expressions and gestures—all the time, honing their meaning in writing, as well.

Working in Groups

See Chapter 1, Learning and Teaching Language Arts, for a description of Avril Font's fourth-grade class, in which all work is done in group workshops. Also see Chapter 7, Teaching with Literature, for ideas about literature groups, in which children read, talk, and write together.

Not every writing workshop group will produce such an authentic and passionate exchange between students. Some students may not care what they're writing about or about who does what work. Children are more likely to care (and even to argue their point) if they're allowed to choose topics they're interested in and people they like to be with. They need many opportunities to have authentic exchanges with each other on issues and topics that interest them, such as:

1. ***Group workshops:*** We've looked at a number of examples of group workshops, in which students collaborate on projects and activities.
2. ***Literature groups:*** Again, we've looked at the success of literature groups, in which children read, talk, and write together.

3. ***Problem-solving groups:*** Children work together to solve problems: setting up class rules, planning a class election, making observations and doing experiments in science, completing research or projects in social studies, or working on a scene in drama production.

Conflicts and Class Court

Conflicts in the classroom can lead to arguments: Whose pencil? Whose turn? Who's right? Who's in charge? Paul Boyd-Batstone, a bilingual teacher in Long Beach, California, uses a "class court" daily to let children discuss and resolve such issues. The court consists of three children each day, selected on a rotational basis. Children put their complaints in writing, which go in a box. Each written complaint is read by the court, who asks questions, listens to answers and opinions, and comes up with a resolution. Paul monitors the proceedings.

Debates

Through debates, conflicting positions can formally be discussed, either between two individuals or among students in a group. Topics can emerge from content areas (e.g., space exploration or the environment), which students can debate after studying them. A panel discussion of "experts" who have studied a field provides a rich context for language interaction. A point/counterpoint format works well for talking about issues with two clearly opposing sides.

Role-Playing and Curriculum Drama

Conflicts and debates can be dramatized, as children role-play important people from history debating issues (e.g., Columbus and his detractors on the shape of the earth) or improvise characters in curriculum drama (e.g., a town meeting between Loyalists and Patriots during the American Revolution).

See Chapter 9, Drama in the Classroom, for ideas about dramatizing history.

In a class debate, students gain control over language as they use it to argue a point.

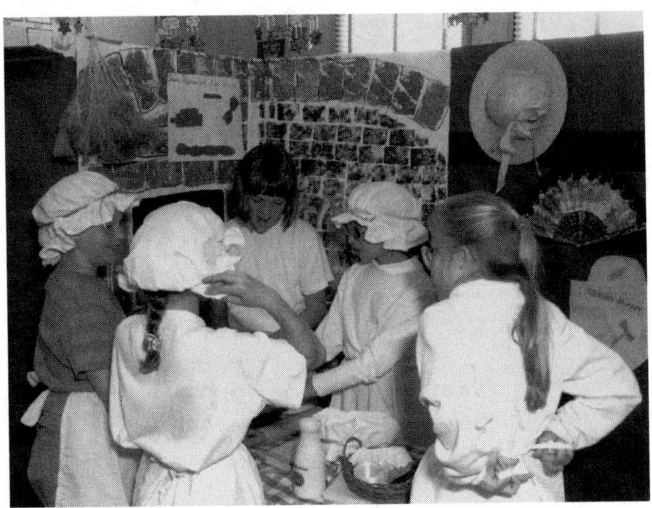

In a curriculum drama activity, students spend the day in a colonial kitchen.

Playing with Words and Sentences

See Linda Gibson Geller (1985), *Word Play and Language Learning for Children.*

Children learn to use language by playing around with it. For example, in the Snapshot, Barbara was playing around (and really annoying Faith) when she made up the word *not-on-purposely* as a synonym for *accidentally*. Children will do this on their own. However, teachers can play on this natural tendency by introducing word and sentence play.

Classifying Words

See Chapter 2, Children and Language, for more ideas on semantic mapping and language play.

This is a variation of semantic mapping in which children look for relationships among words and do visual maps of them. When they classify words, students also look for differences. Words for classification can come up in discussions, be related to learning in content areas, or be introduced by the teacher. Here are several approaches:

1. ***Contrasting Pairs of Words:*** Here are simple dual classifications:

Feelings	*Happy/sad; good/bad; nice/mean*
Descriptions	*Ugly/beautiful; big/little; smooth/rough*
Old and new words	"A word I used to think meant something else . . . but now I know it means . . ."
Personal choices	Favorite words/disliked words

See *Frederick*, by Leo Lionni (1967), which is about a mouse who collects images and words about spring and summer while the other mice gather and store food for winter. When the food is gone and they're mad at him, he cheers them up with a poem about the seasons.

Children often have personal choices of words they love or hate. My son Wyatt has kept a running list of words he hates, including *nougat, snorkel,* and *yawn* (which he says "may be the most mindless word in the world"). Ask children to make their own personal choice lists.

2. ***Groups of Words:*** Here are simple ways to classify related words:
   - *The Four Seasons:* Brainstorm ideas for a chart like the one shown in Figure 11.1.

Name	Winter	Spring	Summer	Fall (or Autumn)
Temperature	Cold	Warm	Hot	Cool
Weather	Snow Ice	Wind Rain	Sunny Humid	Frost Chilly
Holidays	Hanukkah Christmas Kwaanza Chinese New Year Martin L. King, Jr., Day Presidents' Day	St. Patrick's Day Passover Easter Cambodian New Year	Memorial Day Flag Day Fourth of July Labor Day	Halloween Day of the Dead Rosh Hashanah Yom Kippur Thanksgiving
Play	Sledding Snowmen	Kites Puddles	Swimming Beach	Leaves School
Sports	Hockey	Basketball	Baseball	Football
Colors	White	Green	Blue	Brown

FIGURE 11.1 Classifying Words: The Four Seasons

- *The Five Senses:* Instead of a chart, do a minilesson on a triante pattern for writing. The following example was written by third-graders about spring, after doing a chart about each of the seasons:

Triante Pattern	**Senses**	**Poem**
Line 1: One word (Title)		Spring
Line 2: Two words	Smell	Fresh Sweet
Line 3: Three words	Touch	Warm Soft Wet
Line 4: Four words	Sight	Green Colorful Sunny Lively
Line 5: Five words	Sound	Singing Laughing Whispering Gurgling Buzz

3. *Comparisons:* Children can classify words by making comparisons—for example, about what they're able to do in a "You Are Too . . . " pattern. Here are examples from second-graders:

See *George Shrinks*, by William Joyce (1986), which is about a little boy's adventures when he wakes up just a few inches tall.

You are too large to:
fit into a mouse house
swim in a fish bowl
live in a bird cage
You are too small to:
fly to the moon
lift a whale
eat a watermelon whole
You are just right to:
climb upstairs alone
swing up high in a swing

Parts of Speech

It's a simple step from classifying words, in general, to classifying them by their functions and using their traditional names as parts of speech. A few simple writing patterns use and expand on the classifications of words using traditional terms for the parts of speech and the order of sentences:

1. ***Nouns and Adjectives:*** For the "What Next?" pattern, choose a noun and find three adjectives that start with the same letter:

Noun	***Adjectives***
cave	cold, clammy, creepy
dungeon	dark, damp, dreary
swamp	sticky, slimy, slippery

2. ***Verbs:*** For the "My Hands, My Feet" pattern, choose the name of something that can do an action (e.g., hands or feet), and write verbs for what it can do. First-graders wrote these:

My Hands	**My Feet**
squeeze a mop	walk on floors
mess with slop	go through doors
do the dishes	step on bugs
scoop up fishes	play on rug

3. ***Nouns, Adjectives, and Verbs:***

- For the "Concentric Circle" pattern, pick a noun and use three adjectives and five verbs to make a spiral. Fourth-graders created this one:

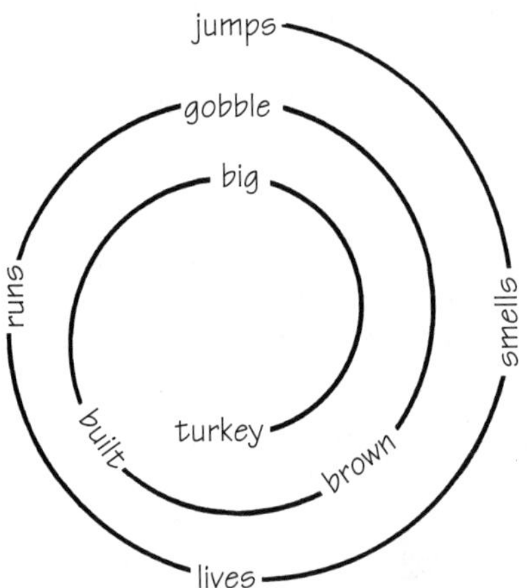

- For the "Diamante" pattern, create a verse in the shape of a diamond, which shifts topic or shows a change in the fourth line. Here's an example written by a fifth-grader, showing his bike before and after he had a wreck on it:

Line 1: Noun	My Bike
Line 2: Adjective, adjective	Black, rubber
Line 3: Verb, verb, verb	Turning, squeaking, fixing
Line 4: Noun, noun/*noun, noun	Wheel, handlebars, chain, pedals
Line 5: Verb, verb, verb	Crashing, bounding, smashing
Line 6: Adjective, adjective	Broken, bent
Line 7: Noun	Bike

* Marks shift in topic or show of change

Here's a list of children's books about language, which focus on parts of speech as well as other language conventions:

Nouns

Merry-Go-Round: A Book about Nouns (Heller, 1990)
Your Foot's on My Feet! and Other Tricky Nouns (Terban, 1986)

Collective Nouns

A Cache of Jewels and Other Collective Nouns (Heller, 1987)
Herds of Words (MacCarthy, 1991)
A Kettle of Hawks and Other Wildlife Groups (Arnosky, 1990)

Verbs

Dig, Drill, Dump, Fill (Hoban, 1975)
I Think I Thought and Other Tricky Verbs (Terban, 1984)
Kites Sail High: A Book about Verbs (Heller, 1988)
Kitten Can . . . (McMillan, 1984)
Seeing, Saying, Doing, Playing: A Big Book of Action Words (Gomi, 1994)

Adjectives

Many Luscious Lollipops: A Book about Adjectives (Heller, 1989)
Super, Super, Superwords (McMillan, 1989)

Adverbs

A Snake Is Totally Tail (Barrett, 1983)
Up, Up and Away: A Book about Adverbs (Heller, 1991)

Prepositions

Over, Under, and Through and Other Spatial Concepts (Hoban, 1973)
Rosie's Walk (Hutchins, 1968)

Constructing Sentences

When children know the names of the parts of speech and what they do, teachers should use patterns that begin with a word or words, and build sentences:

1. ***Noun, Verb, Adverbial Phrase:*** For the "Do What, When, and Where" pattern, write a simple sentence using a noun, verb, and adverbial phrase. These rhyming ones were written by third-graders.

Noun	**Verb**	**Adverbial Phrase**
Snakes	crawl	down the hall.
Kittens	sleep	while I eat.
Witches	zoom	on their brooms.
Bats	soar	outside my door.

2. ***Adjective, Noun, Verb, Adverb:*** Read an alphabet book like *Animalia* (Base, 1987) or *Aster Aardvark's Alphabet Adventures* (Kellogg, 1987) to show the pattern of alliterative sentences. Here is an example written by third-graders:

Letter	**Adjective**	**Noun**	**Verb**	**Adverb**
A is for the	angry	alligator	acting	ambidextrously.

A class book could be made, providing a page for each letter along with an alliterative sentence.

3. ***Adjective, Noun, Verb, Adverb:*** To form a sentence pyramid, begin with a noun and add a word for each line, working down from the top with the base as the whole sentence:

Noun	**Rock**
Adjective/Noun	Big rock
Adjective/Noun/Verb	Big rock sits
Adjective/Noun/Verb/Adverb	Big rock sits quietly

Sentence Games

Model these ways to play games with sentences in minilessons or when the time seems right, in terms of students' needs and interests:

1. ***Name Sentences:*** Choose a name or a special word, and use its letters to start the first words in a sequence of sentences. For variation, use a theme: an advertisement, a slogan, a newspaper headline, or a song, book, or movie title. Here's an example about the movie *Babe,* which is about a pig:

Being a pig wasn't what he wanted to be.
All the other animals thought he should act like a pig.
But he proved that he could herd sheep, like the dogs.
Even the boss thought he was a great herding pig!

2. ***ABC Sentences:*** Each word in a sequence must begin with the next letter in the alphabet. Second-graders wrote this one:

Doughnuts eaten frantically give heartburn.

3. ***Alphabet-All Sentences:*** Challenge children to write ABC sentences using all the letters in the alphabet. Here's an example written by two fifth-graders:

A bear catches dogs, eats frogs, goads horses into jumping kangaroos, likes making new orangutans pretty; "quite right" said the unicorn verifying with x-rays, yams, zebras.

4. ***Newspaper Cut-Up Sentences:*** Have children find interesting words in the newspaper, cut them out, and arrange them in sentences. Variations on this idea include writing ransom notes, nonsense recipes, and hidden messages.

Sentence Combining

Sentence combining is a technique used to increase students' syntactic maturity by having them combine *kernel sentences*—the simplest statements of ideas—to form more complex sentences (O'Hare, 1973; Straw, 1994). Doing so provides a way for students to develop increased control over language conventions and complexity in writing. Three important concepts underlie the technique of sentence combining:

1. ***The Model of Transformational Grammar:*** Recall from earlier in this chapter that Noam Chomsky (1957) proposed a model of grammar with an underlying deep structure, or meaning (language competence), and surface structure, or form (language performance). Understanding the form of language requires awareness of the meaning of language. As Chomsky explains, "To understand a sentence, it is necessary to reconstruct its representation on each level, including the transformational level where the kernel sentences underlying a given sentence can be thought of, in a sense, as the 'elementary content elements' out of which this sentence is constructed" (pp. 107–108).

2. ***A Definition of Syntactic Maturity:*** Kellogg Hunt (1965) created a definition of *syntactic maturity* and a measure called a *T-unit,* which is a "minimal terminable unit," or a main clause plus all modifiers. Using the T-unit, Hunt researched the development of syntactic maturity, showing that as students mature, their written language becomes more complex.

3. ***A Study of Sentence-Combining Exercises:*** John Mellon (1969) did a study using sentence-combining exercises, based on the transformational model of grammar, which showed students' gains in writing maturity and quality.

Materials for sentence-combining practice are available commercially, but children can also work on strategies of sentence combining, changing, and expanding using their own words, phrases, sentences, and ideas. This is what Faith, Barbara, and Lillian were doing in the Snapshot, when they worked together to revise their writing, combining, adding to, expanding, moving parts, and changing their sentences. The word and sentence games described earlier are also excellent ways of teaching students how to combine sentences.

See *Creative Approaches to Sentence Combining,* by William Strong (1986), who explains that "playful attention to language" is the key to language learning. His book provides 20 creative sentence-combining activities, which can be photocopied for classroom use.

Minilessons on Sentence Combining

Teachers can use minilessons and writing conferences to make students aware of the three basic types of sentence transformations: changing, combining, and reducing. The best way to encourage children to develop facility with language structures in real writing contexts is to use their own ideas and writing.

In the list that follows, examples from children's writing are used to illustrate each type of sentence transformation. And those examples come from a prewriting idea list brainstormed by Barbara, Faith, and Lillian (the students in the Snapshot) in preparing to write their story for a kindergarten rebus book. Here's their list:

Boy finds lost cat.
Boy is small.
He's 8 years old.
The cat is a stray.
Cat came from street.
It's in Lancaster, Wisconsin.
The boy's name is Tommy.
Tommy takes care of cat.
Tommy finds out cat is magical.

1. *Changing:* This type of transformation involves turning one type of sentence into another, such as a question or negation:

Basic Sentence: A boy finds a stray cat.

Changed into

Question: Does a boy find a stray cat?
Negation: A boy doesn't find a stray cat.

2. *Combining:* This is putting together several sentences to form a compound sentence:

Basic Sentences: A boy finds a stray cat.
The boy is small.
He's 8 years old.
The cat came from the street.
The cat is magical.

Combined into a Compound Sentence:
A small, 8-year-old boy finds a stray cat from the street, and the cat is magical.

3. *Reducing:* This transformation involves changing some sentences into smaller parts and inserting them into or combining them with other sentences:

Basic Sentences: A small, 8-year-old boy finds a stray cat from the street, and the cat is magical. The boy's name is Tommy, and it's in Lancaster, Wisconsin. Tommy takes care of the cat.

Combined with Other Sentences:
Tommy, a small, 8-year-old boy in Lancaster, Wisconsin, finds a stray, magical cat from the street. He takes care of it.

Literature as a Model for Language Use

When the language of literature sings in children's ears, they will not only understand and enjoy a different kind of language, but they will use a different kind, too. Carol Chomsky (1972) found that the knowledge of complex language structures varies greatly among children from 6 to 10 years old and that this knowledge is not necessarily related to age. The children in her study who developed the greatest facility with language structures sooner were those who had had more exposure to the language of books—both those they had heard read aloud and those they had read themselves.

Teachers in student- and response-centered classrooms can support students' growing acquisition of syntactic structures and use of words by reading aloud. They should do so frequently and from a range of different types of books. Literature provides a model of language, which students will use in their own speaking and writing. For example, when writing about a cemetery at Halloween, Faith (described in the Snapshot) came up with the term *blood curdling,* which impressed her friend Barbara. Then Faith sheepishly confided that she had found the words in a less-than-literary but ever-popular Nancy Drew book.

See Chapter 5, Listening and Talking, for more on reading aloud.

Written Style

Children's books are full of wonderful words and language, which makes them excellent resources for teaching about written style:

- ***Form:*** Children's literature contains sleek but deeply embedded sentence structure forms. This is true even of books for the very young, like the classic *Peter Rabbit* (Potter, 1902): "'Now, my dears,' said old Mrs. Rabbit one morning, 'you may go into the fields or down the lane, but don't go into Mr. McGregor's garden: your Father had an accident there; he was put in a pie by Mrs. McGregor.'"

Other Books by Beatrix Potter
The Tale of Benjamin Bunny (1904a); *The Tale of Flopsy Bunnies* (1909); *The Tale of Jemima Puddle-Duck* (1908); *The Tale of Mr. Jeremy Fisher* (1906); and *The Tale of Tom Kitten* (1904b).

Listening to literature read aloud is another way to support children's growing acquisition of syntactic structures and new words.

Other Books by William Steig
Abel's Island (1976); *Dominic* (1972)*; *The Real Thief* (1973); *Rotten Island* (1984); and *Sylvester and the Magic Pebble* (1969).*
*Also available in Spanish

Other Books by Natalie Babbitt
Bub, or the Very Best Thing (1994); *Tuck Everlasting* (1975); *Phoebe's Revolt* (1968); and *The Search for Delicious* (1969).

See Chapter 7, Teaching with Literature, for more on the Children's Choice awards.

More Books by Paul Goble
Beyond the Ridge (1989); *Death of an Iron Horse* (1987); *The Friendly Wolf* (1974); *Love Flute* (1992); and *I Sing for the Animals* (1991).

• ***Description:*** William Steig has a wonderful way with descriptive words in *Amos and Boris* (1971), a picture book about an improbable friendship between a mouse and a whale who learn to appreciate their differences. Amos, the mouse, is characterized by phrases like "quivering daintiness" and "gemlike radiance," and Boris, the whale, is described as having "abounding friendliness."

• ***Imagery:*** Natalie Babbitt is a master of the use of imagery in children's books. In her book *The Eyes of the Amaryllis* (1977), she describes the ocean at low tide, saying that "it sparkled in the early sunshine, flicking tiny, blinding flashes of light into the air." She characterizes a beautiful day as "a mermaid morning—a morning for sitting on the rocks and combing your long red hair."

• ***Similes:*** Children are aware of how authors use language. For example, in voting for *The Girl Who Loved Wild Horses* (Goble, 1978) to receive a Children's Choice award (given to children's favorite books each year), readers cited use of this simile to describe a herd of wild, running horses: "They swept like a brown flood across hills and through valleys."

Repeated Patterns

Many traditional rhymes, songs, and stories use sentence and story patterns that are repetitive and predictable. Exposing students to such patterns through listening and reading and then responding is a powerful means of promoting facility with different grammatical forms and uses of language.

Sentences Repeated in a Repeated Plot

A familiar example of sentences repeated in a repeated plot is the Scandinavian folktale "The Three Billy Goats Gruff." There are three billy goats in three different sizes, and each repeats the same dialogue in three encounters with a troll when he asks, "Who's that tripping over my bridge?" Marcia Brown's (1957) version of this tale is an excellent story for reading aloud and inviting children to join in on the repeated sentences. This is also a great story for dramatizing by young children.

An example of kindergartners dramatizing "The Three Billy Goats Gruff" is included in Chapter 4, Emergent Literacy. See also Chapter 10, Drama in the Classroom, for ideas about story dramatization.

See Chapter 4, Emergent Literacy, for more on repeated patterns in children's books.

Here's a list of children's books that have sentences repeated in a repeated plot:

A Dark, Dark Tale (Brown, 1981)
Do You Want to Be My Friend? (Carle, 1971)
Have You Seen My Duckling? (Tafuri, 1984)
I Went Walking (Williams, 1990)
The Little Red Hen (Galdone, 1973)
Sheep in a Jeep (Shaw, 1986)
The Three Bears (Galdone, 1972)
The Three Billy Goats Gruff (Brown, 1957)
The Three Little Pigs (Galdone, 1970)
Whose Mouse Are You? (Kraus, 1970)

Sentences Repeated in a Cumulative Plot

Other books use cumulative plots, in which characters, objects, and actions are introduced and then added to previous ones as the story unfolds. A classic example is the nursery rhyme "The House That Jack Built." Here's an adaptation written by first-graders:

This Is the School We Learn In
This is the school we learn in.
These are the children that go to the school we learn in.
This is the book that is read by the children that go to the school we learn in.

Here's a list of books with sentences repeated in a cumulative plot:

The Cake That Mack Ate (Robart, 1986)
Drummer Hoff (Emberley, 1967)
The Elephant and the Bad Baby (Vipoint, 1969)
The Fat Cat (Kent, 1971)
Four Fur Feet (Brown, 1989)
The Gingerbread Boy (Galdone, 1975)
The Little Old Lady Who Was Not Afraid of Anything (Williams, 1986)
The Napping House (Wood, 1984)
Rum Pum Pum (Duff, 1978)
This Is the Bear (Hayes, 1986)

Playing with Stories

Students learn about the form, structure, and conventions of sentences and stories by playing with them and making adaptations. Here are some ideas for playing with stories.

Old Tales, New Versions

A number of children's authors have rewritten familiar folk- and fairytales, using different words, characters, settings, or themes. Students can do this, too. To give them a model of the rewrite, read the familiar tale and then a new variation. The following list shows old tales presented in new versions:

Old Tales	***New Versions***
"Cinderella"	*Sidney Rella and the Glass Sneaker* (Myers, 1985)
	Prince Cinders (Cole, 1988).
"The Emperor's New Clothes"	*The Principal's New Clothes* (Calmenson, 1989)
"The Frog Prince"	*The Frog Prince Continued* (Scieszka, 1991)
"The Gingerbread Boy"	*Whiff, Sniff, Nibble, and Chew: The Gingerbread Boy Retold* (Pomerantz, 1984)
	Pondlarker (Gwynne, 1990)
"Jack and the Beanstalk"	*Jim and the Beanstalk* (Briggs, 1970)
	The Giant's Toe (Cole, 1986)

"Sleeping Beauty"	*Sleeping Ugly* (Yolen, 1981)
"Snow White"	*Snow White in New York* (French, 1988)
"The Three Bears"	*Somebody and the Three Blairs* (Tollhurst, 1990)
	Deep in the Forest (Turkle, 1976)
"The Three Little Pigs"	*The True Story of the Three Little Pigs* (Scieszka, 1989)

Mad Libs

Mad Libs are an adaptation of a commercial word game, consisting of a series of partially completed sentences in a story. Only one student sees the story, and he or she asks another student for a type of word to fill in a blank: a noun, verb, adjective, and so on. Since the student giving the word doesn't know what the story is about, the result is a nonsense adaptation of the original.

Students can write their own stories, make the deletions by inserting blanks with the names of the parts of speech written under them, and play Mad Libs with others. Here is an example written by a fifth-grader (bracketed inserts show where the blanks go):

> **Babies**
>
> Most [plural noun] think babies are cute. They are [adjective] if they don't belong to [pronoun]. If you live with one, you find they [verb] and [verb adverb] and when you [verb] them they smell [adjective]. I am just glad I don't have a [noun], because I think they are [adjective].

Story Frames

Even very young children understand and use conventional story structure, which includes elements like formal openings and closings and the past-tense voice. Children can brainstorm examples of these conventions and write them on separate file cards, which can be classified and kept in separate envelopes (e.g., for openings, characters, closings, etc.). Then, by choosing one card from each envelope and putting them all together, students create correctly constructed but nonsensical stories. The cards provide a *story frame:* something for the students to build on. Here are a few examples:

Openings
Once upon a time . . .
Long, long ago . . .
In a galaxy far, far away . . .

Characters
A poor woodcutter
A wicked queen
A young starfighter pilot

Problems
Didn't have enough food for his children
Hated the beautiful princess
Set out to discover his destiny

Closings
. . . and they lived happily ever after.
. . . and was never seen again.
. . . and saved the universe.

Story Sequence Puzzles

First-grade teacher Phyllis Crawford has used this technique. After a read-aloud story or storytelling session, students discuss the sequence of story events and dictate them to Phyllis. (This can also be done during a reading conference.) She then copies the dictated story on a piece of poster paper, and a child illustrates the other side with a scene from the story. Next, Phyllis cuts up the story into rectangles to form a puzzle. When the puzzle is assembled, the story will be in the correct sequence, and when it's flipped over, the picture will be correct, too.

SNAPSHOT: Revising and Editing Writing in a Fifth-Grade Writing Workshop

I visited Phyllis Fuglaar's class on another day and found Barbara, Faith, and Lillian in better spirits than during my first visit. And this time, I could trace the development of the whole story, which by now had gone through several weeks of revising and editing, session by session in writing workshop:

Session 1. Generating Topics: During the first of several sessions of writing a rebus story for kindergartners, Faith, Barbara, and Lillian talk, interact, doodle, draw, write, rewrite, and reject several topics, words, and names for characters (see their notes in Figure 11.2). Think about the process they're going through. They cross out many rejected ideas, combine other ideas, create new choices, and finally settle on a main idea: *Tommy finds stray cat; Tommy takes care of cat.*

Session 2. Expanding and Elaborating Ideas: During this session, the three girls revise as they write, making needed decisions yet leaving their options open (see Figure 11.3).

Session 3. Moving Sentences and Leaving Blanks for Future Ideas: Now, the girls begin to write a dialogue for their characters, rather than just a narrative of what's happening to them (as they did in Session 2). The girls are also moving whole sentences around within the text. When they're not sure where the story is going next, they leave a space and make a note to themselves about possible options for next time (see Figure 11.4).

Sessions 4 and 5. More Generating, Expanding, Combining, Changing, Moving, and Leaving Blanks: Session 4 is a period of intense writing, during which the girls pause and break when their ideas seem to stop. And Session 5 is another whole idea-generating period, during which they come up with a recipe for a magical mixture of bat's blood, flies, fingernails, toes, eyeballs, and water.

FIGURE 11.2
Session 1. Generating Topics

Session 6. Reconstruction: This is the session described in the first Snapshot: Faith and Barbara argue about grammar during writing workshop, while they try to reconstruct their draft.

Sessions 7 through 9. Reworking a Complete Draft: Barbara has found the missing notes and draft! Each girl works at home on the final draft, and then they work together at school to refine their ideas. They make changes, fill in blanks, change some more, and finally produce a final draft.

Session 10. Final Proofreading: The students check for spelling, grammar, and punctuation before publishing.

Sessions 11 and 12. Publishing the Story: During these two sessions, the girls plan their book, breaking it up into logical chunks for page breaks. Then they lay it out; copy it in large, neat print; and add illustrations and rebus symbols. The final step is binding the story into a book.

Tommy tan or beige
~~Joh~~ cat named Alexander
"When ~~girl~~/boy puts on tee shirt
a glowing cat appears ~~on shirt and finds out~~ and comes Cat back off shirt and starts
They
to take to ~~girl~~/~~boy john~~ ¶Alexander sa sent me here for help. We need a "human to
Tommy
tests
do ~~experioments~~ on, so that we can become more like humans ~~Because it~~ is lonely,
where ~~d~~
we live because there are very few of us."

FIGURE 11.3
Session 2. Expanding and Elaborating Ideas

"After several weeks of testing they ~~make an important~~ found
all
out ~~what~~ they needed to know "

fill blank space

Faith

~~stray cats~~
humans become successful LAST
something else

suggestions

FIGURE 11.4
Session 3. Moving Sentences and Leaving Blanks for Future Ideas

Session 13. Sharing Published Writing: The three young authors read their book to all the kindergarten classes in the school and present it to the kindergarten teachers to place in their class library.

This Snapshot illustrates why students need time and opportunities to write and talk when learning to use written language conventions. This time for talking and revising and editing writing isn't practice for learning how to master language usage; it's actually language in use.

Understanding Writing, Language Conventions, and Meaning

The two Snapshots in this chapter make several important points about teaching writing, language conventions and use, and meaning:

1. ***Writing is recursive, not step-by-step:*** The girls don't follow a simple step-by-step process of producing an idea, writing a draft, and then correcting it for spelling, punctuation, and grammar. We can see how recursive the writing process really is, as they move back and forth throughout the writing process. We can also see how writing is supported by talking, interacting, and having plenty of time to do it. Thirteen sessions weren't too many.

2. ***Language conventions are learned through language use:*** These students' intuitive and underlying knowledge of grammar is what enabled them to express their ideas. What's more, their ideas developed through use. The girls needed time and opportunities to generate ideas, change, elaborate, leave blanks, choose, and play with ideas, words, and sentences. Teachers need to let children know that more ideas are better than few and that they always have options. These are all things that expert users of language do. Teachers should help students realize that they have the power to do these things themselves. They know their language and know how to use it.

3. ***The purpose of language should always be meaning:*** What's most important in this example was the children's drive to create meaning, because that determined the relative importance of written language conventions at each stage of revising. The girls did care about conventions, and so did their teacher. But they cared about them primarily at the point when they became important to the *meaning* of the story—that is, when it was time to share the draft with another writer and, most of all, when they prepared to publish their writing for an audience of kindergartners.

Assessing Language Conventions

Writing portfolios are described in Chapter 10, The Writing Process.

In addition to writing portfolios, much of your assessment will take place during informal observations. Here is a set of questions to consider as you observe children's use of language conventions: grammar, talking, and writing (Lilja, 1980):

1. ***Awareness:*** Does the child demonstrate his or her awareness of language as a method of communication that's used for specific purposes tied to meaning?

2. ***Spontaneous use:*** Does the child demonstrate his or her security with language use by being spontaneous and freely participating in language activities? (Eager hand raising and loud sounds of "Ooh-ooh-ooh, Teacher!" demonstrate this.)

3. ***Nonverbal signs or body language:*** Does the child rely on signals (e.g., pointing, head movements, hand symbols) rather than words to communicate meaning?

4. ***"Baby talk":*** Does the child use obvious "baby talk" in his or her speech patterns, word choices, pronunciation, or sentence structure?

5. ***Thought holders:*** Does the child use substitutes for words (e.g., "uh-huh," "uh-uh," "hmmm") to the point that his or her communication is greatly limited?

6. *Word choice:* Does the child demonstrate that he or she has an ample vocabulary to communicate meaningfully with others and to express ideas clearly? For instance, does he or she use a variety of words and know synonyms for them? Is he or she curious about new words and eager to acquire and use them? Does he or she experiment and play with words?

7. *Sentence patterns:* Is the child able to communicate his or her ideas in appropriate and varied sentence patterns (e.g., questions, negations, exclamations, and sentences with varied word order)?

8. *Thought:* Is the child able to communicate his or her ideas effectively in talking and writing?

Answers to Questions about Language Conventions

1. *What is* grammar?

To different people, *grammar* means sentence structure, usage, description, process, and a set of rules. Historically, teaching grammar has been considered essential because doing so supposedly helps students learn how to use language, conduct an investigative approach, learn a second language, and speak and write in a more socially prestigious way. Even though research over the years has failed to support these reasons for teaching grammar, many educators persist in doing so, for several reasons: Grammar has a long tradition, is viewed as a basic skill, is integral to many textbooks, and is easy to test.

There are three types of grammar: (a) *traditional,* a prescriptive grammar dating back to medieval times; (b) *structural,* an attempt to describe differences among languages; and (c) *transformational,* an attempt to explain the relationship between language and meaning. Current social constructivist and child development theory and research suggests that children learn language and its conventions by using them. Communicating meaning is the purpose of language use.

2. *How should language conventions such as grammar be taught in student- and response-centered classrooms?*

Language conventions such as grammar can be learned through talking and writing in meaningful contexts, in which language is used for real purposes. Teachers can help students develop awareness of the form and structure of language in several ways: talking and interacting while working in groups, settling conflicts and holding class court, debating, and role-playing in curriculum drama. Students can play with words and sentences, through classification, forming patterns, and combining sentences. Children's literature is an excellent model for language use; students should be encouraged to play with the forms and structures of stories. During revising and editing writing is when students apply their underlying knowledge of grammar. Children learn to use language by using it. Teachers must keep in mind, however, that the purpose of all these experiences should be to communicate meaning.

LOOKING FURTHER

1. Examine a language arts textbook. How does it approach teaching grammar? What type or types of grammar does it reflect? What do you think of the approach?
2. Create a pattern based on the functions of words, or find a pattern in literature that does the same thing. Try it out with children, if possible.
3. Start a file of books that you feel are outstanding examples of how words can be used in literature. Create your own classification, including categories like interesting sentence structure, description, figurative language, and imagery.
4. Pick a traditional story you like and rewrite it, changing characters, setting, mood, or theme.
5. Observe children revising their writing while working in groups. Note how they use their underlying knowledge of language.
6. Observe a child and assess his or her language use according to the guidelines listed in the Assessment section of the chapter (see pp. 414–415).

RESOURCES

Geller, L. G. (1985). *Word play and language learning for children.* Urbana, IL: National Council of Teachers of English.

Richard-Amato, P. (1988). *Making it happen: Interaction in the second language classroom.* New York: Longman.

REFERENCES

Applebee, A., Langer, J., & Mullis, I. (1987). *Grammar, punctuation, and spelling: Controlling the conventions of written English at ages 9, 13, 17.* Princeton, NJ: Educational Testing Service.

Braddock, R., Lloyd-Jones, R., & Schoer, L. (1963). *Research in written composition.* Urbana, IL: National Council of Teachers of English.

Chomsky, C. (1972). Stages in language development and reading exposure. *Harvard Educational Review, 42,* 1–33.

Chomsky, C. (1980). Developing facility with language structure. In G. S. Pinnell (Ed.), *Discovering language with children.* Urbana, IL: National Council of Teachers of English.

Chomsky, N. (1957). *Syntactic structures.* The Hague, The Netherlands: Mouton.

Geller, L. G. (1985). *Word play and language learning for children.* Urbana, IL: National Council of Teachers of English.

Heath, S. B. (1983). *Ways with words.* Cambridge, England: Cambridge University Press.

Hillocks, G., & Smith, M. W. (1991). Grammar and usage. In J. Flood, J. M. Jensen, D. Lapp, & J. R. Squire (Eds.), *Handbook of research on teaching the English language arts* (pp. 591–603). New York: Macmillan.

Hunt, K. (1965). *Grammatical structures written at three grade levels.* Urbana, IL: National Council of Teachers of English.

Krashen, S. D. (1981). Bilingual education and second language acquisition theory. In *Schooling and language minority children: A theoretical framework.* Los Angeles: California State University.

Krashen, S. D., & Terrell, T. D. (1987). *The natural approach: Language acquisition in the classroom.* Englewood Cliffs, NJ: Prentice-Hall.

Labov, W. (1972). *Language in the inner city: Studies in the Black English vernacular.* Philadelphia: University of Pennsylvania Press.

Lesiak, J. (1978). The origin of words: A unit of study. *Language Arts, 55,* 317–319.

Lilja, L. D. (1980). Measuring the effectiveness of language education. In G. S. Pinnell (Ed.), *Discovering language with children* (pp. 105–108). Urbana, IL: National Council of Teachers of English.

Mellon, J. (1969). *Transformational sentence combining: A method for enhancing the development of syntactic fluency in English composition.* Urbana, IL: National Council of Teachers of English.

O'Hare, F. (1973). *Sentence-combining: Improving student writing without formal grammar instruction.* Urbana, IL: National Council of Teachers of English.

Richard-Amato, P. (1988). *Making it happen: Interaction in the second language classroom.* New York: Longman.

Straw, S. (1994). Teaching of grammar. In A. Purves (Ed.), *Encyclopedia of English studies and language arts* (Vol. 1, pp. 534–538). New York: Scholastic.

Strickland, R. G. (1962). The language of elementary school children: Its relationship to the language of reading textbooks and the quality of reading of selected children. *Bulletin of the School of Education, Indiana University, 38*(4).

Strong, W. (1986). *Creative approaches to sentence combining.* Urbana, IL: National Council of Teachers of English.

von Bracht Donsky, B. (1984). Trends in elementary writing instruction. *Language Arts, 61,* 795–803.

Weaver, C. (1979). *Grammar for teachers: Perspectives and definitions.* Urbana, IL: National Council of Teachers of English.

CHILDREN'S BOOKS

Arnosky, J. (1990). *A kettle of hawks and other wildlife groups.* New York: Lothrop, Lee & Shepard.

Babbitt, N. (1968). *Phoebe's revolt.* New York: Farrar, Straus, & Giroux.

Babbitt, N. (1969). *The search for delicious.* New York: Farrar, Straus, & Giroux.

Babbitt, N. (1975). *Tuck everlasting.* New York: Farrar, Straus, & Giroux.

Babbitt, N. (1977). *The eyes of the amaryllis.* New York: Farrar, Straus & Giroux.

Babbitt, N. (1994). *Bub, or the very best thing.* New York: HarperCollins.

Barrett, J. (1983). *A snake is totally tail.* New York: Atheneum.

Base, G. (1987). *Animalia.* New York: Harry N. Abrams.

Briggs, R. (1970). *Jim and the beanstalk.* New York: Coward McCann.

Brown, M. (1957). *The three billy goats gruff.* New York: Harcourt Brace Jovanovich.

Brown, M. (1989). *Four fur feet.* New York: Watermark.

Brown, R. (1981). *A dark, dark tale.* New York: Dial.

Calmenson, S. (1989). *The principal's new clothes.* New York: Scholastic.

Carle, E. (1971). *Do you want to be my friend?* New York: Harper & Row.

Cole, B. (1986). *The giant's toe.* New York: Farrar, Straus & Giroux.

Cole, B. (1988). *Prince Cinders.* New York: Putnam's.

Duff, M. (1978). *Rum pum pum.* New York: Macmillan.

Emberley, B. (1967). *Drummer Hoff.* New York: Prentice-Hall.

French, F. (1986). *Snow White in New York.* New York: Oxford University Press.

Galdone, P. (1970). *The three little pigs.* New York: Clarion.

Galdone, P. (1972). *The three bears.* New York: Clarion.

Galdone, P. (1973). *The little red hen.* New York: Clarion.

Galdone, P. (1975). *The gingerbread boy.* New York: Seabury.

Goble, P. (1974). *The friendly wolf.* New York: Bradbury.

Goble, P. (1978). *The girl who loved wild horses.* New York: Bradbury.

Goble, P. (1987). *Death of an iron horse.* New York: Bradbury.

Goble, P. (1989). *Beyond the ridge.* New York: Bradbury.

Goble, P. (1991). *I sing for the animals.* New York: Bradbury.

Goble, P. (1992). *Love flute.* New York: Bradbury.

Gomi, T. (1994). *Seeing, saying, doing, playing: A big book of action words.* San Francisco: Chronicle Books.

Gwynne, F. (1990). *Pondlarker.* New York: Simon & Schuster.

Hayes, S. (1986). *This is the bear.* New York: Lippincott.

Heller, R. (1987). *A cache of jewels and other collective nouns.* New York: Grosset & Dunlap.

Heller, R. (1988). *Kites sail high: A book about verbs.* New York: Scholastic.

Heller, R. (1989). *Many luscious lollipops: A book about adjectives.* New York: Grosset & Dunlap.

Heller, R. (1990). *Merry-go-round: A book about nouns.* New York: Grosset & Dunlap.

Heller, R. (1991). *Up, up and away: A book about adverbs.* New York: Grosset & Dunlap.

Hoban, T. (1973). *Over, under, and through and other spatial concepts.* New York: Macmillan.

Hoban, T. (1975). *Dig, drill, dump, fill.* New York: Greenwillow.

Hutchins, P. (1968). *Rosie's walk.* New York: Macmillan.

Joyce, W. (1986). *George shrinks.* New York: Harper & Row.

Kellogg, S. (1987). *Aster Aardvarks alphabet adventures.* New York: Morrow.

Kent, J. (1971). *The fat cat.* New York: Parent's.

Kraus, R. (1970). *Whose mouse are you?* New York: Macmillan.

Lionni, L. (1967). *Frederick.* New York: Pantheon.

MacCarthy, P. (1991). *Herds of words.* New York: Dial.

McMillan, B. (1984). *Kitten can . . .* New York: Lothrop, Lee & Shepard.

McMillan, B. (1989). *Super, super, superwords.* New York: Lothrop, Lee & Shepard.

Myers, B. (1985). *Sidney Rella and the glass sneaker.* New York: Macmillan.

Pomerantz, C. (1984). *Whiff, sniff, nibble, and chew: The gingerbread boy retold.* New York: Greenwillow.

Potter, B. (1902). *The tale of Peter Rabbit.* London, England: Warne.

Potter, B. (1904a). *The tale of Benjamin Bunny.* London, England: Warne.

Potter, B. (1904b). *The tale of Tom Kitten.* London, England: Warne.

Potter, B. (1906). *The tale of Mr. Jeremy Fisher.* London, England: Warne.

Potter, B. (1908). *The tale of Jemima Puddle-Duck.* London, England: Warne.

Potter, B. (1909). *The tale of Flopsy Bunnies.* London, England: Warne.

Robart, R. (1986). *The cake that Mack ate.* New York: Little, Brown.

Scieszka, J. (1989). *The true story of the three little pigs.* New York: Viking.

Scieszka, J. (1991). *The frog prince continued.* New York: Viking.

Shaw, N. (1986). *Sheep in a jeep.* New York: Houghton Mifflin.

Steig, W. (1969). *Sylvester and the magic pebble.* New York: Farrar, Straus, & Giroux.

Steig, W. (1971). *Amos and Boris.* New York: Farrar, Straus, & Giroux.

Steig, W. (1972). *Dominic.* New York: Farrar, Straus, & Giroux.

Steig, W. (1973). *The real thief.* New York: Farrar, Straus, & Giroux.

Steig, W. (1976). *Abel's island.* New York: Farrar, Straus, & Giroux.

Steig, W. (1984). *Rotten island.* New York: Godine.

Tafuri, N. (1984). *Have you seen my duckling?* New York: Greenwillow.

Terban, M. (1984). *I think I thought and other tricky verbs.* New York: Clarion.

Terban, M. (1986). *Your foot's on my feet! and other tricky nouns.* New York: Clarion Books.

Tollhurst, M. (1990). *Somebody and the three blairs.* New York: Orchard.

Turkle, B. (1976). *Deep in the forest.* New York: Dutton.

Vipoint, E. (1969). *The elephant and the bad baby.* New York: Coward McCann.

Williams, L. (1986). *The little old lady who was not afraid of anything.* New York: Harper.

Williams, S. (1990). *I went walking.* New York: Harcourt Brace Jovanovich.

Wood, A. (1984). *The napping house.* New York: Harcourt Brace Jovanovich.

Yolen, J. (1981). *Sleeping ugly.* New York: Putnam.

Chapter 12

Language Conventions

Spelling, Punctuation, and Handwriting

Questions about Language Conventions

1. *How do children learn the language conventions of spelling, punctuation, and handwriting?*
2. *What are effective ways to teach spelling, punctuation, and handwriting?*

Reflective Response

How do you think you learned spelling, punctuation, and handwriting? Think back to the how you were taught these language conventions in school. If you can remember things that you definitely would or would not do when you're a teacher, write them down, too.

SNAPSHOT: A Fourth-Grade Peer-Editing Group in Writing Workshop

See Chapter 9, The Writing Process, for how to do writing workshop.

Children learn to use the language conventions of spelling, punctuation, and handwriting as a part of the writing process. Here's an example of how this can happen.

Five children are editing and revising writing in a fourth-grade writing workshop peer-editing group. Robert is the student author who's going to read his story, "Mystery of the Witch and Warlock Continues," which is written in a journalistic style for a fictional class newspaper on Halloween. He's new to the class, so Nathan explains to him how editing works in their class. After Robert reads, the other students respond to his writing and make suggestions. (The marginal notes indicate what steps in the writing process and what language conventions are being used and learned.)

Robert, a fourth-grade student author, edits his story "Mystery of the Witch and Warlock" with the help of a peer-editing group during writing workshop.

Explaining Editing in a Writing Workshop

Nathan: Robert, editing means to look through it and see if there's any mistakes, and revising is like changing the words to make it easier to understand. Editing

Robert: It's not going to be the final copy?

Nathan: No.

Robert: After we revise it, do we rewrite it again? Revising

Nathan: Yeah.

Author Reads in a Peer-Editing Group: Robert prefaces his reading by explaining, "This is like a newspaper story about what might happen at Halloween." Then he reads his story: Author reads

Mystery of Witch and Warlock Continues

In Baton Rouge, on the 31st of October which is Halloween, Robert Troll said he saw an evil witch and warlock on a magic broomstick. "It was a scary sight," he said. Robert says that at 8:00 at night while he was taking his son and daughter trick-or-treating he saw the witch and warlock. "My children thought it was scary," says Robert Troll. It was a full moon when the witch and warlock came. They made a scary laughing sound and flew away. His wife said that she had seem something fly up in the sky and she . . . (pause) . . . outside to look at it . . . (pause) . . . outside to see it better but she couldn't see anything. When she came inside it looked like her house had been robbed. "My diamond ring and necklace has been stolen," she screamed. Every Halloween people look outside to see what this flying object is and something gets stolen. Only the most valuable stuff gets stolen. So if you see a flying object do not look outside 'cause if you do something will get stolen.

Peer Editors Respond to the Author: After Robert finishes reading, the other students make suggestions for editing and revising his story, and Robert asks them questions. Peers edit

Melissa: *Evil.* I don't think that word should be there. Maybe you could find a better word to describe them. Word choice

Robert: Or maybe I should leave *evil* out?

Melissa: That might sound better.

Jason: Why don't you put *jewelry* instead of *stuff?* It sounds kinda . . . babyish or something.

Robert: OK. Let's see (looking at story). *Jewelry.* Should I put "'Only the most valuable *jewelry*" or "Her most valuable *jewelry*"? How do you spell *jewelry?* Sentence structure

Melissa: J-E-W-E-L-R-Y. Spelling

Kim (looking at the story): I think you need to indent here to make another paragraph. Paragraph

Melissa: He could give a name to the son and daughter. It could be anybody. You know, it's sorta . . .

Kim: How about using adjectives to describe them? Or grades in school? Or specific age?

Descriptive words

Melissa: Like *evil.* It describes witch.

Robert: OK. How about "His fourth-grade son and baby daughter?"

Punctuation

Jason (looking at story): You need a comma in the middle there. This sorta looks like a period or something.

Handwriting

Robert: Well, it shouldn't. I'll write it neater.

Meaning

Kim: I couldn't really understand the part about his wife. But it's good. It's a good story.

Peer-Editing Group at Work: The students in this fourth-grade peer-editing group continue to discuss all aspects of the story: meaning, word choice, sentence structure, style (it's supposed to be a newspaper article), spelling, punctuation, and handwriting. Their discussion shows that they're aware of the language conventions of spelling, punctuation, and handwriting and know how to apply them when getting a piece of writing ready to publish. These language conventions become important and meaningful when students are writing to communicate to a real audience.

The other peer-editing group members—Nathan, Melissa, Kim, and Jason—all shared their pieces in the same way that Robert did. With the editing and revising advice they received from each other, they spent the next day in writing workshop, rewriting their pieces.

Controlling the Conventions of Written English

The children in the Snapshot demonstrate how students are capable of controlling the conventions of spelling, punctuation, and handwriting when they need to make their meaning clear and communicate effectively through writing for real purposes. Most certainly, these conventions are important. Both the educational community and the general public view correct spelling and punctuation and legible handwriting as characteristics of an educated person.

How well do U.S. students control the conventions of written English? Results of analyses of the writing of 9-, 13-, and 17-year-old students in *The Nation's Report Card* were encouraging (Applebee, Langer, & Mullis, 1987). They showed that "even though American schoolchildren have difficulty organizing and expressing their ideas in a thoughtful manner, they have reasonable control over the conventions of grammar, punctuation, and spelling" (p. 6). Here's a summary of the report's other findings:

1. Students learn to control the conventions of written English.
2. Older students are more proficient than younger ones at both sentence and word levels; likewise, older students use more complex sentences and fewer fragments and run-ons.
3. Spelling improves significantly as children grow older.
4. Students make few errors in word choice and capitalization.

5. Students make very few punctuation errors.
6. There is no consistent profile of a poor writer.

Given these findings, the report makes these recommendations:

> *Students are learning the conventions that they need for writing. . . . However, . . . learning writing conventions is an individual process, with particular skills being learned and practiced by particular children at particular times. . . . Hence, asking an entire class to focus on a particular convention of written English seems unnecessary, even inappropriate. Instead, instruction may be more effective if it treats students as individual language learners, with the teacher relying on each student's own written papers for information about what that student knows and is in the midst of learning.* (p. 45)

Writing versus Skills Approaches

Recall the Snapshot and you can see these recommendations being applied. In the peer-editing group, each student's paper was read and discussed for ideas, organization, and the conventions of spelling, punctuation, sentence structure, word choice, and handwriting. The teacher in this class believes that children learn to write by writing and to control written conventions through editing and revising their own papers. Thus, the time to focus on correcting conventions is during the stages of editing and revising. When students reach these stages, they will inevitably focus on style and conventions in order to make their meaning clear. Again, the purpose of writing is to create and communicate meaning.

The Teacher's Role

The teacher provides students with time to write (as in writing workshop), does minilessons on language conventions, plans teacher- and peer-editing conferences, and offers publishing opportunities. As has been emphasized in other chapters, it's vital that children have a lot of time and opportunities to write.

Another significant part of the teacher's role is to accept and support children's early drawing and scribbling, invented spelling, and attempts at punctuation, all of which are part of developing as writers. The teacher should encourage them just to try—to put down a letter or picture for a word or to leave a blank for a word they can't spell. The teacher should also assure students that they can edit and revise along the way with plenty of help from others.

Keep in mind that children often dislike writing because they're afraid of being criticized for mistakes in spelling, punctuation, and handwriting. Some will only write words they know how to spell or that they can copy from wall charts, books, or other children's papers. Consider how these practices severely limit children's attempts to write authentically, using their own voices and expressing their own ideas.

See Chapter 9, The Writing Process, for a description of writing workshop, including ways to teach language conventions.

Children also often spend much of their time in diversionary tactics during writing because they fear censure for less than conventional practices. For example, they may stop every time they can't spell a word and hold their hands in the air, waiting for the teacher to tell them how to spell it without attempting to do so themselves. Or they may erase the word they really want to use and ask how to spell another. Some students may crumple and throw away the telltale evidence of what they think is chronic illegible handwriting. They may think that the first draft must look like the final copy because teachers have insisted throughout the writing process that spelling, punctuation, and neatness are more important than meaning. Some teachers are so single minded about these topics that their students come to believe that revision means fixing errors, rather than making changes that affect meaning and communication.

This isn't to suggest that correct spelling and punctuation and legibility are not important. Of course they are. But few writers show the world their first drafts or their notes. So the eventual reader doesn't know if the writer had to look up a word to check its spelling or whether someone else edited the draft for punctuation. Authors spend much time revising before anyone sees their work. Moreover, most adults write in private, so few others can witness the errors they make as they go through the stages of writing. But when children write in school, they have an audience—their teachers and classmates—from the start of every piece. Both teachers and students should realize that the beginnings of writing do not represent the final product. Notes, drafts, and revisions are meant to be messy and subject to change.

Given enough time and encouragement from their teachers and peers (as well as a real reason to make their message clear), children will move toward correct written language conventions. Few of them would want their writing put up on a bulletin board or published in a class newspaper if it were full of mistakes. Their awareness of audience and their urge to publish are the greatest incentives to make their writing accurate and understandable. When children have real reasons to write and real audiences to write for, the teacher becomes their collaborator and publisher, rather than merely that person with the punitive red pen.

The following list summarizes ideas about the role of the teacher and offers suggestions to students, as well:

Teachers	***Students***
Encourage all kinds of writing, all the time.	Get your ideas down on paper, even if they're incomplete, messy, or misspelled or lack conventional form.
Accept and encourage invented spelling; learn the stages of spelling development.	Remember that you can have writing without correct conventions, but you can't have correct conventions without writing.
Remember that legibility is what's important for handwriting, and handwriting is important for writing.	
Some writing *doesn't* need editing: journals, notes, idea lists, clusters, outlines, first drafts, informal letters.	Writing does always happen in a straight line; if you can't finish a thought or spell a word, leave a blank and go on.

Some writing *does* need editing: stories for publication, reports, formal letters, newspaper articles, scripts that others need to read.
Model correct writing conventions through minilessons, writing on the board or overhead projector, class charts and posters, and published writing.
Focus on the needs of individual children.
Take into account the developmental level of each child.

Keep the flow of ideas going.
Be confident and enjoy writing. Write for yourself as well as others, using your own voice.
Don't expect a perfect paper the first (one, two, three . . .) times.
Don't apologize for what you've written.
Be proud of what you like about your writing.

Organizing the Teaching of Language Conventions

How do teachers know what and when to teach language conventions if students spend most of their time writing, as in writing workshops? It depends on the grade and developmental level of the students. The best guideline is to teach the skills students need when they need them, but always provide opportunities for students to apply skills in writing. Here are several approaches to teaching conventions:

1. ***Teaching One Skill to the Whole Class:*** Do this either with a skill that should be introduced to the whole class or one that almost everyone is struggling with. Discuss the skill with the class, take volunteers to talk about it in their writing, and do a minilesson for everyone.

2. ***Teaching One Skill to a Small Group:*** Do this when only some students need help, refinement, or special instruction in a skill. For example, if a group is writing a playscript, that would be a good time to talk about quotation marks with them.

3. ***Teacher Conferences:*** The bulk of the teacher's time will focus on assessing individual children's needs and will take place in conferences. Students will master the conventions of writing when they have a real need to get them right—for example, if they're writing a newspaper article that will be published. Conventions gain importance as children develop audience awareness. Thus, the focus of teacher conferences should move from content to editing, as described by teacher Mary Ellen Giacobbe:

- *Content Conference:* I assume the role of learner and by careful listening encourage the writer to teach me about the topic. Once it is established what the writer knows, I ask general questions to help the writer to discover he or she knows even more: "Gee, I didn't know about . . . Could you tell me more about . . . ?" After expanding the topic, I ask questions to help the writer focus.
- *Editing Conference:* When the content is as the writer intends it to be, the child is taught one skill in the context of his writing. For instance, if there is a lot of dialogue in a particular story, I might teach the child

> how to use quotation marks. If the child uses that skill in the next piece of writing, I ask about the usage, and the child decides if it should be added to the list of skills he or she is responsible for during the editing stage of future writing. (Cordeiro, Giacobbe & Cazden, 1983, p. 324)

4. ***Peer-Editing Groups:*** As described in the Snapshot, children meet in groups to edit each other's work.

5. ***Self-Editing:*** Post a list of questions children can ask themselves as they revise and edit their work (which can also be used by peer-editing groups):

Did I start each sentence with a capital?
Did I capitalize the names of people and places?
Did I punctuate the end of each sentence?
Did I use punctuation in other appropriate places?
Did I use quotation marks when someone was talking?
Did I spell correctly or check spelling I wasn't sure about?
Did I indent paragraphs?
Did I use my best handwriting?

Commercial Programs

Commercial programs with textbooks, teacher's guides, and student workbooks have traditionally been used to teach written language conventions. They're easy for teachers to use because decisions about what to teach have been made for them. Frequently, students don't even need teachers' help; they can read a chapter or unit and do the practice exercises on their own.

One type of commercial program teaches spelling. Spelling books are usually divided into units, with lists of words and practice exercises related to particular spelling rules. In the past, the rationale given for using these books was that controlled lists of graded words and direct instruction of rules are necessary for children to learn to spell. However, in an analysis of basal spelling programs, Graves (1977b) showed that students learn the most words from exercises when they apply them in writing. This finding raised serious questions about the real usefulness of spelling books. Graves also found that:

1. Texts used a variety of approaches, with no clear patterns of organization or systematic use of high-frequency words.
2. A test-corrected-test method, involving no formal study with a book, accounted for 95 percent of achievement when compared to the results obtained using a spelling book exercise practice and test-study method.
3. Children spelled better in response-meaning and word study exercises in writing than in exercises on homophones, affixes and inflectional endings, silent letters, initial consonants and blends, vowels, and phonics.

Language arts textbooks have been used to teach grammar, punctuation, and writing. But once again, Graves (1977a) found they did not reflect what research on the writing process tells us about how children learn to write:

1. Texts focused on isolated drills of skills (mainly grammar and punctuation), which increased as students got older.
2. Instruction in writing comprised of the teacher suggesting a writing genre (e.g., prose or poetry), the amount of writing to be done (e.g., a sentence or paragraph), and the topic to write on.

Using spelling books and language arts textbooks to teach writing and written language conventions goes against what research and even common sense tells us about the writing process:

- That children can and will choose their own topics for writing
- That they need time to generate ideas and rehearse and plan for writing through talking, drawing, dramatizing, and the like
- That they can and will write and rewrite many drafts with the help of the teacher and peers through conferences and editing groups
- That the focus on conventions is most appropriate in the final editing stage, when children have a real need to create a correct copy of their work to share with others

The English Writing System

In order to understand written language conventions, teachers should know something about the origins and characteristics of the English writing system. The language conventions of spelling, punctuation, and handwriting represent the rather monumental efforts of literate humans to put the living sounds of language into the symbols of print. Writing first emerged from early people's efforts to record their experiences and leave messages for others; they drew on the walls of caves and carved marks in stone. Later, these pictures and marks became symbols, such as the pictograms of prehistoric cultures and the hieroglyphics of the Ancient Egyptians. Different cultures developed different forms of recording spoken language in writing.

These writing systems, or *orthographies,* have evolved over time. An *orthography* is a code that consists of a set of graphemes (written symbols that stand for a word, syllable, or speech sound in a language). There are several types of orthographies: *logographic,* or word writing, such as Chinese; *syllabic,* or syllable writing, such as Japanese; and *alphabetic,* or sound-to-letter writing, such as English. When we know how to spell, we know how to produce these graphics correctly and we know what they mean.

Many graphemes can represent single phonemes (e.g., the long *a* sound in *way, weigh, wait, fate, ballet, fiancee, lady*), and many phonemes can represent single graphemes (e.g., the *o* in *one, do, dot, open, oven, women*).

Irregularities in English

The most widespread type of writing is alphabetic. The alphabet used for English derives from the Ancient Hebrew, Greek, and Roman languages. Some alphabetic codes—such as Finnish, Turkish, and Spanish—have a one-to-one correspondence between sounds and letters. English, however, has a many-to-many correspondence. More specifically, English has over 40 speech sounds but only 26 letters in the alphabet to represent them. One, two, or more of these letters may function as graphemes—for example, the *-gh* in *laugh,* which represents the phoneme /f/.

Language Changes

Why does English have a many-to-many correspondence, which often makes it highly irregular? The answer lies in a basic characteristic of language: that it changes. Some types of change have made great differences in how English is spoken and written:

The transition from Old to Middle English rendered the *k* sound silent when it preceded a consonant at the beginning of a word, but the grapheme *k* remained in the orthography, resulting in irregular spellings like *knife* and *knight*.

1. ***Sound Changes:*** The pronunciations of sounds and words have changed over the centuries, but their spellings have not always changed accordingly.

2. ***Borrowed Word Changes:*** Many invasions and occupations of the British Isles (notably, by the Romans, the Danes, and the Norman French) as well as British exploration and colonization around the world have made English the "borrowingest" language in the world. Numerous words from other languages have been added to English without changing their spellings. Table 12.1 shows some notable examples.

3. ***Etymological Changes:*** An example of this type of change comes from the influence of classical studies during the Renaissance. Writers of that era wanted to give classical languages a rebirth, so they resurrected some Latin spellings. Many of these spellings reinstated voiced letters that had been deleted in the French pronunciations from which the English words were derived.

TABLE 12.1 Words Added to English from Other Languages

Native American	***French***	***Spanish***	***German***	***Hindu***
raccoon	ballet	mesa	kindergarten	pajama
squash	restaurant	macho	sauerkraut	gymkhana
Norse	***Latin***	***Greek***	***Chinese***	***Japanese***
knife	exit	atomic	tea	kimono
hut	fan	drama	mandarin	typhoon
Arabic	***Russian***	***Italian***	***Iranian***	***Dutch***
algebra	sputnik	umbrella	shawl	wagon
zero	glasnost	piano	sandal	yacht
Hebrew	***Gaelic***	***Portuguese***	***Malay***	***Inuit***
camel	slogan	banana	gingham	kayak
cinnamon	clan	molasses	ketchup	

Learning about the complex orthography of English not only provides a fascinating history lesson; it also suggests the importance of learning about the relationship between words and meaning, rather than simply writing single words in isolation. And although English may seem highly irregular to anyone learning to spell it, the most common words in English have regular spellings about 80 percent of the time (Hanna, Hanna, Hodges, & Rudorf, 1966). What's most important to remember about spelling, punctuation, and handwriting is that they are graphic representations for writing. And writing is for constructing and communicating meaning.

Spelling

Learning to spell is a constructive developmental process, like learning to speak. Children move from the simple to the more complex, making increasingly sophisticated approximations of correct spelling. Individual children seem to move through the same sequence of stages in learning to spell, regardless of when they begin to write. Moreover, they intuitively know a great deal about English orthography, which they use as a foundation in creating a hierarchy of concepts that guide their initial spelling efforts.

See Chapter 4, Emergent Literacy, to review Charles Read's research on the development of young children's spelling and the description of early stages of spelling.

Invented Spelling

Recall from Chapter 4 the discussion of Charles Read (1971, 1975, 1986), who looked at the way children 4 to 8 years old used their knowledge of phonology (i.e., how words sound) to spell. Preschool children were able to name the letters of the alphabet and relate the letter names to the sounds of words. Then

Teachers should encourage students' invented spelling, as they focus on ideas and meaning in writing.

they "invented" spellings for words. Read found that even very young children could do this, and even though they misspelled most words, they tended to misspell them in the same ways. There was a logic to their system of invented spelling. For example, they spelled the sounds of words with the letters that were like those sounds: *BOT* for *BOAT, FAS* for *FACE, LADE* for *LADY.*

Three important ideas were demonstrated by Read's research:

1. Children are trying to make sense of spelling, applying their intuitive knowledge of the sounds of English to writing words.
2. Their understanding of the relationship between sound and writing is qualitatively different than that of adults. Thus, learning to spell and write, like learning to speak, is a developmental process.
3. The spelling errors young children make tell us about the developmental stages of their mental processes.

See Chapter 4, Emergent Literacy, for more on invented spelling.

Stages of Spelling Development

See Table 4.2, Stages of Spelling Development.

Also recall from Chapter 4 the description of how young children begin to hypothesize about spelling based on their knowledge of spoken English. The focus there was on young children, including examples of three first-grade students who were all writing but at different stages of spelling development. The following sections describe these stages for school-age children, kindergarten through middle school. These stages have been described by various researchers (Beers & Beers, 1981, summarizing Beers & Henderson, 1977; Gentry, 1981; Henderson, 1980; Henderson & Templeton, 1986; Read, 1971, 1975, 1986; Templeton, 1979; Zutell, 1979), and I have used the different names they have given to these stages. Each stage is illustrated with a spelling of the word *MONSTER* (Gentry, 1981) and an example from my daughter Elizabeth, who is now in the fifth grade:

Elizabeth writing using invented spelling at age 2

1. *Preliterate Stage (Preschool):* This stage is also called *precommunicative and prephonetic*. Children in it are aware of the purposes of writing but lack the concept of *word* and that words can be divided into *phonemes*. At first, children use scribbles, letterlike forms, and alphabet symbols to represent words. But because they don't know what sounds match the symbols, their writing isn't readable (see Figure 12.1). A child in the preliterate stage spelled *MONSTER* as *btBpA*.

2. *Semiphonetic Stage (Kindergarten through the Beginning of First Grade):* This stage is also called *prephonetic*. Children at this stage understand that letters represent sounds in words. They begin to use letter name spellings to make the association between letters and sounds, making closer approximations to true spelling but omitting major sounds (see Figure 12.2). They also make associations with letters and sounds that are alike. They may use only one or two letters to represent a word (e.g., *D* or *DJ* = *DOG* or *K* or *KDE* = *CANDY*). A child in the semiphonetic stage spelled *MONSTER* as *MSR*.

3. *Phonetic Stage (First Grade):* Children are able to represent all the surface sound features of words and spell words the way they sound to them (*CHROBLE* = *TROUBLE*). They have invented a system of phonetic spelling, based on their awareness that letters and words represent sounds. This system is consistent and reflects a highly sophisticated understanding of the relationship of sounds of speech to symbols of writing. Spelling in this stage can be read by others (see Figure 12.3). Children include all the sound features of the words (e.g., *KADE* = *CANDY*; *SEDRLI* = *CINDERELLA*). A child in the phonetic stage spelled *MONSTER* as *MONSTR*.

FIGURE 12.1 Elizabeth's Preliterate Spelling

FIGURE 12.2 Elizabeth's Semiphonetic Spelling

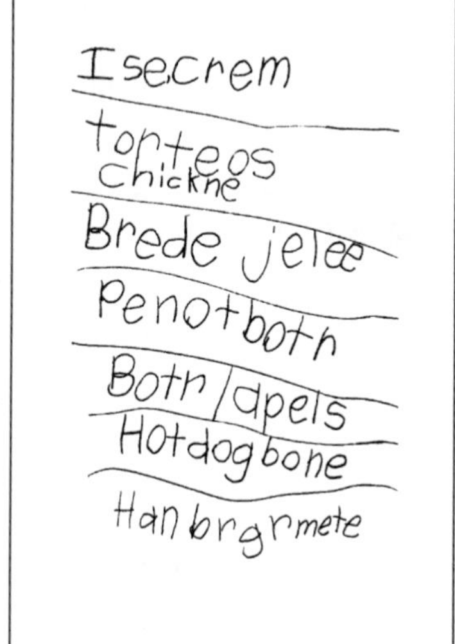

FIGURE 12.3 Elizabeth's Phonetic Spelling

4. ***Transitional Stage (End of First through Beginning of Second Grade):*** Children begin to spell conventionally in this stage. In addition to being able to spell based on their awareness of how words sound, children can now spell based on their awareness of how words look. (Good adult spellers are expert at this when they're able to tell if a word is spelled correctly by whether it "looks right.") At this stage, children put a vowel in every syllable and use e-marker and vowel digraph patterns. They can also use inflectional endings of words correctly as well as letter sequences that occur frequently. Their invented spelling is interspersed with correct spelling (e.g., *DOG* = *DOG* and *CINDARILA* = *CINDERELLA*) (see Figure 12.4). Children at this stage are able to use their morphemic knowledge by comparing one word to another; they can also use their visual memory of words they know how to spell and apply it to new words (e.g., *HIGHCKED* = *HIKED*). A child in the transitional stage spelled *MONSTER* as *MONSTUR.*

5. ***Correct Stage (Second through Fourth Grade):*** In this stage, children are beginning to spell correctly. Their knowledge of word meanings is growing, and they are better able to use complicated vowel patterns in English. They have basically mastered the complexities of English orthography (see Figure 12.5). However, the characteristics and points of change in their spelling in this stage are more difficult to discern now than in earlier stages. They are probably still struggling with consonant doubling and word affixes but may have mastered word roots, past tense, and short vowels; they may still have trouble with the positions of letters, as in the silent *e* that controls vowels. Children's vocabulary is growing, and they understand the meanings of many more words. They have greater familiarity with vowel patterns in relation to stress and meaning in words. A child in this stage spells *MONSTER* correctly.

6. ***Morphemic and Syntactic Stage (Fifth through Tenth Grade):*** By the fifth grade, children increasingly understand how meaning and grammatical structure control spelling in English. They are better at doubling conso-

FIGURE 12.4
Elizabeth's Transitional Spelling

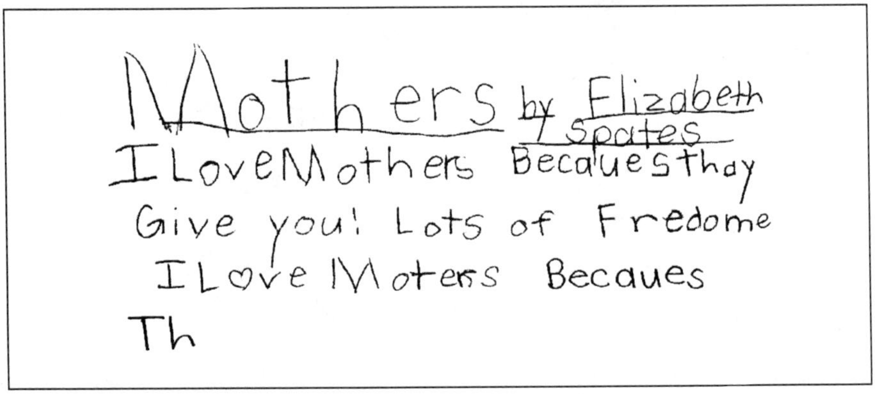

FIGURE 12.5
Elizabeth's Correct Spelling

nants and spelling alternate forms of the same word and at using word endings (e.g., *MANAGERIAL/MANAGE; REPETITION/REPEAT*). Children in this stage are increasingly able to use word meaning (or morphemic) and sentence structure (or syntactic information) (e.g., *SLOWLY; PASSED; FASTER; SLEEPING*). In addition to understanding the underlying phonological rules they gained as young children, older youths now understand and are able to use knowledge about the importance of meaning and syntax in spelling in English (see Figure 12.6).

FIGURE 12.6
Elizabeth's Morphemic and Syntactic Spelling

Teaching Spelling

Traditional versus the Whole-Language and Writing Process Perspectives

Spelling has traditionally been taught using commercial spelling programs that follow the same basic approach. Namely, spelling is treated as a separate subject, with its own book. Instruction focuses on weekly lists of spelling words, which have been chosen because they appear frequently in reading and writing or because they fit a pattern (e.g., words with the long *a* vowel sound). Regardless of how or what words are chosen, all students in the class learn the same words. And the cycle of teaching includes introducing the word pattern, giving a pretest, reviewing the word pattern and conducting word practice, and testing again (usually at the end of the week). Students often practice words they already know how to spell (Zutell, 1994) or are tested before they reach the stage of correct spelling (between second and fourth grade). This is certainly before students can reasonably be expected to use conventional spellings (Gentry & Gillet, 1993).

Advocates of the whole-language and writing process approach have challenged this traditional approach to teaching spelling because of its emphasis on rote memorization and practice of isolated words and skills (Wilde, 1990, 1993). The whole-language/writing process approach takes into account that children have learned to spell most of the words they know by reading and writing. Accordingly, the emphasis should be on children writing. An individualized approach is needed to address the development of spelling in children, invented spelling, and research on controlling the conventions of written English. For instance, *The Nation's Report Card* (Applebee et al., 1987) showed that children in the fourth grade spelled about 92 percent of words correctly in writing; this figure rose to 98 percent by age 17.

Invented spelling should be encouraged. Clark (1988) found that first-grade children who were encouraged to use invented spelling were able to write more independently at the beginning of the year, wrote longer stories with more word variety, and did better when given spelling tests than those who were prompted to use correct spelling. Spelling instruction should be based on a teacher's knowledge of spelling development and a student-centered reading and writing program, including activities that provide students with ways of recognizing word patterns and knowledge about words (Templeton, 1991):

- ***Wide Reading:*** Spelling and reading have a close relationship (Anderson, 1985). Students who are good spellers understand words in print that they would be reluctant to pronounce and spell on the basis of visual as well as spoken representation (Templeton, 1979). In addition, the more words students know, the better they are able to spell and read (Beers, 1980). Providing time and opportunities for wide independent reading, sustained silent reading, and reading across the curriculum is an important component of teaching spelling.

• ***"Word Walls":*** Many teachers display wall charts of words commonly used in children's writing. "Word walls" can also be made with lists of words on special topics, such as holidays or content areas. These "word walls" can help students with spelling and writing and should change according to their needs.

The concept of a "word wall" was introduced in the Lesson Plan in Chapter 1, Learning and Teaching Language Arts.

• ***Spelling Journals:*** Children can keep notebooks, reserving a page for each letter of the alphabet. On each, they can list words they would like to know how to spell, words they have trouble spelling, or words that interest them.

To make their writing more interesting, fifth-graders brainstormed this list of synonyms for *said: asked, spoke, told, begged, stated, declared, pleaded, complained, whined, complimented, informed, screamed, yelled, shouted, hollered, advised, warned, cautioned.*

• ***Dictionaries and Thesauruses:*** Consider the twisted logic of telling a child to look up a word in the dictionary that he or she doesn't know how to spell, when you need to know how to spell the word in order to look it up! Dictionaries and thesauruses are most useful as spelling aids when students are at least at the correct or morphemic/syntactic stage.

Spelling Activities

Kindergarten through Second Grade. For children in these grades, learning to spell should be an integral part of freewriting for meaning; invented spelling should be encouraged. Many school systems establish formal spelling programs by the second and even the first grade. However, one study of first-through fourth-graders suggested that formal instruction in spelling should not begin until children understand word structure through numerous experiences with words in their own writing and reading (Beers, Beers, & Grant, 1977).

In one week, my 4-year-old son asked how to spell his name (*Gordon*), *Mama*, *Elizabeth* (his sister), and *dinosaur butt* (the current popular insult at his preschool).

See Chapter 14, Language across the Curriculum, for more on using dictionaries and thesauruses.

Error patterns of beginning spellers include using letter names for sounds, omitting nasals before consonants, and confusing vowel sounds with similarly articulated letter names. Few of these errors occur after second grade. These normal developmental stages, as described by Read (1971) and others, correspond to Piaget's stages of cognitive development (Zutell, 1979).

Second through Fourth Grades. Common errors of students in these grades include misspelling common words and failing to apply generalizations about some orthographically regular words. Children should still be learning to spell as a part of writing. They may also engage in simple activities with high-frequency irregular words and difficult words from their own writing or spelling journals. Activities that don't require special materials or direct instruction or supervision by the teacher include test-corrected-test method, word games, and minilessons in spelling:

• ***Test-Corrected-Test Method:*** This method accounts for almost all the spelling words learned by students in testing situations. It involves children giving each other tests, immediately correcting them, and rewriting the words they misspelled. Young, less able spellers should confer with the teacher as they correct tests, and the teacher can periodically check the spelling journals of older, more able spellers to note their progress.

• ***Word Study Techniques:*** Gentry (1987) suggests the following for studying unknown words: "visual inspection, auditory inspection, kinesthetic reinforcement, and recall—always with words treated as wholes" (p. 32). He suggests the following two effective techniques for students to learn new words or how to spell words they've missed on tests:

Fitzgerald Method

1. Look at the word carefully.
2. Say the word.
3. With eyes closed, visualize the word.
4. Cover the word and then write it.
5. Check the spelling.
6. If the word is misspelled, repeat steps 1–5.

Horn Method

1. Pronounce each word carefully.
2. Look carefully at each part of the word as you say it.
3. Say the letters in sequence.
4. Attempt to recall how the word looks; then spell it.
5. Check this attempt to recall.
6. Write the word.
7. Check this spelling attempt.
8. Repeat the above steps if necessary.

- ***Word Games:*** Try the following:
  1. *Crossword Puzzles:* Children make them for others to solve. Teachers should make blank grids available.
  2. *Word Searches:* Children write words horizontally, vertically, or diagonally and fill in the blank spaces with random letters. Again, teachers should make blank grids available.
  3. *Cloze Puzzles:* Children write words, deleting certain letters and leaving blanks for others to fill in.
  4. *Rhyming Ping Pong:* Two students or teams of students call out rhyming words (e.g., *cat, bat, fat*), going back and forth as quickly as they can. The winner is the last one to have said a word when the timer goes off.
  5. *Endless Chains:* Play starts with one student or team spelling out a word (or writing it on the board). The next player or team must spell a word that begins with the last letter of the original word.
  6. *Scrambled Words:* In pairs, children try to stump each other by posing scrambled words that their partners have to unscramble.
  7. *Building Words:* Each child in a small group tries to make as many words as possible out of a group of letters.

Commercial word games that enhance spelling are Boggle, Perquackey, Hugger Mugger, Scrabble, Spill & Spell, and Word Yahtzee.

• ***Minilessons:*** During writing workshop, the teacher can introduce some words that follow regular orthographic patterns but that children are still misspelling. Here are useful spelling rules:

1. *Y* rule: For words that end in a consonant plus *y,* change the *y* to *i* before adding *-es* or *-ed* (e.g., *try/tries/tried*).
2. Final, silent *e* rule: For words that end in silent *e,* drop the *e* before adding a suffix beginning with a vowel and keep the *e* when adding a suffix that begins with a consonant (e.g., *skate/skating/skates*).

3. Doubling rule: For words in which the final syllable ends in a consonant preceded by a single vowel, double the consonant before adding a suffix beginning with a vowel (e.g., *hit/hitting*).
4. Plurals rule: Most single nouns become plural by adding an *-s* or *-es* (e.g., *cat/cats; dress/dresses*).
5. *Q* rule: The letter *q* is followed by *u* in English spelling (e.g., *quit, queue*).

• ***Word Sorts:*** Children classify words based on meaning elements, syntactic function, and pronunciation. Words from content areas or any interesting words can be written on cards and sorted according to different features.

1. Letters and sounds: initial letters; consonants; vowels (short, long, digraphs, etc.)
2. Structure: prefixes, suffixes, affixes, inflection, number of syllables, consonant doubling, dropping *e*

Fifth through Eighth Grades. Studies have shown that no formal instruction is just as effective as a formal program for teaching students beyond the fourth grade (Hammill, Larsen, & McNutt, 1977; Manolakes, 1975). Students at this level should focus on better understanding how meaning and form are related in English spelling. They can practice and play with those words that have related forms and roots, especially in studying in the content areas. Activities that are useful include:

• ***Mystery Meaning:*** The teacher uses the dictionary to compile a list of words that students are not likely to know (e.g., *xenophobia, quaff, pyre, mein, entail, cayuse*). Then working in pairs or small groups, students guess the meanings, write them down, and look them up in the dictionary to compare their guesses to the real meanings. Whoever comes closest to the real meaning scores a point.

See Chapter 14, Language across the Curriculum, for more on using the dictionary.

• ***Semantic Maps:*** Create semantic maps, particularly for studying words in the content areas, such as science and social studies. This can be done as a whole-class, small group, or individual activity.

See Chapter 2, Children and Language, for more on semantic mapping.

• ***Word Games:*** Challenge students to make as many words as they can from given phonograms by adding consonants or consonant clusters. Some good phonograms for this include *ace, ade, ate, ill, ine, ight,* and *ost.*

• ***Word Sorts:*** Students classify words written on cards or search for words with similarities. For example:

1. *Grammatical Function:* Parts of speech, stress, inflectional endings (e.g., *-ed, -ing*)
2. *Meaning:* Root families and etymologies, types of words
3. *Phonograms (word parts):* Words that include *mne* (e.g., *amnesia, mnemonic*)
4. *Word Origins (common roots):* Words that include *psych* (e.g., *psychology, psychiatrist, psychiatric*)

Overview of Teaching Spelling

Do

1. Learn the stages of children's spelling development and error patterns for each age in order to view each child's progress individually.
2. Encourage invented spelling.
3. Provide time and opportunities for reading and writing so students can experiment with spelling.
4. Correct spelling in writing through editing and revising real pieces of writing.
5. Plan games for students to expand their word knowledge, exploring similarities and differences among words, meaning elements, and pronunciations.
6. Integrate spelling into writing and content areas.

Don't

1. Assume that:
   a. Spelling is learned through studying phonics.
   b. Copying and rote memorizing of words helps learn them.
   c. Children shouldn't use words they can't spell.
2. Rely on commercial programs, such as spelling books, workbooks, and word lists, while depriving students of time and opportunities for reading and writing.

Punctuation

Punctuation is another graphic feature of written language. Children learn punctuation to set apart syntactic units in English and to provide information about intonation and meaning. In addition to learning about the purposes of individual punctuation marks, students learn about the spaces between words and how to use capital letters and periods to represent proper names and identify the beginnings and endings of sentences.

Development of Punctuation

Instruction in punctuation is usually done in connection with spelling, and both should be taught as a part of the writing process. Children develop control over punctuation as they develop overall writing ability (Hodges, 1991). Thus, knowledge about punctuation develops gradually. Children in the first grade, for instance, may not use punctuation at all. And some students may create their own systems of punctuation because they don't know how to use conventional practices. By the middle elementary grades on, the majority of U.S. students make few punctuation errors. Results from *The Nation's Report Card* (Applebee et al., 1987) showed that even at age 9, 25 percent of students made no errors and 50 percent averaged 1.5 or fewer errors per 100 words in writing.

Teaching Punctuation

Skills versus Writing Approaches

The difference between the skills and writing approaches is illustrated by a study that compared the way two third-grade teachers taught punctuation (Calkins, 1980). One taught punctuation conventions in isolation, using daily drills and worksheets; children corrected their incorrect sentences but did little writing per se. The other teacher taught punctuation as part of the writing process; children wrote for one hour a day, three times a week, and were encouraged to use their own ideas and experiment with punctuation. At the end of the year, the students with the teacher who emphasized daily drills could use an average of 3.85 kinds of punctuation correctly. By contrast, the children with the teacher who emphasized writing could use an average of 8.66 kinds of punctuation correctly. In short, the children in the second group learned more about punctuation because they needed it to write.

Cordeiro, Giacobbe, and Cazden (1983) took an even closer look at how children develop the use of punctuation by studying a first-grade class in which students wrote extensively. For a year, these researchers analyzed children's writing and the nature of writing conferences between the teacher and children. They found that the punctuation marks the teacher explained most often were periods, possessive apostrophes, and quotation marks. Although direct instruction helped some children learn to use possessive apostrophes and quotation marks, many learned them with only half the amount of instruction. Periods were taught and retaught more than any other kind of punctuation but were still used only about half the time they were required.

All the children in the class progressed at about the same rate, but those who didn't receive direct instruction in the correct use of periods actually did better using them correctly. They relied on other sources of information about punctuation, like reading and their own underlying knowledge of how written language works. Even though students didn't always use punctuation by adult standards of correctness, they were developing an intuitive and untaught understanding of phrases and clauses.

Minilessons

Based on the findings of *The Nation's Report Card* (Applebee et al., 1987) on punctuation, minilessons on the following topics should be taught to children in writing workshop:

1. Using capitals, periods, question marks, and exclamation points at sentence boundaries (the most frequently used punctuation marks)
2. Using commas, dashes, colons, and semicolons within sentences (used less frequently by students; better writers make more use of them)
3. Using periods in abbreviations
4. Using apostrophes to show possession
5. Using capitalization of proper names, places, and adjectives
6. Using quotation marks for speech

Self-Editing

Encourage children to edit their own writing, both as they go along and before publishing their pieces. Make a chart of commonly used punctuation marks that students can check themselves against, and display it in the writing center (see Figure 12.7).

See Chapter 9, The Writing Process, for more on teaching punctuation during writing workshop.

Overview of Teaching Punctuation

Do

1. Encourage children to discover and use punctuation as they need it for writing.
2. Explain punctuation conventions based on their functions and meanings, rather than as rote-memory rules (e.g., "a sentence is a complete thought").
3. Remember that a period may be one of the last forms of punctuation to be mastered; first grade may be too early to expect correct use. (Questions or difficulty regarding use of periods may reflect a more highly developed syntactic sense: What is a complete thought?)

Don't

1. Rely on language arts texts, commercial programs, or worksheets or workbooks.
2. Become discouraged with yourself or your students if even after direct instruction in minilessons and using correct forms in their writing, some children make the same errors again. While they gain mastery over one aspect of writing, they may temporarily lose it over another. Progress is real but not always even.

FIGURE 12.7
Commonly Used Punctuation Marks

Period .
1. A period ends a statement.
2. A period is used for an abbreviation and initials.

Question Mark ?
1. A question mark ends a question.

Exclamation Point !
1. An exclamation point shows strong feeling.

Comma ,
1. A comma separates words in a series.
2. A comma comes between a date and year and between a city and state.
3. A comma comes after the greeting and closing in a friendly letter.

Apostrophe '
1. An apostrophe shows where letters have been left out in contractions.
2. An apostrophe shows ownership.

Quotation Marks " "
1. Quotation marks enclose direct quotations.

Handwriting

Despite the wide use of computers for writing by adults, most children begin to write by hand and continue to do so through most of elementary school. Thus, the development of legible handwriting is important to their schooling.

See Chapter 13, Media Literacy, for more on using computers and word processing in writing.

Phases of Children's Handwriting Development

Graves (1983) has described five general phases in children's handwriting development, all of which can occur and overlap during the first grade:

1. ***Get-It-Down Phase:*** Children want to get something down on paper, so they make letterlike forms, letters, and words, often in random order. They have a general idea of writing from left to right.

2. ***First Aesthetics:*** Children are aware of how words are placed on the page and the amount of space needed for their stories. The like to have clean, fresh pages to write on and try hard to get rid of mistakes, which can lead to problems with erasing (e.g., smudging, tearing the page, frustration).

3. ***Growing Age of Convention:*** Children may be less interested with getting their message written down and more concerned with how it looks to others; they take more care with word spacing, margins, and writing exactly on the lines. This concern for appearance also affects spelling and mechanics, as they become more aware of their audience.

4. ***Breaking Conventions:*** As children gain more control over handwriting, spelling, and punctuation, they continue to deal with the content of their writing. Teachers can help them learn that it's all right to change, move, or mess up parts of their writing in the drafting stages.

5. ***Later Aesthetics:*** When children discover they can scratch out rather than erase errors and move and add parts to their writing, they're on their way to understanding that their writing is a work-in-progress. The published piece is where they'll use their best handwriting or word processing, correct spelling and punctuation, clean or special paper, special writing tools (e.g., colored pencils), and illustrations and binding.

During all these phases and throughout their further development in handwriting, children are trying to control the motion of making letters and words on a page and to arrange the page space. Teachers may be tempted to compare children's handwriting to the models in commercial handwriting series, as it seems logical to do so. But unlike spelling, there isn't an agreed on form for handwriting. Legibility should be the standard each child's writing development is viewed against. Students' handwriting may even become less conformist as they get older, which seems to be a natural outgrowth of the preadolescent drive for personal expression. In the fourth and fifth grades, students may adopt a backhand style or a large scrawl with flourishes—perhaps dotting the letter *i* with little circles or even hearts, flowers, or smiley faces. The issue isn't whether it's correct for an 11-year-old to add these personal touches; rather, the issue is whether his or her writing is legible and allows him or her to communicate effectively with others.

Graves (1978) has suggested guidelines for observing change and development in children's handwriting:

What to Look For	*What It Means*
Use of thumb and forefinger together	Children lose control with a poor grip, whether too tight or loose.
Continuity problems	Frequent stops and starts may be due to problems with forming ideas or spelling or inexperience with handwriting.
Position of elbows and body axis	The less elbow motion, the better the speed and ease of writing.
Position of writing surface	Children learn to accommodate paper to the left or right of the midline of the body, rather than straight on.
Inconsistent distribution of strength	Light and heavy lines show how well students can control pressure and suppress large muscles in favor of small muscles.
Use of writing space	Children learn to delineate spaces between words and sentences as they understand what these units mean.

Teaching Handwriting

Handwriting is typically taught beginning with manuscript (i.e., printing) in the first grade and shifting to cursive (i.e., connected letters) between the second and fourth grades. Handwriting charts and books for copying are frequently used, as are minilessons, in which the teacher models letter formations for the whole class.

Modeling Handwriting

Teachers model handwriting when they write on the board, make posters, take dictation on language experience charts, write to students in dialogue journals, or make editorial comments on writing. Handwriting can also be modeled with wall charts of manuscript for first- and second-graders and cursive for third-graders and up. These charts often come in long horizontal strips, which can be mounted above a chalkboard. Students can also look at handwriting books for models of handwriting.

Materials for Handwriting

Teachers should provide many materials for handwriting in the classroom, along with materials for drawing and painting: pens, pencils (including colored pencils), crayons, paints, and brushes and a variety of types of paper (plain, colored, lined, journal). Teachers should also provide other surfaces to write on: wipe-off slates, paper plates, folders, and the like. As mentioned above, handwriting books may also be used.

Two Types of Handwriting

There are two commonly used programs, which present different types of handwriting:

1. Parker Zaner-Bloser is the traditional ball-and-stick style.
2. D'Nealian is an italic style, which attempts to make the transition from manuscript to cursive easier by teaching students to form slightly slanting manuscript letters.

Minilessons

Handwriting is a tool for writing, so children should spend most of their time learning handwriting by using it in writing. Enough direct instruction should be given to enable children to write freely, as they develop fluency and legibility. Topics for minilessons for the whole class or groups in writing workshops include:

1. ***Demonstrate Writing Position:*** Writers of all ages should have comfortable spaces, with tables and chairs at correct levels and enough room to move their arms freely without bumping their elbows. The teacher should demonstrate a good position for the relationship of paper to writer and how to hold a pencil. Guide students to take comfortable and relaxed positions with pencil and paper.

2. ***Introduce Manuscript Letter Forms:*** Figure 12.8 shows a good order and techniques for doing this.

3. ***Demonstrate Transition from Manuscript to Cursive:*** Show the same words written in both styles; then show how cursive letters are connected and the change in slant.

4. ***Introduce Cursive Writing:*** Figure 12.8 also shows a good order and techniques for introducing cursive writing.

For a playful way to introduce letters, see Gail E. Tompkins (1980), "Let's Go on a Bear Hunt: A Fresh Approach to Penmanship Drill," *Language Arts, 57,* 782–786.

Playing with Handwriting

Children can play games with graphic representations of language:

- ***Name Game:*** Encourage children to experiment writing their name as many different ways as possible, making letters that are large and small, fat and thin, overlapping, colored, and so on.

Manuscript

Simple Letters

1. Straight lines | and lines with another stroke t i j k u
2. Circles O and circles with another stroke a d b p g q

Letters with Similar Pattern

1. Open circles C an open circles with another stroke e f
2. Lines and humps n m h r
3. Angles x y v w z
4. A unique letter s

Upper Case

1. Like lower case C O S T K P U V X Z
2. In between F J M N W
3. Unlike lower case A B D E G H I L R Q Y

Transition from Manuscript to Cursive

Show same words in both styles, how they are connected, and the change in slant.

Cursive Writing

1. The numbers and arrows on commercial materials show the order and direction of the formation of each letter.
2. Letters with an undercurve b e f g h i k l r s t u w
3. Overcurve or hump letters m n v x y z
4. Downward curve a c d g o
5. Lower loop j p g
6. Upper-case letters with similarities
7. Note that only six letters are really formed differently in cursive: *b, e, f, r, s, z*.

FIGURE 12.8 Teaching Sequence for Handwriting

Children's Books about Codes
Codes for Kids (Albert, 1976); *Doubletalk: Codes, Signs, and Symbols* (Hovanec, 1993); *The Kids Code and Cipher Book* (Garden, 1981); *Loads of Codes and Secret Ciphers* (Janeczko, 1984); *Super Secret Code Book* (Pickering, 1995)

- ***Creating Codes***
  1. Write a story in which a letter, number, or picture replaces a word.
  2. Create a secret code and write a message in it. Some simple formulas include substituting numbers for letters of the alphabet in order, reversing the alphabet, using the next letter of the alphabet, and creating new symbols for letters.
  3. Create culture codes by finding symbols from the past or other cultures (such as hieroglyphics), and write messages using them.

Overview of Teaching Handwriting

Do

1. Observe children's handwriting development as they write.
2. Keep handwriting in the proper context of writing for real purposes. Remember that legibility is what's most important: Can you read it?
3. Offer many opportunities to explore space: art, constructions, drama, dance, as well as writing.
4. Stock a variety of materials in the writing center.
5. Provide plenty of time for children to write on topics of their own choices.

Don't

1. Use a set of commercial materials with a rigid sequence of isolated drills.
2. Teach handwriting as though it were an end in itself.
3. Restrict young children's use of writing materials (e.g., only letting them use wide-ruled paper or large primary pencils without erasers).
4. Ignore the strong connection made by learning handwriting in the context of real writing.

Children's Books about Hieroglyphics
The Beginning of Writing (Warburton, 1990); *Egyptian Hieroglyphics for Everyone* (Scott & Scott, 1968); *Hieroglyphs: The Writing of Ancient Egypt* (Katan, 1980); *The Riddle of the Rosetta Stone: Key to Ancient Egypt* (Giblin, 1990)

Assessing Language Conventions

Include the following kinds of assessment for language conventions in students' writing portfolios:

Spelling

1. ***Successive Drafts of Student Writing:*** These show students' spelling development over time and from their first drafts through successive revising and editing drafts.

2. ***Spelling Journal:*** Check these periodically. Leave space for children to use the test-corrected-test method, and record results with dates to keep an ongoing record of words practiced. Monitor these records during writing conferences. The spelling journal becomes an individualized record of development: words needed for writing, words causing difficulty, and results of practice through the test-corrected-test method.

Punctuation

1. ***Successive Drafts of Student Writing:*** Successive drafts show how well students have incorporated punctuation before, during, and after completing published pieces of writing.

2. ***Editing Lists:*** Children should keep their own lists of punctuation conventions they have been taught in conferences and mastered in pieces of writing. These checklists should also be used for future editing and become part of students' writing portfolios.

Handwriting

1. ***Anecdotal Records:*** Handwriting is generally assessed through informal teacher observation. The criteria used are legibility (well-proportioned, properly slanted, uniformly arranged letters and words) and fluency (rate).

2. ***Student Self-Evaluation:*** Children should be guided toward self-evaluation in handwriting. Companies such as Zaner-Bloser provide scales of a variety of handwriting samples with evaluative comments and suggestions for improvement that students may use to evaluate themselves.

Answers to Questions about Language Conventions

1. *How do children learn the language conventions of spelling, punctuation, and handwriting?*

Learning the language conventions of spelling, punctuation, and handwriting is a constructive developmental process, like learning how to speak. All are learned best when considered as part of the writing process. In learning to spell, children move from the simple to the more complex, making increasingly sophisticated and similar approximations of correct spelling based on how they hear words. From kindergarten through the eighth grade, children move through the same six stages: preliterate, semiphonetic, phonetic, transitional, correct, and morphemic and syntactic. Individual children seem to move through the same sequence, regardless of when they begin to write.

Children develop control over punctuation as they develop overall writing ability; this is usually done in connection with spelling. Children will discover and use punctuation as they need it for writing in real, meaningful contexts.

Graves (1983) has described five general phases in children's handwriting development, all of which can occur and overlap during the first grade: get-it-down phase, first aesthetics, growing age of convention, breaking conventions, and greater aesthetics. Unlike spelling, there isn't an agreed on form for handwriting. Legibility should be the standard each child's writing development is viewed against.

2. *What are effective ways to teach spelling, punctuation, and handwriting?*

Children should be taught the conventions of spelling, punctuation, and handwriting as part of the writing process. Results of *The Nation's Report Card* showed that 9-, 13-, and 17-year-old U.S. students have reasonable control of these conventions and suggests that individualized instruction using students' own writing is more effective than whole-class instruction in skills. The teacher's role is to provide time and opportunities to write, to encourage invented spelling, and to organize the classroom to provide for whole-class, small-group, and teacher- and peer-editing conferences. Other means to teach spelling and written language conventions include wide reading, word walls, spelling journals, test-corrected-test method, word games, minilessons, word sorts, semantic maps, and self-editing.

LOOKING FURTHER

1. Collect at least three samples of writing from children in the same class. Analyze the stage of spelling development each child is at according to the descriptions in the chapter. If possible, do this for two different grade levels more than one year apart.
2. Do the same as in question 1 but analyze three children's handwriting samples according to Graves's phases of handwriting development, described in this chapter.
3. Ask several teachers how they teach punctuation. Comment on their answers in light of these research findings: (a) the study of how punctuation was learned in two third-grade classrooms (p. 439) and (b) the results of *The Nation's Report Card* (p. 438).
4. Analyze several spelling books according to what Graves found in his analysis of such commercial programs.
5. Observe a group of students in a peer-editing group in a writing workshop. Make notes about ideas you have for using writing workshops when you're teaching.
6. Play one of the word games described in this chapter with a group of children. Talk about it, and see if you can all create a new word game.

RESOURCES

Gentry, J. R. (1987). *Spel . . . is a four-letter word.* Portsmouth, NH: Heinemann.

Wilde, S. (1993). *You kan red this! Spelling and punctuation for whole language classrooms, K–6.* Portsmouth, NH: Heinemann.

REFERENCES

Anderson, K. F. (1985). The development of spelling ability and linguistic strategies. *Reading Teacher, 39,* 140–147.

Applebee, A. N., Langer, J. A., & Mullis, I. V. S. (1987). *Grammar, punctuation, and spelling: Controlling the conventions of written English at ages 9, 13, 17, The nation's report card.* Princeton, NJ: National Assessment of Educational Progress, Educational Testing Service.

Beers, C. S. (1980). The relationship of cognitive development to spelling and reading abilities. In E. Henderson & J. W. Beers (Eds.), *Developmental and cognitive aspects of learning to spell.* Newark, DE: International Reading Association.

Beers, C. S., & Beers, J. W. (1981). Three assumptions about learning to spell. *Language Arts, 58,* 573–580.

Beers, J. W., Beers, C. S., & Grant, K. (1977). The logic behind children's spelling. *Elementary School Journal, 77,* 238–242.

Beers, J. W., & Henderson, E. H. (1977). A study of developing orthographic concepts among first graders. *Research in the Teaching of English, 11,* 133–148.

Calkins, L. M. (1980). Research update—when children want to punctuate: Basic skills belong in context. *Language Arts, 57,* 567–573.

Clarke, L. K. (1988). Invented versus traditional spelling in first graders' writing: Effects on learning to spell and read. *Research in the Teaching of English, 22,* 281–309.

Cordeiro, P., Giacobbe, M. E., & Cazden, C. (1983). Apostrophes, quotation marks, and periods: Learning punctuation in the first grade. *Language Arts, 60,* 323–332.

Gentry, J. R. (1981). Learning to spell developmentally. *Reading Teacher, 34*, 378–392.

Gentry, J. R. (1987). *Spel . . . is a four-letter word.* Portsmouth, NH: Heinemann.

Gentry, J. R., & Gillet, J. W. (1993). *Teaching kids to spell.* Portsmouth, NH: Heinemann.

Graves, D. H. (1977a). Research update: Language arts textbooks: A writing process evaluation. *Language Arts, 54*, 86–90.

Graves, D. H. (1977b). Research update: Spelling texts and structural analysis methods. *Language Arts, 54*, 86–90.

Graves, D. H. (1978). Research update: Handwriting is for writing. *Language Arts, 55*, 393–399.

Graves, D. H. (1983). *Writing: Teachers and children at work.* Portsmouth, NH: Heinemann.

Hammill, D. D., Larsen, S., & McNutt, G. (1977). The effects of spelling instruction: A preliminary study. *Elementary School Journal, 78*, 67–72.

Hanna, P. R., Hanna, J. S., Hodges, R. E., & Rudorf, E. H. (1966). *Phoneme-grapheme correspondences as cues to spelling improvement.* Washington, DC: United States Office of Education.

Henderson, E. H. (1980). Word knowledge and reading disability. In E. H. Henderson & J. W. Beers (Eds.), *Developmental and cognitive aspects of learning to spell.* Newark, DE: International Reading Association.

Henderson, E. H., & Templeton, S. (1986). A developmental perspective of formal spelling instruction through alphabet, pattern, and meaning. *Elementary School Journal, 86*, 304–316.

Hodges, R. E. (1991). The conventions of writing. In J. Flood, J. M. Jensen, D. Lapp, & J. R. Squire (Eds.), *Handbook of research on teaching the English language arts.* New York: Macmillan.

Manolakes, G. (1975). The teaching of spelling: A pilot study. *Elementary English, 52*, 246.

Read, C. (1971). Pre-school children's knowledge of English phonology. *Harvard Educational Review, 41*, 1–34.

Read, C. (1975). *Children's categorization of speech sounds in English.* Urbana, IL: National Council of Teachers of English.

Read, C. (1986). *Children's creative spelling.* London: Routledge & Kegan Paul.

Templeton, S. (1979). Spelling first, sound later: The relationship between orthography and higher order phonological knowledge in older students. *Research in the Teaching of English, 13*, 255–264.

Templeton, S. (1991). Teaching and learning the English spelling system: Reconceptualizing method and purpose. *Elementary School Journal, 92*, 185–201.

Tompkins, G. E. (1980). Let's go on a bear hunt: A fresh approach to penmanship drill. *Language Arts, 57*, 782–786.

Wilde, S. (1990). A proposal for a new spelling curriculum. *Elementary School Journal, 90*, 275–289.

Wilde, S. (1993). *You kan red this! Spelling and punctuation for whole language classrooms, K–6.* Portsmouth, NH: Heinemann.

Zutell, J. (1979). Spelling strategies of primary school children and their relationship to the Piagetian concept of decentration. *Research in the Teaching of English, 13*, 69–80.

Zutell, J. (1994). Spelling instruction. In A. C. Purves (Ed.), *Encyclopedia of English Studies and Language Arts* (Vol. 2). New York: Scholastic.

CHILDREN'S BOOKS

Albert, B. (1976). *Codes for kids.* New York: Whitman.

Garden, N. (1981). *The kids code and cipher book.* New York: Holt, Rinehart & Winston.

Giblin, J. C. (1990). *The riddle of the Rosetta Stone: Key to Ancient Egypt.* New York: Crowell.

Hovanec, H. (1993). *Doubletalk: Codes, signs, and symbols.* New York: Bantam.

Janeczko, P. (1984). *Loads of codes and secret ciphers.* New York: Macmillan.

Katan, N. J. (1980). *Hieroglyphs: The writing of Ancient Egypt.* New York: Atheneum.

Pickering, F. (1995). *Super secret code book.* New York: Sterling.

Scott, H. J., & Scott, L. (1968). *Egyptian hieroglyphics for everyone.* New York: Funk & Wagnalls.

Warburton, L. (1990). *The beginning of writing.* New York: Lucent.

Chapter 13

Media Literacy

Questions about Media Literacy

1. *What is* media literacy?
2. *How should we teach the media in language arts?*

Reflective Response

Think about the media experiences you had in elementary school. What do you think *media literacy* means? What does it have to do with language arts? Jot down your ideas in response to these questions.

Media Literacy Defined

Media literacy was recently defined in the *Encyclopedia of English Studies and Language Arts* (Cox, 1994) and by the National Council of Teachers of English Commission on Media (NCTE, 1994), of which I was the director:

> *Media literacy refers to composing, comprehending, interpreting, analyzing, and appreciating the language and texts of the multiple symbol systems of both print and nonprint media. The use of media presupposes an expanded definition of "text" in the English language arts classroom. Print media texts include books, magazines, and newspapers. Nonprint media include photography, recordings, radio, film, television, videotape, videogames, computers, the performing arts, and virtual reality. On the full range of media channels, all these types of texts constantly interact. They are all texts to be experienced, appreciated, and analyzed and created by students.* (p. 13)

Relationship to Language Arts and Integrated Teaching

Media literacy is part of an expanded definition of *literacy* in general (Cox, in press) and offers great potential as an integrating force in the classroom (Cox, 1994; NCTE, 1994). Traditionally, teachers of English language arts have been concerned with students' ability to read and write print texts. Electronic and artistic media have been used primarily to motivate students to read or to supplement print content. For example, recordings of current songs might be used to introduce a unit on poetry, or a film adaptation of a short story might help students visualize setting and character. But today, students obviously live in a world where more and more information is communicated through listening and viewing. As a result, the meaning of literacy has broadened to include direct education in both print and nonprint texts.

Students who are media literate know how print and nonprint texts function together in the development of thought, language, and knowledge. Media-literate students develop not only the ability to appreciate but to critically analyze all media. These students learn how to create meaning and communicate effectively through multiple media.

In a broad view of literacy, students learn to understand and create messages through varied experiences with many forms of media. Thus, the effective use of nonprint media in the classroom means teaching *about* and *with* rather than simply through media. For instance, students discuss responses to television dramas as well as short stories, retrieve information from computer databases as well as reference books, and compose through filmmaking as well as writing. Active learning experiences with both print and nonprint provide opportunities for students to achieve literacy across multiple media forms.

Perhaps most important, media experiences from both inside and outside the classroom provide access to learning for all students, drawing on a shared media culture as the basis for classroom exploration. This gives children the chance to use what they really experience in talking and writing. The media culture is available, in some way, to everyone. Thus, the media provide an entry point to meaningful language experiences in the classroom for all students. Moreover, different kinds of media provide different kinds of access to a range of students.

If you're not sure about how much attention to pay to teaching with, through, and about the media, consider how much attention the media receive in students' day-to-day lives. By the time a student finishes high school, he or she will have spent an average of 11,000 hours in school but 15,000 hours watching television and 10,500 hours listening to popular music. He or she will have seen hundreds of feature films, been exposed to thousands (perhaps millions) of advertisements, and logged countless hours working or playing on personal computers. The media have a tremendous influence on us, providing information as well as entertainment. They shape our perceptions of the world and ourselves.

Given all this, teachers can teach about, through, and with the media not only to help students become media literate but to use the media as an integral part of the language arts and to integrate teaching across the curriculum. The potential of the media to actively engage children in meaningful listening, talking, reading, writing, and viewing activities across the curriculum is limitless. The media are exciting, motivating, and immediate. They exist everywhere and provide something unique for everyone.

A Model for Teaching Media Literacy

Experiencing Media

Students experience works in a wide range of print and nonprint media as they enjoy, reflect on, discuss, study, and relate works in various media to their own lives. Experiencing media means that students:

1. Use their experiences with media outside the classroom (e.g., print and electronic news, television, advertisements, music, videogames, etc.) as a common experiential basis for classroom exploration through talk and writing
2. Use their experiences with media in the classroom (e.g., film and videotape, audio recordings, computers, etc.) as a common experiential basis for classroom exploration through talking and writing

3. Gain a more equitable access to language-learning experiences through talking and writing about media events outside the classroom and both print and nonprint texts in the classroom

Appreciation and Critical Analysis of Media

Students analyze forms of mass media and other symbolic systems to understand and appreciate their structure and effects. Appreciating and critically analyzing media means that students:

1. Discuss and analyze their own transactions with media texts
2. Discuss and analyze texts in various media to understand their distinctive versus shared characteristics
3. Analyze media to understand biases and values inherent in public media

Creating with Media

Students create their own works in a variety of media, including print, drawings, graphs, diagrams, photographs, films, videos, and performing arts. Creating with media means that students:

1. Create works in varied media so that they have direct knowledge of how language and communications are shaped through different symbol systems
2. Use varied media, such as the visual and performing arts, along with print, in order to extend and express their understandings and feelings
3. Understand the process of creating within a given media through experience and practice with media making

For a review of the research on media and teaching language arts, see Carole Cox (1991), "The Media Arts and English Language Arts Teaching and Learning," in *Handbook of Research on Teaching the English Language Arts*, pp. 542–548.

Books in "The Magic School Bus" series (by J. Cole)
The Magic School Bus, at the Waterworks (1986); *The Magic School Bus, Inside the Earth* (1987); *The Magic School Bus, Inside the Human Body* (1989); and *The Magic School Bus, Lost in the Solar System* (1990).

SNAPSHOT: Third-Grade Limited–English Proficient Students Create a Science Fiction Film

One of my former students, Audrey Eldridge, is now in her third year of teaching limited–English proficient students at International School in Long Beach, California. Here's a day-by-day description of how Audrey introduced a science unit on the solar system, used varied media to teach it, and integrated content and language teaching.

Day 1. Introduce Content Material through Nonfiction Literature

Audrey introduced the topic of space with the book *The Magic School Bus, Lost in the Solar System* (Cole, 1990). The "Magic School Bus" series is extremely popular and a great way to introduce content material through literature. These books use a media-influenced fantasy format to present accurate factual information. A miniaturized school bus goes on impossible fieldtrips led by the teacher, Ms. Frizzle. Students' comments are shown in speech bubbles, like the comics. Their reports on what's happening are shown in inserts, like a split screen on film, and the dialogue takes a humorous tone, like a TV situation comedy.

Audrey read the book aloud, and students discussed it. She said her students were mesmerized by the story and very excited about learning about the solar system.

Days 2 and 3. Wide Reading of Nonfiction and Photographs

Audrey located a lot of nonfiction books about the solar system and put them in a plastic tub in the class library. She read some aloud, and students read others on their own and in pairs and groups. Audrey also used a set of black-and-white photographs of the solar system.

Nonfiction Books on the Solar System
Discovering Mars: The Amazing Story of the Red Planet (Berger, 1992); *Journey to the Planets* (Lauber, 1993); *Meteors and Meteorites: Voyagers from Space* (Lauber, 1989); and *Sun Up, Sun Down* (Gibbons, 1983).

Days 4 and 5. Writing Frame for Nonfiction Report on the Planets

Audrey provided a writing frame for a nonfiction report on the solar system. Students read and did research to find answers to these six questions:

1. What is your planet's name?
2. How many kilometers is your planet from the sun?
3. How many planets is it from Earth?
4. What does it look like?
5. What is special about it?
6. What is the most interesting thing about it?

When the reports were finished, students were even more motivated to learn about the solar system. Audrey noticed this and planned more activities.

See Chapter 14, Language across the Curriculum, for more on research and report writing.

Days 6 through 10. Projects on the Solar System

With Audrey's help, the class brainstormed ideas for the following multimedia group projects, which they researched and carried out:

- *Planet model:* papier-mâché model and written report
- *Planet posters:* picture, written report, and title
- *Plan for a rocket ship:* labeled diagram and written explanation of how it works
- *Rocket ship model:* construction and written report on how it works
- *Model of solar system:* drawn in colored chalk on black butcher paper, with a written description
- *Space suit:* construction and written description

Days 11 through 15. Science Fiction Scriptwriting on the Computer and Making a "Big Book"

Mikey started this next wave of activities when he researched and made a space suit for his project. He was the only one who chose this, and when he did, the other students were very excited. Others wanted to make space suits, so they made costumes for outer space characters. Now that the students no longer felt confined to the facts, fiction took over. A group began calling themselves "Super Mikey and the Evil Aliens."

This round of science fiction projects included writing science fiction stories, doing a puppet show (called "The Cool Aliens"), writing and illustrating a "big book" (*Miss Eldridge on Mars*), and making a film (*Super Mikey and the Evil Aliens*). Here are samples from the "big book" and the film script:

Miss Eldridge on Mars
An Original Science Fiction Book
Written and Illustrated by The Kids in Room 20

Once upon a time Miss Eldridge went to Mars. Seda and Dina were with her in her spaceship. The spaceship turned around and around, and they landed on Mars. All of a sudden an alien saw their spaceship. Then the aliens jumped on their spaceship.

The girls screamed because they were scared of the alien. The alien had four hands, and three legs, and two eyes at the ends of his long antennas and he was green. The girls asked the alien what his name was. He answered, "My name is Tukataka." He wanted to be their friend. Then they all flew back to Earth together.

Video Script for Super Mikey and the Evil Aliens

Super Mikey: We are going to fight the evil aliens.

Hamza: Were are going to go west and we're going to Jupiter and then to Mars too.

Narrator: Then they got to Jupiter. When they got to Jupiter they saw the aliens diging for tresure.

Super Mikey: Oh no. There stiling the gold.

Hamza: We need that gold for the good king.

Narrator: Super Hamza and Super Mikey wen to the good alien king.

King Alien: You need to get that gold.

Queen Alien: We need the gold to pay the rent on the castle.

Narrator: Super Mikey and Super Hamza went to get the treasure on Mars. Thay went to the evil aliens castle. When Super Mikey and Super Hamza went in the castle the aliens saw Super Mikey and Super Hamza fly to get the gold so that the king and the queen could pay the rent.

Alien: Don't move one step.

Narrator: So they did not move a step.

Hamza: Let's fly up.

Narrator: They fly up. They brak the window and went throu the window. They went to the good king and they gave the treasure to the good king and queen. Then Super Mikey and Super Hamza went to thir onw world.

See Figure 13.1, a "ripple effect" of the solar system and science fiction, which shows what happened in Audrey's class, along with other possibilities for teaching language arts with this focal topic. And here's how Audrey

FIGURE 13.1
A "Ripple Effect" of the Solar System and Science Fiction

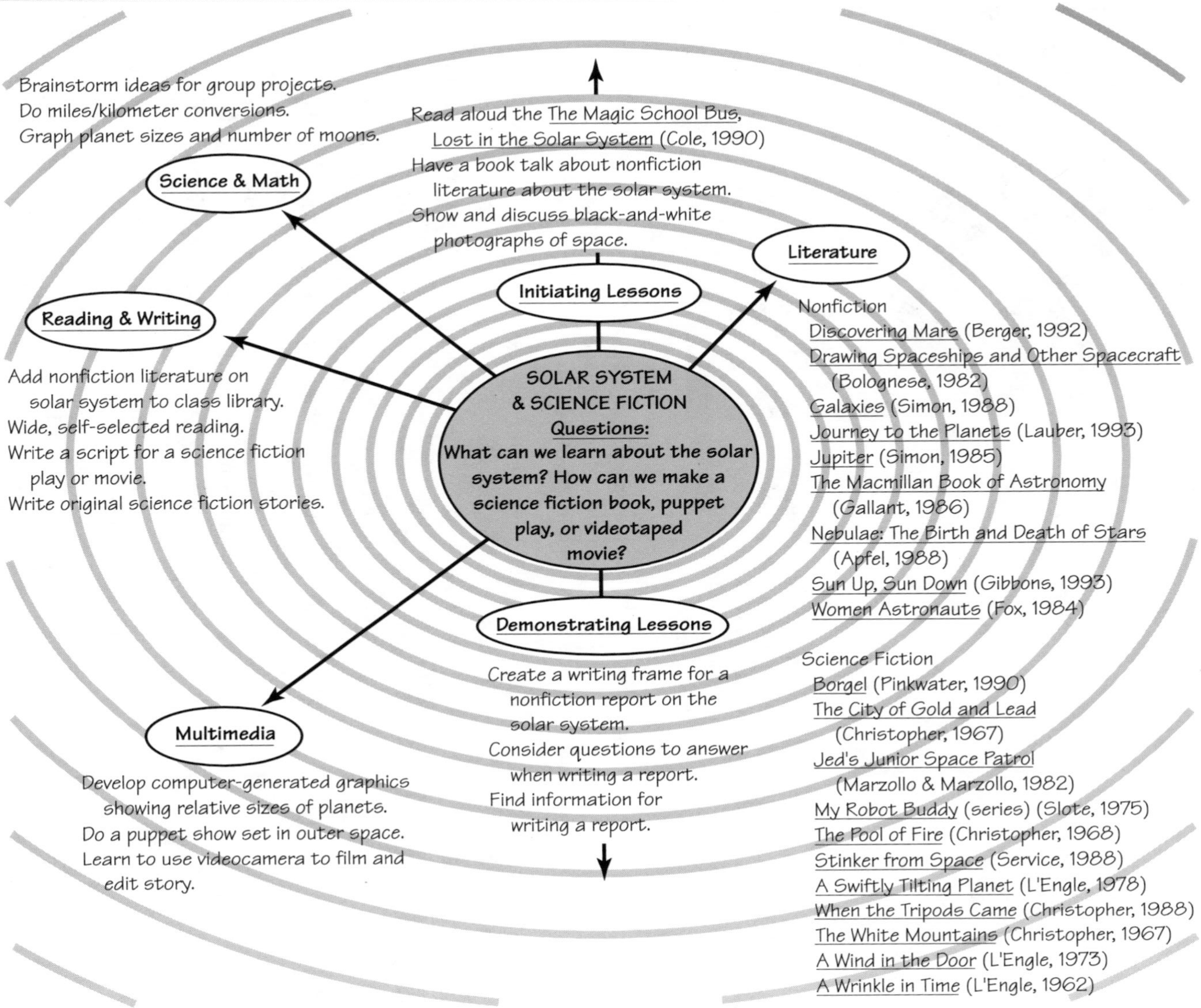

See the list of Children's Books and Films at the end of the chapter for more materials.

SOLAR SYSTEM & SCIENCE FICTION
Questions:
What can we learn about the solar system? How can we make a science fiction book, puppet play, or videotaped movie?

Initiating Lessons
Read aloud the The Magic School Bus, Lost in the Solar System (Cole, 1990)
Have a book talk about nonfiction literature about the solar system.
Show and discuss black-and-white photographs of space.

Science & Math
Brainstorm ideas for group projects.
Do miles/kilometer conversions.
Graph planet sizes and number of moons.

Reading & Writing
Add nonfiction literature on solar system to class library.
Wide, self-selected reading.
Write a script for a science fiction play or movie.
Write original science fiction stories.

Literature
Nonfiction
Discovering Mars (Berger, 1992)
Drawing Spaceships and Other Spacecraft (Bolognese, 1982)
Galaxies (Simon, 1988)
Journey to the Planets (Lauber, 1993)
Jupiter (Simon, 1985)
The Macmillan Book of Astronomy (Gallant, 1986)
Nebulae: The Birth and Death of Stars (Apfel, 1988)
Sun Up, Sun Down (Gibbons, 1993)
Women Astronauts (Fox, 1984)

Science Fiction
Borgel (Pinkwater, 1990)
The City of Gold and Lead (Christopher, 1967)
Jed's Junior Space Patrol (Marzollo & Marzollo, 1982)
My Robot Buddy (series) (Slote, 1975)
The Pool of Fire (Christopher, 1968)
Stinker from Space (Service, 1988)
A Swiftly Tilting Planet (L'Engle, 1978)
When the Tripods Came (Christopher, 1988)
The White Mountains (Christopher, 1967)
A Wind in the Door (L'Engle, 1973)
A Wrinkle in Time (L'Engle, 1962)

Demonstrating Lessons
Create a writing frame for a nonfiction report on the solar system.
Consider questions to answer when writing a report.
Find information for writing a report.

Multimedia
Develop computer-generated graphics showing relative sizes of planets.
Do a puppet show set in outer space.
Learn to use videocamera to film and edit story.

Limited–English proficient students wrote this "big book," Miss Eldridge on Mars, *during a study of the solar system and science fiction.*

described the children's experience making this videotaped science fiction film, which was their first. What she learned about using media with her third-graders is shown in the marginal notes:

Students are self-directed.

> It hardly took any instruction. They wanted to make up a story with the characters of Super Mikey and Evil Aliens and film it on videotape. They wrote the story and then the script. They were ready to film in about a week. I brought the camera, showed them how to start and pan, right to left. They figured the rest of it out as they needed it, made more props and costumes as they needed them. I didn't really know how to do it, so we figured it out together.

Students learn by doing.

> We experimented with things like close-ups. I realized they needed to experience it, try things out, and change things—to just do it. Once the initial excitement was over, they got very professional. I saw lots of good things happening. They practiced hard making their dialogue clear with lots of expression. With video, they get immediate feedback on how they sound or facial expressions. We shot it and played it and made changes immediately. Many times the second take was 100 percent better.

Students work hard.

> They were excited, and I really got work out of them. When I said "If you want to do a video, write the script" they were really writing!

Students need media experiences in school.

> Another plus is that these children are entering a world full of technology, and they will be lost without experience. Many of my students come from very low-income families. They don't have computers and video cameras at home. It's not fair to limit their experiences. They will lose out.

Students are in control.

> The beauty of media is that it is authentic, genuine, and self-created. That's when I learn about my students, their talents. I plan to do more media projects because they're active and students figure things out on their own.

I have expectations. I ask them what they can do; then I expect them to do it. They will always surprise you. I have also learned to let myself off the hook, that I'm not pounding information into them. Just like the students, teachers have to discover their own way rather than just being this rehearsed person. I have learned to give my students freedom of thought and to let them talk. I encourage them to be risk-takers and try to be one myself.

Teachers have expectations, take risks.

Scene 1, Take 2, of Super Mikey and the Evil Aliens

Film

Responding to Film

Students should have experiences with good children's films just as they do with good children's books. In an article I wrote with Joyce Many (Cox & Many, 1989), we discussed children's responses to both literature and film in the context of Rosenblatt's transactional theory:

> *In her transactional model of reader response, Rosenblatt (1985) also takes an eclectic view of the various literary forms and their potential as lived-through experiences. She uses the term "poem" to stand for any literary work of art which she describes as ". . . not an object but an event, a lived-through process or experience" (p. 35). The formal differences between stories, poems, and plays, which she classifies together as literary events, are not less great than the differences between literature and film. Indeed, she suggests that the transactional theory, which seeks to account for the question of "'literariness' or 'poeticity'—i.e., of 'the aesthetic' in 'literature'—has implications for aesthetic education in general" (1986, p. 122). An aesthetic transaction, where the focus of attention is on the lived-through experience and the accompanying ideas, sensations, feelings, and images, can occur*

between any perceiver and any artifact, as between any reader and any text. Thus, the value of the role of the reader, as stressed in reader response theories, can be analogized to the role of the viewer and the same perspective can be used to describe how understanding and literary discourse is created in response to film narrative as well as literature. (p. 289)

Children's Film Interests

Children like the same kinds of things in films that they like in books: storylike narratives, rather than nonnarratives, and live-action films with real-life characters, rather than animated, abstract films (Cox, 1982). Children can be encouraged to respond to films, just as they are to respond to literature, and the same kinds of response options are possible: discussion, writing, drama, and art and mediamaking (Cox & Many, 1992).

See *Martha the Movie Mouse,* by Arnold Lobel (1966), a children's book in rhyme about a mouse who loves movies.

Here's a good selection of children's films to begin with:

Ashpet: An American Cinderella (1989): Set in the rural South in the early years of World War II, *Ashpet* is a humorously touching version of Cinderella. This is one of the many fine films by Tom Davenport in his series "From the Brothers Grimm," all of which are set in the South in different historical periods. Others include *Hansel and Gretel: An Appalachian Version; The Frog King; Rapunzel, Rapunzel; Bearskin;* and *Jack and the Dentist's Daughter.* (Middle- to upper-elementary grades)

Close Harmony (1981): A beautifully done documentary about an intergenerational chorus of young children and senior citizens in New York. (Middle- to upper-elementary grades)

Molly's Pilgrim (1985): Based on the sensitive children's book by Barbara Cohen, this story is about a young Russian Jewish immigrant girl and how she overcomes the insensitivity of her classmates and gains acceptance in her new American environment. (Middle- to upper-elementary grades)

Night Ride (1994): A childhood memoir rich in visual imagery and characterization, based on a story by Kentucky writer Guerney Norman. Ned Beatty, a Kentuckian himself, stars. (Upper-elementary grades)

The Snowman (1982): Haunting original music accompanies this nonnarrated film version of Raymond Briggs's wordless picture book *The Snowman* (1978). (Primary grades)

The Sweater (1983): A young French Canadian boy in the 1940s idolizes professional hockey player Maurice Richard in this story filled with humor, nostalgia, and the universal fears and joys of childhood. The film was adapted to picture book form in *The Hockey Sweater,* by Roch Carrier (1984). (Primary- to upper-elementary grades)

The Tender Tale of Cinderella Penguin (1982): A wonderfully animated spoof of the familiar tale, both poignant and humorous: The glass slipper is webbed, and Cinderella tosses Prince Charming in the air during a torrid tango. (Primary grades)

Film Journals

Students use film journals in groups to discuss films shown in class or films they have seen on television or in movie theaters. In order to give students some basis for rating and responding to films, use the following film preference instrument (Cox, 1985):

1 = I didn't like it at all. (I would rather have done something else.)
2 = I didn't like it very much. (I wouldn't want to see it again.)
3 = It was OK. (I wouldn't mind seeing it again.)
4 = It was good. (I would like to see it again.)
5 = It was great! (I could see it many times without getting tired of it.)

A copy of this rating scheme could be put in the front of each student's ongoing film journal. Students could then give ratings to and write responses about all the films they view.

Film Response Guide

Here's a model for developing ideas for using a film in the classroom:

1. ***Previewing*****:** Teachers should always preview films for suitability and interest; to note concepts, themes, and vocabulary; and to plan how to extend the viewing experience.

2. ***Viewing:*** Children are already enthusiastic about films, so simple introductions are best. Perhaps include a few initiating questions, or suggest that students each remember one thing they saw or heard to talk about after viewing. Teachers should avoid long explanations, vocabulary lists, and questions that sound as if they plan to give a test on the film after showing it. As film critic Pauline Kael put it, "If you don't think you can kill the movies, you underestimate the power of education."

3. ***Postviewing:***

- *Watch-and-Talk Groups:* After viewing the film, let children talk about it in small groups. Observe their responses and then use them for planning response options and extending activities. The children's interests should be the basis for planning, rather than simply the film content.
- *Response Options:* The film-viewing experience is a powerful one. The showing of a 15 minute film—especially if it's one children really like—can create a "ripple effect" of experiences in the class that can last for days or weeks.
- *Resources:* Locate more films, books, and other materials that can extend the viewing experience.

Response Guide to **The Case of the Elevator Duck**

Figure 13.2 shows a sample film response guide developed for use with children's films. The film *The Case of the Elevator Duck*, based on a popular book for children by the same name (Berends, 1984), was rated highest in a study of children's film preferences (Cox, 1982).

PREVIEWING

Title THE CASE OF THE ELEVATOR DUCK **Rating** 4.67

Distributor Learning Corporation of America **Minutes** 17

Circle: (color)/b&w (live)/animated narration/(dialogue) (music)

Audience/Level Middle- to upper-elementary grades

Vocabulary housing project (introduce: genre, synopsis, pilot)

Annotation

The story unfolds around a semiclassic plot: boy finds duck (but can't keep it because of restrictions against pets in the housing project where he lives); boy finds duck's rightful owner (who can't keep it either); and boy finally finds a home for the duck at a day-care center. Characters include: Gilbert, an African American, 11-year-old boy, who's a part-time detective; his mother, who's supportive of his quest to find the duck a home but concerned about the housing authority; a housing policeman; a friend, who can't understand why our hero would rather play detective than basketball; a small Spanish-speaking boy, who can't tell Gilbert the duck belongs to him because he speaks no English; his adult sister, who refuses to take the duck back; and the director of the day-care center, who finally takes the duck in.

PREVIEWING

Introduction

Have you ever found an animal that you couldn't keep? What happened? How did you feel? Have you ever pretended you were a detective or helped solve a mystery? What happened?

POSTVIEWING

Watch-and-Talk Groups

Children's responses included: "I liked it because it was interesting, exciting, funny, etc." They said they liked the duck because they like ducks (in general), because he kept following the boy and appearing in the elevator, and because he was funny. The children liked the way the boy kept trying to find the duck a home; they also liked the boy's voice, thought he was funny, and thought he was nice to the duck. They said the story, action, acting, setting, and music were good. Many said they liked the film because they like animals, stories about children and animals together, and detective stories and mysteries. One child said he liked it because "there was a black boy it, and I'm a black boy, too." Overall response was very positive. Children rated this film extremely high.

Response Options

A. Literature

1. ***Story Synopsis/Genre:*** Write a synopsis based on the book *The Case of the Elevator Duck* (Berends, 1984) or another detective or mystery book you choose. Imagine that this book will become the basis for a new TV series that you will star in called *[Your Name], Young Detective*. Use the following outline to help you determine:

   a. Setting b. Time c. Characters d. Plot

   Write in the style of other detective and mystery stories you have read and viewed.

FIGURE 13.2 Film Response Guide for *The Case of the Elevator Duck*

B. Writing

1. ***Point of View:*** Write the story of *The Case of the Elevator Duck* from the point of view of one of the other characters: Gilbert's mother; the housing policeman; Gilbert's friend, Julio; Julio's sister; or the day-care center director.
2. ***Personification:*** Pretend the duck is a person, and write the story from its point of view. Pretend the elevator is a person, and write the story from its point of view.
3. ***Further Adventures:*** Write about the further adventures of Gilbert or a character from another detective or mystery book. Perhaps start a series of these stories.
4. ***E.T. II:*** Tell about the time you found an animal that you couldn't keep. If this has never happened to you, imagine that you've found an animal or any creature (an extraterrestrial?). What happened?
5. ***Pattern Writing:*** Write a poem about a duck using a pattern such as *cinquain*.
6. ***Concrete Writing:*** Write a poem on a picture or cutout of a duck, or write a poem about a duck in the shape of a duck.

Cinquain and other patterns are described and illustrated in Chapter 10, Reading and Writing, the section on poetry.

C. Drama, Art, Music, and Dance

1. ***Dramatization:*** Dramatize one of the scripts written above as part of a live play, puppet show, videotaped TV show, or tape-recorded radio show.
2. ***Storyboards:*** Using one of the scripts already written, create a storyboard for a Super 8 or videotaped film project.
3. ***Video or Super 8 Filmmaking:*** Make a film from the storyboard.
4. ***"The Duck" Dance:*** Think about how the duck in the movie moved. Describe three or four movements, and do your own versions of them. Choose some music with a good beat, and dance these movements to it, creating a pattern you can repeat and show or teach to others. Then put on the music and do "The Duck."

RELATED RESOURCES

A. ***Books:*** Many mystery and detective books are available for children. Here are a few suggestions:

The Case of the Double Cross (Bonsall, 1980)
Encyclopedia Brown Carries On (Sobol, 1980)
Matilda's Masterpiece (Anderson, 1977)
Nate the Great and the Phony Clue (Sharmat, 1977)
The Rocking Horse Secret (Godden, 1978)

B. ***Films:*** The following live-action films (some of which are book adaptations) follow themes and plots similar to those of *The Case of the Elevator Duck:* a boy or girl and his or her dog, duck goat, horse, kangaroo, extraterrestrial?

Clown (1969)
Being Right, Can You Still Lose? (1976)
Me and You Kangaroo (1973)
Phillip and the White Colt (1973) (adapted from the feature *Run Wild, Run Free,* based on the book by David Rook)
Zlateh the Goat (1973) (adapted from the story by Isaac B. Singer)

Filmmaking with a Camera

See *Ida Makes a Movie,* by Kay Chaoro (1974), about a personified cat who makes a movie and wins an international student film contest.

Filmmaking is a natural outgrowth of film study, just as writing books can follow from literature appreciation (Cox, 1975a, 1975b, 1983). I started making films with children when I started teaching and found the same great benefits that Audrey Eldridge did: Students were self-directed, learning by doing, working hard, and preparing for a world of media. I also found, like Audrey, that I had to take some risks and set some expectations. In the many years I've been doing the media with children, they've never disappointed me or themselves.

Video and Super 8

This discussion of materials and steps in filmmaking will apply to Super 8 and video. Even though video has become more popular than Super 8 in the home movie market, Super 8 is still preferable for color animation and artful editing possibilities. The disadvantage of Super 8 is that the film must be processed before it can be seen, whereas video film can be played back immediately. Other advantages of video are the availability of materials and equipment and ease of editing in the camera. Video is ideal for live-action filmmaking but not for animation. The disadvantages for animation are that it's difficult to shoot a few frames at a time (which is how animated movies are filmed), that shots may have "snow" between them, and that the film will appear jerky.

Film Techniques

As mentioned, the two basic types of films are *live-action* and *animation*. The live-action type includes these subtypes:

- *Documentary:* Students film real events or interviews and put them together in a realistic, documentary style, adding narration, comments, and interviews.
- *Drama:* Students tell a story, which is usually fiction and involves background sets, props, and costumes, and scripted dialogue.
- *Docudrama:* Students combine real events from the present, the past, or somewhere else in the word, adding a narrative story.

Animated films include these subtypes:

See *Make Your Own Animated Movies and Videotapes,* by Yvonne Andersen (1991), a how-to book for children.

- *Three-Dimensional Animation:* Objects are filmed one frame at a time or in short bursts (controlled by a cable release attachment for Super 8) and then moved between frames or bursts; using this technique, inanimate objects appear to move. People can be animated, too, and made to appear doing impossible things, like flying. For elementary students, think about using clay or plasticine, toys, stuffed animals, and puppets.
- *Flat Animation:* A series of drawings are made in which each is just slightly different than the one before. These are arranged sequentially in a flip book and then filmed. Flat cut-out animation can be done using paper shapes cut into pieces or using photographs or cut-outs from photographs.

Materials

1. *Filmmaking Folder:* Each child can use a folder to hold all his or her written materials, such as lists of ideas or supplies, shooting schedules, and notes about equipment, props, and who will do what jobs. Blank storyboard forms should be included, too.

2. *Equipment:* Schools, libraries, and media centers own video equipment. If they don't have a Super 8 camera, ask parents or camera stores about borrowing them. The following equipment is needed for Super 8 and video filmmaking:

- *Super 8:* A Super 8 camera with a cable release; a tripod to secure the camera; for indoor filming, photoflood 250 watt bulbs and clamps to hold them; projector; and splicing equipment.
- *Video:* A video camcorder, which can take just a few frames at a time for animation. (The Sony Video 8 Pro CCD-V220 camcorder will do this if you slide the red button marked "RECORD" forward on the VTR panel, or you can use an accessory remote control, like a cable release. You also need a tripod and photoflood bulbs for indoor animation.)

A *camcorder* is a combination video camera/tape recorder.

3. *Film:*

- *Super 8:* Use Kodachrome 40 for animation with lights or for filming outdoors, unless you can film near a window. For large sets that need more light, use Ektachrome 160. Both must be sent to Kodak for processing. For fast local processing, use Ektachrome 7244, a slightly lower-grade film.
- *Video:* Use any type of videotape.

For processing Super 8 film, send it directly to Kodak.

Steps in Filmmaking

The steps in filmmaking discussed here (Cox, 1983) are illustrated with examples of a film made by fourth-graders, *The Adventures of Planet Man,* using cut-out animation. (Audrey Eldridge's students went through this same basic process in making *Super Mikey and the Evil Aliens,* the project discussed in the Snapshot.)

1. *Brainstorming:* This is a period in which students exchange ideas. When a central theme has emerged, they can continue to work together to refine it or break into groups and work on different parts of it.

The fourth-grade students who made *Planet Man* each made notes on what they would like in the film and then shared them. Their ideas were grouped according to characters, setting, plot, and theme. The students picked the standard science fiction genre but showed great flair for creative names for characters. See Figure 13.3, which shows the cluster the students created in brainstorming about their movie.

2. *Plot Synopsis:* The next step is to pull all the ideas together into one plot, as illustrated by this plot synopsis for *The Adventures of Planet Man:*

FIGURE 13.3 Students' Idea Cluster for Science Fiction Film

A fight between evildoers and heroes. Planet Man is taking Princess Prine to Kandavolin. She is going to bring a top-secret formula for a machine to go back in time to the king there. She is captured by two monsters, the Horlock and the Mudagoo. The secret was handed down from her father before he died. If the evil Dr. Galaxy gets it, he can control the galaxy after he builds the machine. Planet Man is trying to save the Princess but he is vulnerable to Cyplonite. He is stopped by the monsters with Cyplonite.

Meanwhile, the monsters take Princess Prine to another planet, Sisen, and Dr. Galaxy and the Horlock and the Mudagoo torture her. Starben, faithful partner of Planet Man, rescues him. They both go to Sisen to rescue Princess Prine. They have a war in space against Dr. Galaxy's forces. Planet Man and Starben and the good guys barely win, by a hair, a hairsbreadth. They land and have a land fight. They rescue the Princess and get the secret, capture the evildoers and live happily ever after.

3. *Storyboards:* The storyboard is based on the plot summary. Using storyboard forms (which have a sequence of blank squares), students draw an image for each scene in sequence. Space around the squares is for notes about scene summaries, dialogue, sound effects, shooting directions, or whatever is needed to film the scene. The storyboard must show the scenes in the order in which they'll be filmed.

The storyboard for *Planet Man,* shown in Figure 13.4, was prepared by three groups of students; each illustrated one-third of the plot summary on the storyboard. The three groups came together to revise and edit, iron out transitions, and create a satisfying ending.

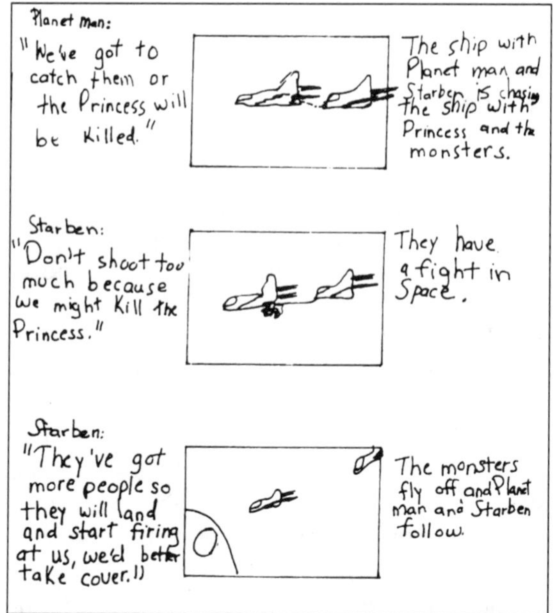

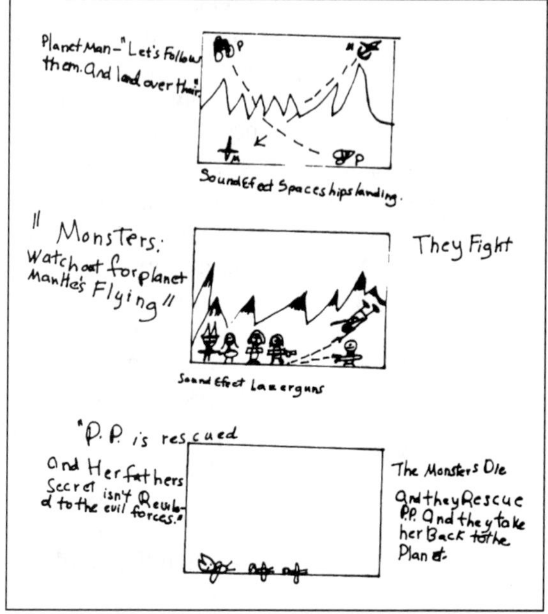

FIGURE 13.4 Storyboard for *The Adventures of Planet Man*

4. ***Backgrounds and Props:*** These can be created from school supplies, such as poster paper, butcher paper, colored paper, paint, crayons, and so on. Avoid white poster paper because it reflects too much light. Black and blue work well.

For *Planet Man,* the students created backgrounds using 22" × 28" poster paper. One background was black with yellow stars cut out of construction paper, which could be moved to show outer space. Another background was blue and had the inside of Planet Man's space ship painted on it. The backdrop for the fight scene on the planet's surface was also blue with mountains painted on it. Props were cut out of construction paper: black letters for title and credits, yellow stars and comets, grey space ships, and characters with separate body parts that could be animated. For instance, facial expressions could be shown with several different mouths in different positions (e.g., a smile, frown, big "O" for surprise).

5. ***Learning to Use Equipment:*** The teacher should demonstrate as much as he or she knows: parts of the camera, basic handling, how to turn it off and on. Then students should be encouraged to experiment, since the only way they will learn to use the camera is by using it. To avoid students' all trying to get their hands on the camera at once, designate one or two (at the most) to be camera persons at any given time. Keep in mind that students will be very motivated at this point.

6. ***Shooting a Film:*** Shooting a film means lights, camera, action—actually, a lot of action, both in front of and behind the camera. Filming is not hard but precise. Young filmmakers learn quickly that the best policy is careful planning. If they're filming a scene with specific characters, costumes, and props, they must be there in advance, ready to go. Students meet this challenge easily because they really want to make films. Here is a step-by-step sequence for filming a shot:

Step 1. Set up backgrounds and props: If children are filming a three-dimensional animated sequence, have them prepare a background that will fill the camera frame for the objects to be animated. Then practice positioning objects and make arrangements for them to stand, sit, or whatever position they are to hold while being filmed. Animation backgrounds can be put on the floor or a table. Live-action scenes can be set up on location in the room or outside and children arrange whatever properties—signs, props, costumes—they need.

Step 2. Secure the camera to the tripod: If filming is done outside, it's better to secure the camera to the tripod before taking it outdoors. A tripod should be used for any staged, rehearsed shots. A hand-held camera is very difficult to control, so it should only be used for on-the-spot events, as when the children are doing a documentary.

Step 3. Set up the camera: Adjust the height, angle, and distance to frame the shot properly. Adjust the distance and focus. Errors in setting up the camera can result in several problems; for instance, the edges may show around an animation scene or the camera may move if not properly secured, making the picture wobbly or out of focus. To avoid problems, the teacher should check the set-up, especially at first. As students become more experienced, they can do this themselves.

In setting up for filming *The Adventures of Planet Man,* the poster paper backgrounds were placed on the floor and the camera, which was attached to a tripod, was angled down. The children who animated the characters sat on the floor and moved the characters' body parts and objects while others filmed each move using a cable release attachment. A light was attached to one tripod leg with an adjustable clamp.

7. ***Editing:*** The simplest way to edit is to do so in the camera; that is, shoot the scenes in the order in which they will be shown. If the scenes don't need reshooting for any reason, the editing will be done when the film is processed or the video is shown. Not all scenes work right the first time, however; retakes are sometimes needed. Or if you're making a film in which several groups are working on different parts, it may not be possible to shoot the film in order.

Sometimes, different groups will make their films on the same roll, which will have to be cut up to separate the films. For video, copy just the scenes you want to use on another tape. You will need two TVs or monitors and an editing controller. For Super 8, physically cut out the scenes you don't want and splice the film back together. This can be done with a Guillotine Super 8 mm tape splicer or a Craig Master Splicer, which uses splicing cement. Here are basic steps to editing Super 8:

Step 1. Cut out the scenes: Children view the entire roll of film and cut out scenes with scissors. Discard scenes that don't work.

Step 2. Editing bags: Drop all the scenes for one film in a large, clean, paper bag. This will keep the film clean and safe from tears or bending.

Step 3. Ordering scenes: Children put the scenes in order by taping each length of film to the inside top of the bag with a big piece of masking tape; a number on each piece of tape identifies the scene number.

Step 4. Splicing: The teacher should demonstrate this to children or let them read the directions and try it themselves using discarded film. After making two good practice splices, students can work on their own films.

8. ***Sound:*** Sound is done simultaneously with video. It can be added to a Super 8 film if a sound stripe is provided during processing, or a tape can be made to go with the film, adding narration, dialogue, sound effects, or music.

Filmmaking without a Camera

A great alternative is to have children draw directly on different types of film stock with thin-tipped, permanent marking pens (Cox, 1980). The images they draw will be projected, just like photoimages. Students can make 16 mm films, 35 mm filmstrips, slides, and transparencies using this method.

Materials and Equipment

In addition to thin-tipped, permanent markers, students will need the following materials to make each of the four types of films:

Good markers for drawing on film: Staedtler Lumocolor S313 permanent thin-tip markers, available in eight colors.

1. *Films:* Clear 16 mm film; reel and can; film gauge; film projector
2. *Filmstrips:* Clear filmstrip or 35 mm film roll; filmstrip can; filmstrip gauge; filmstrip projector
3. *Slides:* 35 mm negatives, film roll, or blank transparency; plastic slide mounts; slide gauge; slide projector
4. *Transparencies:* Blank transparency; mounts

Buy clear 16 mm or 35 mm film stock where art supplies are sold. Or use a solution of bleach and water to strip the emulsion off old films, filmstrips, 35 mm negative strips, or 35 mm rolls of film. After stripping, wipe the film dry and store it in a clean, dry container.

Sources for clear 16 mm or 35 mm film stock: Eastman Kodak, New York, NY (800-634-6101) and Christy's Editorial Film Supply, Burbank, CA (818-845-1755).

Making Films

To make films, children draw directly on 16 mm clear film stock. Younger children can do this as a simple whole-class project, and older children can work in small groups or make individual films in a filmmaking center.

For Younger Children. Try this whole-class project around a holiday, using it to provide a central theme, images, and colors (e.g., red hearts on Valentine's Day, black and orange witches and pumpkins at Halloween, etc.). Follow this sequence:

1. *Brainstorm ideas:* Talk about what images and colors to use.

2. *Prepare surface:* Cover a long table with newspaper, and tape it down.

3. *Set up blank film:* Take a reel of blank 16 mm film, and unroll a strip the length of the table. Use clay to secure the reel upright at one end. Secure the film leader (i.e., the beginning portion) in a few places with masking tape.

4. *Take turns drawing:* Let three or so children stand on each side of the table and draw on the film, making anything they wish or images related to the central theme. When they have covered the length of film on the table, untape it and unroll more film; drop the drawn-on film into a clean, dry paper bag on the floor at the end of the table. Continue this process until everyone has taken a turn drawing on the film.

5. *Rewind film on reel and show:* Wind the finished film from the bag back onto the 16 mm reel by hand, and then show it to the class.

This activity works well even with very young children. I made films with preschool students this way. One done at Valentine's Day was covered with dancing red hearts and children's attempts at writing *love*. When it was done, the teacher used the film in a variety of ways. The class tried out different music with it, sung along with it, and finally danced with it.

See the draw-on films of Norman McLaren, such as *Hen Hop* (1942) and *Begone Dull Care* (1949), distributed by International Film Bureau.

For Older Children. Follow the basic ideas for filmmaking with a camera and for drawing on film. But obviously, older children can go beyond very simple or abstract images, creating representational images of simple shapes changing or even letters and words. In order for a single image to appear for 1 second on the screen, it should be repeated for 24 frames. Repeat the same image with changes done in steps to show a gradual transition: a smiling face to a frowning face, words telling a simple message, and the like. Let children experiment with this technique. To help older students organize their thoughts before filmmaking, have them create a storyboard.

Filmstrips

To make filmstrips, children draw and write on clear 35 mm film stock the same way just described for making films (Cox, 1987). Use the following step-by-step sequence for any age:

1. *Brainstorm:* Filmstrips lend themselves to themes about holidays or simple changes: winter to spring, morning to evening, and so on. Filmstrips are also ideal for telling simple story sequences (e.g., folktales, adaptations of pattern books), creating visual images to go with word images in poetry, or responding to literature (e.g., parts of the story students liked and want to share).

2. *Storyboard:* Make a copy of a filmstrip gauge (see Figure 13.5) but about three times longer than usual. Duplicate the gauge for students to use as storyboard frames. Children draw images on the gauge, and add narration or dialogue on the side. See Figure 13.6, which shows a sample filmstrip story-

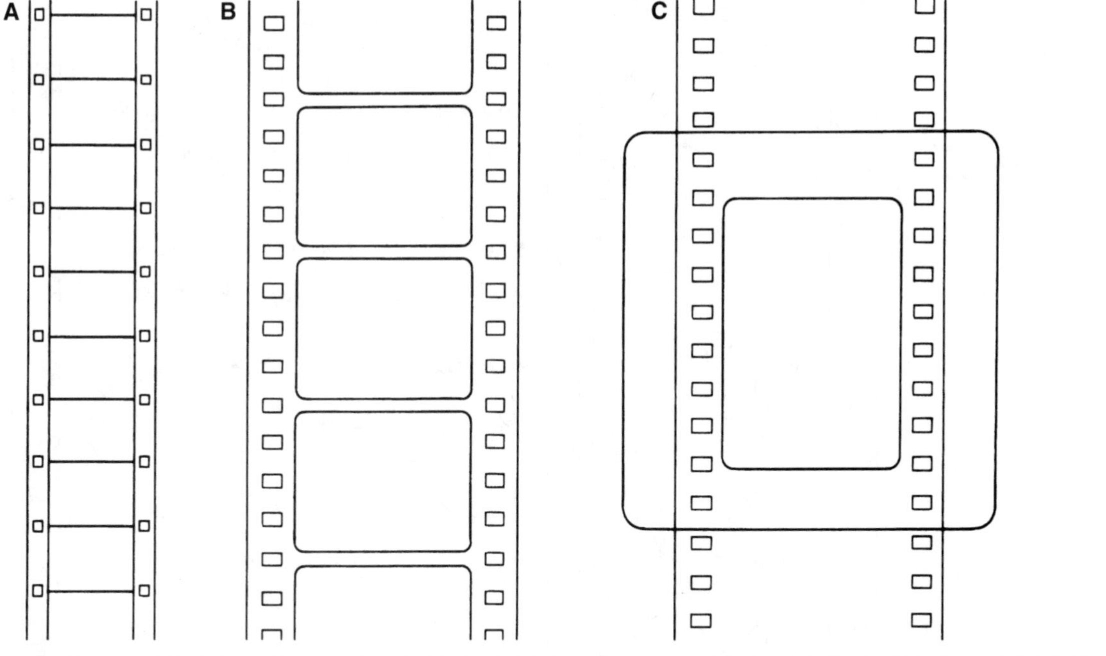

FIGURE 13.5 **Part A:** 16 mm Film Gauge. **Part B:** 35 mm Filmstrip Gauge. **Part C:** Slide Gauge with 35 mm Film Superimposed to Show Relative Size.

board for *The Velveteen Rabbit* (Williams, 1975). The child who made this did so as a response option after his teacher read aloud the book to the class. When the storyboard was complete, the child transferred the images to the filmstrip, as described in the next step.

3. *Transfer images to film:* Tape a strip of clear filmstrip directly over the gauge and trace over the storyboard images with permanent marking pens. Leave about 2 inches of leader at the top as well as frames for opening credits (the title) and directions ("Focus," "Start tape"). Leave room at the end of the film for closing credits ("Made by . . ." and names of filmmakers).

4. *Sound:* Children can narrate the filmstrip while it's being shown or make a tape recording to go with it.

5. *Show the filmstrip:* Show it as you would any filmstrip.

Slides

Use clean 35 mm gauge blank film, and cut it to fit the size of plastic slide mounts. Children can brainstorm ideas, make storyboards showing sequences of images, and transfer those images to film by tracing over them with permanent marking pens. A recorded narrative or music can be added to create a slide/tape show. One advantage to creating a slide show is that the order of the slides can be changed, which can't be done with a film or filmstrip.

FIGURE 13.6
Filmstrip Storyboard for *The Velveteen Rabbit*

Transparencies

Having children draw on blank transparencies works well for reporting information, telling stories, or creating visual aids for telling about a book. One transparency can be used as a visual aid, or several can be used to tell a story. By attaching additional transparencies to the sides of an original transparency, students can create multilayered images. They can lay each added transparency over the original image, telling a story in layers and building up to a scene that includes all the images. These attached transparencies can be cut into two or smaller to make even more possible additions.

This format works well for retelling cumulative tales like *The Napping House* (Wood, 1985), in which a little boy and a lot of animals end up on top of a sleeping granny and then all fly off. This story can be depicted by adding and then removing images of the boy and animals to that of the granny. Transparencies can be stored in manila folders.

Television

Critical Viewing

Neil Postman (1961) has described television as "the first curriculum," given children's experience with this medium before coming to school. Teachers can help children develop critical viewing habits without planning in-class television viewing by simply drawing on students' experiences at home or when an important is televised event (e.g., a presidential inauguration or space mission). Try these activities:

- ***Survey Students' Viewing Habits:*** Have students keep logs for 2 weeks of when, what, and how much (total time) television they watch each day. Based on students' records, discuss their viewing habits. Repeat this activity periodically to note any changes.

- ***Television Journals:*** Have students keep television journals as a basis for thinking and talking about viewing in class. Suggest double-entry journals, in which students note what they watched in one column and their reaction to it in another. Students can write in class as part of regular journal writing. Journals are especially effective as response options to targeted viewing—for example, a documentary related to a content area or an adaptation of literature read in class (e.g., *Sarah, Plain and Tall* [MacLachlan, 1985]).

- ***Television Fact and Fiction:*** Pick a topic and compare how it's depicted on television with what students know about it from their own experience. Use the following frame:

Television Fact and Fiction Frame

Topic	*TV Image*	*Real Experience*	*Explanation of Difference*
Moms	*I Love Lucy:* Lucy stays at home and gets into trouble with crazy schemes.	My Mom works and would never do all those crazy things; she'd be too tired.	Exaggeration is funny sometimes when it's not real.

"Moms" in the frame was written by two of my children—Gordon, 13, and Elizabeth, 10—both great fans of Lucy reruns.

• ***Television and Literature:*** Pick a show or special that's been adapted from a book, such as *Little House on the Prairie* [Wilder, 1935] or a certain genre (e.g., humor, adventure, mystery). Compare how the original book and adapted TV versions are alike and different. Use the following frame:

TV/Book Comparison Frame

	Book	*Television*
Setting		
Characters		
Plot		
Theme		
Mood		

Videorecording

Most schools today have VCR systems that will enable students to do videorecordings. Even very young children know how to use videos and take readily to this easy-to-use medium for recording events and stories. Videos are easy to film, show, and erase. They works well for spontaneous, improvisational, on-the-spot experiences, such as these:

• ***Self-Portraits:*** Have students do self-portraits as part of an "All about Me" project for young children or full-blown autobiographies for older ones. These videos can be shot in school or at home; people from home can come to school, as needed for filming. A buddy system works well, such that one student acts as the crew for the other's self-portrait.

• ***Role-Playing:*** Improvisational situations of all kinds can be videotaped: real-life situations, such as resolving conflicts between friends; scenes from the past, such as interviews with famous explorers or scientists; or scenes from literature, such as the "wild rumpus" in *Where the Wild Things Are* (Sendak, 1963).

"How did you feel when you proved the earth was flat, Mr. Columbus?" Fifth-graders videotape a dramatized interview.

• ***Dramatic Readings:*** Tape a reader's theater presentation of a poem or a story or of students reading their own writing.

See Chapter 6, Drama in the Classroom, for more on reader's theater, story dramatization, and script writing.

• ***Plays:*** Tape story dramatizations or plays written by students.

• ***TV Shows and Commercials:*** Encourage children to create original TV shows, TV show spin-offs, or commercials. Commercials can be spoofs or advertise real products, favorite books, or school events.

• ***News Reports:*** Have students plan and tape a newscast, including headlines, sports, weather, commentary, and commercials. The newscast could have a special focus, such as humor or fantasy (e.g., *News from the Moon*), or relate to content areas (e.g., *News from the Santa Fe Trail, Dateline 1890*).

• ***Oral Histories:*** Have students choose topics and collect first-person accounts about them, creating oral histories of their school or community or a local historical event.

• ***Portraits:*** Ask students to pick special individuals about whom to do documentaries: a family member, classmate, teacher, or community figure.

Photography

Because photography is a pervasive and popular medium—used extensively in books, advertisements, newspapers, magazines, and even at home—it's easy to work with in the classroom. Photographs are easily accessible, and many photographic activities are easy to do in the classroom.

Photoillustration

To introduce the concept of photoillustration, show students examples from children's literature. The following list includes photoillustrators of children's books, characterizing their work and citing titles to consult:

• **Tana Hoban** uses black-and-white and color photographs to illustrate her many concept books: *A, B, See!* (1982); *Count and See* (1972); *Dig, Drill, Dump, Fill* (1975); *Exactly the Opposite* (1990); and *Of Colors and Things* (1989).

• **Bruce McMillan** uses color photographs to illustrate concept and nonfiction books, such as *Mary Had a Little Lamb* (1990a); *One Sun: A Book of Terse Verse* (1990b); and *Time to . . .* (1989).

• **Russell Freedman** often uses archival photographs in biographies and historical books: *Children of the Wild West* (1983); *Franklin Delano Roosevelt* (1990); *Immigrant Kids* (1980); *Indian Chiefs* (1983); *Lincoln: A Photobiography* (1987); and *The Wright Brothers: How They Invented the Airplane* (1991).

- **George Ancona** has illustrated many books with dynamic black-and-white and color photographs: *Handtalk: An ABC of Finger Spelling and Sign Language* (Charlip & Miller, 1974); *Artists of Handcrafted Furniture at Work* (Rosenberg, 1988); and *The First Thanksgiving Feast* (Anderson, 1991).

- **Ken Heyman** uses photographs taken all over the world to illustrate multicultural books co-authored with Ann Morris: *Bread, Bread, Bread* (1989); *Loving* (1990a); *On the Go* (1990b); and *On their Toes: A Soviet Ballet School* (1991).

Students should also be encouraged to bring pictures from home for photoillustration activities focused on themselves or their families. Examples of activities for children of different ages are described in the following sections.

Photo Portraits

Primary students can do photo essays as a part of an "All about Me" project. They can bring pictures from home that document their "early years" and take pictures of themselves at school and home. All these photographs can be compiled in an album, adding captions and stories to go with them. Older students can do self-portraits or portraits of family members, friends, or adults in the school or community.

Students can make photo collages of pictures of themselves on poster paper. One twist on this idea is to trace their body outlines on butcher paper, cut them out, and cover them with photographs and captions.

It's also fun to have students bring in baby pictures of themselves; have them write their names on the backs but keep them secret from one another. Make a bulletin board of the pictures, and add names as students guess who's in each picture.

Photo Essays

Students can use photos from home or taken during the schoolyear and then add words to compose a photoillustrated essay on a topic of interest (e.g., a personal or class pet, a hobby or a science project, or a family trip or school fieldtrip). Students can also do group essays on chosen topics, and their work can be displayed in the classroom or hallway.

Photojournalism

Photographs are used extensively in newspapers and magazines to illustrate stories. Have students examine these kinds of photographs and discuss how they're used and what makes them effective. Try the following activities:

- ***Elements of a News Photograph:*** Select several photographs from the newspaper. Discuss the following elements for each one: choice of subject, details in background, camera angle, and caption. How do these affect the reader? Why?

• ***News Captions:*** Cut out photographs from newspapers with the captions removed. Give the photos to groups of students and ask them to discuss what the stories the photos are from might be about. Then write new captions and compare them to the real captions.

• ***Photo Ads:*** Cut out ads with photographs from magazines. Group them by the products they are selling: soap, shampoo, cars, or whatever. For each group, discuss the features of the photographs highlighted to sell the item.

• ***Collages:*** Have students cut out photographs and ads from magazines and make collages on poster paper. Encourage them to put images together that aren't usually seen together. Students should share their collages in groups and talk about the impact of combining various photographic images, especially if they're not expected to be together.

• ***Historical News Photographs:*** Order duplicated copies of photographs of special events from September 1851 to the present from The New York Times Information Office, 207 West 43rd Street, New York, NY 10036. Discuss these photos with studying the historical period in which they were taken.

Taking Photographs with and without a Camera

Many schools have cameras for students' and teachers' use. In addition, local camera stores and parents might be willing to loan or donate equipment. Polaroid cameras are especially attractive for school use because they provide instant results. Also keep in mind that photographs can be taken with and without a camera.

The Polaroid Education Program provides free Polaroid cameras, film, and teacher training. Contact Polaroid Corporation, 750 Main Street, #2N, Cambridge, MA 02139 (617-577-5090).

With a Camera

Children can write stories that take place in the classroom or school, create storyboards about them, shoot the needed pictures, and write captions and narration. These stories can be published as books or on a bulletin board.

Children can create photo albums of pictures that document special events in their lives, or the class can document an event together (e.g., the class gerbil has babies). To accompany the photos, students should write captions.

Without a Camera

Students can make photographs without a camera, or *photograms,* by placing small objects on light-sensitive paper and exposing it to sunlight. The image, captured on paper, will appear white, and the background will be black. The sharpest images are made from small objects with clearly defined edges: keys, scissors, leaves, and paper clips, for example.

Light-sensitive paper can be purchased at camera stores or where art supplies are sold.

Begin by reading *A, B, See!* (Hoban, 1982), an alphabet book of photograms. Each page shows objects to illustrate a given letter. Talk about the book and how students could make their own photograms or alphabet books. Identify and find objects that fit the theme chosen. Students can write captions and make photo exhibits or a class book of images.

See *Pictures without a Camera,* a children's book by T. J. Marino (1974).

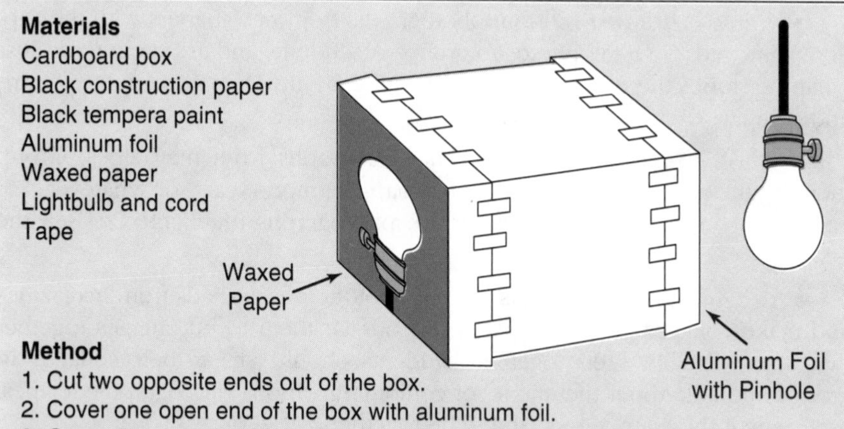

Materials
Cardboard box
Black construction paper
Black tempera paint
Aluminum foil
Waxed paper
Lightbulb and cord
Tape

Method
1. Cut two opposite ends out of the box.
2. Cover one open end of the box with aluminum foil.
3. Cover the opposite open end of the box with waxed paper.
4. Poke the tiniest possible pin-hole in the center of the aluminum foil.
5. Turn on an unshaded lightbulb at one end of a darkened room.
6. Position the box with the aluminum foil side toward the lightbulb.
7. View the projected image of the lightbulb on the wax-papered end of the box. The projected image will be inverted. The pin-hole represents the lens end of the camera, and the wax-papered end represents the film. In a real camera, the image would be projected onto the film.

FIGURE 13.7 How to Make a Pin-Hole Camera

Make a Pinhole Camera

To increase students' appreciation of photography, help them understand how a camera works. Make a pinhole camera, as illustrated in Figure 13.7. This early version dates back to the Ancient Greeks, who discovered that light could pass through a small hole and project an inverted image onto a screen. The Greeks used this discovery to learn about astronomy—for example, to track the sun's movement during an eclipse. Another type of pinhole camera was used during the Renaissance; a hole was drilled into a wall, and the entire room was darkened to create the *camera obscura* ("darkened room").

Xerography

Students can be creative with duplicated copies of photographs: reducing or enlarging size, changing the tone from dark to light, cutting them up and making collages, and so on. Stories can be created to go with these xerographies (based on the word *Xerox*).

Print

Throughout this book, we've discussed the print media usually found in schools: textbooks, children's literature, children's own writing, and teachers' writing. In this section, we'll discuss two types of print media that are prevalent in the community but less used in school: newspapers and magazines.

Newspapers

To introduce the newspaper to students in the middle and upper grades, many schools use a Newspaper in Education (NIE) program. In it, newspapers are delivered to the school, and support materials and inservice training for teachers may be provided, as well. Teachers should contact their local newspapers for information about NIE. Students can also bring newspapers from home.

To help students become familiar with newspapers, set up a Newspaper Center in the classroom. Gather resources (e.g., newspapers, NIE materials, and children's books about newspapers), and prepare a bulletin board displaying parts of the newspaper. Plan time each day for students to read the newspaper and for the whole class to discuss it.

TEACHING IDEA

Introducing the Newspaper

Day 1. Newspaper Makeup

1. As a class and with children sharing newspapers in groups, examine the parts of the newspaper: front page, index, other news pages, editorial, sports, entertainment sections, feature articles, photographs, charts, puzzles, comics, and advertising.

2. Ask each group to find and cut out examples of different types of news stories: local, county, state, national, international; features about people, places, and events; editorials, letters to the editor, and editorial cartoons; display ads; and classified ads. With others in their groups, students should talk about the characteristics of the part they found.

3. Have groups share what they found with the whole class. Repeat this sharing time several times so each group looks closely at another part of the newspaper on different days.

See *Deadline! From News to Newspaper* by Gail Gibbons (1987).

Day 2. Organization of a News Story

1. After everyone has had a chance to read some of the newspaper, discuss the stories they've read and what makes them newsworthy.

2. Discuss the *inverted pyramid pattern* of news stories, in which the most important information is at the beginning of the story. That way, if the length of the story has to be cut, it can be done from the end without losing essential information.

3. Discuss and identify what's contained in the *lead* to the story, the five Ws and one H: What? When? Where? Who? Why? and How? See Figure 13.8, an example of a frame to get children started.

Inverted Pyramid Pattern of a News Story
Most Important Information
Who?
What?
When?
Where?
Why?
How?
:
Least Important Information

(continued)

Read the story and answer each question:

WHAT happened? ______________________________

WHEN did it happen? ______________________________

WHERE did it happen? ______________________________

WHO was there? ______________________________

WHY did it happen? ______________________________

HOW did it happen? ______________________________

FIGURE 13.8 Frame for the Parts of a Newspaper Story

Day 3. Sources of News

1. Discuss how news is gathered, what *datelines* are, and what news agencies do.

2. Have different groups cut out examples of the following types of news item:
   a. Story supplied by the Associated Press
   b. Story supplied by United Press International
   c. Local story with a byline
   d. Syndicated feature
   e. Stories datelined in other states
   f. Stories datelined in other countries

3. Ask the groups to share and compare the different sources of news they've discovered.

Day 4. Headlines

1. Discuss several headlines in the day's newspaper. Ask students: What makes a good headline? Choose one and rewrite it with the whole class.

2. Have each student choose and rewrite a headline, to be shared with the class.

3. Ask students to make up and share fanciful headlines based on class events, nursery rhymes, or stories.

Day 5. Sports

1. Discuss stories in the day's newspaper and whether sports should be included.

2. Have groups find articles about different sports classifications: professional, amateur, spectator, and participation.

3. In groups on their own, have students write sports stories about a local college or professional team, a school sports event, a fictitious sports event, or one from a story.

Subsequent Days: More Newspaper Topics

1. Focus on other parts of the newspaper: comics, entertainment, advertising, business, editorials, advice columns, the weather, horoscopes, and so forth. Have groups study different parts (which have been assigned or selected) and share what they've learned with the whole class.

2. Analyze all the stories on the front page one day. Categorize each as (a) good news, (b) bad news, or (c) neutral news. Note how many end up in each category, and discuss why there is usually so much bad news.

3. Using the 5 Ws and H and the inverted pyramid pattern, have students write a variety of types of news stories about class, school, or community events. Then have students write a reverse version of a typical type of story—for instance, reporting that schools will receive more rather than less money.

Creating a Class Newspaper

After being introduced to the newspaper, students can create their own class, school, community, or fictional newspaper (e.g., based on literature or from another time and place in history). After the class has decided on the type of newspaper, organize the children into a newspaper staff: editor-in-chief, section editors, reporters, cartoonists, layout designers, photographers, and advertising account executives. Children can work in groups to produce the final paper.

To see a historical fiction newspaper created by students, see Chapter 9, The Writing Process, *The Colonial Times* (Figure 9.7).

Look into computer software like The Newsroom, which is a data-based newspaper-producing package for classroom use. With it, children organize their writing into a complete newspaper with banners, a photo lab, copy desk, layout, wire service, and printing press. In addition to explaining what's in a newspaper, this software includes icons, print choices, and clip art; helps students find topics to write about; and prints out the final paper.

See the children's book *The Furry News: How to Make a Newspaper*, by Loreen Leedy (1990).

Magazines

Use magazines from the school library, those available in the class library, or those children bring from home. Use the same techniques to introduce magazines as those described in the Teaching Idea on introducing the newspaper.

Advertising Language

Magazines are ideal for helping children learn about advertising language: namely, how ads make claims that should be interpreted critically. Consider the following types of claims, which are also found on television and in newspapers:

Testimonial	Endorsement by a famous person or organization
Transfer	Qualities of one thing transfer to another
Plain folks	Talking down to people to appear to be one of them
Bandwagon	Everybody's doing it
Snob appeal	Better people are doing it
Facts/figures	Suggests there are statistics to support it
Hidden fears	Playing on people's insecurities
Repetition	Say it often enough so it can't be forgotten
Magic	A special ingredient makes it effective
Weasel words	Misleading customers to think it's good

Since these types of claims are also found in television and newspaper advertisements, this activity could be used in studying those media, as well.

Make an overhead transparency or poster to introduce these common types of advertising claims. Given this list, children can work in groups to look through magazines, find examples, and cut them out. Each group can make a poster to display or share with the class. Children might also write and illustrate or photoillustrate their own advertisements, using advertising language and claims.

Creating a Class Magazine

Children could produce a class magazine in the same way they would a class newspaper. For example, they could report on what they learned in a science or social studies unit and publish it in a magazine with different types of articles: features, fiction, advice and how-to, advertisements, classified ads, and letters to the editor. Or the class could make a literary magazine filled with students' poetry and stories and illustrated with their drawings and photographs.

Here's a list of magazines that publish children's art and writing:

Children's Digest, Box 567, Indianapolis, IN 46206

Cricket, Box 100, La Salle, IL 61301

Ebony, Jr., 820 S. Michigan Ave., Chicago, IL 60605

Highlights for Children, 2300 W. 5th Ave., P.O. Box 269, Columbus, OH 43216-0269

Humpty Dumpty's Magazine, 1100 Waterway Blvd., Box 567, Indianapolis, IN 46226

Jack and Jill, 1100 Waterway Blvd., Box 567, Indianapolis, IN 46226

Language Arts, National Council of Teachers of English, 1111 Kenyon Rd., Urbana, IL 61801

Ranger Rick's Nature Magazine, 1412 14th St., NW, Washington, DC 20036

The Reading Teacher, International Reading Association, 800 Barksdale Rd., P.O. Box 8139, Newark, DE 19714-8139

Stone Soup, Box 83, Santa Cruz, CA 95063

The Weewish Tree, American Indian Historical Society, 1451 Masonic Ave., San Francisco, CA 94117

Computers

With the advent of computers in schools in the 1980s, many people anticipated that they would change the classroom in significant ways. The view today is that computers and school contexts are mutually constitutive and that there is great diversity in how students and teachers actually use computers (Bruce, 1994).

Important variables in determining how computers are used are equity and accessibility, student experience, teacher attitudes, and classroom context. Another issue is the effect computers have on cross-curricular and collaborative learning—for example, several classes or schools using e-mail and sharing information on a topic that links activities in social studies, science, and language arts. Students in Audrey Eldridge's class of third-grade limited–English proficient students used computers to write reports on the planets and to collaborate on scripts for a puppet play and a videotaped film. The key to using computers in the schools is to integrate them into regular language arts experiences, especially writing.

Word Processing and Writing

Word processing and desktop publishing are the most widespread uses of computers in language arts and provide substantial aids to writing (De Groff, 1991; Dublin, Pressman, & Woldman, 1994; Zeni, 1990). Innovations such as word processors that talk with synthesized speech and have speech-to-text capabilities increase access for limited–English proficient students and students with language and learning limitations (Anderson-Inman, 1990; Balajthy, 1988).

Teachers can take dictation from younger students using word-processing programs, which is another way to use the language experience approach. Students can brainstorm ideas, make idea lists, "word walls," and compose, all of which the teacher will record (Barber, 1982; Bradley, 1982). Multiple copies can be printed for students' revising, and then a final draft can be made and printed for illustrating and book making.

Word-processing software for children turns the computer into an elaborate typewriter, except that any piece of writing can be easily revised. Keyboarding (i.e., knowing how to type) should not be considered a prerequisite for writing on the computer (Kahn & Freyd, 1990). Children can readily get their ideas down, revise, and write longer and more detailed stories using word processing (Coburn et al., 1982; Silvern, 1988). Desktop publishing means that students can publish their writing, including graphics. What's more, great benefits come from the social, collaborative, and cooperative environment of groups writing together at computers (Cochran-Smith, Kahn, & Paris, 1988; Daiute, 1983; Dickinson, 1986; Genishi, 1988; Vibert, 1988).

Word-processing software has been developed especially for elementary students (Balajthy, 1989; Gunn, 1990), such as First Writer for younger students and Bank Street for older students. Writer MindPlay Works combines word-processing, spreadsheet, and database programs for use in the classroom.

Integrating Computers in the Classroom

Computer-Mediated Communication

Computer networks, or *computer-mediated communication,* puts a cross-curricular emphasis on teaching the language arts. Both spoken and written language are used, and online communication is often referred to as "talk" or "dialogue," which can encourage students who might otherwise be silent in the classroom, such as limited–English proficient students. Telecommunications allow students to communicate with others using wide-area networks, bulletin board services, and electronic mail (i.e., e-mail) systems like FrEd Mail, Prodigy, and National Geographic Kids Network. Kids Network uses computing and telecommunications to team children from schools in different parts of the United States and to collect and process scientific data (e.g., about acid rain).

Hypertext/Hypermedia

Hypertext is a combination of information on a given subject in both print and visual form; it can be retrieved in any order and with interaction. When hypertext content extends to digitized sound, animation, video, virtual environments, computer networks, and databases, it's called *hypermedia.* In classrooms, this could mean so-called electronic books, or CD–ROM (compact disk–read only memory).

Hypertext authoring systems are software programs that allow creating multimedia essays and electronic databases across subjects. The best known hypertext program is HyperCard, which is being used much more widely in classrooms today to support active knowledge making and critical and integrative thinking. Students can write pieces that combine photographs, sound, onscreen video, and other media. For example, students writing about their families can include scanned-in family photographs, video clips, letters, and family trees.

Hardware and Software

The choices for hardware today are essentially MS-DOS (IBM and IBM clones) and Macintosh. As with most technology, the cost of computers has dropped dramatically in recent years, particularly in terms of the variety and capability of what's available. For instance, color printers and CD-ROM drives are now affordable and even considered standard equipment for many new computer systems.

A greater variety of education software is also available. To assist buyers, new programs are evaluated regularly in journals like *Technology and Learning, Electronic Learning,* and *Media and Methods.* Criteria for choosing software include:

- *Cost effectiveness:* How many students can use it and how often?
- *Flexibility and versatility:* Are multiple uses possible at different levels of grade, ability, and computer experience?

- *Application:* Is it a good fit with the teacher's preferred instructional style?
- *Interactiveness:* Will students be actively engaged? Can they control the software?

Here's a list of software for teaching language arts, including the distributor's phone number for each:

Bank Street School Filer, Sunburst/WINGS for Learning: 800-321-7511
Big Book Maker, Toucan/Educational Resources: 800-624-2926
Calender Creator, Power Up/Educational Resources: 800-624-2926
Children's Writing and Publishing Center, Learning Company/Educational Resources: 800-624-2926
Crossword Magic, Mindscape/Educational Resources: 800-624-2926
HyperCard, Claris: 408-987-7000
KidPix, Brøderbund/Learning Services: 800-877-9378
Kidwriter, Spinnaker/Educational Resources: 800-624-2926
Once Upon a Time, Compu-Teach/Learning Services: 800-877-9378
Playwrite, Sunburst/WINGS for Learning: 800-321-7511
Print Shop, Brøderbund/Educational Resources: 800-624-2926
Storybook Weaver, MECC: 800-685-6322
Timeliner, Tom Snyder Productions: 800-342-0236
Write On! Humanities Software: 800-245-6737
The Writing Center, Learning Company/Educational Resources: 800-624-2926

Organizing for Computers

Teachers can organize their classrooms for computer use in a number of ways. Here are some ideas for one-, two-, and three-computer classrooms:

One-Computer Classroom

1. Groups of two to four students use the computer, while the teacher works with the rest of the class (e.g., for independent writing).
2. Groups of four to six students cycle through a computer center, while the rest of the class works in small, collaborative groups.
3. Peer tutoring, in which more able students help others.
4. Send the computer home over weekends and vacations, especially to families that might not have one.
5. The computer becomes part of a center for study of a special topic (e.g., a science unit on the environment); this will be especially effective with the use of data-based programs.

Two-Computer Classroom

1. Each computer is the focus of a learning center—for example, one in the computer writing center and the other in a center for studying a special topic.

2. Groups of four to six students cycle through each computer in a period of group work, so that all students use the computer within a one- or two-day period.
3. Many of uses described for a one-computer classroom are also appropriate.

Three-Computer Classroom

1. All students have access to a computer in a single lesson or period of group work. The computer is an integral part of the activity, and students rotate to use it.
2. One computer is a permanent part of the writing center; the two others can be used for special topics or other permanent centers, such as art.
3. Many of uses described for one- and two-computer classrooms are appropriate.

Equity, Access, Diversity, and Computers

The flexibility of media can address the challenge of different learning styles, developmental levels, and linguistic and cultural diversity. Electronic discussion through videorecording or filmmaking, collaborative writing with computers, and e-mail all have the potential to encourage students who are sometimes silent because of their social status in school, race, culture, gender, disability, or language-minority status.

Evidence has shown, however, that language-minority children are less likely to have opportunities to use computers than native English-speaking students (DeVillar & Faltis, 1991). In addition to the inequity it demonstrates,

Children collaborate on the computer.

this lack of computer time for language-minority students is also unfortunate because these students have been shown to write more fluently with computers than with paper and pencil and are more willing to revise their work (Dunkel, 1990; Pease-Alvarez & Vasquez, 1990).

The cooperative, collaborative environment that can be created when students write with computers can support the kind of meaningful, context-embedded verbal interaction supported by second-language acquisition theory (Gonzalez-Edfelt, 1990). Many classroom computer and media activities encourage students to work in pairs or groups, to engage in peer tutoring, and to share ideas around the computer. These are both ideal critical-thinking and language acquisition experiences.

Multimedia experiences are also ideal for second-language learners. For example, if the class is reading Mother Goose nursery rhymes, the literature can be presented in dual languages in an interactive HyperCard stack, called *bilingual stackware,* by Ramond Padilla (Padilla, 1990). Students can switch languages and create their own presentations and reports that integrate text, sounds, animation, and graphics. In these kinds of situations, students use all their senses in repetitive, low-risk literacy activities (Chavez, 1990). Perhaps the greatest benefit of multimedia technology for teaching culturally and linguistically diverse students is the motivation and confidence that's possible when students have a sense of control over their own learning and an opportunity for self-discovery.

Assessing Media Literacy

Portfolios can easily expand to include things written by students about media as well as students' own media productions:

1. ***Film/TV/Film Journals:*** Journals provide ongoing records of students' viewing experiences and responses to them. When teachers carry on dialogues with students in their journals, they are constantly assessing students' viewing, thinking, and writing about the media.

2. ***Film/Videotape Productions:*** Use videos to document projects, puppet shows, and dramatizations or to compose by creating and producing stories, storyboards, and scripts. All these items could become part of students' portfolios.

3. ***Computer Use:*** Examples could include samples of children's writing done on word processors, communications through bulletin boards, or uses of database software or hypertext/hypermedia materials.

4. ***Newspapers/Magazines/Photography:*** Include materials produced by students in studying these media as well as records of students' uses of them.

Answers to Questions about Media Literacy

1. *What is* media literacy?

Media literacy is "an ability to comprehend, use, and control the symbol systems of both print and nonprint media, as well as understand the relationship between them" (Cox, 1994, p. 791). Children use a great variety of media. Print media include books, magazines, and newspapers, and nonprint media include photography, recordings, radio, film, television, videotapes, videogames, and computers. Since all these media interact constantly, becoming literate in today's world means that students need to understand how electronic and print media function together. They also need to learn how to discover meaning and communicate effectively through the variety of media available. The media have a tremendous influence on us, providing information and entertainment. They also shape our perceptions of the world and our values.

2. *How should we teach the media in language arts?*

The power of the media to engage children with ideas in meaningful listening, talking, reading, writing, and thinking activities in language arts and across the curriculum is limitless. Teachers have many opportunities to teach about, through, and with the media in language arts. Media experiences from both inside and outside the classroom provide access to learning for all students, drawing on a shared media culture as the basis for classroom exploration. This gives children the chance to use what they really experience in talking and writing. The media culture is available, in some way, to everyone. Thus, the media provide an entry point to meaningful language experiences in the classroom for all students. Moreover, different kinds of media provide different kinds of access to a range of students, encouraging those who are sometimes silent because of their social status, race, culture, gender, disability, or language-minority status.

LOOKING FURTHER

1. Do one of the critical television-viewing activities, and discuss it with others in your college class.
2. Visit a library media center, and ask to preview several children's films for a grade you would like to teach. Start a resource file of film titles.
3. Show a film to children. After viewing, put them in watch-and-talk groups, and listen to them. Plan a film response guide like the one in this chapter.
4. Call or visit the Newspaper in Education office of your local paper to find out what kind of services and materials they offer elementary teachers.
5. Try out and evaluate a piece of computer software for teaching language arts or a word-processing program for elementary school.

RESOURCES

Considine, D. M., & Haley, G. E. (1992). *Visual messages: Integrating imagery into instruction.* Englewood, CO: Teachers Ideas Press.

Dublin, P., Pressman, H., & Woldman, E. J. (1994). *Integrating computers in your classroom: Elementary language arts.* New York: HarperCollins.

REFERENCES

Anderson-Inman, I. (1990). Enhancing the reading-writing connection: Classroom applications. *Writing Notebook, 7,* 6–8.

Balajthy, E. (1988). The Printout: Voice synthesis for emergent literacy. *Reading Teacher, 42*(1), 72.

Balajthy, E. (1989). Holistic approaches to reading. *Reading Teacher, 42,* 324.

Barber, B. (1982). Creating BYTES of language. *Language Arts, 59,* 472–475.

Bradley, U. N. (1982). Improving students' writing with microcomputers. *Language Arts, 59,* 732–743.

Bruce, B. (1994). Computers and school contexts. In A. Purves (Ed.), *Encyclopedia of English studies and language arts* (Vol. 1). New York: Scholastic.

Chavez, R. C. (1990). The development of story writing within an IBM Writing to Read program lab among language minority students: Preliminary findings of a naturalistic study. *Computers in the Schools, 7,* 121–144.

Cochran-Smith, M., Kahn, J., & Paris, C. L. (1988). When word processors come into the classroom. In J. L. Hoot & S. B. Silvern (Eds.), *Writing with computers in the early grades* (pp. 43–47). New York: Teachers College Press.

Coburn, P., Kelman, P., Roberts, N., Snyder, T. F., Watt, D. H., & Weiner, C. (1982). *Practical guide to computers in education.* Reading, MA: Addison-Wesley.

Cox, C. (1975a). Film is like your Grandma's preserved pears. *Elementary English, 52,* 515–519.

Cox, C. (1975b). The liveliest art and reading. *Elementary English, 52,* 771–775, 807.

Cox, C. (1980). Making films without a camera. *Language Arts, 57,* 274–279.

Cox, C. (1982). Children's preferences for film form and technique. *Language Arts, 59,* 231–238.

Cox, C. (1983). Young filmmakers speak the language of film. *Language Arts, 60,* 296–304, 372.

Cox, C. (1985). Film preference instrument. In W. T. Fagan, J. M. Jensen, & C. R. Cooper (Eds.), *Measures for research and evaluation in the English language arts* (Vol. 2). Urbana, IL: National Council of Teachers of English.

Cox, C. (1987). Making and using media as a language art. In C. R. Personke & D. Johnson (Eds.), *Language arts instruction and the beginning teacher.* Englewood Cliffs, NJ: Prentice-Hall.

Cox, C. (1991). The media arts and English language arts teaching and learning. In J. Flood, J. M. Jensen, D. Lapp, & J. R. Squire (Eds.), *Handbook of research on teaching the English language arts* (pp. 542–548). New York: Scholastic.

Cox, C. (1994). Media literacy. In A. Purves (Ed.), *The encyclopedia of English studies and language arts* (Vol. 2). New York: Scholastic.

Cox, C. (Ed.). (in press). *Media literacy: Classroom practices in the teaching of English language arts.* Urbana, IL: National Council of Teachers of English.

Cox, C., & Many, J. E. (1989). Worlds of possibilities in response to literature, film, and life. *Language Arts, 66,* 287–294.

Cox, C., & Many, J. E. (1992). Towards an understanding of the aesthetic stance towards literature. *Language Arts, 69,* 28–33.

Daiute, C. (1983). Writing, creativity, and change. *Childhood Education, 59,* 227–231.

De Groff, L. (1991). Is there a place for computers in whole language classrooms? *Reading Teacher, 43*(8), 568–572.

De Villar, R. A., & Faltis, C. J. (1991). *Computers and cultural diversity: Restructuring for school success.* Albany, NY: State University of New York Press.

Dickinson, D. K. (1986). Cooperation, collaboration, and a computer: Integrating a computer into a first-second grade writing program. *Research in the Teaching of English, 20*(4), 357–378.

Dublin, Pressman, & Woldman. (1994). *Integrating computers in your classroom: Elementary language arts.* New York: HarperCollins.

Dunkel, P. (1990). Implications for the CAI effectiveness research for limited English proficient learners. *Computers in the Schools, 7*, 31–52.

Genishi, C. (1988). Kindergartners and computers: A case study of six children. *Elementary School Journal, 89*(2), 185–201.

Gonzalez-Edfelt, A. (1990). Oral interaction and collaboration at the computer: Learning English as a second language with the help of your peers. *Computers in Schools, 7*, 211–226.

Gunn, C. (1990). Computers in a whole language classroom. *Writing Notebook, 7*, 12–15.

Kahn, J., & Freyd, P. (1990). Online: A whole language perspective on keyboarding. *Language Arts, 67*, 84–90.

National Council of Teachers of English (NCTE). (1994, Summer). Perspective: Media, performance, and the English curriculum—two views. *The NCTE Standard*, 12–14.

Padilla, R. (1990). HyperCard: A tool for dual language instruction. *Computers in the Schools, 7*, 211–226.

Pease-Alvarez, L., & Vasquez, O. A. (1990). Sharing language and technical expertise around the computer. *Computers in the Schools, 7*, 91–107.

Postman, N. (1961). *Television and the teaching of English*. New York: Appleton-Century-Crofts.

Rosenblatt, L. M. (1985). The transactional theory of the literary work: Implications for research. In C. R. Cooper (Ed.), *Researching response to literature and the teaching of literature*. Norwood, NJ: Ablex.

Rosenblatt, L. M. (1986). The aesthetic transaction. *Journal of Aesthetic Education, 20*, 122–128.

Silvern, S. B. (1988). Word processing in the writing process. In J. L. Hoot & S. B. Silvern (Eds.), *Writing with computers in the early grades* (pp. 43–74). New York: Teachers College Press.

Vibert, A. (1988). Collaborative writing. *Language Arts, 65*, 74–76.

Zeni, J. (1990). *WritingLands, composing with old and new writing tools*. Urbana, IL: National Council of Teachers of English.

CHILDREN'S BOOKS AND FILMS

Anderson, J. (1991). *The first Thanksgiving feast* (G. Ancona, Photoillus.). New York: Clarion.

Anderson, M. (1977). *Matilda's masterpiece*. New York: Atheneum.

Andersen, Y. (1991). *Make your own animated movies and videotapes*. Boston: Little, Brown.

Apfel, N. (1988). *Nebulae: The birth and death of stars*. New York: Lothrop, Lee, & Shepard.

Apfel, N. (1991). *Voyager to the planets*. New York: Clarion.

Ashpet: An American Cinderella [Film]. (1989). Available from Davenport Films.

Barton, B. (1988). *I want to be an astronaut*. New York: Crowell.

Bearskin [Film]. (1983). Available from Davenport Films.

Begone dull care [Film]. (1949). Available from International Film Bureau.

Being right, can you still lose? [Film]. (1976). Available from Walt Disney Educational Media.

Berends, P. B. (1973). *The case of the elevator duck*. New York: Random House.

Berger, M. (1992). *Discovering Mars: The amazing story of the red planet*. New York: Scholastic.

Bolognese, D. (1982). *Drawing spaceships and other spacecraft*. New York: Watts.

Bonsall, C. (1980). *The case of the double cross*. New York: Harper & Row.

Branley, F. M. (1983). *Saturn: The spectacular planet*. New York: Crowell.

Briggs, R. (1978). *The snowman*. New York: Random House.

Cameron, E. (1954). *The wonderful flight to the mushroom planet* (series). New York: Little, Brown.

Carrier, R. (1984). *The hockey sweater*. New York: Tundra Books.

Case of the elevator duck, The [Film]. (1974). Available from Learning Corporation of America.

Chaoro, K. (1974). *Ida makes a movie*. New York: Seabury.

Charlip, R., & Miller, M. B. (1974). *Handtalk: An ABC of finger spelling and sign language* (G. Ancona, Photoillus.). New York: Four Winds.

Christopher, J. (1967a). *The city of gold and lead*. New York: Macmillan.

Christopher, J. (1967b). *The white mountains*. New York: Macmillan.

Christopher, J. (1968). *The pool of fire.* New York: Macmillan.

Christopher, J. (1988). *When the tripods came.* New York: Dutton.

Close harmony [Film]. (1981). Available from Coronet/Learning Corporation of America/MTI.

Clown [Film]. (1969). Available from Learning Corporation of America.

Cole, J. (1986). *The magic school bus, at the waterworks.* New York: Scholastic.

Cole, J. (1987). *The magic school bus, inside the earth.* New York: Scholastic.

Cole, J. (1989). *The magic school bus, inside the human body.* New York: Scholastic.

Cole, J. (1990). *The magic school bus, lost in the solar system.* New York: Scholastic.

Fox, M. V. (1984). *Women astronauts: Aboard the shuttle.* New York: S & S Trade.

Freedman, R. (1980). *Immigrant kids.* New York: Dutton.

Freedman, R. (1983a). *Children of the wild west.* New York: Clarion.

Freedman, R. (1983b). *Indian chiefs.* New York: Clarion.

Freedman, R. (1987). *Lincoln: A photobiography.* New York: Clarion.

Freedman, R. (1990). *Franklin Delano Roosevelt.* New York: Clarion.

Freedman, R. (1991). *The Wright brothers: How they invented the airplane.* New York: Holiday.

Frog king, The [Film]. (1981). Available from Davenport Films.

Gallant, R. (1986). *The Macmillan book of astronomy.* New York: Macmillan.

Gibbons, G. (1983). *Sun up, sun down.* New York: Scholastic.

Gibbons, G. (1987). *Deadline! From news to newspaper.* New York: Crowell.

Godden, R. (1978). *The rocking horse secret.* New York: Viking.

Hansel and Gretel: An Appalachian version [Film]. (1975). Available from Davenport Films.

Hen hop [Film]. (1942). Available from International Film Bureau.

Heyman, K., & Morris, A. (1989). *Bread, bread, bread.* New York: Lothrop, Lee & Shepard.

Heyman, K., & Morris, A. (1990a). *Loving.* New York: Lothrop, Lee & Shepard.

Heyman, K., & Morris, A. (1990b). *On the go.* New York: Lothrop, Lee & Shepard.

Heyman, K., & Morris, A. (1991). *On their toes: A Soviet ballet school.* New York: Atheneum.

Hoban, T. (1972). *Count and see.* New York: Macmillan.

Hoban, T. (1975). *Dig, drill, dump, fill.* New York: Greenwillow.

Hoban, T. (1982). *A, B, see!* New York: Greenwillow.

Hoban, T. (1989). *Of colors and things.* New York: Greenwillow.

Hoban, T. (1990). *Exactly the opposite.* New York: Greenwillow.

Jack and the dentist's daughter [Film]. (1984). Available from Davenport Films.

L'Engle, M. (1962). *A wrinkle in time.* New York: Farrar, Straus, & Giroux.

L'Engle, M. (1973). *A wind in the door.* New York: Farrar, Straus, & Giroux.

L'Engle, M. (1978). *A swiftly tilting planet.* New York: Farrar, Straus, & Giroux.

Lauber, P. (1989). *Meteors and meteorites: Voyagers from space.* New York: Scholastic.

Lauber, P. (1993). *Journey to the planets* (4th ed.). New York: Crown.

Leedy, L. (1990). *The furry news: How to make a newspaper.* New York: Holiday House.

Lobel, A. (1966). *Martha the movie mouse.* New York: Harper & Row.

MacLachlan, P. (1985). *Sarah, plain and tall.* New York: Harper & Row.

Marino, T. J. (1974). *Pictures without a camera.* New York: Sterling.

Marzollo, J., & Marzollo, C. (1982). *Jed's junior space patrol: A science fiction easy-to-read.* New York: Dial.

McMillan, B. (1989). *Time to . . .* New York: Lothrop, Lee & Shepard.

McMillan, B. (1990a). *Mary had a little lamb.* New York: Scholastic.

McMillan, B. (1990b). *One sun: A book of terse verse.* New York: Holiday House.

Me and you kangaroo [Film]. (1973). Available from Learning Corporation of America.

Molly's Pilgrim [Film]. (1985). Available from Phoenix Films.

Night ride [Film]. (1994). Available from Northfork Films.

Phillip and the white colt [Film]. (1973). Available from Learning Corporation of America.

Pinkwater, D. (1990). *Borgel.* New York: Macmillan.

Pratchett, T. (1989). *Truckers.* New York: Chivers North America.

Rapunzel, Rapunzel [Film]. (1978). Available from Davenport Films.

Rook, D. (1967). *Run wild, run free.* New York: Scholastic.

Rosenberg, M. (1988). *Artists of handcrafted furniture at work* (G. Ancona, Photoillus.). New York: Lothrop, Lee & Shepard.

Sendak, M. (1963). *Where the wild things are.* New York: Harper & Row.

Service, P. (1988). *Stinker from space.* New York: Scribner's.

Sharmat, M. (1977). *Nate the Great and the phony clue.* New York: Coward, McCann.

Simon, S. (1979). *The long view into space.* New York: Crown.

Simon, S. (1985). *Jupiter.* New York: Morrow.

Simon, S. (1988). *Galaxies.* New York: Morrow.

Singer, I. B. (1966). *Zlateh the Goat and other stories.* New York: Harper & Row.

Slote, A. (1975). *My robot buddy.* New York: Lippincott.

Snowman, The [Film]. (1982). Available from Weston Woods.

Sobol, D. J. (1980). *Encyclopedia Brown carries on.* New York: Four Winds.

Sweater, The [Film]. (1983). Available from National Film Board of Canada.

Tender tale of Cinderella Penguin, The [Film]. (1982). Available from National Film Board of Canada.

Wilder, L. I. (1935). *Little house on the prairie.* New York: Harper & Row.

Williams, M. (1975). *The velveteen rabbit.* New York: Avon.

Wood, A. (1985). *The napping house.* New York: Weston Woods.

Zlateh the Goat [Film]. (1973). Available from Weston Wood Studios.

Chapter 14

Language across the Curriculum

Questions about Language across the Curriculum

Learning to Use Language and Using Language to Learn

Thematic Teaching

SNAPSHOT: ***Thematic Teaching in Willa Richardson's Third Grade***

Tools for Using Language across the Curriculum

Finding Information

TEACHING IDEA: ***Student-Created Reference Books***

SNAPSHOT: ***Third-Graders Research How to Build an Aquarium***

Recording Information

Organizing Information

Sheltered Content Instruction for Limited–English Proficient Students

Content-Based English Language Development

Specially Designed Academic Instruction in English

Guidelines for Sheltered Content Instruction

Assessing Language across the Curriculum

Answers to Questions about Language across the Curriculum

Questions about Language across the Curriculum

1. *What does* language across the curriculum *mean?*
2. *How should we teach language across the curriculum?*

Reflective Response

Think of a special theme you learned about in elementary school. In what ways did you learn to use language in learning about that theme? Jot down your ideas.

Learning to Use Language and Using Language to Learn

Language across the curriculum means teaching the language arts of thinking, listening, speaking, reading, writing, and viewing within the context of the content areas, such as social studies, science, mathematics, and music and the arts (Froese, 1994). Language across the curriculum is based on three principles:

1. All genuine learning involves discovery.
2. Language has a heuristic function (that is, language is a means to learn).
3. Using language to discover is the best way to learn (Bullock, 1975).

In a student- and response-centered classroom, language across the curriculum means using an integrated approach to teaching. Students ask questions, identify and solve problems, use research and study skills, and discover the interconnectedness of subject matter. And teachers plan experiences that enable students to do these things, initiating themes of learning and collaborating with and modeling for students. Sometimes, both students and teachers initiate themes or identify topics of interest for individual inquiry.

I'll never forget the thematic unit we did when I was in the fourth grade in Mrs. Canaday's class. When Hawaii became a state, everything we did was related to Hawaii. I got to lead the hula when we presented what we learned for parents and other classes. It was great!

Thematic Teaching

Thematic teaching has a long history in education. Sipe (1994) notes that "educational practice dating back to Socratic discussions reflects the value of organizing instruction around meaningful questions as both a method for examining existing knowledge and for generating questions that may lead to the development of new knowledge" (p. 1213). Educational reform movements since the eighteenth century have advocated integration of subjects. John Dewey promoted units in the 1920s and 1930s as part of progressive education. And in the 1960s and beginning again in the 1980s with the whole-language movement, we have seen teaching around themes (Buckley, 1994).

This approach has been called various names, such as *units* and *thematic units.* Today, the terms used include *theme study, theme cycles* (Altwerger &

TABLE 14.1 Examples of Language across the Curriculum in This Text

Grade	*Chapter*	*Theme: Activities*
K	4	The zoo: fieldtrip, reading, writing, and drama
K–1	9	Pigs: shared "big book" experience, art, and drama
K–2	9	Author unit on Eric Carle: focus on his books about insects and animals
1	4	Apples: experiences with and about apples
2	5	Creatures: fantasy creatures, film, and literature
2	9	Genre unit on folktales: focus on a type, or genre of literature
3	3	Columbus and the Taino people: events of 1492 from different perspectives (those of Columbus, Europeans, and Native Americans)
3	14	Solar system and science fiction: science, writing, and filmmaking
3	14	The environment and ecology: focus on wetlands, building an aquarium
3	14	Independent projects: child chooses and learns about a theme
3–4	10	Mealworms: observing, reading, and writing about their behavior
3–4	11	Colors: in nature, poetry, art, music, people (cultural and racial diversity in U.S.)
4	1	Our community: adaptable to any community
4	8	Southwest United States: geography, history, and culture (Native, Hispanic, and Anglo Americans)
4–6	9	Core book unit on *Treasure Island:* intensive study of a classic; related topics
K–5	6	The Renaissance and Shakespeare: a schoolwide cross-curricular event

Flores, 1994), and *integrated, cross-curricular,* and *thematic teaching. Whole language* generally means integrated teaching, as well. I call these *"ripple effects" of response-themed learning,* because I know that they're not totally planned by teachers. Rather, one idea or activity will be like a pebble thrown into a pond, generating ripples that grow and spread across the curriculum, depending on the ideas, interests, and experiences of students.

The idea behind all these terms is the use of language across the curriculum. Specifically, children will learn to use language as they use language to learn in other subjects (Thaiss, 1986).We've already looked at many examples of language across the curriculum in this text, many of which I've referred to as "ripple effects." Table 14.1 list examples of language across the curriculum presented in this text.

I've explained the "ripple effect" in more detail in Chapter 1, Learning and Teaching Language Arts.

SNAPSHOT: Thematic Teaching in Willa Richardson's Third Grade

Willa Richardson teaches the third grade in Baton Rouge, Louisiana. She teaches students to use language across the curriculum during a year-long focus on problem solving, research, and study skills. Willa believes that "we must help children learn how to solve problems themselves. I enjoy it, and I think my enthusiasm spills over into the classroom, and whatever we are

Students in Willa Richardson's "outdoor classroom" make observations, take notes, talk, and solve problems using the scientific method.

researching spills over into all other areas of the curriculum. I want to stimulate children to be observant, identify problems, and then know how to gather the data to solve them. I think they learn to use language by using it."

Here's a step-by-step description of how Willa applies her philosophy from the first day of school, when she initiates a theme on the environment and ecology, through the rest of the schoolyear, when students learn about topics that they choose to study.

A Theme on the Environment and Ecology for the Whole Class

• ***Observing in an Outdoor Classroom:*** Willa has created an "outdoor classroom" in the area outside her class, where students have planted trees and plants and kept animals. At first, Willa asks students to spend time there just using their eyes, observing things that interest them and talking together about what they see.

• ***Learning the Scientific Method:*** After several days, the class talks about what they have observed. As students begin to ask questions based on their observations, Willa introduces the scientific method, which involves these five steps:

1. State the problem.
2. Form a hypothesis (or guess).
3. Collect data.
4. Interpret findings.
5. Draw conclusions.

• ***Minilesson on Notetaking:*** Willa makes a "word wall" of things the children have been observing and does a minilesson on notetaking. "I tell them to be quick, concise, and pick out the main idea." She uses the overhead projector to demonstrate and asks questions like: "What did you see?" "Why do you think it was there?"

• ***Continued Observations, Inquiry, and Language across the Curriculum:*** Willa says she encourages students to observe everywhere, correlate their observations with what they already know, and share what they see and read when they come to school. She says even though this appears to be science, she tries to integrate it with all other subjects. This is language across the curriculum.

• ***Building an Aquarium:*** Next, Willa sets up a real problem for her students to solve: building an aquarium and creating an environment that fish can live in. "This is my way of creating a learning environment where children are in charge of the information they are processing." Here's how Willa plans building an aquarium:

1. *Trips to the Library:* They all go to the library and look for information on tropical fish. The librarian shows filmstrips and films on fish and demonstrates how to find information in the library using the real topics of fish and aquariums, which the students are trying to investigate.
2. *Choosing the Water Environment and Fish:* Next, the class must do some serious research to select (a) the type of water environment they want to create and (b) the type of fish that will be compatible with it.
3. *Using Language in Several Content Areas:* As the children create the aquarium and solve problems, they're using language across the curriculum.
   a. *Math:* The class has a limited budget for buying materials, so they must figure out how much everything is going to cost and where to get the best prices.
   b. *Writing:* After they get the fish, Willa introduces poetry patterns, such as haiku, and students write about the fish.
   c. *Social Studies and Science:* Willa tries to extend the aquarium topic by locating nonfiction books about it and relating it to anything on the environment and the ecology of living things. She encourages her students to ask their own questions ("not just the questions that they think I want them to answer") and then to read to answer them. She explains how to look for the main idea when reading and to use the scientific method applied to reading for information. "I want them to begin to think this way."

• ***A Trip to a Wildlife Refuge:*** In January, the environment/ecology theme involves planning and taking a trip to a wildlife refuge, Sabine National Park and Holly Beach in southern Louisiana. Since the students live in Louisiana, the emphasis has been on wetlands. Here's what happens:

1. *Writing Letters to Parents:* This is a big project and requires a lot of parental involvement. Fifteen parents need to go along on the trip. As a group, students write a letter to send home to parents, asking for their support.

2. *Writing Letters Asking for Information:* Students write letters to the National Park Service and other governmental agencies, asking for brochures, pamphlets, and other materials on wetlands.
3. *Learning Map Skills:* The children use maps of Louisiana to learn where they're going and to picture how they will get there. In doing so, they learn map skills.
4. *Planning an Itinerary:* Willa duplicates a map of the area for each student to write on. Together, they plan a route and figure mileage, places to stop, and a timed itinerary. They have the most fun planning their menus and what they will take to eat!
5. *Visiting a Wildlife Refuge:* The students gather information from the primary source: the Sabine National Park. They're given tours by the park rangers, see slide shows and view exhibits in the visitor's center, and participate in other activities to learn about the park. At nearby Holly Beach, the children use microscopes (which they brought along) to do observations, take notes, and collect specimens (e.g., water plants, shells, etc.).
6. *Using Language Back in the Classroom:* Willa says the best part of the trip is after they return to the classroom:

> The children have this great wealth of impressions, ideas, and data to draw on. The writing that follows is wonderful. They are perfectly primed up to write across the curriculum. Until I began to do this, I didn't know children had such insight. And it all expands and gets bigger. In reading and spelling, they become intensely interested in books on the subject, correctly spelling words they will use to write thank you letters, and letters of inquiry for more information. There is so much opportunity to learn so many things when students have real experiences they are interested in and use language across the curriculum.

When Willa talks about how "it all expands and gets bigger," she's referring to the "ripple effect" of ideas and interests that develops in a student- and response-centered classroom like hers. See Figure 14.1, which illustrates this "ripple effect" of the environment and ecology, for ideas about teaching this and other themes.

Each Child Chooses a Theme: Independent Projects

This is an opportunity for individuals to choose themes they really want to learn more about, using the research skills they have acquired to work on independent projects. Here's how Willa helps her students do this:

- ***Idea List:*** Willa asks students to make lists of things they're interested in.

- ***Teacher Conferences:*** Willa schedules a conference with each child to talk about his or her interests and help pinpoint a topic. "It takes a while to focus, and they haven't always been asked to do this." With Willa's help, each student narrows it down to three choices.

FIGURE 14.1
A "Ripple Effect" of the Environment

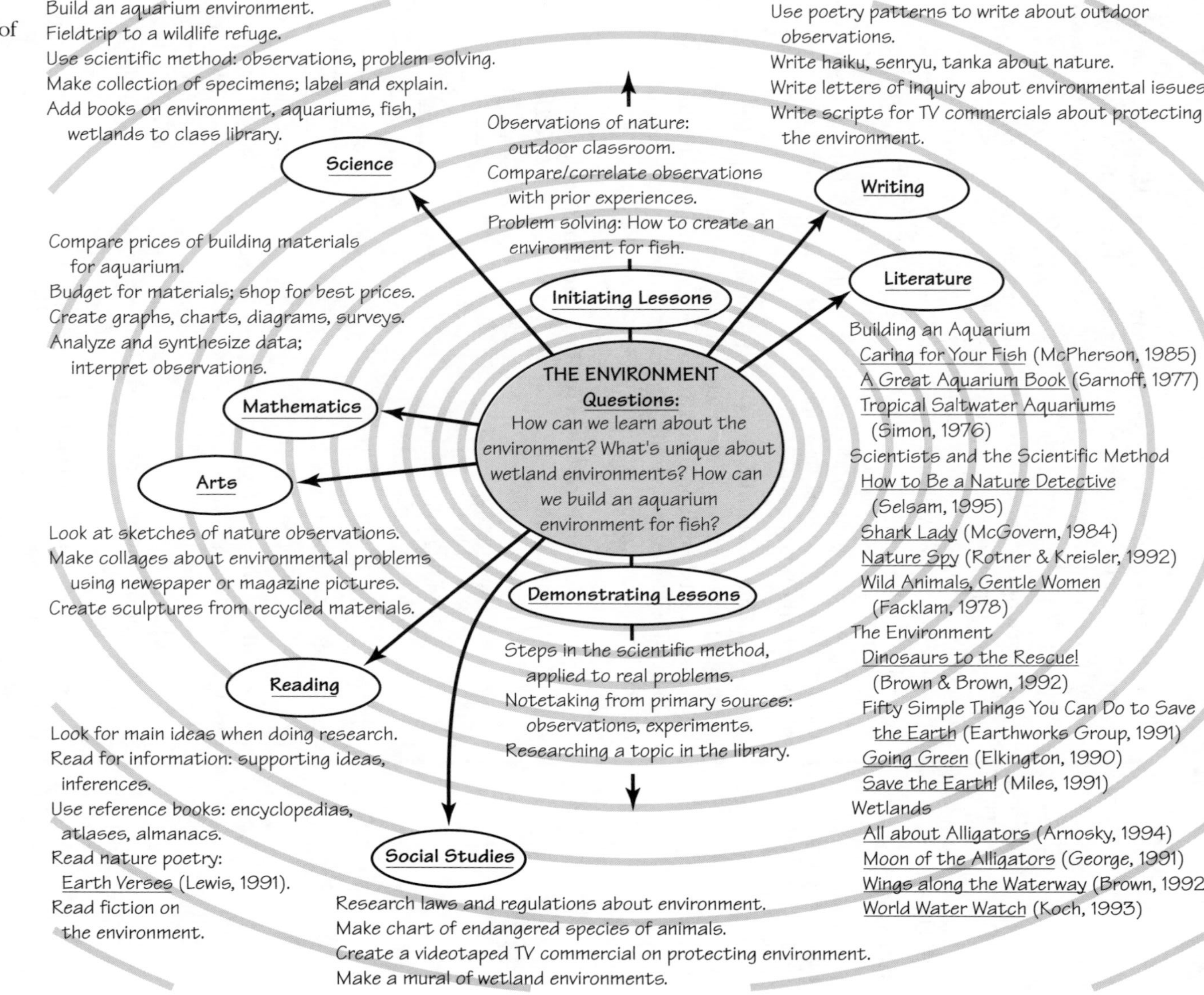

See the list of Children's Books at the end of the chapter for more materials.

• ***Parent Conferences:*** Next, students talk over their ideas with their parents because this is a big project and they will probably need help gathering materials and going to the library. A three-way team is formed: child/parent/teacher.

See Chapter 13, Media Literacy, for analyzing and writing newspaper articles using the 5 Ws and H.

See Chapter 1, Learning and Teaching Language Arts, to see how to use a K-W-L chart for developing questions with a class or group.

• ***Developing Questions:*** After the students have done some reading on their topics and developed files of references on 3" × 5" index cards, Willa helps them develop focus questions. They talk about the five Ws and H: When? Where? Who? What? Why? and How? Every child writes down 10 or 12 questions about their subject to talk about with Willa. She helps them ask questions that are broad enough, because if the questions are too narrow, the students won't find enough information. "It's hard at first to get them to think big, to look for underlying ideas. They get picky. When was someone born? When did they die?"

• ***Setting a Schedule:*** Willa and her students set a project schedule, allotting a number of weeks for each part and then filling in the dates. Each child takes a schedule home to have his or her parents read it; to acknowledge that they have, the parents sign a tear-off sheet, which is returned to school. The schedule for the entire project looks like this:

Schedule of Dates for Independent Project

	Step	***Week***	***Due Date***
1.	Choose topic	Week 1	___________
2.	Develop questions	Week 2	___________
3.	Parent library trip	Week 3	___________
4.	Finding information	Week 4–5	___________
5.	Rough draft	Week 5–6	___________
6.	Outline & bibliography	Week 7	___________
7.	Creative product	Week 8–9	___________
8.	Cover & illustrations	Week 10	___________
9.	Completed report		___________

• ***Parent Library Trip:*** The students learned a lot about using the library during the unit on the environment and ecology. Now, Willa schedules an evening in the public library with parents to explain the project and to start looking for information. The librarian demonstrates how to find various sources of information, and students begin researching their topics with their parents.

• ***Five Types of Information:*** Students in Willa's class must use five different types of information:

1. *Magazines:* Students find information in magazines by using the *Reader's Guide to Periodical Literature.*
2. *Encyclopedias:* These reference books are available in the classroom, school, and public libraries. Many libraries now have "electronic" encyclopedias on CD-ROM.
3. *Books:* Students find books on their topics using their library skills.

4. *Newspapers and Pamphlets:* Willa brings a newspaper to class everyday, which the students use to look for information related to their own topics and those of others in the class.
5. *Interviews:* Each student must do one interview. He or she develops a list of questions to ask, tape records and transcribes the interview, and takes pictures. Willa has developed a file of people to interview on different topics. Over the years, her students have interviewed the head coaches of Louisiana State and Southern Universities in Baton Rouge, the mayor, the head of the zoo, and others. The children may also interview their parents or other teachers for relevant information.

Use the Yellow Pages for ideas about people to interview.

• ***Taking Notes:*** Students record each source of information on a 5" × 7" card, which they number. They jot down the same number for each source when they take notes from it on more 5" × 7" cards; this is an easy way of keeping track of which notes came from which source. Students also use the computer and set up files to take notes when they're using sources in the classroom.

• ***Writing the Report:*** Students begin to write their reports when they feel they have enough information. First, they begin to draft parts of their reports. They learn to summarize and organize the information they have found. They conference with Willa and other students in peer-editing groups. During their weekly conferences with Willa, she discusses their progress and where they are on the schedule. When each student has completed his or her rough draft, he or she does an outline, bibliography, cover, and illustrations. Here's a list of all the parts of a report:

Title Page
- Title
- Name
- Date

Table of Contents
- Outline
- Page numbers

Introduction
- Why they chose theme
- What they did

Body
- Section for each part of outline
- Illustrations

Bibliography
- Author and title (third and fourth grades)
- Author, title, publisher, year (fifth and sixth grades)

• ***Creative Products:*** Students brainstorm to come up with ideas for a creative product based on what they wrote their reports about. Parents can become involved, making this a family project, and it might even extend into the community. One child had the whole LSU School of Veterinary Medicine helping on a project about animals. Other children made films and videos, overhead projector transparencies, and slide shows. One girl wrote a song for her project on music. The possibilities are endless!

Sandi Kim's Independent Project on Korea

Sandi Kim was learning to use language and using language to learn when she did her independent project on Korea. On the day she reported what she'd learned, she and her mother rode the bus to school in traditional Korean costume, which created a sensation on the bus. They created another sensation at school when Sandi shared her mother, their traditional dress, and special Korean food. She also reported on how she chose her topic and found information, how she determined which questions she wanted to answer about Korea, what answers she found to some of these questions, and how she felt about doing this project.

> **Choosing Korea as a Topic and Finding Information**
> My parents are Korean, but I was born in Alabama. I wanted to find out more about Korea. We have lots of books about Korea at home, and I got a lot more from the library. I also read the encyclopedia, magazines, the newspaper, and some pamphlets.
>
> I interviewed my Dad. He was a captain in the Marines and told me all about the war of North and South Korea. He was shot during the war and has a little scar on his neck, but his hair hides it.
>
> ***Questions about Korea***
>
> 1. What are the people in Korea like?
> 2. How do the people in Korea live?
> 3. What is the Korean alphabet and language like?

Sandi Kim and her mother share traditional Korean dress and food.

What Sandi Learned about Korea

1. ***What are the people in Korea like?*** People always have to bow low because long ago, they began to bow to important people like adults and parents. They used to wear very complicated clothes, like my mother and I are wearing today, but now it's more simple and they wear the same kind as we do. They wear these costumes just on holidays. It's fun to wear the costumes, though. When you raise your arms, the sleeve looks just like a bird's wing.

2. ***How do they live?*** The people of Korea aren't very rich because of all the wars they've had. Sometimes, they feel like just a little shrimp between the two big whales, China and Japan.

Seoul is very crowded, and most people live in apartments. Children would be lost for sure if they went alone to the markets. There are few cars. Just buses, like in China.

Girls and ladies like my mother don't have freedom. They can't just walk around anywhere as we can here.

3. ***What is their alphabet and language like?*** They used to write Chinese or Japanese but King Sejong didn't like that because it took lots of pages for one sentence, so he invented a new alphabet that was simple.

When a child says "I love my mother" in English, a child would say "I love our mother" in Korean in case they had a brother or sister who would feel sad if they said only "my mother."

How Sandi Kim Felt about Her Project

It was fun to do this. I especially like wearing the traditional dress and coming to school with my mother. If it had been something the teacher had made me do, I wouldn't like it as much. But I liked it a lot, so I made it long.

How Other Students Felt about Their Projects

I asked several other students in Willa Richardson's class how they felt about doing independent projects. Here's what they told me:

Matthew on Moviemaking

I liked writing the report and making the movie, even though the rough draft was hard and it took me two whole times of doing the whole thing to get it right. But it took me five times to get the movie right, and now I want to start another report and movie. Fiction this time. A space monster movie.

See Chapter 13, Media Literacy, for examples of making films with children.

Amy on Cats

I've done reports before, but this was the only time it was fun. It was a better topic because I got to pick it. I got an idea for my next report after my cat got run over and killed. Bones and fossils and stuff like that.

Thomas on the Chicago Bears
This was a good thing to do because I wanted to do it because I like the Bears and because I didn't have to have a lot of help. Me and my father got the materials, and I found out a lot I didn't know until I read a lot of books about them. It was fun. I want to study a baseball team next.

Robert on Killer Whales
I liked the report the best this year because I liked the writing. And I didn't have any homework. I just worked on the report every night!

Tools for Using Language across the Curriculum

Finding Information

Many sources of information are available to elementary students. *Primary sources* are those that students discover and experience firsthand: going on trips, hearing speakers, doing experiments, and the like. *Secondary sources* are those created or compiled by others, such as books, magazines, newspapers, reference books, software, films, tapes, and so on. Table 14.2 summarizes the sources of information available to elementary students.

Interviews

Interviews are an excellent primary source of information. As noted in the Snapshot, Willa Richardson requires her third-graders to conduct interviews as part of their independent projects. When I interviewed them about their projects, they all said they enjoyed doing the interviews the most.

Sample Interview Questions. Willa suggests the following sample questions, which each child can adapt for the person he or she chooses to interview, either on tape, by taking notes, or both:

- What is your job title?
- What does your job involve?
- What special training or experience did you need for your job?
- How did you find your job?
- What did you like about your job? dislike?

Young children can do interviews in a whole-class situation with a guest, such as a parent, or on a fieldtrip in the community. But older children are capable of and interested in finding their own interviewees.

TABLE 14.2 Primary and Secondary Sources of Information

	Primary Sources			
	Personal Experiences	***Fieldtrips***	***Guest Speakers***	***Experiments***
In School	Memory Ongoing Classroom School	Library Cafeteria Principal's office Maintenance	Teacher Other teacher School personnel	Observations Hypotheses tested Data analysis
Out of School	Trips Extracurricular activities Community events	Business Government agencies Parks and zoos Museums Monuments Entertainment events	Professionals Experts in field (develop a resource person file; check Yellow Pages)	Surveys Interviews Oral history

	Secondary Sources				
	Children's Literature	***Periodicals***	***References***	***Vertical File***	***Media***
Library/ Media Center	Fiction Nonfiction Biography Magazines	Journals Newspapers Reports	Dictionary Thesaurus Encyclopedia Atlas Hypertext/ Hypermedia	Pictures Pamphlets Clippings Miscellaneous	Study pictures Slides Filmstrips Films Tapes Videotapes Games Transparencies Dioramas Models Specimens

Benefits of Interviewing. Haley-James and Hobson (1980) described a first-grade class in which all the children interviewed a police officer during a unit on "community helpers" and cited these benefits of doing so:

- Students assume adult language roles.
- The drive to communicate is encouraged, as students ask questions.

- Students are eager to write and read the results of the interview.
- Students are in control of their own language and learning.
- Every child can succeed.
- Interviewing unifies all the language processes.
- Children discover language rules and conventions about language based on their own experiences and observations.

Another observable outcome in this first-grade class is that the children wrote longer personal and group language experience stories. In addition, they used more sophisticated language and learned to spell the special vocabularies of the police officer. Finally, their desire to communicate was reinforced as they shared what they'd written with others.

Initiating an Interviewing Program. Haley-James and Hobson (1980) suggest the following guidelines for teachers:

1. *Practice interviews:* Simulate practice interviews, perhaps having students interview the teacher about one of his or her interests. The teacher should bring an object to prompt students' interest and questions.

a. Give students only the information they ask for. If they ask only yes/no questions, give only yes/no answers. Help them develop broader, higher-level questions.
b. Evaluate the interview. Ask which questions solicited the most information, and develop more practice questions.
c. Have the students interview each other in pairs, and evaluate their interviews the same way.

2. *Write up interviews:* Help students clarify meaning during conferences, and teach needed spelling and conventions in context.

3. *Share interview results:* Students can read interviews in class or at home. Other ways to share interviews include through research reports, bookmaking, mediamaking (documentaries, audio recordings, or photo essays), and student-produced newspapers and magazines.

Children's Literature

Children's literature provides the richest source of information, both fiction and nonfiction. Of course, teachers should have classroom libraries. But if they plan to focus on themes, as Willa Richardson did, they should supplement their class libraries with temporary collections of books from school and public libraries and encourage children to bring books from home.

References that list books by subject, or theme, include:

See Chapter 7, Teaching with Literature, for more subject guides to children's literature.

Children's Catalog (H. W. Wilson, Annual)
The Elementary School Library Collection (Bro-Dart, Annual)
Subject Guide to Children's Books in Print (R. R. Bowker, Annual)

Textbooks

Willa Richardson selected all the chapters on the environment, ecology, and building an aquarium in available social studies and science texts to supplement children's observations and children's literature. Students should know how to use the following parts of a textbook to locate information accurately and easily:

1. *Table of Contents:* Ask students to locate a specific topic and tell what unit, chapter, and page it's on.
2. *Glossary:* Ask students to find words in boldface print (darker than the others). Look them up in the glossary at the back of the book, and tell what they mean.
3. *Index:* Ask the children to turn to the index at the back of the book. Give them a topic, and let them find it in the index. Then have them locate the pages with that information on it and read what they find to the class.
4. *Maps:* Go over a map and find the places listed in the legend, or key.
5. *Photographs:* Look at a picture and read the caption. Talk about what's going on in the photo and why it's in that part of the book.
6. *Diagrams, Charts, Tables, Graphs:* Look at these types of graphics, and discuss how to find information using them.
7. *Study Questions and Aids:* Read and answer some of the questions, and review what other study aids are provided. Discuss how these features help readers use the book.

The skills children learn in using textbooks become tools for using any nonfiction or reference sources, including many electronic media.

Encyclopedias

Teachers shouldn't underestimate children's ability to use reference materials; it's amazing what they can master when they're interested in something. Students learn to use reference books by using them. Thus, teachers should introduce types of reference books and explain what kinds of information can be found in each. Establish a classroom library of reference books. Garage and library sales are good sources of used reference books.

Students should understand that encyclopedias are a good place to start finding information because they summarize the most important facts on a topic and often list related topics at the ends of entries, for readers who want to find out more. The teacher should demonstrate how to look up a topic by letter and explain how many are cross-referenced. Let each student do this on a topic he or she is interested in.

Here are types of encyclopedias appropriate for different levels and an "electronic" encyclopedia on compact disc:

Late Primary
Britannica Junior Encyclopedia
The New Book of Knowledge

Middle Elementary
Challenger: The Student's Encyclopedia
The World Book Encyclopedia

Upper Elementary and Middle School
Collier's Encyclopedia
Compton's Encyclopedia
Encyclopedia International

Electronic Encyclopedia
Compton's Multimedia Encyclopedia

Electronic Publishing

Students may also have access to information produced electronically, such as CD-ROM. This technology allows volumes of text (about 300,000 pages) to be stored on a single disk. Hypermedia/hypertext creates "hyperdocuments," which can include text, video, and sound.

Electronic publishing also means computer networks, which are becoming alternatives to print publications. Libraries, schools, companies, and universities are linked in networks that provide access to electronically published documents. Electronic publishing often provides more graphic, aural, and animated techniques to present information visually and auditorially. As noted earlier, an example of an electronic encyclopedia is *Compton's Multimedia Encyclopedia* (Rickelman et al., 1991).

Specialized Reference Books

The following reference books are commonly used by children and normally found in school libraries:

Atlas of American History
Bartlett's Familiar Quotations
Book of Junior Authors
Contemporary Authors
Information Please Almanac
Who's Who in America
World Almanac and Book of Facts
World Atlas

Dictionaries

Here are dictionaries ranging from the simplest to more complex, for students of different grade and ability levels:

Picture Dictionaries for Primary Grades
The Cat in the Hat Beginner Book Dictionary (Random House)
The Golden Picture Dictionary (Western)
My First Picture Dictionary (Lothrop/Scott, Foresman)

Elementary School Dictionaries
The Charlie Brown Dictionary (Random House)
Macmillan Dictionary for Children (Macmillan)
Scott, Foresman Beginning Dictionary (Doubleday/Scott, Foresman)

Middle School Dictionaries
The American Heritage School Dictionary (Houghton Mifflin)
Macmillan School Dictionary (Macmillan)
Thorndike-Barnhart Intermediate Dictionary (Random House)

Teach students to use dictionaries as sources of information about word meanings and as general reference tools. But don't refer children to the dictionary to find the spelling of a word. (Obviously, if they don't know how to spell the word, they won't be able to find it in the dictionary.) Introduce dictionary skills in connection with themes students are already learning about. For example:

The Scott Foresman Beginning Dictionary provides an excellent introduction to the dictionary around the theme of zoo animals and ecology.

1. *Alphabetical Order:* Students should know the alphabet. A simple check is to have them write out the letters in order.

Try reading aloud Juster Norton's (1961) children's book *The Phantom Tollbooth,* which is about the imaginary land of Dictionopolis, full of word and dictionary humor—really!

2. *Guide Words:* Knowing how to use guide words (i.e., the words at the tops of the pages) can save the frustration of looking through an entire letter section. Show a sample page on the overhead projector, and demonstrate where the guide words are and what they indicate. Make a list of words around a theme, and find the guide words for the page of each entry. Children could do this in groups, each with a different list of words.

3. *Parts of a Dictionary Entry:* Using a word related to a theme, go over the parts of a dictionary entry. Use an overhead projector transparency, and check to see if the librarian has materials that might be useful.

4. *Multiple Meanings:* Choosing the correct meaning of a word is a critical aspect of dictionary use. Students often think all the meanings for a word are interchangeable, which is not always the case. Encourage students to pinpoint different meanings to see that they're not all the same.

5. *Reference Use:* The dictionary can be an excellent source of information on themes by giving multiple meanings of related words as well as word origins.

Thesauruses

A thesaurus is an excellent tool for writers of all ages. Here are four, listed in order from easiest to most difficult:

In Other Words: A Beginning Thesaurus (Scott, Foresman)
Roget's Thesaurus (Random House)
Synonym and Antonym Dictionary (Scholastic)
Words to Use: A Junior Thesaurus (Sadlier)

TEACHING IDEA

Student-Created Reference Books

A good way to introduce students to reference books is to have them create their own. Here are several ideas:

• ***Class Telephone Directory:*** The children make an alphabetized list of their names, telephone numbers, and addresses. This can be reproduced, sent home, and actually used.

• ***Encyclopedia on a Theme:*** Students create their own encyclopedias on themes that interest them. Their encyclopedias should include the information the students have learned and be alphabetized according to topics and subtopics.

• ***Thesaurus: Primary Grades:*** Phyllis Crawford, a former first-grade teacher and now a principal in Baton Rouge, Louisiana, had her students create their own thesauruses using pattern writing. She used the "If I Were" pattern and worked with the class theme of farm animals. Students had to find other words for some of those in the pattern. Then they made a page in the thesaurus for each word, showing other words as well as the pattern they wrote. Here's the page first-graders created for the word *filthy:*

Filthy: Dirty, unclean, grimy, grubby, messy, yucky, icky, gross

If I Were a Pig

If I were a pig, a plump <u>filthy</u> pig,
If I were a pig, this is what I would do.
I would grunt, grunt, grunt, grunt, grunt.
That's what I would do.

• ***Thesaurus: Upper Grades:*** Phyllis Fuglaar, a fourth-grade teacher in Baton Rouge, asked her students to use the thesaurus to find substitutes for words in the titles of well-known stories. Groups of students picked titles, found words to substitute, and then read the revised titles to the rest of the class, who had to guess what they were. Can you guess?*

1. Trio of Diminutive Hogs
2. The Petite Scarlet Fowl
3. Slumbering Symmetry
4. The Treasure Effect
5. Mouser in Soles
6. The Diminutive Vermilion Biddy
7. Elderly Belle That Dwelled in a Pump

***Answers:** 1. The Three Little Pigs 2. & 6. The Little Red Hen 3. Sleeping Beauty 4. The Golden Touch 5. Puss-in-Boots 7. The Old Woman Who Lived in a Shoe

Library Media Center

Teachers should walk their students through the library and identify the locations of the circulation desk, card catalogue or online catalogue, and vertical file (pamphlets, etc.) as well as shelves or sections for these kinds of materials: picture books, easy-to-read books, oversized books, fiction, nonfiction, biography, reference books, periodicals, and audiovisual materials. Describe the types of materials in each category. Students can make a map of the library, with a key to identify the parts.

Card Catalogues. Traditionally, information is retrieved in a library by using a card catalogue, and many schools still use this system. To introduce the card catalogue, show students enlarged versions of the three types of cards (subject, title, and author) on poster paper or an overhead transparency.

Explain that if you're looking for a book by title, look under the first letter of the first important word in the title. You will be using the *title card*. You can also look up the author of the book (using the *author card*) or the general subject (using the *subject card*). All three types of cards include the same basic information but in a slightly different arrangement. And all the cards are arranged in alphabetical order in the card catalogue by the first important word in the first line: the title, the author's last name, or the topic.

Online Catalogues. Many libraries have replaced their card catalogues with computer databases and online catalogues. An *online catalogue* includes all the resources available in a library or combination of libraries accessible through that computer. Most college and university libraries have their holdings online, making access quick and easy, and more and more public libraries are converting to this system, too. Some school libraries also have online catalogues and library-to-class networks (such that students can access information in the library from the class computer).

The Dewey Decimal System. The Dewey Decimal System groups nonfiction books in categories with corresponding numbers, known as *call numbers*. (University and public libraries usually use another system, the Library of Congress system, but most elementary schools use the Dewey.) Once students have located the call number for a book (which is found on the card catalogue card or online entry), they will be able to go to the place in the library where the book is stored. For instance, a book with a call number of 921 will be a biography.

Periodicals. Information can also be found in various types of *periodicals*, which are publications that come out on a regular or periodic basis, such as newspapers and magazines. The *Reader's Guide to Periodical Literature*, indexed and bound in annual volumes, lists articles from such publications by author and subject. Not all elementary school libraries have the *Reader's*

Guide, but most middle schools do. Since her school library didn't have a *Reader's Guide*, Willa Richardson scheduled a fieldtrip for parents and students to the public library to show them how to use it and to encourage them to use the public library as well as the school library.

Cricket is a literary magazine, but each issue is filled with fiction, poetry, nonfiction articles, and hands-on science and art activities related to themes—for example, Native Americans, Antarctica, and famous women.

Each school library will have its own collection of magazines. Common titles include *National Geographic World, Cricket, Ranger Rick,* and *Zillions* (a child's *Consumer Reports*). Consult a listing of these magazines, usually provided near the *Reader's Guide,* to know which ones the library has.

Study Guide for Library Use. Students should learn to use the library to find information when they are actually researching a theme. For example, students in groups could answer questions they developed by using different parts of the library. Groups could rotate so that everyone has a chance to try out all possible sources of information in the library.

SNAPSHOT: Third-Graders Research How to Build an Aquarium

Willa Richardson's third-grade class split into small groups and set off for the library. Each group had the following study guide:

Study Guide for Using the Library: Building an Aquarium

Questions

1. What kinds of water environments for aquariums are there?
2. Which kind should we create in our aquarium?
3. What kinds of water, plants, and fish belong in this kind of aquarium?
4. Where can we find them?
5. How do we put them together in the aquarium?
6. How can we maintain the aquarium?
7. What do we need to know about each of the fish?

The groups were assigned to do research in these parts of the library:

Group 1: Card Catalogue or Computer Files/ Dewey Decimal System

1. Look under the topics *aquarium, fish,* and *tropical fish.*
2. List some books you could use to make an aquarium.
3. Locate three of these books. Make a note card on each.
4. Identify the authors. List other books by each author on this subject.
5. Locate the books on the shelf and check out the ones you think will be useful.

Group 2: Periodicals

1. Check the newspaper for information on *fish*.
2. Use the *Reader's Guide* to find articles on *aquarium*, *fish*, and *tropical fish*. Make a note card on each.
3. List two magazines that might have information on *fish*.
4. Look through several issues for information. Take notes.

Group 3: Encyclopedias and Other References

1. Make a list of all encyclopedia book sets and electronic encyclopedias in the library. Locate them.
2. Look up *aquarium*, *fish*, and *tropical fish*. Take notes.
3. At the end of each article, you will find related topics.
4. Look up at least one more article.

Group 4: Vertical File

1. Check the vertical file for pamphlets, clippings, and other materials under headings *aquarium*, *fish*, and *tropical fish*.
2. Check out any useful material you find.

Group 5: Media

1. Find media on *fish* (picture sets, filmstrips, films, audiotapes, videotapes, computer software). Take notes.

Group 6: Dictionary and Thesaurus

1. Make a list of dictionaries and thesauruses in the library.
2. Look up *aquarium*, *fish*, and *tropical fish* in each one.
3. Take notes. Compare what you find.

Recording Information

Underlining

Students can underline on their own notes, on copies of pages of books, or on newspaper or magazine articles not in the permanent library collection. Do a minilesson on the overhead projector, emphasizing the following:

Minilesson on Underlining

1. Look for *main ideas.*
2. Look for *keywords* you will want to remember and find again.
3. *Underline* words you don't know meanings of, and put a *question mark* next to each in the margin. Look up their meanings.
4. *Note questions or ideas* in the margin.

Media Recording

Information can be recorded by various electronic and visual media: audio and videotape recorders, data-processing computer programs, and photographs. Interviews, for example, can be recorded electronically and visually.

Notetaking

There are two approaches to notetaking:

- *Teacher Takes Dictation:* Teachers of younger or limited–English proficient students can take notes for them. Language experience charts are one way to do this—for example, a chart on a trip to the zoo.
- *Students Write Notes:* Have students use 3" × 5" or 5" × 7" index cards, small pieces of paper, loose-leaf notebooks, or computer databases or text files. Do a minilesson on notetaking:

Minilesson on Notetaking

1. Look for *main ideas*—things that are important or interesting to you.
2. Put those ideas in *your own words.* Avoid just copying.
3. Identify important *names, dates,* and *specific facts:* size, quantity, technical names.
4. Note *ideas of your own* as you read.
5. Note *questions* that occur to you as you read.
6. *Combine ideas* as you note them. Look for *themes.*

Summarizing

Synthesizing information requires more thought by students than just writing down information, and to do so effectively takes a lot of practice. Have students practice by:

- *Summarizing What Others Say:* Do this at the beginning of the year with simple class procedures or rules (e.g., household chores or management techniques).

- *Summarizing What They Say for Others:* Provide opportunities for sharing, current events, and oral reporting so that students can summarize what they've said as a sort of conclusion.

- *Summarizing What They or Others Have Written:* Students may summarize their own writing before reading it to others or summarize what they have understood as others read their own writing (e.g., during peer-editing conferences).

- *Summarizing What They Have Read:* Students can summarize books for reading conferences or to recommend them to others during a sharing period or as part of an individualized reading record. For an independent project, key information can be recorded on a chart by breaking it down into important parts before summarizing. The chart gives the central question and has columns for noting the 5 Ws and H.

Organizing Information

Note Card File

As noted earlier, Willa Richardson's third-graders began to organize the information for their independent projects from the very beginning, using index cards. They jotted down the source of the information and what they thought was important, based on the questions they were answering.

Data Charts

Help students make charts to organize information. A *data chart* can be as simple as folding a large piece of paper several times to make squares, putting a question in each square, and adding information that answers it.

Loose-Leaf Notebooks

Students can organize information in loose-leaf notebooks, which have removable pages, more easily than spiral-bound notebooks. They can write questions on separate pages and put down all the information that answers that question on that page, adding pages as they need them.

Computer Files

The organizational method described for loose-leaf notebooks will also work with computer files. Set up separate pages in a text file and record and answer questions.

Students' Own Organizational Schemes

Jacobs (1984) notes that students intuitively develop their own organizational schemes and don't respond well to rigid formulas for organizing their writing. Peer-response groups in writing workshop might be a good time for students to talk to others about organizing their writing, sharing their individual methods and getting feedback on them.

Outlining

Outlining is a way to synthesize main ideas and establish the relationship among them. Outlining should be taught using a topic or event the children have experienced, rather than an abstract concept.

- ***Outlining an Experience:*** Phyllis Crawford teaches middle-elementary students outlining as they plan and do cooking experiences, such as making tacos:

Students make tacos as Phyllis Crawford teaches outlining based on a real experience.

Outline for Making Tacos

I. Preparing the ingredients
  A. Lettuce
    1. Wash
    2. Pull off dead leaves
    3. Slice fine
  B. Tomatoes
    1. Wash
    2. Peel
    3. Chop fine
  C. Cheese
    1. Take off wrapper
    2. Cut in chunks
    3. Grate
  D. Meat
    1. Turn on electric frying pan
    2. Put meat in
    3. Poke meat with wooden spoon until brown, not pink
  E. Onions
    1. Peel
    2. Close your mouth (to keep from crying)
    3. Chop fine
II. Putting the tacos together
  A. Food
    1. Put all of one kind of food on a big plate
    2. Put plates in a line on a long table
    3. Open box of taco shells and put at beginning of table

B. Making the tacos
   1. Get a plate
   2. Get a taco shell
   3. Put in the ingredients (you don't have to eat onions or other things you don't like)

C. Eating
   1. Go to your seat
   2. Start to eat
   3. Use your napkin

• ***Blank Outlines:*** After students have practiced making an outline together, they can use blank outlines for independent work:

Subject

I. A main topic
   A. Subtopic
      1. Detail
         a. Subdetail

Sheltered Content Instruction for Limited–English Proficient Students

Limited–English proficient students learn English through learning in the content areas: social studies, science, math, health, or any activity in which the purpose is to learn something other than language (Krashen & Terrell, 1987). Activities for content instruction might include sharing, music, media presentations and productions, guest lecturers, readings and discussions, and individual student reports.

See Chapter 3, Language and Cultural Diversity, for more on teaching limited–English proficient students.

Limited–English proficient students make a life-sized model of a jaguar while studying the rainforest.

Recent studies on the academic achievement of language-minority students have indicated the need for content instruction in the primary language without translation (Ramirez & Merino, 1990). Thus, Spanish-speaking students should be taught the content areas in Spanish, at least in part. In addition, classroom teachers can meet the needs of language-minority students in learning both content areas and English through two other approaches: content-based English language development (ELD) and specially designed academic instruction in English (SDAIE). Let's look at each.

Content-Based English Language Development (ELD)

In the ELD approach, content is the focus of instruction, but the primary goal is to increase English language proficiency. This approach can be used with students at all grade levels.

ELD Lessons

These stages of language proficiency were described in Chapter 3, Language and Cultural Diversity.

Here's an example of a content-based ELD lesson on geography, which could be adapted to any state. The teacher uses a map of the United States and asks questions and gives prompts geared toward each child's stage of language proficiency:

1. ***Listening Comprehension, or Preproduction:*** Silent stage, active listening:
   "Point to *your state* on the map."
   "Point to *your city* in *your state*."
2. ***Early Production:*** Single words and short phrases:
   "Which state is north of *your state?"*
   "Which state is south of *your state?"* (and so on with other directions)
   "Is it usually hot or cold in *your state?"*
   "Name the states that border *your state*."
3. ***Extending Production:*** Sentences, longer narratives:
   "What are some things you would take on a trip to *a state that borders your state*?"
   "What are some places you have visited in *your state*?"
   "What do you like to do in *your state*?"

Three-Step Interview

The three-step interview was described as a cooperative learning strategy in Chapter 5, Listening and Talking.

As students become more fluent, use the three-step interview for content-based ELD. In it, students form pairs, one interviews the other, and then they reverse. After that, each child shares about the other with the whole class. Students could do interviews like this to talk about their state. For instance, use these questions/prompts:

"If you could live anywhere in the United States, where would you live?"
"Tell about a vacation you would like to take in the United States."

Specially Designed Academic Instruction in English (SDAIE)

The key idea of SDAIE is to make content material as accessible to limited–English proficient students as it is to monolingual English students (i.e., native speakers) and language-minority students who have become fluent in English. Another term for the SDAIE approach is *sheltered instruction*.

Let's discuss this approach using terms from second-language acquisition theory and practice. SDAIE experiences should be *context embedded* (James Cummins's [1984] term) and provide *comprehensible input* (Stephen Krashen's [Krashen & Terrell, 1987] term). These experiences should provide a bridge from content taught in the student's primary language in a bilingual program (or where there is a bilingual aide and materials) to mainstream English classes. The goal is for limited–English proficient students to learn the same content as fluent language-minority students and monolingual English students.

SDAIE Lessons

There are four main components of an SDAIE lesson:

For a literature-based lesson about the moon, see the picture book *Armadillo Ray* (Beifuss, 1995), a combination of a pourquoi tale and hard facts.

1. *Content:* Identify the main ideas and key vocabulary of what will be taught, and choose appropriate materials.

2. *Connections:* Make links with students' personal experiences and cultural heritages. Draw on their prior knowledge. Show relationships by using outlines, webs, semantic maps, clusters, and "word walls." If possible, use an aide to preview and review the lesson in each student's primary language (i.e., L1). This is called *L1 preview/review*.

3. *Comprehensibility:* Align the activity to each student's stage of English proficiency. Modify what's said to provide comprehensible input, considering rate (slow down), enunciation (speak clearly), vocabulary (avoid idioms), and contextualization (use gestures and facial expressions.) Use extralinguistic clues: visual aids, realia, maps, manipulatives, graphs, and teacher modeling. Check for comprehension: monitor student understanding, ask questions throughout activity, and review frequently.

4. *Interaction:* Allow students to use their primary languages. Use cooperative learning strategies and group work. Plan for multiple interactions: student/teacher, student/student, student/content, and student/self.

Guidelines for Sheltered Content Instruction

In sum, here are 10 guidelines for sheltered content instruction:

1. Teach content but plan lessons related to students' lives; ask them what they already know about a subject. Also utilize a lot of visuals and provide hands-on involvement: drawing, labeling, and constructing.

2. Make everything you say as understandable as possible; avoid complicated words or sentences, speak slowly and keep intonation normal, avoid idioms, and use body language. Communicate individually with students as much as you can.

3. Avoid forcing students to speak.

4. Reassure students that their own languages are acceptable and important.

5. Make any corrections indirectly by repeating what the student has said in correct form.

6. Try to answer all questions, but avoid overly detailed explanations.

7. Check to see whether what you're saying is understood. Ask questions: "Do you understand?" "Do you have any questions?" Be aware of feedback, particularly blank stares and puzzled expressions.

8. Reinforce key concepts over and over in a variety of situations and activities.

9. Use aides and tutors who speak students' native languages, and request that content books be provided in native languages, as well.

10. Become as informed as possible about the cultures of your students. Respect and enjoy what's unique about each culture by making it part of the classroom.

Assessing Language across the Curriculum

1. ***Checklist and File for a Report:*** Create a checklist for a report, including all requirements and expectations. Students can check off activities as they complete them, and the final checklist will become a part of their portfolio, along with the report and any creative products. Figure 14.2 shows a checklist that Willa Richardson required her students to complete when they did independent projects.

2. ***Checklist for Library Use:*** Here's an informal assessment checklist for experiences and abilities expected of students at different grade levels:

Kindergarten

- Introduce the library: the librarian, pleasures of the library, books to look at, storytelling, films, filmstrips, records, and special programs such as puppets, guest speakers, book fairs, and displays
- Care of books: how to hold a book, turn pages, use a bookmark, replace on shelf, place on desk, care for books taken home

NAME ______________________		
Check if:	*Completed*	*Attached*
1. Idea list	______	______
2. Teacher conference	______	______
3. Questions (10–12)	______	______
4. Schedule	______	______
5. Parent sign-off	______	______
6. Five types of information	______	______
a. Magazines	______	______
b. Encyclopedia	______	______
c. Books	______	______
d. Newspapers/pamphlets	______	______
e. Interview	______	______
7. Note cards	______	______
8. Completed report	______	______
9. Creative product Describe here:	______	______

FIGURE 14.2
Checklist and File for Independent Project

- Locate a picture book and easy-to-read book: by the first letter of the author's last name
- Use of media and technology: independent use of computers, tape recorders, and filmstrip projects

Primary: Grades 1 and 2

- Locate books: in fiction section, by author
- Use reference materials: primary dictionary, picture dictionaries, thesaurus, encyclopedia, atlases
- Basic skills to build study skills: alphabetizing, using table of contents and index
- Sharing creative work in library: art, models, books they've made, reading to younger children, creative dramatics

Picture books are usually grouped on the shelf according to first letter only.

Middle, Upper-Elementary, and Middle School: Grades 3 through 8

- Learn to use card catalogue or computer files
- Learn to use Dewey Decimal System
- Learn to use *Reader's Guide to Periodical Literature*
- Prepare displays, based on research conducted in library
- Use library independently: during class, before and after school

nswers to Questions about Language across the Curriculum

1. *What does* language across the curriculum *mean?*

Language across the curriculum means teaching the language arts of thinking, listening, speaking, reading, writing, and viewing within the context of the content areas: social studies, science, mathematics, music, and the arts. Language across the curriculum is based on three principles: (a) all genuine learning involves discovery, (b) language has a heuristic function (i.e., language is a means to learn), and (c) using language to discover is the best way to learn it. In a student- and response-centered classroom, this means an integrated approach to teaching, in which students ask questions, identify and solve problems, use research and study skills, and discover the interconnectedness of subject matter.

2. *How should we teach language across the curriculum?*

Teachers use thematic teaching, which has a long history and has been called by various names: *units, thematic units, theme study, theme cycles,* and *integrated and cross-curricular teaching*. According to this approach, teachers plan and initiate themes, and collaborate and model for students so as to initiate themes for individual inquiry. Students learn about the library and how to find information their from primary and secondary sources. They also learn to record and organize information, often preferring their own organizational schemes. Sheltered instruction for limited–English proficient students can take two approaches: lessons for content-based English language development (ELD) or specially designed academic instruction in English (SDAIE).

LOOKING FURTHER

1. Brainstorm ideas of creative products that students could make as independent projects.
2. Choose a theme or an area of the curriculum (e.g., social studies, math, science, or fine arts)—something you might want to introduce to children or that interests you. Develop a bibliography of related children's books.
3. Visit a school library or media center, and develop a study guide for a grade level you would like to teach. Pick a specific topic to plan the guide around.
4. Plan a SDAIE lesson for limited–English proficient students and try it out, if possible. Describe what happened.

RESOURCES

Gamberg, R., et al. (1988). *Learning and loving it: Theme studies in the classroom*. Portsmouth, NH: Heinemann.

Richard-Amato, P. A. (1996). *Making it happen: Interaction in the second language classroom* (2nd ed.). White Plains, NY: Longman.

REFERENCES

Altwerger, B., & Flores, B. (1994). Theme cycles: Creating communities of learners. *Primary Voices, K–6, 2,* 2–6.

Ausubel, D. P. (1963). Cognitive structure and the facilitation of meaningful verbal learning. *Journal of Teacher Education, 14,* 217–222.

Buckley, M. H. (1994). Integrated English language arts curriculum. In A. Purves (Ed.), *Encyclopedia of English studies and language arts.* New York: Scholastic.

Bullock, A. B. (1975). *A language for life.* London, England: Her Majesty's Stationery Office.

Cummins, J. (1984). *Bilingualism and special education: Issues in assessment and pedagogy.* San Diego, CA: College-Hill.

Froese, V. (1994). Language across the curriculum. In A. Purves (Ed.), *Encyclopedia of English studies and language arts.* New York: Scholastic.

Haley-James, S. M., & Hobson, C. D. (1980). Interviewing: A means of encouraging the drive to communicate. *Language Arts, 57,* 497–502.

Jacobs, S. E. (1984). Investigative writing: Practice and principles. *Language Arts, 61,* 356–363.

Krashen, S. D., & Terrell, T. D. (1987). *The natural approach: Language acquisition in the classroom.* Englewood Cliffs, NJ: Prentice-Hall.

Ramirez, J. D., & Merino, B. J. (1990). Classroom talk in English immersion, early-exit and late-exit transitional bilingual education programs. In R. Jacobson & C. Faltis (Eds.), *Language distribution issues in bilingual school* (pp. 61–103). Clevedon, England: Multilingual Matters Ltd.

Rickelman, R., et al. (1991). Electronic encyclopedias on compact disc. *Reading Teacher, 44,* 432–434.

Sipe, R. B. (1994). Thematic units. *Encyclopedia of English studies and language arts* (Vol. 2). New York: Scholastic.

Thaiss, C. (1986). *Language across the curriculum in the elementary grades.* Urbana, IL: National Council of Teachers of English.

CHILDREN'S BOOKS

Arnosky, J. (1987). *Drawing from nature.* New York: Morrow.

Arnosky, J. (1990). *A kettle of hawks.* New York: Lothrop, Lee, & Shepard.

Arnosky, J. (1991). *Secrets of a wildlife watcher.* New York: Morrow.

Arnosky, J. (1994). *All about alligators.* New York: Scholastic.

Baylor, B. (1976). *Hawk, I am your brother.* New York: Macmillan.

Baylor, B. (1978). *The other way to listen.* New York: Macmillan.

Beifuss, J. (1995). *Armadillo Ray.* San Francisco: Chronicle Books.

Bramewell, M. (1992). *The environment and conservation.* New York: Prentice-Hall.

Brown, L. K., & Brown, M. (1992). *Dinosaurs to the rescue! A guide to protecting our planet.* New York: Little, Brown.

Brown, M. B. (1992). *Wings along the waterway.* New York: Watts.

Douglas, M. S. (1986). *Everglades: The river of grass.* New York: R. Bemis.

Earthworks Group. (1991). *Fifty simple things you can do to save the earth.* Berkeley, CA: Earthworks Press.

Elkington, J. (1990). *Going green: A kid's handbook to saving the planet.* New York: Viking.

Facklam, M. (1978). *Wild animals, gentle women.* New York: Harcourt, Brace, Jovanovich.

George, J. C. (1991). *Moon of the alligators.* New York: HarperCollins.

Guiberson, B. Z. (1992). *Spoonbill swamp.* New York: Holt.

Holmes, A. (1993). *I can save the earth: A kid's handbook for keeping earth healthy and green.* New York: S & S Trade.

Koch, M. (1993). *World water watch.* New York: Greenwillow.

Lewis, J. P. (1991). *Earth verses.* New York: Macmillan.

Lewis, J. P. (1991). *Water rhymes.* New York: Macmillan.

McGovern, A. (1984). *Shark lady.* New York: Scholastic.

McPherson, M. (1985). *Caring for your fish.* New York: Troll.

Miles, B. (1991). *Save the earth! An action handbook for kids.* New York: Knopf.

Milgrin, H. (1990). *The ABC of ecology.* New York: Davenport.

Norton, J. (1961). *The phantom tollbooth.* New York: Random House.

Peet, B. (1974). *Wump world.* New York: Houghton Mifflin.

Pringle, L. (1990). *Saving our wildlife.* New York: Enslow.

Rotner, S., & Kreisler, K. (1992). *Nature spy.* New York: Macmillan.

Seuss, Dr. (1981). *The Lorax.* New York: Random.

Sarnoff, J. (1977). *A great aquarium book.* New York: Scribner's.

Selsam, M. E. (1995). *How to be a nature detective.* New York: HarperCollins.

Simon, S. (1976). *Tropical saltwater aquariums: How to set them up and keep them going.* New York: Viking.

Simon, S. (1977). *What do you want to know about guppies?* New York: Four Winds.

Simon, S. (1988). *How to be an ocean scientist in your own home.* New York: HarperCollins.

Van Allsburg, C. (1990). *Just a dream.* New York: Houghton Mifflin.

Appendix

Activities for the Schoolyear

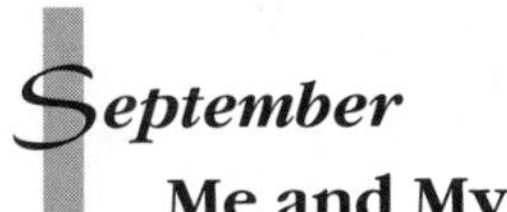

September

Me and My Family

Language and Literacy Experiences

Sharing

- *Scheduled Time Each Day:* 15–30 minutes
- *Establish Guidelines:* Individual times; taking turns; good questions for other students

Journals

- *Private Diaries:* Students write anything they want or in response to prompts: "What's new in your life?" "Tell your feelings today." "Make a wish."
- *Dialogue Journals:* The teacher, an aide, or another child writes in response to a journal entry.
- *Community Journals:* Anyone in class can write in open journals; keep them by the window (to observe weather, the playground), by the class pet, in centers, and so on.
- *Electronic Bulletin Boards:* Students correspond within the class, school, community, country, or world.
- *Emerging Writers:* Students copy the date from the calendar and draw pictures, which the teacher labels.

Star of the Week

- *Model:* The teacher tells about himself or herself, shows family pictures, and shares mementos.
- *Bulletin Board:* A child is featured on a "Star of the Week" board; post his or her name, mount pictures and papers, and position a table underneath to hold favorite objects (e.g., books, handmade things, awards).
- *Interviews:* Students in the class ask the Star of the Week questions, which the teacher writes on a language experience chart. Sample questions: "Where were you born?" "Who's in your family?" "What's your favorite . . . ?" "What's your greatest dream?"
- *Books:* The Star picks two other children to copy the interview on computer, a few sentences on each page; the pages are then printed, illustrated, and bound as a book.

Writing about Ourselves

- *Autobiographies:* Students create timelines, describe special events, write their life stories, talk about their families, or dream about the future.
- *Emerging Writers:* Children make outline collages; the teacher traces the outline of each child's body on butcher paper, and then he or she illustrates it through writing, gluing on pictures, adding mementos, and the like.
- *Effigies:* The teacher traces each child's body on butcher paper and cuts it out; the child draws on features and clothes, making a front and back; the edges are stapled together on three sides; the "body" is stuffed with newspaper and the remaining side is stapled shut; the effigy can sit in a chair.
- *Self-Portraits:* Students draw their own portraits; the teacher can write their names or take dictation, as needed.
- *Memoirs:* Children write about something they remember, like a special event or person.

Writing about Others

- *Interviews:* Students develop questions in class to ask each other or family members, school teachers or staff, or community helpers.
- *Recording Interviews:* During the interviews, students take notes or audio- or videotape them.
- *Sharing Interviews:* Students write biographies or edit and show the videotaped interviews.

Lesson Plan: *I Like Me!*

Level: Primary to middle grades

Purpose: Listen to, enjoy, and respond to literature of self-esteem.

Teaching Sequence:

1. Read aloud the book *I like me!* (Carlson, 1988), about a "pretty pink pig" with good self-esteem who tells all the things she likes about herself and is her own best friend.
2. Use aesthetic, open-ended questions and prompts to discuss the book:
   - "What did you think of the book?"
   - "What was your favorite part?"
   - "What are some of the things you like about yourself?"
3. Create a "word wall" on chartpaper by writing down the children's ideas. Use the heading "WHAT I LIKE ABOUT ME!"
4. Using the "word wall" as a model, children do a cluster of ideas of what they like about themselves, draw pictures to illustrate them, and write captions. Emerging writers can write their names and then give dictation to the teacher to label or write captions on their pictures.

Extending Activities:

1. Students in middle- and upper-elementary through middle school can write *biopoems:*

BIOPOEM

First name

Four words that tell about you

Child of
Lover of (3 things)
Who feels (3 things)
Who needs (3 things)
Who would like to see (3 things)
Resident of
Last name

2. Read *Something special* (McPhail, 1988), *Amazing Grace* (Hoffman, 1991), *The day of Ahmed's secret* (Heide & Gilliand, 1990), or *Cleversticks* (Ashley, 1992).

Children's Books

Ashley, B. (1992). *Cleversticks.* New York: Crown.

Carlson, N. (1988). *I like me.* New York: Viking.

Cisneros, S. (1994). *Hairs/Politos.* New York: Knopf.

Frasier, D. (1991). *On the day you were born.* New York: Harcourt Brace Jovanovich.

Friedman, I. (1984). *How my parents learned to eat.* Boston: Houghton Mifflin.

Heide, F., & Gilliand, J. (1990). *The day of Ahmed's secret.* New York: Lothrop, Lee & Shepard.

Hoberman, M. A. (1991). *Fathers, mothers, sisters, brothers: A collection of family poems.* New York: Penguin.

Hoffman, M. (1991). *Amazing Grace.* New York: Dial.

Lomas Garza, C. (1990). *Family pictures: Cuadros de familia.* New York: Children's Book Press.

McPhail, D. (1988). *Something special.* Boston: Little, Brown.

Rylant, C. (1985). *The relatives came.* New York: Bradbury Books.

October

Fall

Language and Literacy Experiences

Drawing and Writing Observations

- *Nature:* Students record weather observations in a community journal kept by a classroom window; take a nature walk and record observations on paper on lap boards outside; bring samples of fallen leaves or dried plants to class and draw and write about them.

Pattern and Poetry Reading and Writing

- *Poetry Collections:* The teacher reads aloud poetry collections and students write Halloween poems. Suggested books include *It's Halloween* (Prelutsky, 1977), *Hey-how for Halloween* (Hopkins, 1974), and *Halloween poems* (Livingston, 1989). Or the teacher may read *The thirteen days of Halloween* (Greene, 1990) and everyone writes a class version.
- *Hands-On Experiences:* Children make crayon rubbings of fall leaves; create a "word wall" about leaves changing color, texture, and shape; write diamante patterns (see Chapter 10) about leaves; carve pumpkins; create a "word wall" of describing words; write triante patterns (see Lesson Plan).

Arts and Crafts

- *Drawing and Painting:* Through the month of October, students draw or paint trees in the schoolyard that change color once a week and then write about the changes. Students can also examine a piece of popcorn under a microscope; draw it; and write describing words on it to create a concrete poem (see Chapter 10).

- *Masks:* Children create masks using manila folders, paper plates, or construction paper. See *Traditions around the world: Masks* (Earl & Sensier, 1995) and *Pablo remembers: The fiesta of the Day of the Dead* (Ancona, 1993).

Drama

- *Story Dramatization:* Students dramatize a story such as *Where the wild things are* (Sendak, 1963), *Clyde monster* (Crowe, 1964), *There's a nightmare in my closet* (Mayer, 1968), or *Esteban and the ghost* (Hancock, 1983).
- *Shakespeare:* Do the witches scene from *Macbeth* (see Chapter 6). See *Shakespeare & Macbeth: The story behind the play* (Ross, 1994).

Lesson Plan: *Popcorn*

Level: All grades

Purpose: Talking, writing, and concept and vocabulary development.

Teaching Sequence:

1. Pop popcorn and pass it out on paper napkins for children to eat. Ask them for words that describe the sight and touch of popcorn. Record the words on chartpaper under these headings: "Smell," "Sound," "Sight," "Touch," and "Is like/reminds me of."
2. Ask the children if popcorn reminds them of anything (e.g., going to the movies, a family story), and record their ideas on a "word wall."
3. Write a class triante using words from the "word wall" on chartpaper:

   Line 1: One-word Title
   Line 2: Two words Smell
   Line 3: Three words Touch
   Line 4: Four words Sight
   Line 5: Five words Sound

4. Writing options: Emerging writers can draw pictures and label them, using describing words from the "word wall" or giving dictation to the teacher or aide. Older students can write their own triantes using the class triante as a pattern and words from the "word wall." Students can also write popcorn stories: what popcorn reminds them of, family experience, and so on.
6. Read *The popcorn book* (de Paola, 1978).

Extending Activities:

1. Do some of the things suggested by *The popcorn book*: Compare the numbers of kernels that pop after the popcorn has been kept in the refrigerator in an airtight container versus exposed to the air; record observations. Cook popcorn using the two different recipes in the back of the book.
2. Read and write *pourquoi* tales like the Native American one in *The popcorn book:* Africa, *Why mosquitoes buzz in people's ears* (Aardema, 1985); Brazil, *Feathers like a rainbow: An Amazon Indian tale* (Flora, 1989); Cambodia, *Judge Rabbit and the tree spirit: A folktale from Cambodia* (Wall, 1991).

3. Make collages by gluing popcorn on black construction paper and write about the images.
4. Grow popcorn seeds; soak them overnight and plant in a plastic cup. Observe and measure plant growth, and record changes in a journal.
5. Read *Popcorn* (Selsam, 1976) or *Corn is maize* (Aliki, 1988).

Children's Books

Aardema, V. (1985). *Why mosquitoes buzz in people's ears.* New York: Dial.

Aliki.(1988). *Corn is maize.* New York: Harper & Row.

Ancona, G. (1993). *Pablo remembers: The fiesta of the Day of the Dead.* New York: Lothrop, Lee & Shepard.

Crowe, R. (1964). *Clyde monster.* New York: Dutton.

de Paola, T. (1978). *The popcorn book.* New York: Holiday House.

Earl, A., & Sensier, D. (1995). *Traditions around the world: Masks.* New York: Thomson Learning.

Ehlert, L. (1991). *Red leaf, yellow leaf.* New York: Harcourt Brace Jovanovich.

Flora. (1989). *Feathers like a rainbow: An Amazon Indian tale.* New York: Harper & Row.

Greene, C. (1990). *The thirteen days of Halloween.* New York: Children's Press.

Hancock, S. (1983). *Esteban and the ghost.* New York: Dial.

Hirschi, R. (1991). *Fall.* New York: Dutton.

Hopkins, L. B. (1974). *Hey-how for Halloween.* New York: Harcourt Brace Jovanovich.

King, E. (1990). *The pumpkin patch.* New York: Dutton.

Krull, K. (1994). *Maria Molina and the Days of the Dead.* New York: Macmillan.

Livingston, M. C. (1989). *Halloween poems.* New York: Holiday House.

Mayer, M. (1968). *There's a nightmare in my closet.* New York: Dial.

Prelutsky, J. (1977). *It's Halloween.* New York: Greenwillow.

Ray, M. (1992). *Pumpkins.* New York: Harcourt Brace Jovanovich.

Ross, P. (1991). *M and M and the Halloween monster.* New York: Viking.

Ross, S. (1994). *Shakespeare & Macbeth: The story behind the play.* New York: Viking.

Selsam, M. (1976). *Popcorn.* New York: Morrow.

Sendak, M. (1963). *Where the wild things are.* New York: Harper & Row.

Simon, S. (1993). *Autumn across America.* New York: Hyperion Books.

Titherington, J. (1986). *Pumpkin, pumpkin.* New York: Greenwillow.

Udry, J. (1957). *A tree is nice.* New York: Harper & Row.

Wall, L. M. (1991). *Judge Rabbit and the tree spirit: A folktale from Cambodia.* New York: Children's Book Press.

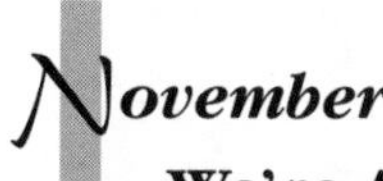

November

We're All Pilgrims

Language and Literacy Experiences

Oral Histories

- *Interviews:* Students ask parents or grandparents about the countries of origin of their families. Questions to ask: "Where were you born?" "Where were your parents born?" "When did they come to United States?" "How old were they?" "Why did they leave their country?" "What was life like in the native country?" "How was it like/unlike life in the United Sates?" "Tell any special memories." Read *Grandfather's journey* (Say, 1993), a story about Japanese American immigration.
- *Family Trees:* Using the information from the oral histories, students make family trees.

- *Map of Where We're All From:* On a wall-sized world map, children locate and label where their grandparents, parents, and other relatives are from. Then they make a border around the map with photographs or drawings of themselves. Their pictures can be connected to their families' countries of origins on the map with yarn and pins.

Documentary Interviews

- *Role-Playing:* Each child chooses a family member who came from another country and finds out some interesting facts about him or her. In pairs, children take turns role-playing their family members and interviewing them, like they're TV reporters. Read *The lotus seed* (Garland, 1993), which is about a Vietnamese woman who brings an important seed with her to America.
- *Videotaping:* Videotape students' interviews and create a documentary about immigration, emphasizing how we're all pilgrims.

Curriculum Drama

- *Ellis Island:* Students split into two groups: one portrays the staff at Ellis Island and the other portrays immigrants from different countries. Turn the room into Ellis Island with signs: "Medical Exams," "Money Exchange," and the like. The "immigrants" arrive and go through the process of entering the United States, which is run by the "staff." Then students switch roles, so everyone plays both roles. Students discuss and write about their experiences. Read *I was dreaming to come to America: Memories from the Ellis Island oral history project* (Lawlor, 1995); *Ellis Island: Doorway to freedom* (Kroll, 1995); or *Ellis Island: New hope in a new land* (Jacobs, 1990).
- *The First Thanksgiving:* Younger students can dress as Pilgrims and Native Americans, decorate the room (e.g., with dried corn and cornstalks), set a table (e.g., make placemats and centerpieces), and prepare food: raw vegetables, simple batter bread and butter, popcorn, and vegetable soup. Read *Across the wide dark sea: The Mayflower journey* (Van Leeuwen, 1995); *Sarah Morton's day: A day in the life of a Pilgrim girl* (Waters, 1989); or *The first Thanksgiving feast* (Anderson, 1989).

Lesson Plan: *Memory Boxes*

***Level*:** Middle through upper grades

***Purpose*:** Discuss, write, and construct a box based on family experiences.

***Teaching Sequence*:**

1. Using family oral interviews as a basis for discussion, ask: "Where did they come from?" "What was the country they left like?" "Why did your family leave that country?" "Describe a special family memory of that country."
2. Record children's responses on chartpaper, using a large grid:

We're All Pilgrims

	Europe	**Africa**	**Asia**	**The Americas**
Describe country				
Reasons for leaving				
Special memories				

3. Discuss differences and similarities among children's family experiences.

4. Ask children to think about what special memories or things they would take with them if they were to leave their homes now. Discuss in groups.
5. Make folded boxes out of construction paper (see Chapter 8).
6. Have children decorate their boxes with labels and drawings of things they would take and draw and cut out things to put inside their boxes.

Extending Activities:

1. Children write about leaving a country, based on their experience or that of someone in their family. Write the account as a story or in journal form.
2. Show the film (16 mm or video) *Molly's Pilgrim* (1985; 24 min.).

Children's Books

Anderson, J. (1989). *The first Thanksgiving feast.* Boston: Houghton Mifflin.

Atkin, S. B. (1993). *Voices from the fields: Children of immigrant farmworkers tell their story.* Boston: Little, Brown.

Bunting, E. (1988). *How many days to America?: A Thanksgiving story.* New York: Clarion.

Bunting, E. (1994). *A day's work.* New York: Clarion.

Cohen, B. (1983). *Molly's pilgrim.* New York: Lothrop, Lee & Shepard.

Friedman, R. (1980). *Immigrant kids.* New York: Dutton.

Garland, S. (1993). *The lotus seed.* New York: Harcourt Brace Jovanovich.

Groff, N. (1993). *Where the river runs: A portrait of a refugee family.* Boston: Little, Brown.

Jacobs, W. (1990). *Ellis Island: New hope in a new land.* New York: Scribner's.

Kroll, S. (1991). *Mary McLean and the St. Patrick's Day parade.* New York: Scholastic.

Kroll, S. (1995). *Ellis Island: Doorway to freedom.* New York: Holiday House.

Lawlor, V. (Ed.). (1995). *I was dreaming to come to America: Memories from the Ellis Island oral history project.* New York: Viking.

Lord, B. B. (1983). *In the year of the boar and Jackie Robinson.* New York: Harper & Row.

Molly's Pilgrim. (1985). Distributed by Phoenix Films.

Sandler, M. W. (1995). *Immigrants.* New York: HarperCollins.

Say, A. (1993). *Grandfather's journey.* Boston: Houghton Mifflin.

Surat, M. 1983). *Angel child, dragon child.* New York: Carnival/Raintree.

Van Leeuwen, J. (1995). *Across the wide dark sea: The Mayflower journey.* New York: Dial.

Waters, K. (1989). *Sarah Morton's Day: A day in the life of a Pilgrim girl.* New York: Scholastic.

Winter, J. (1992). *Klara's new world.* New York: Knopf.

December

Celebrations

Language and Literacy Experiences

Sharing Family Experiences

- *Discuss:* Students talk about different types and ways of celebrating this time of the year (e.g., Hanukkah, Christmas, Kwanzaa). Do a "word wall" of different celebrations, noting how individual families celebrate each.
- *Write Memoirs:* Children do a cluster of ideas about special memories of celebrations as a basis for writing their memoirs.
- *Read: Too many tamales* (Soto, 1993); *Christmas tree memories* (Aliki, 1991); *Elijah's angels: A story for Chanukah and Christmas* (Rosen, 1992); *Tree of cranes* (Say, 1991); or *Seven candles for Kwanzaa* (Pinkney, 1993).

Reading and Writing for Information

- *Doing Research:* Children go to the library and find books on these celebrations for reading aloud, self-selected reading, and reading for information—for example, *Light the candles! Beat the drums!* (Sarnoff & Ruffin, 1979).
- *Compiling Information:* Make a large wall chart on butcher paper about each celebration and how members of the class might celebrate:

	Hanukkah	Christmas	Kwanzaa
Who			
What			
Why			
How			
Where			

- *Celebration Posters:* In small groups, children create posters with information and illustrations about celebrations, based on their own family experiences and what they've learned reading. Groups share posters with the class.
- "*Big Book of Celebrations*": Bind students' celebration posters into a "big book" or make a book of writing and drawings about celebrations.

Reading and Writing Poetry

- *Read Poetry on All Celebrations: Celebrations* (Livingston, 1985); *Poems for seasons and celebrations* (Cole, 1961).
- *Write Poetry about Family Celebrations:* Children write free verses, patterns, or name poems (i.e., write the name of a holiday vertically on the left side of the paper, and add a phrase beginning with each letter).

Lesson Plan: *Celebration Filmstrips*

Level: Primary through upper grades

Purpose: Talk, read, draw, and write to create celebration filmstrips.

Teaching Sequence:

1. In cooperative groups of four to five, children brainstorm ideas for making draw-on filmstrips about celebrations with several options:
   - *Celebration Poem or Song:* Students choose their favorites and write and illustrate a few lines or stanzas on each filmstrip frame (e.g. "The Night Before Christmas").. Sources of poems are *Las navidades: Popular Christmas songs from Latin America* (Delacre, 1990) and *Poems for Jewish holidays* (Livingston, 1986).
   - *Celebration Memoirs:* Students show the sequence of events of their special memories, adding narration to go with all frames.
   - *All about a Celebration:* On all frames, students illustrate things about the celebration, including information about it as the narration.
2. Each group uses a filmstrip gauge (see Chapter 13) to draft drawings for each frame in sequence, with narration, sound effects, or music to go with it.
3. When the drafts are complete, children take blank filmstrip stock and tape over their filmstrip drafts. Then they use permanent marking pens on acetate to trace over drawings (e.g., Staedtler Lumocolor 8313 permanent thin-tip markers).

For blank filmstrip stock: (1) clean off old filmstrips, 35 mm negative strips, or 35 mm rolls of film in a solution of bleach and water, or (2) order from a film supply company (e.g., Christy's Film Supply, Burbank, CA (818) 845-1755).

4. The groups present their filmstrips. Narration, sound effects, or music can be live or taped.

Extending Activities:

1. *World Premiere of Celebration Filmstrips:* Children plan and host a premiere for other classes and parents, making posters, writing announcements (which can be delivered via loud speaker or computer bulletin boards), and drawing and writing invitations. Show the filmstrips in a darkened room or auditorium. Serve popcorn. Give Participation Awards to everyone.
2. *Make More Filmstrips, Films, Slides, or Transparencies:* Students draw on 16 mm films, slides, or transparencies (see Chapter 13) to illustrate other themes, using poetry, stories, or personal experiences.

Children's Books

Aliki. (1991). *Christmas tree memories.* New York: HarperCollins.

Ancona, G. (1995). *Fiesta U.S.A.* New York: Lodestar.

Baylor, B. (1986). *I'm in charge of celebrations.* New York: Scribner's.

Chocolate, D. (1992). *My first Kwanzaa book.* New York: Scholastic.

Cole, W. (1961). *Poems for seasons and celebrations.* New York: World.

Delacre, L. (1990). *Las navidades: Popular Christmas songs from Latin America.* New York: Scholastic.

Drucker, M. (1992). *Grandma's latkes.* New York: Trumpet Club.

Howard, E. (1989). *Chita's Christmas tree.* New York: Bradbury Books.

Hoyt-Goldsmith, D. (1993). *Celebrating Kwanzaa.* New York: Holiday House.

Livingston, M. C. (1985). *Celebrations.* New York: Holiday House.

Livingston, M. C. (1986). *Poems for Jewish holidays.* New York: Holiday House.

Manushkin, F. (1989). *Latkes and applesauce: A Hanukkah story.* New York: Scholastic.

Pinkney, A. (1993). *Seven candles for Kwanzaa.* New York: Dial.

Riehecky, J. (1993). *Kwanzaa.* New York: Children's Press.

Rosen, M. (1992). *Elijah's angels: A story for Chanukah and Christmas.* New York: Harcourt Brace Jovanovich.

Ryder, J. (1994). *First grade elves.* Mahwah, NJ: Troll.

Sarnoff, J., & Ruffin, R. (1979). *Light the candles! Beat the drums!* New York: Scribner's.

Say, A. (1991). *Tree of cranes.* Boston: Houghton Mifflin.

Soto, G. (1993). *Too many tamales.* New York: Putnam's.

Spier, P. (1983). *Peter Spier's Christmas!* New York: Doubleday.

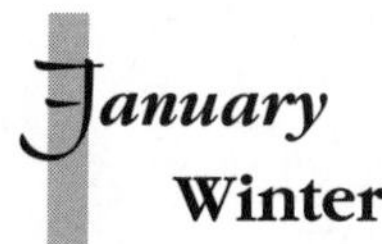

January

Winter

Language and Literacy Experiences

Writing and Illustrating Images

- *Talk about Winter Images:* Children talk about gray skies, leafless trees, brown grass, snow, and so on.
- *Read:* The teacher reads aloud *The snowy day* (Keats, 1962), for younger students, or *Stopping by woods on a snowy evening* (Frost, 1978), for older students.

- *"Word Wall":* Students creates a "word wall" of winter images based on their experiences or in response to words and illustrations from the two books.
- *Write and Illustrate Winter Images:* Children write haiku, cinquain, poetry, prose, or captions and illustrate them using tempera paint (white paint on dark paper, cotton balls for gluing, torn paper collage as used by Keats), tissue paper applied with starch, or construction paper.

Read about and Dramatize Different New Year's Celebrations

- *Read: New Year's poems* (Livingston, 1987); *All in a day* (Anno, 1986); *Lion Dancer: Ernie Wan's Chinese New Year* (Waters & Slovenz-Low, 1990); *Chinese New Year* (Brown, 1987); *Chinese New Year's dragon* (Sing, 1992); *Chin Chiang and the dragon dance* (Wallace, 1984); *Hoan Anh: A Vietnamese-American boy* (Hoyt-Goldsmith, 1992); or *Dara's Cambodian New Year* (Chiemruom, 1992).
- *New Year's Celebrations Day:* Children form groups, choosing one type of New Year's celebration to read more about. Then they choose one aspect of it to dramatize through reader's theater, role-playing, puppets, story dramatization, music, or dance. All groups share their celebrations on one day.

Lesson Plan: "I Have a Dream"

Level: Primary through upper grades

Purpose: Read, talk, and write in response to ideas of Martin Luther King, Jr.

Teaching Sequence:

1. In connection with celebration of the Martin Luther King, Jr., holiday, read about his life and ideas: *I have a dream: The life and words of Martin Luther King, Jr.* (Haskins, 1993).
2. Ask students to respond to his ideas in class and small cooperative group discussions.
3. Ask students to consider what their dreams for the future are, and record them on a "word wall" cluster for the whole class: "I HAVE A DREAM."
4. Students write clusters of dreams, using the class "word wall" as a model and choosing one or a few words to expand on in writing (a few sentences or up to a paragraph). For emerging writers, the teacher takes dictation.
5. Students illustrate one or some of their dreams and display their drawings with their writing on a class bulletin board: "I HAVE A DREAM."

Extending Activities:

1. Display students' writing and drawing on a class bulletin board ("I HAVE A DREAM") or bind them into a class book for the classroom library.
2. Read the following: *A picture book of Martin Luther King, Jr.* (Adler, 1989); *Martin Luther King Day* (Lowrey, 1987); *Meet Martin Luther King* (DeKay, 1969); *My life with Martin Luther King, Jr.* (King, 1993); or *Martin Luther King, Jr., and the freedom movement* (Patterson, 1989).
3. Create a timeline and mural of major events and ideas in the life of King.
4. Read about other famous African Americans. Then compare their lives and ideas to those of Martin Luther King, Jr. (e.g., *Malcolm X: By any means necessary* [Myers, 1993]), or with those of leaders of other minority groups

in the United States (e.g., *Caesar Chavez* [Concord, 1992] and *Cesar Chavez* [Franchure, 1988], the Chicano American union leader).

5. Read aloud *The dream keeper and other poems* (Hughes, 1994).
6. Read and do a reader's theater or chorale reading of *I am a man: Ode to Martin Luther King, Jr.* (Merriam, 1971).

Children's Books

Adler, D. (1989). *A picture book of Martin Luther King, Jr.* New York: Holiday House.

Anno. (1986). *All in a day.* New York: Philomel.

Briggs, R. (1978). *The snowman.* New York: Random House.

Brown, T. (1987). *Chinese New Year.* New York: Holt.

Burton, V. L. (1943). *Katy and the big snow.* Boston: Houghton Mifflin.

Chaffin, L. (1980). *We be warm till springtime comes.* New York: Macmillan.

Chiemruom, S. (1992). *Dara's Cambodian New Year.* Cleveland: Modern Curriculum Press.

Concord, B. (1988). *Caesar Chavez.* New York: Chelsea.

DeKay, J. (1969). *Meet Martin Luther King.* New York: Random House.

Franchure, R. (1988). *Cesar Chavez.* New York: Harper & Row.

Frost, R. (1978). *Stopping by woods on a snowy evening.* New York: Dutton.

Haskins, J. (1993). *I have a dream: The life and words of Martin Luther King, Jr.* Highland Park, NY: Millbrook.

Hirschi, R. (1990). *Winter.* New York: Dutton.

Hoyt-Goldsmith, D. (1992). *Hoan Anh: A Vietnamese-American boy.* New York: Holiday House.

Hughes, L. (1994). *The dream keeper and other poems.* New York: Knopf.

Keats, E. J. (1962). *The snowy day.* New York: Viking.

King, C. S. (1993). *My life with Martin Luther King, Jr.* New York: Holt.

Kroll, V. (1994). *The seasons and someone.* New York: Harcourt Brace Jovanovich.

Livingston, M. C. (1987). *New Year's poems.* New York: Holiday House.

Lowrey, L. (1987). *Martin Luther King Day.* Minneapolis: Carolrhoda.

Menendez, P. (1989). *Black snowman.* New York: Scholastic.

Merriam, E. (1971). *I am a man: Ode to Martin Luther King, Jr.* New York: Doubleday.

Myers, W. D. (1993). *Malcolm X: By any means necessary.* New York: Scholastic.

Patterson, L. (1989). *Martin Luther King, Jr., and the freedom movement.* New York: Facts on File.

Prelutsky, J. (1984). *It's snowing! It's snowing!* New York: Greenwillow.

Radin, R. (1982). *A winter place.* Boston: Little, Brown.

Sing, R. (1992). *Chinese New Year's dragon.* Cleveland: Modern Curriculum Press.

Wallace, I. (1984). *Chin Chiang and the dragon dance.* New York: Atheneum.

Waters, K., & Slovenz-Low, M. (1990). *Lion dancer: Ernie Wan's Chinese New Year.* New York: Scholastic.

Yolen, J. (1988). *Owl moon.* New York: Philomel.

February

Black History Month

Language and Literacy Experiences

Read Biographies

- *Read Aloud and Discuss: A weed is a flower: The life of George Washington Carver* (Aliki , 1988), about the man who demonstrated multiple ways to use sweet potatoes and peanuts; *Rosa Parks* (Greenfield, 1973), about the woman who sparked the civil rights movement; and *Harriet Tubman and black history month* (Carter, 1990), an introduction to biographies of African Americans and black history month.

- *Literature Groups:* These are good books for literature groups to choose, read, and do projects on: *Amos Fortune, free man* (Yates, 1967); *Anthony Burns: The defeat and triumph of a fugitive slave* (Hamilton, 1988); *Matthew Henson, Explorer* (Gilman, 1988); *Thurgood Marshall: A life for justice* (Haskins, 1992); *Ray Charles* (Mathis, 1973); and *Space challenger: The story of Guion Bluford* (Haskins, 1984).

Reader's Theater

- *Scripts:* Students adapt reader's theater scripts based on the words of African Americans at different periods of history. Sources include *To be a slave* (Lester, 1968); *Rosa Parks: My story* (Parks/Haskins, 1994); *Shirley Chisholm: Teacher and Congresswoman* (Scheader, 1990); *Malcolm X* (Adoff, 1970); *Jesse Jackson* (McKissack, 1989); and *The Black Americans: A history in their own words, 1619–1983* (Meltzer, 1984).

Curriculum Drama

- *Recreating History:* Students read about and dramatize scenes from important moments in African American history. Sources include *Runaway slave: The story of Harriet Tubman* (McGovern, 1968), which is about helping other slaves to freedom; *The freedom ship of Robert Smalls* (Meriwether, 1971), about a slave who hijacked a ship and with a slave crew sailed it to freedom during the Civil War; and *Rosa Parks and the Montgomery bus boycott* (Celsi, 1991), about the famous incident on the bus.
- *Read and Play:* Children read and play scenes. Sources include *Langston: A play* (Davis, 1982), about the African American poet Langston Hughes, and *Take a walk in their shoes* (Turner, 1989), about the lives of African Americans.

Black History Timeline Mural

- *Create a Timeline:* Children in groups research different periods of African American history and make an illustrated timeline on a wall-length mural of butcher paper, adding paintings, cut-out figures, photographs, writing, and artifacts.
- *Display on Tables beneath the Timeline:* Books about African Americans and black history, related student writing, art, and projects.

Lesson Plan: *Black History Newspaper*

Level: Middle through upper grades

Purpose: Read, talk, write, report on black history in a newspaper format.

Teaching Sequence:

1. After a period of reading, talking, writing, and doing projects on African American history, students plan a newspaper to report what they have discovered.
2. As a class, brainstorm ideas for sections and topics for each section. Record them on chartpaper, leaving space under each topic: Articles, Editorials, Letters to Editor, Sports, Entertainment, Book Reviews, Cartoons & Comics, and Classified Ads.

3. Small groups are formed and assigned sections. Groups brainstorm ideas, choose section editors, decide who will write what, and begin drafts.
4. In a final class discussion, each section leader shares topics and ideas, which the teacher records on the chart under each section head. The chart is a working plan for the production of the newspaper. Note section editors and group members on the chart.

Extending Activities:

1. Students continue to read, write, illustrate, and produce the newspaper.
2. Use software such as The Newsroom, designed for newspaper production.
3. Read accounts of African American history: *The march on Washington* (Haskins, 1993); *Freedom's children: Young civil rights activists tell their own stories* (Levine, 1993); *Escape from slavery: The boyhood of Frederick Douglass in his own words* (McCurdy, 1994); *The civil rights movement in America from 1865 to the present* (McKissack & McKissack, 1991); *A long hard journey: The story of the Pullman porter* (McKissack & McKissack, 1989); *Now is your time! The African-American struggle for freedom* (Myers, 1991).

Children's Books

Adoff, A. (1970). *Malcolm X.* New York: Crowell.

Aliki. (1988). *A weed is a flower: The life of George Washington Carver.* New York: Simon & Schuster.

Carter, P. (1990). *Harriet Tubman and black history month.* Columbus, OH: Silver Press.

Celsi, T. (1991). *Rosa Parks and the Montgomery bus boycott.* New York: Milbrook.

Davis, O. (1982). *Langston: A play.* New York: Delacorte.

Feelings, T. (1995). *The middle passage: White ship/black cargo.* New York: Dial.

Fox, P. (1973). *Slave dancer.* New York: Bradbury Books.

Gilman, M. (1988). *Matthew Henson, explorer.* New York: Chelsea House.

Greenfield, E. (1973). *Rosa Parks.* New York: Crowell.

Greenfield, E. (1989). *Nathaniel talking.* New York: Black Butterfly Children's Books.

Hamilton, V. (1988). *Anthony Burns: The defeat and triumph of a fugitive slave.* New York: Knopf.

Hamilton, V. (1993). *Many thousand gone: African Americans from slavery to freedom.* New York: Knopf.

Haskins, J. (1984). *Space challenger: The story of Guion Bluford.* Minneapolis: Carolrhoda.

Haskins, J. (1992). *Thurgood Marshall: A life for justice.* New York: Holt.

Haskins, J. (1993). *The march on Washington.* New York: HarperCollins.

Lester, J. (Ed.). (1968). *To be a slave.* New York: Dial.

Levine, E. (1993). *Freedom's children: Young civil rights activists tell their own stories.* New York: Putnam's.

Mathis, S. B. (1973). *Ray Charles.* New York: Crowell.

McCurdy, M. (Ed.). (1994). *Escape from slavery: The boyhood of Frederick Douglass in his own words.* New York: Knopf.

McGovern, A. (1968). *Runaway slave: The story of Harriet Tubman.* New York: Four Winds.

McKissack, P. (1989). *Jesse Jackson.* New York: Scholastic.

McKissack, P., & McKissack, F. (1989). *A long hard journey: The story of the Pullman porter.* New York: Walker.

McKissack, P., & McKissack, F. (1991). *The civil rights movement in America from 1865 to the present.* New York: Children's Press.

Meltzer, M. (1984). *The Black Americans: A history in their own words, 1619–1983.* New York: Crowell.

Meriwether, L. (1971). *The freedom ship of Robert Smalls.* New York: Prentice-Hall.

Myers, W. D. (1991). *Now is your time! The African-American struggle for freedom.* New York: HarperCollins.

Myers, W. D. (1993). *Brown angels: An album of pictures and verse.* New York: Harper & Row.

Parks, R. (with J. Haskins). (1994). *Rosa Parks: My story.* New York: Dial.

Porter, C. (1994). *Meet Addy* (and other Addy books). New York: American Girl.

Ringgold, F. (1993). *Aunt Harriet's underground railroad in the sky*. New York: Crown.

Scheader, C. (1990). *Shirley Chisholm: Teacher and Congresswoman*. Hillsdale, NJ: Enslow.

Turner, G. (1989). *Take a walk in their shoes*. New York: Cobblehill.

Yates, E. (1967). *Amos Fortune, free man*. New York: Dutton.

March

Women's History Month

Language and Literacy Experiences

Family Women's History

- *Interviews:* Each child interviews family members about women in his or her family: "Who were they?" "Where were they from?" "What did they do?" "What was their life like?"
- *Timelines:* Children create timelines of the women in their families.
- *Scrapbooks:* Using black construction paper, each child makes a scrapbook about women in his or her family, including (for each woman) information, photographs, drawings, and mementos. Individual students' pages are assembled into a class scrapbook or mounted on a bulletin board.
- *Mother's Day in Class:* Children invite mothers or other women family members or friends to come to class to talk about their lives and those of other women in their families, describing backgrounds, jobs, and special talents.
- *Read Aloud:* The teacher reads aloud to students *Childtimes: A three-generation memoir* (Greenfield, 1979), an intergenerational childhood memoir by three African American women.

Reading Biographies, Scriptwriting, and Drama

- *Read Aloud:* The teacher reads aloud *Taking flight: My story by Vicki Van Meter* (Van Meter/Gurman, 1995), about a 12-year-old girl who piloted a plane across the Atlantic.
- *Literature Groups:* Students in groups choose and read books such as *Queen Eleanor: Independent spirit of the medieval world* (Brooks, 1983); *Demeter's daughters: The women who founded America 1587–1787* (Williams, 1976); *Founding mothers: Women of America in the Revolutionary era* (De Pauw, 1994); *Susette La Flesche: Advocate for Native American rights* (Brown, 1992); *The last princess: The story of Princess Ka'iulani of Hawaii* (Stanley, 1991); *Louisa May: The world and works of Louisa May Alcott* (Johnston, 1991); *Eleanor Roosevelt: A life of discovery* (Freedman, 1993); *Amelia Earhart* (Pearce, 1988); and *Women astronauts: Aboard the shuttle* (Fox, 1984).
- *Drama:* Each group writes and plays a scene in the life of a famous woman.

Women Visual and Performing Artists

- *Read:* The teacher reads aloud books such as *Inspirations: Stories about women artists* (Sills, 1989); *Visions: Stories about women artists* (Sills, 1993); *Frida Kahlo* (Turner, 1993); *Georgia O'Keeffe* (Turner, 1991); *An actor's life for me!* (Gish/Lanes, 1987); *Barefoot dancer: The story of Isadora Duncan* (O'Connor, 1994); and *Big star fallin' Mama: Five women in Black music* (Jones, 1995).

- *Recreate:* Students do paintings and performances in the styles of women visual and performing artists (e.g., Georgia O'Keefe's paintings, Isadora Duncan's dancing).

Women's History Museum

- *Create a Museum:* Collect books about women, including student-written stories, and add student projects (writing and drawing, dioramas, posters, artifacts with labels and captions) about women's contributions to history.

Lesson Plan: *Women's History Quilt*

Level: Middle through upper grades

Purpose: Read, talk, write, and draw about the lives of famous women.

Teaching Sequence:

1. Read aloud and discuss *Good Queen Bess: Queen Elizabeth I of England* (Stanley & Vennema, 1990).
2. Do a "word wall," clustering ideas from children about Queen Bess's characteristics.
3. Based on reading the biography of a famous woman, each child or children in cooperative groups create a cluster of ideas and images about her.
4. Based on their cluster of ideas, each child or group sketches a quilt square (12" × 12" is a good size) about their famous woman. The squares could be created by using liquid embroidery pens to draw on cloth (e.g., muslin); by gluing on appliqués of scraps of cloth, felt, yarn, buttons, feathers, and so on; or by using construction paper.

Extending Activities:

1. The quilt squares are sewn, stapled, or hole-punched and tied together with yarn to create a class women's history quilt.
2. Read books with quilt motifs: *Eight hands round: A patchwork alphabet* (Paul, 1991); *Tar beach* (Ringgold, 1991); *The Josefina story quilt* (Coerr, 1986); *Sweet Clara and the freedom quilt* (Hopkinson, 1993); *Sam Johnson and the blue ribbon quilt* (Ernst, 1983); *The patchwork quilt* (Flournoy, 1985); *The keeping quilt* (Polacco, 1988); *Tonight is Carnaval* (Dorros, 1991); *The Canada geese quilt* (Kinsey-Warnock, 1989); and *Nine in one Grr! Grr! A folktale from the Hmong people of Laos* (Xong, 1989).
3. Read aloud *The always prayer shawl* (Oberman, 1994), the story of a shawl that is passed down through several generations of Jewish men, which shows that textiles can be important to men as well as women.

Children's Books

Ashby, R. (Ed.). (1995). *Herstory: Women who changed the world.* New York: Viking.

Brooks, P. S. (1983). *Queen Eleanor: Independent spirit of the medieval world.* Philadelphia: Lippincott.

Brown, M. M. (1992). *Susette La Flesche: Advocate for Native American rights.* New York: Children's Press.

Coerr, E. (1986). *The Josefina story quilt.* New York: HarperCollins.

De Pauw, L. (1994). *Founding mothers: Women of America in the Revolutionary era.* Boston: Houghton Mifflin.

Dorros, A. (1990). *Tonight is Carnaval.* New York: Dutton.

Ernst, L. C. (1983). *Sam Johnson and the blue ribbon quilt.* New York: Lothrop, Lee & Shepard.

Flournoy, V. (1985). *The patchwork quilt.* New York: Dial.

Fox, M. V. (1984). *Women astronauts: Aboard the shuttle.* New York: Messner.

Freedman, R. (1993). *Eleanor Roosevelt: A life of discovery.* New York: Clarion.

Gish, L. (told to S. Lanes). (1987). *An actor's life for me!* New York: Viking.

Greenfield, E., & Little, L. J. (1979). *Childtimes: A three-generation memoir.* New York: Crowell.

Hopkinson, D. (1993). *Sweet Clara and the freedom quilt.* New York: Knopf.

Houston, G. (1992). *My Great Aunt Arizona.* New York: HarperCollins.

Johnston, N. (1991). *Louisa May: The world and works of Louisa May Alcott.* New York: Four Winds.

Jones, H. (1995). *Big star fallin' Mama: Five women in Black music.* New York: Viking.

Kinsey-Warnock, N. (1989). *The Canada geese quilt.* New York: Cobblehill.

Klein, N. (1975). *Girls can be anything.* New York: Dutton.

Oberman, S. (1994). *The always prayer shawl.* Honesdale, PA: Boyds Mills.

O'Connor, B. (1994). *Barefoot dancer: The story of Isadora Duncan.* Minneapolis: Carolrhoda.

Paul, A. W. (1991). *Eight hands round: A patchwork alphabet.* New York: HarperCollins.

Pearce, C. A. (1988). *Amelia Earhart.* New York: Facts on File.

Polacco, P. (1988). *The keeping quilt.* New York: Simon & Schuster.

Ringgold, F. (1991). *Tar beach.* New York: Crown.

Sills, L. (1989). *Inspirations: Stories about women artists.* New York: Whitman.

Sills, L. (1993). *Visions: Stories about women artists.* New York: Whitman.

Stanley, D., & Vennema, P. (1990). *Good Queen Bess: Queen Elizabeth I of England.* New York: Four Winds.

Stanley, F. (1991). *The last princess: The story of Princess Ka'iulani of Hawaii.* New York: Four Winds.

Turner, R. (1991). *Georgia O'Keefe.* Boston: Little, Brown.

Turner, R. (1993). *Frida Kahlo.* Boston: Little, Brown.

Van Meter, V. (with D. Gurman). (1995). *Taking flight: My story by Vicki Van Meter.* New York: Viking.

Williams, S. R. (1976). *Demeter's daughters: The women who founded America 1587–1787.* New York: Atheneum.

Xong, B. (1989). *Nine in one Grr! Grr! A folktale from the Hmong people of Laos.* Emeryville, CA: Children's Book Press.

Language and Literacy Experiences

Observing and Writing about Experiences

- *Planting:* Children plant bean seeds (soaked in water first) in plastic tumblers or flower or grass seeds or bedding plants in pots, window boxes, or patches of earth.
- *Hatching:* Locate eggs and kits for the classroom (e.g., chickens, ducks, butterflies). Children keep observation journals of the progress of growing and hatching things, making drawings, labels, captions, measurements, graphs, and diagrams.

Poetry Walk and Journals

- *Poetry Walk:* Children take a walk on the schoolgrounds or in the neighborhood during spring and stop at intervals to write in poetry journals about sights, sounds, smells, feelings, images, similes, and metaphors.

- *Poetry Journals:* Use poetry journals as sources of ideas for children writing spring poetry and songs.
- *Read: In a spring garden* (Lewis, 1989).

Puppets and Props

- *Read:* Read picture books about animals, insects, and plants in spring, such as *Make way for ducklings* (McCloskey, 1941) and *The very hungry caterpillar* (Carle, 1969).
- *Making Puppets and Props:* Students make puppets and props of the characters from the book to retell or dramatize the story: for example, ducks (paper bag puppets with orange construction paper beaks), caterpillars (egg cartons split in half, painted, with pipe cleaner attenaes), and butterflies (butcher paper cutouts [one each front and back], painted, stapled and stuffed with newspaper).

Story Dramatizations

- *Stories: The carrot seed* (Krauss, 1945); *The great big enormous turnip* (Tolstoy, 1968); and *The little red hen* (Galdone, 1973).

Photograms

- *Making Photograms:* Place small spring objects like seeds, leaves, and flowers on light-sensitive paper and expose to sunlight for a few minutes; rinse the paper in water and see the impression made by the object.
- *Read: A, B, See!* (Hoban, 1982), which is illustrated with photograms.

Lesson Plan: *Sing and Dance a Spring Poem*

Level: Primary through upper grades

Purpose: Compose poetry, songs, and dances based on experiences in spring.

Teaching Sequence:

1. Do a class "word wall" of children's observations, associations, and images of spring, based on classroom or outdoor spring experiences (described earlier, e.g. planting, hatching, poetry walk): "IMAGES OF SPRING."
2. Use a familiar tune like "Frere Jacques" and count the number of syllables in each line. Fill in a chart organized according to the number of syllables per line with phrases from the "word wall" that have the same number of syllables:

   "Spring Song" (to the tune of "Frere Jacques")
   Line 1: 4 syllables ________________________________
   Line 2: 4 syllables ________________________________
   Line 3: 3 syllables ________________________________
   Line 4: 3 syllables ________________________________
   Line 5: 6 syllables ________________________________
   Line 6: 6 syllables ________________________________
   Line 7: 3 syllables ________________________________
   Line 8: 3 syllables ________________________________
3. Sing the song together.

Thanks to Paul Boyd-Batstone for this idea.

4. Add simple movements to each line that have the same number of syllables (e.g., waving arms in air, turning around with arms outstreched). Dance and sing the poem. Add simple rhythm instruments: bells, tambourines, maracas, sandpaper blocks, rattles (e.g., dried beans inside two paper plates stapled together).

Extending Activities:

1. Create individual song sheets so children can write their own songs and create their own dances, or have children work in small groups.
2. Add props to dances, such as scarves, lengths of nylon net, and ribbon sticks (e.g., attach colorful ribbons to the end of a piece of dowel or an empty paper towel tube).
3. Plan a program for children to sing and dance their poems for other classes or parents. Make posters, programs, and ads for the school bulletin.
4. Make illustrated books of songs written by individuals or small groups.
5. Other tunes for songwriting: "Somewhere Over the Rainbow," "Row, Row, Row Your Boat," and "Old MacDonald Had a Farm."
6. Music for spring dancing poems: Grieg's "Little Bird," "Papillon" ("Butterfly"), and "To Spring"; Respighi's "The Birds," Rimsky-Korsakov's "Flight of the Bumble Bee," Beethoven's Sonata no. 5 for Violin and Piano ("Spring") and Symphony no. 6 ("Pastoral"); Mendelssohn's Melody in F ("Spring Song"); and Vivaldi's "Spring" from "The Four Seasons."

Children's Books

Arnosky, J. (1987). *Sketching outdoors in spring*. New York: Lothrop, Lee & Shepard.
Carle, E. (1969). *The very hungry caterpillar*. New York: Philomel.
Galdone, P. (1973). *The little red hen*. New York: Clarion.
Gibbons, G. (1989). *Monarch butterfly*. New York: Holiday House.
Gibbons, G. (1991). *From seed to plant*. New York: Holiday House.
Hirschi, R. (1990). *Spring*. New York: Dutton.
Hoban, T. (1982). *A, B, See!* New York: Greenwillow.
Horton, B. (1991). *What comes in spring?* New York: Knopf.
Krauss, R. (1945). *The carrot seed*. New York: Harper & Row.
Lauber, P. (1991). *Seeds: Pop-stick-glide*. New York: Crown.
Lewis, R. (1989). *In a spring garden*. New York: Dial.
McCloskey, R. (1941). *Make way for ducklings*. New York: Viking.
Rockwell, A. (1985). *First comes spring*. New York: Crowell.
Tolstoy, A. (1968). *The great big enormous turnip*. New York: Watts.

Ecology

Language and Literacy Experiences

Think about the Earth

- *Read Aloud and Discuss:* The teacher reads aloud *Miss Rumphius* (Cooney, 1982), about a woman who tries to make the world a more beautiful place, and asks the children how they might make the earth more beautiful.

Brainstorm Research Questions

- *Read Aloud and Discuss:* The teacher reads aloud *The lost lake* (Say, 1989), about a Japanese American father and son who find their vacation destination overrun by too many people, and asks children to discuss it.
- *Questions:* List students' questions of concern about ecology (e.g., preserving the environment, endangered animal species) and how to take action.

Reading for Information

- *Small Groups:* Children form groups around questions and read to answer them: *Fifty simple things you can do to save the earth* (Earthworks Group, 1991) and *The big book for our planet* (Durrell, George, & Paterson, 1994).

Letter Writing

- *Write for Information:* Children write to the Sierra Club (730 Polk St., San Francisco, CA 94109) or the National Wildlife Federation (1400 16th St. N.W., Washington, DC 20036).
- *Write to Take Action:* Contact local, state, and U.S. representatives (Conservation International, 1915 18th St. N.W., Washington, DC 20036).

Photo Essays

- *Creating Photo Essays:* Children photograph problems in the local environment and create photo essays, adding titles, captions, and actions to be taken.
- *Read Photoillustrated Books:* *Saving the peregrine falcon* (Arnold, 1985) and *Where do birds live?* (Hirschi, 1987).

Lesson Plan: Story Dramatization of *The Great Kapok Tree* by Lynne Cherry

Level: Primary through upper grades

Purpose: Read, discuss, and dramatize a story with an ecology theme.

Teaching Sequence:

1. Read aloud *The great Kapok tree* (Cherry, 1990), a picture book about the animals, plants, and Yanomamo people of the Amazon rainforest and what could happen if it were destroyed. Discuss with children, asking: "What did you think of the story?" "What was your favorite part?" "What do you think will happen to the rainforest?"
2. Plan a story dramatization based on the book. Make a chart, and fill in as students continue to discuss the story and how to dramatize it:

   The Great Kapok Tree

   Setting: Amazon rainforest, around large kapok tree

   Characters: Narrator, boss, woodcutter, Yanomamo child, rainforest animals (boa constrictor, bees and butterflies, monkeys, birds [toucan, macaw, cock-of-the-rock], frogs, jaguar, tree porcupines, and sloth).

   Plot:

   (1) Boss tells woodcutter to chop down tree.
   (2) Woodcutter starts to chop down tree but falls asleep.
   (3) Animals tell him why he shouldn't chop down tree.
   (4) Woodcutter wakes up and leaves without chopping down tree.
3. Cast the characters and make a large space for playing the story.

4. Play the story: The narrator (student or teacher) reads the narrative part of text aloud, and the characters speak their parts to the sleeping man. Play the story several times, so children can play different characters.
5. Ask students how they felt about playing the story, what they liked about how different children acted out the characters and plot, and what they might do next time to make it better.

Extending Activities:

To order this musical version, write Paul Boyd-Batstone, 2890 Cedar Ave., Long Beach, CA 90806.

1. To produce a musical of the book, use the cassette tape *The great Kapok tree* (music by Paul Boyd-Batstone), which has lyrics for 12 songs based on the book and a teacher's guide with a rainforest unit, music, ideas for staging the book as a musical, making props, and a bibliography of resources.
2. Read *One day in a tropical rainforest* (George, 1990); *Rain forest secrets* (Dorros, 1990); *Nature's green umbrella: Tropical rain forests* (Gibbons, 1994;) *Make your own rainforest* (Johnston, 1993); and *Welcome to the green house* (Yolen, 1993).
3. For information or advocacy about protecting the rainforests, write letters to Children's Rainforest (P.O. Box 936, Lewiston, ME 04240) and Rainforest Action Network (450 Sansome, Suite 700, San Francisco, CA 94111).

Children's Books

Arnold, C. (1985). *Saving the peregrine falcon*. Minneapolis: Carolrhoda.

Baylor, B. (1976). *Hawk, I am your brother*. New York: Scribner's.

Cherry, L. (1990). *The great Kapok tree*. New York: Har-Brace.

Cooney, B. (1982). *Miss Rumphius*. New York: Penguin.

Dorros A. (1990). *Rain forest secrets*. New York: Scholastic.

Durrell, A., George, J., & K. Paterson (Eds.). (1994). *The big book for our planet*. New York: Dutton.

Earthworks Group. (1991). *Fifty simple things you can do to save the earth*. Kansas City, KS: Earthworks.

George, J. (1990). *One day in a tropical rainforest*. New York: Crowell.

Gibbons, G. (1994). *Nature's green umbrella: Tropical rain forests*. New York: Morrow.

Hirschi, R. (1987). *Where do birds live?* New York: Walker.

Hughes, T. (1995). *The iron woman*. New York: Dial.

Jeffers, S. (1991). *Brother Eagle, Sister Sky: A message from Chief Seattle*. New York: Dial.

Johnston, D. (1993). *Make your own rainforest*. New York: Lodestar.

Jonas, A. (1990). *Aardvarks disembark*. New York: Greenwillow.

Lauber, P. (1988). *Summer of fire: Yellowstone, 1988*. New York: Orchard.

Say, A. (1989). *The lost lake*. Boston: Houghton Mifflin.

Seuss, Dr. (1981). *The lorax*. New York: Random House.

Yolen, J. (1993). *Welcome to the green house*. New York: Putnam's.

June

The Future

Language and Literacy Experiences

Picture the Future

- *Read and Discuss:* The teacher reads aloud *Just a dream* (Van Allsburg, 1990) and asks students to discuss it.

- *Drawing and Writing:* Students draw pictures of and write about what the future might be like.

Time Capsule

- *Creating a Time Capsule:* Students brainstorm a list of things to include in a time capsule that would show children in the future what the world is like today. Choose things to place in a metal box, with a written explanation and messages from all the students, and bury it.
- *Bulletin Board:* Children display the project on a bulletin board, including the list and photos of things in the time capsule, copies of the written explanation and messages, and photos of the children burying the capsule.

Reading and Writing Future Fiction

- *Read Aloud:* The teacher reads aloud *The green book* (Paton, 1982), for younger students, or *The giver* (Lowry, 1993), for older ones.
- *Write:* Children write stories about what life in the future might be like.

Future Filmmaking

- *Scriptwriting:* Students develop scripts for filmmaking based on reading and writing future fiction.
- *Producing:* Children make videotaped films, filmstrips, or computer displays with hyperstudio.

Local History Project

- *Changes over the Years:* Students learn how their town has changed by interviewing people who have lived in the area for a long time, finding photographs of the area taken over time, and reading accounts of what it used to be like (e.g., in old newspapers, magazines).
- *Changes to Come:* Children make predictions about what the area will be like in the future, based on how it has changed in the past. Invite a city council person or official to talk to the class.
- *Mural:* The class makes a mural—"Our Town: Past, Present, and Future"—displaying what they've learned.
- *Read: Where the forest meets the sea* (Baker, 1987); *Window* (Baker, 1991); *The little house* (Burton, 1942); *Story of an English village* (Goodall, 1989); *New Providence: A changing city scape* (Von Tscharner & Fleming, 1987); *Toddlecreek post office* (Shulevitz, 1990); *The changing countryside* (Muller, 1977b); *The changing city* (Muller, 1977a); *Shaker Lane* (Provensen & Provensen, 1988); *My place* (Wheatley, 1990); and *Heron Street* (Turner, 1989).
- *Write:* Students write memoirs as though they lived in an earlier time.

Lesson Plan: *Future World Theme Park*

Level: Primary through upper grades

Purpose: Imagine, draw, write, and construct a model of Future World Theme Park.

Teaching Sequence:

1. After a period of thinking, talking, reading, and writing about the future, make plans for Future World Theme Park, to be constructed in the class-

room. Brainstorm ideas and record on chartpaper for "What Future World Would Be Like" and "How to Create Future World."

2. Categorize ideas and form groups to make plans for creating Future World, such as signs and murals, maps, models and dioramas, exhibits, computer demonstrations, and interactive displays (e.g., hyperstudio, videos, photo essays, live shows and dramatizations, and rides).
3. Each group makes (a) a diagram of what they want to make, with a written explanation of how they will do it, (b) a time frame for doing it, and (c) a list of materials they will need.
4. Groups report to the class what they will do and record ideas on a "wall chart" as a plan for building Future World.

Extending Activities:

1. Over a 2- to 3-week period, groups carry out their plans to turn the classroom into Future World, continuing to read, discuss, write, plan, and construct parts of it.
2. Invite other classes and parents to visit Future World: make posters advertising its opening, write announcements for the school bulletin and electronic bulletin boards, videotape a commercial to show in other classrooms, and make tickets and free passes.
3. Invite the local newspaper to visit and report on Future World.
4. Take pictures for a book students will write: *How We Made Future World.*
5. Use Sim City software to create a future simulation.

Children's Books

Alcock, V. (1988). *The monster garden.* New York: Delacorte.

Baker, J. (1987). *Where the forest meets the sea.* New York: Greenwillow.

Baker, J. (1991). *Window.* New York: Greenwillow.

Bunting, E. (1990). *Fly away home.* New York: Clarion.

Burton, V. L. (1942). *The little house.* Boston: Houghton Mifflin.

Christopher, J. (1967a). *The city of gold and lead.* New York: Macmillan.

Christopher, J. (1967b). *The White Mountains.* New York: Macmillan.

Christopher, J. (1988). *When the tripods came.* New York: Dutton.

Dickenson, P. (1989). *Eva.* New York: Delacorte.

Durrell, A., & Sachs, M. (1990). *The big book for peace.* New York: Dutton.

Goodall, J. (1989). *Story of an English village.* New York: McElderry.

Lowry, L. (1993). *The giver.* Boston: Houghton Mifflin.

MacDonald, C. (1989). *The lake at the end of the world.* New York: Dial.

Muller, J. (1977a). *The changing city.* New York: Atheneum.

Muller, J. (1977b). *The changing countryside.* New York: Atheneum.

O'Brien, R. (1975). *Z for Zachariah.* New York: Atheneum.

Paton, J. (1982). *The green book.* New York: Farrar, Straus, & Giroux.

Provensen, A., & Provensen, M. (1988). *Shaker Lane.* New York: Penguin.

Shulevitz, U. (1990). *Toddlecreek Post Office.* New York: Farrar, Straus, & Giroux.

Turner, A. (1989). *Heron Street.* New York: Harper & Row.

Van Allsburg, C. (1990). *Just a dream.* Boston: Houghton Mifflin.

Von Tscharner, R., & Fleming, R. (1987). *New Providence: A changing city scape.* New York: Harcourt Brace Jovanovich.

Wheatley, N. (1990). *My place.* Melbourne, Australia: Australia in Print.

Index

Subjects

Children's Books and Films